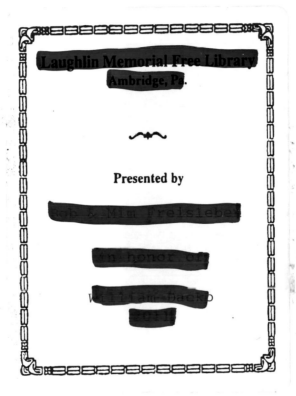

ALSO BY SCOTT EYMAN

Ingrid Bergman

Lion of Hollywood: The Life and Legend of Louis B. Mayer

John Ford: The Searcher 1894–1973

Print the Legend: The Life and Times of John Ford

The Speed of Sound: Hollywood and the Talkie Revolution, 1927–1930

Ernst Lubitsch: Laughter in Paradise

Mary Pickford, America's Sweetheart

Five American Cinematographers

With Louis Giannetti

Flashback: A Brief History of Film

With Robert Wagner

Pieces of My Heart: A Life

EMPIRE *of* DREAMS

THE
EPIC LIFE *of*
CECIL B. DEMILLE

SCOTT EYMAN

SIMON & SCHUSTER
NEW YORK   LONDON   TORONTO   SYDNEY

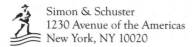

Simon & Schuster
1230 Avenue of the Americas
New York, NY 10020

First Simon & Schuster hardcover edition September 2010

SIMON & SCHUSTER and colophon are registered trademarks
of Simon & Schuster, Inc.

For information about special discounts for bulk purchases,
please contact Simon & Schuster Special Sales at
1-866-506-1949 or business@simonandschuster.com.

The Simon & Schuster Speakers Bureau can bring authors
to your live event. For more information or to book an event,
contact the Simon & Schuster Speakers Bureau at
1-866-248-3049 or visit our website at www.simonspeakers.com.

Designed by Nancy Singer

Manufactured in the United States of America

10   9   8   7   6   5   4   3   2   1

Library of Congress Cataloging-in-Publication Data

Eyman, Scott, date.
    Empire of dreams : the epic life of Cecil B. DeMille / Scott Eyman.—
1st Simon & Schuster hardcover ed.
        p.   cm.
    Includes bibliographical references and index.
    1. DeMille, Cecil B. (Cecil Blount), 1881–1959.   2. Motion picture
producers and directors—United States—Biography.   I. Title.
    PN1998.3.D455E94   2010
    791.43023'3092—dc22
    [B]   2010027710
ISBN 978-0-7432-8955-9
ISBN 978-1-4391-8041-9 (ebook)

In Memory of Richard deMille

1922–2009

And for Lynn Kalber Eyman,

whose love sustains me.

The dynamic, ambitious young Cecil B. DeMille, with eyes
that leave no doubt about his determination to master fortune.

"Cecil Blount DeMille . . . rode the fluctuating business deeps as on a surfboard, with gaiety and bravado. If he had any doubts as to his own ability or scope, he never expressed them. He had doubts about his colleagues; he expected the worst in business dealings and was always ready. He was himself a phenomenally shrewd man who augmented an instinct for popular taste with bold and astonishing business coups. His success was a world success, and he enjoyed every minute of it, and it lasted. He kept sex, sadism, patriotism, real estate, religion and public relations dancing in midair like juggler's balls for fifty years."

—*Agnes deMille*

CONTENTS

EMPIRE *of* DREAMS

DeMille (right) takes direction from Billy Wilder
on the set of *Sunset Boulevard*, as Gloria Swanson
looks on in character as Norma Desmond.

PROLOGUE

On the morning of May 23, 1949, at the Paramount studio on Marathon Street in the heart of Hollywood, Cecil B. DeMille was busily engaged in polishing Billy Wilder's dialogue.

May 23 was the first of four scheduled days of work for DeMille on a film called *Sunset Boulevard*. Although DeMille had wrapped up work on *Samson and Delilah* in January, a set from the biblical spectacle had been reconstructed to give the impression that the director had been caught during production by the visit of his onetime protégée Norma Desmond, played by Gloria Swanson, a star DeMille had discovered.

Wilder's films were noted for their pungent dialogue and merciless examination of human cupidity, while of late DeMille's had been noted for the splendid vastness of their images and the frequently silly lines his actors were paid to speak.

But if there was anything Cecil B. DeMille knew, it was how Cecil B. DeMille should sound.

His first scripted line was "It must be about that appalling script of hers. What can I say to her? What can I say?" In his rushed but legible handwriting, he changed "appalling" to "impossible," and gave the second sentence a more rhythmic quality: "What can I tell her? What can I say?"

He turned his attention to the flat line: "You'll pardon me, Norma. Why don't you just sit and watch?" On a separate piece of paper, he wrote a couple of variations. "Excuse me a minute Norma, will you? Why don't you just sit here and watch?" was one. Another was "I won't be a moment, Norma. Why don't you just sit here and watch?" And he added, "Pictures are different now, you know."

He marked moments that didn't carry dialogue but nevertheless needed some kind of actor's accent. At Norma's line "That's no excuse. You read the script, didn't you?" he added a parenthetical "(Look)" to indicate a glancing expression of dismay. Likewise, at his line "Get me Gordon Cole on the phone" he needed

1

to know what kind of transition Wilder was planning before he could decide on his delivery: "I presume camera pans off me, or I exit?"

After a line from an assistant director: "I hear she was a terror to work with," DeMille's scripted line was, "She got to be. A dozen press agents working overtime can do terrible things to the human spirit." He cut "She got to be" and added "Not at first. Only toward the end. You know, a dozen . . ."

He noted pieces of physical business ("glasses") and refers to himself in the third person: "holding her hand in his." He added stage directions, which the script itself lacked. "Searching for words" he notes of himself at one point.

DeMille's rewrite always stayed within the sense of Wilder's original dialogue. He made only one outright objection. His first line to Norma Desmond was originally "I haven't seen you since Lindbergh landed in Paris and we danced on the nightclub table."

"I never go to nightclubs," DeMille told Wilder. "And if I did I wouldn't dance on a table, even if Lindbergh flew to Paris twice. And if I did dance, it would be with Mrs. DeMille." The lines were reworked.

Throughout his revision, DeMille's polish lessens the staccato rhythm of Wilder's dialogue into something more conversational, more graceful, with special attention paid to cadence.

At 10 A.M., DeMille was called to the set, and Wilder began shooting the sequence that would place Cecil B. DeMille in historical context as much as any of the seventy films he directed.

Wilder placed all sorts of personal DeMille totems throughout the picture as in-jokes. A miniature statue of Dagon, the pagan idol whose destruction serves as the climax of *Samson and Delilah*, is featured in the New Year's party at Norma Desmond's house. The bed that Desmond sleeps in was hauled out of the prop room at Paramount, where it had lain since DeMille used it twenty-five years earlier.

Throughout DeMille's four days of shooting, Paramount's A. C. Lyles was on the set, and said, "It was wonderful to see the affection and the respect DeMille gave Gloria Swanson off camera. He was . . . gallant with her all the time."

After his work on the picture was completed, Wilder patted DeMille on the back and said, "Very good, my boy. Leave your name with my secretary. I may have a small part for you in my next picture." DeMille told a reporter, "I was an actor once, you know. . . . The public had had a look at me as an actor on Broadway before I came out [to Hollywood] and I decided to let the matter rest. Discretion is the better part of valor."

He was, of course, being unnecessarily modest. DeMille was in fact a good actor, and as the millions who have seen *Sunset Boulevard* can attest, when it came to playing Cecil B. DeMille, he was a great actor.

Sunset Boulevard captures DeMille as he undoubtedly saw himself, and as his family knew him . . . at his best. "The thoughtful side, the compassionate side—the Old Man at his best—emerges through Billy Wilder's eyes," his associate producer Henry Wilcoxon said. "I'm not ashamed to say I cry when I watch that scene."

"DeMille was very good," remembered Billy Wilder with satisfaction. "Much better than a lot of the actors in his pictures. He took direction terrifically. He loved it, he understood it. He was very subtle."

Sunset Boulevard was not the first time Cecil B. DeMille appeared in a movie. Thirty-six years earlier, in *The Squaw Man*, his very first film as a director, he played a faro dealer in order to save the $3 it cost to hire an actor. There had been a half dozen other cameo appearances over the years, always playing the part of Cecil B. DeMille.

But they were all innocuous movies, made to be seen for a season and forgotten. *Sunset Boulevard* was a serious movie by a serious director about two constructions—Hollywood and the delusions of celebrity—that DeMille knew more about than most. That is undoubtedly why there was really only one choice if a movie director was to be featured in Wilder's film—the most famous director of his time, the man who symbolized Hollywood to America and the world at large.

DeMille might have been expected to object to the script's scathing portrayal of the town he had found as a rural backwater and helped build into a world production center. But Billy Wilder had an edge. Wilder's first wife had been Judith Iribe, the stepdaughter of DeMille's longtime art director Paul Iribe. Besides that, DeMille liked Wilder's films a great deal, and they both worked at Paramount, the studio DeMille had co-founded.

Wilder was a man who jealously guarded the primacy of his scripts, but he quietly assented to all of DeMille's dialogue changes. In fact, he more or less gave him carte blanche, because DeMille is the heart of the film's crucial scene—he's the conscience of the film. Without DeMille, the audience has no knowledge of the Norma Desmond that used to be: "A lovely little girl of seventeen with more courage and wit and heart than ever came together in one youngster"—or what led her to become the fascinating gargoyle we see: "a dozen press agents working overtime . . ." etc. As one critic noted, DeMille is the only character in the film with an "uncorrupted heart. In his compassionate regard for Norma Desmond, he seems more human than any hero in a DeMille epic."

The other director in the cast, Erich von Stroheim, was a creatively frustrated man. He beseiged Wilder throughout production with all sorts of suggestions, some excellent—it was von Stroheim's idea that his character write Norma Desmond all her fan mail—and some bizarrely tangential—he wanted to be shown washing her lingerie. But DeMille was, as a psychiatrist would say, a completely actualized personality, so offered no broader suggestions about his portrayal or the film as a whole.

Wilder remembered that DeMille accepted the part with alacrity, pausing only to say, "Very good. $10,000." Actually, DeMille bartered his services on the picture, although the $10,000 figure was nearly accurate. DeMille's remuneration was contractually specified as "a new 1949 black Cadillac seven (7) passenger limousine, costing approximately Six Thousand Six Hundred Dollars, ($6,600)." Five months later, when he was called back for a day of retakes, DeMille's contract was extended to include a cash payment of $3,000.

★

Cecil Blount DeMille was five foot ten and a half inches tall and 178 pounds. He was never classically handsome, but all of his life he was the dominant figure in any room he entered because of his strong, compellingly masculine personality, radiant energy, and the warm, almond-shaped brown eyes that had once been attractively set off by a thick thatch of curly brown hair. Unfortunately, the hair first thinned, then disappeared by the time he was twenty-five.

At the age of sixty-eight, DeMille still gave an impression of indomitable but gentlemanly strength, anchored by a voice that compelled attention. It was an actor's voice, formed by years of theatrical trouping that had preceded his entry into the movies. It was also a famous voice—by the time he came to shoot his sequence in *Sunset Boulevard*, DeMille's fame as a radio star was the equal of his fame as a film director. "His name was like Walt Disney's, in that it meant as much as any of the stars in the picture," said A. C. Lyles, who rose from Adolph Zukor's office boy to become a producer on the lot.

Although *Sunset Boulevard* has come to be acknowledged as the only great Hollywood movie about Hollywood, at the time DeMille's very presence seemed to eastern critics to be a symbol of the film's implicit corruption. In *The New Yorker*, Philip Hamburger even went so far as to (purposely?) get details wrong when he wrote that "DeMille—wearing, so help me, directorial puttees—says to her, 'Norma, you must realize that times have changed in pictures.'"

Besides the misquotation of the dialogue, DeMille is clothed entirely in a conservative business suit—puttees are nowhere in evidence.

But that was typical of the condescending and willfully inaccurate critical attitude that DeMille had endured for twenty years and that would prevail until his death in 1959 and beyond. It was partly his own fault. He understood the power of personal publicity as few filmmakers have, and devised and executed a command personality that made him one of only two or three movie directors known to the general public—a personality that existed above and beyond his films: he was the Patton of the movies, fearlessly pushing his army of actors, extras, and technicians through the enemy lines of indifference and industrial ennui, inexorably moving toward the promised land of audience satisfaction.

In Kevin Brownlow's lovely phrase, "He directed as if chosen by God for that one task," but underneath the display and showmanship of the later years was one of the half dozen most distinguished careers in silent movies, which segued into commercial dominance in the sound era.

Because of his imposing personality and dozens of equally imposing films, for generations of fans DeMille *was* the movies—their opulence, their excess, their *movieness*. But it hadn't always been that way.

After an initial apprenticeship of a year or so, DeMille directed a series of nervously brilliant intimate melodramas before his films evolved into sly marital comedies and often outlandish melodramas. A flirtation with epics around World War I began to harden in the 1920s, and by the 1930s, DeMille movies had attained their perfect state: must-see spectacles for the masses, a Victorian child's idea of the American West or Roman times or biblical days—larger than life, with heroic heroes and dastardly villains, far more spectacular, far more splendid, and far, far more romantic than any historical or behavioral reality.

DeMille was mounting the movie equivalents of the great pageant-plays of his childhood, which meant that he was serenely ignoring the general trend toward naturalism that followed the introduction of sound.

Although he was the son of one successful playwright and the brother of another, DeMille's spiritual father was really David Belasco, the theatrical impresario of the late nineteenth and early twentieth centuries who favored melodrama that blew right past matters of plausibility as if logic were merely a word in the dictionary.

At their worst, the films of DeMille's commercial maturity were colorful and entertaining; at their considerable best they were physically impressive and dramatically thrilling, floridly nostalgic, occasionally preposterous visions of the distant past. Either way, he retained the great popular artist's gift of compelling the audience to wonder what was going to happen next to people in whose existence they did not really believe.

Lost to the critics who disdained him were the great accomplishments of his early days, when he was one of the most inventive and ceaselessly energetic filmmakers of his generation. Lost to those same critics was anything other than a grudging recognition of the talent it took to reliably provide pleasure for audiences of four generations—from the nickelodeon era to widescreen and stereophonic sound.

Throughout the changing times and corresponding changing styles, DeMille rarely attempted to craft his films to suit contemporary styles. He made what he liked, made it straight and without winking. Take it, he implicitly said, or leave it. The public took it, but as his career advanced, the critics tended to leave it.

In truth, DeMille's dramatic tastes and his imposing visual sense were far more suited to silence than sound, when The Image slowly but surely became leashed to The Word. As critics began to judge movies as much by how they sounded as how they looked, it was only natural for DeMille's standing to suffer.

But critical disdain necessitated a willful ignorance of the span and content of most of DeMille's career—the spectacular series of innovative melodramas of the early years that birthed Paramount Pictures; open-minded marital comedies that observed, with withering accuracy, that the chains of marriage are often so heavy they sometimes require three or four people to carry them; the unsurpassed brilliance of his command of scale in screen spectacle; and an entrepreneurial vision that invariably attracted the best art directors, costume designers, cameramen.

What all this meant was that DeMille was far more aesthetically influential than he was ever given credit for. DeMille's comedies of marital misalliance set the pattern for those of Ernst Lubitsch, as well as Chaplin's *A Woman of Paris*; DeMille spectacles such as *The Crusades* certainly influenced Sergei Eisenstein's *Alexander Nevsky*. As for epics, DeMille's example impelled dozens of filmmakers to throw themselves into the fray, even those who had no affinity for the form. As Howard Hawks, Nicholas Ray, Joseph L. Mankiewicz, and George Stevens would discover, it's harder than it looks.

Yet many remained convinced that he was nothing but an empty, cynical showman.

"Cecil B. DeMille simply vulgarized everything that D. W. Griffith did," snapped Sidney Lumet. "He was the cheap version of D. W. Griffith's work. I don't think he had an original bone in his body, nor an original thought in his head. Anything else you would like to know?"

Charlton Heston, who starred in the last two pictures DeMille directed, recognized how DeMille was regarded. "[He was] terribly unfashionable and dismissed pejoratively as a corn merchant," Heston said. "I think he was much more than that."

Certainly, DeMille's movies embodied a strange combination of qualities: an enthusiastic obsession with lavish detail, and a boyish gusto that produced luscious surfaces, often lacquered over very basic characters and themes.

Yet, as film critic Michael Sragow has noted, "see him at the right age, and the size and the velvet artwork skies and yes, even the self-importance will stay with you for the rest of your life." About half of Steven Spielberg derives from Cecil B. DeMille, pretty much uncut, up to and including *The War of the Worlds*—at one time, a DeMille project.

The totality of DeMille's career is among the most remarkable, if not aesthetically consistent, in American movies. Although he eventually typed himself as a director of epics, in the broad range of a forty-six-year directorial career that encompassed seventy films, he directed every kind of movie: comedy, fantasy, social preachment, western, suspense, war, musical comedy.

He created two great stars (Gloria Swanson, Charlton Heston) thirty years apart, and gave many other stars (Bebe Daniels, Wallace Reid, Sessue Hayakawa, Claudette Colbert, William Boyd, Joel McCrea, Robert Preston) the boosts that led to major careers.

His primary ingredients were a remarkably elastic Edwardian morality combined with a splendid sense of composition and display. Critics thought his films were pure commercial calculation, and there was undoubtedly an element of that involved, but in fact the components of DeMille's career were an authentic representation of his own psychological tensions.

Cecil B. DeMille was a preacher's kid who genuinely believed in God and His word. At the same time, he almost never attended church. He became increasingly conservative as he aged, eventually becoming a pillar of California's political right wing, yet serenely maintained two private lives: a sincerely adored wife and children in a household of correct Episcopalian probity, balanced against a revolving trio of devoted mistresses.

DeMille's personality embodied unresolvable tensions bred by a devout Episcopalian father and a flamboyant Jewish mother—lust mixed with God, God mixed with Mammon, with a strangely naive sophistication informing the life choices of a sincere moralist who contained a strong dose of libertine. All these contradictions seeped from his life into his work. It is these dichotomies that animate DeMille's best films, and that make both the man and the work so fascinating.

DeMille was always a populist filmmaker, in the same sense as Frank Capra, but one who, at least in the silent days, took serious, entirely successful flyers at Art. But his increasing social and political conservatism tended to be most successful when embedded in genres that could be read as archetypal narratives of good and evil: the higher law of the Old or New Testament, the epic western, and so on.

At the same time, he was a strange kind of conservative. His silent film *The Volga Boatman* gives a surprisingly sympathetic account of the Russian Revolution; he spent several months touring Stalinist Russia in the early 1930s and found it fascinating; he regarded Congress' political investigation of Hollywood in the late 1940s with appropriate contempt for the publicity mongering it was.

No simple characterization of left or right, artist or hack, can encapsulate the life of this extraordinary man.

Through the various phases of his career, one thing remained the same: DeMille's image of the director as emperor. He introduced his own trailers, narrated his own movies—the work was personalized to an extent that no other Hollywood director ever attempted. Neither Gregg Toland nor Bernard Herrmann was absorbed into Orson Welles the way that everybody who worked with him was absorbed into Cecil B. DeMille. If nothing else, DeMille provides a capsule confirmation of the auteur theory.

In a sense, this was a logical extension of DeMille's instinct for command. By 1915, after directing movies for little more than a year, DeMille had mastered movie narrative, the process of storytelling, more than any other director alive—yes, even more than Griffith. DeMille understood that, on its most basic level, narrative can be an irresistible freight train. He became adept at planting the seeds of each scene to come in the preceding scene—the basis for scene three occurred in scene two, the question resolved by scene four had been introduced in scene three, and so on through to the end of the picture.

DeMille's plots could be goofy, but his narrative often produced inexorable dramatic thunder. Because his films were the most vivid, the most immediately *legible* in the business for child and adult alike, they were also the most popular.

And in his early years, in movies like *Kindling, The Cheat,* and *The Whispering Chorus,* he displayed a knack for brutal realism and a taste for unhappy or ambiguous endings that would have destroyed the career of a filmmaker with less control of his career and of the public. But he was also a furiously moving target, throwing a film onto the marketplace six, eight, ten times a year. In these early years, he never made the same movie twice.

By his own intent, DeMille's career is inseparable from Hollywood itself. By 1956, when he released *The Ten Commandments,* his last, most commercially successful film, the Lasky Barn, where he had made his first film in 1913, was California Historical Landmark No. 554. He was no longer just a director; he had ascended to the realm of history and myth, at least partially because of his own efforts. His meticulously maintained archives entail more than two thousand boxes, and forty-five of DeMille's fifty-two silent films survive because he took the responsibility of preserving them himself.

Because of his own sense of history, through DeMille the story of the Hollywood film industry can be traced, from its beginnings as a bastard stepchild of the New York theater, through the revolutions of sound and widescreen, and on to the battles with broadcast and pay television.

DeMille often acted as if he had invented modern Hollywood perhaps because, in a very real way, he had. It was not merely the fact that DeMille headed west in 1913 and found a sleepy little retirement town, which he helped convert into the world's center for the movie industry; it was that DeMille's silent films showed the world how movies could be speedily manufactured on a commercial basis without sacrificing pace, style, technical and narrative innovation, or aesthetic excellence. DeMille built an empire for DeMille, but he also built an empire called Hollywood.

D. W. Griffith was the first directorial superstar, but DeMille was right behind him. By the early 1920s, Griffith was washing out, unable to compete with changing tastes. DeMille was barely into his second wind, and there would be a third, a fourth, and a fifth to follow. No other director has been a major commercial force in the movies for as long.

By the mid-1920s, the critics had started to write him off, pointing to aesthetics they regarded as kitsch, as well as the conventional themes and the implicit—later overt—anti-totalitarian ideology made explicit in his spoken prologue for the 1956 version of *The Ten Commandments*: "The theme of this picture is whether men are to be ruled by God's law, or whether they are to be ruled by the whims of a dictator like Rameses. Are men the property of the state, or are they free souls under God?"

It's easy to overlook the fact that his films reflect a turbulent, manifestly sexual imagination usually involving an incessant struggle for power; there is the branding of a dishonest woman in his legendary *The Cheat*, there are whips and disfigured faces in *Something to Think About* (1920), chained bodies in *The Golden Bed* (1925), women dragged by their hair in several films, and women being clothed to suggest what critics Paolo Cherchi Usai and Lorenzo Codelli call "coercion, aggression and deceit."

For DeMille, the spiritual values represented by the Bible would be compensation for the barely sublimated sexual war in his depictions of men and women. DeMille saw life as a struggle for control, for dominance—morally, politically, sexually.

The themes of his pictures were matched by the themes of his personality. "He seemed to have an innate aura of power," said one woman who worked with him. "Everything around him was quiet. So quiet he had to be powerful."

"He appeared to be a very genial, congenial man," said Angela Lansbury, "but he was also very demanding. He surrounded himself with a coterie of people who waited on him hand and foot, he demanded absolute attention, and he ruled the set with an iron hand, and an iron voice, I might add. He carried a microphone man with him all the time, and he simply put his hand behind him and took the microphone and spoke to the entire assembled group of people on the set, and in this way he could command attention and he could also direct the extras, and the actors, and the animals, all at the same time.

"He needed always to have this kind of control. He also had a man who was always there with a chair, and when he wanted to sit down he simply kind of glanced over his left shoulder, and the man shoved the chair under his bottom."

Many people within and without the industry disliked him and his work precisely because of the display, the ceremony, the sense of importance that Lansbury would characterize as "pukka, as in the British Raj." Others would characterize his on-set demeanor and manner with the Yiddish word *ferbissana*—cold.

Yet this same man was noticeably quiet, almost passive, at home, usually deferring to his wife and daughter. For the secret of Cecil B. DeMille was not just that he had an actor's voice, he had an actor's gifts. On a soundstage, he created and seamlessly played the part of Cecil B. DeMille with unfailing brio. There he could be brutal, with sarcastic monologues that spiraled into arcs of contemptuous eloquence. Often, these diatribes were feigned for the sake of imposing greater control of a vast production.

A. C. Lyles tells a story about DeMille coming upon an extra in the Paramount commissary. "I remember you," said DeMille. "You worked for me about ten years ago on a picture. You were great, you were wonderful, and that was ten years ago. Why didn't you ever come back and want to work for me again?"

"Mr. DeMille," said the man, "I never got over the first time I worked for you."

Yet DeMille staff people stayed for decades, not just because he carried them between pictures on full salary, but because he could be and often was delightful. Lyles kept a parrot in his office, and DeMille made a habit of stopping by in order to broaden the parrot's vocabulary. In due time, the parrot began repeating, "Hello, C.B., Hello C.B. I'm an eagle, I'm an eagle, I'm an eagle." Then DeMille taught it to say "Ten Commandments!"

"He had more fun with that parrot, trained by Cecil B. DeMille," said Lyles.

Surveying his life, objectively appraising his career, one can honestly say that Cecil B. DeMille was afraid of nothing except boring an audience.

"We had stars," said Lyles. "We had Mary Pickford and Rudolph Valentino and Bob Hope and Bing Crosby and Claudette Colbert, but the mainstay in picture-making here for years was Cecil B. DeMille. He was the mountain in the [Paramount] logo."

One thing is inarguable: there was never a career like DeMille's before, and there has been none like it since. DeMille's importance transcends his individual films, and even transcends his achievements, because he embodies the story of the American motion picture and its rise to world preeminence. It is the story of the acquisition and maintenance of more power than was held by any of his directorial contemporaries; of the birth of the vertically integrated movie studio, where production, distribution, and exhibition were centrally controlled, where exhibitors took the complete output of a studio in order to get those few pictures that they knew would pay the bills—the films directed by Cecil B. DeMille.

All of this was possible only through the indomitable drive of one man with the surest instincts of any director in the history of the movies.

★

This book is the first to be written with complete access to DeMille's archives, which give an unmatched record of the theater of the late nineteenth century and the movies of the first half of the twentieth.

This is how Hollywood became the center of world movie production, both literally and metaphorically; this is how Cecil B. DeMille became the most famous director of his time.

This is Cecil B. DeMille.

Before he became the most successful film director
of his generation, DeMille was a struggling actor in sundry repertory
and touring companies. Here he is in rehearsal with his wife, Constance,
for one such production circa 1903. (Motion Picture Associates)

PART ONE

1881–1913

"The old Belasco plays are like religious plays.
The story is nothing; it's what you breathe into it."

–CECIL B. DeMILLE

1

In 1871 Sylvester Samuel came to New York from Liverpool with his family, to act as a buyer for his family's retail stores in England. The Samuels became successful in both mercantile and emotional terms, settling in Brooklyn, where their English accents and Central European Jewish background gave them a touch of aristocratic distinction. Their eighteen-year-old daughter, Beatrice, caught the performing bug and joined a Brooklyn literary and performing organization that was an outgrowth of the Chautauqua movement. On November 4, 1872, Beatrice's group presented an evening's entertainment that included her reading of a poem entitled "The Vital Spark," and a comedy in which she played a flirtatious Irish heroine, complete with accent.

In the audience that evening was a young man named Henry Churchill deMille. Henry, born September 4, 1853, was the eldest of ten children of William deMille, the mayor of Washington, North Carolina, and Margaret Blount Hoyt. The family name had been deMill until William added an "e" to the end for visual symmetry. They traced their ancestry back to Holland and the Meld, a Celtic tribe living along what is now the Belgian coast, mentioned by Julius Caesar in his *Gallic Wars*.*

The deMille family survived the Civil War, although their home had been burned and they were left with nothing.

Henry deMille had been enchanted by the theater since childhood. His first appearance on the boards came in 1866, in an amateur production of a farce called *Nan the Good for Nothing*. That same year, Henry gave up a trip to New York rather than miss declaiming a two-line part in *Pocahontas*, which in time led to his being sent to attend Columbia College by a grant of $175 from something called the So-

---

* As will be clear in these pages, there are variations on the spelling of the family name—deMille, de Mille, DeMille, De Mille, etc. Cecil himself, when writing in his own hand, spelled the name "deMille," but used "DeMille" professionally in the movies. To avoid confusion between Cecil and the other members of the family, as well as to impose some much-needed consistency, I refer to Cecil as "DeMille."

If anybody lived an uppercase life, DeMille did.

ciety of New York for the Promotion of Religion Through Learning. He promptly joined Columbia's Drama Society. In these years, Henry was a habitual theatergoer, as well as a weekly vistor to Barnum's Museum on Broadway near Broome Street.

His lack of resources made Henry's college life difficult. Most of his fellow students had money and, as he remembered, "it made it a little hard—not that I wanted the money so much, as that I wanted friends, companions. I was cut to the heart to find out how pitiable human nature sometimes is to find myself neglected, thrown aside, because I had not money."

Henry was a Democrat, a compulsive reader, "interested in everything," as his younger son would remember. Physically, he looked like a prim Victorian school-master, with pince-nez glasses and a high forehead that would only get higher with the passing years, an unfortunate genetic trait that would be passed on to his sons, along with other, more desirable ones.

He retained his theatrical passions, but, as his younger son would observe, "Boys from nice southern families, with strong religious leanings, did not go on the stage in the 1870s." When Henry asked his mother, "What would you say to my becoming an actor?" the quick response was, "It would break my heart." Neither did boys from nice southern families with strong religious leanings break their mother's hearts. The theater was out.

For almost a decade, Henry cautiously studied theology, church history, and the sermons of Charles Kingsley, while writing plays and short stories in his spare time.

So it was that on November 4, 1872, two people in love with the theater met at the 14th Weekly Entertainment of the Philokalia Musical & Literary Association in Brooklyn. We know this because Henry preserved the printed program. After Miss Samuel's recitation, Henry introduced himself to the young actress. Although her family generally called her Tillie, Henry informed her that he would prefer to call her Beatrice, after Dante's beloved.

Henry was obviously a smooth talker, but his intentions were strictly honor-able. Physically, Beatrice wasn't any more than presentable, but it was her person-ality that made her what she was: outgoing and vivacious, in contrast to Henry's more contemplative nature. He was smart, but she was street-smart and adventur-ous—two traits that would characterize their younger son.

The families were not thrilled with their children's choice: Henry had chosen a Jew; Beatrice a Gentile. Neither of them cared. When Henry spoke on the topic "What's in a Name" at a Columbia Semi-Annual in 1875, Beatrice threw him a bouquet. That night, Henry wrote in his diary, "Beatrice was with me."

Henry graduated with his bachelor's degree from Columbia in 1875. After several years of the deepening relationship, Henry's mother said that it might work out if Henry would agree to pack away his aspirations for a career in the theater and wait a full year before marrying his girl.

The dutiful son said yes, while the crafty young man set about obeying the letter of the promise, if not its spirit. Henry accepted a job at a prep school in

Brooklyn where, in a stunning coincidence, Beatrice had recently been hired as an elocution teacher. Henry's salary was $700 a year, which he supplemented with another $550 worth of private tutoring. "I used to meet Beatrice every morning," wrote Henry, "and walk with her to the school, a distance of two miles."

Game, set, match.

On July 1, 1876, Henry and Beatrice were married, without her parents' consent or presence, at St. Luke's Church in Brooklyn. "Our marriage had been bitterly opposed by her father because of our different religions," wrote Henry. "But she had for over a year been baptized into the Christian faith. In that very church she had been baptized, confirmed, and had partaken of her first communion."

The breach between father and daughter would not be permanent; when her father died, he left her a full share of his estate. The honeymoon was spent in Washington, North Carolina, with Henry's family, then it was back to Brooklyn, where they took an apartment on Madison Street.

Beatrice's original religion, and her abandonment of it, became something of an issue for the family. Richard deMille, Cecil's son, would say that "She loved Henry deMille more than she loved religion, so she had no difficulty at all becoming an Episcopalian Christian." For his part, Cecil tended to speak of "my English mother who is an Episcopalian," although he never pretended she hadn't been born Jewish. As with other great talents born in that era such as Douglas Fairbanks and Fred Astaire, a part-Jewish heritage was something to downplay, not proudly proclaim. For Cecil, Beatrice's true religion was her family, which neatly obliterated both the religion she was born into, as well as the religion she chose.

Despite Henry's religiosity, their marriage was one of earthly passion. In a diary entry, Henry wrote that "In evening I felt very—on the—thinking of my wife. It seems as though our spirits came specially together that night. Is there not a spirit's voice that speaks in spite of the body? I certainly felt the sweet influence of her spirit that night. I have never had a greater proof of the sympathy of soul with soul."

Henry was also seriously pious; his diary for 1878 records that when he went on a trip to Coney Island, he took along a volume of the sermons of Charles Kingsley. That same year, he was accepted by the Long Island Diocese as a candidate for Holy Orders in the Episcopal Church. Henry would be listed as a candidate for the priesthood for eight long years, until 1885, but he was never ordained, for life was soon to take him in the direction of his initial enthusiasm.

William Churchill deMille, Henry and Beatrice's first son, was born "after a day of great anxiety" in Washington, North Carolina, at the home of Henry's paternal grandparents, on July 25, 1878. It was a difficult delivery, and there were some complications for Beatrice; Henry's diary alludes to her being "terribly ill" and to a resulting operation that had to be performed in the fall.

In the autumn of 1878, Henry and his wife and son returned to New York, where he took a job teaching at Columbia Grammar School for $900 a year. He also made $400 from *Leslie's Weekly* for an eighteen-part serial he wrote, but money was still tight. The census of 1880 finds the family at 408 W. 23rd Street in Manhattan, lodging with a family named Lewis.

In the summer of 1881, Beatrice was once again pregnant, and Henry took her to the Berkshires to escape the New York heat, while he served as a private tutor in Latin, Greek, and mathematics for four young students. It was in a boardinghouse on Main Street in Ashfield, Massachusetts, that Cecil Blount deMille entered the world in the large upstairs front room of a home owned by a Mrs. Bronson. Henry deMille was teaching a class downstairs at the time. Henry marked the day in his diary: "August 12 my little boy Cecil was born. The 1st of Sept. the pupils and I returned to N.Y., where I [stayed] at the flat, which I refitted with curtains and hall carpet and dining room carpet all new for the reception of my sweet wife, and her two precious boys."

When school started—Henry was now making $1,000 a year—he was working on a play called *Robert Aclen* in addition to teaching. The play involved Episcopalian principles, and it brought Henry to the attention of the Reverend George S. Mallory, who, along with his brother, co-owned the Madison Square Garden Theatre. Beginning in April 1882, the Mallorys hired Henry as a play reader for $1,500 a year, plus an extra $1,000 for any play he wrote, provided it ran two hundred nights—a very long run in those days.

It was in his capacity as a dramaturge that Henry met the stage manager of the Garden Theatre, a young man named David Belasco. Born in 1853, Belasco was vital, bombastic, and determined to be successful in the theater on his terms. He had been secretary to Dion Boucicault, had collaborated with the playwright James Herne, and had a modest success with a play he wrote called *Hearts of Oak* in Chicago in 1879.

That same year, Belasco had staged a version of *The Passion Play* in San Francisco that featured James O'Neill as Christ, along with a cast of four hundred. Outside the theater, Jews were attacked in the streets, which seems to have left Belasco uninterested despite his Jewish heritage—a fact he never emphasized.

Belasco and Henry became friends and set about rewriting a play called *Elsie Deane*. Henry's own play, *John Delmer's Daughters*, was produced in December 1883, and closed after six performances despite Belasco's direction. A month before that, on November 24, Henry had pasted a program for a play called *The Rajah* in a scrapbook and wrote beside it, "Baby Cecil's first entertainment at the M.S. Theatre."

If his diary is any indication, most of Henry's attention seems to have gone to his wife and elder son. "Many pleasing traits were observed in my boy William," he wrote after a family trip to Virginia for a wedding. "His good behavior, adherence to the truth, etc. His mother had forbidden his eating any candy, and he kept a piece which had been given him and brought it all the way to N.Y. to ask whether he might eat it."

There are no comparable admiring notations about Cecil.

When Charles Frohman and his brother Daniel hired Belasco away, the partnership with deMille temporarily broke up. Henry went back to being a drama-turge and supplementing his income by acting in road companies. Times were hard, but Beatrice's father died and her inheritance was enough for them to rent a summer house in Echo Lake, New Jersey, which gave William and Cecil a healthier summer environment than the stifling urban jungle of New York. The Echo Lake house dated from pre-Revolutionary days—the floors were held together by wooden pegs instead of nails. Local rumors had it that the place was haunted, and that was probably one reason it cost only $50 a year to rent. For money like that, ghosts could be dealt with.

Cecil would remember the Echo Lake house with something approaching rap-ture all his life. It was at Echo Lake that he first became entranced by the world of nature, which would always remain a passion. The boys soon had a dog, then they got a strawberry roan horse named Jack, and Cecil was soon on a first-name basis with every cow and horse in the neighborhood.

In later years, Cecil enjoyed telling a story about the time Beatrice took the two boys fishing for bass on Echo Lake. Bill was rowing while Beatrice and Cecil fished. Beatrice got a strike, but Bill stopped rowing because the boat was heading into the reeds. *"Keep rowing, you stupid boy, keep rowing!"* Beatrice bellowed. For the rest of his life, whether catching mountain trout or marlin, Cecil never caught a fish without thinking of Beatrice and her imitation of Lord Nelson.

Henry was always hustling. In his diary he would note that through the winter and spring of 1884–1885 he was rewriting plays and staging and acting in some-thing called *Sealed Instructions*, which he played in Chicago at the Grand Opera House for three weeks, "receiving excellent notices for my performance." Money was tight, but Henry was painfully responsible, and his account books reveal that he took out a $5,000 life insurance policy in December 1884.

In this period, Henry told his diary, "I had to get along by borrowing and other such doglike means of living." In December 1885, he was acting with Bea-trice in New Orleans, where they hated the food but loved the atmosphere. "At the French Market we saw the patent medicine man advertising with snakes. . . . Small alligators were for sale around the market and streets. . . . Then we went to Metai-rie cemetery. The avenues are lined with orange trees laden with fruit; the tombs are of white marble and all built above ground. This singular inscription struck me: 'Jonas Pickles—the elements were so mixed in him . . . ' Mixed pickles!"

Henry's letters home when he was on the road with a play are usually undated, but always ardently emotional and enveloping: "God bless and keep you all, my darlings. I take you *all* in my arms and press you close against my heart. A kiss for each of you from Your Dearest." He paid attention to new technology, as in a note about Bradford, Pennsylvania, where, "natural gas burned everywhere, even for heating the rooms."

Sometimes the letters allude to domestic disagreements, and Henry is always apologetic:

"My Darling Loved One, I am safe and well, on my way to Boston, where I shall soon arrive. I followed you in my mind last night, to the theater. . . . You are always in my thoughts. I wish I could let you see how much you are to me. Such love as I have for you, any woman might be glad to have, for it is unmixed with anything that savors of earth. Do you think I don't realize what you have done for me and my poor little one? Do you think I can ever forget it? Do you think I don't love you ten times more for it? I love you now more than I ever did in my life. You are still my stand-by, my Beatrice, my Agnes. . . . Always remember that when you are tempted to judge me by my unfortunate temper. Judge me by what I say to you when I am writing, because it is then that my heart speaks. . . .

"I hope my boys will have a good time. You might judiciously let them have what they want in the way of fishing tackle, etc. and charge it to me. Kiss my precious little bright-eyed angels every night and morning for me. And let one kiss that you give the boys, be always for me. . . . I take you in my arms and kiss you and pray God to make you see how much you are loved, admired and cherished by your Devoted Husband."

In 1886, Henry and Belasco reunited on *The Main Line* ("An *Idyll of the Rail-road,"*), a play Henry wrote with Charles Barnard, which was presented at the Lyceum Theatre, directed by Belasco. The play's principal dramatic distinction was the hero's revulsion when he discovers that the woman he loves plays cards; its most impressive scene represented a snow blockage in the Rocky Mountains, with a full-size reproduction of a locomotive tearing across the stage. The reviews for *The Main Line* were quite good, especially for the innovative staging. The play closed in a month, but it managed a tour in a production that Henry and Belasco staged.

Belasco was now a rising star and he indicated to Henry that he intended to allow him to hitch his boxcar to Belasco's powerful locomotive. Belasco remembered Henry with obvious affection and some pride. "We were successful because our way of thought was similar. We were frank in our criticism of each other. Henry excelled in narrative and had a quick wit. I acted while he took down my speeches. When a play was finished it was impossible to say where his work left off and mine began."

For the tour of *The Main Line* in the fall of 1886, Henry acted, and Beatrice did as well, under the stage name Agnes Graham. The tour lasted for twenty-eight weeks, 235 performances, and ended with debts of between $6,000 and $7,000. "My condition was desperate," wrote Henry in his diary. "It seemed as if I should never get my head above water again."

But riding to Henry's rescue was Daniel Frohman, who asked deMille and Belasco to write a play together, and offered $25 advance apiece. It was the best offer on the table—actually, it was the only offer on the table—so the two men returned to Henry's house in Echo Lake and went to work.

During the next four years, Henry deMille and David Belasco were to collaborate on four plays: *The Wife* in 1887, *Lord Chumley* in 1888, *The Charity Ball* in 1889, and *Men and Women* in 1890. Each of them was successful, each toured the country, each was a society play taking place in Fifth Avenue and Newport drawing rooms.

In 1887, Cecil was six, just old enough for David Belasco to make an impression—one of Belasco's greatest gifts. Cecil remembered him as a "slender young man, with his shock of coal-black hair, his deep, dark eyes, and the high-standing clerical collar he always wore. . . . He had the spirit of fun that children love, and with it the rarer gift of taking children seriously, treating them as persons."

For the deMille boys, Belasco became a heroic uncle figure. He wore a cape, made a spectacular entrance, and sustained it—a figure from one of the throbbing melodramas he would put on the stage and altogether bigger than life.

Belasco and Henry worked out a pattern for their relationship: they sat at desks that faced each other, wrote longhand, and talked for about four hours every day. Then they would hand their scribblings to Beatrice, who would make a fair copy, after which Bill and Cecil would be called in to listen to a reading of the day's work. The boys were always encouraged to voice their opinions, and Cecil was proud of the fact that some of their suggestions were actually adopted. It was a lesson he never forgot: in later years, he would take a suggestion from anyone, from a mailman to a grandchild.

After a day of writing, Henry would relax at night by reading aloud a chapter from the Bible and an accompanying chapter from history. Henry liked to have his head rubbed while he read, and the boys would take turns in order to keep their father reading as long as possible. The result was, as Cecil would remember, "the heroes of the Bible and world history were as much alive to us as Superman and Hopalong Cassidy are to youngsters today."

Cecil loved these evenings, consisting of literary stimulation that ranged from the Bible to Thackeray to Victor Hugo. "Father had a beautifully modulated voice. . . . He made everything real. . . . *The King of Kings* and *The Ten Commandments* were born in those evenings when father sat under the big lamp and read and a small boy sat near his chair and listened."

The family remembered Cecil as a habitually rambunctious child who was always launching himself into the house with a breathtaking discovery that demanded everybody drop everything and pay attention.

Belasco liked the boys, but he had a mercurial disposition. When Cecil was seven or eight, Belasco promised him that he would give him a pony for his birthday. As August 12 approached, so did Cecil's agitation, and on the morning of his birthday, he flew to the window to look into the yard.

No pony.

The barn?

Nothing.

Cecil waited all day in vain. The pony never showed up and its absence cast a deep pall over the other presents he got. Belasco had forgotten a promise made to a child.

"It was a bitter experience," the child remembered when he had grown to be an old man, "as only a childhood sorrow can be bitter." Characteristically, it strengthened Cecil's resolve. "I learned from it not to expect the world to be as sure or as dependable a place as the family circle with father and mother at the center and all the grandparents, aunts and uncles making a comforting circumference. Every child learns that sooner or later. . . . I am glad, in a way, that I learned it from a man whom I have so many other and great reasons to respect."

★

Charles Frohman remembered that Belasco and deMille were seamless collaborators. "DeMille . . . was primarily a literary person, while Belasco, with his strong natural sense of drama, worked less with lines and situations than with action and stage effect. He saw human nature only from the footlights."

After Belasco and deMille wrote a script, they would get it on its feet in rehearsal, where it would be rewritten. Belasco would walk through the movement on stage while deMille sat at a table in the front row furiously rewriting. "Now Henry," Belasco would say, "give me a speech that begins here and takes me over here. Then I turn suddenly like this—and see the woman I love."

In a Belasco play, the curtain went up on a scene featuring completely appointed rooms—windows that opened and shut, real flowers in window boxes, real food cooked on real stoves, rooms that gave every appearance of having real people in them, with exquisitely painted and lit backdrops. Pine needles would be strewn on the floor of a set so that the audience would smell the aroma. But all these authentic physical details would be put in the service of conventional story structures and a happy ending.

The Wife opened at the Lyceum on November 1, 1887. The reviews were good, but business was ordinary. Frohman wanted to close the show, but Belasco supposedly grabbed the producer by the throat until Frohman consented to give the show a chance. (That's the way Belasco told it, anyway—he was always the hero of his own life.)

Henry's version of the show's survival was less dramatic and more likely: "Its fate was for some nights in doubt until David and I took off our coats and went to work revising. We reduced it from 5 acts to 4. Rewrote the comedy . . . and immediately after the new version was put on business jumped up and it passed its 200th performance. I had a very bad time during this winter paying up the debts of *The Main Line* so that the royalties of *The Wife* were largely consumed in that quarter." *The Wife* ran for 239 performances, an excellent run in that era. With a hit under their belts, Henry and David were commissioned to write another play for the Lyceum.

The Wife was Henry's first taste of success, and it churned out just enough money to provide a new apartment for the family, a three-room flat on Waverly Place. Henry and his family could finally begin to enjoy New York. He took his boys to the theater, to rehearsals, and to the Metropolitan Museum, where William was fascinated by the paintings, especially Lepage's *Joan of Arc*, while Cecil stared at the Egyptian gallery's mummies and statues.

Henry also spent the winter of 1888–1889 as associate director of the New York School of Acting, previously the Lyceum School of Acting, previously the Empire School. Henry renamed the school yet again. This time, the name stuck and the American Academy of Dramatic Arts continues to turn out superb talents 120 years later. Among Henry's projects there was the translation of Sophocles' *Elektra* from the Greek, which was performed at the academy on March 11, 1889.

Cecil attended kindergarten at Houseman's School, 9 University Place in Manhattan. The arch in Washington Square was under construction at the time, and Cecil remembered proudly coming home with chips from it in his pocket.

The stories Cecil would tell his own family of his childhood tended to involve the formation of his interests and his intellect. Listening to his father reading the Bible at night and learning to read it himself; absorbing the illustrations of Doré, Rackham, Dulac; observing Belasco with unalloyed awe. Surviving correspondence from this era indicates an extremely confident and self-possessed child who adored his mother and had problems with spelling, as he would all his life.

"Dear Sweety," Cecil wrote on June 22, about 1888, from Echo Lake, New Jersey. "I hope you are well. Tuesday I was sitting in a tree in the orchard when a pretty oriole came in the tree that I was sitting and he began to sing, but then I scared hem. I am having a nice tine. The two trunks have come. The girl [written over the first attempt, which was gril] has arrived safely. A kiss to all.

Cecil B. DeMille

your loving son."

★

Henry's next collaboration with Belasco, *Lord Chumley*, was written for a young actor named E. H. Sothern. It was another hit, as was *The Charity Ball*, their third play. Then Henry worked on the translation and organized the first American production of *Lysistrata*, which Belasco directed in March 1889.

With success came pressure, and it appears Henry could be pettish, as his correspondence often apologizes for being short-tempered, possibly because he and Belasco were now going away to get most of their work done and Beatrice felt left out. In his letters, Henry is usually placating Beatrice, lathering her with emotion, and there are occasional references to things like her "tearful face" and her "poor, suffering letter." It's possible that Beatrice was unsure of her husband, but, given Cecil's memories of his mother and the personality indicated by her correspondence, it's more likely that Beatrice was a drama queen, playing at being insecure in order to provoke the desired response.

There was also evident tension between Beatrice and her mother-in-law, as Henry addressed his mother in the tones of a rapt Momma's Boy: "I love you, I admire you more than any woman on earth. My poor little child wife is full of faults beside you. I know she has no better friend than you. You are truer to her than her mother, and I love you for that, too. You are the guiding angel of our lives. She will know it someday—not in this world, because she is too weak."

In letters to his wife, Henry took the exact opposite tack: "Poor little M—thinks *she* is the flower. I am afraid she is not. But let her think so, if it is her happiness. You and I know who the flower is. You know whom I really trust and depend upon, for all my contradictory actions. Kiss my boys . . ."

At times, Henry runs back and forth between his mother and wife like a classic henpecked man, always trying to smooth over trouble. "I wouldn't cease writing, my Darling. I couldn't quite stand that. Let me have a letter or so, that I can show to M—. I must hear from you. Make your letters so she can read them. I will make mine so nobody can read them but you. Kiss my sweet ones, my precious babies, give love to all . . ."

Working with the tempestuous Belasco, living with the tempestuous Beatrice, and attempting to mediate between his wife and his tempestuous mother must have been exhausting for Henry deMille.

★

William remembered one episode from childhood as a definitive metaphor for the differing personalities of himself and his brother. Beatrice had taken her boys to the New York Athletic Club, then located at the corner of 55th and Sixth Avenue. Cecil and William were part of a demonstration about how to save nonswimmers from drowning. The boys, neither of whom could swim, were instructed to jump into the deep end of the pool and wait to be rescued.

Cecil, "with an immaturely regal gesture, tossed aside his robe, took a good look at the crowd, rushed out on the springboard and leaped blindly into space. He knew he was going to land in deep water, but had sublime faith that he would be pulled out amid tumultuous applause, which was exactly what happened."

William started out with an equivalent bravado, but, just before he got to the end of the board, suddenly realized that it would be tragic if he were to drown right in front of his mother. Looking over, he saw that "Mother's expression conveyed a mixture of gentle understanding and regret. At this point, I jumped, for the simple reason that I was afraid not to."

The brothers' personalities never altered—Cecil was forever drawing his sword and charging, while William hung back and grudgingly followed his younger brother, making saturnine comments the entire time.

As an old man, Cecil B. DeMille kept a childhood photo in his bedroom. It was taken in 1888, at Echo Lake. The seven-year-old Cecil, with curly hair at shoulder length, is holding a bouquet of flowers, while ten-year-old Bill is holding

Homer Q. Putnam, the family dog, gifted with the name of a character in one of Henry's plays.

In those sylvan days, the woods were alive with a bird the boys called "the chewink-chewee," after his evocative call. The chewink-chewee tended to establish a nest on a bank on the way to Strubel's brook, and Bill and Cecil watched several generations of chewink-chewees sent out into the world.

For exercise, there was a Swimming Club, which was run by a young reporter on the New York *World* named Albert Payson Terhune, later the author of famous dog stories. DeMille would always be grateful to Terhune for not only teaching him and Bill the manly arts of boxing and fencing, but for giving them an intimate knowledge and love of nature.

Along with his affinity for nature, Cecil was also a natural, not to mention original, storyteller. Witness this effort, written when he was nine:

MY HUNTING STORY

When I was nine I had a verry small gun. I whent out to see what I could shout. I was about five miles from home when it began to snow. I found no game, one little bird. It was snowing verry fast when I started for home. I had to pas by a house that had a verry saveg dog. It was no fun to here that big dog barking in the snow. Some years ago I had a fine mastif pup. I only had it about four months, when it was stolen. I had nat senn him for three years. And so the dog came running for me, and I mistoke his joy for hate, and shot. He gave a yelp, and quickened his speed. I drew my knife and waited for him, when suddenly I huerd a noise behimd me. I turnd half round to see a large Panther crouching behind me. On came the dog, but to my joy he sprang past me and caut the Panther by the throat and speedily put an end to him and then turnd to receve my knife blow. When he fell deing at my feet I saw to my sarowe that it was my pup come to my aid. I neeld down by him. He looked up in my face and liced my hand, but I could not save him. He died a minit affterwrod from my gun shot. I thrwe him ofver my back and carid him home. And now he stands in are parler in the same possichon he was in when he saved my life.

Cecil possessed certain attributes from birth: a devotion to simple but compelling lines of melodramatic action, and a wretched sense of spelling.

Aside from his adored parents, Cecil was also entranced by his father's brother Richard, who spelled his last name with the uppercase D and who lived on Patchen Avenue in Brooklyn. Richard's most exotic quality was that he could play a game of chess without being in the room. "He would sit writing," remembered Cecil, "and he would just call the moves to you. You would call back your move to him and he'd never stop writing, or whatever he was doing, and he would beat you. He had an amazing mind."

2

Near century's end, America was awash in extravagance. The country's architectural taste ran toward turrets and gingerbread cornices on houses, ostrich
feather boas and stiff bustles on women. Formality was de rigueur; people dressed
up to play croquet or badminton. Similarly, the theater was a place for spectacle
rather than simplicity. Meeting this need was the dramatic team of Belasco and
deMille.

Belasco brought dramatic lighting and elaborate, three-dimensional sets to
the theater. His carefully designed stage pictures and adherence to the star system
resulted in something that might be termed romantic realism—absolute authenticity of environment propping up plays that relied on the rip-roaring melodrama of
the post–Civil War era.

The writing didn't necessarily service the acting, or even the characters.
Rather, it serviced the direction—Belasco's rhythms and beats, Belasco's miraculous control of color and sets, all of which obscured the fact that his taste in plays
wasn't any good.

It's probable that Henry was attracted to Belasco for many of the same reasons he was attracted to Beatrice: energy, a sense of command, instinctive intelligence, and an absolute ability to deal with whatever circumstance threw at him.
Henry and his partner were opposites emotionally as well as physically—Henry tall
and graceful, with thinning reddish hair and measured voice; Belasco a dynamic
fireplug with black hair turning prematurely white, abrupt speech, and a fiery,
sensual temperament.

For the young Cecil, who stood in the wings and watched his father and Belasco rehearse their plays and who wept at the performances, these shows were a
passage into a world of glamour that transcended even the throbbing theatricality
embodied by Belasco himself.

Three hits in a row lifted Henry up into the loftier precincts of the theater;
in November 1889, he was proposed for membership in the Players Club by

26

Daniel Frohman, and seconded by E. H. Sothern. "I was elected a member of the Players Club, 16 Gramercy Park, November 14, 1889," noted Henry proudly in his diary. With money came responsibility, and Henry took out more life insurance—$10,000 worth in August of 1890, and another $10,000 in February of 1893. A little while after that, Henry took his younger son to lunch with famed actor Edwin Booth. Cecil would remember that lunch all his life.

Three of the four Belasco-deMille collaborations played at the Lyceum Theatre in New York, and each of them was more popular with the public than with critics. William Winter, the first serious American theater critic, called *The Wife* a "sentimental confection" and said that it owed more to "the far inferior and much easier method of literary and theatrical photography" than to the standards of Sheridan and Congreve. On the other hand, the *Times* and the *Herald* loved *The Wife* and said that it was an important American play.

The Belasco-deMille partnership soon attained a position of power and influence, but there was a serpent in the tree. In mid-1890, Belasco became infatuated with Mrs. Leslie Carter, who had just been divorced by her husband on the grounds of energetic adultery with five men. Belasco was thunderstruck by the possibilities of her personality on the stage and the possibilities of her body in his bed. He determined to turn her into the greatest actress of the American stage. This painstaking instruction took a while—Belasco's technical rehearsals alone could last for weeks—so Henry was left to his own devices, although he seems to have had some nominal Belasco-related duties, possibly instructing Mrs. Carter.

"Yesterday I found time to call on Mrs. Carter," Henry wrote his wife on Lyceum Theatre stationery. "Oh! My! but she can persuade. I did not yield, however. I will tell you all about it . . . A long embrace and sweet, sweet kisses from your Devoted, Ever Loving, Ever Longing, Ever Trusting Husband."

While Belasco was otherwise occupied, Henry set to work adapting a German play called *The Lost Paradise*, but was called back to work by Belasco. Henry and David set up shop in Washington, North Carolina, to work on their new play. William was with them, but he fell ill with scarlet fever and was very sick for nine long weeks. Once William was out of the woods, Henry and Belasco finished the play in July.

Men and Women opened in October 1890 and ran until the end of March 1891—another hit. But it was the last collaboration between the two men. With his wallet fortified, Belasco returned to the instruction of Mrs. Carter. Their initial collaboration was *The Heart of Maryland*, in which the climax involved the star hanging by the clapper of a giant bell to keep it from ringing, thereby saving the life of her lover. As the curtain came down, the audience erupted in tumultuous cheers.

Belasco had found the final piece of his formula: a dramatically sensational climax of action rather than personal revelation. He was now the dominant purveyor of theatrical melodrama in America and would remain so until about 1915, when he would be overtaken theatrically by Eugene O'Neill and cinematically by Cecil B. DeMille.

With Belasco occupied with matters dramatic and erotic, Henry returned to *The Lost Paradise*, which proved successful. He used most of his accrued royalties for seventy-six acres on a hill above Pompton Lakes, New Jersey, and an estate that would be called Pamlico. The house was finished by Easter 1892, a three-story Victorian with turrets and a wide porch overlooking a lake, on the east side of the road leading from Pompton to Oakland, all of it surrounded by the Ramapo Mountains.

A new friend of the family was the bandleader John Philip Sousa whom Cecil remembered as a stuffy, pompous man, although he enjoyed riding horses, which was a plus to the young boy. Another neighbor in Pompton was none other than Annie Oakley, and Cecil remembered throwing mud balls into the air so she could practice her shooting.

Cecil's first crush was on a girl named Olive Reimer, whose father enjoyed telling the children magnificent stories drawn from literature—"The Murders in the Rue Morgue," Balzac, and so forth. It wasn't until years later that Cecil realized that Mr. Reimer became a storytelling sage only when he was roaring drunk.

It was around this time that Cecil devised an alternate heroic persona for himself. He called this alter ego the Champion Driver—Cecil's amalgamation of Robin Hood, Ulysses Simpson Grant, and Samson. This dashing figure would eventually be incarnated in the movies by Douglas Fairbanks Sr. and Errol Flynn, but for Cecil the Champion Driver resembled no one but Cecil. In his mind, the Champion Driver was the man of action who saved the fair damsel and, by extension, America, destroying his enemies in the process—or, in one unfortunate case, Beatrice's lovingly tended artichokes, decimated as Cecil laid waste to imaginary enemies. Cecil would carry this alter ego around with him for the rest of his life, partly in jest, partly seriously.

In February 1891, it was announced that the successful Belasco-deMille partnership was no more. Henry deMille's politely veiled comment to his diary was, "It was during the last few days of this year [1890] that I found that David's interest and mine no longer lay together, and in perfect amity and with mutual regard for each other we determined not to work together for the present."

The theatrical trade papers suggested that Belasco's obsession with Mrs. Leslie Carter was the cause of the breakup. Henry's refusal to elaborate—which would not have been the case had the issue been creative or financial—would tend to confirm the suspicions of the trades. As Henry's letters to his wife show, he was not averse to discussing his worries and fears, but, to a high-minded Victorian gentleman, an argument about a friend's mistress was not a fit subject to be aired.

In any case, Belasco was leaving Henry and his family in a much stronger position than he had found them. The deMilles' third child, Agnes, was born on April

23, 1891. It was a difficult birth; Beatrice nearly died, and Henry had to clear his desk so the doctors could use it to lay out their surgical instruments.

In a spectacular example of the strange synchronicities of fate, in 1892 Henry wrote a fan letter to the social philosopher and economist Henry George. George had published *Progress and Poverty* in 1879, a dense, idealistic book that advocated the abolition of all taxes save a tax on land. George was probably the first American economist to be taken seriously in Europe, and *Progress and Poverty* became one of the most popular nonfiction works of the nineteenth century, attracting admirers that ranged from Leo Tolstoy to Pope Leo XIII. George Bernard Shaw gave Henry George credit for converting him to socialism. George ran for mayor of New York in 1886, and came in second, ahead of a young Theodore Roosevelt— an admirer of the land tax. (George's ideas still attract a thousand students a year to the Henry George School of Social Science in New York.)

Henry could have had no way of knowing that his oldest son would marry the daughter of Henry George, or that the marriage would prove an epic mismatch primarily because George's daughter actively embodied her father's high-minded ideals, while Henry's son lived in the world.

At the end of 1892, Henry paid $5,062 on the mortgage of Pamlico, $4,300 of that being a loan from his mother. Henry's first—and last—Christmas in his new house was a happy one. William, Cecil, and Henry cut down their own Christmas tree on the land surrounding the lake. "The boys decorated it," wrote Henry in his diary, "and none of us were permitted to enter the parlor until Sunday after service; when the room was darkened, the tree lighted and the presents distributed. My own [present] was a complete set of Ruskin's works . . . this great soldier of the Truth."

On January 8, 1893, Henry deMille delivered a sermon at the Pompton Christ Church. On January 25, he went into New York to see the new Belasco play starring Mrs. Leslie Carter at Charles Frohman's Empire Theatre. Henry stayed at the Ashland House, and complained that the club's sewage problems upset his digestion.

The last entry in Henry's diary is dated Thursday, January 26: "Attended second performance of the Theater of Arts and Letters with Mildred and Stammie, 'The Harvest' by Clyde Fitch and 'Squirrel Inn' by Frank R. Stockton and Gene Presbrey at 5th Ave. Theater. The morning of Thursday, lectured to the Senior Class at the American Academy of the Dramatic Arts. That night went to the Lambs Club, 8 West 29th Street, with Wilton Lackaye, Tom Oberle and R. C. Cotton. Sat talking until 7:30 next morning."

About February 1, Henry became ill at home. Initially, it was not regarded as serious, but then he began hemorrhaging. A Dr. Colfax of Pompton and a Dr. Tartaball of New York did what they could, but it soon became clear that Henry deMille was dying of typhoid.

"He sent for me and he saw the family one at a time," remembered Cecil. "It was in our house at Pompton, New Jersey—and he asked me a question. And I couldn't answer because I was choked and I couldn't answer—I did not know that he was dying—I didn't know how sick he was even. I was a little boy, but something prevented my talking because my throat was tight as you are when you're about to cry—so I couldn't answer and he waited for a few minutes and he said, 'Well, run along and play.' I've never forgotten that and I never could get it from my mind—that he couldn't understand that I wanted to—I'm sure that he did—but he couldn't understand at the time what I wanted to tell him. I wanted to express my love and affection for him but I couldn't. I couldn't speak."

The halting phrasing of a man who customarily spoke in polished paragraphs is striking, as is the pain and guilt over his perception of having failed his father. DeMille would return to this episode again and again over the years, fearful that his dying father took silence for indifference. The possibility that he had failed his father haunted Cecil, and the implicit self-reproach grew until he could barely complete the story.

Henry deMille died in his house on Pompton Lake at four in the morning on February 10, 1893. He was thirty-nine years old. His sons were fourteen and eleven, his daughter was two.

The next day his casket was in the center of the living room. Beatrice brought the boys in to see their dead father. "She put her arms around us and spoke, not to us but to him: 'May your sons be as fine and noble and good as you were. May they follow in your steps . . . ' "

The obituaries in the New York papers paid tribute, although they were dutiful rather than inspired, and none of them offered any quotes from David Belasco: "Mr. deMille was a slender, scholarly looking man, and was liked by the people of the dramatic profession," said one. "He was very exact and methodical in business dealings, and he and Belasco made a large amount of money out of their popular plays."

Another asserted, "the idea that he wrote the Belasco-DeMille plays . . . and that his collaborator merely dramatized and staged them, is a fallacy. They were joint workers in every sense of the word, alike as to invention, wording and formation. . . . In personal bent and habits he was a literary man and socially was of unspotted character."

Henry died intestate, so Beatrice had to get busy. What she had to work with was the house, which was free and clear, and $20,000 in life insurance. Her granddaughter, the choreographer Agnes deMille, would characterize her as "a domineering and aggressive woman, with the clothes sense and some of the business scruples of a Gypsy." All in all, a fairly necessary set of qualities for a young widow with three small children at the end of the nineteenth century.

At first, she and Bill wrestled with an uncompleted play Henry had left, but the results were not satisfactory and Beatrice knew it. Just a few months after her husband died, Beatrice converted part of the house into the Henry C. deMille

Preparatory Boarding and Day School for Boys and Girls. (Cecil had been attending another school, where he was beaten up by a boy named Lester Smith, who held a baseball bat in his right arm while hitting Cecil with his left. "Don't use the bat!" begged Cecil. "I don't need to," replied Smith.)

Beatrice used some of the insurance money to build an addition to the house for the boarding pupils, and she also added a tennis court and baseball diamond. She finagled references from Dr. Nicholas Murray Butler of Columbia, and the Episcopal bishop of Newark. On February 10, 1894, she added a postscript to her husband's diary: "Just one year since the death of my dear husband, of typhoid hemorrhages of the intestines!

"I shall try and keep up this narrative of the family for the sake of my dearest children William, Cecil, and baby Agnes Beatrice, to all of whom, in the years to come, it will undoubtedly prove of interest. I shall take up the narrative where their father left it in January, 1893."

But there were no more additions to the diary; Beatrice didn't have the time. She had to take care of her children, and take care of them she would.

★

An ad in the *Pasquannock Valley Argus* announced that the deMille school offered "full classical and scientific courses, modern languages, theory of music, drawing, painting and physical culture." Also offered were "tennis, baseball, rowing, skating and coasting." Tuition and board came to $500 a year.

Beatrice was setting a viable, intelligent course for herself and her children. But vicious fate wasn't done with her just yet. On February 11, 1895, Agnes came down with what seemed to be a cold. By the next morning it was clear that something else was happening, something much worse. Beatrice sent Bill on horseback through a blizzard to get a doctor, but it was too late. Agnes died—not of a cold, but of spinal meningitis.

Like her father, Agnes was laid out in a coffin in the hall of their home. Beatrice took Bill and Cecil down to the hall lit only by candlelight. She made them kiss the cold, dead face of their little sister and swear that they would never in their lives do anything to any woman that they would not have wanted done to Agnes.

This scene, somewhere between Dickens and Poe, would never be forgotten by either of the brothers—how could they, even if they had wanted to? Although he would eventually depart from both the spirit and the letter of the vow, Cecil probably remained a virgin until his wedding night. Bill, precocious sexually as well as professionally, had far more personal history than his younger brother.

Agnes was cremated and her ashes placed next to those of Henry deMille. Beatrice kept the letters and telegrams of condolence for Agnes all her life. After her death, Cecil kept them for all his life. Moreover, he kept a miniature of Agnes on his watch chain, honoring her and his parents at the same time.

★

Cecil would say that his mother was a fine teacher but a bad businesswoman. He might also have paid tribute to her as a superb role model of industry and diligence. It was her example as well as her personality that would form his own life. Like many men brought up primarily by females, he adored women, was comfortable with them and perfectly capable of deferring to them.

It was, however, difficult for him to be equally conciliatory with men. With men, he would tend toward the peremptory and he would have only a couple of intimate friendships with male peers because other men were potential challengers. Cecilia, Cecil's daughter—whose name indicates the breadth of his very secure ego—would tell her cousin Agnes, Bill's daughter, that "Father has no friends, hundreds of admirers, but no friends, not one in the world." It was an exaggeration—Jesse Lasky, for one, would become a true friend—but not by much.

Beatrice couldn't have been too terrible a businesswoman, for the deMille school lasted for more than ten years, even if things were a tight squeeze for much of the time. Evelyn Nesbit, the mistress of Stanford White, was a student at the school for a time, and remembered it in her memoirs as "a large, yellow, rambling structure set on a hill in the beautiful Ramapos. . . . [Beatrice] ruled over less than 20 pupils and never did manage to make the place financially successful. And yet it was a splendid school; the girls enjoyed a homelike atmosphere and the best of teachers."

At Christmas, Beatrice threw a party that lasted from December 25 to New Year's. Students could invite relatives or close friends, and young male guests were domiciled in a separate building, so the proprieties were observed at all times. Nesbit remembered that Beatrice was "a woman of distinct personality [and] had her own ideas of dress." She noted that Bill reigned as the family intellectual and was busy writing a play called *Strongheart* in a study called "The Dreamery" located at the top of the house.

Nesbit had not come there for an education, but to get out of New York. Stanford White had recently discovered that she was having an affair with John Barrymore.

With his randy theatricality, Barrymore referred to Nesbit as his "quivering pink poppy." To get her away from the dashing young actor, White spirited Nesbit away to Pamlico and Beatrice. To keep her busy, Bill gave her fencing lessons, and Nesbit referred to him in her diary as "Bill deMille, that pie-faced mut who is in cahoots with Stanford to keep me prisoner."

Harry Thaw, another young blade about town in love with Nesbit, followed her to Pamlico, as did Barrymore. Beatrice did her best to keep her young charge away from her suitors, but Barrymore left love notes scattered on the tennis court and other places around the property.

Nesbit and Beatrice became close, and Beatrice counseled her to avoid Barrymore—the actor was mad, bad, and dangerous to know. She should think about Harry Thaw; he was wealthy and good-looking. Avoid the frying pan; jump right into the fire.

Nesbit had her doubts—her diary revealed that she was suspicious of Thaw's sexuality, and with good reason—but she ended up marrying him anyway, although continuing her relationship with White. This juicy triangle culminated in Thaw's murder of White in 1906, on the roof theater of Madison Square Garden.

Introduced at trial was sworn evidence that Nesbit had three operations that had all been listed as "appendectomies"—the standard euphemism for an abortion. One of the said "appendectomies" had taken place at the deMille School. When the prosecutor asked, "Was the operation performed on you at Pompton a criminal operation?" Thaw's attorney jumped up and said that Nesbit could hardly testify to that as she had been under anesthesia.

★

Bill did his best to fill a paternal role for his younger brother. He went out of his way to familiarize Cecil with Wagner's operas, which forever after remained Cecil's idea of the pinnacle in music.

When he was fifteen, Cecil was sent to the Pennsylvania Military College—a glorified boarding school. Beatrice bartered his tuition for the tuition of the daughter of the academy's commandant at Pamlico. Cecil had to wear a military uniform and engage in military practice. "Oh, the long and dreary winter!" he scribbled in a workbook. "Oh, the cold and cruel winter!" Next to "auxiliary unknown quantity," he writes, "What in pink hell is the meaning of this?" Under the phrase "binomial formula," he writes, "If x = my dinner, and y = the cavity my dinner should fill, then x is negative and y is very possitive." At one point, he amuses himself by drawing a naval battle in his algebra book.

While he attended the military college, Cecil was designated Cadet No. 214, which was only one of the reasons he hated the place. Cold baths, drills at dawn, and long lectures on manly virtues were other reasons. On the other hand, he learned to ride, to shoot, and to box—all necessary skills for surviving in show business. He also learned the value of discipline, the thrill of command, and an emphasis on physical fitness, all of which he would practice throughout his life and which would come in handy sooner rather than later.

Cecil's letters from the military college are typically idiosyncratic in matters of punctuation. They're also boyishly charming and funny, as this, from April 16, 1897: "I am just in the middle of 'Quo Vadis' and I think it is one of the finest books I have ever read, but I nearly lost a front tooth trying to pronounce the author's name." A month later, he wrote, "Tomorrow we go to Chadsford [sic] on horseback, that is eighteen miles from Chester (the cavalry I mean, not the whole corps). Well at any rate we all had to pay half and the college paid half, it was 90 cents, when I heard this I refused to go, but a friend of mine named Rhinstrom paid for me in spite of all I could do, I told him I did not know when I could pay him back but he said, I could go plum to —! and he paid my 90 cents, and I won't ask Mother for anymore money, so what am I to do?"

Obviously, money was tight. Cecil washed carriages for spare change and tried to pretend he was interested in the curriculum. "We are to be addressed this morning by the Rev. Dr. Somebody from Phil. and this afternoon by the Rev. Dr. Somebodyelse. That is the program for the day as nearly as I can find out. . . . Will you, if you have time, send me a list of the misspelled words in this letter."

Beatrice clearly favored William, just as Henry had. It was William who studied at a *gymnasium* in Freiberg, Germany, while Cecil made do with Pennsylvania Military College. Later, when Bill was stranded in Germany, Beatrice used some of Cecil's share of his father's estate to get her older son home. Still later, Bill would attend Columbia, while Cecil enrolled in the American Academy of Dramatic Arts, where his tuition was waived because of Henry's seven years of service there. Bill lived in New York while attending Columbia, while Cecil commuted from New Jersey every day—a four-hour round-trip.

Because Bill was manifestly the Young Prince, he developed a sense of his own innate worth that would lead him to develop a noncompetitive personality, as well as eventually provoke serious conflicts with his mother. Beatrice and Cecil would always hustle, while Bill waited for the world to come to him; besides that, Beatrice was a profligate spender, and Bill would come to resent her constant desire for reimbursement for all that she had done for him.

Perhaps because nobody put a very high value on Cecil, Cecil didn't either. Despite his clear second-string status within the family, he was generous in spirit. Although he never got first choice of anything throughout his childhood and adolescence, it was Cecil who would take care of his mother and pay all her expenses as soon as financially feasible.

Cecil's audition report at the American Academy of Dramatic Arts, filled out by AADA president Franklin Haven Sargent, captures his character as well as any single piece of paper could:

Age: 17

Height: 5-10½

Weight: 152

Proportions: Good (Athletic)

Parentage: Henry C. deMille

Personality: Pleasing, aesthetic

Esthetic Taste: Probably good

Dramatic Interest: Undeveloped

Personality: Nervous-making

In that era, the AADA held classes and rehearsals at Carnegie Hall, and for performances used the Carnegie Hall Lyceum and the Empire Theatre at 40th and Broadway. It was a two-year program, with the first year including technical subjects such as fencing, pantomime, diction, stage mechanics, makeup, and stage business, and the final examinations consisting of complete performances.

The second year mostly consisted of mounting and performing productions at the Empire Theatre. In either year, the classes were enlivened by guest lectures from such famous talents as John Drew, Joseph Jefferson, and Daniel Frohman. The catalogue stated that the cost of living in New York was between $5 to $15 a week for the school year, which, in Cecil's senior year of 1899–1900 ran from September 15 to May 14.

While Cecil was learning the rudiments of the theatrical profession, Bill graduated from Columbia in 1900; among his classmates was Upton Sinclair. Professor Brander Matthews encouraged his students to go to the theater often and keep notebooks of observations, and Bill took him seriously; his notebooks fill six scrapbooks. On *The Squaw Man*, with Theodore Roberts and William S. Hart, which Bill saw on December 5, 1905, and which Cecil made into a movie in 1913–1914: "Very good. Tricky in places but effective. Faulty in technique as to one use of coincidence in meetings etc. First act: conventional but interesting. Second act: crude—boring Englishman there. Third and Fourth: strong, and the real stuff. Good scheme following the newer technique of writing a five-act play and leaving out the fifth act."

★

At the academy, Cecil clashed with the legendary teacher Charles Jehlinger, who had been a student in the first academy class in 1884, returned to AADA in 1896, and would remain there until his death in 1952. Despite his fear of Jehlinger ("the only man in the world I was ever frightened of," Cecil would remember shortly before he died) he nevertheless absorbed some of the teacher's temperament and approach.

Jehlinger was a neatly turned-out little man, with wire-rimmed glasses and a center part in his hair. Accompanying the pinched look was a cutting manner. His approach to the profession was peremptory: "Stop acting" was one of his favorite bromides, which would usually be followed by "Don't think of acting, think of living." He hated overtly dramatic acting and taught his young charges that to be a successful actor you had to have the hide of a rhino and the heart of a baby.

He was a hard taskmaster who might greet a scene with "Crude, but there are possibilities."

Jehlinger's approach was intensely practical, with none of the soul searching for Truth that would accompany the efforts of many acting teachers. Cecil's main objection to Jehlinger was his habit of imposing his own conception of a part on an actor, making them little more than ventriloquist's dummies. Cecil believed this was a bad way to teach the art of acting; besides, Cecil didn't like being told what to do. Others did. Besides DeMille, some of Jehlinger's acting students included William Powell, Spencer Tracy, Edward G. Robinson, and Hume Cronyn—actors of charm as well as substance, with an overriding commitment to craft and professionalism.

Among the faculty was the fine character actress May Robson, and one teacher who met with Cecil's wholehearted approval: Wellington Putnam, an elocutionist who emphasized the vowel sounds and helped turn DeMille into a superb speaker. Cecil's own memory of his youthful self was of a student who kept mostly to himself, had few friends, and needed self-confidence, the Champion Driver notwithstanding. One of the friends Cecil made at the academy was Wilfred Buckland, who had been a student of Henry's and who was on the faculty teaching makeup. Buckland would later become Belasco's art director and, later still, Cecil's, revolutionizing the art of motion picture design.

Cecil graduated from the academy in 1900. The graduation exercise involved a full-scale production of a play called *The Arcady Trail*. In the audience was Charles Frohman. Cecil was hired by Frohman for a small part in a play entitled *Hearts Are Trumps*, which opened at the Garden Theatre on February 21, 1900, and ran for ninety-three performances. The only other actor of note in the cast was Claire McDowell, who would play a lot of parts for D. W. Griffith. In all respects but one, it seems to have been an unremarkable production, but a notation in the playbill strikes an eerie chord: "Moving pictures in Act III, Scene 4, made by William Paley and reproduced by the famous Kalatechnoscope."

Cecil was only eighteen years old when he made his Broadway debut. He must have thought he was one of the chosen; he must have thought it was going to be easy.

3

After *Hearts Are Trumps* completed its New York run, there was a summer hiatus, but the show went on tour in the fall. When they got to Washington, the cast was joined by a girl who, DeMille remembered, "wasn't a very good actress, but there was something about her that quite attracted me—her breeding, charm and good taste." One scene in the play took place at a modiste shop, and every night after DeMille finished his part, he would sit out front and watch the young girl play her scene.

The girl's name was Constance Adams, the eldest of five children of Judge Frederick Adams of East Orange, New Jersey. Born in 1873, she was eight years older than Cecil and carried herself with a statuesque self-confidence that was emphasized by the long brown hair that she wore in the becoming manner of the Gibson Girl. After Constance's mother died, her father married his former sister-in-law, after which Constance rebelled and went on the stage against the Judge's express wishes.

In Newark, DeMille and the young actress met at a restaurant and began a conversation. She told him that when the tour got to Boston she was staying at a boardinghouse at 9 Beacon Street. DeMille hadn't booked a room there, but he immediately changed his plans. It was, he remembered, a very old house with lavender-colored windowpanes, and the theater they played in was the Boston Museum. "I played the part of a young barrister," DeMille remembered, "and was very bad."

By then the two were in love, and on the last day of 1900, as the clock struck midnight and they sat on the steps of the boardinghouse at 9 Beacon Street, Cecil proposed and Constance accepted.

"Where do you suppose we will be at the beginning of the next century?" she asked.

"I can't tell you the place," he replied, "but I know we will be together."

As proposals go, it was not only smooth, but romantic and prophetic.

While Cecil and Constance were beginning the process of becoming experienced theatrical troupers, they were also working on getting Judge Adams to agree
to the marriage. Constance's father was appalled; an itinerant actor was not his
idea of a suitable son-in-law. But Constance was, in her ladylike way, immovable.

★

Between the school and starting up a literary agency—her latest brainstorm—
Beatrice somehow found time to write a feminist play. It was called *The Greatest
Thing in the World*, and opened in Washington in February 1900. It was obviously
a projection of Beatrice's feelings about herself and her situation: a widow with
two sons—one named Cecil—goes out into the world to make her fortune in business. She is condemned and faces losing custody of her children, but fights back
and wins both her children and a successful career.

"This is the woman's age," Beatrice announced in an interview, assuming the
same stentorian tone her son would use for his public pronouncements. "Every
relation between the sexes has changed because woman has changed. Hereafter
no woman is going to be married without feeling that she is getting as much as she
gives. That may sound like a crude statement of the matter, but expresses pretty
clearly what I mean. . . . This theme, women's intrinsic equality—lies very close to
my heart."

Beatrice's dynamism moved outward in every direction, at least partially because it had to—the deMille School would eventually close in December 1907.
Beatrice threw herself into her literary and theatrical agency, convincing Belasco
to let her handle the plays Henry and he had co-authored, then opened an office
in the Knickerbocker Building on Broadway.

Belasco continued to be a presence in the deMille family, and Cecil believed
that he helped them out financially on occasion, although both Beatrice and
Cecil would carry some surreptitious bitterness about Belasco to the end of their
lives.

Beatrice developed a solid client list; she became the agent for, among others,
Mary Roberts Rinehart, James Montgomery Flagg, Wilson Mizner, Zoë Akins,
Beaulah Marie Dix, and Avery Hopwood. And she found a couple of pretty good
actors, among them the future silent movie star Milton Sills.

★

After the tour of *Hearts Are Trumps* closed, grim reality set in. For several months,
Cecil lived on 45 cents a day. He and another man rented a room for $2 a week,
and had to share the bed. As he remembered from the lofty vantage point of
1920, "The Sixth avenue elevated ran over the foot of our bed." His next professional engagement was in Chicago and paid $20 a week, out of which he had to
pay all his expenses except railroad fare. It was the first time he had ever been so
far away from home. DeMille and an actor he had met at the American Academy

of Dramatic Arts named Carl Eckstrom shared an upper berth on the train to Chicago.

Their boardinghouse was on Michigan Avenue, and their room was on the top floor. Cecil and Eckstrom bought 10 cents' worth of ice cream, but since the room didn't come with silverware they had to scoop out the ice cream with some cardboard they tore out of a box. That first night, a murder was committed outside their apartment building—two men pulled another man out of a hansom cab and beat him to death while the stunned actors watched from a window.

The spring of 1901 brought Cecil parts in a couple of Frohman productions (*To Have and to Hold* and *Are You a Mason?*). DeMille began to learn some of the coping strategies unknown to those outside the profession. Chewing gum was good for emergency radiator repairs; if you didn't have an iron, you could still press a newly washed handkerchief by pasting it flat onto a bathroom mirror. In the morning, it would not only be dry, but suitable for folding.

During the summer, Cecil was at liberty; in the early winter, he was again called by Frohman for a play called *Alice of Old Vincennes*. By this time, Constance had somehow convinced her father of Cecil's suitability as a son-in-law. On August 16, 1902, they married at the Adams family home at 77 Washington Street in East Orange. It was a small wedding, just the immediate family; Cecil's best man was his brother. The flowers were lilies of the valley.

Marrying Constance was the most crucial decision Cecil ever made. Constance Adams DeMille was serene, beautiful, steadfast, absolutely reliable, remembered by everyone who knew her as a perfect Victorian lady. Cecil's niece, Agnes deMille, who didn't like a lot of people in the family or, for that matter, out of the family, remembered Constance as "softspoken, regal, trailing soft velvet or chiffon. . . . Her voice was halting but soft and had the modulation of a trained actress. Her humor was superb, though quietly expressed." Cecil's pet name for his wife would be Gretchen, probably deriving from the name of Faust's true love.

As Anne Edwards noted, "with her full bosom, small waist and smoldering, somewhat Latinate looks, Constance might have been suspected of possessing a sensuous nature." Evidently, the reverse was true. Constance was smart, observant, cool-headed, and deeply religious. She had immense dignity, a natural reserve, and nobody in her long life ever called her "Connie." She was the sort of woman whose entrance into a room is invariably met by gentlemen standing up. Men respected her, women trusted her.

Constance's calmness gentled Cecil's rambunctious temperament. Cecil sensed that he needed that gentling, and valued Constance all the more for it. Agnes deMille summed up the relationship between her uncle and aunt: "He *adored* her."

Over the years, Constance would endure several long-term extramarital relationships on Cecil's part, but she learned to live with them—and with him. She instinctively understood that she was part of a family concern, very much in the

French manner. She would always be the dominant part of Cecil's emotional life, as well as his professional life. Cecil's attorney Neil McCarthy would write, "I consider her counsel and advice as valuable as that of anyone in the business, not alone because of her knowledge of the business, but because of her ability to think clearly."

★

As soon as the reception was over, the newlyweds were off to join the E. H. Sothern company, with Cecil playing Osric in *Hamlet*, a supporting role in his father's play *Lord Chumley*, and another part in *If I Were King*. Cecil was later to pay tribute to Sothern by saying that working with him was "like going back to school, the best school a future director could attend."

Once something went wrong with a performance; at eleven, immediately after the final curtain, Sothern ordered a full rehearsal of the second act. Needless to say, the second act ran like a clock thereafter. DeMille said that everything he ever knew about directing crowds he learned from Sothern: "Sothern gave every single extra an appropriate, distinct, individual line to say. The audience could not hear the lines but they saw and heard a crowd of real people talking and acting like real people."

Over the next several years, Cecil and Constance became experienced itinerant actors, the migrant workers of the theatrical profession. As an old man, Cecil would reminisce with intense nostalgia about the rickety wooden railroad coaches, with windows that were referred to as "poker windows," because it took jacks or better to get them open. Then there was the time in West Virginia when a train crashed. Constance had been admiring the wildflowers on the side of the tracks when the collision occurred. A fire extinguisher came down on Cecil's head and exploded, covering him with toxic chemicals. People were screaming, Cecil was furious and in pain, and all Constance said was, "Oh, now we can get out and pick wildflowers."

"From that moment," he would remember, "I have never lacked confidence in her ability to handle any situation calmly."

One post-Sothern jaunt took them through Canada, and DeMille remembered that for the entire tour they were never warm, because they didn't have enough money to stay in hotels with heated rooms. The hotel lobbies and corridors were heated, but the rooms themselves were icy.

On another tour, Cecil and Constance stayed at a boardinghouse run by a woman who kept a python as a ratter. The python enjoyed wrapping himself around the stair banister at night, so when Cecil and Constance came in after their performance they had to be careful not to grab the banister on the way up to their room, lest the python wake up angry. "He would tell that story with such obvious joy," remembered his granddaughter Cecilia, "that I felt it was a very happy time in their marriage."

While on the road, Cecil and Constance kept in touch with their families via postcards. Most of the messages were about their adventures rather than their plays. On May 25, 1903, Cecil sent his mother a postcard of Pikes Peak: "Great Scott, have you ever spent a night 14,147 feet high. You wake up every 15 minutes gasping for breath. It is 5 above zero and the 25 of May. Yesterday we could see the New Mexico range 250 miles away. We have many strange things to tell. Love from C. & C."

On June 16, Constance wrote Beatrice on a postcard of Mount Tamalpais, "Dear Mother, Cecil took the trip with Mr. McCloskey up this mountain yesterday. It was very beautiful and most interesting. I stayed at home to study . . . as there had been a row and the understudy left the company but she has been taken back now so my virtue was all for nothing. Lots of love. Constance."

A day later, Constance chimed in from Oakland: "Dear mother, we left San Francisco yesterday afternoon. Oakland is a lovely place much more my idea of California than anything we have seen yet. We are both well. Lots of Love, Constance."

Cecil and Constance were again in E. H. Sothern's company when they opened the Mason Opera House in Los Angeles on June 18, 1903, with *If I Were King*. Sothern played François Villon, with Cecil in the role of Colin De Cayeulx. (Constance seems to have been along for the sightseeing, as she doesn't appear in the cast list although she might have appeared under a pseudonym.)

The young DeMilles were nothing if not well traveled. By July 6, they were in Butte, Montana. "Dear Mother, it is the fifth of July and we are bundled up in our heaviest overcoats. And today we had a little flurry of snow. Butte is the wildest yet. Love to all will write soon. Cecil."

It's obvious that DeMille adored performing in front of an audience, any audience. Years later, one of his employees asked him about his youthful years on stage: "Doesn't an actor get tired of playing the same role in the same play night after night?"

"You're not an actor if you do," he replied succinctly.

These years of trouping had some practical benefits—much later, DeMille would assert that he could name at least one hotel in practically any town in America. Constance's memories of those hotels often focused on the problems they had because of Cecil's refusal to part with the only pets they could afford: a couple of little squirrels in a basket cage.

The life of a roving actor could be terribly grim, but DeMille was observant and sensitive, and he learned the rough but emotionally sincere life of America between the coasts. DeMille would believe, with considerable justification, that theatrical actors, directors, and producers began to lose touch with the mass audience once the age of touring shows died out a few decades later. The touring years would be invaluable to him, for the America between the coasts would constitute the primary audience for the movies he would make.

★

Part of the reason that Cecil adored his mother was her ardent spirit. "She was always for anything new," he would remember. "Anything that had adventure in it, she was for." In so many ways, Cecil was his mother's son—always ready for a new challenge, always ready to venture outward or put himself at risk. (A close friend would later compare Cecil to the intrepid foreign correspondent Richard Harding Davis.) So it was no surprise that Cecil loved the West as soon as he saw it; indeed, he loved the *idea* of the West *before* he saw it.

"We wanted to come out west, because we loved it out here," DeMille would remember in 1933. "Mrs. DeMille and I were travelling with E. H. Sothern in 1903—opened the old Mason Opera House, played in *If I Were King* and *Hamlet*. I loved the west so much and thought of every excuse in the world to get out here—even of giving up the stage to come out here and maybe buy a ranch. Both Mrs. DeMille and I were so completely lost in the whole idea of the west."

DeMille remembered that on that 1903 trip he was making $35 a week and Constance was making $20 a week, the Pullman berth cost them $27, and there wasn't a lot left over. "The first time I saw the Rocky Mountains, I woke her up quickly and said to look at that sight. We knew then that the west would be the place for us."

During a Canadian tour of Henry deMille and David Belasco's play *Lord Chumley*, Cecil came down with the measles, and Bill came out from New York to play the part. He took no salary and after a couple of weeks when Cecil was back on his feet, Bill was hit for $200 to keep the company going.

Richard deMille, Cecil's son, would obliquely refer to "difficulties" in the marriage in these early years. "Constance was quietly dismayed at Cecil's luxurious notion of marital bliss. She yearned to give him all he wanted, but it went against her nature and against her background. Disappointed by her restraint, he accepted invitations from more excitable young women ready to give and glad to receive sharper if less loving pleasures."

Other family members, including Agnes deMille, asserted that the marriage was happy for years, and that signs of a sexual misalliance weren't evident until after the birth of their daughter Cecilia in 1908.

★

While Cecil was tussling with railroad timetables and enduring unheated boardinghouses, his brother was finding success. William took a stand against prejudice in his play *Strongheart*, first performed in 1905, the story of an Indian who goes to an eastern college, falls in love with the sister of one of his white classmates but cannot maneuver past the prejudices of his friends. He returns west without the woman he loves.

Meanwhile, Cecil appeared in a play called *The Prince Chap* in New York and received a decent review: "Cecil B. DeMille was capital as the Earl and received a hearty round of applause, which was well-deserved." But Cecil wasn't sitting around waiting for the next audition. He also wrote an unproduced play entitled *The Pretender*, set in seventeenth-century Russia, as well as *Son of the Winds*, about a mythical Indian civilization. It also failed to earn a production.

Bill and Cecil collaborated on a play called *The Genius* years before Theodore Dreiser used the title for a novel. Beatrice retitled it *The Genius and the Model* and did a polish. It was produced in 1906 but ran for only twenty-one performances. During one particularly desperate moment, Cecil went on to tour with the Standard Opera Company in productions of *The Bohemian Girl, Martha, The Chimes of Normandy,* and *The Mikado.* He remembered that he acted, sang, booked theaters, managed, and even filled in when the conductor was indisposed. In between engagements, when times got bad, Cecil would get a loan from Bill, and it's a safe assumption that Beatrice helped out as well.

Probably at Beatrice's urging, David Belasco took on William as a collaborator, and William was credited alone for one big hit that Belasco produced and directed in 1907, *The Warrens of Virginia.* Bill thoughtfully wrote a part for his brother, and Belasco thoughtfully agreed to hire Cecil. Cecil signed a contract with Belasco on April 27, 1907, for the 1907–1908 season. It was a standard boilerplate contract—Belasco had to pay only half salary for Holy Week and the week before Christmas, the sort of arbitrary cheating that led to the formation of Actors' Equity. There was only one specific addendum: Belasco was obligated to pay for a sleeper compartment for Cecil while on tour. Cecil's salary was set at $65 a week in New York, $75 a week on tour, with rehearsals free, as was the norm in those pre-Equity days.

Although he was working steadily that year, Cecil was still paying off old debts, and was continually borrowing money from his brother. He borrowed $1,000 from Bill in March (at 5 percent interest), another $500 (also at 5 percent) two weeks later, $300 in April, another $200 a few weeks later, $200 in June, and $100 in October. All of the loans would eventually be repaid.

Until *Sunset Boulevard, The Warrens of Virginia* would serve as the height of Cecil's acting career, but since it was loosely based on an adventure of his grandfather, and was written by his brother, it's possible that his casting was not entirely due to his stage technique. Also in the cast was a young Canadian actress who had recently dumped her original name of Gladys Smith for the more aristocratic Mary Pickford. Actually, it was a good cast from top to bottom—also featured were Frank Keenan and Blanche Yurka.

Pickford recorded a spectacular example of Belasco's singular directorial techniques in her memoirs. During one rehearsal lasting far into the night, Belasco was working on the set of the dining room of a Virginia mansion. Belasco picked up a jar that was supposed to contain molasses and tasted it. Bellowing for the prop man, he commanded him to taste the contents.

"What is that?" he demanded.

"Maple syrup, sir."

"And if you please, what does the manuscript call for?"

"Molasses, sir."

"And you dare waste my time and the time of the ladies and gentlemen of my company with maple syrup?"

At that point, Belasco smashed the jar onto the stage floor, and began jumping up and down on the sticky mess. He ordered the prop man to clean it up and screamed, "Never, never presume to take such liberties with me again!"

While the prop man was mopping up and thanking God he still had a job, Belasco sidled over to Pickford and asked what she thought of his performance. "I find it absolutely necessary to break something at least once before an opening night in order to keep the cast on their toes," he told her.

The Warrens of Virginia opened December 3, 1907, and was an immediate smash hit. It ran for fifteen months in New York, then spawned a succession of touring companies. William deMille was now a name to conjure with in the American theater. Once again, Cecil studied Belasco's manner. "There was never a rigid Belasco formula, but there were Belasco ingredients that the public came to expect from him always, and he did not disappoint them."

Cecil learned Belasco's lessons well.

Belasco was now operating as a mogul, essentially devising star vehicles; it was less important that the play be good than that it showcase the personality and attributes of its leading player. With the exception of *Madame Butterfly* and *The Girl of the Golden West*, two plays turned into operas by Puccini, Belasco's shows were locked in their time, largely because he always made sure that his scripts were injected with the maximum dose of melodrama. But there was always an eye for the luscious emotional effect; in his production of *Madame Butterfly*, Belasco and his faithful electrician Louis Hartmann, who worked for him for nearly thirty years, used colored rolls of silk behind the set's translucent screens to give the effect of a slow fade from day to night, with results that ravished critics and audiences.

★

Cecil and William stepped up their collaboration. Shortly after *The Warrens of Virginia* opened, the brothers offered *The Royal Mounted* (1908), a florid tale of murder and a manhunt. *The Royal Mounted* closed after thirty-two performances, but Cecil believed that every failure had the nugget of a potential success buried deep inside it, and, in any case, he never threw anything away. *The Royal Mounted* would serve as the basis for his highly successful film *North West Mounted Police* more than thirty years later.

Nearly a year after the premiere of *The Warrens of Virginia*, on October 5, 1908, Constance gave birth to their only biological child, a daughter they named Cecilia. Cecilia was born in her grandparents Adamses' house, undoubtedly because the Judge wanted his daughter to have better medical care than Cecil could afford.

While one son flailed—Cecil attempted yet another Indian play called *The Stampede*, which earned a single production from the Chicago Stock Company—and another was thriving, Beatrice was gaining some momentum in her field. By 1910, she had turned her agency into the DeMille Play Company, and Cecil was working as her general manager. In January of that year, Cecil directed Owen Davis's play *The Wishing Ring* on Broadway, and he would produce a couple more plays in the next few years, including *Cheer Up*, written by Mary Roberts Rinehart, Beatrice's most successful client. The runs were short, the reviews mediocre.

In an undated, handwritten note from much later in his life, Cecil defended himself against potential criticism from an overly harsh future biographer—an astonishing message found, not in a bottle, but in a file folder: "The reason most of the plays I produced were failures is that I had no money myself and had to find an actor or a writer who had money to finance their own work."

In the summer of 1910, Cecil approached David Belasco for a loan with an idea for a play as collateral. At first Belasco wasn't interested, then agreed to pay DeMille a stipend for six weeks during which he would write the play; if it was any good, Belasco had the rights to produce it. Cecil went up into the woods of Maine and wrote his play. The idea revolved around life after death—a hard-driving businessman returns from the dead to right the wrongs he committed in life. A similar idea had worked for Dickens, so there was no reason to think that it wouldn't work for DeMille.

That, at least was the chronology as DeMille remembered it. But DeMille's own copy of the play carries the notation "Completed July 6, 09" and notes that it was delivered to Belasco on September 18, 1909.

Whatever the dates, the play was eventually called *The Return of Peter Grimm*, and it was about a man who comes back after death to observe what his descendants have made of their lives. Belasco rewrote it, keeping the central idea, but changing most of the characters. DeMille's wealthy, independent paper manufacturer named Martin Best was converted into a gentle, lovable nurseryman named Peter Grimm. Yet DeMille's original script—titled *In the Midst of Life*—invents the play's masterfully dramatic ending: a young boy dies and goes off with the old man to adventures beyond. Belasco added the touch of the old man singing a nursery rhyme the child always loved. Belasco took sole credit as author. When the play opened, with David Warfield in the title role, buried in the small print was the credit "Suggested by Cecil B. DeMille," which seemed radically unfair, as DeMille created about 60 percent of the play.

In his autobiography, DeMille acknowledged that Belasco was contractually within his rights, and said that "I do not for a moment believe that Belasco deliberately chose to cheat. He was not small. . . . Perhaps it was like the pony he promised me when I was seven or eight years old. Perhaps he just forgot."

Perhaps, but perhaps not. DeMille was dictating nearly fifty years after the event, and he was never one to admit that anybody had bested him. The play was a great success and a credit on it would have made a big difference in his struggling life in the theater. What made it worse was that a month before *The Return of Peter Grimm* opened at the Belasco Theatre, DeMille had produced a play called *Speed*, which closed after thirty-three performances.

The Return of Peter Grimm opened in Boston on January 2, 1911, with a young actor named Thomas Meighan in a supporting part. Some reviews mentioned DeMille, some didn't. DeMille was outraged at what he clearly regarded as Belasco's arrogation of his rightful credit. Counting the episode of the pony—and we can be sure that Cecil did—it was the second time Belasco took advantage of him.

DeMille proceeded to take on Belasco in the pages of the newspapers. The *New York Times* reported a story headlined "Cecil DeMille Charges Belasco Takes Credit Due Him as Author of David Warfield's Play." The article said that "Belasco further strengthened that idea [that he was solely responsible] . . . by his curtain speech at the opening in Boston, when he declared that the play was the result of an experience which he asserted that he had on the night of the death of his mother. He averred that on the night that she departed this life in San Francisco, he awakened suddenly in New York and saw his mother standing beside his bed, and that she spoke to him as when in the flesh, bidding him good-bye, and saying she was about to leave for another world. . . . It is no new thing, of course, for Belasco to be charged with irregularities in the matter of claiming credit as author of plays produced by him."

Beyond the competing claims and counterclaims of two magnificent egotists, what actually happened?

In the contract between Cecil and Belasco, dated September 18, 1909, Cecil is to be paid $2,940 up front, and an additional $5,000 at the rate of $100 a week. By signing the contract, Cecil "sells, assigns, transfers and gives over to Belasco, all his rights, titles and interest of every name, nature and kind in and to the play and . . . expressly sells, assigns, transfers to Belasco, all ideas, inventions, originations, matter and material of every name, nature and kind." The contract also specifies that the program of said play shall contain the acknowledgment that the initial idea of the play was suggested by Cecil B. DeMille.

Belasco would never have forked over $8,000—a great deal of money in 1909—for a mere idea. Cecil was being paid, and paid well, to ghost a play about a ghost for Belasco. But it was a flat fee, what is called "work for hire," with no royalties involved. Somewhere along the line—probably when the show became a great hit—Cecil realized he had sold himself and his play far too cheaply.

Belasco was perfectly capable of stealing credit, although in his mind he was simply the godhead through whom all ideas flowed, therefore entitled. Agnes deMille believed that, in spite of his denials of bitterness, Cecil deeply resented

Belasco's piracy for the rest of his life. The evidence bears her out. Cecil's copy of his original script carries this notation in his hand, documenting what he always believed was Belasco's perfidy: "This is the first draft of the play I wrote with David Belasco 1908-9-10, later called *The Return of Peter Grimm*—some of the pages were copied by a secretary, the balance are in my handwriting. Cecil B. deMille, July, 1942."

As Agnes deMille put it, "He thereafter spent his life proving, first, that he was as smart as his older brother, second, that he was as smart as Belasco, and third, that he was smarter than anyone else."

DeMille's eventual revenge would be finely calibrated. Cecil would appropriate Belasco's image and surroundings—the cathedral-style office complete with vaulted beams, bear rugs on the floor, baronial manner—and transport it wholesale to Hollywood, where he performed the part of the impresario better than Belasco had done it in New York.

Beyond that, Cecil would replicate Belasco's working methods: "Belasco surrounded himself with a permanent staff, as loyal as they were efficient. . . . Personal loyalty stood high among his values. He was a benevolent despot. He fought the advance of organized labor . . . but he kept his own people on the payroll even when there was nothing for them to do. He confidently expected actors to work for him for less money than other producers would pay them; and the wisest among them did, and profited by it more than the difference in money."

All exactly replicated by Cecil, as was the efficacy of the carefully calibrated managerial tantrum.

When *The Return of Peter Grimm* was made into a silent film by Fox in 1926, and later as a Lionel Barrymore vehicle by RKO in 1935, the credit reads "From the Play Written and Produced by David Belasco." Cecil ground his teeth quietly.

★

In March, 1903, Bill married Anna George, the daughter of Henry George, the man to whom Henry deMille had written a fan letter years before. Marrying the daughter of Henry George gave the deMille family a patina of intellectual seriousness to go along with the moral seriousness inculcated by Henry. Bill's marriage soon produced two daughters: Agnes, born in 1905, and Margaret in 1908.

Bill continued to have success in the theater, although his work hasn't stood the test of time. "He was a journeyman craftsman," opined Agnes, "who could tailor a well-made plot . . . and turn out dialogue which acted very well and which was sometimes extremely funny. His work possessed, however, no real distinction or style. He knew his rules: he could hold attention, build suspense, and make a point. That's a lot, but it doesn't last."

Neither did love. Anna deMille was sexually repressed, and it wasn't long before her husband sought passion elsewhere. Shortly before her death, Anna told her daughter Agnes that her distinction in life lay in having been her father's daughter, her husband's wife, and her daughter's mother—a life so devoted to the service of others that it was essentially self-obliterating.

✴

In 1911, Mary Pickford made a momentous decision to leave the stage and go into the movies. On July 25, William deMille wrote David Belasco a letter: "Oh, by the way, you remember that little girl, Mary Pickford, who played Betty in *The Warrens of Virginia*? I met her again a few weeks ago and the poor kid is actually thinking of taking up movie pictures seriously. . . . It does seem a shame. After all, she can't be more than seventeen and I remember what faith you had in her future . . . and now she's throwing her whole career in the ashcan and burying herself in a cheap form of amusement. There will never be any real money in those galloping tintypes, and certainly no one can expect them to develop into anything which could . . . be called art. I pleaded with her not [to go into films] . . . but she says she knows what she is doing. So I suppose we'll have to say goodbye to little Mary Pickford. She'll never be heard of again, and I feel terribly sorry for her."

William sounds like a terrible snob, but he was only articulating the conventional wisdom of his time and class. He was also a snob with a sense of irony; he enjoyed telling this story on himself.

Cecil, meanwhile, was barely getting by. In April, he formed a theatrical partnership with one Nathan Spingold for the representation of plays, actors, and writers. A few months later, he signed a deal with the actor Robert Ober to play in something called *Baxter's Partner*, for which Cecil contributed four weeks' labor in exchange for one third of the nonexistent profits. He directed a play called *The Marriage-not*. He wrote a couple of plays that didn't get produced, wrote additional dialogue for Mary Roberts Rinehart's *The Water Cure*, and worked with Bill on a play called *After Five*.

If Cecil's own productions were gasping for air, he was breathing deeply of the theater of this period, which affected him more profoundly than any other dramatic art he would experience. When he was well into middle age, he would respond to a newspaperman's question about the ten most memorable plays he ever saw. His list, carefully annotated by hand, included Richard Mansfield in *Cyrano de Bergerac*, William Gillette in *Secret Service*, *Hamlet* with Johnston Forbes-Robertson and E. H. Sothern, Gillette again in James M. Barrie's *The Admirable Crichton*, Pauline Lord in *The Late Christopher Beane*, Dustin Farnum and William Faversham in *The Squaw Man*, Doris Keane in *Romance*, and (immodestly) David Warfield in *The Return of Peter Grimm*.

There were other plays and performances he loved—H. B. Warner in *Alias Jimmy Valentine*, Mrs. Leslie Carter in *Zaza*, Henry Irving in *The Bells*, Sothern again in *The Prisoner of Zenda*, Frank Keenan and Blanche Bates in *The Girl of the Golden West*. But of all the plays DeMille admired, only two derived from what might be termed the modern American theater that began around World War I: Jeanne Eagels in *Rain* and Alice Brady in Eugene O'Neill's *Mourning Becomes Electra*.

It was Henry Irving who made DeMille realize that the most important quality an actor needed—at least a DeMille actor—was authority, and DeMille would cite authority as his reason for hiring talents as varied as Gloria Swanson and Yul Brynner. In a scene in *The Bells*, Irving was told that a murder his character had committed was about to be solved, and all the actor did was continue to methodically drop coals into a stove, without any show of emotion. That was for the audience to supply.

"A great actor, like a great orator, never gives the impression that he is using all his emotional power," DeMille would assert. "He gives just enough for what the role or scene demands, but he leaves the audience with the unconscious conviction that he has still more to draw upon, an untapped depth of which he remains the master . . . He should let the audience take up the emotion where he leaves it, and let them carry it the rest of the way."

In terms of his aesthetics, DeMille would remain his father's son, a nineteenth-century man of the theater—his greatest strength, as well as his greatest limitation.

4

Jesse L. Lasky was atypical for an early movie mogul. For one thing, he was a native Californian; for another, his early life was dotted with success as a vaudeville producer, whereas most of his peers treaded water waiting for movies to be invented.

"In retrospect," said his daughter Betty, "it's easy to see that he had the wrong background to succeed in Hollywood as far as financial success. Money didn't mean anything to him, whereas the others were grasping because of their background. They crawled out of ghettos and when they reached the top they were insecure. 'Who can I trust? Who's going to stab me in the back?' My father trusted everyone, loved everyone. Possessions meant nothing, money meant nothing. If you walked into his office and admired something, he'd say 'Take it, take it.' "

Jesse Lasky was born in San Francisco in 1880. When his father died before Jesse finished high school, he lied about his age to get into the musicians' union and got bookings as a cornet player. His fantasy was that he would be discovered by John Philip Sousa, but Sousa never heard of him. Lasky's other hero was Jack London, so Lasky joined the Alaska gold rush. He came back empty-handed, played his horn in saloons, then in vaudeville in tandem with his sister Blanche, who married a man named Sam Goldfish, later Goldwyn. "She immediately regretted it," remembered Betty Lasky. "He was not husband material; very argumentative and quarrelsome."

Lasky segued into producing vaudeville acts, which brought him his first success. He lost his first nest egg—his brother-in-law would remember the loss as $100,000, while others put it at $150,000—with the Folies Bergère, a lavish theater-restaurant on Broadway that charged $2.50 admission, the highest in New York other than the Metropolitan Opera. Cabaret was the rage of Europe, but Lasky was ahead of his time. The Folies Bergère failed in four months in 1911.

Cecil and Lasky met because of Beatrice. Lasky approached her about hiring Bill to write the libretto for an operetta by Robert Hood Bowers called *California*.

Bill being otherwise engaged, Beatrice steered Lasky to her younger son, who was barely keeping the wolf from his family's door. Technically, Cecil remained his mother's general manager, although he would say later that "she was the real general." His business expertise was of little help to his invariably improvident mother, who was usually no more than a month from insolvency.

Lasky knew Cecil by sight and didn't like his manner, or the way he seemed to stare right through him on the occasions when they met. Lasky thought Beatrice was attempting to help out the brother who wasn't a success and whom nobody wanted. "Cecil and I surveyed each other seriously," remembered Lasky. "Much against my better judgment I hemmed and hawed through the story thread of my operetta. But Cecil's eyes were taking on a glint of insight and I could sense his imagination was filling in the gaps, mentally picturing how he would dramatize it. When I finished, he leaned forward and exclaimed, 'Say, I like that!' The minute he said, 'I like that,' I liked him. And I've never stopped."

On October 12, 1911, Cecil and Jesse signed a deal to produce *California*. Cecil received $100 in advance, $100 to stage the play, and $25 for every week the show ran. Cecil and Jesse wrote the book, William LeBaron—later a very successful producer at Paramount—wrote the lyrics, and Blanche Lasky designed the costumes. *California* showed off the Belasco influence, as the set featured a live orange tree, from which the actors picked fruit.

DeMille and Lasky became close friends, lunching daily at the Claridge Grill, taking vacations together—sans wives and children—in Maine. Cecil wrote and staged a couple of one-act plays for Lasky, who successfully booked them.

"He and Mr. DeMille hit it off right away because they were very much alike," said Betty Lasky. "They were only a year apart in age, and they seemed to have many similar qualities—they both had an enormous zest for life and they loved to go away on weekends together on hunting trips. They were like blood brothers from the minute they met in 1911. They had everything in common. Unfortunately, my father lacked one strength of DeMille's: business."

In May 1912, Lasky hired Cecil to write and stage another Bowers operetta unpromisingly called *In the Barracks* for a royalty of $40 a week. In September, Lasky hired him to "stage book and production" of *The Little Parisienne* by William LeBaron for $250 plus $12.50 royalty for each of the first ten weeks played, and $15 a week thereafter.

None of this was enough, because none of these shows ran very long. In April 1912, Cecil had been sufficiently desperate to list himself as co-author of both *Strongheart*—written by his brother—and *The Return of Peter Grimm*—Belasco be damned. That same month, Cecil received a letter from an agent letting him down easy: "I sincerely hope the stock royalties you receive this spring will pay the balance due you from us. It is a good play, but apparently the public is not much interested."

Cecil also authorized one Lillian Buckingham to adapt *The Stampede* for vaudeville for a royalty of $20 a week "in the small time" and $30 a week "in the big time." As Lasky remembered, "these mild adventures weren't enough to satisfy Cecil's high-spirited nature. . . . I could see that he was getting restless." He could also see that they were both going broke.

"What should we do now?" asked Lasky rhetorically one day.

"Let's go down to Mexico and join the revolution," suggested DeMille, referring to Pancho Villa's uprising, and in later years both men insisted he was quite serious. Show business, Cecil pointed out, wasn't really working out. Maybe they needed to take a break; maybe they needed to try something entirely different.

"No," said Lasky, clinging to the rational. "If you want excitement, let's go into pictures."

"All right, let's," said Cecil.

"We were in Claridge's Grill," DeMille remembered shortly before he died, "and we turned over our bill of fare and started to form a company." And so what Cecil called "refugees from bankruptcy" began the process of creating show business history.

After lunch, heads still together, Cecil and Jesse walked down 44th Street to the Lambs Club and ran into Dustin Farnum, who had made a hit on Broadway in *The Virginian*. DeMille and Lasky asked Farnum if he'd like to make a movie. Farnum looked around and spotted Edwin Milton Royle, who had written *The Squaw Man*, which had been a hit ever since it was first produced in 1905. The play, which starred William Faversham, had spawned a novel, been a successful road show, and came back to Broadway in both 1907 and 1908. Royle, smelling royalties, thought it was a good idea too.

Just like that, they were in business.

Both DeMille's and Lasky's accounts of their momentous lunch are fairly synchronous. But according to a self-serving interview Sam Goldwyn gave DeMille's staff in the mid-1950s, the Lasky and Goldfish families lived together in a large apartment, and it was Sam who nudged his brother-in-law toward the movies. "Jesse was not too interested in my idea and the thing that finally attracted him was the fact that I was going to use his name as President of the company. I told Lasky I would like Cecil (we called him 'C') associated with us. . . . We used to play roulette for nickels at Cecil's or William's or my house every Saturday night."

What Sam didn't mention was that he thought Cecil would be a good man in the firm, but not as a director; for that, he suggested, someone—anyone—with experience. Supposedly, Goldfish made a run at D. W. Griffith, but Griffith wanted to see a good bank balance in the coffers of any company he was going to do business with, and a good bank balance was something none of the proposed partners had.

Terry Ramsaye's account in *A Million and One Nights*, written in 1926, adds another *Rashomon*-like perspective. In Ramsaye's telling, it was attorney Arthur Friend who was the instigator of the entire affair, talking up movies relentlessly beginning in the spring of 1913, and gradually convincing Sam Goldfish, Blanche Lasky Goldfish, and Jesse of their importance. All this, of course, confirms that success has a million fathers.

The night after the Lambs Club meeting, Jesse Lasky went home and calmly, casually told his wife, "Bess, we are going into the picture business." She was properly horrified by such a déclassé decision and asked him to repeat what he had just said.

"Yes," he said. "It's true."

"You can't be serious. Those horrid flickers—I can't bear them, they hurt my eyes." Jesse soothed Bess; Cecil was his best friend, and it was what he wanted to do. It had more to do with Cecil than it did with him, Jesse explained. It would be all right; she would see.

★

After the first few days of the partnership, reality dawned and there was some confused throat clearing. None of the principals had any experience in the field of motion pictures; in fact, they barely knew what they were talking about. William deMille would later write that Cecil never actually saw a movie until the proposition began to take shape. Cecil stoutly insisted he had seen movies, at least three of them—he specifically recalled *The Great Train Robbery*, a brief actuality that featured a bullfight, and something about a durbar in India.

Jesse, Sam, and Cecil promptly went together to the nearest nickelodeon. After they came out, Jesse asked Cecil what he thought. "Well, I don't know anything about pictures," he said, "but if I can't do better than *that*, I ought to be shot at sunrise."

While Cecil had remained blissfully unaware of the primary competition to his profession—DeMille and his brother obviously regarded themselves as scions of theatrical royalty who didn't have to bother with the passing fancies of the nickelodeon—the movies were progressing from amusement to something approaching an art form, led by a man named David Wark Griffith and a slew of rivals.

Like Cecil, Griffith had been a predominantly unsuccessful actor and playwright; like Cecil, Griffith went into the movies as a last resort; like Cecil, he was a man who learned very quickly.

The primary difference between the two men was aspirational. Griffith's writing for the theater consistently attempted vast accomplishment. For Griffith, the goal was to be an artist, or nothing. But Cecil's work in the theater, like his mentor Belasco's, was primarily about entertainment, not artistry.

In the beginning, in 1908, Griffith's pictures for the Biograph Company were only marginally better than the competition, but he immediately grasped film's plastic nature—the way two pieces of film spliced together could make something greater than the sum of their individual parts. By 1909, while Cecil was still floundering in the theater, Griffith was making the occasional compressed miniature masterpiece, such as *A Corner in Wheat*, then, moving on through his years at Biograph, *The House With Closed Shutters, An Unseen Enemy, The Musketeers of Pig Alley, The Mothering Heart*—films that are close to being the equal of the epic features Griffith would begin making in 1914—*The Birth of a Nation, Intolerance*, etc.

Another contributing factor in Cecil's sudden interest in the movies was the production of films of Bill's plays *Classmates* and *Strongheart*, both made in the late summer of 1913 by director James Kirkwood, as well as films of Henry deMille and David Belasco's plays *Men and Women* and *The Wife*, that were made that fall. Clearly, there was money to be made in the movies by the deMille clan.

Cecil ran the whole idea past Constance, who had, through more than ten years of marriage, endured an unremitting struggle for solvency.

"Do what you think right and I will be with you," she replied simply.

No wonder he loved her.

To get an idea of how movies were actually made, Goldfish made an appointment with Thomas Edison and drove down to West Orange, New Jersey, where he found the inventor trying to synchronize sound with motion pictures—an obvious fool's errand. Edison was nearly deaf by this time, but managed to hear enough of what Goldfish had to say to give permission to have Goldfish's director watch production at Edison's studio.

Goldfish told Cecil to go over to the studio on East 188th Street, near Bronx Park, and watch how movies were made. "I thought he would stay there a week or two," remembered Sam, "but after the first day he called me and said, 'If that is the way they make pictures I think I will be knighted after one year.' He never went back there again."

DeMille remembered what he had observed. "The director called for action. The cameraman cranked. A girl emerged from a hedge, climbed the wall, and ran down the road, looking back in terror from time to time at some unseen pursuer. A man met her, stopped her, and they talked, in pantomime of course, with much emotive gesticulation."

While Goldfish's insertion of himself as the central figure of whatever happened to be going on at the time is probably self-serving—both Lasky and DeMille remembered Lasky as far more critical to the alliance—his characterization of DeMille's imperial self-confidence seems exactly right. DeMille was always a man of acquisitive intelligence; he must have sensed that the movies played to his strengths—drive, a big-picture sensibility, industrial savvy—more than the stage ever could.

The Jesse L. Lasky Feature Play Company roster included Sam Goldfish to sell movies, Arthur Friend to handle the corporate and legal responsibilities, Jesse as producer, and Cecil as Director-General—whatever that was. Although DeMille always reported that Dustin Farnum turned down 25 percent of the company in lieu of a flat $250 a week salary, Farnum's contract in fact called for $250 a week *and* 25 percent of the net profits from the release of *The Squaw Man* throughout the world.

As far as Bill deMille was concerned, Cecil was committing cultural vandalism. Bill was so reflexively contemptuous of this not-all-that-new medium that he hadn't bothered to see a one-reel movie adaptation of one of his own plays. Bill remembered that the news that Cecil was going into the movies had the same impact on him that a southern colonel would have felt if his son had announced that he was going to join the Union Army. "The name we bore had been honorably known to the theater for two generations, and now he was going to drag it in the dust of a vulgar, unworthy scheme of coaxing nickels away from poor little children."

On September 3, 1913, from his summer place at Merriewold Park in New York, William wrote his brother a letter.

> I was quite disturbed to get your letter of last week telling me that you, Jesse Lasky, Sam Goldfish and [lawyer] Arthur Friend have formed a company to go into the moving-picture business. I knew, of course, that your last two productions in the theater had divested you of everything except your ambition and personal charm, but I did not suspect that you had reached the point of utter desperation. After all, you do come of a cultured family, two of whose members have made honorable names in the field of drama, and I cannot understand how you are willing to identify yourself with a cheap form of amusement and which no one will ever allude to as art.
>
> I do not blame Jesse so much, as his years in vaudeville have probably made anything else seem attractive; nor do I censure Sam, whose experiences as a high-pressure glove-salesman might easily stimulate a wild desire to bite the thousands of hands which have fed him. Arthur's work as a lawyer has naturally made him familiar with the depths to which human beings can sink in their desire to acquire wealth, so to his legal mind, teasing nickels and dimes out of the mentally immature by making photographs leap and prance is no doubt a vast improvement on murder or highway robbery.
>
> But you—who were born and raised in the finest traditions of the theater—you who have undoubted dramatic ability and stand more than an even chance of making your name known in all the big cities of the United States—to throw away your future; end your career before it is well started and doom yourself to obscurity if not, indeed, to oblivion, seems to me a step which calls for protest from those who really care about what happens to you . . .

I suppose Mother is heartbroken. This must be a terrible blow to her for I know what hopes she had for you. . . . When you get stranded out there in the West I will send you your railroad fare—as usual.

William signed off "With love (which is akin to pity)."

Few men have so fervently seized an opportunity to make a colossally condescending fool of themselves.

The movie trade papers announced that the Jesse L. Lasky Feature Play Company had contracted for sufficient material to keep the firm busy for three years, and the company would be making a picture a month for the first year. This was nonsense; the company had only enough money to make the first of those pictures and, as a matter of fact, there was a shortfall even there, because Cecil had no money. The company was capitalized at $20,000, but could raise only around $15,000. As Cecil remembered, "Sam put up $5,000, Jesse put up $5,000, Arthur Friend put up $5,000, and I was to put up $5,000, but I didn't have the $5,000."

Bill flatly refused to throw $5,000 in the hat. Cecil turned to the only person he knew who might be able to raise money—his mother. Beatrice sold Pamlico, the house in Pompton, for $30,000. Beatrice was encouraging her boy to cast his lot "with the despised and infantile movies," much as she had encouraged Henry to preach from the stage rather than the pulpit, except this time her encouragement was accompanied by money.

Two very important components of what Cecil brought to the company were the family name and the plays his father had written for Belasco. DeMille's contract specified that he would obtain the movie rights to the "plays and scenarios . . . controlled by the . . . DeMille Agency and the . . . plays and scenarios owned and controlled by the legal representative of the late Henry C. deMille."

Between loaning her son the money for his investment and providing Henry's plays as likely story material, Beatrice was really a silent partner in the firm. In addition to his mother having to underwrite his investment, Cecil was very clearly on probation. He agreed to work "without salary or other compensation of any nature whatsoever until such time as the board of Directors of the said corporation shall, in their absolute judgment, conclude to give to [DeMille] a regular salary for his services."

This meant that he needed expense money. Cecil took the family silver to Simpson's on 42nd Street and got either $75 or $175 (his memory wavered on the amount). Either way, it was enough to pay his railroad fare west.

Cecil had one last theatrical project, the play he and Bill had written called *After Five*, which opened in New York on October 29, 1913, and closed after thirteen performances. That made it official: in the thirteen years since his debut in *Hearts Are Trumps*, and excluding the disputed *The Return of Peter Grimm*, Cecil had been involved in thirteen Broadway shows as an actor, writer, director, or producer. One show had run ten months (*The Warrens of Virginia*), two had run three months (*Hearts Are Trumps* and 1905's *The Prince Chap*), five had run a month, and five had run less than a month.

It was a record of theatrical futility worthy of Max Bialystock. Without touring, work in stock, or loans from Bill—and, undoubtedly, help from Beatrice and Constance's parents—Cecil, Constance, and Cecilia would likely have starved to death.

It was change or die. As Cecil observed in a November 10, 1913, letter about the theater's continual state of crisis, "The present conditions, theatrically, are the most unfavorable in the twelve years that I have been associated with them. The pieces that are absolute knock-outs are doing business. Nothing else is. Business on the road is ghastly." It's a mark of Cecil's bumptious nature that problems were always in circumstances, never with himself. His mother had raised a son whose primary personal trademark would be self-confidence, the belief that he would always succeed so long as he kept trying.

★

The plot of *The Squaw Man* concerns a wealthy, educated Englishman pursued by the law. He escapes to the American West, where he falls in love with a young Indian woman who saves his life and takes care of him. She becomes pregnant and they marry. When he is informed he can come back to his inherited wealth, he compromises to the extent of staying with his wife but sending his son to England to be educated. The Indian wife commits suicide, neatly ripping off *Madame Butterfly*.

There was no way the story could be filmed in the East; the landscapes of New Jersey, which were the setting for early films that required outdoor scenery, were far too woodsy for the necessary contrast between the genteel English settings of the beginning and the rest of the film. DeMille and Lasky set about figuring out a likely location spot.

Then there was the question of a director, someone to back up—or front for—Cecil. William Haddock, who had been working at Eclair and had directed Dustin Farnum, remembered meeting with Jesse, Cecil, and Sam on the night before Thanksgiving 1913. They offered Haddock $300 a week and stock in the company to make the picture. Haddock thought about it for a couple of days but turned them down; scuttlebutt had it that the Lasky company had enough money to make only one movie and would fold immediately thereafter, which would make the stock worthless.

It was at that point that all eyes in the room must have turned to Cecil. Even though his total tutorial in the craft had come from that half day at the Edison studio, "I thought it was very simple." Of course, from DeMille's point of view, he had nothing to lose; as he remembered, he "had a proven ability to support myself, my wife and our child on an income of $20 a week or less." He could always go back to New York and earn $20 a week again. But the partners were not about to give their entire nest egg to a man who had spent a half day behind a movie camera, so they hired a man named Oscar Apfel to co-direct with Cecil.

So it was that five people set out for the West—the perfect place to make a western, or so the thinking went: directors Cecil B. DeMille and Oscar Apfel, cameraman Al Gandolfi, star Dustin Farnum, and the star's dresser and secretary, Fred Kley. Constance and Cecilia stayed behind in New York—just in case Bill was right, and he had to front Cecil's return fare to New York, there was no sense paying two and a half fares when it could just as easily be one.

The destination was Flagstaff, Arizona, more or less because Flagstaff, Arizona, *sounded* western and because Tom Mix was making successful westerns in nearby Prescott. More to the point, the distant location was a way of avoiding the Motion Picture Patents Company, a consortium founded in 1909 that controlled the license to make or sell movies in America. The Patents Company was opposed to feature production, which was yet another reason the Lasky company had to find an exotic location.

Jesse did not know much about movies, but he was certain the future was with feature-length pictures of an hour or more. He had made what he remembered as a systematic survey of the field, noted the lavish new theaters that were being built, and compared the business they were doing with the business being done by the reliable nickelodeons that relied on daily changes of one- and two-reel shorts. If the movies were to triumph, he sensed, they had to snare the middle class as well as the working class. The Lasky company, Jesse decided, would aim for the carriage trade.

General Film—an important component of the Patents Company—warned the Lasky company that even if they made their film, they wouldn't be able to sell it because there was no one to sell it to but them and they wouldn't buy it. "I said," remembered DeMille, "I can make a picture out of this play because I've never seen what I want to do on the screen. . . . [Other pictures] were all one or two reels, some three reels. One of the things [General Film] told me was that people wouldn't stay in a theater that long."

As the train made its way west, Cecil and Oscar Apfel wrote a rough shooting script. As Cecil described the division of labor, "Apfel knew a great deal about motion pictures, 1913 vintage; I was supposed to know something about dramatic construction."

DeMille and company appear to have taken the Southern Pacific via New Orleans to Arizona, leaving on or about December 12, 1913. The trip was uneventful until they got to Flagstaff. It was raining. "When we got off the train in Flagstaff," remembered Cecil, "it was colder than when I left New York." It also appeared uninteresting—barren and flat. "We looked around and said this doesn't look like the type of country *The Squaw Man* was laid in, so we got back on the train and came out to California."

In later years, DeMille would tell his associate Henry Wilcoxon that bailing out of Flagstaff because it was raining was a publicity story. "Actually, to tell the truth, the terrain was uninteresting and I didn't like the light. The quality of light was so important, especially in those days. Now film is a great deal faster."

Cecil wanted a variety of terrain, and there was not enough variety to be had in Flagstaff. As the train began puffing for its leavetaking, Cecil had to make a quick executive decision. He remembered that the end of the line was Los Angeles and that other moviemakers had been working there in a casual manner for years. Cecil had played Los Angeles in his touring days and he knew that the sun shone all the time, there was a variety of beautiful land, from seashores to mountains, and it was even further from the Patents Company than Flagstaff.

As the train pulled away from the Flagstaff station, the members of the Jesse L. Lasky Feature Play Company were on it, all but one of them undoubtedly questioning the sanity of their Director-General.

★

On the train west, probably around December 17, feeling lonely and, it seems, horny, Cecil sat down and wrote his wife a remarkably honest letter.

Dearest Gretchen,

All day long, in fact ever since the train left western Kansas, I have been looking for a permanent home for us. For in spite of my harem numbering hundreds of the most beautiful women in the land, I love you.

1st because you are you, generous, good, self-sacrificing and lovable in more ways than I have time or space to write.

2nd because you love me, with all the strength and bigness of a big heart a loving nature and a sharp mind. And the next glorious thing to loving is being loved.

3rd well the third shouldn't be written. It should only be suggested on nights when the moon is wonderfully clear and that strange throb that passes the heart of all living things is felt. Or when it is storming terribly and that cosy feeling of warmth and snugness comes to us sitting before a fire dry and warm. I said it shouldn't be written, but it occured to me that by writing I can, forever frustrate any intention on your part to publish this letter after I am dead and famous. third then I love your body. I like your cool solid flesh. I like your strong pretty legs. I like the round firmness of your brests. I love the passion in you. I love the thought of your body taught by me for me. I love the thought that it is mine. and never has been nor could be another. I love to have you want me and to show me that you want me. I love the deep look that comes into your eyes, when you are mine this way. I know that no one on earth has ever seen that look, or ever will see it but me. It gives me a barbaric desire to hurt you—(thats when I pull your hair).

I love to feel your body next [to] mine and pressing close, and to hear what you and I only know and to feel a kiss far from the ordinary kiss on my lips. So do we cut the strings of all reserve from all the senses. I believe there is nothing more improper than mentioning these terrible things to ones wife, these little tributes are always kept for the mistress. She alone hears such shameful words.

But what am I to do? I find myself in the unique position of prefering my wife's body to that of any other woman. Here then is a predicament. I must teach my wife those things which the mistress usually provides. But, shrieks the horrified god of morals, she is a good woman, she is pure, she has no right even to know that such things exist, [to] feel such violent and evil passion.

Then weakly I reply but it is her body I want to feel pressed close to mine. It is her passion I want to feel respond to mine, it is her breath I want to feel warm and quick against my cheek. It is the sound from her lips I want to hear when for a heavenly moment she is transported onto the hights of passion.

You libertine, replies the god of morals, would you so debase your wife. It is for this I have created the mistress. Then I look the god straight in the face and laugh—you two faced idiot I call him. I don't care what other women feel, it's what *my* woman feels that pleases me. Let other men go in to their wives in the dark and steal silently and with hallowed dignity their frigid nights of love and save themselves and their passion for their mistresses. My wifes my mistress and I'll teach her all a mistress knows. And we'll have light, liberty and passion with our love. And to our hearts content. And I'll pull her hair to *my* hearts content and you can go to the devil with your morality and your mistresses. Horrible gasps the god. I shall hide my face from you forever. You can't I call as he departs for if you turn your back I see your double face. That little mother is the third way I love you that way that should never be written.

And now as to our home I have selected some ten or twelve places each one more impossible than the last. Right now we are at one. It's a great table land miles and miles in area surrounded by high mesas and mountains and queer red rocks of fantastic shapes, some of them I am sure looking like the god of morality. One great monster of a rock with a great broad summit that must be a mile around on top and two thousand [feet] high, we'll call a monument to our love, a love that was strong enough to grow stronger through each of its trials. In case I forget the place It is somewhere near Taltic or Bluewater, New Mexico. There being no water I presume it was named after a mirage . . . The only occupants of this entire territory seem to be a few indians and Im sure heards of rattlesnakes and gila monsters. I saw one deer which means there are also mountain lion, wild cat and wolves. doesn't it sound like the ideal place for us. We'll take up a large tract of land, get the water and every thing on in and be ready for my retirement in three years at which time I shall have money enough put away to live comfortably and write whatever I please—if only for you to read. Until tomorrow at three.

Adios—Da

DeMille's desire for sex unleavened by propriety, his desire for erotic variety, are unusual sentiments for a man of his generation to commit to paper. Even more unusual, he and Constance had been married for more than eleven years at this point, and he was still speaking of teaching her to be the kind of lover he needs.

DeMille had been attracted to Constance because of her emotional solidity, her deep reserves of sense—she completely lacked the improvisational, slightly scatty qualities of his mother. Constance was *sound*. But Constance could not shut off her reserve in bed. And it was that more than anything else that would eventually send Cecil out into the world, looking for those qualities he could not find in his wife.

Despite the sexual misalliance indicated by the letter, Constance kept it for the rest of her life, along with some other letters and notes from Cecil in an envelope on which she wrote:

CA de Mille

Private letters

(To be opened only by CB de Mille)

otherwise burn.

★

Cecil and company arrived in Los Angeles on December 18, 1913. It was a Thursday, and they set up shop at the Alexandria Hotel downtown at 210 West Fifth Street. Word quickly got around town that new people at the Alexandria were going into the movie business, and DeMille was soon visited by two men named L. L. Burns and Harry Revier, who wanted the lab work these rich easterners would be needing. Their lab was in a town called Hollywood, about ten miles north of downtown Los Angeles.

As the discussions continued, it became clear that the Lasky company was going to need a more practical production headquarters than the Alexandria Hotel. Burns and Revier also had a building in Hollywood that could be used as company headquarters that included a small stage. It all sounded too good to be true, but it wasn't.

Revier had worked in production for both American Gaumont and Universal before joining with Burns in 1912. Burns was the founder of Western Costume and the two men had leased a barn in Hollywood from a man named Jakob Stern. This was the structure they were trying to sublease to DeMille. Cecil wisely thought he'd better take a look at the prospective studio.

After a long drive through the outskirts of Los Angeles, they turned off a sparsely settled main drag then known as Prospect Avenue, drove down a broad shady avenue called Vine Street, and found a ramshackle group of wooden structures on the southeast corner of Vine and Selma.

"It was a barn," DeMille remembered. "Unmistakeably, it was a barn." DeMille was not disturbed; as he put it, "I expected to be working like a horse: what did it matter being housed like one?"

The single-story barn had been built in 1895. It had a forty-by-sixty-foot wooden platform outdoor stage jutting out from a wall. One of the wings of the barn ran along Vine, the other stretched back parallel with Selma. Slightly to the south was an orange grove.

Revier and his partner had already built six dressing rooms and a modest laboratory for processing film. There was a small carriage house on the premises that Revier also rented for his office. When DeMille and his company arrived on the lot, the premises were uninhabited, and Revier was eager for tenants.

On December 22, less than a week after arriving in Los Angeles, DeMille signed a letter of understanding to sublease the Burns and Revier "studio." The lease was for four months at $250 a month, with an option to extend for three years. (The Lasky company would eventually purchase the entire block, paying Jakob Stern more than $100,000, which included another city block immediately to the east.)

Burns and Revier agreed to enlarge the shooting stage to forty by seventy and to erect "new and modern diffusers," i.e., muslin drapes over the stage. In addition, they agreed to build a second stage, which the DeMille company could use when it was not in use by somebody else.

Burns and Revier also offered to develop the Lasky negatives and make the first print for 1.5 cents a foot. DeMille could negotiate, and by the time the contract was formalized on Christmas Eve, Burns was promising to "extend all partitions to the ceiling in all dressing rooms now on said premises." The price for lab services had been reduced to three-fourths of a cent per foot, including "tinting, toning and dyeing of the positive film."

★

There was a fair amount of movie production going on in and around Hollywood. Biograph had been sending cast and crew out every winter since 1906, Selig had established a permanent studio by 1909, while other studios opened in Edendale and Santa Monica by 1911. The February 1, 1910, issue of the *Los Angeles Times* reported that "with three of the largest companies in the country here, the mountains, the valleys, the orange groves and the seashores teem with persons riding, running and posing before the motion camera. . . . The reason Southern California has been chosen by the motion picture companies is that the background for any kind or style of picture may be found here. If the requirements demand snow, a party of picture actors or actresses may be seen ascending Mt. Lowe. If, on the other hand, the sand or seashore is necessary in bringing out a scene in the picture, coves and stretches of sand are at hand."

The *Times* reported that Biograph alone employed more than fifty people, and that the total number of actresses and actors working in the movies in L.A. ran to about two hundred. By 1912, Vitagraph, Kalem, Universal, and even Edison all had ancillary studios operating in southern California, but they were largely satellite operations for eastern studios established for the sole reason of maintaining production during winter.

By 1913, there were over forty companies operating in Los Angeles county, most of them seasonally, and with one other crucial proviso—nearly all of them were making shorts for the Motion Picture Patents Company trust. Only the Jesse L. Lasky Feature Play Company set itself the task of the exclusive manufacture of features.

Other than the warmth and the sunlight, Cecil's environment was not appreciably improved from the week before. He was still hustling, and he was still broke; moreover, he had the responsibility of knowing that his mother had bet her nest egg on her younger boy. Yet, DeMille was invigorated by the town, the quality of the light, and by the task he was about to undertake.

Cecil B. DeMille had experienced struggle and he had experienced failure. Now, finally, he would experience success.

Cecil B. DeMille in his office in 1914, in front of a poster for
The Squaw Man, already sporting the working wardrobe
of the next forty-five years—boots to support his ankles,
riding breeches, and a soft, open-necked shirt.

PART TWO

1914–1928

"Imagine, the horizon is your stage limit and the sky your gridiron. No height limit, no close-fitting exits, no conserving of stage space, just the whole world open to you as a stage; 1000 people in a scene do not crowd your accommodations . . . I felt inspired, I felt that I could do things which the confines of a theater would not permit."

–CECIL B. DeMILLE, 1914

"We were like the English garrison in India; speaking a different language, isolated, intent only upon our objective. We talked, breathed, lived and ate pictures."

–WILLIAM DeMILLE

5

Cecil had stumbled on a town only a few people had heard of, and for a good reason. Hollywood had been founded in the 1880s by Methodist temperance advocates who banned liquor and, twenty-five years later, the movies. Neither ban succeeded.

Cecil would recall the Hollywood he first saw as "a lazy little village . . . in its shining pink stucco dress, dreaming peacefully at the foot of gentle green hills." Agnes deMille later described it as "a country town of the southwest and . . . very lovely and romantic and attractive. . . . The streets ran right into the foothills and the foothills went straight up into sage brush and you were in the wild, wild hills. Sage brush and rattlesnakes and coyotes and the little wild deer that came down every night. And all of it was just enchanting. Franklin Avenue absolutely arced with pepper branches, and Vine street had their palm trees and pepper trees lining them."

It seemed like paradise. "[There were] orange trees all over," remembered DeMille. "The Los Feliz district was all prairie and brush. Vine Street was one of the most beautiful streets in the world then. There were pepper trees and great stands of eucalyptus, magnolia and jacaranda trees."

Cecil was carrying $10,000 of the company's money, but couldn't find a bank that would handle it. "There was a little bank on the corner of Cahuenga and Hollywood Boulevard. . . . They would not take a motion picture account—you couldn't put in your own money if you were a motion picture man—just like you were a horse thief from Utah. You were regarded with a great deal of suspicion if you were a motion picture man." Since the local bank refused to accept any deposits from the Lasky operation, DeMille and company opened a line of credit with a grocer named Hall, on Cahuenga.

The suspicion of the population derived from the fact that most of the inhabitants were midwesterners who had come west to die, but had been given a new lease on life by the extraordinary climate—perfect, warm days, brisk, cool nights. It

67

was a leisurely life, and sometimes a wild one; sitting on a Hollywood patio after dark, you could hear the coyotes howling in the mountains.

The environment may have been idyllic, but Cecil had come here to work, and work fast. The Lasky business plan was viable but there was little room for error. Because the trust refused to handle the picture, the Lasky company was going to have to sell *The Squaw Man* on the states rights market—selling prints outright to exhibitors who would pay a license fee to show the film in a given geographical area or state. It was going to be critical to make the movie for a price, for the states rights market could bring only a limited amount of money.

Total income for thirty to forty prints sold around the country was likely to be in the neighborhood of $50,000, so the movie shouldn't cost more than $20,000. Less was better, but the film couldn't be a cheater, had to deliver what it promised, or the exhibitors wouldn't buy it. Cecil was going to have to thread a needle, and if that worried him, he didn't show it. While Cecil was gearing up production in the West, Sam began to sell a movie that didn't exist . . . yet.

Oscar Apfel, Cecil's co-director, was described in the *New York Dramatic Mirror* as "well-known in film circles." In fact, he had been making movies since 1911 for Edison, Mutual, and Pathé, where he usually worked from his own scripts. Before entering the movies, he had worked as a stage manager, stock company director, and with Belasco—the magic credential! Cameraman Al Gandolfi began in the movie business in his native Italy and had also worked at Pathé, as well as with Apfel.

It's probable that Apfel was delegated to handle the camera and that Cecil's charge included the acting and ramping up production. DeMille would describe their division of labor this way: "Apfel knew the technique of the screen, I knew the technique of the stage." At least once he went even further: "Oscar Apfel . . . was a good motion picture director, and I never even directed [a] picture. Apfel . . . really did most of the direction for which I got the credit. He went though this, my first picture, with me, and I [got] the technicalities of direction—a great many of them—from him."

✶

DeMille's first local hire was a secretary named Stella Stray, who, he remembered, "was delightful. She had worked for one of those companies around Hollywood that was making westerns. They went broke and, not having any cash, paid her off in physical assets of the company. They owed her about $300. So they gave her twenty cow-ponies and two mules. There was a tribe of Indians that had been used, but they didn't owe them very much so they gave them a typewriter. She thought she was rich. And suddenly she discovered that ponies eat. And she made a quick swap with the Indians. She gave them the ponies and took the typewriter!"

Stella Stray remembered that an office for DeMille was partitioned off in the barn, as well as smaller spaces for Fred Kley and a casting office run by Ethel

Wales, who was also an actress. Across the back of the barn was a huge sign: "ABANDON ALL HOPE YE WHO ENTER HERE." This amused Cecil for a while, but he eventually had it taken down.

A few months later, when DeMille had to effect some economies, he told Stella he had to reduce her salary of $15 a week. She refused to take the cut and quit on the spot. DeMille realized that losing Stella meant he would also lose her typewriter, which was the only one in the office, so he kept her on at $15. His first editor was another woman, Mamie Wagner.

Somebody—probably Cecil—had a sense of history; just before shooting began on December 29, 1913, a panoramic photograph was taken of the cast and crew of *The Squaw Man* lined up outside the barn. As the film historian Marc Wanamaker has observed, the crudeness of the weathered old barn and the costumes of the cast gave the proceedings the look of a western ghost town. Another photograph that was taken on the first day of production shows Oscar Apfel directing, while DeMille stands offstage with a small group of people. If he wasn't actively directing in those first months, the surviving evidence makes clear that he was heavily involved in everything else.

DeMille remembered that on the first day of production, someone playfully touched a cigarette to a small piece of waste film, which exploded in a quick burst of flame. The extreme volatility of the nitrate film stock frightened Cecil, and he decided that the company would use two cameras so as to have two negatives, just in case, and hang the expense. Cecil took the second negative back to his rental house every night for safekeeping.

DeMille found that California was cheaper than New York. The wages for carpenters and other service personnel were 25 percent to 50 percent less than back east. Not that he was encouraged to splurge on staff. "We had one painter, one property man, one grip," DeMille remembered. "We did not have an electrician because there were no electricians at the time."

Stories in the *Moving Picture World* would later claim that the *Squaw Man* company ranged all over the Southwest and north as far as Wyoming in search of exotic locations. Actually, the company never left southern California. Locations included Mount Palomar, San Pedro harbor, Idyllwild, and Hemet. The English manor house was in the then fashionable West Adams district of Los Angeles, and a scene of the English Derby was stock footage intercut with scenes of Dustin Farnum and a few other actors in a hastily constructed back lot grandstand.

Another bit of bogus publicity asserted that *The Squaw Man* was the first feature motion picture. Actually, a more accurate claim might be that it was one of the first features made in Hollywood—there had been at least one feature made in Hollywood, *The Sea Wolf*, in 1913—before DeMille and company even got on the train for Flagstaff.

Although the existing documents make no note of it, DeMille insisted that the original rental agreement allowed Jakob Stern to keep a horse, a cow, and a car in half of the barn. Out of necessity, the Lasky company put a partition down the middle. DeMille's part contained the drain, which meant that "When [Stern] watered [the horses] down, as he did daily, we placed our feet in waste baskets and waited until the streams subsided."

For people used to the dim light of New York winters, California presented unexpected delights. In those early days of moviemaking, the filmmakers hung lengths of muslin sheets on ropes strung over the wooden stage. When fully spread out, the muslin not only diffused the sunlight but formed a cloth roof, making the stage a shaded oasis that was cooler than the surrounding space. The muslin gave the bright California sun an amber tone, and the light's strength varied according to the time of day and year. In the hot summer, the light would be watery, because of the shimmering heat. Year round, as the afternoon wore on, the stage would get perceptibly darker, fading to a yellow glow by twilight.

"It was like San Francisco in the Gold rush days," remembered DeMille. "Pictures in the beginning were exciting." Other than the muslin for diffusion, for reflectors they used conventional bedroom mirrors. "At first they didn't even put muslin over them or cheesecloth. They just reflected the straight light, which was like a ray of sunshine breaking through the house."

The production was flying blind. "We didn't see dailies," remembered DeMille. "I don't remember any dailies. You looked at the film in your hand—you looked at the negative, to see what was there." Because they were shooting in the winter, they were bedeviled by static, flashes on the film that looked like lightning and were caused by cold. There wasn't enough money to reshoot every scene that contained static, so DeMille and Apfel had to cut around it. "When you see the picture," said DeMille, "you'll know that it's a little bit abrupt at finding the squaw dying in the snow. That's why it was abrupt. All the other [shots] had static."

For eighteen days, production ground on. If the sun went behind a cloud, work stopped. If the day was cloudy, work stopped for a long time, but as soon as the sun broke through, the actors and crew would come rushing back to the set. DeMille broke some ground and gave his film an added dose of reality by actually casting a Native American actress to play the film's heroine. Lillian St. Cyr, who usually went by the stage name of Princess Red Wing or Lillian Red Wing, was a Winnebago who had been born in Nebraska in 1883 and had worked for many of the East Coast film companies, among them Biograph and Kalem.

Cecil had rented a house at 6136 Lexington Avenue. His companion was a tame gray female prairie wolf he had bought from a newspaper ad and would bring to the studio on a leash. (Even Belasco never thought of a pet wolf!) The wolf ate what Cecil ate, and seemed to appreciate his cooking. After dinner, as Cecil would sit reading, often falling asleep in his chair, the wolf paced around the perimeter of the living room, hour after hour, all night long. She must have slept, but Cecil never saw her doing it. He and the wolf were very happy together.

Stella Stray remembered losing a couple of days to the weather: "We had to perforate our own stock, and it rained, and the roof leaked . . . day after day, and it was either the printing machine or the perforating machine that we had to hold an umbrella over! This was still inside the barn."

There was only one apparent instance of sabotage from the trust; after a couple of days of shooting, Cecil came into the cutting room to find the negative unspooled, lying on the floor and ground into the dirt. "That would have finished us—that was the end. There was no way of fixing a negative, no way of repairing a scratched negative." But DeMille's second, protection negative saved them. After that, there were some threatening letters, and Cecil bought a revolver to replace the smaller gun he had brought with him from New York.

It was like the Wild West in other aspects too. One day Cecil was riding home on horseback through the Cahuenga Pass when he heard a sharp crack and the unmistakable sound of a shot flying past his head. He drew his gun, but there was nothing to be seen.

"When the shot was fired, I was sort of non-plussed . . . and the horse looked around as though he were saying, 'Well, are you going to stay here all night? Why don't we get out? When do we move?' Both the horse and I were anxious to get back to dinner—at least I used that as an excuse. . . . That to me was not as important as making the picture."

Cecil said that there was a second shot taken at him a few days later, but that was the end of it. DeMille believed that the person shooting at him was using a rifle; if so, that meant they could probably have picked him off had they wanted to, so the shots were an attempt at intimidation, not murder.

The last day of production was January 20, 1914. "We were shooting the scenes set in England at a red brick house on West Adams street," DeMille would remember with Proustian detail nearly fifty years later. "It looked like a castle. The house is still there. It was Mother's birthday. I always remembered. I was sitting there and I happened to be thinking about her, I was probably going to send her a wire; I was thinking how lovely and sunny it was, that she ought to be out here where she could have the sun."

Discounting the $20,000 paid for the rights to the property, The Squaw Man cost $15,450.25 to make—more or less on time, more or less on budget. Cecil gave Apfel credit for the efficient production. More importantly, he had fallen in love with this strange new art form. As he told a New York reporter the day after the movie opened, "It was a new feeling, a new experience and I was enamoured of the way Mr. Apfel went about focusing his camera, getting his actors and actresses within range of the lens and the way in which our cameraman followed every move, studied the sun, tried to dodge a cloud, edged his camera into a more advantageous position."

A day after the film was finished, Cecil began cutting, without Apfel's assistance. DeMille remembered the entire editing process as "a very utilitarian procedure," and the equipment was equally basic: "The cutting paraphernalia consisted of a pot of film cement, an electric light over a piece of ground glass and two rewinds—that was the cutting paraphernalia."

Cecil looked at a rough assembly of negative and wired Goldfish:

RAN SQUAW MAN COMPLETE FOR FIRST TIME. ALL WHO SAW IT VERY ENTHUSIASTIC. FARNUM WILL DELIVER TO YOU SUNDAY NIGHT. PROPER CUTTING TAKES A GREAT DEAL OF TIME. RUNS JUST SIX THOUSAND FEET. WOULD SAVE SEVERAL HUNDRED DOLLARS EXPRESS DIRECT TO BUYERS. YOU MAY BE SATISFIED YOU HAVE GOOD PICTURE. HAVE NOT BEEN TO BED FOR SIXTY HOURS AND STILL UP. C.B.

Another DeMille cable followed:

JUST COMPLETED OUR EIGHTY SEVENTH CONSECUTIVE HOUR OF ASSEMBLING AND CUTTING WITHOUT SLEEP. FARNUM LEAVES WITH FILM 1 O CLOCK TODAY ARRIVES NEW YORK PENNSYLVANIA [STATION] 5 THIRTY SUNDAY EVENING. HE WILL COMMUNICATE IMMEDIATELY WITH YOU SO YOU MAY RUN PRINT SUNDAY NIGHT. THE OFFICE AND LABORATORY FORCE WOULD APPRECIATE A WIRE FROM YOU.

Another wire followed:

HOW ABOUT ONE THOUSAND DOLLARS. BILLS TO MEET SO GET THE OTHER THOUSAND TO ME AT EARLIEST CONVENIENCE. C.B.

An anxious Goldfish replied the next day:

GIVE US BY RETURN WIRE SOME IDEA HOW MUCH MONEY YOU WILL REQUIRE TO START [the next picture on their schedule] AS UNTIL SQUAW MAN IS RELEASED WE HAVE VERY LOW FUNDS AND CANNOT PROCEED EXCEPT VERY CAREFULLY. SAM G.

Just before they shipped the picture back east, the Lasky company decided to screen the finished movie at the barn. And thus began the first great crisis of Cecil B. DeMille's movie career.

Jesse Lasky, who had taken the train from New York for the grand unveiling, remembered about fifty people present for the screening. Soon after the credits, the image began to slide up the screen—Dustin Farnum's head kept rising out of the frame. Cecil thought that the projectionist was asleep but in fact he was adjusting the machine. There was still something wrong—no matter how often the projectionist fixed the frame, the picture would get the jitters and slide out of frame. As DeMille would recall forty years later, "every scene didn't climb off. It was an accumulation that would go wrong."

Cecil and Lasky first started to sweat, then felt the cold hand of fear squeeze their stomachs. The image was clear enough but it simply wouldn't stay on the screen. Failure loomed; bankruptcy knocked. Cecil went back with the projectionist to find the source of the problem. It was the projector, right? No, the projector seemed fine. It was . . . the film itself. The damn thing just wouldn't stay on the screen.

DeMille refused to panic. "I couldn't believe it was a disaster because I don't believe there's anything you can't fix," he remembered with the security of hindsight. That said, Lasky must have cast some dark looks Cecil's way, because he remembered that "I would say I was not at the height of my popularity. If it were a popularity contest, what I would have been was not the top. Sam . . . might have gone to jail, Jesse might have been ruined and I might have had to actually have gone down to Mexico this time and really joined the revolution."

Jesse and Cecil stayed up until three or four in the morning trying to figure out the problem. If the negative stock was defective, they were ruined, but Cecil knew that couldn't be; it had run through the camera just fine, and the images were clear as he and Mamie Wagner had cut the negative. It had to be something else. But what? They had spent all their capital making the movie, and what they had to show for it was a film that wouldn't project. They were afraid to tell Sam for fear that he would have a stroke.

Cecil kept circling around the problem. It had to be something basic, so basic that they had all simply overlooked it.

What had happened was a function of what DeMille would call his "Dutch thrift," undoubtedly exacerbated by Sam's yammering about saving money. Cecil had purchased a secondhand British sprocket-punching machine to perforate the negative stock with sprocket holes. The problem arose because the British machine perforated the negative stock at sixty-five sprocket holes per foot, while the Lasky company's camera equipment and positive stock was perforated at the American standard of sixty-four sprockets to the foot. Neither Cecil, Oscar Apfel, nor anybody else was aware of the slight but crucial variance. The persistent jittering and rolling of the frame line was the result of the misalliance between positive and negative stocks.

Cecil and Mamie hadn't noticed the problem earlier because they hadn't looked at any dailies, which would have necessitated striking positive prints, which would have cost money. Cecil and Mamie had screened and edited negative. The screening at the barn was the company's first look at the movie printed on positive stock.

And now the floundering began.

A panicked Cecil wired Eastman Kodak in Rochester:

CAN WE PROCURE FROM YOU POSITIVE STOCK PERFORATED SIXTY FIVE HOLES TO THE FOOT—ANSWER COLLECT. LASKY COMPANY, SIXTY TWO EIGHT FOUR SELMA AVE. HOLLYWOOD, CALIFORNIA.

The answer was evidently negative, because Cecil was soon wiring Jules Brulatour, a sales agent for film:

MUST HAVE FIFTY THOUSAND FEET POSITIVE PERFORATED SIXTY FIVE TO MATCH FIRST TEN THOUSAND FEET NEGATIVE WHICH WAS DELIVERED TO NEW YORK OFFICE THAT WAS LOT NUMBER FIFTY EIGHT EIGHT. NO PRINTER WILL TAKE A SIXTY FOUR POSITIVE ON A SIXTY FIVE NEGATIVE. FIRST STOCK WAS EASTMAN SUPPLY . . .

On January 23, DeMille wired Goldfish,

THINK I HAVE ARRANGED TO PERFORATE THE FIFTY THOUSAND FEET OF SIXTY FIVE HERE. WON'T KNOW DEFINITELY UNTIL MORNING. IF NOT YOU HAD BETTER PURCHASE SECOND HAND PERFORATOR WITH TWO DIALS—ONE PERFORATING SIXTY FIVE AND ONE SIXTY FOUR HOLES TO THE FOOT AND I WILL PERFORATE ALL STOCK HERE. TELL ME WHERE YOU GOT FIRST NEGATIVE GANDOLFI BROUGHT. . . . SEND THE HUNDRED THOUSAND FEET OF SIXTY FOUR. CAN YOU SPARE MORE MONEY—HAVE ONLY SMALL AMOUNT IN BANK AFTER TOMORROW'S SALARIES. IF POSSIBLE WIRE ME ENOUGH TO KEEP FAIR BALANCE. AM HOLDING OFF BILLS HERE BECAUSE YOU SAID SHORT OF CASH.

That night, Sam sent a telegram:

OF VITAL IMPORTANCE SHOULD KNOW YOUR OPINION ON SQUAW MAN. WHEN CAN WE EXPECT FIRST PRINT?

On January 24, Cecil frantically wired back:

CAN'T ARRANGE PERFORATION UNLESS YOU CAN FORCE EASTMAN TO GIVE YOU POSITIVE TO MATCH FIRST NEGATIVE. RUSH PERFORATING MACHINE . . . WITH FIFTY THOUSAND FEET UNPERFORATED POSITIVE. . . . SQUAW MAN A GREAT PICTURE. CAN SEND FIRST PRINT FIVE DAYS AFTER RECEIVING PERFORATOR OR SIXTY FIVE POSITIVE.

DeMille was under the misapprehension that matching the sixty-five perforations on the negative to the same perforated positive would solve their problem. But the projector sprockets were still turning at sixty-four to the foot, so the picture would still roll upward.

He finally broke down and wired Sam in New York:

SOMETHING TERRIBLY WRONG WITH PRINT. PLEASE ADVISE. REGARDS, CECIL.

"Please advise"? What could Goldfish possibly do at a distance of three thousand miles? Actually, he did quite a bit. He telephoned Cecil and they went over the problem inch by inch. Sam then said he would sleep on it. Sam knew considerably less about the technical aspects of movies than Cecil did, but Sam also knew Sigmund Lubin of Philadelphia, who had a lab as well as a production facility and was an expert at everything photochemical.

What made Sam's idea of seeking help from Lubin dangerous was the fact that Lubin was a member of the Trust, and theoretically forbidden from taking any work from an independent. But Lubin had a checkered history with the Trust; at one point he had violated Edison's patents and been forced to leave the country to avoid lawyers. As film historian Robert Birchard would observe, Lubin "was in the establishment, but not of it."

Goldfish explained the situation to Lubin; Lubin told Goldfish to get him a print of the film. Cecil and Jesse got on the first train to Philadelphia—it must have been an agonizing trip. Cecil decided to use the train trip to edit the spare negative of the film to match the first. (He was probably hoping that the problem had been in the first camera, and the negative from the second camera would be fine.) He rigged up a cutting apparatus that lay across the seat opposite him in the compartment. As the train worked its way east, Cecil spliced the movie together without the help of a screen, holding the film strips up to the window to identify the action. As he put it, he was "poring over the tiny pictures until my head was reeling."

When the train pulled into Philadelphia, Cecil had worked for forty-eight hours straight, but the second negative was almost finished. They arrived and handed the film to Lubin. He held a strip of film up to the light, turned it around, called in a technician, and handed it to him.

After fifteen agonizing minutes, the technician came back. "Nothing wrong with the negative, it's just the sprocket holes." Lubin's technicians cemented unperforated film over the edges of the film, and then reperforated the film.

For his trouble, Lubin asked only to be given the business of supplying release prints for the Lasky company's productions. And just like that they were back in the movie business. For the rest of his life, DeMille always had a soft spot for Sam, and no wonder. He habitually drove everybody crazy with his manic, querulous ways, but he had been cool in a terrible crisis, and he had saved their company.

In the three weeks before the press screenings of The Squaw Man, the Lasky partners had to raise about $3,000 to pay for the lab work and additional prints. Harry Reichenbach, the Lasky press agent, asserted that after being turned down by George M. Cohan, Arthur Hopkins, and B. F. Albee, they got the $3,000 from a bottom-feeder named Harry Cohn, who was given a piece of the company in return. Four months later, Cohn sold his piece of the company back to Jesse, Cecil, and Sam for $55,000, which Cohn later used to establish Columbia Pictures.

(Reichenbach was a legendary fantasist, so Cohn's payout figures are undoubtedly high.)

Beatrice finally saw the film she had helped finance on February 16, in the theater downstairs at the Longacre Building, where the Lasky company had taken offices.

> JUST RETURNED FROM SEEING PICTURE. IT'S WONDERFUL HEARTIEST CONGRATU-
> LATIONS TO EVERYBODY CONCERNED. FARNUM GAVE ME THE KISS YOU SENT . . .
> I'M PROUD OF YOUR MOVIE KISS THE WIFE AND BABY FOR MOTHER.

Bill saw the picture with his secretary, a woman named Anne Bauchens. She would remember from the vantage point of 1956 that "I was a very naïve young lady. . . . I had worked in real estate offices and as a switchboard operator. . . . I had never been among the literary and more intelligent groups [so] I just thought it was the most wonderful thing I'd seen."

The Squaw Man had an exhibitors' screening on February 17; within two weeks, the Lasky company had sold the movie in thirty-one of the forty-eight states. A week later, every territory except Missouri, Kansas, Nebraska, and Iowa was sold, and eventually they all fell in line. *The Squaw Man* would amass a net producer's profit of $244,700—an amazing return for the period, although a lot less amazing when you subtract Dustin Farnum's 25 percent.

Louis Reeves Harrison of the *Moving Picture World* wrote that *The Squaw Man* was "one of the best visualizations of the stage play ever shown on the screen . . . a source of surprise and delight for me." *Variety* said that it "may be set down as a genuine 'masterpiece' in moving picture productions."

The *New York Dramatic Mirror* wrote that "*The Squaw Man* [is] among the few really satisfactory film adaptations of plays. In point of sustained interest it gives place to none; the acting offers no cause for criticism, the settings are notably appropriate and, best of all, there is a real story told in photographed action, not in lengthy subtitles, illustrated by fragmentary scenes."

The *Dramatic Mirror* critic stumbled over Cecil's great gift, already present in chrysalis form in his beginning picture, for which he didn't even bear sole responsibility. In more than a century of movies, there have been few directors with DeMille's gift for narrative—his ability to move a story forward, not just with every scene, but with every shot. From the very beginning, DeMille movies *moved*.

And something else: Jesse and Cecil chose for their first vehicle a sympathetic story about Indians, and Cecil went out of his way to cast an Indian actress to play an Indian character—something that wouldn't become the norm for another seventy-five years. Over the years, DeMille would be saddled with—and occasionally saddle himself—with a reputation as a reactionary, but in this case, he was far ahead of his time.

Dustin Farnum fell in with the prevailing line of sweetness and light and forgot to mention the torments of production—the sabotage, the gunshots, the chaos wrought by inexperience. He told the *Moving Picture World*, "The success of *The Squaw Man* is due to the manner in which it was made—the cleverness of direction and the way the whole thing was handled by everyone concerned."

The Squaw Man ("Picturized by Cecil B. DeMille and Oscar C. Apfel," as the main title announces) is mostly up to the standards of the period. There's no sense of the tight budget, or, for that matter, the inexperience of the filmmakers working at a lonely outpost on the edge of the continent. The titles tend to announce the action before we see it, in the manner of Griffith's Biographs: the title "Henry plunges heavily on the Derby" is followed by a race scene and the character filling out IOUs. Later on in the film, that tendency is curbed. Most of the film is played in medium shots like most movies in 1914—not imaginative, but safe.

Where Cecil and company excel is the locations; there are real mountains, real snow, and there is some dynamic staging. The set of a stateroom in a ship beset by stormy seas rocks back and forth effectively, there's a split screen shot, and the set of a saloon is built adjacent to railroad tracks, so a train can roll by and actors can walk from the set in the foreground and climb onto the train in the background, and vice versa, a staging strategy replicated by Abel Gance in *La Roue*. (In his career-long tightrope walk between nervous, intimate melodramas and gargantuan epics, Gance would be one of DeMille's most ardent acolytes.)

Only one or two brief scenes betray the palsy that drove the Lasky company toward the rocks. On the other hand, there are numerous telltale flecks of white in the shape of Lubin's newly punched sprockets salting more than a few scenes.

DeMille was always sentimental about *The Squaw Man*—he would remake it twice—and around the lot it was known as the mortgage lifter. From today's vantage point, the first release from the Lasky company is a picture that doesn't transcend its time.

Transcendence would come soon enough.

6

DeMille and company didn't start shooting *The Virginian*, their second picture, until April, two months after *The Squaw Man* was released and it was increasingly obvious that it would be a big hit. As the money rolled in, production ramped up. *The Virginian* was, of course, an adaptation of Owen Wister's famous novel, and was made for $17,022, bringing back slightly more than $110,000 in receipts.

The Virginian was the first movie for which DeMille took sole credit ("Picturized by Cecil B. DeMille"), and it once again focuses on the beefy charms of Dustin Farnum. At the same time, it's a far more fluid film than *The Squaw Man*. There are very tight close-ups, an almost total reliance on locations, and some very creative use of the camera. One scene is lit only by a campfire, and at one point DeMille mounts the camera on the back of a stagecoach to get a dynamic shot looking down on the driver and the leading lady as they ride through a canyon. When the Virginian's friend Steve is hanged for rustling cattle, DeMille shows the swinging body in shadow form.

There is an overriding sense that DeMille is presenting not theater, but figures in a landscape. Already present is a strong sense of how to effectively dramatize commercial material. *The Virginian* features some of the low-key lighting that is nowhere to be found in Oscar Apfel's work and would become one of DeMille's signatures—a prominent stylistic device that undoubtedly owed a great deal to his new cameraman. Al Gandolfi, who had shot *The Squaw Man*, stayed with Apfel as he made other pictures for Lasky, so Cecil hired a thirty-six-year-old named Alvin Wyckoff. Wyckoff and DeMille would form a seamless team for nearly ten years.

During the production of *The Virginian*, the company was on location in the San Fernando Valley when they came across another movie company. The director sent DeMille a tart note saying that the frame buildings DeMille had thrown together for a set had ruined the planned compositions. DeMille sent a snippy note back, and he remembered that the mood of the letters "might easily have led to gunplay between both groups if it hadn't presently become apparent that the other director was a woman." DeMille capitulated to the extent of letting the competition shoot its scenes first, but he refused to raze his sets.

The female director's name was Jeanie Macpherson. She was eventually fired for taking too long in production and showed up at the Lasky barn carrying a book of stills and some of her reviews. Cecil kept her waiting, which led to another exchange of unpleasantries, but they finally got down to cases.

Cecil didn't really need an actress. Nor did he need another director—DeMille and Apfel were quite enough at the moment. "Why don't you learn something you can do at 80 as well as 18?" he asked her. "Learn to write—and not the sort of tripe you've been writing up to now, but genuine dramatic material. Or would you rather be a leading woman for a few years and then do a permanent fadeout?"

Macpherson got huffy—she always got huffy when challenged, which was why DeMille enjoyed challenging her—and stormed out. She was back the next day, asking for a job at $25 a week. And so began the second most important relationship of Cecil B. DeMille's life.

Jeanie Macpherson was born in Boston in 1887. She had a journeyman's show business career that included chorus work at the Chicago Opera House, and small parts for Sir Johnston Forbes-Robertson. She had also been in the touring company of Bill deMille's play *Strongheart*. By 1908, she was working in the movies at both Edison and Biograph. At the former, she had been directed by Oscar Apfel; at the latter, she had appeared in a long list of Griffith's best, most innovative Biograph films: *The Curtain Pole, A Corner in Wheat, The Message of the Violin, The Lonedale Operator, Enoch Arden.* She had also written and produced movies at Universal and Balboa. Some thought that love letters she had written Griffith helped break up his marriage.

Macpherson was an all-arounder, with a strong, vivid personality. She was a tough, feisty creature, and in common with most of the women in DeMille's life, more striking than beautiful. He pronounced her name "Jinny," and she would stay with him for the rest of her life.

"After Constance, Jeanie was the great love in his life," said DeMille's granddaughter Cecilia. "He talked about her a lot. She shared with him that most important time; when you are young and you're going up. He would talk about the thrills he and Jeanie had had in what they were doing together—the films, the pioneering in a new industry, watching the major successes of their collaboration. He once told me that there were three women aside from my grandmother—who was always in a separate category—who could have had anything they wanted from him: my mother, Gladys Rosson, and Jeanie."

All this came about because of a shift in his marriage to Constance. In 1914, at the age of forty-one, Constance suffered a miscarriage, and that, coming after the difficult birth of Cecilia, impelled her to remove herself from the marriage bed. The ardent letter that Cecil wrote her during his trip to California to make *The Squaw Man* carries some indication that sex may not have been her cup of tea in the first place. In 1914, Cecil was only thirty-three, and not of a celibate disposition. There is no indication that he had ever had an extramarital affair until now—both Jesse Lasky and William deMille believed him to have been an absolutely loyal husband, and they would have known—but he began one with Macpherson.

Outside of the bedroom, nothing changed. Cecil regarded Constance with something approaching adoration. As for Jeanie Macpherson, Cecil respected her tenacity, both professionally and personally. "She was like a tarantula," he would remember admiringly years later. "When she got her fangs into anything you couldn't shake her loose."

Jeanie understood the rules of the game she had entered into: "I don't believe that an old wife who has helped a man to succeed should be turned in like a second-hand car," she would tell a journalist, with more personal insight than readers could have guessed.

★

Cecil felt secure enough in his new profession to send for Constance and Cecilia. The family moved to another rental, this time on Cahuenga. Cecil's pet wolf seems to have made Constance nervous, so Cecil gave the animal to the zoo at Universal, where he would occasionally visit her.

Artistically, the Lasky company's great leap forward came when it signed Wilfred Buckland as supervising art director just before Cecil began shooting *The Call of the North* in June. Buckland was born in 1866 and had worked as a lighting designer and stage manager for David Belasco for twelve years. Not only did Buckland design and light Belasco's plays, he had decorated Belasco's theater. Belasco bestowed on him the lofty title of "General Stage Director." Buckland was convinced by Beatrice DeMille to give the movies a try, and signed an eighteen-month contract on May 19, 1914, that started at $75 a week and escalated to twice that. Beyond his professional expertise, Buckland was practically family; he had been a pupil of Henry's, had acted in Henry's play *The Main Line*, had taught Cecil and William at the American Academy of Dramatic Art.

From Buckland's point of view, the Lasky company seemed to offer something more than just an opportunity to hop from the stage to the movies. "I was seeking an opportunity to picturize in a more 'painter-like' manner," he would write a few years later, seeking to apply "to Motion Pictures the same rules which govern the highest art of painting." He was also counting on the Lasky company eventually opening a New York branch, which would presumably need Wilfred Buckland as supervisor. (It is unclear whether this satellite production facility was in fact floated as an inducement to Buckland, or was just a personal fantasy.)

When Buckland arrived at the studio, he found an unroofed wooden platform, two feet off the ground, and the adjoining barn. At one end was a telephone pole that had a boom attached to it, and the muslin sail that would be spread over the stage as a diffuser for the sunlight. If Buckland was appalled at the conditions, which were Stone Age compared to the bountiful lighting boards he had in New York, it wasn't for long. *The Call of the North* features one knockout visual effect: a beautiful night scene of a cabin in the woods that involves a backdrop painting, a miniature cabin built in forced perspective, and a foreground of pine trees—a shot far beyond the capabilities of the carpenters that had been building the Lasky sets before Buckland.

Buckland would build spectacular sets then and afterward (Douglas Fairbanks's *Robin Hood* was Buckland's greatest post-Lasky achievement) but all that pales next to his bringing the Belasco technique of designing with light to the movies, where it could be more heightened than in the theater. At that time, as DeMille remembered, cameramen were rated according to "how clearly you could see under the table . . . how clearly you could see the back corner of the room—both corners." DeMille had something else in mind, and he knew that Buckland could help him realize it.

"Buckland is a man who has not been given credit that he deserves," DeMille stated near the end of his life. "Belasco's productions were something nobody in the world could equal, and that was because of Buckland."

A month after signing Buckland, in June 1914, the Lasky company bought the movie rights to ten Belasco plays for what Lasky remembered as $100,000 against 50 percent of the profits, an outlay of cash that indicates how successful the little company had been in just six months. Besides using the Belasco plays as presold properties, DeMille sought to find a screen equivalent for the luxurious physical environments that Belasco had created on stage; the extensive panning shots across Buckland's sets in a film like *The Girl of the Golden West* have nothing to do with story, everything to do with DeMille's pride in his new art director.

What Buckland brought to the Lasky pictures was detail and theatricality. He abandoned painted backdrops and most T-shaped sets; his interior sets were elaborately dressed, and DeMille felt comfortable with the art director's taste for verisimilitude. "I will challenge anyone to find an incorrect detail in *The Call of the North*," he wrote Sam Goldfish. "In matters of detail, there is no stone left unturned."

Buckland constituted a one-man art department—he was designing, painting, set decorating, and doing a lot of the lighting as well. Buckland was a mandatory hire because in May 1914, the Lasky company agreed to turn out thirty pictures a year. By mid-1914, Lasky pictures were rolling out more or less on schedule, and the profits were rolling right back in. Cecil and Jesse were a dynamic team, united in their mutual enthusiasm and volcanic energy. All his moviemaking life, DeMille had a military capacity to create and instill unit discipline, and within six months of arriving in Hollywood, he had designed and staffed a smooth production facility.

The Call of the North was shot in June and rushed out in August. It was the first example of Cecil's penchant for self-promotion, as he appears in the credit titles with the authors, conjuring up images of the actors playing their parts.

"*The Call of the North* is the latest and beyond question the best of the Lasky photoplays produced under the direction of Cecil B. DeMille and Oscar C. Apfel," wrote the *New York Dramatic Mirror*, while the *Moving Picture World* said, "The dominant characteristic of the play is lavishness. A lofty ambition to attain the highest ideals in the motion picture art gave birth to this feature, which I am tempted to describe as one of the greatest classics ever produced on American soil."

Next up was a charming little film called *What's-His-Name*, shot in July, released in October. It's based on a novel by George Barr McCutcheon that is actually a comic rewrite of Dreiser's *Sister Carrie* as it might have been written for an expert light comedian such as Sidney Drew. DeMille's showmanship kicks in with the credits, as playbill pages with the actor's pictures dissolve into the actors themselves. The star, a popular Broadway comedian named Max Figman, advances toward the camera and bows left, right, and center. *What's-His-Name*—the title refers to the dubious status of a shopkeeper husband once his wife makes it to the theatrical big time—offers some behind-the-scenes insights into the pre–World War I theater, and features a delightful performance by little Cecilia DeMille—one of several she gave in her father's films in this period. It's a zesty, solid film that cost only $12,233, and grossed slightly more than $61,000.

Cecil was still learning his craft in this period—he relies too much on medium shots—but every film he makes has some compelling, exploitable, or dramatic element: a famous source play, attractive stars, or innovative handling, sometimes all three.

By the middle of 1914, the Lasky company had joined a releasing combine called Paramount, organized by a man named W. W. Hodkinson. Paramount was a distribution mechanism releasing pictures from a group that included Famous Players, Bosworth, and Lasky. Famous Players was run by a bright, highly acquisitive man named Adolph Zukor. Zukor liked the pictures the Lasky company was making; he also liked the name Paramount.

★

The Lasky company proposed to solve the printing problems that had bedeviled *The Squaw Man* by having Cecil run their own lab to make the master print that Lubin in Philadelphia would duplicate in bulk. "I have bought the laboratory for $2,250 and am paying [Harry] Revier $250 for nine weeks," Cecil announced. "He has given me the formula of the secret toning process and will be on hand to give what technical advice I require. I think, however, that I have fairly well mastered the work sufficiently to direct others in doing it."

As William deMille would observe, "One thing I have always admired about my younger brother is his ability to bite off more than he can chew, and then chew it."

In the memories of all who experienced these first years in Hollywood, this was a golden time. They were young, deeply emotional friends and lovers engaged in something that felt like summer camp, but actually went beyond a goofy lark into the realm of an astonishing artistic conspiracy. They were pushing, daring each other to accomplish something available to only a few people in any century: to simultaneously create an art form and a business empire.

★

Although Cecil wrote a number of the scripts for the first batch of Lasky productions, he was frank about his own gifts. "I did not and do not consider myself a writer," he would admit. "I think better in visual images and dramatic situations rather than in words." He needed someone he could count on to take charge of the Lasky script department.

He needed Bill.

On July 30, Cecil cabled his brother:

HAVE GOT GOOD OPENING HERE TO COLLABORATE ON SCENARIOS WITH ME LEAVE YOU PLENTY TIME FOR OWN WRITING. WOULD YOU CONSIDER COMING HERE IMME-DIATELY AND WHAT SALARY WOULD YOU ACCEPT. YOU WOULD FIND ATMOSPHERE HERE CONDUCIVE TO INSPIRATION IN YOUR OWN WORK. COME ON IN WATER IS FINE. WIRE ANSWER. CECIL.

Over the next few months, Cecil kept nudging. Bill wanted $200 a week to start, which Cecil thought rather high, especially as Sam Goldfish was cage-rattling about budgets. Finally, on September 17, Bill took the plunge: "Dear C.—Answering yours of September 10th, by the time this reaches you, I will be on the train bound for Hollywood. . . . I am coming, prepared to jump right in and if I fit stay a year or two. . . . I will not bring the family until I am sure that there is a place there that I can fill with credit to myself and the company. . . . I expect to leave New York on Tuesday, the 22nd, on the Santa Fe Limited, which shall bring me to Hollywood, I think, on Saturday evening. Billy."

Almost a year to the day after writing his condescending letter to Cecil about his impending career suicide, William deMille was en route to California to work as a script supervisor for the Lasky company. In a letter to Sam written the same day Bill agreed to head west, Cecil expressed some doubts. "Tickled to death at his coming out here, but, at the salary named, it will be necessary for him to produce to pay for himself, as I believe $200 per week for a scenario writer will not be, in itself, a paying proposition, because if you are counting on this shorting the time consumed in producing you are utterly wrong. Not in a single instance has the scenario held the play up a day. . . .

"I can make Zukor productions for you in three weeks; in fact, I will guarantee to turn you out a half dozen *Eagle's Mates* [a Mary Pickford vehicle for Famous Players] weekly . . . Griffith has now been working for four months on *The Clansman* and is not nearly finished. He is the man we are trying to top and I think we are succeeding. I, personally, cannot give you any good work by rushing. Jesse has been on the ground for a week and he should know that it is practically a physical [impossibility] to cut down the time consumed in making a production. . . . Again let me express my thanks to you for securing Billy. It will be a pleasure, as well as an assistance, for me to have him here, but he has got to produce to earn that salary."

Bill arrived in Hollywood on September 26. When he saw his brother, he realized that movies agreed with Cecil. "He had bronzed and hardened, he was about twenty pounds heavier with not an ounce of fat. He seemed to glory in the excitement of the work—the dust, the dirt, the heat and general confusion."

Cecil was about to begin shooting *Rose of the Rancho* on location, so Constance and Cecilia met Bill's train. "Hollywood itself," Bill wrote his wife the next day, "is a suburban town, with lots of tropical vegetation, tremendous Palms, etc., but it all has to be nurtured very carefully; the country being really desert and supporting best those things which grow in the desert. But the general effect is rather tropical luxuriance with wild desert just outside & in plain view. . . . I don't think however you need to fear our remaining here permanently, as the social life is practically limited to our own people, and the artistic & musical life is nix."

It was Bill's first day on the set of *Rose of the Rancho* when he heard a familiar voice boom, "Hello, William."

"I looked toward a quiet chap in riding pants, hat, sun-glasses and a mass of blonde, wavy hair," remembered William. "He turned out to be Wilfred Buckland, the company's art director, who had designed all the scenery for 'The Warrens of Virginia' when I worked with Belasco, and was destined to be one of my best friends in the many hectic years to follow."

William said that he hadn't believed that anything could have separated Buckland from the theater, and Buckland said he thought the same thing about Bill. Then Buckland threw his arm out toward the valley and the mountains beyond. "You see, this is the first time in my life I ever had a stage big enough to work on."

Besides plunging into scripts, Cecil also pressed Bill into work as an actor on *Rose of the Rancho*, where Bill played a sharpshooter as well as a rider. Bill noted in a letter home that Cecil played off battling groups of movie extras against each other, telling one group to get to the top of the stairs, and another group to absolutely refuse to let them get to the top of the stairs. Result: "a few scratches & bruises & a bloody nose or two no one was hurt. We were much relieved, for we fully expected some broken bones & even had a doctor there to be ready in case. . . . This is a wonderful, healthy life in the open air," exulted Bill in closing.

In the next two weeks, Cecil gave Bill a crash course in moviemaking, culminating in Cecil's script for *Rose of the Rancho*. The task, Cecil told his older brother, was to write completely for the eye and disregard the ear.

On October 29, a telegram was sent to Sam Goldfish in New York that revealed both Bill's acquiescence to the world of the movies and his own financial travails:

> ADVANCE BILLY'S WIFE ANNA DE MILLE TRANSPORTATION AND TWO HUNDRED DOLLARS. CHARGE THE WHOLE AMOUNT TO BILL HAVE ARRANGED SO AMOUNT WILL BE HELD OUT OF HIS SALARY. BILLY IS FORCED TO DEPEND ON THIS SO DON'T FAIL HIM.

✳

Rose of the Rancho concerns land grabbers and claim jumpers in Spanish California, and the supposed stars were Bessie Barriscale and Monroe Salisbury—with a very early appearance by Jane Darwell, John Ford's Ma Joad.

But the actual star was Wilfred Buckland. Amidst some frantic emoting, Buckland created a lovely atmosphere of adobe missions, arbors, and dappled sunlight. The sets are lived-in, and, while studiously paying attention to Belasco's plot, Cecil made sure to experiment with staging, notably with deep focus, which enabled characters to make an entrance in the background and walk to the foreground, all in sharp focus.

David Belasco was delighted. "It was like a dream to sit in my theater," he wrote Cecil, "and see my production of *Rose of the Rancho* unfold in all its beautiful color and with all its dramatic action. You have caught the very shadows of the land of my childhood."

While Cecil was turning out a series of pictures that are still watchable a hundred years later, New York was putting pressure on him as Director-General for the company's West Coast output. Sam Goldfish wanted Lasky pictures to cost less, but DeMille stoutly thought that was impossible.

> If you will go over my salary sheets, you will appreciate the impossibility of any reduction there, with the exception of the one you name, Apfel. With this exception, a cut anywhere in the salaries is an impossibility, for the reason that the cut was made at the time of employment. For instance: Do you realize that two of the princip[al] parts in *The Man from Home* received a weekly salary of $15? In [*The Circus Man*] the star receives $100.00 and the leading woman $15.00 and the leading juvenile $25. Comparatively, the rest of the salaries are the same. We pay from 30% to 60% less, per capita, in salaries than any company operating on the Coast. In other words, I am giving you features that have taken first place in the country at a less price than Universal can make its one reel

abortions or Ford Sterling his one reel grotesques. . . . I defy Man, God or Devil to accomplish even one half as good results for that amount of money. . . .

I feel that you are entirely inappreciative of the fact that I have given the company work that can compete with Griffith, at a cost that theatrically can compete with the 5 and 10 cent store. . . .

I am utterly helpless at this end. In fact the suggestion that I reduce from here had rather made me feel, "What's the use?"

Cecil halfheartedly threw out some suggestions—get rid of the character actor Theodore Roberts, even though "he is one of the strongest cards we have," or do away with Wilfred Buckland "and go back scenically. . . . I'm free to confess that the problem has got me stumped. With best regards, Yours 'Until death us do part.' "

If there was any bending to be done, it wasn't going to come from Cecil.

Later that month, it was DeMille's turn to be on a tear, as he was furious about the quality of the lab work Lubin was doing on the Lasky pictures. "These pictures are full of light effects, which have cost us several thousand dollars to produce and I should hate to see them made worthless by Lubin not following the sample print. Some scenes are to be printed too dark. This is purposely done and unless they go by our sample print, they will try to bring out the detail of background, which will ruin the effects. Also, we have spent many weeks in perfecting a certain color to resemble artificial light. I am sending Lubin . . . a formula of this color. This must be carried out exactly. No substitute color will do. It is simple and inexpensive and there is no excuse for its not being fulfilled. . . .

"I have gone to the tremendous expense of diffusing the entire stage with light yellow diffusers, which give the soft gold sunlight effect of California. This can be made absolutely worthless by Lubin printing with too light or too heavy a light. . . . Also, we must find some way of preserving the impressionistic effects we are beginning to get."

When *Rose of the Rancho* was nearly ready for release, DeMille was still fretting. "There is one scene in *Rose* where the murder is committed that is so dark that only a square of light on the floor is discernible. The entire action of the murder is lost in the blackness of the background. This must be carried out this way. There are many instances of shades of printing of this kind and the man who sets the lights for the printing must have the sample print before him to follow. Corcoran, the manager, and the entire Lubin plant will inform you that it is ridiculous and the public won't and don't like it and many other things of the sort, but I want my sample print followed and followed exactly."

A month later, an unmollified DeMille wrote to Goldfish that the Lubin print of *Rose of the Rancho* "is best he has done for us but far from right. Amber color much too light looks like black and white print. Daylight patio scenes much too contrasty. Scene where Negro servant sends Larkin back for soldiers so light it is undiscernible. . . . You say someone saw this print run. That's the place to begin cutting salaries."

Two days later, DeMille took his grievance directly to Lasky: "I will not consent to have Lubin print *Girl of the Golden West*. Shall try firm here? Hold consultation on this at once and advise. As I am through with Lubin that is positive so let us avoid unnecessary delay on the subject."

DeMille's relentless drive was paying off. Besides that, the alliance with Belasco was noted in the advertising: "Jesse L. Lasky in association with David Belasco presents . . ." heralded *Rose of the Rancho* as well as *The Warrens of Virginia*.

★

For the first nine months of his time in Hollywood, Cecil hedged his bets by maintaining his New York apartment at 241 West 108th Street, but he gave no signs of being focused on anything but movies. "I saw the picture *Judith of Bethulea*," he wrote Blanche Goldfish, Sam's wife. "It is a fine piece of work, but under our methods of producing, would not run more than two reels."

Practically the entire family was now busily engaged in movies. Even Constance threw herself into a western called *Where the Trail Divides* directed by James Neill and released in October. She was billed as "Constance Adams" and the main feature of her performance was her thick brown hair cascading down Pre-Raphaelite style, as an Indian slung her over his horse.

Just as Cecil was everywhere in this period, so was Constance. To go along with her primary part in her husband's emotional life, she was also becoming a very important part of his business life. Jesse Lasky wrote her, "Your stock is now worth fifty seven thousand three hundred and some odd dollars. As I hold the original stock, I am now turning it in so as to secure the new stock certificates which I will hold until I come to California. . . . I think our company is going to be a very prosperous one. Don't you agree with me?"

At the end of 1914, Lasky hired Blanche Sweet away from Griffith through Jeanie Macpherson. Sweet had no actual contract with Griffith—none of his stars did—so signing her was more a matter of breaching loyalty to Griffith than of money. Not that money didn't matter.

"I am still holding out on Blanche Sweet as I hate to pay her over $300," wrote Jesse to Sam Goldfish on November 4. "I will not lose her and, if by the time I leave I cannot bring her around, will give her more money." By December 4, Sweet was working for the Lasky company on *The Warrens of Virginia*.

Cecil's debts began spilling over into the company. On September 11, Jesse wrote him that "some of your creditors are beginning to bother Mr. Friend so I wish you let us know if, after three or four weeks you could let us deduct, say $30 per week out of your [$250] salary as Mr. Friend [the Lasky company's lawyer] thinks he probably can make some arrangements to pay them small sums until the debts are settled. . . . We will continue to pay [Beatrice] $50 per week which [will also be deducted.]"

Besides being engaged in her usual struggles, Beatrice was also angling for an invitation to see her boys on the West Coast. Beatrice was seen by others as a somewhat tiresome personality, but DeMille always smiled when he talked about her in later years. He recognized her eccentricities and found them amusing. She had a way of always needing money, and was perfectly willing to interrupt her son in the middle of production or anything else. She was his mother, and that meant she didn't have to wait.

According to his daughter Agnes, William was a little leery of her "bleeding the boys for money. She spent money on her personal adornment like nothing I've ever known. She was not so much large as portly, and she dressed like the Gypsy Princess in an operetta. Her taste was so abominable that it was a kind of taste in itself. She found someone in Hollywood that could make realistic poinsettias out of plastic, and realistic wild roses and realistic honeysuckle, and she had lamps of this, with twines and loops and traps. Now that wouldn't be enough—she put a *veil* over it. With *beads*. She was a quite handsome woman with *beautiful* silver-gray hair in masses and coils, with big combs, with big feathers . . . red silk petticoat, green silk petticoat, silk stockings and gloves with lace inserts. *Nothing* was left unadorned."

The New York office had been dunning Cecil's salary to pay the bills he had incurred before heading west for the Lasky company. But those deductions, plus Beatrice's expenses, left Cecil with insufficient liquidity to take care of his needs in Los Angeles.

If Cecil wasn't wrangling over money with his mother, he was doing so with the equally stubborn Sam Goldfish. Sam wanted Cecil to spend less money, while Cecil would explain in detail why that wasn't possible. After a bunch of hectoring letters all saying the same thing, DeMille took a deep breath and responded, not to "Dear Sam," but to "Dear Sir":

You will note that my end, as per your letter of Sept. 1st, averages about $14,000 and your end $17,000, out of which I am paying $5000 for a star, making two positive prints, paying for the stock consumed therefor and for negative stock, have purchased three automobiles and maintained a large plant without any overhead expense charge. If you deduct the star's salary you get the total cost of production $9,000. This amount is inclusive of every production expense, including rent and, for that, we are turning out the best pictures being made today.

I have looked about carefully for a means of reducing our average expense, but consider it practically an impossibility to come much below this figure and maintain our present standard, which, of course, is the very heart and soul of the company. . . .

If our standard is to remain at its present height and climb higher, which is the desire of you and Jesse and myself, it will be an absolute impossibility to reduce on this end. The only suggestion I have to offer along this line is that as far as the artistic merits of our work here is concerned, we do not need the $1000 a week stars. Whether or not you need them for the value their names give, is a matter that you are more competent to judge than I.

By mid-October, the Lasky company was the mass production elite of the nascent Hollywood film industry. Cecil was offered $120,000 a year to throw in with another company and turned them down flat, even though it was far more than he was making from Lasky. "Many companies are going to fail," William wrote, "but it is because companies like ours are putting them out of business. We'll have to wait a bit for the big money—but it is here—if we can deserve it. . . . C will be better off eventually with this Company."

In October, the company took an inventory of the prop department—one detects the fine hand of Sam Goldfish in this—that revealed Lasky, after ten months of production, owned one organ, with stool, valued at $6.00; twenty-seven law books, valued at $6.75; three rat traps, valued at $3.00; a single feather duster worth 75 cents; two miniature trains worth $20.40; ten dozen whiskey bottles worth $2.00; a stereopticon set worth $2; and last but certainly not least, one what-not worth $3.00. The total value of the company's props came to $1,400.62.

More importantly, the Lasky company also occupied three city blocks of prime Hollywood real estate, and had a new ranch with twenty thousand acres of land for location shoots, not to mention offices in New York.

★

Beatrice worked hard at placating Cecil's creditors and seems to have done a good job of it. He owed $2,000 to one Thomas Higgins, and there was also $300 owed to Mr. Pincus, the landlord of Cecil's New York apartment. In addition, there was $703.62 to Max Josephson—Cecil's attorney in his theatrical years—$1,000 owed to a Mr. Rolnik, and $70 owed to J. F. Taylor and Co. publishers and importers.

Then there was $562.50 due the Wagenhals & Kemper Company for the leasing of their play *Seven Days*, to Beatrice, as head of the DeMille Company. "From what we have learned of the financial situation of the DeMille Company," wrote Messrs. Wagenhals and Kemper, "we shall not consider . . . a suit against it, as we understand that it is still indebted to several creditors and is without assets sufficient to meet such claims."

Since Cecil had been a manager of the company before the siren call of Jesse Lasky, they wanted their $562.50 from him. They got it, at the rate of $50 a month.

"I am besieged by your creditors," Beatrice wrote to her son. "Next week I will make out a list of the most important and the most importunate. What shall I do about the Encyclopedia Britannica? They are threatening all kinds of fearful things. Also a bill from your garage. Now my dearest child take up your pen *this moment* and write to Mr. Higgins. . . . If Mr. Higgins has plenty of time to fix up things with the proper people to be consulted . . . he will surely extend the time. But for Heaven's sake write him the moment you get this."

Higgins was willing to settle for $50 weekly. Jesse Lasky insisted that Cecil not sell any of his Lasky stock, which he correctly insisted was the basis of Cecil's future fortune. Jesse advanced the $50, and Cecil lowered his salary draw to $100 a week. I WILL CLEAR YOU OF DEBT AND WE WILL DIVIDE AFTER WE ARE FREE OF DEBT, wired Beatrice. THIS IS MY YEAR AND YOU MAY TRUST YOUR MOTHER.

Then there was the matter of an unspecified amount of debt to a Mr. Carey—"have just had a long talk with his man. Better pay him a little, to show good will. It would be a pity to have a new judgment filed at this stage of the game."

But Cecil's checks to Higgins failed to arrive, and said Mr. Higgins was dropping by Beatrice's office. "He was astonished and hurt, and doesn't think much of the business methods of the present young men of today . . . he made me promise I would write you today without fail, and tell you what he had said. Please let me know what you are going to do and for mercy's sake, child, answer an old man's letters when he takes the trouble to write on the run. . . . Your loving but worried Mother."

For the next two years, until the debts were all paid off and Cecil began amassing the assets that would make him the richest director in Hollywood, there are several constant refrains in Beatrice's correspondence:

1. Cecil didn't write often enough.

2. Cecil was in terrible financial trouble.

3. Beatrice was in terrible financial trouble.

4. Cecil should thank God he had Constance. "You are blessed beyond your desserts—so far—in having such a wife, but she loves you and you can make it all up to her—every atom—in the years to come and—now!!!"

Despite the often frantic worry reflected in her letters to California ("Haven't paid either office rent or office telephone yet this month. Can you help a little from the front?"), Beatrice never seems to have doubted Cecil's eventual success. "Once started clear we'll soar right up to success and happiness" is the way she ends one letter. Another closes with "This year is going to be a big one for all of us." Still another ends with, "It does me good to the very soles of my toes to know you are going to be on Easy Street some time in the very [near] future."

She passed along compliments from friends and also pointed out ideas that seemed to her fallow, as with a couple of pictures Cecil made about a Bowery character named Chimmie Fadden—"I have come to the conclusion that the 'Chimmie Fadden' type of picture will probably never do business, and therefore I think it might be well to try an entirely different type of subject for [Victor] Moore."

When Cecil did write back, he told her, "Always at all times tell me exactly what you think. Real opinions are the only ones of any value."

*

When not directing, writing scenarios, supervising the other directors, juggling his debts, and running the lab—in spare moments he probably grabbed a broom and swept the studio—DeMille kept an eye on what other producers were doing and occasionally offered some boyishly enthusiastic wild schemes:

> Last night Hobart Bosworth invited me to see his private running of *The Valley of the Moon*. Here again, is a case of fine photography killed by bad scenario. The direction is fine, but the people would not stay through to the end. Dusty [Farnum] and I were bored to extinction, yet the book is full of drama and could have been a fine picture. . . .
>
> I had a long talk with Bosworth recently at Mary Pickford's reception which we attended in all our glory, and suggested to him that we join our forces for South America. From all I can learn, South America is almost virgin soil and the man that gathers enough strong feature stuff together, can control the field. It seems to me with ourselves, Bosworth and one or two other concerns which I am confident would go into the scheme, you could [send] some one down to South America and exhibit these pictures and make a very good clean up. . . .
>
> I am still in complete ignorance of the affairs of the Lasky Company in New York and the rest of the world other than Hollywood.

These were years when Cecil was gathering around him the nucleus of the professional family that would stay with him for the rest of his life. Another crucial hire was a young girl who came to work as DeMille's secretary on December 13, after Stella Stray moved over to the editing table. Gladys Rosson was a prim little woman who wore steel-framed glasses, dressed like a provincial schoolteacher, and looked like the popular conception of a spinster. But Gladys was a ferociously organized, determined, and—above all—focused woman whose focus was always resolutely on Cecil B. DeMille. She worked for him all her life, and was one of the few admitted to the trusted inner circle of his business and family. Gladys's brothers Arthur and Hal followed her lead and became notable members of the movie community, the former as a director, the latter as a cameraman of genius.

That same year, Jesse Lasky brought a stocky, energetic young lawyer to DeMille's office in the barn. Back in New York, Cecil's legal affairs, which mainly involved fending off creditors, had been the province of Max Josephson. But Neil McCarthy was handling a real estate deal for Jesse, and DeMille took an immediate liking to him. He was alert, very smart, and had the grin and sense of humor befitting an Irishman. DeMille's granddaughter would remember McCarthy as charming and handsome, "an Irish rogue." He became DeMille's lawyer and intimate friend, and remained so for the rest of DeMille's life. Beginning with DeMille, McCarthy developed an exclusive list of clients that eventually included Louis B. Mayer and Herbert Hoover.

The inner circle was completed by Bill's secretary, Anne Bauchens. Cecil put her on the payroll at $10 a week, and she organized the secretarial department at Lasky. After becoming one of the first script supervisors, she found her metier as a film editor.

Bauchens worked almost exclusively as Cecil's film editor from 1918 until his death. The relationship was always strictly professional; he would remember that in over forty years, he only roused her to passion once. A car Cecil was driving spun out so that its back end was hanging over a precipice. "I hung onto the brake and Anne threw her arms around my neck and said, 'Oh, Cecil!' That was Annie's only burst of emotion toward me in the forty years that we've been working together." DeMille trusted both McCarthy and Bauchens absolutely; neither of them ever gave him reason to regret that trust.

★

Eight days after finishing *Rose of the Rancho*, Cecil was shooting another Belasco play, *The Girl of the Golden West*, converted into an opera by Giacomo Puccini in 1910. Cecil shot his film in precisely eight days, which perhaps explains why the opera is better. Cecil didn't take much time for niceties, although there are several moments when the camera tracks in from a long shot to a medium shot. The story is a Bret Harte–ish tale of early California, the leading lady (Mabel Van Buren) is homely, but Jeanie Macpherson, who acted in the film, is noticeably charming. Cecil spent $15,109 making the film, which earned $102,224.

From *The Girl of the Golden West*, Cecil segued to an adaptation of Bill's hit play *The Warrens of Virginia*. Cecil and Bill were able to quickly cobble together an adaptation of the play because they knew the material so well. As he was readying the production, Cecil wrote the playwright Stewart Edward White, "I am about to produce The Warrens of Virginia, and expect to kill a lot of perfectly good actors and some good horses. Why don't you come down and see the fun?"

White responded: "Nothing would please me better . . . especially if you will guarantee to kill a lot of actors."

Cecil began *The Warrens* on December 5, finished it on January 9, 1915, and it was released on February 15. Cecil remembered that it was on that picture that he devised what he referred to, with some exaggeration, as "the birth of artificial [screen] lighting."

"When we first went to California, everything was sunlight. No artificial light was employed. Having come from the stage, I wanted an effect, so I borrowed a spotlight from an old theater in Los Angeles [DeMille later remembered it was the Mason Opera House] when I was taking a photograph of a spy. The spy was coming through a curtain and I lighted half of his face [with] only just a smash of light from one side, the other side being dark. I saw the effect on the screen and carried out that idea of lighting all through the rest of the picture, that is, a smash of light from one side or the other."

When DeMille sent the finished picture east, Sam Goldfish sent a violent telegram: "Have you gone mad? Do you expect us to be able to sell a picture for full price when you show only half of the man?"

"This isn't an exaggeration," DeMille would insist when telling the story in later years. "This is exactly as it occurred. . . . I was really desperate. As I told you, the director has to go through; he has to do something. So Allah was very kind to me and suggested the phrase 'Rembrandt lighting.' I sent a telegram to New York saying 'If you fellows are so dumb that you don't know Rembrandt lighting when you see it, don't blame me.' The sales department said, 'Rembrandt lighting! What a sales argument!' They took the picture out and charged the exhibitor twice as much for it because it had Rembrandt lighting."

The story sounds a little too well rounded, the stuff of anecdotal history, but both DeMille and Lasky remembered the same set of circumstances and the same responses. Actually, "Rembrandt" lighting soon became "Lasky" lighting, because early filmmakers understood the importance of what a later generation called branding.

"I was trying to get composition and light and shadow," DeMille would recall, "and I would say to [Alvin Wyckoff] 'You mustn't make this part so light, under the table mustn't be light—it should be dark and the back corner of the room shouldn't be light—it should be dark.' So they all said, 'He likes it *contrasty*'— contrasty!—that was the phrase. There were some terrible battles because of that, because that meant expose it for contrast. It didn't mean shadow it, it just meant make the whites whiter and the blacks blacker."

DeMille films began to use spotlighting for dramatic effect, in the same way that it was used on the stage: to guide the viewer's eye and to heighten a dramatic moment with harsh pools of light in the midst of darkness. The result, as historian Lea Jacobs noted, is "confined and shallow areas of illumination, sharp-edged shadows and a palpable sense of the directionality of light."

DeMille's lighting was innovative for the movies, although it seems likely that he was adapting the techniques of David Belasco to the screen. Take the lighting directions for a wealthy banker's library in the third act of *Men and Women*, written by Belasco and Henry deMille in 1890:

From the doors . . . are windows through which is seen a low balustrade
and trees completely shutting out the view of the street beyond, with
the exception of a portion of one house, which is seen through the
branches of the trees. At the back of the room, running obliquely to
the R. is a large fireplace. Above the fireplace is a niche in which is set
a stained-glass picture of the Magdalen at the feet of the Saviour. The
picture is not discernible at first, that part of the room being in the
shadow. A soft red glow proceeds from the fire in the grate. The hanging
lamp sheds a subdued light over the room. A lamp with a dead green
shade stands turned down. Everything outside is covered with snow. The
storm has ceased. The clouds have broken in places, showing small portions of a cold moonlit sky, a dull blue light pervading the atmosphere
outside.

Throughout Belasco's scene, the light levels alter as the characters turn lamps
up or down. Finally, a character turns out all the lights so that moonlight can be
seen through the windows. The climax comes when the moonlight illuminates
the stained glass window, gradually revealing the Magdalen over the fireplace.

As with his mentor, DeMille would use lighting not only to create striking
images, but to heighten already dramatic situations. DeMille would rarely be interested in dynamic camera movement per se, was considerably more expert in
abrupt, volatile editing, but his concern with composition and lighting made him
a true innovator in moviemaking of this period, where the primary concern was
in recording a clean, unambiguous image.

From a major effort, Cecil downshifted to a quickie: *The Unafraid*, a Balkan
story with some nice castle sets shot in three weeks. After a year of making movies,
Cecil is achieving fluency; he still relies too much on medium shots, but the medium shots are tighter than they had been, and better lit. *The Unafraid* is on a par
with the pictures other companies were making, which is to say slightly beneath
the standards of the Lasky company. (In a handwritten letter that provides a plot
point, "niece" is misspelled "neice." It would have been easy to retake, but either
nobody noticed or nobody cared.)

But Cecil was doing more than just making pictures; he was building an
organization, not to mention putting together the pieces of a stock company that
would provide at least as much pleasure as the nominal stars—prominent character actors such as Raymond Hatton are appearing in DeMille's pictures, as they
would for the next decade. Cecil never tired of telling the story of Hatton's introduction to the splendid facilities of the Lasky studio.

"I can't dress there," Hatton yelled.

"Why not?" innocently inquired DeMille.

"Why not? Come in and taste this atmosphere yourself. . . . Who's been
using this dressing room anyway? Who was the last person to use it?"

"It was a horse," confessed DeMille.

"A horse?" Hatton repeated, with a you-must-be-joking look on his face.

"Yes," said DeMille. "We couldn't afford a new dressing room, so we used a box stall. See, we tacked the door on the front there."

★

The Unafraid cost $14,226, and returned $63,944. It was the beginning of Cecil's greatest period of accomplishment. In 1915, he directed thirteen of the Lasky company's thirty pictures and wrote eighteen of them as well, including a couple of masterpieces.

In early 1915, while shooting *The Captive*, Jeanie Macpherson's first script for Cecil, an extra died. DeMille wanted a shot where a door would first be hammered by gun butts, then splintered by bullets. They rehearsed with empty guns, then loaded the guns, but when Alvin Wyckoff had a camera problem, DeMille ordered another rehearsal and ordered the guns to be unloaded. Everybody complied but one man. As they rehearsed the shot where the extras pound on the doors with their gun butts, the loaded gun went off and the bullet entered the forehead of one of the extras, blowing a hole in the back of his skull. "I got some of his brains on my coat," remembered DeMille.

One of the extras began sobbing, explaining that he had thought unloading his gun was a waste of time. DeMille told him to pull himself together and leave Hollywood after the inquest, at which he did not reveal the guilty party's name. The dead man's name was Bob Fleming; DeMille and Lasky felt honor-bound to keep his widow on the payroll for years.

"Sitting at home that night, Jesse and I, that's where Mrs. DeMille was wonderful," remembered Cecil years later. "She knew we felt terribly. You can't help but feel that perhaps in some part it must be your fault—for not having checked everything first, or taken [the guns] away. Or for . . . trusting that people followed your instructions. We had the inquest. Nobody knew who killed him. Nobody knew whose gun had been loaded. The coroner's jury brought in a verdict of accidental death."

Production was suspended for the day, putting the pell-mell Lasky production schedule behind. According to leading man House Peters, DeMille refused to close down production yet again so the cast and crew could attend the funeral of the dead extra. But Peters put his foot down and said he was going to the funeral and everybody else would have to come along too, as there weren't any scenes to shoot that didn't include Peters.

This was a particularly stressful period for Cecil. Blanche Sweet was starring in *The Captive*, and she remembered coming across Jeanie Macpherson passed out behind a pile of lumber next to the barn. DeMille mentioned the same incident in a tape he made with Art Arthur for his memoirs. "I found her . . . I don't know. It might have been Blanche. It was when I was at the old studio on Vine

Street. Jeanie and I had been working and I said good night to her. She went out to leave and I worked till about—I guess another hour or hour and a half. . . . I picked her up and carried her in—either to my office or hers, I don't remember, or Gladys', and put her in my car and drove her home, carried her upstairs and gave her to her mother. But she was not well then."

More than ten years later, Macpherson also talked about a time when she was very ill and not expected to live. "Once I saw Cecil DeMille cry. It was when I was lying very ill in a hospital. Everyone thought I was going to die, but myself. I was vaguely conscious that Cecil was sitting beside my bed, crying. I heard him say, and it seemed to come from a million miles away, 'I can't do anything to save my little pal.' That's the way he is about his 'pals.' Friendship means more to him than love to most men."

All this transpired about nine months after Cecil and Jeanie met. It's possible that a flu bug was involved, but the extreme emotion recalled by both makes that unlikely. She could have been pregnant and miscarried; but the cause of her illness remains unknown.

By this time, Cecil was free to make other sexual arrangements so long as it was clear that Constance's position was to remain unchallenged. "As long as I live, there will never be another Mrs. Cecil B. DeMille," Constance told her sister-in-law. Constance once told her niece Agnes, "You know, sex and love have nothing to do with one another. They are entirely different concerns in human life."

Most people who knew DeMille believe that he would have been a very happy man if he could have gotten everything he needed from one woman. But Constance was steadfast in her decision to abstain from marital relations. Her only inadequacy was sex; other than that, she was a wife and partner in every possible way.

In fact, the situation was not all that unusual for the period; Jesse Lasky and his wife, Bessie, also had an understanding. "Jesse's affairs were quiet, in secret," remembered his daughter Betty. "He and my mother lived separate lives. They didn't divorce because it wasn't necessary. If you were rich you could lead your own life. They had separate wings of the house and private phones. It was a strange marriage; he adored her, but at the same time she didn't fill his needs, and he went elsewhere. All those men had mistresses scattered about. Mr. Zukor was the only exception."

For Macpherson, DeMille could be misguided but never wrong. She was an adoring apologist, regarding his bursts of temperament as armor for "an extremely sensitive nature. Actors didn't like him, and I have seen them tremble before his sarcasm and often cry with humiliation. But . . . he would forgive anyone anything if a person would only admit his error. But try to tell him that the other fellow was to blame, or insinuate another department was responsible for your blunder, and you were in serious trouble with him."

DeMille loved Macpherson as a woman but didn't particularly respect her as a professional. "She wrote like a plumber," DeMille recalled. "I am sure I was frightfully insulting to her, but that kid took it and plugged along." Another time, he bluntly said that "She was not a good writer. She would bring in wonderful ideas but she could not carry a story all the way through in writing. Her name is on many things because she wrote with me. I carried the story and she would bring me many, many ideas."

Other screenwriters agreed with DeMille. Beulah Marie Dix didn't think of Macpherson as a writer, but as "an exceptional collaborator for an exceptional man." Bertram Milhauser was driven up the wall because "Jinnie" couldn't punctuate; he theorized that she stood across the room and threw periods and commas at the title cards as if they were darts.

Yet Macpherson would become Cecil's most important screenwriter of the silent era. "She was more of an inspiration in conversation than she was in the writing," he said. ". . . But she was a very, a very brilliant woman."

For Blanche Sweet, newly signed as the company's leading lady, DeMille suffered by comparison with her previous director. "Nothing could be as exciting as Griffith," Sweet told film historian and author Kevin Brownlow. "Poor Cecil DeMille didn't have any experience to go on. . . . He had come from the theater and so he had a background of that, but there was nothing exciting about Cecil DeMille and his work."

Sweet left the distinct impression that the entire stint at Lasky was a misalliance. "We used to laugh when it was all over and we knew each other socially. He [DeMille] told me, 'I was terribly afraid of you, because you'd come from this great director, and I wasn't a great director,' and I said, 'Well, I was scared of you.' We were both looking at each other, and trying to understand the other and we never did succeed in understanding each other."

After a couple of films that no longer survive, in late May 1915, Cecil began shooting his own script for *Kindling*, the closest he ever came to a socialist tract. It's about life in the slums, and the sets are so disgustingly atmospheric as to be worthy of a German film from five years later. Crooks and whores surround a poor couple, played by Thomas Meighan and Charlotte Walker, introduced as "Victims of the city." A baby in their tenement building dies, surrounded by flies, his bottle full of gin. Walker's character is pregnant, but conceals the fact from her husband because he refuses to bring a child into such a world. "Half of them die," he snarls, "the rest grow up to be crooks."

Their tenement is owned by a rich dowager, who hires the pregnant woman to sew for her. Class resentment boils over and the seamstress attempts to rob her benefactor to get the money to go west, where she and her husband can start over. The crime is discovered and the mother makes an angry plea for her unborn child that shames the dowager, who gives her $100 and sends the family west.

It's a film of indictments, savagely directed, as unyielding and Zolaesque as one of Griffith's perfectly chiseled Biographs; Cecil shot it in two weeks, and it was released a month after he finished shooting. It grossed six times its $10,039 cost and some of the critics sat up and took notice.

"I do not hesitate to say that this is one of the best samples of the Lasky school of motion picture art," wrote Stephen Bush in the *Moving Picture World*. "When at its best this new school beggars comparison. . . . It scores in every scene and there are no weak links." Nearly a hundred years later, the compliment holds true.

★

Then and later, Jesse Lasky was distinguished by his capacity for appreciating and encouraging artistry. "He had this [talent] more than some of the other pioneers," said director Rouben Mamoulian, "because he was an idealist, and when he saw something beautiful, he gave you a tremendous reaction to it. . . . He was always burning about something, always excited about something."

To Jesse's conceptual fire was added Cecil's organizational genius and sense of drama. Around this time, Sam Goldfish asked Cecil to expound on why he had left the theater for the movies. Ignoring such mundane motivational factors as impending bankruptcy, Cecil came up with some very good reasons: "Because where one member of the paying public will see a play, there are two thousand who will see a picture; whereas one or perhaps two countries would see my play, practically all the countries in the world will see my pictures. Again, and as has been probably said before, the scope of the photoplay is so much wider than that of the legitimate drama. In the first place, we DO things instead of acting them. When a big effect is necessary, such as the burning of a ship, the blowing up of a mine, the wrecking of a train, we do not have to trick the effect with lights and scenery, we DO it."

He mentioned the joy he found in the outdoor life that early moviemaking entailed, then returned to the fulfillment he was finding in this new art form.

"In the play we have two, three and sometimes four settings and can spend months in working out the details. In one picture we may have one hundred and fifty interior settings alone, and even though each may be on the screen but a few moments, each has to be correct to the smallest detail. . . . Again, the smaller cities get exactly the same form of productions as the five great cities of the world. I simply give you a few of these points to show why I don't expect to return to work on the legitimate stage, ever.

"I could go on till my stenographer fainted from exhaustion."

Cecil closed this unusually revealing letter by telling Goldfish that he would soon be forwarding some new publicity photographs. The photos, he wrote, showed "two new hairs which have recently appeared upon my dome of thought, called Maude and Clariesse respectively."

★

In December 1914, perhaps as a result of a recent miscarriage, Constance brought home a fifteen-month-old baby the DeMilles called John, who was the son of a man named Ralph Gonzales. When John turned three, Constance and Cecil legally adopted him. Unlike the other two children that the DeMilles would eventually adopt, the truth of John's parentage was never discovered by him. "John didn't fit," remembered Richard deMille. "John was a Mother Teresa gesture on the part of Constance; she would always be big on saving young women, as when she founded the Hollywood Studio Club with Mary Pickford."

★

Because he was on his feet most of the day, Cecil took to wearing laced boots to support his ankles and protect him from the brush and snakes on locations. His working wardrobe also included riding breeches—because they were loose-fitting—and open-necked shirts—because he disliked neckties. For the rest of his life, even after most of his films were made in the safe confines of the studio, he would wear variations on this wardrobe.

Throughout this period, the Lasky company was overwhelmed trying to keep supply in some equilibrium with spiraling demand, and breathless telegrams were constantly flying east and west. The cash flow had improved, but as far as Beatrice was concerned, there was never enough cash flow.

"Dearest Boy," she wrote Cecil on December 2, 1914, "I have this moment sent you by registered mail the two rings as instructed by your letter of November 27. . . . I am terribly short all the time. So far I have squeezed through, and I trust in God. I don't write because you never answer. . . . Have you forgotten that Mr. Pincus is still waiting patiently for his three hundred dollars? At the present time he is calling me up daily to know if the promised 'wired money' has arrived." Beatrice closed by asking "Does William really like it out there? He writes no oftener than you do. . . . Your handwriting this morning did me good, even if it was only a line—literally. My heart's love for you all. Mother."

In January 1915, Jesse Lasky noted that Cecil owed the Lasky company $4,400, and was preparing to sell some of his stock to get another $1,000 to pay off some back debts. Cecil told Lasky that the weekly debt reduction he was committed to meant he couldn't send his mother her $50 a week stipend, so he asked Goldfish to send her the money from the company and add it to his tab.

In February, Cecil wrote his mother to ask if she was actually using the car he had bought her for $375. If so, fine; if not, sell it. He reported that he had paid some debtors a large sum of money and paid another debtor $1,000 in addition to $70 interest, "so he ought to be happy. . . .

"Constance is going East in May for a month. Why don't you return with her? Just because I am working day and night is no particular reason why I should not hear from you."

In April, Cecil's old attorney Max Josephson wrote him about $703.62 Cecil had owed him for several years. "On July 21, 1913, you wrote me as follows: 'I as-sure you it has not been negligence that has prevented my making the payment due you for services rendered. You know I struck a line of failures last years . . . and if you will stick a while longer you will not be the loser. . . .'

"If it is too great a tax on you to remit the whole amount now, may I ask you to send a check for a substantial part, and thereafter remit to me weekly a further sum, until your obligation is liquidated."

Scribbled on the letter is the notation, "Paid–C. B. deM."

☆

DeMille had discovered that after editing a picture, it helped to put it on the shelf for a week or two, then take another look. That way, he came to the picture fresh, and could usually find some cuts that he hadn't seen before. This cutting accounts for the hurtling pace of most of the early Lasky pictures. They're not always great, or even good, but they're never dull. Cecil took to movies so quickly, adapted to them with such alacrity, because they matched up seamlessly with his own ardent emotional makeup: Show me. Interest me. Dazzle me.

Jesse Lasky's correspondence mostly concerns business, but he often had to spend time refereeing between DeMille and Goldfish. At the same time, there are occasional notations about the care and feeding of DeMille that indicate the implicit respect Lasky felt for his friend and partner: "I wish," Lasky wrote Sam Goldfish, "whenever there is an article published concerning Cecil, you would see that they are forwarded to him. He never reads any of the magazines or papers. As a matter of fact, he does not get time to read at all. He produces and runs the plant all day and depends on his nights to write his scenarios, so he will never get any time to do any reading."

Bill had taken charge of the scenario department, and Jesse pronounced himself "absolutely delighted . . . with the results Billy is obtaining. He is proving himself so vitally important that I wonder how we ever tried to get along without a man of his ability. You can feel safe that any picture that he undertakes to write will be a dramatic masterpiece of its kind."

Bill was perennially rushing to get scripts finished, sometimes in less than a week, so they could be put into production immediately. He couldn't do it alone, so he started hiring other writers: Marion Fairfax, the wife of the actor Tully Marshall, would write movies until the end of the silent era; Hector Turn-bull was the former drama critic of the *New York Tribune*, and would write *The Cheat* for the company, as well as marry Blanche Lasky after she divorced Sam Goldfish; Turnbull's sister Margaret was also one of Bill's hires, as was Edgar Selwyn.

Production was bursting at the Lasky company. Besides DeMille, there were now three other directors (George Melford, James Neill, and Fred Thompson), five cameramen, and a stock company of eighty actors. A row of orange trees was leveled to make space for dressing rooms. Outside on Vine Street, there were benches beneath the pepper trees where unemployed picture people congregated, so Cecil could always pick up an actor, an assistant, or a prop man.

Cecil was still doing much work besides directing. Sometimes there was no script girl, because Cecil would make the shooting notations himself: "Have drawer closed first take" and "Open 2nd take." He would scribble "OK" next to each shot as it was completed, or draw a line through it. For shots he decided he didn't need, he would scribble "Out."

The early scripts Cecil was working from and often writing are little more than shot lists, with telegraphic lists of actions. Take this example from his script for *The Warrens of Virginia*: "Exterior, Federal Trenches. Men in trenches. Officer, Arthur and Bill Peavey come on carrying flag of truce. Arthur asks to be taken to General Griffin. Officer takes him off scene—Bill remains at trench, seats himself on breastworks. He and Northern soldier talk. Bill pulls out quid of tobacco, asks Northern soldier if he will have a chew. He takes some . . ."

Decor, lighting, costumes, staging were all at the discretion of the director, but then with his own scripts Cecil presumably already knew what he wanted to do, so didn't need to put it on paper. Occasionally, he'd jot a sarcastic remark about someone else's literary efforts: "It must have been lunch time when this was written and the author was hungry."

William wrote a more sophisticated script, as befitting his more literary sensibilities, as with this scene from *The Wild Goose Chase*, with Ina Claire, shot by Cecil in a pell-mell ten days in 1915:

"Scene Two. The front of the town opera house, over the drug store. The Opera house being on the second floor. Stairway going up to it and a large sign, which reads, 'One Night Only. The Eminent Shakespearean Actor Horatio Brutus Bangs as Romeo. Admission 15-25-35.' Next to this is a poster of Blanche Sweet in 'The Warrens of Virginia' at the Photo Play Theater. Horatio is an actor of the old school, trying to look prosperous. He wears a heavy fur overcoat, but looks rather seedy, smokes a cigar and carries a cane. He is reading the sign with satisfaction . . ."

The overwhelming impression of dynamism in DeMille's vocabulary—the "smash" of lighting; "the director has to go through . . ."—and the state of mind that vocabulary indicates, explains a great deal of the success he was earning. While he would increasingly shoot his pictures in a visually sophisticated manner, in terms of story and stars he and Lasky were hedging their bets, seldom deviating from theatrical properties and theatrical stars. Not until he was a grizzled veteran with nearly six years of moviemaking under his belt did Cecil discover that an actress with no stage experience whatever could have more resonance on screen than any stage-trained actress.

★

As DeMille's films began to be noticed, so did he, and people who knew his mother in New York began to wonder about his consistent emphasis on his Episcopalian half. This gradually led many to assume a covert anti-Semitism, a stance that would only be strengthened by his future status as a pillar of California's right wing.

But the America of a hundred years ago was a very different place than it is now. Both Cecil and William embodied the typical prejudices of their Victorian childhoods. Agnes, William's daughter, believed that both Cecil and William were anti-Semitic; she quoted her father referring to "your Broadway Jew manager." Yet Bill told his stepdaughter that he was "very proud of his Jewish heritage." Agnes would also report that she heard Cecil say, "I don't like the Jewish people out here." And then he would smile and say, "Of course, I have to stop and remind myself, I'm one of them."

Cecil's own private feelings about Jews seem to have settled on an old saying he remembered from his childhood that sounds suspiciously like something from (the Jewish) David Belasco: "Every salad is helped by a little dash of garlic, and every man is helped by a little dash of Jew."

In most cultural and religious respects, DeMille was egalitarian, promoting women into positions of power and influence very early in his career and displaying no noticeable prejudices about homosexuals. Once, when he was going to be introduced to someone on the set of one of his films, he was told, "They are colored."

"I don't care about the color of their skin," he snapped. "I only care about the color of their soul."

He once said, "I can understand being bored by a bore. I can understand being thrilled by a brilliant man. But you can never say, 'This man can't be brilliant because his skin is black.' . . . I haven't the smallest antagonism about race or color. I haven't bad feelings about any man because he's black, white, red, brown, green or blue."

Ultimately, as Cecil's longtime screenwriter Jesse Lasky Jr. would note, "He did not heavily identify himself with Jews—or much with anyone else. He had a suspicion that most people might not be worth identifying with anyway. He served his own Gods . . . but he was enormously loyal to those who served with him (the military phrase is deliberate) and proved it on many occasions."

★

When Cecil wasn't making his own movies, he was riding herd on the rest of the Lasky production. He wrote Jesse about a problematic picture that had drawn titters in a screening. "Without question, it is the absolute fault of the scenario . . . [which has] blunders which a five year old child would hardly make. . . .

"In my opinion, Billy should be absolutely exonerated for this reason: it is impossible for him to write scenario after scenario, under pressure, and guide the work of his department as well." Overlooking the fact that what was impossible for Bill was a daily task for Cecil, he switched around the department. Billy would supervise and collaborate with the three staff writers on scripts, with the other writers deferring to Billy's judgment. "In this way, he collaborates on three scenarios at once. . . . It leaves one scenario writer for each director which is ample to keep nicely ahead. This mode of procedure will continue until such time as we can think the scenario department can stand sufficiently on its own legs to allow Billy to continue writing again."

As for the bad picture, Cecil and Bill spent a Sunday recutting and retitling to make it releasable.

★

DeMille enjoyed Sam Goldfish a great deal for his energy and humor, some of it unintentional. But Goldfish had been born in Poland, had a thick accent, a high-pitched voice, and a shaky command of English grammar. Once, DeMille impatiently asked Goldfish if he had any concept of what a double negative was. Immediately, he was seized by regret.

"There was a film [in Goldfish's eyes] that I knew I could never wash away," DeMille would tell a family member. "I have regretted all my life saying that." Yet there were times when Sam's compulsive nattering drove DeMille to abrupt explosions of fury. When *Chimmie Fadden* opened in mid-1915, Sam wrote Cecil a letter complaining that people don't usually pour cocktails on the carpets in nice homes. DeMille fired back that "it is the criticism of a fool. You might say it is impolite for people to be sick on a carpet. It is generally supposed that there are certain conditions which cause people sometimes to forget that they should be polite. In fact, your transmitting any asinine criticism of this sort to me, I should say, shows a slight wave of mental aberration on your part. A sensible criticism I always want. A fool thing of this sort, please spare me."

Cecil was also in receipt of a letter from his mother that, after relaying some information about the purchase of a property, went into a recent Lasky release. "The last third was somewhat tedious and the end was wicked in all you left undone—a real begging of the question. If William is at the head of that department—how could it get by him?"

Everybody's a critic.

7

In 1915, the Lasky company opened negotiations with Geraldine Farrar, the great diva of the Metropolitan Opera. An opera singer in silent movies would seem to be intrinsically absurd, but Farrar would prove the exception to the rule, just as she had been since her debut as Marguerite in *Faust* in Berlin in 1901. Farrar was not exactly beautiful, but striking, vivid, and self-possessed in a way that gave her an aura of sexuality. When David Belasco saw her in Puccini's *Madame Butterfly*, he said, "If she lost her singing voice today, she would still be the greatest dramatic actress in America." Farrar's fees and royalties earned her as much as $130,000 a year, and her personality drew a wide variety of men into her orbit.

She had relationships of varying degrees of seriousness with Puccini—who wrote *Suor Angelica* for her—and with the baritone Antonio Scotti, but her most serious affair was with conductor Arturo Toscanini. Unfortunately, Toscanini was married, and Farrar was not interested in the role of mistress. She gave Toscanini an ultimatum, he chose his family, and that was that.

The contract she signed with the Lasky company mandated eight weeks of work for a fee of $35,000, and further stipulated that "The star shall not work more than six hours a day, this period to be broken into morning and afternoon sessions of three hours each, with an intervening period of two hours at midday for rest." The Lasky company was to furnish her a house and a car. Although the initial thinking had been to spend the eight weeks making just one movie, someone came up with the idea of cramming three films into the summer.

The news that Farrar was going to make a movie of *Carmen* struck the industry like a thunderbolt. Back east in New Jersey, a young director named Raoul Walsh read the news in the trade papers and went to his boss, William Fox. He told him that they had enough standing sets in Fort Lee to do a quick knockoff version with Fox star Theda Bara and scoop the DeMille version. "You're still that damned Irisher with the Yiddisher *kopf* [head]," exclaimed Fox. According to Walsh, two days later they were shooting. The Fox knockoff of *Carmen* opened simultaneously with DeMille's, undoubtedly skimming off some money.

Farrar arrived in Hollywood on Friday, June 11, and Jesse made sure she felt welcome. Schoolchildren were recruited to meet her at the Santa Fe train station, and there was a carpet of flowers leading from her private railroad car to her automobile. Her welcoming gift was a large basket of oranges.

The studio rented her a house, with a staff of four. After she toured her living facilities, she was taken to the studio, where she was shown her bungalow, the first one Jesse and Cecil built for a star. There was wicker furniture, a piano, chintz drapes. The rooms were full of flowers—roses, poinsettias, carnations, poppies. Farrar adored it all, as well she should have. Cecil strode in, dressed in puttees and workshirt with the sleeves rolled up. One tough pro eyed another, and they instantly knew they could work together.

The next night, at ten, there was a formal welcoming dinner at the Hollywood Hotel. Among the attendees were Cecil and William with their wives, the Dustin Farnums, the Douglas Fairbankses, the Wilfred Bucklands—all of the early Hollywood settlers. Even Sam Goldfish came out from New York to attend.

"The decoration consisted of awkward bowls of poppies, wisteria and roses," remembered Bessie Lasky. "The wives stood in lines with their husbands, introducing everyone to the guest of honor and her family. Miss Farrar looked ravishing dressed in a white brocaded satin evening gown trimmed in black Chantilly lace. Her jewels were worn with great dignity. She had a heavy necklace of emeralds and pearls and her smile enchanted even the old ladies who were peering through the lighted windows of the porch."

When the grand march was announced, actor John Drew took Farrar's arm and everybody marched into the ballroom. As the night wore on, the case of champagne was gradually emptied. Eventually, Farrar sang an aria from *La Bohème*, after which everybody ate—platters of chicken, bread and butter sandwiches, and salad.

On Monday, Farrar came to the studio at dawn, made up and raring to go. The only problem was that she was practically the first person at the studio. "Where's Mr. DeMille," she wanted to know. "Where is everybody?"

On her second day of work, DeMille met Lasky at his office in the morning and said, "I want to show you something you'll never forget." He proceeded to lead Lasky through the orchard to the shooting stage. Everyone on the staff, from stars to secretaries, was standing transfixed around Farrar's bungalow next to the stage, listening to her sing an aria from *Madame Butterfly*.

In spite of her accomplishments and reputation, Farrar was approachable, charming, and a fierce worker. Soon, she was universally known as "Gerry." Blanche Sweet got into the habit of leaving her dressing room door open so she could hear Farrar singing between setups.

Farrar never complained, was never in a bad mood. It was Farrar who might have been responsible for what soon became one of the more pleasing affectations of silent film production. "I asked Cecil if we might have music during our scenes, as I was so accustomed to orchestral accompaniment for certain tempi and phrasings," Farrar remembered. It wasn't just for the proper mood; she used music as a timing mechanism, to give a sense of rhythm to her movements.

DeMille hired a piano player named Melville Ellis, who kept up a steady stream of classics—according to Farrar's friend Edward Wagenknecht she hated music from Tin Pan Alley and Broadway. Although contemporary trade journal stories indicate that director James Kirkwood had used an orchestra and singers to help his cast maintain the proper mood as early as January 1914, it was Farrar's modest request that opened the floodgates; soon, every silent movie had set musicians playing for the actors.

Although Farrar in *Carmen* was the centerpiece of the summer's activities, Cecil insisted that she make a different movie first, in order to get used to the demands of the camera. She was put in a picture entitled *Maria Rosa*, as a sort of glorified screen test. William deMille contributed the script, about Catalan peasants beset by torrential jealousy.

Farrar presented only one problem—her gray eyes photographed blank. She began to panic, but DeMille had a solution. For the rest of her movie career, Farrar always had to look at a piece of black velvet held in her sightline but out of camera range. Her retinas expanded and her eyes looked normal to the orthochromatic film.

In *Maria Rosa*, Farrar shows herself to have already grasped most of the essentials of screen acting, although Wallace Reid is far more beautiful than she is. Then it was on to *Carmen*, which was based not on the opera libretto—too expensive—but on the original Prosper Mérimée story, which was in the public domain.

Moviemaking struck Farrar as basic but fun. "The cosmetics applied were more or less of a white grease paint, with an overlay of Rachel powder, a little eye-shadow, all applied by my own hand. I used no lip rouge. I wore my dark, abundant hair which I dressed myself, parted and coiled at the nape of the neck. I needed no seamstress, make-up specialist, consultant or other specialist in my preparations to meet the camera."

"I thought DeMille was a genius," Farrar told Kevin Brownlow, "and I was very fond of him. He would never shoot you in a close-up against white, and he would never allow a moving background behind a close-up. He wanted all the attention focused on the expressive moment."

After *Maria Rosa* and *Carmen*, Farrar made *Temptation*. She felt comfortable with the camera, although she had qualms about the modern-dress *Temptation*. "She is terribly disappointed at her appearance in modern clothes," Cecil wrote Jesse Lasky on August 2. "She has intimated, now that thirty-nine scenes have been taken, that maybe we ought to change the scenario and do *Tosca*; but I have succeeded in convincing her that she was very beautiful. There is a great deal in what she says. So far, she seems a little flat in modern stuff. She is so big and strong and powerful that she needs a part which will take care of her particular emotions. As a sweet, little innocent virgin, she isn't much to shout about."

At the end of the eight weeks, Farrar regarded the entire experience as "a most pleasant one." Just before she headed back east on the train, she threw a party at her house and invited everybody from the studio. It was a Saturday night, and the party began at eight. The spread was bountiful, the liquor was of superlative quality, and the hostess was ravishing; she danced with everyone, never sat down and never stopped moving. At six on Sunday morning, the dancing finally stopped, and Bill deMille noticed Farrar walking barefoot on the dew-covered lawn, accompanied by the handsome actor Lou Tellegen.

The critics fell in line with Farrar's co-workers and adored her. Julian Johnson in *Photoplay* wrote that whatever her successes in opera, "the furnace heat of this tropic, exotic characterization [in] the *Carmen* film will, in its own way, stand alongside *The Birth of a Nation* as an epochmaker. . . . Cecil DeMille must have enthusiastic mention for his direction of this photoplay, and Alvin Wyckoff for his photography. The artistry of both is beyond criticism." The *New York Dramatic Mirror* said that she "has proved herself one of the greatest actresses of all time" and said that her Carmen "will live long after her operatic characterization has died in the limbo of forgotten singers."

Carmen is good, but not distinguished—nothing to compare to the movies DeMille would make in just a few months. It's cunningly made, with two or three fine sets, two or three nominal ones, and some good locations. Alvin Wyckoff's lighting in the close-ups prefigures film noir and Farrar, unlike most opera singers, moves like a cat. She carries herself like a star because she *is* a star. DeMille knows what he's got and gives Farrar a lot of close-ups. He isn't afraid of the story's sexuality—at one point, Wallace Reid cups Farrar's breast in his hand and leaves it there—it's no accident.

Most of Cecil's pictures had been costing from $10,000 to $18,000, but Lasky spent $23,429 on *Carmen*, and earned $147,599 in receipts—more than doubling the usual returns, and the highest gross of the three Farrar films made in 1915. Clearly, presold titles were a good idea then as now.

★

In these early years, Cecil was Lasky's rock. On October 12, 1915, Jesse wrote Goldfish that he, Cecil, and Blanche Sweet had a four-hour meeting trying to cope with their problems, among them a shortage of releasable films, and Cecil had stepped up and volunteered to make two pictures at once. This meant that George Melford could start another picture, and Frank Reicher another. As for the physical stress, Lasky wrote that "Cecil is feeling very fit and we are planning everything so carefully that he will be able to do the two pictures in three or four weeks time and his doing them will insure of them both being good."

DeMille being DeMille, in later years he would claim he undertook this Sisyphean task "just to show that it could be done. Critics were saying that not enough time was given to the preparation and production of motion pictures. To show that pictures, effective enough for the time, if necessary could be turned out almost like short orders in a one-arm lunch, I put *The Cheat* and *The Golden Chance* in production simultaneously."

On top of all this, he was still in charge of hiring and firing, maintaining and expanding the physical plant, not to mention dealing in a rather steely fashion with his mother's sense of entitlement.

After Cecil and Beatrice had some discussions about her coming to live with them in Hollywood, she returned a check that Cecil had sent her because it struck her as insufficient for her needs. In a letter that defines passive aggression, she intimated that she was rethinking her future housing requirements: "Several times in the stress of shortage I have had to borrow from Sam Goldfish who each time bade me be of good cheer because you having landed would so fix matters the last borrow from him would end the ghastly worry. I have paid back to him the different amounts and will borrow no more—from him! Life is a deadly nuisance, dear Boy, but here's good luck for you and Constance and Cecilia."

DeMille was in Mojave directing Victor Moore in a minor but charming sequel called *Chimmie Fadden Out West*, which featured good New York street atmosphere as well as a scene-stealing mule, when his mother's letter arrived. He quickly replied. "Dear Mother, Your rather remarkable epistle with its enclosures has just arrived. . . . I cannot believe that you would take an attitude of this sort toward me because I had made you a present of $175 instead of $250 as intimated in your letter you would have preferred.

"I had always been inclined to think that the difficulty between you and Billy had been probably more Billy's fault than yours; but again, your letter to me has changed my views on that point . . . you are in full possession of all your faculties and know best what course you choose to pursue toward your own sons. . . . I regret exceedingly that our plans for the future together should have fallen through."

He appended a deadly P.S.: "I note that the last line in your letter suggests that life is a deadly nuisance. I do not believe the fault is life's."

Late 1915 saw the beginning of a period during which the Lasky company leased the entire block on Selma Avenue in order to keep the production line supplied with films of a high quality. Jesse wrote Sam about their problems.

"Regarding [Raoul?] Walsh, the director, whom you wired about, Cecil knows him and doesn't think he can amount to very much. We will try to see one of his pictures and will then advise you further. You see, there is no use of our hiring a director unless we can get one as good as Cecil. We can get a good mediocre director out here; but what we are looking for is the biggest man in the game. [Jules] Brulatour has two such men. One by the name of Turnaer [Maurice Tourneur] and the other, a Frenchman, who produced *Les Miserables* [Albert Capellani]. . . .

"*The Cheat*, scenario by Hector Turnbull, with Fannie Ward, promises to be a great production and is well underway. The Goodrich picture, Cecil will start tomorrow. It has been held up on account of the scenario, which is also by Hector Turnbull. Cecil finally gave up trying to put the scenario into shape and he and Jeanie wrote an original which looks very good."

Lasky's initially lofty appraisal of Bill as head of the scenario department had come crashing to earth. "We discovered that William was useless as the head of the Scenario Department. Something had to be done and before taking the next step, we decided to see if he might not develop into a good director. While I am by no means sure that his first picture will be good, it is quite good judgment to give him a chance. . . . We are up against it in all departments, and occasionally have to take a chance like this."

★

This is the way it was: Visitors stayed at the Hollywood Hotel, a wooden building at Hollywood and Highland that ran half a block fronting on Highland. It looked like a slightly shopworn summer hotel, with rocking chairs lined up on the front veranda. The lobby was small, and in the dining room food was served in white porcelain bowls that looked like bird baths. The rooms had matting instead of carpeting, the beds were iron, the windows had white net curtains, and there was a small closet with three hooks.

"The odor," remembered Bessie Lasky, "was like left-over food that had been fried in stale bacon fat." The atmosphere was sleepy and depressing, the boarders "looking blank and useless, rocking alone on the porch, filling the air with futility and gloom, transparent in their shabby clothes."

To get to the studio, people would either be picked up by the studio car, or rent horses and ride down Vine Street and tie the horses off in front of the barn with a large wooden sign: "Lasky Studio." Directly across the street was an orange grove with an old stucco house in the middle. People who had never been far west—or far south—would marvel at the orange blossoms and the way their scent could perfume the air for hundreds of yards, or the way the pepper trees on Vine swayed in the breeze.

The hotel would send over box lunches: cold chicken, a hard-boiled egg, a piece of tomato, a bread and butter sandwich, and salt and pepper. Chairs would be placed around the perimeter of the set. There, remembered Bessie Lasky, "the handsome, picturesque young director in puttees, boots and cap . . . acted out the scenes for the people and put on the best show himself."

Bessie and Constance would place themselves so they could see the company's director outperforming the actors. "Sometimes we sat cheerfully in the blazing sun on a ladder, all day, just to see a few extras ride into a desert scene to make a few gestures. Of course we had to read what they called the 'Script' and spent evenings before the fire trying to choose the most fitting title. All the wives competed [to write] inter-titles and were privileged to go to the barn where they had rough-cut the film. It was strewn all over the floor of a tiny room where recently a horse or cow had serenely slept."

The hunt for locations was likewise a communal endeavor; the rented car roamed all over canyons, mountains, and narrow dirt roads, looking for spots where Cecil could stage his scenes. "We would wind and wind into the wee small hours, searching for spots for the next picture. It was excitingly dangerous because if an accident occurred, such as a wheel slipping off, we had to sleep in the car until someone came along by chance to help us out of the dilemma."

It was rural, rough, without niceties. It was everything Cecil and Jesse had dreamed of and more. "It was so exciting we could hardly wait for the next telephone call to be on the lot for a still greater experience," remembered Bessie Lasky.

In that large, dark green barn on Vine and Selma, you walked in through an office that had a wicker gate. A young cousin of Jesse's named Mervyn LeRoy might be sitting there and could tell you whether or not you could go in. Passing through the office, you came to the open stages. There were dressing rooms made of plasterboard and just enough wood framing to keep everything from collapsing in a stiff Santa Ana wind. There were no provisions made for heat, so during late nights or chilly winter weather everyone froze. But always they worked, and worked hard.

"The atmosphere of the silent film studio was not conducive to real emotion, or to concentration," remembered DeMille. "It was noisy and there was banging going on—sets were put together. It was very different from the modern studio as you know it."

Agnes deMille would have a difficult relationship with her Uncle Ce all their lives, but when she talked about him at work in those early days, her reservations melted away and she remembered only a force of nature, a man with a conquistador's energy who subtly made her feel as if she "had to give an absolute reason for being a woman, for being alive, for being there, for occupying air space. . . .

"I saw him directing, and he had the most tremendous energy of anyone I've ever known, and for longer stretches. As you look at his pictures, the old pictures, I think they are miraculous. When they say he's marvelous with crowd scenes, what does that mean? It means that everybody is doing something intelligent, something pertinent, and something different, and that there's a great vivacity and liveliness and invention right through it, the way there is naturally with people."

In this rough-hewn environment, Cecil was creating not merely some fine films and his own legend, but the industrially based Hollywood film industry. Bill remembered that sixteen-hour days were the rule; in his first year in Hollywood, he was away from the plant on only seventeen days, including Sundays.

"We thought pictures, ate pictures, dreamed pictures. No work was too hard to attempt; no sacrifice too great to make. One picture trod on the heels of another, and all had to be ready to meet their release dates. A call from the studio would take a bridegroom away from the altar, a mother from her children's Christmas tree, a winning golfer from the 17th hole. Our families knew us mostly by reputation and no hostess expected us to be less than an hour late for dinner." No detail was too small; Bill remembered long, Jesuitical conversations with Cecil about whether or not spoken titles should contain quotation marks. (Yes.)

"There was great excitement and great fervor," said Agnes deMille, "and a great sense of romance, romantic adventure. They didn't know what they were working in, they didn't know what the future would be, they didn't know what they were doing. They knew that every picture broke boundaries. Some one new thing would be done, a new way of handling the camera, a new way of cutting, a new way of lighting, and they'd be so excited by it. . . . There was a communal sense in the group. Whenever they finished a picture, they'd paste it together and ask everybody, all the families, all the children, all the cousins, neighbors sometimes, 'come in come in and see our picture, we're running it,' and then they'd ask everybody what they thought.

"I cannot believe it was that simple, but it was, and I think some of the simplicity and some of that fervor and excitement is in the films and that's why they're valuable and lovely."

✳

There is no reason to suspect that DeMille regarded The Cheat as anything more than a rip-roaring melodrama. He didn't take much more care in production than he had with less distinguished pictures—it was shot between October 20 and November 10, and released on December 13. The script itself is halfway between the telegraphic approach of The Warrens of Virginia and the far more specific work of William deMille.

Six days after he started The Cheat, Cecil began simultaneously shooting The Golden Chance, but after about a week, he made up his mind to fire the lead actress. Her name was Edna Goodrich and she was a drunk. "Cecil has a fine story," Jesse Lasky wrote Sam Goldfish on November 2, 1915, "but he claims she is killing it. She cannot act and also screens very poorly." Cleo Ridgely was cast in the part and Cecil began reshooting The Golden Chance on November 5, finishing on the 26th.

Cecil directed The Cheat from nine to five. Then he ate dinner and lay down until eight, when he began directing The Golden Chance until two in the morning. Most nights he grabbed a few hours of sleep in his office before starting all over again, but when he did go home, Constance was waiting up for him. After this unbelievable marathon was over, he took a grand total of three days off before going back to work.

Initially, DeMille was slightly unsure of *The Cheat*. "When [screenwriter] Hector [Turnbull] talked to me about that I was a little leery of it at that time—whether he could do it." But once he read the script—stark, sexually drenched material about miscegenation and power, resistance and submission—he decided to go with it.

The Cheat is an authentic landmark movie, beginning with the frankness of its story: a silly socialite gambles away her money and accepts $10,000 from a Japanese admirer in return for a promise to sleep with him. When she reneges, he brands her like a piece of livestock and she shoots him. Prosecuted for attempted murder, she exposes her brand, the court riots, and she is acquitted.

The script's introduction to Sessue Hayakawa's character reads: "Tori is discovered seated near tables, reading magazine or newspaper, and smoking. He is dressed in smart American flannels." DeMille's changes are handwritten: "Scene dyed *Red*—Black Drop—oriental lamp—brazier of coals—Tori takes iron away from object he is branding—turns out light—replaces iron in brazier—his face shown in light from coals—when he puts lid on brazier, screen goes black."

DeMille throws out the script's suggestion of Tori's assimilation and chooses to emphasize his "Asian" characteristics, as well as his trait of branding his possessions—in this case an objet d'art, later in the film the leading lady. For a scene of Tori and the woman together, DeMille scribbles a note: "Baby spot two face in light together." The script doesn't mention the smoke from her burning flesh, but DeMille has it wafting into the shot as Tori brands her out of frame.

DeMille structures some of his editing by thought rather than action. In other words, he ignores physical space in favor of psychological space. When the husband confronts his wife with her extravagant bills, she thinks of her lover, who is equally focused on her. DeMille does not cut from husband to wife, the actual scene of the moment, but from wife to lover, even though they are miles apart. For 1915, this is innovative; given the sexual implications of the cutting, it's truly remarkable.

As the eminent film scholar James Card wrote, "the lighting is advanced, creative and sophisticated beyond any other film of 1915. . . . The dramatic utilization of Japanese decor (shadows and blood on the shattering wall screens) did not reappear in the United States until Kurosawa. The ambivalent approach to the chief protagonist as played superbly by [Sessue] Hayakawa awaited the emergence of the anti-hero of the 1950s for a comparable directorial outlook."

For his star, DeMille used the legendary stage actress Fannie Ward in only her second movie. Ward wasn't famous for her acting, but for her youthful appearance in spite of the fact that she was at least forty-three years old and working in a medium whose harsh lighting could make thirty-year-olds look fifty. Geraldine

Farrar characterized her as "a baffling ingenue [who] carried the inevitable parasol to shade her baby-like complexion, which she candidly confessed 'took hours to fix up.' " Besides a complicated makeup regimen, Ward also endured several face-lifts as did her husband, Jack Dean.

DeMille's casting instincts led him to the young Japanese actor Sessue Hay-akawa, who responded with an astonishing portrayal keying on sexual malice. In outline, Hayakawa's character is the heavy, but the actor's sexual magnetism is so intense, his acting so contained, that the audience's sympathy invariably gravitates toward him rather than Ward's silly society bitch.

Hayakawa remembered that DeMille and Lasky "knew the psychology of [the] actor, not like a businessman who doesn't know the heart of an actor. . . . They *were* actors [italics added].

"Mr. DeMille . . . never showed me what to do, how to do it. He explained the situation—'All right, Sessue, you do it, the way you feel'—and I do it, exactly, without any rehearsal, the film going on." DeMille had a five- or six-piece orches-tra playing throughout the scenes, and he wouldn't talk during the take itself—"then we become mechanical," according to Hayakawa.

The actor remembered that Marshall Neilan, with whom Hayakawa also worked in this period, "didn't care much about your psychology." For Neilan, acting in movies was based on externals, mostly movement. "For DeMille, it was mainly to make you understand the motive, why you must shout, why you are sad, why you must do that—you have to feel motive first." For Hayakawa, DeMille would always be "the greatest of the great."

The Cheat was a hit in America—a gross of $96,389 against a cost of $17,311; foreign would bring in another $40,975—and the critics were impressed as well. The *Moving Picture World* declared that "pictures like this put the whole indus-try under obligations to the Lasky company. . . . The feature is of such extraor-dinary merit as to call for the highest term of praise." In England, *The Bioscope* declared that "as a work of art, *The Cheat* has the hard and glittering brilliance of a diamond."

The Cheat survives only in prints from a 1918 reissue, which entailed some minor changes, most notably involving the nationality of Hayakawa's character. In 1915, he was clearly identified as Japanese, causing angry protests from the Japanese community, but in 1918, when Japan was America's ally in World War I, the titles changed him to Burmese. In addition, the original subtitles, which were brief in 1915 ("One of Long Island's Smart Set") became more flowery ("Haka Arakau, a Burmese ivory king to whom the Long Island smart-set is paying social tribute.").

A sensation in France, *The Cheat* seems to be the only silent movie that was converted into both a play and an opera (Camille Erlanger's *Forfaiture* in 1921). Louis Delluc detested movies before World War I, but *The Cheat* and the com-edies of Charlie Chaplin converted him from a theater critic to a movie critic; he compared *The Cheat* to *Tosca*, and wrote that "Paris has received *The Cheat* with violent admiration . . . it sees here for the first time a film which merits the name of film."

Even Colette rhapsodized, writing, "Let our aspiring cine-actors go to see how, when his face is mute, [Hayakawa's] hand carries on the flow of his thought. Let them take to heart the menace and disdain in a motion of his eyebrow and how, in the instant when he is wounded, he creates the impression that his life is running out with his blood, without shuddering, without convulsively grimacing, with merely the progressive petrifaction of his Buddha's mask and the ecstatic darkening of his eyes."

The French were enthralled by the film's production values, a sensuality that extended beyond the subject matter to the decor and costumes: lace, silk, furs. *The Cheat* synthesized all the strengths of the American movie, and of DeMille. Not analysis, but action; not tracking, but cutting: drama that is primarily theatrical conveyed through means that are purely cinematic—the best of both worlds. In France, DeMille would always be regarded as a major filmmaker, and several laudatory monographs were published about him over the years, in stark contrast to what would become his critical standing in his native country.

The Golden Chance, released at the end of January 1916, is nearly as remarkable as *The Cheat*. It features Wallace Reid as a young millionaire who falls in love with Cleo Ridgely, an Ingrid Bergmanesque actress playing a poor woman from the slums burdened by an alcoholic husband. She works as a seamstress but fills an empty chair at a society dinner party, where she meets Reid. Noticing Reid's interest, her employer begins pimping her out in order to attract Reid's money for a business venture. Not only is he gorgeous, he's a millionaire. Afterward, the mistress of the house pays the seamstress her day wages for her time and asks for her jewels back.

The seamstress can't help but compare her possibilities to her present— DeMille shows her gazing in a mirror at the tonsorially perfect Reid, who dissolves into her drunken, dissolute husband. The seamstress's husband burgles the house and is conveniently killed by the police, ostensibly leaving her free to marry Reid. But DeMille pulls off a stunningly ambiguous, lady-or-the-tiger ending: Reid leaves her, then comes back, but there's no embrace. She looks away from him, he looks away from her, then down at the ground. Neither of them knows what to say or do. Fade out.

The picture carries several in-jokes—the girl is the daughter of a judge, just like Constance, and a newspaper headline carries the dateline "Pompton, New Jersey." The Cinderellaish upstairs/downstairs machinations are played for absolute psychological reality. Unusually for this period, but not unusually for DeMille, the actors behave rather than act, and after little more than a year and a half of filmmaking he is absolutely fluent with both his camera and his actors.

Both *The Cheat* and *The Golden Chance* are sexually charged, emotion-drenched dramas of the real world, intimate chamber dramas on a very realistic level. *The Cheat* could only have been made by Cecil, but *The Golden Chance* is more like the quietly observational movies that William would soon begin directing, except it has a propulsive drive that William's films rarely had.

The Golden Chance grossed $83,504 against a cost of $18,719 and the *New York Dramatic Mirror* said that "The master hand of Cecil B. DeMille is evident throughout the whole picture. His is the bigness of vision that can see and appreciate the value and importance of little things. . . . Even this story, good as it is, could have been irretrievably spoiled in the hands of a poor director. As it is, the original strength of the story is increased and accentuated, made more human and more appealing by the delicate touch of the man responsible for its production."

Taken together, *The Cheat* and *The Golden Chance*, shot simultaneously, released a month apart, are DeMille at his protean best, innovatively illuminating his actors with stark shards of light. DeMille's mise-en-scène in this period is never casual; each sequence has its own texture, its own visual theme: soft, dappled sunlight for romantic exteriors, heavy brocades for the interiors inhabited by the aristocracy; high-contrast lighting for scenes of threat; and so forth. It was craftsmanship ascending toward art, and only the very best directors of the period were indulging in this kind of painstaking visual detail.

In an interview with the *Moving Picture World*, Jeanie Macpherson explained how she and Cecil achieved such a sense of dramatic compression combined with headlong pace. It all had to do with construction: "Each scene must be a drama in itself. The whole picture must be made up of a series of small dramas. This makes the completed picture a mosaic of little ones. Scenes that have no dramatic value in them, or say nothing, must be eliminated. So the scenario writer must bear in mind at all times not what he can put into a picture, but what he can leave out."

★

By the end of 1915, DeMille was making films that can still be watched with appreciation and, occasionally, amazement. He was among the premier talents of this period, although Cecil had his doubts, at least in retrospect. When DeMille pulled the low-key but charming *What's His Name* off the shelf for Cecilia's twenty-first birthday party—she played a supporting part—he watched the movie with horror. "This is without doubt the worst movie ever made," he told his daughter, "and there is no hope for the man who made it."

If, as Sessue Hayakawa said, "his art was a business," in this period the emphasis was on art. But success also enabled Cecil to live up to the ideas he had always had about himself.

In July 1915, Jesse Lasky wrote Sam Goldfish that "Cecil showed me a copy of a letter he had written to you on publicity for himself. It seems that this has been in his mind for some months. . . . Cecil has proved his value to the firm in many ways and . . . there can be no question of his loyalty to us. . . . You know the public go to see a Griffith production, not because it may have a star in the cast, but because Griffith's name on it stands for so much. It seems to me that the time has come for us to do the same with Cecil's name. . . . In a word, he is the biggest asset we have, so let's use it for all it is worth."

In most cases Lasky adopted Cecil's point of view about the company's strengths and liabilities. Lasky's tone in his letters to Goldfish is that of a patient older brother pointing out nuances to an impulsive sibling. Lasky's giddy enthusiasm occasionally led him to overlook things—he would refer to the sadomasochism of *The Cheat* as "a wonderful, absorbing love story"—but he always tended to business.

"I am just in receipt of your long letter . . . in which you ask us to wire our opinion of a possible future amalgamation of our producing companies with the Paramount," Jesse wrote Sam on November 2, 1915. "On account of Cecil working day and night it is impossible to get his mind onto any business matters right now. This is so important, I am going to take time, so that we can all consider it, and I will advise you of our opinion as soon as possible."

There were recurring problems, mainly temperamental actors and the impossibility of finding good directors. For the former, "we are having trouble with Wallace Reid. He has apparently received an offer from some other firm of more than twice the money we are paying him, and although we have a cast iron contract, he has informed us through his attorney, that he is not going to continue with us after the picture he is now in is finished."

Wallace Reid was finessed—his problems, Lasky wrote later, were "of a personal nature. He was in a desperate situation." The company advanced $1,000 to get him out of his troubles, which may or may not have involved the drug addiction that led to his early death.

The quality of Lasky's films was attracting other actors; Lasky ebulliently reported that Marie Doro wanted to work for them solely because of Cecil, "whom she considers the greatest of all picture directors and that means more to her than money. . . . Of course you realize that if Cecil directs her and we only pay her by the week when she works, many of her pictures will be finished in two weeks. You can see that she will be a very cheap star."

With the money rolling in, Lasky suggested to Cecil that they give it a couple of more years and then call it quits—retire. Go hunting in Alaska, fishing in Florida, be beach bums in Hawaii, but get off the treadmill. DeMille eyed Jesse speculatively, then told him he could never hold himself to such a deal. "Write it down now, I'll sign it," retorted Lasky. DeMille wrote out an abdication agreement for the two of them, they both signed it, and it was stowed away in a drawer.

★

By 1916, the insecurities and debts of 1914 were past, and Cecil finally began to moderate his pace. In the frantic year of 1915 he directed thirteen pictures; in 1916, he would direct only four, largely because he wanted to devote more time to preparation and production. The studio was already engaged in block booking, selling fifty-two pictures a year to exhibitors, and they seldom had fifty-two properties on hand by the time the sales campaign began. For years, there were phantom properties that were always listed as being part of the next year's production plans. *Her Great Sacrifice* was one such generic title; another was *Hell and High Water*. Cecil remembered that these titles were announced and sold for years without ever being made.

Cecil had been working reflexively, on the run, but with the company becoming increasingly successful, he also began to devote time to his family life. Early in 1916 Cecil and Constance found the house they would live in for the rest of their lives. It was high up in an area called Laughlin Park, just south of Griffith Park, in the Los Feliz district. In a 1915 prospectus in the *Los Angeles Times*, Laughlin Park was described as "practically the highest ground in Hollywood . . . the last word in residential masterpieces, a replica of Italy's finest landscape gardening. . . . The late Homer Laughlin worked out the plans of this residential paradise."

DeMille's new residence had been owned by a widow named Ada Perry. It was only a couple of years old, handsome and large, with a colonial-pillared portico and plentiful plantings of olive trees, where DeMille would shoot a scene for *The King of Kings* in ten years' time. The price was $27,893, the mortgage was for ten years. The main floor had a large but simple and homey parlor, and an oak-paneled formal dining room with exuberantly carved teak chairs surrounding a long oak table. The second floor was largely given over to bedrooms.

Constance decorated it in a conventional combination of Chippendale and Victorian furniture—some authentic antiques, some reproductions. There were fine Oriental carpets for the living room and dining room, printed linen curtains for the windows.

In 1918, Charlie Chaplin rented the house next door for about a year from a Mr. and Mrs. William Dodd. In 1920, DeMille bought the Dodd house and joined it with his residence by means of a long loggia designed by Julia Morgan, the architect of San Simeon. The total property encompassed only 2.5 acres, but it was enough for DeMille and his growing family for the next forty-odd years.

The Chaplin house—that was how it was always referred to—held the DeMille office, a screening room, and a guesthouse. Beyond the loggia were several arcades filled with books, Bibles, and bibelots, until you came to an enormous paneled room dominated by a large carved desk and a pink-fabric highbacked chair from which DeMille ruled his business empire.

Underneath the desk was a group of fly-swatters that DeMille kept for reducing the surplus population, and there was a Chinese brass bowl, originally used for opium, that DeMille used as a receptacle for pipe ash.

The wall across from the desk was reserved for plaques and trophies. Below those, on a bookshelf, were leather-bound copies of his scripts and some of the research that had gone into them. To DeMille's right was a large movie screen that was always permanently in place, and on a low table in front of the screen was the original battered Pathé camera with which he had shot *The Squaw Man*. While the room was large, the heavy furniture meant that it could hold no more than two dozen people for a screening; DeMille himself would sit in a large leather chair in the corner of the room.

Laughlin Park was never a fashionable address for the movie colony—that would be, in order of evolution, the Hollywood Hills, Beverly Hills, Bel-Air, and Brentwood—but DeMille didn't care. When he found something he liked, he stuck with it. The move to Laughlin Park signaled a new phase of Cecil's life; cutting back on filmmaking meant there was more time to devote to civic and political activities.

Cecil served on the board of directors of the nascent Motion Picture Relief Fund, along with Donald Crisp, Hal Roach, Douglas Fairbanks, William S. Hart, and Jesse Lasky. And Constance had been an active supporter of the Children's Hospital in Los Angeles—where she had found John DeMille—since arriving in Los Angeles in 1914.

★

While Cecil was going from success to success, Beatrice was still having trouble. She wrote Cecil to congratulate him on his accumulating accomplishments, while fretting over the fact that William wasn't getting much publicity, and revealed an abiding bitterness concerning her late husband. "Two deMilles at once BOTH MAKING GOOD seems to be more than a city—any city—can absorb. Never mind deMILLE is DE MILLE and what does it matter which letter of the alphabet makes good? It isn't BELASCO swallowing another deMille as he did your father. And it takes the good work of many deMilles to make up for the many mistakes of the mater deMille."

Beatrice invariably complained about the absence of money in her life, and she wasn't exaggerating. Arthur Friend wrote Cecil that his mother had given Friend a complete rundown of her financial affairs. Friend wrote, "I find . . . no hope of being able to gain anything for her unless you volunteer to help her. I think if you could arrange to send in to me on her account a small amount every week, I shall be able to make a satisfactory adjustment for her on the installment plan . . . your mother requires assistance immediately." Friend suggested that a remittance of perhaps $25 to $50 a week could, over time, resolve her situation.

Cecil responded by writing her back, at a slight but perceptible emotional arm's length. "I appreciate your imploring me not to work too hard, but it is very necessary at the present moment, as our program has been a little weak recently and we all feel that it needs a couple of solar plexus blows which I am endeavoring to give it, in order to bring it up and put it in fighting condition.

"Don't fail to see *The Cheat* with Fannie Ward. Think I have made a very good picture and I know I have made Fannie Ward . . . I notified Arthur Friend that I would send him $25 weekly on which to feed the howling mob."

Then Cecil discovered that Beatrice had borrowed money from the same Thomas Higgins who had been one of Cecil's most aggressive creditors. "I need not say that I was astonished," Cecil wrote Higgins, "and the purpose of this letter is to ask if you have received in full the $2,000 which I sent you, and which I believe was paid in full just a year ago."

Cecil had sent Beatrice $50 a week to pay off his debt to Higgins, and was clearly concerned that Beatrice might have diverted some or all of the money to her own uses. "I do not understand the necessity of Mrs. DeMille having borrowed from you," Cecil concluded, "but I am not closely in touch with her private affairs."

Beatrice's incessant neediness about money and her accompanying scatty financial sense eventually caused William to refuse to have anything to do with her financially. It also is probably the cause for the occasionally distant tone of Cecil's letters to his mother.

"We played that game for years," Cecil would say as an old man. "She would rather cheat me out of $5 than get a check for $1,000. Her most famous remark—once she wanted a carryall—to pick up children who were attending the [deMille school for girls]. Bill and I said, 'You can't pay $300 for this, it is only worth $150. Just offer $150 for it.' She said, 'Pay them what they want—they must learn I will not haggle with them.'

"She always had a scheme for making large sums of money. Once she had a cactus, withered and old, in a pot on her porch. She said, 'That is my secret—it is wealth. We will ship it to Australia where they have lots of cattle. This is a spineless cactus. They will plant it there and have food for the whole country.' The cactus was shriveled and dead in a week. Bill would never play the money game with her. She couldn't get any from him."

Once, when an interviewer—who hadn't known her—characterized Beatrice as "lovable," Cecil quickly interjected, "She was not so lovable. That's what made her a great woman. She was a brilliant, brilliant woman."

★

At the studio, DeMille's office assumed baronial proportions. As William would remember, the top of the desk began "to suggest a bargain counter at the Metropolitan Museum. The beamed and vaulted ceiling, the Gothic stained-glass windows admitting a dim religious light, the heavy old-English furniture, the floor covered with skins of polar bears. . . . Siberian wolves, timber wolves and a buffalo, always made me uncertain whether I was entering Westminster Abbey or the sitting room of Eric the Red."

In addition to the accumulation, the trappings of success, there were signs of arrogance in an interview Cecil gave to *Photoplay* and Adela Rogers St. Johns on the topic of marriage. "If a woman has the mental strength to stand the gaff, her husband will always come back to her. . . . If she just has the moral poise to weather his yieldings to the beast within."

From the general, Cecil moved to the specific. "I have been married eighteen years. In eighteen years I have never passed a Saturday night at home. In eighteen years I have never said where I was on a Saturday night, nor what I was doing, nor with whom I was. And in eighteen years, I have never been asked."

Cecil was bloviating—he never habitually spent weekends away from his family until much later—but it was still a disconcerting display of sexual belligerence, one he would be careful never to repeat.

Cecil's changes were mirrored by those of Hollywood. The rural nature of the town was slowly disappearing; fruit orchards were chopped down, bungalows built, and dirt roads paved. Banks, jewelry stores, dentists, and doctors suddenly appeared. Residents dressed in white all January, as if they were in Newport and large mansions began appearing in the previously deserted canyons of Beverly Hills and in the hills above Hollywood.

★

The Heart of Nora Flynn, released in April of 1916, is one of the strongest of Cecil's pictures of this period, featuring Maurice Tourneur–like split screens, and a strong performance by the luscious Marie Doro as Nora, an Irish nursemaid with a crush on Elliott Dexter's chauffeur. The lady of the house is having an affair with a society wastrel, but Dexter thinks Nora is having the affair. Comes the confrontation, Nora takes the fall for her mistress because of her affection for the family's child. The husband demands that his wife fire Nora as an unsuitable employee for a good household. There's a devastating farewell scene between Nora and the child, and as she leaves the house for the last time, the chauffeur asks her to marry him.

It sounds simpler than it plays; besides being an attack on the social hypocrisy of the upper crust, the film is very emotionally fraught. There's little sense of healing in the last-minute marriage proposal—these innocent people have been put through a wringer by an arrogant, hypocritical morality. *The Heart of Nora Flynn* cost $21,988 and earned $87,738.

As spring gave way to summer in 1916, discussions got underway about a possible merger between Adolph Zukor's Famous Players and Lasky. While the merger was still hanging fire, Goldfish got wind of changes that angered him. "Have wire from Jesse stating he will claim first vice-presidency which it was de-

cided when I was with you and him was to be my office," wired Goldfish to
DeMille on April 28, 1916. "Don't propose to give Jesse his way on this please wire
me straight message how you will vote on this proposition."

"If the election of First Vice President is a reward of merit," replied DeMille
two days later, "then I consider that I am entitled to it as I believe my own efforts
have done more to make the Lasky company than any other individual influence
but I believe the First Vice Presidency is offered to the Lasky company because
of the merit and efficiency of the company and not because of the value of any
one member and that therefore the position should go to the President of this
company and Jesse as such will have my vote." Sam didn't take this well, but Zukor
made a Solomonic decision—he said he would make Jesse first vice president and
Sam the chairman of the board.

Jesse began rearranging the company's finances in a series of wires that also
indicate Constance's crucial place as Cecil's not so silent partner. He wired Cecil
on May 26,

INCREASING CAPITAL STOCK TO HALF MILLION. ALL BUT HUNDRED THOUSAND
GOES TO PRESENT STOCKHOLDERS AS DIVIDENDS. FIFTY THOUSAND IS BEING SOLD
AT PAR BALANCE TO REMAIN IN TREASURY. HAVE CONSTANCE EXECUTE POWER OF
ATTORNEY RUNNING TO ME AUTHORIZING ME TO SIGN HER NAME TO CONSENT
OF STOCKHOLDERS TO INCREASING OF CAPITAL STOCK. RUSH THIS. WIRE WHEN
MAILED. INCREASE AS ABOVE VITALLY NECESSARY TO FINANCE BUSINESS SUCCESS-
FULLY THROUGH SUMMER.

Lasky wired DeMille on June 24:

HAVE ZUKOR'S CONSENT TO FIFTY FIFTY BASIS WHICH WE FEEL MAKES ATTRACTIVE
PROPOSITION. ALL OF US INCLUDING YOURSELF WILL BE OFFICERS AND DIRECTORS
AND WILL HAVE FIVE YEAR CONTRACTS WITH NEW CORPORATION TO BE CALLED
FAMOUS PLAYERS LASKY CORPORATION. CONTROL OF PRODUCING END WILL VEST
IN US SO THERE WILL BE NO CHANGE IN YOUR POSITION OR PLANS FOR SPECIAL
RELEASES BUT FEEL CERTAIN MERGER WILL MAKE EVERYBODY'S STOCK MORE VALU-
ABLE. . . . THIS DEAL JUST BETWEEN FAMOUS AND US, NO BANKER, NO BROKERS OR
OTHER LEECHES. . . . ANXIOUS YOUR APPROVAL.

DeMille liked the idea.

APPROVE MERGER. RELY ON YOU TO REPRESENT MY PERSONAL INTERESTS.
PRINCIP[AL] POINTS ARE: 1 TO REMAIN IN COMPLETE AUTHORITY OF WHATEVER
STUDIO AM CON[N]ECTED WITH AND THAT I MAY NOT BE MOVED FROM CALIFORNIA
WITHOUT CONSENT.

On June 29, Jesse wired DeMille:

THE STORY OF THE MERGER OF LASKY AND FAMOUS WAS WIDELY PUBLISHED IN TO-
DAY'S NEW YORK DAILYS THE TRADE GENERALLY HAVE BEEN CONGRATULATING US
ON THE NEW COMBINATION WE ARE ALL VERY MUCH PLEASED AND CONGRATULATE
THE NEW DIRECTOR GENERAL OF THE FAMOUS PLAYERS LASKY CORPORATION.

And so it was that the Lasky Company (primary asset Cecil B. DeMille) merged with Adolph Zukor's Famous Players (primary asset Mary Pickford) to form Famous Players-Lasky. Zukor, along with Daniel Frohman, had formed Famous Players in 1912 expressly to distribute the Sarah Bernhardt film *Queen Elizabeth*. Although *Queen Elizabeth* was a hit, the follow-up features were less successful, and the firm flirted with bankruptcy throughout early 1913. It was saved by the signing of the young actress from Toronto whose growing popularity was soon pulling the entire Famous Players train.

Lasky's production policy was much more broadly based than Famous Players', and the results showed in their respective balance sheets, and with the critics. The firm that took first billing in the merger had not been doing that well: the operating profit for the Lasky company for the six months ending June 30, 1916, was $447,321, while Famous Players' profit for the same period was a far more modest $129,560. That year, Julian Johnson wrote in *Photoplay* that Famous Players "for months . . . has sent out the dullest, most conventional plays."

Jesse Lasky would confirm that diagnosis when he wrote Cecil in June 1916, "The real reason why Famous Players finally gave in to coming in with us on an even 50-50 basis was because they finally realized that they were in a hole regarding scenarios, stories and productions and could not keep up pace." Yet, forty years later, Lasky's characterization of the merger in his memoirs was contrary to the historic facts, as though Adolph Zukor had gradually brainwashed him: "Famous Players was making more pictures than we were at the time and their assets were considerably greater than ours. . . . However, Zukor was satisfied to split the stock fifty-fifty between both companies in order to make the proposition attractive to us."

Cecil always had a wary respect for Zukor, if only because he had the true entrepreneurial spirit and was obviously a very cagey customer. Zukor was tough and smart. He was the kind of man you want in the foxhole with you. If he had a fatal flaw, it was that he was endlessly calculating and gave off no heat, always a problem for DeMille. When DeMille spoke of Jesse Lasky it was always "Jesse," and Sam Goldfish was "Sam." But Adolph Zukor was "Zukor."

Within the industry, the merger was regarded as a win-win. "Through the merger," editorialized *Picture Play* magazine, "it becomes possible for Lasky, which is located on the West coast, to borrow from Famous Players any player needed for a production which should necessarily be made in the West because of its atmosphere. Famous Players, being located in New York, may exercise the same privilege over Lasky players wanted for plays which are essentially Eastern. . . . This approaches perfection in photo-play making. . . . It is at least a big step forward, and in a new direction."

Eventually, Famous Players-Lasky would adopt the considerably loftier name of Paramount, but the merger brought so many problems that the future was far from assured. Mainly, Adolph Zukor and Sam Goldfish couldn't get along. Zukor was cold and appraising, while Goldfish was querulous and loud. He was also hungry for a public profile, and griped about "Jesse L. Lasky Presents" on the credit titles of the company's films. Goldfish would later tell *New Yorker* writer Alva Johnston that in the early days Lasky did not want to be bothered with the workings of the company, that he, Goldfish, was the "only full time worker," an egocentric spin on history made ridiculous by the profusion of surviving cables and night letters between Lasky and DeMille.

It would be considerably more accurate to say that Goldfish did a brilliant job running the sales and business departments while chafing about being barred from supervising production because DeMille was already doing it. In spite of the mutual affection that the two men would always have for each other, Goldfish never entirely trusted DeMille when it came to money. "He sensed that strain of unbridled extravagance that surged through the DeMille veins," was the way Jesse Lasky Jr. put it.

After the merger, there was a great deal of Sturm und Drang about the delegation of power, a lot of it stemming from the fact that Goldfish wasn't shy about letting Zukor know that his company was far more successful than Zukor's—Famous Players got first billing in the merger only because of a coin toss.

Since the old Motion Picture Patents Company had collapsed, both Lasky and Famous Players had been distributing their films through the distribution organization known as Paramount, which also handled three other producers. Each producer received 65 percent of the revenues for their films, with Paramount taking 35 percent for distribution. This struck Zukor as excessive, and the fact that somebody besides Zukor was running Paramount struck him as a miscarriage of justice.

Goldfish's inability to get along with Zukor made him the odd man out after the merger. Another contributing factor to the collision was the fact that Lasky's sister Blanche divorced Goldfish in early 1916 on grounds of adultery.

But Lasky and Zukor got along well. "He was a creator," remembered Zukor. "Every morning he arrived with a brisk step, full of enthusiasm, loaded with new ideas." Conversely, "every hour on the hour, and sometimes the half hour, Sam . . . sent a shock through the organization, in the manner of those pneumatic drills which shake all the buildings in the vicinity. It was Sam's nature."

The situation came to a head during a conference between Lasky and Mary Pickford about her next picture. Goldfish burst into the room and unhelpfully said, "Jesse, don't let Zukor butt in on this picture. He's OK as an executive, but we've always made better movies than Famous Players, so see that you keep the production reins in your hands." Goldfish was right—Lasky's pictures *were* better than Zukor's, better than almost anybody's—but it was a fatally impolitic thing to say.

Pickford naturally told Zukor about Goldfish's remarks, and Zukor got his back up. He informed Lasky and DeMille they had to make a choice, Zukor or Goldfish, and they had a weekend to make it. "I did not agree with [Zukor]," Lasky wrote to DeMille,

> but rather took issue with him and supported Sam. Little by little, how-ever, the fact was made clear to me in a thousand ways that there was no question but what Zukor was right, absolutely . . .
>
> Fortunately at about the moment I came to this conclusion, Arthur departed for the coast, and I was left in a splendid position to work side by side with Zukor. During this period our company never had more vital business or more business to take care of. Decisions of great importance of every kind had to be made. All kinds of situations arose in the Famous Players Studio that had to be met. Finances had to be taken care of and so while working in constant touch with Zukor, daily, I had the chance to study him as against Sam. . . .
>
> First . . . [Zukor] is an all around better business man—has better foresight—is a better financier and has a broader and bigger grasp of the picture business, than Sam. These facts, combined with the fact that I found he is considered the biggest man in the motion picture industry and incidentally that his reputation for honesty and integrity is remark-able—impressed me. . . . Instead of being hindered I find Zukor is help-ful. You know the pleasure of working without argument and for the first time in the history of our company I feel that there are no inside politics. . . .
>
> Sam resigned yesterday."

It had to be a tougher decision than Lasky was letting on, but business was business. Goldfish was bitter and stayed bitter. He sold his ten thousand shares of the company for $700,000 cash and set up a company in partnership with the theatrical producer Edgar Selwyn. They called the company Goldwyn, which had a more salubrious ring to it than Goldfish, so he took the company's name for his own.

DeMille always respected Sam, and even arranged a bank loan for him a few years down the road that would enable him to enter independent production, where he would finally achieve great success because there was nobody to fire him when he became impossible.

"When I left the company," remembered Sam, "the one man for whom I carried affection and respect was Cecil. He behaved very honorably but there was nothing he could do because Jesse stepped over the line." Sam didn't speak to Jesse Lasky for more than forty years, and he always characterized Zukor as a "rat."

In December 1916, Zukor secretly purchased the shares of Paramount board member Hiram Abrams, which, with his own shares, gave him controlling interest. He promptly deposed Paramount president W. W. Hodkinson, fired Abrams, and became the unchallenged president of the world's largest production and distribution combine, with Jesse Lasky as vice president in charge of production.

The amalgamation meant that Paramount would be responsible for releasing around 104 pictures a year—enough to supply the complete needs of any theater that booked their product. This cornering of the market was Zukor's most brilliant strategy; in essence, he devised a company that replaced the Motion Picture Patents Company.

★

By the end of 1916, Cecil had paid off his own debts as well as his mother's, and was supporting her financially, which Beatrice took as her due. Cecil could afford it. Success hadn't changed either mother or son. Cecil had always acted like the Grand Seigneur, even when he didn't have cab fare. Now there was enough money to buy his own cab company.

In 1916, Cecil was earning $500 a week until his salary was doubled that August. Dividends from Lasky stock brought in another $18,515, and assorted small investments brought his income to a total of $55,584. Over the next two years, his earnings remained stable, but his investment income declined, and he would write off as bad debt the $100-odd a week he was giving Beatrice, as well as $2,937 to Jeanie Macpherson. In 1919, however, his income shot up to $96,471, which remained Cecil's income floor for the near future. The firm foundation of Cecil's fortune was not his percentage of the great box office successes he was making; it was his stock in Famous Players-Lasky, which by 1919 was selling for a whopping $60 a share.

Cecil was also beginning a second career as an independent banker; in October of 1916, he lent Wallace Reid $7,500. By the end of 1919, the man who had gotten out of New York in December of 1913 just one step ahead of a slew of creditors would have total assets of $796,064.

★

Geraldine Farrar happily signed up for another summer of moviemaking in 1916. This time, Cecil would devise something different—instead of ramming the diva through as many program pictures as possible, he would use her star power in the service of something different—one special, spectacular movie.

"You will be engaged on special productions from now on, almost continually," wrote Jesse Lasky to Cecil. "In order to concentrate and be able to write and direct them in a proper manner, you should be relieved from the necessity of corresponding with and wiring to New York office, and all responsibility." Lasky delegated some of DeMille's tasks to a general manager over whom Cecil, as Director-General, still had authority. The assumption was that DeMille, along with five other directors, could supply the volume of films the company needed.

DeMille took the increased responsibility as his due. The matinee idol De-Wolf Hopper, who had known Cecil since his threadbare theatrical days, was shown around the Lasky lot when he arrived in Hollywood to make a stab at a movie career. Hopper asked about DeMille's closed office door. "Shhhh," he was told. "Mr. DeMille is thinking."

"Is that possible?" asked Hopper.

Cecil bought his mother a house on Argyle Avenue in Hollywood, but Beatrice rented an apartment in Long Beach for her writing. He gave her a respectable car for transportation, but she traded it in for a large Packard and remained game for any get-rich-quick scheme. "Life with mother was always adventurous," sighed DeMille late in his life.

In late middle age, Beatrice's hair looked, said one friend, "like hammered silver," and her startling black eyes still carried the gold flecks that had enchanted Henry years before. Her two-story bungalow had a furnace to ward off the cold California nights and an innovative mix of styles and colors: a blue Chinese rug, built-in chairs, benches, and shelves, an incense burner shaped like a miniature volcano, and a sort of altar rail around the fireplace. The dining room had a cabinet that was carved and inlaid with niches, and there was a sideboard that held a bronze lady astride a horse with a couple of guards. Magically, there was a panel in the floor that, when stepped on, opened the kitchen door.

Beatrice was a lot of fun, but, like most of the DeMilles, there was a point beyond which it was unwise to go. She once took an obstreperous child aside to explain that adults had rights, high among them the right to be free of other people's noisy children.

Beatrice's theatricality could not have been further from Constance's serene disposition. Constance was appraised by Evelyn Scott, the daughter of the playwright and screenwriter Beulah Marie Dix, as "very calm and quiet . . . just a bit preoccupied. When she spoke, she hesitated slightly, a habit which I loved, perhaps because a child would only hear friendly things from her: She never was unkind. She was beautiful as well."

✦

DeMille now began to focus on *Joan the Woman*, the first of the "special productions" about which Lasky was so enthusiastic. *Joan the Woman* is usually regarded as DeMille's response to Griffith's *Intolerance*, but work on *Joan* began long before *Intolerance* was ready to be shown. It's more likely that the template was Thomas

Ince's *Civilization*, released in April 1916, as well as Mark Twain's unreadable *The Personal Recollections of Joan of Arc*, which Cecil bewilderingly claimed was "the most moving book ever written on the subject of that wonderful soul."

On May 18, 1916, while he was in New York, Cecil received permission to go ahead with *Joan the Woman* and immediately wired property master Fred Kley back in Hollywood,

WIRE ME STRAIGHT MESSAGE IF BURNS CAN MAKE TWENTY ETCHED SUITS ARMOR. . . . GET ESTIMATE ON ARMOR FOR TWENTY HORSES. TELL BUCKLAND I THINK BOTET DEMONVILLE COURTROOM TOO PLAIN. WANT ELABORATE SET. ALSO PLAN CITY SQUARE FOR BURNING AT STAKE. GET ESTIMATE ON FRENCH MAID COSTUMES APPROXIMATELY SAME NUMBER AS TO HAVE AND TO HOLD SAY THREE FIFTY OR FOUR HUNDRED COSTUMES IN ALL EXCLUSIVE OF ARMOR. TRY AND LOCATE OR START DUVAL MAKING SPEARS, LANCES, ETC. FOLLOWING ILLUSTRATIONS OF BOTET DEMONVILLE.

DeMille wrote to Lasky with a boyish enthusiasm about his plans: "[The two battle scenes] will, I think, make them sit up and take notice. One is the storming of LaTourelle where the Maid raises the siege of Orleans and is wounded. This action brings in one hundred knights in armour and seven hundred fighting men, bowmen, spearmen, pikemen, etc., and eight pieces of old artillery throwing round stone balls. This army is against two hundred English, defending the Castle, headed by Wally Reid. Of course, the French will be led by Farrar. You can see that there will be something doing.

"There are many tremendous and elaborate sets—both interiors and exteriors—all of which have to be built. In two or three days I will send you a summary of the cast. . . . I wish you could run out here for the big battle scenes which I will take early in August, as I know you will not have seen anything like them before. I am taking every precaution possible but, of course, a scene like this, will have its toll of injured, so if you happen to hear of my sending a good many men to the hospital, don't become unduly alarmed."

Although he was deep in the planning for his biggest picture to date, Cecil still found time to keep an eye on the box office. "I believe we are inclined to be a little too high-brow [in the matter of titles for pictures]. I have noted two pictures that are playing opposite each other this week—one at Tally's, called *Going Straight*, and one across the steet, at Woodley's, called *A Gutter Magdalene*. *Going Straight* has been jammed all week and *A Gutter Magdalene* has been starving to death. . . . The doorkeeper explained that the people didn't know what the hell a Magdalene was, but that they did know what *Going Straight* meant. I believe that this point is worthy of most careful consideration."

DeMille had never made a film on the scale of *Joan the Woman* before, and the script he and Jeanie Macpherson wrote indicated as much. For the scene of the gathering before the great battle, he noted, "The entire field of men kneel at the same time—not a SEE-SAW kind of kneeling, some up and some down—but with an entirely concerted movement. Sun sinks lower and lower in this scene as Joan prays to Almighty God, until she is standing in the last rays of the dying sun."

He designed shots that referred to artists that had influenced him, a habit that he would maintain for the rest of his life. "Scene 21: Country road near Joan's house (LONG SHOT) Joan is driving sheep toward camera—back lighting on her head if possible. (NOTE: This scene should suggest a 'Millet.')" Later in the script, for a scene with Raymond Hatton's Charles, DeMille notes, "His attitude should suggest a picture of Maxfield Parrish's."

His workday went from ten in the morning to about seven at night. Then he attended to business for an hour, ate at eight o'clock, then worked on the next day's plans till one in the morning. Geraldine Farrar had asked for an extra $10,000 because of two weeks' postponement in shooting, and DeMille had grudgingly given it to her. "She seems to have lost a little something of the great spark of genius that animated her last year," DeMille wrote Lasky. "Although she is tremendously enthused over the story and says it is the greatest work of her life, at the same time, that little spark seems missing. She may get it as we go on in the work; also, she has gotten pretty plump."

Actually, Farrar's problems were centered on Lou Tellegen, whom she had married in February. Tellegen was a tall, handsome, petulant boy toy who had risen to leading man status through attributes that had nothing to do with acting. Tellegen assumed the basic right of the gigolo and began interfering in his wife's films. Cecil and Jesse had to invent things to divert him; eventually, against their better judgment, they let him direct. The marriage would end badly after seven years and Tellegen would end badly as well, via suicide.

Beyond that, Farrar was tired; the film's emotionally and physically exhausting production ran from June 19 to October 7. It was the most expensive picture that Lasky had made, consumed the most time, and monopolized the company's most important star and director.

By early September, *Joan the Woman* was heading into its third month of production. Farrar was afraid of horses, so Cecil had to hire a stuntwoman named Pansy Perry to double for her, and there was pressure to get Farrar's scenes finished so she could return east for a concert tour. Despite a brutal heat wave, the singer remembered the picture as "a thrilling experience. . . . The entire company was obedient and enthusiastic to Mr. DeMille's inspired direction. . . . It was a supremely lovely film—and I never played any screen part that inspired my love and enthusiasm as did this beautiful story."

She didn't mention it in her memoirs, but DeMille made demands on Farrar that a lot of actresses, let alone opera stars, would have rejected out of hand. For the sequence where Joan is confined to her cell, DeMille suggested that he could take some white mice, paint them brown so they'd look like rats and have them run over and around Farrar. If she didn't want to do it, he wouldn't insist, but it was an idea, wasn't it? "Well, he was so nice about it, I couldn't refuse," she remembered. "And I told myself, if I live through this, let's hope he won't want a retake."

On September 6, 1916, Jesse Lasky informed Cecil about the latest news from New York:

GRIFFITH PICTURE INTOLERANCE OPENED LAST NIGHT. IT IS BEING SEVERELY CRITI-CIZED ON ALL SIDES AND OPINION EVERYWHERE IS THAT IT DOES NOT COMPARE WITH BIRTH [OF A NATION]. THE LACK OF CONSECUTIVE STORY IS THE PICTURE'S WORST FAULT IN FACT IT PROVED A DISAPPOINTMENT AS FAR AS THE FIRST NIGHT AU-DIENCE WAS CONCERNED. HOWEVER THE PART OF THE PRODUCTION WHICH DEALS WITH THE FALL OF BABYLON IS WONDERFUL AND IN MY OPINION THE PICTURE WILL BE A GENERAL SUCCESS. SINCE WATCHING THE GRIFFITH PICTURE MR. ZUKOR AND I ARE CONVINCED THAT YOU HAVE A WONDERFUL CHANCE WITH THE FARRAR PIC-TURE. YOU WILL BE COMING INTO NEW YORK AT JUST THE RIGHT MOMENT, AND IF YOU HAVE A STORY YOU WILL BE GIVING THE PUBLIC JUST WHAT THEY ARE CLAMOR-ING FOR.

DeMille's attitude toward Griffith was typically admiring—"Griffith had no rivals," he would write. "He was the teacher of us all"—but also analytical. DeMille understood that Griffith's great gifts did not include a knack for business, saying "like many another fine artist of the stage or screen, he did not fully understand the truth of Sir Henry Irving's statement that the theater 'must be carried on as a business or it will fail as an art.' "

Beyond that, DeMille distrusted Griffith's penchant for shaggy narratives that were so diametrically opposed to his own streamlined dramatic arrows that drove straight through to the heart of the story. He always dated the beginning of Griffith's decline to *Intolerance*, although his ultimate consideration of Griffith culminated in sincere graciousness: "When the history of motion pictures is writ-ten a hundred years from now, Griffith will have his honored pages in it. I hope that DeMille may have a footnote."

Geraldine Farrar was twenty years too old for the part of Joan, and at least that many pounds overweight, but her essential dignity and charisma work for the part, especially as she faces impending death. Her Joan is manifestly ahistorical—she's in love with an English soldier played by Wallace Reid—and oddly, there's no scene where Joan hears voices and is called to the sword.

Joan the Woman is the first film where DeMille expands his work to the scale of the epic and, despite the characteristically excellent art direction by Wilfred Buckland, in some respects it's an uneasy film. It feels illustrated more than dra-matized, and DeMille hadn't yet mastered Griffith's knack for balancing the in-timate with the epic. The film is too diffuse and impersonal, but then, with the exception of Carl Theodor Dreyer's eccentrically claustrophobic *The Passion of Joan of Arc*, all films on the subject encounter dramatic problems.

DeMille does better work with the battles, which build in savagery, and in the apparition of a black horseman that Joan sees riding in front of her—a presentiment of death. But DeMille saves his best for the last. It is early morning in the town square, and a man with a cart arrives and begins to stack hay around the stake. A small dog frolics at the man's feet as he cheerfully goes about his business, oblivious to the moral consequences. When the hay is set afire, DeMille transitions to a lithographic color process which gives a startlingly beautiful image. How Farrar managed to survive without third degree burns or, at the very least, smoke inhalation remains a mystery.

The financial disappointment of *Intolerance* made Lasky and Zukor nervous about *Joan the Woman*. Cecil's picture had a flashback structure, and it was ten reels, much longer than the usual Famous Players-Lasky film. A publicity man named Roswell Dague wrote a long, well-reasoned memo to DeMille and Lasky two weeks before the premiere arguing for the removal of framing sequences that invoked the then-raging world war, which he felt seriously detracted from the spectacle of the main story. He even invoked the confusion wrought by *Intolerance*'s attempt to make a connection between ancient Babylon and World War I–era America.

In response, Jeanie Macpherson wrote an impassioned memo saying that the removal of the framing device would result in leaving the audience with the memory of a dead Joan, which would defeat the purpose of the picture. Besides that, there was the ambition of the piece, which would be seriously compromised if the picture was to be treated as just another piece of yard goods. The picture stayed long, but exhibitors in the Midwest wrote the studio complaining about the financial bath they were taking and asked for cuts that would bring the running time under two hours.

Joan the Woman was released through a company called Cardinal Film Corporation, which Zukor, Lasky, and DeMille set up for the road shows. The picture was exhibited in primarily legitimate houses, with a schedule of only two shows a day and a large orchestra on hand to play the score by William Furst. There was an intermission of ten minutes "between the First and Second Epoch," according to the program.

It soon became obvious that *Joan the Woman* was not going to be a great success, even though it was to serve as the blueprint for the latter stages of DeMille's career: a broadly absorbing story of humanity against a background of great historical events, re-created on a massive scale.

Despite the indifferent public response, the critics loved the picture, especially Julian Johnson in *Photoplay*: "*Joan the Woman* is the best sun-spectacle since *The Birth of a Nation*. . . . To me the great moment . . . was the episode in Charles' shabby court where Joan pleads for soldiers to save France. As she talks the dim and shadowy figures of great knights on armor, on battle chargers which would have upborne the Norse gods, plunge over them all, through the hall. This is . . . handling a camera as Michelangelo handled his chisel."

"It has really puzzled us all," Jesse Lasky wrote DeMille. "I mean the fact that everyone is talking about the picture and praising it in the highest terms and yet the business is nothing like it should be." Lasky was heavily papering the house at all performances in order to give the impression that the film was a big hit.

Joan the Woman would eventually gross $605,731 against a cost of $302,976, but a lot of the gross was eaten up by the expense of the road show release. Overall, the film was considered merely a succès d'estime, and not worth the investment.

In any case, both Jesse and Cecil were tired of keeping up with the staggering release schedule of 104 pictures a year for the combine. "I am wondering," wrote a wistful Jesse to DeMille, "if, after your efforts in producing 'Joan' you have any soul left or if the business is getting you as it has got me and you have turned into a regular machine."

★

After more than three years of unrelenting labor, DeMille needed a getaway, and he got one—a place that would become his favorite spot on earth. DeMille saw an advertisement for a tract of land up in the Little Tujunga Canyon, and took Constance and Cecilia to meet Neil McCarthy there. "You might as well turn around," McCarthy told them when they arrived. "You wouldn't want it."

DeMille asked what the problem was. McCarthy went on to explain that there was nothing there but rocks and mountains, and the only way in was through a narrow canyon. The land couldn't be subdivided, couldn't be developed. There was a stream that ran through it, but it wouldn't provide enough water power for electricity.

"It's completely surrounded by mountains?" asked Cecil. "The only way in is through this narrow canyon? It's really wild country?"

McCarthy said it was an uninhabitable hell hole.

"Go back and buy it," said DeMille. "It's exactly what I want."

Paradise, as DeMille would call his vacation home, was about twenty-five miles from Hollywood, near a crest of the Sierra Madre, straddling Alder Creek, near the top of Little Tujunga Canyon. To get there, you took Osborne Street to Little Tujunga Road, turned off on Gold Creek Road, then turned again on Alder Creek Road. Over the years, DeMille would buy up adjacent properties when they came up for sale, and by the end of his life Paradise encompassed the entire end of a box canyon, surrounded by the mountains of the Angeles National Forest.

The only timber cut at Paradise was for fire trails, and DeMille refused to allow shooting of any kind, either with a gun or a camera. As a result, the place became a sanctuary for animals as well as for DeMille. (Late in his life, he made an exception for Yul Brynner, who took some lovely photographs of DeMille on the grounds.)

When DeMille wasn't in production on a picture, he would often leave for Paradise on Thursday and come back on Sunday. It was a place where he could work, a place where he could relax, a place where he could spend time with Jeanie Macpherson or Gladys Rosson. The main house was designed by Buckland and furnished in Western style, with a large stone fireplace, log furniture, and Navajo blankets for color as well as authentic totem poles. It was essentially a giant log cabin, and was built around a large tree that grew through the roof of the veranda. The walls held a moose head from Canada and a grizzly shot by DeMille. As with every other place Cecil called home, there was a profusion of trinkets and totems: Navajo belts, blankets and curtains, coat racks made of antlers, a pipe organ built into a wall. Because Cecil didn't play, it was a player model, with a selection of organ rolls stacked nearby.

In another corner of the sixty-foot-square living room was a pool table, while a table that comfortably sat sixteen served for meals. A Victrola with a large selection of records was also available. There was one small bedroom, two large bedrooms, and a large kitchen, with quarters for the help upstairs. Outside, there was a path down to DeMille's stone cottage, out of sight of the main house. The furniture throughout was rustic, with bed frames made out of rough-hewn logs, and wicker furniture.

The first thing Cecil did every morning was to plunge naked into a spring-fed pool. Beyond Cecil's cottage was a rising path to three more guest cottages, and beyond that a caretaker's cottage. In total, DeMille owned seven hundred acres.

DeMille adored the animals at Paradise, and soon trained deer to eat apples out of his hand, while a fox joined him for breakfast every morning. Feeding would be announced by banging on an empty can. Cecil grew especially fond of a frog that had somehow found its way into a toilet. When the occasional cascade of water was released, the frog would gallantly stroke through the waterfall, then triumphantly surface as the waters fell back, usually startling those who didn't know of his presence. "Paradise is the reason I'm alive," Cecil would say as an old man.

There were no phones at Paradise until the 1930s. That said, the linen was the highest thread count, and the crystal wasn't shabby either. As one guest would observe, "There were no wives ever invited to Paradise. Or husbands."

Female guests would find a vial of custom-made perfume called "Paradise" by their dinner plates. Women guests could bring evening clothes, but male guests were requested to bring only trousers. In their rooms, they found Russian silk shirts that were color-coded to indicate the wearer's eminence: red (ordinary gentleman), white (producer), or purple (director, government official, corporate head). Since red was by far the most flattering color, nobody minded being outranked. Gold or silver chains were also offered as an accoutrement.

On Saturday nights, there was an additional ceremony. A valet would carry in a three-tiered basket lined with velvet and full of costume jewelry, French perfume, compacts, and other baubles. The women could look but not touch. Later, they would roll billiard balls to determine the order in which they could choose their gifts. Occasionally, DeMille would toss in a ruby or other unset gem worth far more than the sum total of the material in the basket, but those were hardly ever chosen.

"Paradise wasn't San Simeon," said Agnes deMille, who was there precisely once, when she graduated from college, "but it was a good pocket-size sample of the same thing, set in the sagebrush amid the cicadas, with the silent, soft-footed cougars coming around nightly to raid the chicken coops. . . . A family treat of this nature was rare. On most weekends Cecil took his own guests, and what went on there, goodness only knows. No gentleman talked; Cecil's family never asked."

In November 1917, Cecil wrote Lasky that Jesse had made a serious mistake in allowing his chauffeur to drive to Paradise, as he had been talking to the other chauffeurs, "with results that may not be entirely pleasant. I should have greatly preferred that you had kept the knowledge of this Camp entirely to yourself—as we had originally outlined."

Although the family believed that Constance never set foot in the place, it seems she did. In a reminiscent mood, DeMille once told a story about Constance standing in Paradise and admiring "the beautiful, beautiful mountains." Suddenly, DeMille noticed a rattlesnake coiled next to her feet. Telling her not to move under any circumstances, he got a stick and killed the snake.

Constance stepped back, looked down and said, "They're cruel mountains, aren't they?" A pensive Victorian lady, Constance preferred a more controlled environment.

By 1920, Cecil's domestic arrangements were generally known in Hollywood and the occasional item appeared, even in a company town like Los Angeles: "Wonder why—so many film men go to Tia Juana incognito? William D. Taylor always is immaculately dressed? Ruth Roland doesn't marry her husband? . . . Cecil B. DeMille never goes home on Saturday nights? . . ."

The eroticized atmosphere, the positioning of DeMille by DeMille as a sultan dispensing largesse, and the fact that so many of the details were generally known are some indication of his self-confidence and the freedom he enjoyed.

*

After considering the fact that *Joan the Woman* had monopolized DeMille and Farrar for an entire summer, and that several movies could have been made for the same time and money, Jesse Lasky began a concerted campaign to nudge Cecil away from his historical side trip.

"We all of us still feel that if instead of doing a period play for your next special, you could get a subject modern in theme, our chances for success would be much greater." Lasky suggested a story about the Boxer Rebellion, with Farrar as an American girl in love with an Englishman attached to the British legation. It was the beginning of dozens of cables and letters trying to dissuade DeMille from going back to the past.

In line with this, Lasky virtually demanded that Cecil take on Mary Pickford, whose last couple of pictures had been regarded as critical and commercial failures. He even sent DeMille a copy of *Rebecca of Sunnybrook Farm*—could any story have been less interesting to a man like DeMille? "We will not allow her to go to the coast," Lasky told DeMille, "unless she consents to be managed and guided by you in everything pertaining to her plays as well as the choice of her stories . . . she has insisted on doing typical Pickford stuff until the public has become tired of it. She needs a director with force and you need not be afraid to do a DeMille type of piece rather than the Pickford type. . . . Pickford is still the greatest star on earth and the eyes of the motion picture world are on her—yet there can be no doubt but what she has reached the pinnacle of her success and her popularity is about to wane purely because the standards of her pictures have not improved."

The problem was not that Pickford's box office had fallen off; as Lasky told DeMille, the results on *The Pride of the Clan* and *Less than the Dust* were up to snuff, although *The Poor Little Rich Girl* had died in the screening room. The problem was that Pickford was spending more money on her pictures than the company had budgeted. "We are a couple of hundred thousand dollars in the hole," reported Lasky. DeMille was expected to bring in a couple of Pickford pictures for far less than she had been spending, thus bringing costs in line with returns.

The problem was exacerbated by Pickford's new contract. In June 1916, Zukor had signed her to a contract that paid her $10,000 a week, with a $300,000 bonus for signing, 50 percent of the profits of her films, and an additional $40,000 for the month it took to negotiate the contract. All this at a time when the average Paramount picture cost around $40,000.

"I am going to make an effort," Cecil assured Lasky, "to hand you the two Pickford pictures for $150,000, which I believe is about 75% of the cost of any one of her pictures up to the present time." He went on to pepper Lasky with questions about business being done by *Joan the Woman* and plans for the next Farrar picture, and noted the emphasis on money by closing the letter with an embarrassed P.S.: "This communication sounds much like a letter from one fat millionaire to another."

It was decided that Pickford would trek out to California and put herself in DeMille's hands. To ensure obedience, Zukor instructed Pickford to put it in writing: "I have no desire to interfere in the choice of stories, in the casting of the different actors, including myself, and in the final editing. I am placing myself unreservedly in your most capable hands."

In January 1917, Pickford, her mother, brother, and sister, not to mention her sister's baby daughter, left for California to make two pictures for DeMille, despite the fact that Cecil and Jesse still hadn't agreed on the pictures. "I am convinced that it would be grave mistake for me to do a light subject with her," wrote Cecil on January 18. He asked Jesse what he thought of "A strong western dealing with the vigilantes, starting in the east and bring character alone into the conditions of California in [eighteen] fifty-two. Second: somewhere in Belgium, showing conditions of present German occupation of Belgium, English prisoners are kept in detention camps—deportation of Belgian men and forced labor of the women, omitting battles and all war stuff possible. . . . A girl left alone to fight the present conditions. . . . I can promise a Pickford picture that will do for her what *The Cheat* did for Ward. I do not mean to make the picture anti-German in any way. This would be my choice."

Jesse responded that he thought the western was a great idea but the war picture was problematic; the market was flooded with war pictures and it might alienate the foreign market, especially "Germany and Austria where Pickford was and is very popular. . . . We prefer Vigilante story first and then *Rebecca of Sunnybrook Farm* or something similar but more dramatic. We only want fifty five hundred or six thousand feet at most and picture should not be elaborate in production."

But there was no way DeMille was going to make *Rebecca of Sunnybrook Farm* or any other prototypical Pickford picture; he convinced Lasky to go ahead with the war picture, eventually titled *The Little American*.

In spite of the fact that Pickford and DeMille had known each other for years—she having acted in Bill's play *The Warrens of Virginia* in 1907—their collaboration was a forced march. Aside from having to write what she regarded as a humiliating letter, Pickford was insecure, and happiest when being jollied along by an ebullient director like Marshall Neilan. DeMille's fiery earnestness unnerved her.

"I was quite honored to work with a man of DeMille's stature," she remembered in 1962, "but I never escaped, through all the years up to his death, the feeling of uneasiness with him. Even under the most delightful social conditions, I could not feel comfortable in his presence. But I lived up to my word with Adolph [Zukor]. If I didn't agree with the way Cecil was doing a scene, I didn't let him know it. . . . It was like being in an iron cage. I determined to never again appear under his direction. I always had a great respect for Cecil, and valued our friendship—but we were simply not professionally compatible."

It's probable that she could not be comfortable with any personality to whom she felt subservient; she would claim similar feelings of unease with Ernst Lubitsch, a more gemütlich personality than DeMille, but of equivalent command on a film set.

DeMille was in no mood to coddle her; he wrote to Lasky, "If she refuses to work we are convinced we have a perfect law suit against her for heavy damages, etc. We will instantly stop paying her immense weekly stipend, which will be a relief."

Pickford arrived in Los Angeles on February 14, and Cecil told Lasky that "I shall probably disappear from view for the next two months, so I am bidding you an affectionate farewell."

★

The success of the company necessitated a lot of new hires, some of whom would be with DeMille for the rest of their lives, while others would move on rather quickly. On March 16, 1916, Cecil hired a young man named Cullen Tate, who would become DeMille's longest-serving—and longest-suffering—assistant director. Tate was hired for $15 a week, with overtime payable after midnight every day but Sunday.

Helping out in the summer of 1917 was a young man on summer vacation from Cornell named Howard Hawks. Hawks was up in the rafters of a set representing a French château that was to be bombed as part of the action of *The Little American*. Hawks's job was to drop a lot of cement pieces onto the floor below. But when the flash powder representing the explosions went off, Hawks couldn't breathe, lost his balance, and fell onto a table in the middle of the set. DeMille shook his head in disgust.

Hawks seems to have had a sneaking affection for DeMille. "He was *filled* with—oh, the greatest ego," he later told Peter Bogdanovich. "When he came onto the stage in the morning, it was like God walking on the set. Everybody was quiet, there was a hush. He had this huge office with a vaulted ceiling and stained glass, the lights all fixed, with uncomfortable places for everybody else to sit, or else they had to stand. . . . When you think of some of the scenes he made—and yet, when you put them together, they worked. . . . He was by far the most popular director that ever lived."

Hawks would claim in later years that his entire career was based on doing the exact opposite of DeMille; the older man would emphasize melodrama and bang the drums, while Hawks downplayed the drama and had his actors move through everything with resolution and stiff upper lips. When Hawks tried to do his version of a DeMille spectacular—as almost every A list director did at one time or another—he emerged with *Land of the Pharaohs*—the worst movie of his career.

Another DeMille assistant of this period who would go on to bigger, if not better things, was Sam Wood, who shared with his boss a taste for adventure—Wood had once hitchhiked across the country. Wood was a real estate broker and had never thought much about the movies until 1906, when a film company rented one of his properties. Closing his real estate company in 1910, Wood worked his way up to the position of DeMille's assistant director until he graduated to directing his own pictures in 1919. He went on to a long and successful career bereft of personal style until he hired William Cameron Menzies to design pictures like *The Pride of the Yankees*, *King's Row*, and *For Whom the Bell Tolls*—a property that was purchased for DeMille.

★

A Romance of the Redwoods, the first of the DeMille-Pickford films, was shot in five weeks beginning February 17, in Santa Cruz County in northern California. Cecil was at his best, punching over the drama, which has more than a few resemblances to *The Girl of the Golden West*, and catching resplendent moments of physical beauty.

DeMille's treatment is more authentic than in *Rose of the Rancho*, where he seems to have been hemmed in by respect for Belasco's rather ordinary original show. On the other hand, the increase in realism means less photographic beauty. There's a lot more romance than redwoods, and the requisite happy ending feels provisional, if only because of the picture's predominantly grim tone.

The Little American, which began shooting only three weeks after *A Romance of the Redwoods* was completed, was a hate-the-Hun war movie put over with tremendous panache. The film's dramatic centerpiece was a re-creation of the sinking of the *Lusitania* shot in the studio with a large tilting set, and in San Pedro Harbor, with the frantic survivors illuminated only by searchlights sweeping the water.

Captured by the Germans when she makes her way to France, Pickford's Angela is forced to clean the mud-covered boots of German soldiers, which DeMille shoots and Pickford acts in such a way as to make the task a metaphor for rape. Jack Holt, with his ridiculous Fearless Fosdick jaw, is converted from a pleasant young man to the Beast of Berlin by enlisting in the German army, but is reconverted to decency by Mary Pickford. As Brownlow notes, "Everything about *The Little American* was carefully calculated. The titles were designed to attract storms of applause. Even the names of the characters were of a nationalistic nature."

Released just as America was entering the war—DeMille's timing often verged on the supernatural—*The Little American* was a tremendous hit, costing $166,949—Pickford's salary accounted for $86,666 of that—and earning $446,236, for a net profit after all costs in the $140,000 range. The returns for *A Romance of the Redwoods* were similar—a cost of $134,831, a gross of $424,718.

The company was watching costs, even for pictures with A list stars.

ARTCRAFT PICTURES [a subdistributor that handled key films from key filmmakers at increased rental prices] IN THE FUTURE MUST NOT EXCEED FIFTY FIVE HUNDRED FEET

Lasky informed DeMille.

THIS APPLIES TO FARRAR AND PICKFORD. DO YOUR UTMOST TO HOLD PRESENT PICK-
FORD PICTURE TO AT LEAST SIX THOUSAND FEET. [AM] GIVING YOU FIVE HUNDRED
FEET LEEWAY ON ACCOUNT OF THIS INFORMATION REACHING YOU SO LATE.

Cecil was always a total professional; the final length of *The Little American*
came to 5,900 feet.

The top-down supervision that Pickford was enduring was also being ladled
out to Cecil. In January, Jesse Lasky had forwarded a memo from the New York
publicity department that stated, "What the public demands today is modern
stuff with plenty of clothes, rich sets, and action. Nothing prior to the Civil War
should be filmed, until such time as the artists among our audience shall com-
prise more than the present 10 per cent."

DeMille bridled at this and other lowbrow nudgings and fired back: "While
there is no question in anybody's mind that the New York office is the seat of
government, there is considerable doubt in our minds that it is the seat of great
literary and dramatic discernment."

Cecil's next picture, *The Woman God Forgot*, was a farrago about the Aztecs
with Geraldine Farrar and Wallace Reid. It opens snappily with a human sacrifice, features lots of acting from the shoulders up, and some stunning Buckland
art direction. Despite the terrible acting and silly plot, DeMille tosses off some
truly spectacular shots that are fully the equal of Griffith or, in a few years, the
German epics of Lubitsch.

Besides *The Woman God Forgot*, Farrar also made *The Devil-Stone*, the story of
which was co-written by Beatrice. But the strong relationship between Cecil and
Farrar was beginning to break down. There was the picture Lou Tellegen had
directed, which in both DeMille's and Lasky's accounts was appalling. "Tellegen
chose to get very upset about the whole matter," remembered Farrar. "Naturally,
my interest and support were his, and whether right or wrong, I did not renew a
further engagement with Lasky on his account. . . . In this instance, wifely loyalty
prevailed over professional discretion."

The miffed Farrar signed a contract with Sam Goldwyn's new company,
where she made seven pictures, three of them co-starring Tellegen, none of which
she thought distinguished. They have all disappeared. When Goldwyn told her
that her recent pictures were not doing well, she suggested they simply tear up her
contract, which still had two years to run. She quit the movie business in 1920
and returned to opera until her retirement in 1922.

Although the company was now swimming in money, there were personnel
problems stemming from ambition. Wilfred Buckland had once again become
restless with Cecil's definition of his job. Cecil wanted his art director to be an
artisan who created sets at his command; Buckland wanted to collaborate on cam-

era positions, actors, everything related to the physical act of filming. In essence, he wanted to be what William Cameron Menzies would become—not an art director, but a production designer, a planner of the movie's entire visual scheme.

Buckland's messages to the front office must have raised some eyebrows: "The company must realize my value has increased as the value of their stock has. . . . It is impossible to get results which will advance firm's interests and my own unless given more scope, and a voice in formulating new projects. [D. W.] Griffith agrees with me that time has come when Picture Industry will suffer unless new methods I advocate are adopted. . . . To one of my education and experience the designing of Motion Picture sets alone does not give the mind sufficient occupation."

DeMille managed once again to calm Buckland, but the roots of their parting in a couple of years—and of Buckland's eventual estrangement from the movie industry—were clearly visible.

Buckland would stay at Famous Players-Lasky until 1920, although whether he quit or was fired is unclear. If the latter, Cecil welcomed him back a few years later to work on *Adam's Rib*, as well as a film or two later in the 1920s. After Buckland's triumph with Douglas Fairbanks's *Robin Hood*, his career gradually slowed, and by the late 1930s he was a hanger-on in the production department at MGM, drawing layouts of minor props and architectural details for Cedric Gibbons.

*

While assiduously laying the foundation for his own long-term career, DeMille was also watching out for his big brother and backed up Bill's tentative suggestion to sell the Lasky company his own plays. "It seems to me very short-sighted and criminal, with authors as scarce as they are . . . for us not to utilize one of the best writers in the country, whom we have with us, whose whole heart and soul is in the work and whose only desire is our welfare."

Beneath their unflinching mutual loyalty, Bill and Cecil were very different men. As Agnes deMille would remember, "Uncle Cecil's attitude was patriarchal, loyal, and deep, but he lived with the grand gesture and exuded emotional protestations like eau de cologne. Pop never permitted himself demonstrations of any kind or even affectionate assurances. He was shy for all his articulateness and diffident and very proud. . . . Cecil stood stocky and straight, with his legs planted like a wall, a barricade, a mounted gun, but Pop sprawled and crumpled."

It followed that Lasky, who adored Cecil's strong, dramatic style, was not all that pleased with Bill and his penchant for rewriting scripts before he would begin production. In one letter, Lasky told Cecil, "I have resented Billy's putting us in this position with each script that he takes hold of. I feel that he should make a very strenuous effort to do the best he can with the material given him and begin shooting in something like reasonable time after the scripts have been received by him. . . . I am all for Billy. I believe he is the best director we have but that will avail us nothing unless he can shoot pictures in a reasonable space of time and with reasonable preparation. In fact, he must produce as many pictures a year as each of the other directors."

★

The Famous Players-Lasky studio now covered the entire block bounded by Vine, Sunset, Argyle, and Selma. There was a second lot a square block to the east that was known as the Argyle Lot, which held standing sets: a New York street, a slum street, a few mansions—baseline sets that could be redressed to represent nearly anything.

When America entered World War I in April, Famous Players-Lasky organized a Home Guard, a military company under the jurisdiction of the National Guard. Cecil, by dint of his time at the Pennsylvania Military College and natural predisposition toward command, was captain, while Bill was sergeant. They drilled three nights a week throughout the war, and were equipped with uniforms, rifles, even two machine guns—"everything except experience," noted Bill. Every other Sunday, everybody piled into studio cars and went out to the country for field drills and machine gun practice.

When the Home Guard was promoted to battalion status by the adjutant general of the state of California, it began to recruit from other studios. The outfit now included a band, a signal unit, two machine gun sections, a field ambulance, and guns that, Cecil said, he "cheated the company into buying. I knew I might get into a discussion if I asked for guns for the Home Guard, so I asked for guns for [a] picture, and they said, 'Anything you want.' " The barn that had birthed the studio was now called into service as a barracks.

Cecil took to the Home Guard as he took to movies. He posted a notice on the walls of the studio:

Attention:
From: Capt. Cecil B. DeMille
Subject: Inefficiency of Non-Commissioned Officers.

It has come to my notice that some of the non-commissioned officers have no copy of the *Infantry Drill Regulations*. Understand that the possession of this Manual, and a complete knowledge of the Schools of the Soldiers, Squad and Company is essential to the retention of your offices.

I suggest that each non-commissioned officer give at least half an hour each day to a study of the Drill Regulations.

"They drilled very faithfully," remembered Agnes deMille, "and then they had a final drill out at the Lasky ranch and some of the men went to France. Mary

Pickford presented them with their colors, and I remember Mrs. Pickford saying she'd had it all made out of silk, the finest silk, and all the stars were hand embroidered. Mary had a special couturier's outfit of patriotic grey, with a little veil down the back. She looked splendid. When he said goodbye to the boys, Cecil's voice broke and he was really overcome with it. Mary, however, like a little soldier, stood up and sent them to their death very valiantly. The grisly part is that some did go to their death."

In August, DeMille wanted to take a couple of portable generators, projectors, and films to Europe and set up a circuit of movie theaters for the troops. He figured between fifty and sixty machines would supply entertainment for nearly the entire French front and asked the company to donate prints of its movies.

Lasky replied that the idea was certainly worthy and patriotic but business was terrible—the Spanish flu epidemic would cut grosses by as much as 25 percent—and the company couldn't stand to lose him. If DeMille could set up the theater circuit in France in an absolute maximum of two months, it was okay, and the company would cheerfully donate the prints.

Unbeknownst to Lasky, DeMille was thinking about enlisting, although his ability to do the job he was best qualified to do was hampered by his innate imperiousness: "I am taking the position that I am very willing and anxious to go out and fight in any rank or place the Government may be able to use me, but if they desire me to do motion picture work—that is a very different matter; inasmuch as I stand at the head of my profession, my thought is that the Government must recognize me as such, and agree to my forming alone the department of military motion picture photography."

That was not all DeMille did for the war effort. He became a volunteer representative of the Justice Department's Intelligence Office, a rough precursor of the FBI. DeMille investigated individuals he employed, reported on people he met at parties, and used the network of Famous Players-Lasky offices to investigate people in other cities. It was the same job he would do, expending considerably greater effort and with much more impact, during World War II.

As it happened, the war ended before DeMille and the government could negotiate an agreement for his contribution. By that time, the industry was aflame with the news of the new First National Exhibitors' Circuit, a scheme by which a group of exhibitors went into production by making the biggest splash possible—signing both Mary Pickford and Charlie Chaplin to make movies for them.

★

DeMille's position as Director-General for the studio meant that he had to listen to a lot of complaints about the overall quality of the company's movies. "I have asked Mr. Zukor to talk to you at great length on the subject of trying to improve the Lasky productions," wrote Jesse. "The Famous Players stuff is holding up very well . . . the majority of complaints today from Exhibitors are directed against the Lasky product. This is very serious. The remedying of the situation is in your hands."

Lasky's continual struggle with questions of artistic quality while engaging in mass production was part of the reason for his response when Cecil showed him the contract they had signed a couple of years earlier, the one about retiring and traveling, hunting in Alaska, fishing in Florida, etc.

"Come on," said Cecil, calling Jesse's bluff. "I'm ready."

Lasky looked at the piece of paper as if he had never seen it before. There were other men sitting in the office, and Lasky was clearly not disposed toward talking about it. "Very funny," he said with a notable lack of humor, "very funny."

DeMille left the room and quietly closed the door.

8

The Lasky stock company kept expanding. Theodore Roberts flourished partially because he was liked by both Cecil and Jesse. Roberts was a very amiable man who specialized in elderly diamonds in the rough—Lionel Barrymore before Lionel Barrymore. Roberts had been a protege of James O'Neill, and was successful in stock and vaudeville, especially in a one-act play called *The Sheriff of Shasta*, written for him by Bill deMille.

Cecil had met Roberts in stock in 1906 or 1907. Cecil remembered that Roberts' wife made marvelous spaghetti, until they split up and she threw him into jail for nonpayment of alimony. "We used to correspond," remembered DeMille, "and he used to ask me to do one or two things for him when he was in jail, because he needed tobacco or cigarettes.

"He knew Geronimo. He went down to talk to Geronimo at whatever prison he was in . . . Somewhere in Kansas. He had two wives there. And his wives were washing clothes . . . and [Theodore Roberts] took out a little burning glass that he had and lit his cigarette with it. Geronimo watched and was so fascinated by this thing that Theodore gave it to him. He had a wonderful time focusing it, and then he saw that he could throw the spot at a long distance. These wives—they were bare to the waist—he focused it on his wives' backs and finally she gave a yell and reached around to grab but there was nobody anywhere around. Geronimo was sitting stone-faced. Then he'd try it on the other one. Then she would give a yell, and reach around, and Geronimo, sitting far away, would be stone-faced. Theodore said he got a better idea of Geronimo's nature from that than from anything else he ever heard or saw."

After arriving in Hollywood in 1914, Roberts bought a house at the top of Vine Street where he kept goats along with chickens and ducks. Because of his willingness to play large parts, small parts, or whatever was needed, Roberts appeared in 103 films in 15 years, including 23 movies for Cecil.

Then there was Julia Faye, born on a farm outside Richmond, Virginia, in

1893 and brought up in St. Louis. She was feminine and charming, and she got into the movie business by a stroke of luck. She was visiting an aunt in Hollywood and wanted to see a movie studio. While waiting in the lobby, she heard someone call for a "Mr. Cabanne," who turned out to be Christy Cabanne, a director who had lived next door to Faye when she was a little girl. Through this connection she played small parts in a few Keystone Triangle comedies of 1916; the cameraman Karl Brown distinctly recalled that she had also worked as a stuntwoman, with a specialty in jumping out of burning buildings and into a fire net.

Faye wrote an unpublished memoir that gives a reasonably discreet version of how her relationship with DeMille began. "It was just after lunch," she remembered, "while I was sitting on the set with a group of girls that a rather tall, broadshouldered man wearing a slouch hat, green riding breeches, puttees and shirt open at the throat, walked by. His shoulders were bent slightly forward, his head held down and this gave the effect that his head was at least a foot in front of his body."

Julia was immediately struck by him, and asked the other girls who he was. "That's Mr. DeMille, the Director General of the company," said one. "Say, there isn't one of us girls that wouldn't give our all for him but he never gives us a tumble." They went on to complain that he looked at women "like one looks at a horse to buy it, and that's only when he's looking for girls for his next picture."

DeMille heard the girls whispering and turned around, asking Julia if her name was Jean Johnson. No, she replied, her name was Julia Faye. She was called away to rehearsal, but later that evening Wallace Reid, who had worked with Faye, formally introduced them. DeMille asked her to sit down by him and they began talking. She gave him the potted history of her career, and told him that what she really wanted to do was write.

Very well, he said. "I want just an idea. Do you know what I mean by just an idea? It is a story told in ONE line. THAT is your situation upon which you build your story. Unless you can do that you haven't a dramatic story!"

"Every line of that conversation is indelibly written in my memory," gushed Faye. "I shall never forget the thrill of it! It started a friendship that has lasted over 40 years. He has never failed to stimulate my mind to better work in all of those years."

A few days later, she took her story idea to his office, and he asked her to sit in the leather chair by the side of his desk. She walked across the white bearskin rug to DeMille's desk. Behind him there were two stained glass windows. The precisely calibrated effect was of a lord in his Gothic castle. "He liked that idea of being, shall I say, remote from you," wrote Julia. "He told me later that he got his desire for such an office from David Belasco, for whom he had worked as a young man."

He glanced at her story idea. Faye wondered if there was a part for her in his next picture. "Yes, I think so," he told her, "but you will never be a star in pictures. You should try to write instead. This is a good idea."

"Why do you think I will never be a star, Mr. DeMille?"

"Because you haven't the right kind of personality. You are the 'cute' type. In the theater we call them soubrette. Also, your face is too round, your nose too long and I want you to write." He told her that he thought she might be able to alternate with Miss Macpherson as a scriptwriter.

But Faye could never get in to present her completed story to DeMille, and Gladys Rosson told her she might never manage it "because of Miss Macpherson." It seemed that Faye had blabbed about her meeting with DeMille, and Macpherson had heard about it. "I found out later that Miss Macpherson was very much in love with the Chief and that she was very jealous of her position as his writer. She . . . was very clever, had a splendid mind, a strong will and dominating personality and was urged forward by an even more dominating mother. To my knowledge she was the only enemy I have ever had."

Shortly thereafter, Faye was swimming in the studio pool during her lunch hour. "Several times I saw the Chief stand and watch the swimming and diving for a few minutes but he never talked to any of us beyond a formal nod in the morning."

Finally, DeMille made his move: "If you aren't busy tonight, Julia, would you like to dine with me here in the studio?" he asked her. "I have work to do on my scenario tonight and since I am dining alone I thought you might like to join me."

Faye said she'd love to but she'd have to call her mother. That nominal task accomplished, the two had dinner, during which DeMille talked and Faye listened. "I was a good listener and since he was a brilliant talker, I became more and more interested in this fascinating man, which made me a splendid audience, a characteristic not missed by the discerning eye of my host. Could THAT be one of the reasons we have been friends for years?"

After dinner, he took her back to his office where he showed her his collection of armaments, a head of the Buddha, the uses of Japanese shields, and, presumably, his etchings. "I had dinner with him many times when he found that he was going to be alone and I always enjoyed discussing art, music and religion in which we were both greatly interested."

Shortly after this, he told her that perhaps it would be better if she stuck to acting, in order to accumulate experiences that she could write about when she was older. It was also more convenient if she wasn't in direct competition with Jeanie Macpherson, who by this time would undoubtedly have been perfectly happy to drive her fountain pen deep into Faye's skull.

It was and is a fairly typical situation: an attractive, ambitious, emotionally callow young woman arranging things so that she couldn't help but be noticed by a powerful, attractive man with a strong sex drive. Agnes deMille thought Julia was on the level of a chorus girl, while Richard deMille would appraise the members of DeMille's harem thusly: "Julia was the most glamorous, although not very. Jeanie was older, and quite handsome as a young woman. She also had more on the ball than Julia, who was simply an actress, a companion. Jeanie was a writer and really worked with Cecil. And Gladys [Rosson] was the person who made it all work. Gladys was very bright and totally devoted to Cecil and guarded him like the hounds of Cerberus."

Also falling into DeMille's orbit at this time was Theodore Kosloff, who had anglicized his name from Fedor Mikhailovich Koslov. Kosloff had graduated from the Moscow Ballet School, been a member of Diaghilev's Ballets Russes, and had founded the Imperial Russian Ballet, a twelve-member company that achieved an initial success. Kosloff made a point to accept young female students who came from monied families, and he also made it a point to sleep with as many of them as possible, in spite of a wife and child in Bournemouth, England. Kosloff was small, lithe, and beautiful, with longish hair and a Russian accent that lent him an exotic air. Jeanie Macpherson had studied ballet with Kosloff around 1911, and in a few years, Cecil would arrange for his niece Agnes to take lessons from him as well.

In Agnes's carefully considered and undoubtedly accurate opinion, Kosloff was an atrocious choreographer, but he could reproduce Fokine's dances at will and call them his own. Cecil DeMille cast Kosloff as an Aztec prince in *The Woman God Forgot*. Kosloff's grace and high cheekbones photographed well, and he coached Wallace Reid in how to move gracefully in costumes.

The Russian Revolution bankrupted Kosloff—he had invested in apartments in Moscow—so DeMille used him in two more pictures, allowing Kosloff to design his own costumes. Actually, Kosloff *told* DeMille that he had designed his own costumes, but Winifred Hudnut, a young Utah girl who had been his student, then his lover and whom he had rechristened Natacha Rambova, had designed them. Kosloff and Rambova had a torrid relationship that supposedly ended with Kosloff shooting her in the leg for having the temerity to leave him. Rambova would later marry Rudolph Valentino.

DeMille's taste for the exotic would have been stimulated by Kosloff, and they undoubtedly shared a mutual respect over their ability to control several women at the same time. Kosloff would eventually establish a virtual ballet empire in Los Angeles, and even franchised his brand nationally, with satellite schools in Dallas, San Francisco, and Chicago.

DeMille was building a core staff with continuity—a studio within a studio. This meant that the staff's loyalties were always with him rather than with Famous Players-Lasky. DeMille was amassing corporate power to go along with his creative power—rather more of the former than any other director until Alfred Hitchcock.

★

Jesse Lasky continued to put pressure on DeMille to steer clear of epics and "get a subject modern in theme" for his next special production. Lasky made these points several times, in several different letters, recommending that DeMille and Macpherson "write something typically American . . . that would portray a girl in the sort of role that the feminists in the country are now interested in . . . the kind of girl that dominates . . . who jumps in and does a man's work." Jesse bought a novel called *Old Wives for New* for $6,500 and wrote Cecil about the property, strongly suggesting but stopping well short of ordering—Jesse knew his man well.

The pressure that DeMille was under was kept out of sight. Around the lot, he still functioned as the Director-General; in November 1917, he had a come-to-Jesus meeting with the alcoholic Marshall Neilan. The results were satisfactory: "[I] received his entire apologies and promises of good behavior in the future. He blames Pickford throughout for all the difficulties but now says he is perfectly willing to work with her or with anyone else and wherever the company dictates: and he has also agreed to be on time, etc. . . . In other words, he is much chastened—I hope it takes."

An old friend from New York who obviously knew DeMille very well wrote him about this time. "At last, I should say, you are in your element. Life has always been a story book to you, and now you can make a story book come to life. It must be glorious. I can think of nothing lacking. A wonderful outlet for your energies, a glorious country all about, thrills everyday, no monotony, work that's worthwhile, for it makes happy countless thousands. . . .

"You are—well, all I've always known you to be. I won't thank you for the helping hand stretched across thousands of miles. Your 'Come out, we'd really like to have you,' means more than you can possibly imagine. And if, by hook or crook, I can manage, I'll come. . . . My love to Constance and the baby, and please write again."

★

The year 1918 would see "A Cecil B. DeMille Production" added to the main titles of his pictures, and his films would constitute a separate series under the Artcraft banner. Joseph Henabery, who was directing Douglas Fairbanks at the time, remembered that DeMille maintained about half the small buildings on the Argyle Lot for his personal headquarters, including a private dining room.

Henabery didn't quite understand the riding breeches and boots, mainly because those clothes were hot and would attract too much attention if you ventured off the lot. "To see him up on a camera platform surrounded by his staff was much like looking at a king on his throne surrounded by his court," remembered Henabery, who found him personally "somewhat aloof, but in conversation . . . pleasant and affable. He was a gentleman.

"[But] when he handled groups or made scenes with large crowds, he would use a megaphone of appropriate size to shout instructions. Then he became a dynamic and forceful person. He was a fine director."

Both Henabery and Fairbanks were amused by the trappings, and enjoyed sitting outside DeMille's dining room window at lunchtime and making remarks about his movies and the way he dressed, in tones just loud enough to be overheard. "He ignored us completely," said Henabery. "We never got a rise out of him."

Henabery would undoubtedly have been surprised to find out that DeMille's prerogatives when it came to material weren't much more expansive than his. On December 7, 1917, Jesse wrote Cecil that New York had peremptorily decided that their films had to be shortened. Exhibitors, he told Cecil, were complaining that the movies were too long—sometimes the theaters couldn't end the last show of the day until 11:30 at night. Artcraft pictures, said Jesse, should not be more than five thousand feet, or five reels, and all Paramount pictures should be held to 4,500 feet. If everybody cooperated, Lasky figured that the company could save somewhere between $200,000 and $300,000 a year in release prints. "By the above lengths, we do not mean average but *every* picture must be within the above footage."

Cecil said he would give Jesse what he wanted, although he probably had no intention of actually doing so. But first, he had to direct one of his greatest films: *The Whispering Chorus.*

The film concerns the nicely named John Tremble, a disgruntled bank cashier who's making $25 a week resulting in "the slow acid of discontent stealing into a man's heart," as a title has it. Tremble goes to buy his wife a dress, but gets into a card game instead, where he loses $20.

Blaming the world for his Bob Cratchit–like existence, Tremble first steals money from the bank, then abandons his wife. Living in the woods, he discovers a dead body in a lake. He switches clothes with the dead man, and puts his wallet in the corpse's pocket. Then he smashes the corpse's head so that identification will be superficial. When the disfigured body is discovered, his wife and everybody else believe Tremble to have been murdered.

Tremble is now free to enjoy the good life, and DeMille devises an audacious sequence in which he cross-cuts between Tremble's wife remarrying and Tremble shacking up with a whore.

Time goes on; Tremble is lamed by an accident and becomes a dissolute alcoholic. When he goes home to visit his dying mother he's arrested as a tramp, and executed for his own murder. He's holding a rose given him by his former wife. But Tremble refuses to tell the truth about his identity, which would make his wife a bigamist and ruin her life. He's strapped into the electric chair, and as he convulses, the rose petals fall.

The film is strong in theme, unrelentingly grim in execution—von Stroheim would have taken a human life in order to direct the Zolaesque story.

There has always been an urban legend that the financial failure of *The Whispering Chorus* drove DeMille in a radically different direction. ("It lost a great deal of money," claimed Agnes deMille. "Cecil had to make money or he couldn't survive.") But the figures say something else entirely. Shot between December 10, 1917, and January 31, 1918, for a reasonable cost of $72,499, *The Whispering Chorus* grossed $242,109 worldwide. If DeMille swerved toward more commercial areas—and he did—it had nothing to do with the supposed financial failure of this utterly uncompromising film.

The footage for *The Whispering Chorus* totaled 6,555 feet. Despite Jesse's pleas, no DeMille film of this period was less than 5,600 feet, and most were around the same length as *The Whispering Chorus*. Cecil had learned the invaluable trick of agreeing to executive pleas, then going ahead and doing what he wanted.

Beginning with *The Cheat, The Golden Chance,* and continuing through *The Whispering Chorus*, DeMille discovered his true gift: large themes of passion and elemental conflict, scripted and—sometimes—acted in a theatrical manner, but directed with a pure moviemaker's pacing and style. The core conflicts would change little over the next forty-odd years—Man and God, Man and Society, Man and Woman—but they would be dramatized through action rather than thought or even emotion. Primarily a storyteller, DeMille would express his poetic emphases through his gift for striking, crowded images.

Not everybody was impressed by *The Whispering Chorus. Motion Picture Classic* recommended it to "anyone desiring a wholly miserable afternoon or evening," and said that it was "guaranteed to take the joy out of life." *Photoplay* strenuously objected to the proposition that two people (Tremble's ex-wife and her new husband) "may base their happiness upon a lie. Also, the final scenes are unnecessarily terrible, with awful, subtle suggestions that will drive sensitive spectators almost into hysterics."

Despite the financial success of *The Whispering Chorus*, Jesse informed Cecil at the beginning of 1918 that "Our policy for 1918 is a simple and clear one. We will hold down expenses everywhere."

*

Gloria Swanson remembered with photographic specificity the impression DeMille made on her the first time they met.

"He was of the Belasco school," she remembered, "and nobody else in the movies had anything like it. There were stained glass windows behind him and as you approached him you were blinded by the light and he could see you and you couldn't see him. There were many firearms and weapons on the wall and polar bear rugs and things like that for you to trip over.

"But here was a man that to me is one of the most fascinating characters I've ever met because his strength of mind and will is fantastic. When he talks to you or looks at you you know he's looking at you, you sense it, you feel it. You could have your eyes closed and you would feel his eyes in your head. Of course, I was nervous and I was impressed and I was excited with the idea of making a picture for him."

DeMille would discover other stars, and he gave a leg-up to many talents who had been languishing in small parts or inappropriate vehicles. But his supreme discovery was this young actress whom he spotted in a Mack Sennett comedy. "I liked the way she leaned against a doorway," was the way he remembered the moment. Gloria Swanson didn't make the jump from Keystone slapstick to DeMille immediately—there was a brief period where she was anchoring a series of program pictures at Triangle—but her vivacity and that vaguely defined but unmistakable thing called star quality made her an obvious bet.

Swanson had heard the rumors about DeMille's harem, and noted just where the exits in the office were in case she had to make a run for it, but he never gave her a reason to do that. Swanson told DeMille that she had no actual contract with Triangle; she was getting $100 a week and had verbally accepted a renewal but the contract itself hadn't come through yet.

As DeMille's old partner Sam Goldwyn once observed, a verbal contract isn't worth the paper it's written on. After an interim period in which she went back to Triangle, Cecil entered into negotiations with Swanson for a Famous Players-Lasky contract. The young actress signed a deal on December 30, 1918, that paid her $150 a week for four months, $155 for another four months, with raises continuing until she would be making $350 a week in her second year. There was a company option for two more years, with her salary eventually rising to $550 a week at the end of the contract.

To young Gloria—she was eighteen when she met DeMille, nineteen when she signed the contract—it was wealth beyond the dreams of avarice. "She was so excited she didn't know what to do," remembered Adela Rogers St. Johns. "And she said, 'The thing in my life I've always wanted the most is a beautiful, elegant automobile painted orchid-color.' And I said, 'Gloria you can't have an automobile painted orchid color.'

" 'Yes I can, and what's more I'm going to.' And right then, Miss Gloria Swanson set the fact that she did not do what other people did, she was to do something that made other people do what Gloria Swanson did."

"[DeMille] was an extraordinarily fascinating man," Swanson recalled in a series of tape recordings she made in the early 1950s. "He had such a powerful way about him. Anyone that ever worked with D. W. Griffith . . . seemed to have the stamp of their director on them—they all more or less had traces of mannerisms. Whereas with Mr. DeMille, he would say to an actor, 'Now look here, I'm not running a school. I am paying you to act. So act!' He would allow me to try to work a scene by myself, give my own interpretation of it and then he would stand there like a maestro and make criticism of it and tell me what to add or omit, whether to slow it down or speed it up, and I think that did more for me than any other experience I have had.

"He terrified everybody [but] somehow he didn't terrify me because he never said a cross word to me in the . . . years I worked for him. . . . There was always a great deal of awe with Mr. DeMille, because, as I say, he frightened people, and if you didn't do the job demanded of you, you simply got hell, there was no question about it. . . . He would take off his coat, hold his arm out—he had a Filipino who would be there to pick it up—then he would start to sit down, wouldn't even look behind him, and there would be a chair stuffed under him, and there was a kind of bugle sound as I recall just when he was going to arrive, so everybody got into position and got ready to work."

On his end, it was a combination of fatherly affection and sublimated ardor. She loved his understanding of the materialist aspects of female psychology—he let her pick out the jewelry she wore in every scene. He gave her the nickname of "Youngfellow," and it became a running in-joke between them for the rest of their lives. (He calls her Youngfellow in *Sunset Boulevard*, and she always signed her birthday telegrams and occasional letters to him with the same name.)

Swanson returned the feeling. "There was no other director like him in the world. When I came on a new set, we had a set up. I would familiarize myself with it. If [the set represented] my home, I'd fix the cushions and the magazines and make it look lived-in and then he'd say to me, 'Youngfellow, when you do that in the scene, when you were walking around with the telephone and the telephone cord, do that again.' And sometimes I didn't even remember what I'd done. He was inclined to say very rude things to people, [but] in my whole association with him . . . he never said anything that was rude, that hurt my feelings. He was absolutely incredible with me."

Swanson, who began working with Cecil on *Don't Change Your Husband*, would be the vehicle through which DeMille would project an entirely unexpected vision—the postwar American woman, eager for emancipation and pleasure. As film historian Jeanine Basinger wrote, "he turned [Swanson] into a symbol of a particularly new kind of American woman: sophisticated, soignée, and definitely not a virgin . . . she was out in the world, ready for something to happen, riding in fast cars, shopping, dancing, smoking, doing pretty much whatever she felt like."

Cecil had undoubtedly wanted to feature Swanson in *Old Wives for New*, the picture that Lasky had been urging him to make, but she was still tied up at Triangle when he had to begin production in March 1918. He shot it quickly, in five weeks, spending a minimal $66,241. Although it's not much of a picture, it started DeMille on one of his most innovative phases and gave birth to an entirely new genre—call it the comedy of divorce—that anticipated the work of Ernst Lubitsch.

DeMille started his comedies where most directors end them—with marriage.

They all take place after the glow has worn off and the partners are growing bored with each other. After the couple have experienced sexual (mis)adventures outside of marriage, they reconcile, now realizing that the partners in a marriage have to expend some effort to please each other. As DeMille put it, "The little things that you do over the breakfast table, and how you tell your wife goodnight and so forth can have just as much effect on a family and on a human story as how quick you can draw a gun."

Aside from introducing sexual intrigue into marital drama without actually challenging the core institution—the titles of the films give away DeMille's sympathies—the marital comedies have a relation to DeMille's own life in that they deal in a very cosmopolitan and modern way with realities that had always been swept under the rug in conventional Edwardian households.

The DeMille marital comedies were perfectly calibrated to appeal to a nation in flux. Between 1880 and 1930, the number of salaried employees increased eightfold, amounting to 60 percent of the middle class. Women were heavily involved in this new economy—from 1890 to 1930, the percentage of women in the workforce rose from 19 percent to 25 percent. As women worked, household expenditures tripled between 1909 and 1929. Likewise, the amount spent on cosmetics, beauty aids, and home decoration increased eightfold between 1914 to 1924. As money spread, so did sex. One survey found that 74 percent of college women born between 1890 and 1900 were virgins at marriage. For those born after 1913, the percentage dropped to 31 percent.

DeMille was fascinated by the delicate emotional calibrations of romantic and erotic love and their trinity—marriage, temptation, infidelity. He carefully structured his films to reflect what the sociologist Lary May called "an internal domestic revitalization." The conventional solution to a couple attracted by extramarital adventures would be a climactic return toward Victorian conventionality, but the characters of DeMille's films usually preserve their marriages by integrating various allures into their domestic relationship.

As DeMille well knew, tolerance, understanding, and a sense of humor go a long way toward sustaining a marriage. So does endeavoring to stay sexually appealing to a partner.

In the years after World War I, propriety was less attractive than the promise of freedom. Mary Pickford and Lillian Gish would inevitably give way to Clara Bow and Louise Brooks—a transition anticipated by DeMille. The DeMille films manage to have it both ways—they confront the anxieties implicit in abandoning old behavior patterns, but they tend to reaffirm the original marital transaction. At the same time, they're problem pictures in which the premise carries more weight than the characters; DeMille doesn't give his women the room for authentic emotion as would directors who came out of a different cultural tradition such as Lubitsch or Josef von Sternberg.

The DeMille marital films (*Old Wives for New; Don't Change Your Husband;*

For Better, for Worse; Why Change Your Wife?; and, arguably, *Male and Female*) were all enormously popular, movies that seemed to be more than movies: a reflection, comment, and articulation of current life itself. "They were sought in every American town for their lessons in manners and etiquette," wrote Lewis Jacobs from the vantage point of 1939. "How to order in a restaurant, what to wear on all occasions, how to conduct oneself at all times. The audiences accepted this film society as the real thing."

The plot of *Old Wives for New* features Elliott Dexter as Charles Murdock, a businessman with a fat, blowsy wife and two indifferent children. In flashback—done with direct cuts—we see the slender, vivacious girl he fell in love with and married. On a hunting trip, he meets a young girl (Florence Vidor) who's as good a shot as he is. Love blooms, but she refuses to have anything to do with him because he's married. But not for long.

The acting is naturalistic, but something is missing—mainly, sex. That would come when Cecil introduced Gloria Swanson into the mix. Cecil devises one scene that's brilliant in its antitheatricality. Theodore Roberts plays an old roué who's cheating on his mistress. When he's shot in the chest, we see only a small pinprick of blood on his dress shirt. He seems confused more than hurt, and goes to sit down. He stumbles slightly, and the blood on his shirt begins to spread. He gets up, goes to the bed, collapses and dies with a complete lack of histrionics.

Old Wives for New is full of reversals of character and convention that were startling in 1918. The fat wife stuffs herself while reading the Bible and ignoring her family; the girlfriend is an independent businesswoman who would prefer a man but doesn't need one; divorce is a viable solution to a bad marriage. If the public was shocked, they were shocked in great numbers—the film grossed nearly four times its cost.

It is these films that began DeMille's reign as a master of voluptuous display, and began to define him as a supreme showman at a time when showmanship was a way of life. In *Male and Female*, we see maids preparing Swanson's tub and douche—bath crystals, powder puffs, and rose-scented toilet water are poured into the shower cistern. Gloria rises. Her sheet slips away from her while the maids raise a towel with perfect timing—we don't see a thing. She steps into the tub and crushes a bouquet of roses against her lips while the water cascades down. The luscious sensuality nearly provides the scene with color and sound.

The narrative stops dead while we watch this lovely young woman take a bath, an act preceded by a title: "Humanity is assuredly growing *cleaner*—but is it growing more artistic? Women bathe more often, but not as beautifully as did their ancient Sisters. Why shouldn't the Bath Room express as much Art and Beauty as the Drawing Room?" DeMille's implication that Swanson is continuing an example of sanitary splendor begun by the ancient Romans makes her the symbolic luxury bather for her generation.

The bathtub scenes seem odd today, but it has to be remembered that around

World War I most of America was still rural; indoor plumbing was something of a luxury. For those in the cities, the *luxe* settings of the DeMille marital comedies were purely aspirational; for those in the country, they were guided tours to an exotic foreign country. DeMille understood this; as he was shooting Gloria Swanson's bathtub scene, he yelled at her, "Prolong it! Relish the smell of the rosewater. More rapture!"

Critics thought he was being exploitive, but there was a sense in which DeMille was taking a form of personal revenge. "I remembered our bathroom from Waverly Place—a little apartment on Waverly Place when I was a little boy, a very little boy. That was when the Washington Arch was built, in that period. The Belascos lived in an apartment right opposite us, and the bathroom was a dark, dingy room that had a tin tub in it which was boxed in with wood and had a little closet underneath that you opened and all the dust pans and dust cloths and dust brushes and everything were kept under there, and of course, every cockroach in miles—it was their recreation ground.

"You could hear the laughter and shouts of these cockroaches, having a wonderful time, and it created a sense of something that wasn't nice, in my mind, which I never forgot. I could draw you a picture of that bathroom now, and I wouldn't miss it by much. And this was 70 years ago. So that when I got the chance to really do some beautiful bathrooms . . ."

DeMille actually favored bathrooms that were spartan. Once, Constance gave a tea at Laughlin Park for some club ladies. Two of the visitors asked her if they could possibly take a look at Mr. DeMille's bathroom. "They were terribly disappointed," remembered Cecil. There was not "a square inch of onyx or ermine, without even a tap over the tub for rose water or milk."

DeMille surrounded Swanson's essentially playful personality with gorgeous gowns, up-to-the-minute hairstyles, sensuous settings, and provocative themes. After the stop-and-start successes of the early costume period, the seven films they would make together over the next three years would constitute a commercial and critical validation for the director. Beyond that, the DeMille-Swanson films would bracket them together in the public mind—a pairing that *Sunset Boulevard* would emphasize.

Don't Change Your Husband and *Why Change Your Wife?* are playfully sardonic about the implicit boredom of marriage, as well as virtually everything else. In *Don't Change Your Husband*, the image dissolves from the spit-shined shoes of a lover to the scuffed, untied shoes of the husband, from the lover's immaculate necktie and jawline to the open neck and flabby jowls of the husband. It's a sequence that could be dropped intact into any of the pointed, lethal comedies Lubitsch would begin making in a few years.

Lubitsch took it an extra step, of course; his women are smart, knowing, and usually understand exactly what to do and why; they can hold their own with any man. DeMille's tendency toward paternalism would be exemplified by *Why*

Change Your Wife?, where Gloria Swanson (the first wife) and Bebe Daniels (the second wife) fight over the inert Thomas Meighan. For DeMille, men were the priapic suns around which women worshipfully cluster for warmth. But taken together, these films add progressive social values to what DeMille had already accomplished with the stylistic astonishments of *The Cheat*, *The Whispering Chorus*, and a half dozen other small gems that exemplified what critic Dave Kehr would call his "great formal inventiveness." Cumulatively, the marital comedies are among DeMille's finest achievements—James Card called them "the most valid sociological examination of sex and marriage that was ever undertaken in American silent motion pictures."

DeMille was presenting a new world, one where women's prerogatives were the same as men's. He's functioning not as a social critic but as a sociologist, with his analytical but always discerning delight in decor and furnishings. DeMille's eye captures America at a time when it was shifting radically, with altering rules of admission. There would still be an in-class and an out-class, but no longer would the social circles be mutually exclusive.

His true subject, then as well as in the later religious films, is worldliness, its attendant delights and exacting costs.

At Grauman's Million Dollar Theatre in downtown Los Angeles, *Don't Change Your Husband* broke all attendance records and critics were impressed; "a masterpiece of artistic direction," said one trade paper. *Don't Change Your Husband* is directed with an admirable insouciance, and played naturalistically—Gloria Swanson and Elliott Dexter embody a rueful humanity. The title sounds moralistic, but the point the story makes is that changing spouses doesn't make much difference. DeMille was a sensible sophisticate; he knew that no matter where you go, there you are.

At the end, when Swanson and Dexter reconcile, Swanson's lover Lew Cody takes out his key chain, removes the key to Swanson's front door, tosses it on the table, and leaves. It's a lovely piece of fatalistic business.

The crowds for *Why Change Your Wife?* were so large that Sid Grauman had to schedule a 10:45 P.M. show at his Rialto theater, and Paramount boasted that it had broken box office records in every city in which it played. The film grossed just over $1 million on a cost of $129,349. Tellingly, it was far more commercial in America (a gross of $759,228), where all this was news, than in Europe ($250,000), where it was conventional wisdom.

These films also brought to fruition a frequent DeMille theme: the inevitable rightness of social class. In DeMille movies like *Male and Female*, and even into the sound era with *Four Frightened People*, people may fall in love and marry across class lines, but it doesn't work out; happiness is to be found only when like marries like.

It's a commonplace theme of the time, but it's also obvious that DeMille approves of such class consciousness; it's one of the reasons that some of these movies date. While he may have gone out of his way to marry above himself, he also held himself slightly aloof from most of the people he worked with. He had two sets of friends: studio friends and house friends, with the demarcation line being their suitability to Constance.

★

The shipwreck scenes of *Male and Female* were shot on Santa Cruz Island. The voyage over was complicated when Gloria Swanson's Pomeranian fell overboard, although they managed to save the dog. Then rough seas washed over the deck and made most of the cast seasick. As always, DeMille's primary focus was the picture when he warned Swanson to avoid sunburning her "long Swedish nose."

For the shipwreck sequence, DeMille used six cameras, and the outcropping where Alvin Wyckoff was shooting was so precarious that two assistants held on to his legs to steady them while the waves washed over them. Swanson was wearing a $3,000 gown of gold point lace and satin with gold bugles, sequins, and beads hanging in chains from the waist, along with a scarf banded with sable. It was just what you don't want to wear when swimming, but it was Thomas Meighan who got hurt when he cut his leg on some rocks.

It was DeMille's idea that the studio change the title of James Barrie's play *The Admirable Crichton* to *Male and Female*. For one thing, he noticed that Lasky twice called it "Admiral Crichton," even though Lasky knew the correct title. When DeMille suggested the title change, New York reacted with writhing unease, mostly because they were afraid of offending the eminent author.

"Practically the whole office objects to the title chosen for *Crichton*," wrote Lasky. "We are making great progress in negotiating . . . for all of Barrie's plays [including *Peter Pan*], and they fear he would be offended if we changed the title of the play. . . . I think the New York office is right . . . it really isn't right or proper to change the title of a Barrie play."

But Barrie was an experienced man of the theater, and he knew a box office title when he heard it. When Lasky hesitantly explained the proposed title, he cheerfully exclaimed, "Capital! I wish I'd thought of that myself!"

Male and Female begins with elemental force—shots of the sky, the sea, the Grand Canyon, and quotes from Genesis. Overall, the film is an impeccably designed, beautifully shot presentation of late Edwardian mores, done in a sprightly and charming manner that portrays useless aristocrats and the industrious and resourceful serving classes personified by Crichton. After the shipwreck, the women compete for the honor of waiting on the admirable Crichton—the male principle paramount. Crichton and Gloria Swanson's Lady Lasenby are about to be married—a minister is conveniently among the shipwrecked—when a ship hoves into view and rescues everybody. Back home, the old order is restored: "Crichton serves again."

Besides featuring the most enticing of Swanson's bathroom displays, *Male and*

Female suggests, with admirable equanimity, that it is a good idea for masters to marry their servants, and that it is a bad idea for masters to marry their servants. When Crichton saves the life of Swanson's Mary, DeMille inserts a flashback to an Oriental dream kingdom, the motivation for which is a quoted line that Barrie drops into the play once, and DeMille drops into the movie several times: "If I were a King of Babylon . . ."

The flashback is dramatically irrelevant, but it gives DeMille a chance to get away from shipwreck wardrobes and into some costumes representing ancient Babylon, where they are entertained by a troupe that includes the young Martha Graham, and a group of Ruth St. Denis dancers.

If you take movies as a reflection of the real world, the flashback is the sort of thing that can drive you wild; if you take movies as escapist fun, it's wonderful. In fact, as critic David Thomson has noted, the entire film, and most of DeMille's work in this period, is made with enormous zest and good humor. DeMille was evolving into a filmmaker who wanted it both ways, and would have it both ways: he wanted to use escapism to point up moral lessons that would help the audience lead a godly and prosperous life.

Male and Female, aside from being a deliciously provocative title, also provided another colorful fragment of the DeMille legend. The prop man had supplied a stuffed leopard for the flashback in which Thomas Meighan was to manfully dominate Gloria Swanson. Meighan was to play the scene with the cat, which he had supposedly killed, hanging over his shoulder. The stuffed animal looked phony, so DeMille ordered that a real dead leopard be found. The prop man found a circus leopard that had killed a man and was going to be put down, but DeMille was struck by the cat's beauty and decided to let it live. He ordered it chloroformed instead. The prop man insisted that it would never work; the cat would need too much chloroform to render it unconscious, which would kill it anyway.

DeMille persisted. The animal's cage was covered with a cloth and a dozen sponges were dipped in the chloroform and stuffed into the cage. "The cage started to go—started to rock, back and forth," remembered DeMille.

"The leopard, of course, didn't enjoy being chloroformed. There was this roar of rage and the cage rocking back and forth and Tommy [Meighan] sitting with his eyes glued on this thing saying, 'My God, my God.'

"Gloria sat there with no emotion at all, just waiting patiently for the scene. . . . Tommy, watching this thing, began to run with sweat. Finally, it got less and less and less and the cage stopped rocking. When it was perfectly quiet—I had the scene all rehearsed—I said, 'All right, get in place.' "

The unconscious leopard was hauled out of the cage and draped over Meighan's shoulders. The only sound that could be heard was the cat's sibilant breathing. That, and the occasional drip of drool hitting the ground.

"Tom had a slightly greenish look, due, no doubt to the mingled odors of leopard and chloroform right under his nose," remembered DeMille. "And he was to play [the scene] as if they weren't there. This was a hell of a love scene." A rifleman was positioned to pick the leopard off just in case it woke up.

"I want you to be entirely unconscious of the animal," instructed DeMille. "Play the scene just as if she wasn't there."

In the middle of the love scene, the leopard's stomach started to make grumbling sounds as the chloroform wore off. "Mr. DeMille, he's coming to," muttered Meighan as he manfully kept the scene going. "Mr. DeMille! *Mr. DeMille!!*"

"Go on, damn it, go on!" yelled DeMille. "Never mind that little cat, *go on!*"

The cat began to reflexively knead its claws. DeMille was unfazed. "Perfect," he snapped. "Dying agony. *Go on.*"

For Swanson's scene with a lion, a large piece of canvas was placed on the actress' body, with the cat atop the canvas. Swanson remembered that the experience of being under the big cat when he roared was like a hundred vibrators covering every part of her body. The shot completed, Swanson was told she had to change into another costume for another scene. At that point, she broke down and began to cry. "Thank Goodness," DeMille said. "At last a woman!" He brought out his tray of semiprecious jewels, purses, and pins and let her choose, like a good little girl. Thus mollified, she and the show went on—a great deal of tension and struggle for a single shot.

The entire episode was DeMille at his best and worst—danger, grandeur, self-induced absurdity, and a boyish, self-conscious delight in all of it.

Everything about *Male and Female* enchanted the front office, especially the title.

A THOUSAND CONGRATULATIONS,

wired executive John Flinn.

IT IS NOT ONLY THE FINEST PICTURE IN EVERY PARTICULAR OF LOVE STORY AND SPECTACLE THAT YOU HAVE EVER MADE IT IS THE FINEST PICTURE EVER PRODUCED. OUR WHOLE DEPARTMENT IS KEYED TO A PITCH OF INTENSE ENTHUSIASM.

The film was another spectacular hit (cost $168,619, gross $1.2 million), but there were beginning to be dissenters in a press corps that had always bestowed lavish praise on Cecil. *Photoplay*'s Julian Johnson wrote that *Male and Female* was "a typical DeMille production—audacious, glittering, intriguing, superlatively elegant and quite without heart. It reminds me of one of our great California flowers, glowing with all the colors of the rainbow and devoid of fragrance."

★

The gradual accession of DeMille as the prime selling point in DeMille movies was demonstrated by the first remake of *The Squaw Man* in 1918. In 1914, DeMille had been an unknown quantity, and the advertising focused on the renown of the play and the presence of Dustin Farnum. The advertising for the 1918 version featured a full-face close-up of DeMille looking imperious, and the legend, "Cecil B. DeMille's Production *The Squaw Man*." The actors were listed, but not pictured.

While Cecil was in the midst of the marital comedies, Lasky suggested Joseph Conrad's *Victory* as likely screen material. DeMille didn't like it. "I have, by gluing myself to it, managed to read 293 pages of *Victory*," he wrote Jesse on January 23, 1919. "On page 298, I have found the first thing of interest. It may be from here on it will improve; but Conrad's dry and uninteresting style is a hard test for the nerves." A day later, he told Lasky he had finished the book, and page 298 was as good as it got. No sale.

Cecil also had some business concerns. DeMille fired off a letter protesting the overhead charges on *Don't Change Your Husband*, which added $20,127 to its actual cost, as opposed to the $12,000 DeMille thought was fair, thereby cutting into his percentage of the profits. "I have gone into this matter at great length with Mr. Garbutt and he admits that the charge of overhead on my last picture is unjust but says that there were no other companies working and that they don't know how else to charge it."

This was one of the first flashes of an ongoing business disagreement about the manner in which Zukor and Lasky would seek to insulate the studio from Cecil's ever-increasing budgets. But DeMille was operating from a position of strength, and everything seemed to be going his way. Even DeMille's mail was interesting, as when Marshall Neilan wrote a long, woozy fan letter about *Don't Change Your Husband*. "Despite all this praise in my heart, I think I am a better director than you, my mother thinks the same and I am going to do my damndest to make a better picture than Don't Change Your Husband."

DeMille wrote back that "Your words of praise . . . are all unquestionably true, and the only fault I have to find with the opinion expressed in your splendid letter is that you say you are a better director than I am; but on this point, I am sure, that more sober thought will produce a reversal of your opinion. However, if on further consideration, you find that you still sincerely believe that I am not as good a director as you are, I shall be very glad to meet you personally and carefully explain to you, beyond a shadow of a doubt, that I am really a very much better director than you are. Anyway, I am sure we will both concede that there are no directors who are better than we are."

★

After the innovative comedies of divorce came a period that might be termed romantic evangelism, in which DeMille touched on some of the closely observed moral squalor of von Stroheim, taking care to sugarcoat the realism that Americans always equate with pessimism by applying moralistic overtones.

At the same time, DeMille began to develop more outside interests. In 1917, when the Lasky company needed some aerial shots, they hired a young aviator named Al Wilson. DeMille climbed into the cockpit and felt a stirring of interest. When America launched itself into World War I, DeMille bought a Curtiss JN-40 so he could be certified as an aviator. It seems that DeMille's 1913 plans to follow the Mexican Revolution, to do anything so long as it could be considered an adventure, were dormant but not dead.

As DeMille would later admit, there was another motivation for all this, which was to overcome a lifelong terror of heights. For Cecil, fear was something to be confronted, then overcome through force of will. He was also intrigued by flying's simplicity. "There were only two instruments," he would remember. "A fuel gauge in the plane and an altimeter on your wrist: with those, you could tell how high you were and how long you might stay there. There were no parachutes. Your first serious mistake was, as a rule, your last."

In May 1919, DeMille and some partners launched Mercury Aviation, California's first official commercial airline. Along for the investment ride was George Flebbe, the husband of Beulah Marie Dix, as vice president, and DeMille's attorney, Neil McCarthy, as secretary and treasurer. Al Wilson was chief pilot and hired former World War I aviators to fly Curtiss Jennies to cities between San Diego and San Francisco. Mercury constructed landing fields in San Diego, Long Beach, Pasadena, Bakersfield, Fresno, and San Francisco. Locally, they used the southwest corner of Melrose and Fairfax for their central airfield. (Neil McCarthy remembered they had an option to buy the property for $1,500 an acre.)

Mercury made the first commercial flight between Los Angeles and San Francisco on June 12, 1919. The flight took an overnight stop in Fresno, and needed seven hours and twenty-one minutes of flying time. DeMille got his pilot's certification and in 1920 he bought one of the first all-metal planes from Germany. Eddie Rickenbacker flew the plane into DeMille Field Number Two at the intersection of Fairfax and Wilshire.

DeMille remembered that his equivalent of a teenage joyride came when he buzzed the flagpole at the opening of Sid Grauman's Million Dollar Theater. "If I had come a little closer to the flagpole, I would have opened the roof and literally brought down the house."

A lot of people thought airplanes were ridiculous, but Cecil was always interested in the latest thing. "I myself, when very young, laughed with derision at the thought of a horseless carriage," DeMille told the *Los Angeles Examiner*, "and in my youthful stupidity made the remark that one would never be invented. Now, I hear on all the sides the same stupid remark made with regard to aviation which once I made concerning the automobile, and which my great-great-grandfather made regarding the locomotive. In spite of this common disbelief in the practicality of aviation we are on the verge of a great aerial age."

After much propagandizing, Cecil finally convinced Jesse Lasky to go up with him. Lasky was in the front seat, but couldn't hear what Cecil was shouting at him. At that point, the motor suddenly stopped. Lasky's heart skipped several beats—he believed he was about to die. Actually, Cecil had just shut down the motor so he could explain to Lasky the turns he was about to do, but that was small consolation to his friend. The engine restarted without a problem, but Lasky claimed that it was years before he could bring himself to go up in another airplane.

All this greatly irritated Adolph Zukor, who believed that aside from endangering a primary corporate asset, DeMille was distracting himself. On the other hand, he didn't want to antagonize the Director-General, because, as Zukor remembered, "The worst thing you could do was tell Cecil not to."

DeMille's enthusiasm for aviation didn't alter, but his enthusiasm for Mercury did. Mercury flew people, horses, Holstein calves, got a great deal of publicity, but did not make money. As DeMille put it, Mercury's major financial contribution was to "the [company] that manufactures red ink."

The airline's start-up costs totaled $59,155 and that, plus operating costs, would have necessitated an awful lot of $10 sight-seeing trips before break-even. Part of the problem may have been that DeMille was running Mercury with his left hand while directing a steady stream of pictures with his right hand. A larger problem was simply that Mercury was ahead of its time; commercial aviation wouldn't succeed until years after Charles Lindbergh's Atlantic crossing in 1927. In September 1921, after a few years of near-obsession about aviation, and under pressure from Zukor and Lasky, DeMille and his associates sold Mercury Aviation to Rogers Airports. Mercury was a lovely, romantic idea, but Cecil was always a man who could cut his losses and move on, and in this case they really were his losses; Neil McCarthy recalled that DeMille insisted on paying back the other investors himself. For years, Cecil kept an old wingless Spad in his garage as a sentimental memento of his flyer in flying. The last time he actually took the controls of a plane was in 1934, when the great stunt pilot Paul Mantz asked him to take over while he took a nap. Although DeMille greatly enjoyed flying, his preferred method of transportation remained railroads, generally the SuperChief, until the 1950s, when commercial airplanes had become the standard.

In addition to airplanes, DeMille became increasingly interested in the banking business. DeMille would become a board member of the Federal Trust and Savings Bank of Hollywood, as well as president of the Culver City branch of Attilio Giannini's Bank of Italy (later Bank of America). Cecil's gradual accession to an elite level of intimacy with one of his industry's primary financiers put him on an entirely different level from any other director. DeMille might have said that this was entirely appropriate; after all, he was earning more money than any actor save Pickford, Fairbanks, and Chaplin, but such relationships also worked to the advantage of the Bank of America. Including moguls such as Louis B. Mayer and the Schenck brothers, also board members, along with DeMille in their management structure meant that the payroll accounts of many of the Hollywood studios, not to mention a lot of their employees' money, would naturally gravitate toward Giannini's banks.

All this high finance meant that actors were seldom entertained on DeMille Drive, while Bill's circle of friends and visitors included nearly every concert artist who passed through southern California: Rosa Ponselle, Efrem Zimbalist, and Lawrence Tibbett, for example. Writers at Bill's house might include Somerset Maugham or Rebecca West, while Charlie Chaplin was a regular, bringing Douglas Fairbanks with him for regular party turns in which they would improvise one-act plays in nonexistent languages.

★

In 1920, Constance brought home another child, a nine-year-old named Katherine, who would join Cecilia and John. Katherine Lester had been born in Canada to a schoolteacher father named Edward Lester, who was killed at the battle of Vimy Ridge, and a mother who was diagnosed with tuberculosis. Katherine's mother wanted to take her daughter to her late husband's parents before her death, even though they had disowned their son. The mother was failing fast on the trip, and took the precaution of pinning a note to her daughter's clothes. In case of her death, she asked that the child be transported to her grandparents in California. But when they got to California, the grandparents couldn't be located. When her mother died, Katherine was placed in the orphanage of which Constance, providentially, was a director.

Constance was bewitched by the child's dark beauty, and by a story that seemed like a terrible fairy tale. This was a life in desperate need of someone willing to save it, and Constance was determined to be that person. As he did in all domestic matters, Cecil acquiesced, although he was worried about Katherine's ability to communicate—all she seemed to do was read. Cecil had Katherine's genealogy traced and put between hard covers. When she was older, he gave her the family history and told her, "This is for you to keep, so that you will always remember that you had a fine father who was a brave man."

At first, Katherine didn't blend well with Cecilia and John. At mealtimes, Katherine sat quietly, while the rest of the family leafed through books and magazines for citations to back up their after-dinner conversations about a dozen different subjects. Katherine seemed to be in a shell until someone mentioned Grimm's Fairy Tales, which happened to be her passion. She then asserted her opinions, and Constance realized that Katherine would indeed fit in.

Katherine always remarked on Constance's kindness, but was more drawn to Cecil's bright personality. When Katherine was still fairly new to the family, Cecil invited her to the studio. When a story problem arose, Katherine piped up with her suggestions. Instead of hushing her, DeMille invited her to attend a story conference, and he treated her ideas with the same consideration he did everybody else's. To the end of her days, Katherine was pleased that her adoptive father was genuinely interested in her. Not only was she his daughter, she was a member of the audience, and her opinions were valued.

★

DeMille was now among the most desired directors in Hollywood, and he did not lack for offers. Cecil was flattered but he assured Zukor and Lasky that he was a company man. "There is not the smallest foundation for the rumors you have heard regarding myself and First National or any other concern except Famous Players-Lasky," wrote DeMille on February 26, 1920. "You must know by now that so long as the company is represented by you and Jesse I will belong to it until old age or locomotor ataxia sever my connection. You can make any announcement you wish regarding the matter; in fact, you have authority to speak for me at all times."

On April 19, 1920, he wrote a long telegram to Jesse outlining his offers and his needs, prefacing it by saying, "I hope I do not have to assure you of my loyalty to the organization and of my intention of remaining with it. I have not in any way changed my attitude since our conversation, but I do believe that I should share somewhat more in the success of my pictures than we outlined."

Cecil went on to enumerate his options. United Artists had offered him $300,000 on any picture grossing in excess of $750,000. He had gone over the U.A. books and liked what he saw. Pickford's *Pollyannna* had taken in $606,000 domestically. "If I only made two pictures per year and the United Artists only lasted two years I could make more than under five years contract outlined between us." Besides that, First National had offered him a million dollars a picture, but he would have to pay his production costs from that lump sum.

> When Fairbanks' and Pickford's pictures were earning far less than my pictures are now earning, the company deemed them worth ten and fifteen thousand per week against a profit of one half of their pictures. The company pays [actress] Mary Miles Minter ten thousand per week with her pictures scarcely breaking even.
>
> I am sure it is not the intention of you, Zukor or the company to penalize me for my desire to remain with you and because of my past loyalty to the company but it seems to me to resolve itself into one of two things: either the company is rewarding me on our newly proposed basis of five thousand per week for my past services only and not for my present earning power believing that my pictures are not financially strong, in which case the offer is too large and I should not want to remain, or else they are deliberately paying me on a different basis *from the other stars* [italics DeMille's] because I am regarded as one of the family.
>
> My desire would be to have the cash remuneration exactly as we last

discussed it starting May first and to receive in addition a percentage of the profits beginning with the new contract next year. All I ask is that you do not figure on the basis of what [you] can get him for but on what is he worth. I have produced thirty seven pictures with but two that were not successes. Can any star or director show as good a record?

When it came to business, DeMille's arguments were always rigorously logical. The only thing he failed to take into account was that his pictures were increasingly expensive to produce, while, at this point in their careers, Pickford's and Fairbanks's entailed only nominal expenditures over and above their salaries; the profits on their pictures might very well have been greater than the profits on DeMille's because of his high overhead. And by lumping himself in with actors, he was doing himself a disservice, because the company had a habit of seriously underpaying many actors, as Gloria Swanson—currently making around $500 a week—could attest.

DeMille thought it wise to remove some of his eggs from a single basket. By 1920, he formed Cecil B. DeMille Productions, with Constance, Ella King Adams (Constance's stepmother and Cecil's script reader) and Neil McCarthy as full partners.

The rest of the industry was increasingly aware of DeMille's remarkable knack for knowing what the public wanted to see before they did. "From my observation," wrote production supervisor Sol Wurtzell to William Fox in April of 1920, "the productions that are making the biggest success today are not propaganda pictures, but rather pictures of the type Cecil DeMille is making . . . [DeMille's] productions are not propaganda, they are rather . . . a certain type of picture that depend, not so much upon the stories, but rather upon the artistic settings, the cast and the manner in which the production is made; and last but not least the titles of the pictures."

Commensurately with Cecil's prestigious status, he began pushing back against the company's hurry-up-and-shoot-it mentality. The man who had made two pictures simultaneously in 1915 would strenuously resist rushing *For Better, for Worse* to completion in order to meet an early release date: "Think it very serious mistake to try to make me finish this picture for March release. . . . If you want me to make good pictures I absolutely cannot be rushed in my work. If our policy is to really make good pictures and fewer of them let's start now. I cannot possibly make more than five pictures in a year and have them of the kind we all want."

The emphasis on speed and regimentation was causing dissension on other levels as well; the always touchy Wilfred Buckland was again bridling. "As for coming back here I strongly advise you not to do it," he wrote to a former employee of the art department. "Conditions are changed. We have been Commercialized by Frank E. Garbutt into a Film Foundry Factory. Draughtsmen all specialized and no opening anyway until one of them dies of overwork. . . . It's a new game all around and you would not like it. I don't myself. . . . You could do much better making Christmas Cards for publishers."

★

In Paradise, Cecil had his getaway place, and now he added yet another accoutrement of wealth: a yacht. In 1921 he bought *Seaward*, a magnificent 106-foot twin-masted Gloucester fishing boat that he refurbished inside and out. She was a thing of sizable beauty, and Cecil would carefully maintain and use her regularly until World War II. The *Seaward* had a single-screw 65 horsepower auxiliary motor, and could do 7.5 knots. She carried a crew of eight and seven passengers. The hull was white with gold trim, her decks were oak, and the interior was black and white walnut.

Each private stateroom had electric lights, hot and cold running water, showers, and heat. The salon had a library and phonograph with a good selection of records, and there were electric refrigerators so the ship could carry fresh meat and vegetables. There was also a state-of-the-art wireless rig that could send voice messages 250 miles or coded messages a thousand miles. The decor was by a young man named Mitchell Leisen, who cleverly devised lamps that rested on gyroscopes—no matter how rough the seas, the lamps remained upright.

Leisen was brought to DeMille by Jeanie Macpherson. DeMille liked him and put him on the payroll as a costumer. Leisen played around with wardrobe for a while, but he had studied architecture and thought that something in the art department might be a better fit. "Anybody can design a beautiful palace," said DeMille, "but can you make a livery stable that smells?" DeMille assigned him to work with brother Bill as a set dresser on two pictures. Leisen found that Bill was "very studious, very conscientious. He was having a quiet love affair with his scriptwriter, Olga Printzlau."

For Leisen, it was the beginning of his movie education. In time, Cecil would trust Leisen sufficiently to use him as art director, costume designer, and occasional second unit director. In addition, Leisen would design and install some of the architectural features at Paradise, such as custom-made lamps and wall brackets in the shape of rattlesnakes.

Another new addition to the staff was the diminutive Chinese-born Wong Tung Jim, who became the great cinematographer James Wong Howe. He was originally hired by Alvin Wyckoff to keep the camera room clean, and when DeMille needed some extra cameras on *For Better, for Worse*, Howe was put on as a slate boy. Howe smoked cigars that were nearly as large as he was, and the combination of his round face, tiny body, and large cigars amused DeMille.

"Alvin, who's that?"

"It's Jimmy Howe. He's one of the extra assistants I put on."

"He looks very funny. It gives me a laugh. Keep him on with me."

DeMille gave Howe the job of cranking the camera during the final rehearsal of every scene. When it was over, Howe would give DeMille the total footage he had shot, and DeMille would either speed the performances up or slow them down, depending on the scene's importance in the overall film.

In this pre-union era, DeMille would arrive at the studio about ten in the morning, lunch around three, work till about nine or ten. Howe had the job of unloading the movie and still cameras after the shooting day was over, then filling out the reports of footage shot. This meant that he usually wasn't through till after midnight, which was when the last streetcar ran. Since Howe couldn't afford a nightly hotel room—he was making $10 a week—he took to sleeping on the luxurious DeMille sets, which meant that he was always the first man on the set in the morning.

"It was on the corner of Vine and Sunset," remembered Howe, "surrounded by orange and lemon groves and at a certain time of the year, when the orange and lemon blossoms would bloom, the fragrance would be wonderful and the sleeping would be very restful." DeMille didn't know that Howe was sleeping on his sets, so was considerably impressed by the young man's admirable work ethic. He told Wyckoff to give him a raise.

Another new hire was a photographer named Karl Struss, who had been part of the circle around Clarence H. White and Alfred Stieglitz and their salon, 291 Fifth Avenue. After some unpleasantness about the photographer's supposed expression of pro-German sentiments during World War I, Struss packed up his still cameras and went to California.

DeMille hired Struss as a still photographer, but after only a few days it became apparent that Struss's sophisticated knowledge of light, filters, and lenses could produce the same pictorialist effects in movies that it did on stills. Struss was put on the third camera as a supplement to Alvin Wyckoff, who lacked Struss's technical knowledge.

DeMille was increasingly interested in a softer, more modern look than the harsh contrasts and inky blacks of Lasky lighting. James Wong Howe confirmed that DeMille's interest in chiaroscuro lighting had vanished. "I remember he used to tell Alvin Wyckoff, 'Look, I spent a lot of money on this set; I want to see every corner of it.' " Wyckoff would light the set and handle the camera shooting the master shot, while Struss and another cameraman handled closer shots.

When Cecil remade his 1915 masterpiece *The Golden Chance* as *Forbidden Fruit* in 1920, the influence of Struss on the texture of DeMille's work became obvious. The earlier film was made at the stark height of Lasky lighting, while *Forbidden Fruit* is elegant and glossy. In every other aspect, the remake is markedly inferior to the brilliant original—a harbinger of Cecil's erratic work in the early 1920s. The earlier picture played for keeps—a real sense of emotional desperation and tenement squalor. The remake is played for society swank pure and simple, complete with lovely but irrelevant Cinderella flashbacks that pad the running time.

In a couple of months, DeMille signed Karl Struss to a personal contract. Since Alvin Wyckoff's time was increasingly taken up with running the camera department for Famous Players-Lasky, Struss earned screen credit within a year. DeMille stopped using Wyckoff by 1923.

It's possible that off-screen activities played a part in the gradual move away from Wyckoff. Charles Rosher told Kevin Brownlow that "Wyckoff finally wrecked himself with DeMille when he founded the cameramen's union." Wyckoff, along with Rosher, was one of the founders of the Association of Screen Cameramen, the ASC, as well as being instrumental in the formation of IATSE Local 659. Wyckoff's union activities would not have been met with approval, for DeMille's politics were growing more conservative . . . as, for that matter, were Karl Struss's.

Struss and DeMille maintained a mutual admiration society; when Edward Steichen came to Hollywood in 1932 to shoot some portraits, DeMille looked at some of his work and said, "I'll take Struss anytime." DeMille always retained an interest in quality still photography; in 1923, he hired Edward Curtis to shoot some spectacular stills for *The Ten Commandments* and *Adam's Rib*. He also became interested in early color and 3-D, and owned a Realist 3-D camera. There are three-dimensional stills extant from *The Affairs of Anatol, Something to Think About*, and *Why Change Your Wife?*, among others, and Yousuf Karsh would do portraits for the 1956 version of *The Ten Commandments*.

"The photography was independent of the direction," Struss would remember of his first movie boss. "He was concerned mainly with the actors. At times he would put his fingers in his ears so he wouldn't be able to hear what they were saying and just look at them to see if the pantomime was strong enough to carry the action. That was his inheritance from the stage—the narrative interest.

"Whenever he had a lot of people on the set, he would assert himself. I didn't like that attitude at all. He would say, 'Where are my 27 useless assistant directors?' Well, why would he employ useless assistant directors? Why insult them?" Julia Faye told Struss that DeMille admired him because he was always a gentleman yet once he made up his mind he stuck to it. "Vacillation infuriated him," said Struss. "Years later, after he went over to the old Ince studio on his own, he had several different Directors of Photography. They'd make about 12 takes of a scene and then the photographer would want to go in and change the lighting. Oh, that used to burn him up."

When Struss left after a couple of years, the director gave him a glowing letter of recommendation: "There are few better photographers," DeMille wrote. "His still work is more than excellent. He is highly artistic and I cannot too highly recommend him."

★

Not quite forty, DeMille was a devilishly attractive man, extremely masculine and vital. Gloria Swanson was a beautiful young woman whose sexual taste ran toward older men. There are stills showing her gazing adoringly at him that resound with sexual attraction, but Cecil maintained a rigid self-control.

As he would later tell his granddaughter Cecilia Jr., one night he and Swanson were looking at rushes of *Male and Female* when she got up, sat down in his lap, and put her arms around him. "I sat there, I never moved," he remembered. "I never put her back in her seat or expressed any emotion. I kept my hands to myself. I think it was the hardest thing I ever did." After a few moments, a deflated Swanson got up and returned to her own seat.

"Why did you do that?" asked his granddaughter.

"I had a star who was in love with me. I could pull more out of her in a day if we remained friends. If we became lovers, I would have lost some of my control."

For DeMille, sex had its place, but that place was firmly behind larger issues of command.

Swanson had talent and personality. She might very well have become a star under any circumstances, but DeMille presented her impeccably, surrounded a young girl with luxurious trappings that convinced the audience—and Gloria. "I do things under the guise of Gloria Swanson that me, Gloria, doesn't want to do but I do it because it's expected of me," Swanson explained. "I use her most of the time to support me. She's been a tool."

Cecil's next-to-last picture with Swanson was an indigestible stew called *Something to Think About*. Vaguely reminiscent of Mary Pickford's *Daddy-Long-Legs*, it's the story of a wealthy cripple in a small town who finances the education of a blacksmith's daughter. Eventually, she agrees to marry him, but runs away with another man, who is killed in a subway accident. Now a mother, she returns to the small town and marries her original benefactor.

The title is explicitly moralistic, as is the treatment. "As if the Divine Fire on the Forge of Life had failed to weld the Steel of his Splendid Mind to the Brass of a Crippled Body . . ." is the title that introduces Elliott Dexter. More damagingly, DeMille turns the sleek society leopard that he and Swanson had developed into a confused working-class ninny.

DeMille devised a far more effective send-off for his last collaboration with Swanson. Jesse Lasky bought Arthur Schnitzler's 1893 play *Anatol* and suggested that Cecil make it "a sort of sentimental farewell appearance of Swanson, Daniels, Hawley and Ayres" as nominal parts of the DeMille stock company. DeMille didn't like losing such a large nucleus of talent, and he didn't particularly like Schnitzler's play, explaining that the round-robin nature of the erotic merry-go-round would be difficult to do effectively. Lasky insisted; DeMille acquiesced. He also acquiesced in the matter of the title. Cecil's preference was *Five Kisses*, but Lasky wanted something close to Schnitzler's original. It was called *The Affairs of Anatol*.

Again DeMille filled it with a light irony that seems slightly literary, although its explication is visual. Our first view of the title character is of his feet, which are tapping nervously while he waits for his wife to make breakfast. Our first view of his wife is also of her feet—she's getting a pedicure. In two shots, we are informed that the wife is more concerned about her feet than her husband's stomach—this marriage is in trouble.

The Affairs of Anatol became an exercise in physical beauty because of the work of DeMille's new art director Paul Iribe, a French expert in Art Nouveau. Iribe came to America in 1917, and was soon working at Vogue magazine, after which he designed the clothes for a Broadway musical called The Rose Girl. He was snapped up by Lasky and DeMille. Iribe would be DeMille's art director for the rest of the silent era, often working in tandem with Mitchell Leisen.

It wasn't easy work; DeMille was a man who believed in miracles, and expected his staff to perform them often. Arnold Gillespie, later to be head of special effects at MGM, worked as a draftsman for DeMille in the early 1920s, and recalled that DeMille "was thoroughly detested by everyone—until they got to know him." Gillespie remembered one time when DeMille was displeased with a prop gun and told the prop man, "Why don't you go out and shoot yourself with it." A few minutes later, the company was startled by the sound of a bang off the set. DeMille turned pale, but the prop man had just shot off the blank to scare DeMille.

Those who could stand up under the barrage were permitted to introduce their own ideas, and by using Iribe, DeMille became one of the first filmmakers to introduce America to cutting-edge French decorative art.

Wallace Reid stars as the philandering Anatol, and he fits right in among the ravishing art direction and particularly delicious use of color, which Cecil pressed for because "I believe special color to be of great importance."

A temporary problem was presented by Somerset Maugham, who felt that DeMille was using some ideas he had suggested during a recent visit to Hollywood. "I wish to put it on record immediately," wrote Maugham, "that I told the theme to Cecil DeMille in the presence of [Edward] Knoblock and my secretary on the afternoon of the evening on which I told it to you and you asked me to write the picture."

Lasky fired back rather curtly. "I am wondering if you are aware of the fact that Mr. deMille and his co-authors were working on the theme of the Anatol story for many weeks before your arrival in Hollywood. Mr. deMille has plenty of records, I feel sure, to prove this fact. If you still have any doubts after you read this letter, I wish you would bring the matter directly to Mr. deMille's attention." The matter was dropped.

The Affairs of Anatol was thoroughly worked over by four different screenwriters (Jeanie Macpherson, Elmer Harris, Lorna Moon, and Beulah Marie Dix). A bored married man (Reid) looking for relief from his fatuous babydoll wife

(Swanson) seeks excitement, which eventually encompasses an encounter with a two-timer named Emilie (Wanda Hawley) who is, remarkably, from Pompton, New Jersey. Then there's Annie (Agnes Ayres), who steals Anatol's wallet and tells her overly trusting husband that a kind old man gave her the money. Finally, there is Satan Synne (Bebe Daniels), who lives at "The Devil's Cloister." She wears a dressing gown that looks like an octopus and sleeps in a single bed with a live leopard at its foot. She's actually Mary Deacon, a desperate woman earning money to pay for surgery for her husband—a plot lifted by von Sternberg for *Blonde Venus*. Startled and chastened by the procession of female misfits in pain, Anatol goes back to his wife.

It's a sly, charming picture, with a sumptuous production that feels appropriate. Anatol may be prowling, but he's also a boob—when he learns he's been two-timed, he breaks up his girlfriend's apartment in a rage, just as Charles Foster Kane will do in *Citizen Kane*. This action only amuses Theodore Roberts's observant old roué, who looks askance at such an expenditure of misplaced energy and who is as close as the movie actually gets to decadence. Poor Anatol barely has a flirtation, let alone a mistress, as DeMille presents a worldly facade that doesn't extend to anybody the audience cares about. The film is only slightly titillating but it's good-humored and amusing and much smarter than its reputation would indicate.

With a surefire box office title and Reid and Swanson in the leads, *Anatol* was bound to be a hit, but even Cecil must have been surprised. Made efficiently for an adjusted cost of $176,508 (one episode was removed and later amplified into a separate feature by Sam Wood, with the $44,127 it cost being deducted from the total), *The Affairs of Anatol* grossed $1.1 million, nearly a tenfold return on investment—just like the old days.

Adapting a highbrow play into a movie is a surefire way to get bad reviews, as Lubitsch found out when he did *Design for Living* in 1933, and it is right about here that the critics begin to turn on DeMille. While *Anatol* is, on its own level, very enjoyable, it doesn't get near Schnitzler's bittersweet tone, because that wasn't DeMille's business. Frederick James Smith wrote in *Motion Picture Classic* that there was "nothing left of Schnitzler but the title. The subtle craftsmanship, the sentimental melancholy and the humorous cynicism have given place to crudity and even clumsy vulgarity . . . the worst massacre since Custer's forces were wiped out by the redskins."

Robert Sherwood, reviewing movies for *Life*, wrote that [*Anatol*] "should be enormously popular with those who think Schnitzler is a cheese," while an English film critic named G. R. Doyle would write that *The Affairs of Anatol* was the worst film he had ever seen. The response was similar in France, where Cecil had been a favorite ever since *The Cheat*. The modern critical response isn't much better; the normally perceptive Jeanine Basinger complained that the DeMille-Swanson movies are "really about only three things; sex, women, and clothes." As if that particular trinity is trivial; as if show business empires haven't been built on much less.

A more realistic appraisal would be to credit DeMille for showcasing the new woman that made her appearance after World War I. No longer did a wife need to be devoted solely to family and community; now she could be interested in clothes, in sexual experimentation, in using a man for whatever she could get. The DeMille brothers, of course, had it both ways—their wives were focused on their husbands and families, and their mistresses were devoted to their lovers, which accounts for the conflicting impulses of infidelity and domesticity that animate these films.

The critical revolt against DeMille's work of this stage derives from a generalized impression that the movies of his middle period betray the integrity of his earlier work. It's curious, because today these films of the 1918-1921 era are often quite pleasurable. It's not until films like *Saturday Night* and *Manslaughter* that DeMille made truly terrible movies—and reaped even greater financial rewards.

The critics had no way of knowing the extent to which DeMille's movies played out his own youthful dreams of success—and excess. As he would confess, "your poor person wants to see wealth, colorful, interesting, exotic—he has an idea of it many times more brightly colored than the reality. How do I know? Because, when doing twenty weeks solid of one-night stands, without baths . . . my dreams of wealth . . . [had] color, lights, fun."

Agnes deMille observed the transition in Cecil's work from muscular melodrama to flamboyant display and said that "I think he was filming his own daydreams. I think he was very young in some ways. He always thought of all of us, even his little nieces, as young women. He always gave us presents of very fine French perfume, or French underwear, beautiful lingerie and all that. Father gave us books.

"I said to my father once, 'Look at this splendid perfume that Uncle Ce gave me,' and he said, 'Well, have you ever tried soap?' I mean it was quite a different point of view. But I think Cecil found all these things extraordinarily lovely. He really did like voluptuous young women. He really did like them all rolling around in his bed, and he had been raised quite differently. He dallied in the thoughts of it."

There was indeed a transition taking place in DeMille's work—between movies that had dealt in a melodramatic but recognizable way with social and sexual reality and movies that represented a complete fantasy. Soon, he would embark on the movies that would make his name synonymous with spectacle and display, movies that portrayed elemental human passions amidst settings of such splendidly enlarged dimensions that they could fire the imaginations of the dullest member of the audience.

The art decoration might be ostentatious, the morality might derive from the thunderous strictures of the Victorian theater, but the commercial response would be reliably enormous and it would be stimulated by DeMille's portrayal of the fluid sexuality of the Jazz Age—success justifying Cecil's certainty in his own Christian rectitude.

Cecil Blount DeMille was not a man to be defeated by his internal contradictions; he was, rather, a man who was fueled by them.

9

On a trip to Oregon, Cecil wrote Constance one of the calming letters that were an occasional part of their relationship, a letter steeped in reminiscence (and containing a few misspellings):

> "Dearest—I am sitting up in my berth watching the majestic shaster [Mount Shasta] with the morning sun playing on the great snow fields on her sides and thinking of the last time we saw her together. I know you will remember the thrill it gave us. I feel that the manner in which these great peaks affected us then has had much to do with our lives. These peaks are not unlike the effection that we feel for each other, great and imovable, peaceful yet powerful. Though the sun is sparkling on the snow, beneath are great volcanis fires. We can feel secure standing on such a height for even the clouds are rolled back when they attempt to smother it. And the storms that may sweep about it only make its surface a little smoother and makes us surer of its own power.
>
> Love is really the greatest thing in the world.
>
> C.

While Cecil was busily maintaining his empire, Constance kept busy with good works. She headed up a committee to build an elaborate new structure for the Hollywood Studio Club, designed in attractive Mediterranean style by Julia Morgan. The club was finally completed in 1926 at a cost of $250,000, and for the next fifty years the club on Lodi Place provided a safe haven for more than ten thousand young women who launched themselves into the movie business. The women paid nominal rates of around $10 a week for room and board, and notable alumnae included Ayn Rand, Donna Reed, Linda Darnell, Dorothy Malone, Kim Novak, and Sharon Tate.

★

Fool's Paradise tells the story of Arthur Phelps (Conrad Nagel), a man wounded in World War I who is nursed back to health by a young nurse (Mildred Harris). But she cares only for display and excess, and he goes back to work in the oilfields of the Mexican border, where he falls in love with a saloon dancer with the dazzlingly unlikely name of Poll Patchouli (Dorothy Dalton).

When he's blinded, he mistakes Poll's imitation of a French accent for his long-lost nurse. Poll pays for the operation that restores Phelps's vision, after which he leaves Poll and his Boston bull terrier to search for his lost love. Poll responds by first burning his poetry manuscript, then his house. Phelps finds his idealized nurse living as the kept woman of a Javanese prince. She throws her glove into a pit of crocodiles and offers to go away with the man who retrieves it. At this point, Phelps realizes that his true love waits for him in El Paso.

It's a surreal plot that prefigures elements of *A Farewell to Arms, City Lights,* and *Vertigo,* and it's hampered not at all by its B level cast. DeMille punches it over with absolute conviction, vividly re-creates the visceral hurly-burly of a bordertown, and draws engaged, committed performances from the cast. The film again emphasizes his status as a child of Belasco—story was far less important to DeMille than theme, not to mention lighting, sets, and the overall physical impact of the production.

As Mitchell Leisen was to say of DeMille, increasingly he "had no nuances. Everything was in neon lights six feet tall: *Lust, Revenge, Sex.* You had to learn to think the way he did, in capital letters."

Of DeMille's employees, both Cullen "Hezi" Tate and Anne Bauchens had the nerve to tell him he was wrong. "DeMille respected anybody who would do that," said Arnold Gillespie. "A lot of [DeMille's behavior] was tongue in cheek. It was an act; he was showing off."

One day, DeMille asked a young costumer named Edith Head to design gold-plated riding boots, which caused her to shudder. "DeMille . . . had horrible taste," she would say. "He liked flocky things; he liked things that made people say, 'What the hell is that?' He told me, 'I never want anything shown to me as a design that you could possibly buy or wear. I want something original.' "

★

August 12, 1921, was DeMille's fortieth birthday, and his mother remembered her baby boy's celebration with a poem: "Not a step can I see before my son/As he heads on his fortieth year/But we've left the Past in God's Keeping/And the Future God's mercy will clear/What now looks dark in the distance/Will lighten as Cecil draws near.

Knows his Mother"

Beatrice wasn't writing anymore. She was, rather, enjoying herself, and her younger son had no secrets from her. One day Beatrice brought home an armload of new dresses that, she told her friend Beulah Marie Dix, were charged to Cecil. "He buys other women clothes," she said. "Why not me?"

While the critics thought DeMille was declining to bread and circuses, those same critics thought that William was doing the finest work of his life. Movies like *Conrad in Quest of His Youth* and *Miss Lulu Bett* are melancholy, almost existential contemplations of the past, of unfulfilled lives. William worked very much in the manner of a theatrical director, as Lois Wilson, the star of *Miss Lulu Bett* remembered. "We rehearsed a bit before we started making the picture. In the silent days that was most unusual. We always knew our script ahead of time. . . . He was really still in the theatre. I learned more from William deMille . . . than any [body else] I ever worked with."

William's sensibility was obviously influenced by James M. Barrie and Booth Tarkington, and many of William's films touch on themes explored by the modern novelist Anita Brookner. Paolo Cherchi Usai believes that William's films represented a subdued "dark" side of the DeMille sensibility that Cecil could no longer acknowledge as his own films grew more grand—and grandiose.

Certainly, Cecil was conscious of his brother's newly emerging status as a critic's darling. DeMille wired Adolph Zukor: "In my opinion it is very important that we find some means of differentiating William deMille's brand from my own . . . William deMille's pictures are of such a different type from mine that an audience going to theater expecting to see a [Cecil B.] DeMille picture is disappointed. . . . As the matter is very delicate for me to handle I wish you would see if some method of differentiating between the two brands can be worked out."

While DeMille unquestionably loved his brother, his highly competitive nature is on full display in this letter. He knew his work was more commercial than his brother's and he meant to maintain his reputation with audiences. At the same time, each of the brothers was sensitive to the other being slighted. When one critic praised Bill as "the subtle and intelligent member of the de Mille family," Bill told his daughter Agnes, "I wish they would not use me as a hammer with which to whack Cecil." Agnes would recall that "The only thing that made Father lose his temper . . . was criticism against Cecil, artistic, moral or spiritual. . . . He simply would not have his kid brother picked on, no, not even when kid brother sat astride Hollywood . . . and was one of the very rich men in the business."

Those people who were friendly with both brothers noted the differences in the emotional temperature around their respective houses. "It was interesting at William de Mille's," remembered Evelyn Scott, the daughter of screenwriter—and Beatrice's pal—Beulah Marie Dix. "Aunt Anna had her group (distinguished guests), Agnes and Margaret had the young men, and Uncle William had his study. . . . Uncle William once expressed to Mother a wish that he could have a long and plumy tail to drape across one arm, for making entrances . . .

"At the Cecil DeMilles', there was never any sense of being brushed aside, and no stern formality, although there was a butler. . . . We had every Christmas dinner there, bringing presents to put under the big tree. . . . Uncle Cecil's presents could be fascinating. One year he gave me a small pearl pin, which I liked even better than the sapphire ones he gave his nieces. . . .

"Any dinner was fun, with Uncle Cecil storytelling and Aunt Constance being kind. Any evening, where we talked around the snores of Sloppy, the English bull, by the living room fire, was a merry time. Often we played games, word games such as 'I Packed My Grandmother's Trunk' or 'My Minister's Cat.' Both required lots of memory and lots of words."

In time, Sloppy met his maker and was replaced by another bulldog named Angie. This one was all white, but had a touch of blackness in his heart. Like most bulldogs, he snored horribly, which could be disconcerting during screenings, so DeMille banished the dog from the room. The dog would trudge upstairs and position himself in the bedroom directly over Cecil's chair and continue snoring, which resonated right through the floor.

Bill had ended his affair with Olga Printzlau and began sleeping with the novelist and screenwriter Lorna Moon. Moon was born and raised in the lowlands of Scotland. She had red hair, the vivacity that often accompanies it, as well as talent. Her husband was killed in the war, and she left their child with relatives while she pursued a career. She came to Hollywood and began working at Famous Players-Lasky, where she met and fell in love with Bill. That was all more or less normal for Bill. What wasn't normal was that Moon became pregnant.

Moon's pregnancy occurred at just about the same time as her tuberculosis was diagnosed, but she refused to abort the child and gave birth on February 12, 1922. Nine months after the child was born, she came to the conclusion that she had to give him up.

Bill certainly couldn't take the boy—"I think [Anna] simply would have dropped him off the balcony one day—I mean, how can you raise a mistress's child?" asked one family member, who sounds a lot like Agnes. But the child was a deMille, and, even more to the point, he was a boy, the only boy the brothers would father. Something had to be done.

Cecil undoubtedly thought long and hard about how to explain the situation to Constance. It must have been a fascinating conversation. Soon thereafter, Neil McCarthy publicly announced that someone had left a baby inside Cecil's car. The first person McCarthy called upon this stunning discovery was Constance, because of her work with foundlings. Constance decided on the spot to adopt the child, who was named Richard, after Cecil's uncle who could play chess while out of the room. Cecil and Bill struck a deal: as far as the world and the child were concerned, Richard was adopted; when Cecil or William died, the survivor agreed to tell the child the truth about his parentage.

The business about the car was an unfortunate choice of a cover story, if only because just the year before Chaplin's *The Kid* had featured a mother leaving her illegitimate child in a randomly chosen automobile. "The brothers had to deal with it," said Richard deMille. "So they invented a very careful and deliberate plan to carry it out. Lorna Moon was advised very strongly to have an abortion, but she had made up her mind to have me, and the brothers simply had to adjust.

"The key to the entire arrangement was that the wives were Victorian and the husbands were Edwardian. It's a highly unusual case where a man can make these arrangements work. For William, they didn't work at all, but for Cecil they worked beautifully. That's because William was not trying to manage everything, he was just expressing himself and indulging his appetites.

"Cecil was a much more systematic, controlled personality. On the surface, it looked like it was the other way around, because William played the philosopher and Cecil played the tribal chief. But Cecil was the careful planner, very aware of risks, costs and benefits. For instance, Cecil resisted the desire to have very beautiful mistresses. He didn't have very beautiful mistresses because they didn't fit into his plan: women who loved him, did what he told them to do, and would not make any trouble. They were available, and they were trustworthy.

"The ultimate reason Cecil's life worked was because Constance knew everything about the other women and accepted it. They had a bargain that he would be free to do what he needed to, she would be his wife in all other respects, and he would never embarrass her. It was a conspiracy of propriety."

Within the family, only Cecil, Constance, and Bill knew the truth of the new adoption. Anna never knew, neither did Bill's other children, or Cecil's. Outside Hollywood, the adoption was the occasion for much heartwarming press coverage. Inside Hollywood, it was generally believed that the baby was Cecil's. And for the next thirty-three years, that was the way it stood. In the meantime, Lorna Moon's tuberculosis went into remission. She remarried and came back to Hollywood, then wrote the bestselling novel *Dark Star*, which was eventually adapted into the MGM picture *Min and Bill* by her friend Frances Marion.

Cecil could not have been thrilled about Bill's behavior, but he was even more irritated about another affair that Bill began a few months after Richard was born. The woman was another screenwriter, named Clara Beranger, and the relationship eventually resulted in Bill divorcing his wife, which caused one of the few overt arguments between the brothers. "When a man has been married 23 years," announced Cecil, "he must not leave his wife. Besides, I don't think your Clara Beranger is talented."

In fact, Clara Beranger had gone to Goucher College, and had worked in newspapers and magazines until she went to Hollywood. She had fallen in love with Bill and stood quietly by during his affairs with Olga Printzlau and Lorna Moon. According to her daughter Frances Triest, she was told "Look out for the DeMille boys" when she began working at Famous Players-Lasky. As she eventually told her daughter, "I did look out; I married one."

Frances Triest remembered her mother as "extraordinarily beautiful, but very

strong-headed. I came to like and respect her more as I grew older. I think I became an actress because it was something she would never have considered; it was
a form of rebellion."

Anna deMille had driven her husband crazy; she was a fussy perfectionist
with a compulsion to supervise. Besides that, as one family friend noted, "Aunt
Anna's mind was still a great deal on her father, Henry George." But that in itself
probably wouldn't have resulted in a divorce, certainly not after nearly a quarter
century.

What finally broke the marriage was Bill's taste for sex, presumably far less
inhibited varieties than he had been experiencing at home. "Mother could have
discovered sex too, but not without help," wrote Agnes deMille. "And there was
no help for our mothers. The ignorance of our fathers was abysmal and rigid; the
ignorance of our mothers, total."

It was a painful and protracted divorce. Bill and Clara Beranger weren't actually married until August 13, 1928. Frances was seven when her mother married
Bill, and spent the first years of the marriage shuttling back and forth between
her father in New York and her mother in Hollywood. At first, William and Clara
lived on Marmont Lane, opposite the Chateau Marmont. It was a Tudor house
with a garden and a workroom for Clara. Eventually, they moved to Playa del Rey.

★

Under the contract he signed with Famous Players-Lasky in August of 1920,
DeMille received 30 percent of the net profits on his pictures. He believed, with
some justification, that the bigger the picture the bigger the gross, hence the bigger the net. On May 21, 1921, Lasky had written DeMille: "At this moment it
seems absolutely unwise to invest more than $290,000 in the average DeMille
production," and attached a précis of a meeting of the executive and finance
committees. The memo asserted that business was bad, Canadian business was
down 66 percent, and the Criterion Theatre in New York hadn't made any money
all year. Paramount's problem was that to make any money on a $290,000 nega-
tive, given DeMille's percentage of the profits, the picture had to gross around
$900,000, which, given the deteriorating market conditions, seemed difficult.

Although the memo carries no attribution, one can detect the fine hand of
Adolph Zukor in some of the points: "We have been able to take advantage of
the times and have cut the costs at our Long Island City Studio enormously; for
instance, Elliott Dexter was glad to play a part which will consume about three
weeks for $1250, and my recollection is that we paid him $1000 a week. Even
where you have contracts with such people as Paul Iribe, you ought to call them in
and we think when you explain true conditions you can get them to adjust their
contracts."

DeMille could squeeze a dollar with the best of them, but any economizing on DeMille pictures was going to emanate from DeMille; economies imposed by New York would always result in fiery exchanges. DeMille had spent the last eight years of his life affirming and reaffirming his loyalty to the organization, so he undoubtedly felt that Zukor was trying to take advantage of him.

This was the opening salvo in a war that would rage for three years.

Zukor and Lasky offered Cecil a salary of $6,500 a week and a sliding percentage of the gross, with a production budget of $290,000 a picture. DeMille agreed, but he didn't like it.

★

Around August 1921, DeMille took off for a hunting trip and kept Constance—or "Gretchen" as he addressed her—up to date on his doings with the guides Fritz and Chester: "Fished in the afternoon frequently getting two trout at a cast. The nights are gorgeous. Wonderful moon as I lie in my sleeping bag. All the troubles in the world fade into a wonderful skyline of rugged mountains with pines silhouetted against the moon . . .

"I got the scare of my life today, as I was hunting downstream with my eyes on the mountain side above, something prompted me to look down. My right foot was forward and about two feet on each side of it was a large rattler. Both of them with heads poised ready for business, but neither of them making a sound. I believe I hold the world's record for a backward broad jump and I know the beating of my heart frightened the game for miles around. However I killed them both and took the rattles as trophies. Fished in the afternoon, had an early dinner and then climbed the opposite wall of the canyon . . . and waited until dark for the grizzly. No luck . . .

"Rose at 4:15 and climbed the canyon wall before daybreak. . . . Returned to camp and breakfast before sunrise. . . ."

Fritz fell off a ridge onto a rock about 15 feet below and was much the worse for wear. The next day, Fritz was in such pain he didn't want to get out of his sleeping bag, but DeMille bandaged his ribs tightly, which relieved some of the pain.

Finally, just as the trip was winding down, DeMille got his grizzly: "As I got [to] the big rock it was light but the sun had not risen. Against the white rock of a dry waterfall I saw the grizzly. He had finished breakfast and was starting back up the canyon. A second more would take him out of sight behind some great rocks, so I fired quickly hardly taking aim, and I over shot him. The bullet struck the white rock about an inch over him. He turned like a flash and started in my direction at a full run.

"He had according to Fritz and Chester about fifty yards to travel. The night before it had seemed to me about one hundred—with him coming in my direction like a race horse it seemed about ten. I fired again and hit him in the foot. This did not seem to even slow him up. The shooting was very hard as I could only get flashing glimpses of him among the big rocks and manzanita bushes. I decided I had better shoot straighter as I was not going to get many more shots. I got the third shot broadside to him as he was tearing around a bush. He had shorted the distance between us by about half. This shot struck well and he fell rolling down hill about ten feet, then got up and started towards me again. I fired but he was behind a rock and the bullet plastered on the face of it as he came around the rock travelling much slower but still surly.

"I took careful aim for his head and fired. He went forward in a heap. I fired two more shots to be sure and then gave the boys the three shot sign. I started to do this with my revolver and found the spring was injured so not a shell fired. This made me weak-kneed for a minute as I had counted on it in case we came to close quarters as the magazine of my rifle was empty. However no signal was necessary . . . Fritz and Chester skinned him—an hour and a half, which is going some for a man with a broke rib. We packed the skin and headed back and were at breakfast by seven thirty but it had been some busy morning."

In September, Cecil started catching up on the movies he had missed and wrote Jesse his opinions: "Having seen *The Sheik* and remembering your opinion of it, I want to tell you mine, and then let's watch and see who is right.

"I think it is a very stupid, uninteresting picture, with not a moment of reality, and it bores one throughout. Agnes Ayres is very bad, and with the exception of a few scenes, much of her beauty is gone. Valentino was apparently so made to over-act in his big close-ups that my children screamed with laughter as each close-up of him came on the screen. In this picture, there are some of the most beautiful shots of Arabs riding that I have ever seen, but I saw so many Arabs riding for so long that I would take little naps and wake up to find them still riding.

"I know you thought the picture was a winner. Don't go too strong on it, as I have a fifty dollar bill that says it is a lemon—any takers?" DeMille underestimated the potency of Rudolph Valentino, hammy close-ups or no; the picture reaffirmed his stardom from *The Four Horseman of the Apocalypse*.

In January 1922, Paramount took out a full-page ad in a trade paper advertising "Cecil B. DeMille's Horn of Plenty for Exhibitors" the cornucopia made up of the titles of all of DeMille's films since *Old Wives for New* up through *Fool's Paradise*, with money tumbling out of the large end. These were the DeMille films Jesse Lasky loved—produced at a reasonable price, with no particular production problems, guaranteeing profits.

Jesse and DeMille remained close, although hunting trips were largely a thing of the past because Lasky was too busy with the press of business. DeMille hosted Lasky's family on many occasions. Betty Lasky remembered that "DeMille was very theatrical, dramatic and he had a great deal of charm—a wonderful family man. As children, we would go on his yacht to Catalina, and we would go to Paradise, and he would point out the deer to me that would come up to the kitchen. He had a wonderful, fatherly side to him. After dinner at Paradise, he would wear robes, like something out of the Arabian nights, and he would bring out his collection of precious stones and we could look at them and he would talk about them."

⋆

DeMille could justify Jeanie Macpherson's presence on his payroll, but Julia Faye was something else again. She just wasn't star material, although she probably thought she was. As most mistresses do, Faye began agitating for a more central part in her lover's life. In 1922, DeMille assigned her to do some story analyses, and the reports she turned in showed she wasn't an analytical thinker either. Her reports were also ungrammatical and full of misspellings.

On the other hand, she undoubtedly had latent talents. An undated letter to Cecil provides a glimpse into her kittenish charm:

> Dear—These are the pine nuts I picked for you, over nine thousand feet high. They have been roasted and the shells are easily cracked with the teeth. Like peanuts, you can't stop eating them once you start. I hope you like them.
>
> No doubt you are very busy with your writers and secretaries, so I'll not bother you, but do let me know how you are progressing and when I may come to see you again, won't you?
>
> The days are probably not unpleasant but how are the nights?
>
> I'm praying for you—Love, Julia.

Constance had been able to accept Jeanie's presence in Cecil's life because of their shared affinity for their work. But it was impossible to understand Julia's importance on any level other than sex. It was clear that Cecil had no intention of ever divorcing Constance, but neither did he have any intention of dropping Julia at Constance's request. All this meant that Julia's presence constituted a direct blow to Constance's pride.

According to Agnes, Constance consulted her father about Cecil's affair with Julia, and he counseled her as a good Victorian father would: "If you must leave him then you will get a divorce. But if you go back you must accept him as he is." And so Constance trooped back to Laughlin Park, and contrived to defuse the rumors by inviting Jeanie and Julia to her house for tea.

This gambit fooled no one—everybody at the studio, everybody in Hollywood knew that Jeanie and Julia were Cecil's mistresses. One actress remembered chatting with Julia on a set when she saw Constance walking toward them. The actress began to panic—Will she slap Julia? Will she slap me for being Julia's friend? But Constance came up to Julia, put her arm around her and complimented her on her beauty in scenes she and Cecil had screened the night before.

⋆

It had long been obvious that DeMille was an inspired businessman. "He went to a business conference the way my father went to a tennis match," observed Agnes deMille. "Don't think of your opponents as people," he told his niece. "You can't do that. They're your opponents in a game." He never drank during a business meeting, and he wouldn't smoke or even have tea or chew gum, lest he be momentarily distracted by anything other than the matter at hand.

Among the deals he transacted was buying William's share of their father's literary estate. Cecil paid Bill $2,500 for his sixth interest in *The Wife*, *The Charity Ball*, *Lord Chumley*, *Men and Women*, *Classmates*, and *Royal Mounted*. In the same agreement, Cecil undertook to pay all of Beatrice's living expenses, and Bill also transferred to Cecil his future inheritance of his mother's percentage of Henry deMille's plays.

Could Bill have been completely uninterested in their father's work, was he less emotionally bound to Beatrice than his younger brother, or was it merely an acknowledgment that Cecil was better able to take care of her, financially as well as psychologically?

Richard deMille theorized that "Cecil was interested in preserving his father's legacy, and he may have thought that William was not in a position to do so. And he might have thought that William's marriage was problematic and he didn't want the assets tied up [when the marriage failed.]"

★

Among DeMille's major tasks was to find a replacement for Gloria Swanson, who had become too valuable to be monopolized by one director. He settled on an actress named Leatrice Joy, née Zeidler. Like Swanson, Leatrice was dark, charming, and had a background in two-reel comedies. DeMille liked comediennes, because he believed they always overacted, and it was a lot easier to tone down a large actor than it was to inflate a smaller talent.

Like Swanson, Joy was quite young—twenty—and terribly impressed. She was impressed by the way DeMille would always stand up when a woman entered the room, impressed by his absolute control on the set. Other than DeMille's ritual reading of the script for the cast and crew a day or two before production began, Joy never saw a script again, and let DeMille explain each scene, which he would do in great detail, emphasizing emotional coloring.

She was also appreciative of the way he let actors be actors, never demanding or imposing a performance, often simply saying, "Do it as you feel it." If Joy didn't satisfy him, he would suggest "I'd go a little deeper if I were you."

DeMille inveigled Joy into taking a pay cut from the $750 a week she was making at Goldwyn, which caused her boyfriend, John Gilbert, to explode. "How can you work for that silly son of a bitch? He treats people like cattle and acts like he's doing them a favor by paying them anything at all for the privilege of working with him. . . . You think he'll make you a star, but the fact is no one is going to notice you on those epics of his unless he has you riding around naked on the back of a Bengal tiger or wallowing in one of his sunken bathtubs."

DeMille's feelings about Gilbert were nearly identical to Gilbert's feelings about him, albeit pithier. "I wouldn't use him as a fertilizer on my plants," DeMille indelicately told Joy. His feelings were only amplified after the actor went through a Mexican divorce from his first wife in order to marry Leatrice. It was then discovered that the divorce probably wasn't legal in America, and the first wife began dark mutterings about bigamy.

As so many people would, Joy went to DeMille for his strength and knowl-edge of the mechanics of negotiation. First, he made her acknowledge his position as arbiter. On office stationery, she wrote, "Dear Mr. DeMille, In connection with a personal affair of which we both know, I agree to be guided by your judgment in the matter. And to follow your instructions in connection therewith."

DeMille told Gilbert to pay off the ex-wife and be quick about it. She wanted $500 a month on top of the $5,000 Gilbert had given her to go away, but settled for $250 a month. Gilbert agreed, then changed his mind. This ridiculous situa-tion went back and forth through all of 1922 and into early 1923, with DeMille demanding that Leatrice Joy use whatever influence she had with her bad-boy hus-band to make him live up to his promises. At one point, Jesse Lasky wondered if it would really be so bad if the whole thing came out in the press, but Cecil wasn't so blasé. Years later, after Gilbert's triumphant success in *The Big Parade*, he and DeMille were on the same elevator, and as the actor got off, he turned to DeMille and said, "Pretty good fertilizer, eh, DeMille?"

For a time, Joy was Cecil's favorite actress, and he gave her the leads in all of his personally directed productions. He also made sure other directors presented her as he wished them to. When Marshall Neilan cast her as a household drudge, he outfitted her with a large facial wart. DeMille took one look at Neilan's rushes and told him to get rid of the wart—Neilan was ruining the image of his beautiful new star.

Joy's first film for DeMille was *Saturday Night*, which told the story of two par-allel romances revolving around class distinctions. To cut to the chase: Never the twain shall meet. Like many of Cecil's movies of this period, *Saturday Night* has a B movie cast (Edith Roberts, Jack Mower, Conrad Nagel) and a rote, improbable story. It gives every indication of a director who is going through the motions. Yet the picture made money (cost $224,635, gross $753,807), for, as far as the public was concerned, Cecil remained an authentic celebrity as well as a directorial co-lossus. He made a guest appearance in James Cruze's film *Hollywood,* and when the movie's theme song was issued, the lyric included "Cecil B. DeMille, and gaze upon his brother Will."

Saturday Night was mainly notable for introducing a young actor to DeMille's attention. During a swimming party sequence, the top of Julia Faye's bathing suit came apart when she hit the water. The young actor held Julia with her back to the camera until DeMille called "cut." With the actor's coat around her shoulders, she told DeMille what had happened. He thanked the young man, whose name was William Boyd, and made room for him in his stock company.

DeMille took a fatherly interest in the young actor, and decided to build Boyd up into a star. When Boyd broke his ankle and was unable to work for a month, DeMille wrote him a personal check for $300 to tide him over. In the years to come, Boyd would achieve stardom twice, once while working for DeMille's independent production company in the late 1920s, and later as Hopalong Cassidy. He became one of the few actors to be regularly invited to DeMille's house, and the two men became lifelong friends.

After completing *Saturday Night*, DeMille, his valet, Yamabe, and Paul Iribe took off for Europe. Iribe was very French, a good traveling companion, and a wonderful raconteur. One of Iribe's anecdotes became a favorite of DeMille's. It involved Iribe's aged uncle, who felt the night drawing near but decided to have one last sexual fling. Taking himself to a brothel, he engaged the services of a girl. When Iribe asked how they had gotten along, the uncle said she was "very nice, very charming. And then I felt a terrible pain in my back, and I knew I had come." DeMille told the story often among male friends, complete with French accent.

The trip itself seems to have been dogged by misfortune. On January 22, 1922, in Rome, Iribe and DeMille arrayed themselves in formal clothes and presented themselves at the Vatican for their scheduled audience with Pope Benedict XV, only to be told that the pope had just died. In Paris, DeMille contracted rheumatic fever and for the first time in his life was seriously ill. Confined to his bed, too sore to move, unable to eat, he felt as if he were dying. By the time he was well enough to travel, his stomach was still queasy, and the ocean crossing was debilitating. By February 3, he was still quite shaky, and he wasn't able to walk around the grounds of Laughlin Park until April.

★

DeMille was sufficiently pleased with his new discovery to use Leatrice Joy in *Manslaughter*, one of the least of his films. "I want you to be a lady in this," he told Joy, "but I don't want you to be a *real* lady, I want you to be what a housemaid *thinks* a lady is. Do it for *them*."

Every once in a while, DeMille's peremptory personality would come under assault. Louise Beavers, later an actress, but then working as Leatrice Joy's dresser, attached a nineteen-yard gold-encrusted mantle to Joy with a couple of safety pins. The scene was a flashback to ancient times featuring live Bengal tigers. DeMille's preparations for the scene involved two pearl-handled revolvers, the better to imitate Frank Buck, a well-known big-game hunter. DeMille was irritated by the tacky safety pins and asked Beavers what she thought she was doing.

"Mr. DeMille, when them big cats start running around and biting people and you start firing them guns, I don't want my baby hindered by no 19 yards of train."

Later, DeMille was showing off in front of a group of bankers that were touring the set. "Where are my 1000 assistants?" he thundered over the loudspeaker, whereupon Hezi Tate walked over. "Here's 999 of them," he said, "what do you want, boss?"

On *Manslaughter*, Mitch Leisen decorated a library with false bindings. DeMille pulled them all down onto the floor in a display worthy of Belasco, and demanded that Leisen put real books on the shelves. But authenticity went only so far. Since the film had an important courtroom scene, Joy attended some trials by way of research, and noted that there were few histrionics when someone was found guilty. During the scene in the film where she was to be found guilty, Joy stayed motionless, then closed her eyes and collapsed. DeMille called cut and said, "When are you going to start acting, Miss Joy?"

"You don't appreciate what I gathered from my experience," said Joy, explaining that she was only doing what a woman she had observed at trial had done. "Well," said DeMille, "I'd like it a little bit more—*portrayed* is the word." Joy batted her eyes and gave a conventional representation of female grief.

Manslaughter is heavy on production values and negligible in most other areas. Joy plays a willful, wild society girl, Thomas Meighan a handsome, stalwart, dull district attorney. During a race on pogo sticks at a party, a brooding Meighan intones, "This dance—with its booze and license—is little better than a Feast of Bacchus." Dissolve to a Roman orgy with gladiators, dissolve back to modern times, complete with a female prizefight.

Lois Wilson, a maid with a sick child, asks Joy for a loan. When it's refused, she steals a ring and, when Joy doesn't show up at a clemency hearing, is sent to jail. When a policeman is killed chasing a speeding Joy, Meighan prosecutes the woman he loves. Cue another flashback in which Meighan, transformed into a Visigoth, takes Rome and, by extension, Joy.

The jail sequences carry some of the starkness of *The Whispering Chorus*. Meighan, wracked by guilt, hits the bottle. Joy does two years hard time and emerges to find Meighan destitute. The two reunite, with regeneration not far behind.

The problem with *Manslaughter* and most of the other movies DeMille made in this period is not the subject matter. The problem is that DeMille is selling rote degradation followed by rote moral uplift and selling it too hard.

Manslaughter cost $384,111, and grossed $1.2 million.

Joy believed that her career with DeMille broke up her marriage to John Gilbert, who came to believe she was having an affair with her director. It wasn't true, but Gilbert had an obsessive personality and couldn't be convinced. The arguments became constant, and the domestic strife began to negatively affect Joy's work. It got to the point where DeMille would drop newspaper clippings about her failing marriage into her lap. Finally, DeMille threatened to reshoot her scenes with another actress. "Your acting is terrible, your mind is so distracted that I can't reach you. . . . Miss Joy your work must come first. If it doesn't, then you and I will have no reason to continue together. Is that perfectly clear?"

Joy took the hint and left her husband. Later, they reconciled and had a child before finally divorcing. "DeMille didn't want her having sex," remembered Leatrice Fountain, Joy's daughter, "he didn't want her fighting, didn't want her coming to the studio with circles under her eyes."

Leatrice Joy put up with all this because, as her daughter said, "She loved being a star more than she loved being an actress. And she loved authority. She was quite tolerant of DeMille's relationship with Julia Faye; it was show business. Mother admired him—when he made a movie that had jewels and furs, he got the finest jewels and furs. There was never anything cheap about his work. The only criticism mother ever leveled at him was that she didn't think he gave Julia Faye enough money."

Although Joy was a delightful, humorous woman, on screen she tended toward dignity; as a result, her natural, spunky charm didn't quite come across and she didn't have the career she seemed destined for.

★

DeMille's recent pictures only increased the proportion of bad reviews. "He makes me think of a manufacturer of luxurious automobiles," wrote the French critic Louis Delluc in 1922. "When a Rolls, a Cadillac, a Hispano is built, it is likely they have claim to no other aim but to please . . . the public, and to give it what it wants. But it is equally likely that this servility and self-effacement strikes a blow at imagination and inspiration."

Local critics were even less respectful. "DeMille looks like action," noted Allene Talmey. "Large, broad shouldered, preposterously healthy, his face and scalp have been burned a dark red-brown, his almost totally bald head rimmed by a band of curly gray hair." Talmey noted the "grave theatricality" with which Cecil went about his work, and the fact that "he has made many stars, much money. . . . He is president of one bank and director of another. His pictures have been successful, always an exaggeration; for in his mind's eye he sees everything as more tremendous than reality."

Talmey's piece gives a good sense of the slowly pyramiding doubt wrought by Cecil's cascading series of successes, and the manner in which he basked in his glory. Yet DeMille's images became part of cinema's DNA, and, as already noted, many of his plots had a strange way of turning up in later years as well. As the film historian Robert Birchard pointed out, *The Little American* is clearly a forerunner to aspects of Rex Ingram's *The Four Horsemen of the Apocalypse*; characterizing a long relationship at a dinner table is most famously done by Orson Welles in *Citizen Kane*, but DeMille did it first in *Something to Think About*; in *The Ten Com-*

mandments, a dying Nita Naldi pulls a curtain off its rings, which Hitchcock—a great DeMille admirer—lifted for Janet Leigh's death throes in *Psycho*.

☆

In the early summer of 1922, Will Hays, the newly hired head of the Motion Picture Producers and Distributors Organization, made his first official trip to California. Hays had been the managing partner of Hays and Hays of Sullivan, Indiana, the law firm representing the corrupt oil baron Harry Sinclair. Hays had also been chairman of the Republican National Committee, and when Republican Warren Harding was elected president, Hays had been rewarded with the job of postmaster general.

Hays had accumulated and laundered an illegal $8 million slush fund for Harding, and he had been up to his elbows in the Teapot Dome scandal. Greasing the political pole has always been a lucrative job, but it paled next to being the front man and chief lobbyist for the movie industry, a job that brought with it a Manhattan penthouse, a salary of $150,000, and an expense account.

Hays was ridiculously homely—he looked like a large rodent—but he was an experienced and expert power player, which is why he had been hired: to forestall any kind of national censorship in the wake of the Roscoe (Fatty) Arbuckle manslaughter trial and the William Desmond Taylor murder—both scandals emanating from Famous Players-Lasky. It was the devout hope of everybody in the movie business that Hays could lend an aura of small-town American probity to an industry increasingly regarded as Sodom on the Coast.

Hays was the right man for the job, assuming that the job was bobbing, weaving, and paying lip service to lofty but vague ideals. As his ghostwriter, Raymond Moley, would observe, Hays "used language mainly not to reveal but to conceal thought."

In the midst of his speeches and meet-and-greets Hays spent a weekend at Paradise along with Cecil and William, Jesse Lasky, and William S. Hart. "We all gathered in the big living room and talked until the early hours both nights," remembered William S. Hart. "Mr. Hays got plenty of rest, but not much sleep." The brandy-and-cigars atmosphere and man-to-man understandings that resulted from such meetings would prove invaluable whenever Cecil or the studio needed a favor.

☆

The first few months of 1923 were difficult for DeMille. On January 18, Wallace Reid died at the age of thirty-one from the effects of drug addiction. It was the last of the scandalous body blows that Famous Players-Lasky would endure, at least publicly.

What made Reid's death particularly notable was the fact that his wife, actress Dorothy Davenport, had gone public with his addiction on December

17, 1922, just after committing him to a sanitarium for treatment. Davenport told two different stories about Reid's addiction. The first involved a back or head injury while on location for the 1919 picture *The Valley of the Giants* (Reid did mention "how we were all 'messed up' " by a train wreck in a July 1919 interview); the second involved a 1921 picture called *Forever*, based on *Peter Ibbetson*. Reid, according to his wife, got sick and began to worry that his "illness was delaying production and adding to the expense." He supposedly then asked a doctor for morphine in order to "nerve him for his daily and arduous task."

It is, of course, possible that an injury contributed to Reid's drug addiction; so might overwork. In both 1920 and 1921, Reid had made six pictures per year; in 1922, he made nine—twenty-one pictures in three years, about twice as many as equivalent stars. Paramount worked their primary young leading man and his $2,500 weekly salary frantically before he collapsed in late 1922. DeWitt Bodeen reported that in his last few pictures Reid looked notably ill, and in *Thirty Days*, his last picture, he looked "ghastly." At any rate, it's highly probable that heroin was involved rather than morphine; in November 1920, *Variety* reported that a "dope peddler" who had said he was delivering heroin to a well-known star was arrested, and it was widely assumed within the industry that the star in question was Reid.

While the impact of Reid's death reverberated through Hollywood and America, DeMille was desultorily engaged in defending his new picture, *Adam's Rib*, from critics within the studio who thought the picture was "Too long . . . people are not *enthusiastic* about the picture . . . last reel gets quite a few laughs, as the people refuse to take same seriously."

Photoplay magazine piled on for multiple hits: a feature review by Frederick James Smith said, "This seems to mark the complete collapse of the man who could once intrigue audiences with his daring, albeit garish boudoir revelations. *Adam's Rib* is a mass of utter absurdities with a good box-office title. . . . Very badly acted stuff, this." Another New York critic wrote that *Adam's Rib* "was a star example of the kind of thing which made intelligent people laugh at the motion pictures."

It's a strange response for a mostly lighthearted picture, with the tone set by an introductory title: "The dangerous age for women is from three to seventy." Anna Q. Nilsson plays a bored wife who's been married to Milton Sills for nineteen years—no wonder she's bored. Theodore Kosloff, playing the King of Morania, tries to seduce her. Livening things up is Elliott Dexter, adept and funny as a single-minded paleontologist with pince-nez glasses focused only on a hall of dinosaur skeletons—a character and setting later stolen by Howard Hawks for *Bringing Up Baby*.

Dexter wants nothing to do with her: "You are an inexcusable, impertinent product of the movies—women's suffrage—and the war," he tells her. "And you don't belong in a museum except for purposes of research." But he's overmatched by her coquetry. The plot thickens when Sills bribes Morania to recall their randy king, while at the same time his daughter, determined to preserve her parents' marriage, decides to seduce the king.

Adam's Rib begins as high comedy about adultery and deceit and ends as a conventional melodrama. Stylistically, it's negligible—brightly lit, no camera movement, and not an awful lot of dramatic involvement. But it shows DeMille trying to build a bridge between the films he had been making and the next stage, not quite getting there, mostly because he seems not to have had a clear goal in mind.

Adam's Rib is best viewed as a smorgasbord—take what you like, ignore the rest—and is marred only by an interminable flashback to the forest primeval that stops the film dead in its tracks, not that the audience minded overmuch. The film, which cost slightly more than $400,000—DeMille was cheerfully ignoring his supposed budget ceiling of $290,000—grossed nearly $881,206.

★

Besides a clear case of career blahs, DeMille was engaged in a defense of the industry from calls for censorship brought about by scandals and movies by people such as Cecil B. DeMille. His feelings about censorship were the stirrings of a libertarian stance that would garner considerably more attention in the 1940s: "Censorship, whatever its expressed aim and purpose, resolves itself into a rule of the minority over the majority. It is the rule of one man or a small group imposed upon a city or state, a state of affairs autocratic, undemocratic and un-American. . . . Censorship means creative art shall be limited in range by limits imposed by people who set themselves up as censors. Shakespeare, Byron and Ibsen and hosts of other artists would not have written their masterpieces if censorship had its way. . . . Let the artist establish his own standards—the people can feel safe in relying upon his judgment rather than that of a censor, apt to be of a narrow and cramped vision."

But aesthetic theoreticals were quickly forgotten when DeMille was called in to defuse a catastrophic threat.

For some time, Gloria Swanson had been engaging in enthusiastic adultery with Marshall Neilan under the eyes of her husband, Herbert Somborn. Swanson was a lusty woman; there were also more transient relationships with the married Thomas Meighan and the unmarried Rod La Rocque around this time, and she remembered the La Rocque episode as being particularly "hectic . . . we had lovers' quarrels all the time."

Swanson's recollection was that she had been living apart from her husband for as long as nine or ten months and that she was, she believed, morally free.

Legally was another matter entirely. "I had talked to the studio about getting a divorce on the grounds of desertion," Swanson remembered, "[and] the studio begged me not to do anything about it. . . . They begged me not to have a divorce because they felt it would be, at this time, inopportune, and to wait, and unfortunately I waited." When Swanson went to Europe, Neilan went with her.

Now Swanson was being blackmailed by Somborn, with a figure of $150,000 being thrown around, and a custody fight for their two-year-old daughter, Gloria, on the horizon. Somborn's complaint listed a roster of thirteen or fourteen co-respondents, Lasky, DeMille, and Zukor among them. Most of the men had never slept with Swanson, and some of them had never even met her, but that wasn't the point. Coming on the heels of the Arbuckle, William Desmond Taylor, and Wallace Reid scandals, a sex scandal with Swanson could further damage the industry and the studio.

DeMille was first stunned, then alarmed. On February 14, 1923, he wired Lasky,

HAVE HAD LONG TALK WITH IMPORTANT ATTORNEY REPRESENTING HUSBAND OF STAR IN PRODUCTION NUMBER 273 SCANDALOUS PUBLICITY BOMB WILL EXPLODE WITHIN WEEK OR TEN DAYS RECENT ACTIONS IN EUROPE WITH DIRECTOR OF *STELLA MARIS*. WILL RECEIVE FULL PUBLICITY. . . . PLEASE TREAT MATTER VERY CONFIDENTIALLY AS ONLY AFTER GREATEST DIFFICULTY HAVE I OBTAINED PERMISSION FROM INTERESTED PARTY TO TELL YOU LADY HERSELF DOES NOT KNOW STORM IS ABOUT TO BREAK. . . . [WILL] ENDEAVOR TO MAKE SOME SETTLEMENT AS MATTER WILL PROBABLY REOPEN ATTACKS ON WHOLE INDUSTRY STOP HAVE LITTLE HOPE HOWEVER OF BEING ABLE TO AFFECT ANY COMPROMISE AS REVENGE PLAYS IMPORTANT PART.

On February 17, DeMille wired Lasky to tell Will Hays to send a wire that he could present to Swanson:

HAVE HAYS WIRE ME MY HOUSE LAUGHLIN PARK TOMORROW SUNDAY SO THAT I RECEIVE SAME BEFORE ELEVEN O'CLOCK TELEGRAM STATING THAT IF THIS AFFAIR COMES OUT PRINCIPAL STAR WILL BE BARRED FROM PICTURES AND PERMANENTLY KEPT FROM SCREEN. IT MUST BE MADE STRONG AND MUST POSITIVELY REACH ME BEFORE ELEVEN O'CLOCK IN MORNING.

The next day, as Swanson was leaving DeMille's house after a conference during which he urged her not to let the matter go to court under any circumstances, a Western Union boy arrived. DeMille opened the telegram, read it, and handed it to Swanson.

LET THERE BE NOT A SHADOW OF DOUBT IF THIS AFFAIR BECOMES KNOWN THE PRIN-
CIPAL STAR WILL BE BARRED FROM PICTURES AND PERMANENTLY KEPT FROM THE
SCREEN.

It was signed, "Will Hays."

"If I got hit with a hammer between my eyes I couldn't have been more taken aback," remembered Swanson. "I must say I was floored, and I left there quite weakened." Swanson trusted DeMille implicitly; he could ask her anything and she would comply. When she had given birth to her daughter, Gloria, in October 1920, DeMille bought her a string of beautiful pearls with a diamond clasp and asked her to make an appearance in *The Affairs of Anatol*. Swanson agreed, even though she wasn't due back at the studio for two months.

Paramount representatives fanned out across the United States and Europe trying to build a plausible defense, obtaining depositions from hotel managers that Swanson and Neilan did not share rooms while they were registered there. The testimonies must have been insufficient, because DeMille began negotiating a settlement.

Somborn wanted a small fortune, predicated on Swanson's earnings since 1920, a contract he had overseen. On February 20, Cecil wired Lasky MEETING LASTED ALL NIGHT. BELIEVE OUR PRINCIPAL SAFE. PARTICULARS LATER. Somborn was ask-ing for 10 percent of Swanson's earnings since 1920, or about $120,000 over the length of the contract, which was still in effect. Both Lasky and DeMille figured that Somborn might accept a discount for cash.

For the next two weeks, proposals flew back and forth. On March 6, Cecil wired Lasky:

MATTER WILL BE ADJUSTED FINALLY TOMORROW NIGHT. HAD CLOSED FOR TWENTY
FIVE THOUSAND BUT ON NEW DIFFICULTIES ARISING, I OFFERED TEN THOUSAND
ADDITIONAL PROVIDED MATTER COULD BE DEFINITELY CLOSED BY WEDNESDAY
NIGHT AND WE BE ABLE TO START PICTURE THURSDAY MORNING. THIS HAS BEEN
SATISFACTORILY ARRANGED AND ALL PARTIES SEEM HAPPY EXCEPTING ME AND I AM
GOING TO A COMFORTABLE INSANE ASYLUM IF YOU CAN TELEGRAPH ME A GOOD
ADDRESS.

Swanson agreed to the price but didn't have the cash. "So [DeMille] said, 'Well, don't worry about that. The Famous Players-Lasky will give you the . . . $35,000, but of course you will have to do some extra pictures.' So it sort of rang a bell in my mind because this was what they were after and had been after for some time . . . they had always wanted me to make one more picture a year which automatically would reduce the price of my salary per picture." (At this point, Swanson was earning $2,500 a week for four pictures a year.)

After some more back and forth, DeMille wired Lasky on March 16:

WILL REQUIRE THIRTY FIVE THOUSAND TO CLOSE RECENT MATTER. AS WE ARE PAY-
ING IT FOR EXTRA PICTURE DOES NOT NEED TO BE PRIVATELY ARRANGED. ADVISE
ME HOW YOU WISH TO DRAW AS WILL NEED MONEY UPON SIGNING OF AGREEMENT
WHICH WILL PROBABLY BE TOMORROW SUNDAY.

On March 22, 1923, a check for $35,000 was made out to Gloria Swanson
Somborn, and that same day she gave a personal check for the same amount
to Herbert Somborn. With the money safely in hand, Somborn gave the studio
an affidavit asserting that "affiant has had investigations made of his said wife's
conduct since May, 1921, and that the results of all such investigations have been
reported to affiant from time to time; that affiant does not know of his said wife
having committed adultery with any man at any time, nor does affiant know of his
said wife having placed herself or allowing herself to be placed in a compromising
situation with any man, nor does affiant know of any time when his said wife has
not acted with decorum and in accordance with the universally accepted idea of
social propriety."

That same day, Swanson signed an addendum to her contract with Famous
Players-Lasky that added a picture to her contract for which she was to be paid
$7,000 a week, with her salary garnisheed by $431 a week until the money was repaid. The last clause in the addendum was a beauty: the company could discharge
Swanson for any reason if "at any time in the future, through no fault of [Fa-
mous Players-Lasky] and/or without its connivance and consent, first party shall
be charged with adulterous conduct or immoral relations with men other than
her husband, and such charges or any of them are published in the public press,
the waiver herein contained shall be null and void and of no force and effect." In
other words, if the situation recurred, the company would hang her out to dry.

Shortly after the matter had been settled, Swanson was sitting with Will Hays
at a social function. When Swanson broached the subject of the telegram sent to
DeMille's house, Hays looked bewildered. When she explained further, he convincingly swore up and down that he had never sent any such telegram.

"This was quite a shock" remembered Swanson. "I suppose I could have gone
to Mr. DeMille, but I didn't. I approached Mr. Lasky about it . . . but he, smiling,
said, that it was the only way they knew of getting me to settle this thing." Because
of the surviving telegrams, we know that Hays was a skillful liar and did indeed
send the telegram, but had probably demanded plausible deniability. Lasky took
the fall.

Business, as Chaplin observed in *Monsieur Verdoux*, is a ruthless business,
and DeMille's first loyalty would always be to the increasingly vast company he
helped found. Years later, an employee of DeMille's would note his "unwavering

allegiance" to Paramount. "He had a very, very intense sense of responsibility to Paramount."

DeMille's political and filmmaking instincts would come in handy many times over the years—not that Zukor always took advantage of them. One day a young man named Irving Thalberg came in to talk to him. Thalberg was running production at Universal and was ramrodding a massive version of *The Hunchback of Notre Dame*, starring Lon Chaney. DeMille was impressed—Thalberg was young, looked younger, believed in the movies, thought big, and acted on those thoughts. He probably reminded DeMille of himself.

"Jesse, this boy is a genius," DeMille said. "I can see it. I know it." But Lasky didn't like Thalberg's *Hunchback* and balked at Thalberg's request for a raise over the $450 weekly he was getting at Universal. Thalberg would be heard from, and very soon.

★

Katherine deMille remembered life on DeMille Drive in this period: "When I first came we were all young children, and we sat first at a little table and then we were allowed to sit up till Father came home, talk to him, ask him questions—but he was usually pretty late 'cause he worked late and then he would go see the rushes, and he would come home very tired—park the car down in the garage and walk up the long hill. We always said, 'This is ridiculous. Why don't you drive up here and one of the servants will park the car.' But 'No,' he said, 'it's refreshing. I like it.'

"That was an occasion, when he came in that front door and we went to see him. We'd kiss his cheek and it was cold from the night air. You remember those little things. He brought a surge of excitement into the house. We'd sit around—if it was very late, he'd eat off a tray in the living room. We'd have a fire going or something, and we would sit on the sofas and ask him questions."

The children rarely went to Paradise, but trips on the *Seaward* were frequent: Catalina, Santa Cruz, Santa Barbara. "Father let me bring a friend," remembered Katherine. "He was usually working—most times. Jeanie would come along. She was a very bright woman. Now Julia [Faye] his other lady friend, was not too bright. We children used to do a rather mean imitation of her."

At Christmas, the children would open their presents first, then Cecil would take an entire morning to open several mountains of presents, piled on five or six tables that surrounded him. The family sat around watching with amazement at the luxurious gifts he received from actors and other peers. Cecilia, as the heir apparent, also received a profusion of presents from people at the studio, and would generally be saved from throwing up from excitement only by being marched off for a nap.

The children's birthdays were also generously celebrated. One birthday Richard received a set of toy boats, which he proceeded to bring into the bathroom as DeMille was taking a bath. The boats were set sail in the tub around Cecil, and he took his washcloth, captured a big bubble of air, and let it go underwater. The bubble rose to the surface and nearly knocked the boats over, greatly exciting Richard. DeMille enjoyed Richard's enjoyment and kept rocking the boats, forgetting about his bath.

★

DeMille and Sam Goldwyn had remained friends, and it's probable that on some level DeMille always felt indebted. In 1923, DeMille repaid the debt when, in his capacity as a director of the Bank of Italy, he okayed a $250,000 loan to Sam. A. P. Giannini complained: "He has no assets." Giannini also could have pointed out that since leaving Famous Players-Lasky in 1916, Goldwyn had amassed an unbroken record of failure in motion picture production.

"You're right," replied DeMille. "He has no assets, except talent, which is the only asset worth anything in the motion picture business. I made that loan on talent and on character." DeMille went on to say that if Giannini only wanted him for window dressing, not his judgment about motion picture loans, there was no point in remaining with the bank. Giannini relented and said, "It's all right, C.B. But don't do it too often."

That $250,000 was the seed money for Samuel Goldwyn Productions, which would become one of the most successful independent filmmaking companies in Hollywood history.

Sam being Sam, he returned the favor a few years later, when he offered to loan Cecil the services of Vilma Banky. Banky was earning $250 a week, and he proposed to charge Cecil $25,000 for her. "It was natural to Sam," said a resigned DeMille. "He didn't know he was just being a dirty stinker. To himself he was just being a good businessman . . . and I had saved Sam's life. . . . I had put up my own personal standing and gotten him a $250,000 loan—that was his response! 'Tis in my memory and locked—and I myself shall keep the key to it!"

Ever since the commercial failure of *Joan the Woman*, Zukor and Lasky had been assiduously working to make sure that DeMille's grandiose notions for future films remained just that—notions. Perhaps DeMille's most enticing idea of this period was a production of *Romeo and Juliet* with Valentino and Leatrice Joy. Lasky clutched his chest and wrote back the same day, saying he "would jump on a train and come across the continent and try and lock you up rather than let you make such a terrible mistake."

But for some in the early 1920s, bigger was better. Von Stroheim made a splash with *Foolish Wives* in 1921; Jesse Lasky himself went to bat with New York and got a $500,000 budget for James Cruze's *The Covered Wagon*. By the time the Cruze western was finished, it had gone considerably over budget, but the resulting critical and commercial success made the issue moot.

On October 8, 1922, DeMille ran a contest through the *Los Angeles Times* asking the public to suggest the idea for his next picture. First prize was $1,000, and the letters flooded in. The winner came from F. C. Nelson of Lansing, Michigan, who manufactured lubricating oil. Nelson's letter began, "You cannot break the Ten Commandments—they will break you." Finally, a subject worthy of the son of Henry deMille, and one that fortuitously meshed with the new public fascination over Egypt begun by the discovery of King Tut's tomb in 1922.

As it happened, seven other respondents had also suggested the Ten Commandments as a theme for the picture. They hadn't submitted a usable story along with the theme, but DeMille felt honor-bound to pay them all $1,000 apiece. And so it was that *The Ten Commandments* went over budget at its inception.

Lasky went into sales overdrive. HAVE SUCCEEDED AROUSING CONSIDERABLE EN-THUSIASM IN MINDS OF ZUKOR AND KENT OVER COMMANDMENTS IDEA, he wired Cecil. Marshall Neilan had observed the story contest, and he fired off one of his amusing telegrams to DeMille, offering as a story suggestion the idea that the devil is not a man, but a woman—a proposition he was prepared to endorse based on personal experience.

The more the New York office thought about it, the more they realized that the last time Cecil had taken on costume epics, he had made *Joan the Woman* and *The Woman God Forgot,* neither of which made much money. As far as Zukor was concerned, Cecil was returning to the bad old days and he wasn't happy.

CECIL'S PRODUCTION WILL IN ALL LIKELIHOOD HAVE AN EGYPTIAN AND PALESTINE ATMOSPHERE,

cabled Zukor to Lasky.

IT WILL HAVE TO HAVE A TREMENDOUS LOVE INTEREST IN ORDER TO OVERCOME THE HANDICAPS OF ATMOSPHERE I SUGGEST THAT YOU AND CECIL GO OVER THE STORY CAREFULLY.

Zukor was also alarmed that the initial budget was $700,000 and the picture hadn't even started shooting yet.

Trying to placate Zukor, on May 10, 1923, DeMille waved a flag of financial truce: "I fully realize the responsibility of the enormous sum of money I am spending," he wrote Zukor. "I can assure you that to the best of my belief the picture will have those qualities of love, romance and beauty which you so rightly suggest are necessary to any picture, and as an evidence of my appreciation and of my faith in this picture, I hereby waive the guarantee under my contract on this picture, other than the regular weekly payments."

Cecil's waiving of some of his contractual rights gladdened Zukor's mercenary heart, and he replied that he was "very pleased . . . appreciate your expression regarding guarantee . . . you have our co-operation one hundred percent." The studio nervously approved a budget of $750,000—the final cost of *The Covered Wagon.* But James Cruze shot film quickly, and DeMille had developed a taste for elaboration that went hand-in-hand with increasingly luxurious standards of production.

The script, which involved a Biblical prologue preceding a modern story, was written between April and June of 1923, and the cast was largely made up of contract players: Theodore Roberts as Moses, the French actor Charles de Rochefort as Pharaoh, and, for the modern story, Richard Dix and Leatrice Joy. A newcomer to the DeMille troupe was a young actor with the deliriously silent-movieish name of Rod La Rocque.

On May 21, 1923, four open trucks holding twenty-one immense concrete sphinxes twenty-five-feet high and weighing five tons apiece arrived in Guadalupe, 170 miles north of Los Angeles. The sphinxes were slowly unloaded—each of them was in two parts so they could be driven under bridges—and arranged in two long lines before the scaffolding that in six weeks' time would become the gates of Pharaoh's city.

When it was completed, the great gate was 109 feet tall, the side walls were 750 feet long and covered in bas-reliefs of rearing stallions pulling chariots. On either side of the gate were thirty-five-feet-high colossi of Pharaoh—clay and plaster over metal framing. DeMille didn't use any matte paintings or glass shots for ancient Egypt, because he wanted freedom to choose camera angles, and optical effects would limit his visual choices.

When the sets were finally ready, the cast and crew met at Union Station in Los Angeles for an 11 P.M. train and arrived about four in the morning at Guadalupe. Even the cast for the modern section of the story went on location as assistants and extras. By the same token, when the modern section was shot, the cast of the Bible sequence worked in small parts. The result was a feeling of emotional integration between the cast and crew, despite the fact that the only connection between the stories was metaphorical.

Everybody disembarked at Guadalupe to find an entire town built for the 2,500 people and three thousand animals DeMille had gathered for his location shoot—a medical tent, tents for the actors, cabins for the leading actors, a large mess tent. DeMille's own tent featured authentic Persian rugs, and Leatrice Joy said that the atmosphere resembled that of an Arab prince, or a shah. "He was elegant. He knew elegant things and he just loved them."

Among the assembled multitude were Orthodox Jews brought from Los Angeles for reasons of authenticity, but a problem arose when it was discovered that there had been no preparations made for Kosher observance. DeMille thus set up a Kosher kitchen.

The mess tent featured a raised dais for DeMille's table, and the superb military-style planning struck the child actor Pat Moore as entirely typical, as was the hierarchical nature of the mess tent, where people sat in order of importance.

"Being a small boy, I could sit anywhere, so I'd get to sit next to Mr. DeMille," remembered Moore. "You couldn't order anything, you had to eat what you were given because he was feeding thousands of people, literally, and it was the middle of the Guadalupe desert. It was all handled like clockwork. They had a bugle that would wake you up in the morning, and another bugle when things were ready to go, and they had a team of four horses pulling these great tubs that they would mix concrete in, because cars would not go in the sand. The horses would tow these things up to the location. It was *fascinating* to see all this going on in a tent town outside of Guadalupe."

The young Mervyn LeRoy was still hanging around after a failed trial as a cameraman that led DeMille to call him the inventor of soft focus—LeRoy could never keep an image sharp. LeRoy was happy to take a job as an extra and observed with wonder how Cecil organized his troupe. "Everything was planned and routinized, and the huge machine functioned like an army," remembered LeRoy.

Reveille was at 4:30 A.M. The extras lined up for breakfast at mess tents, then divided into groups, which were called companies and platoons, with assistant directors in charge. DeMille had a military-style field telephone to communicate with every area of the tent city. Between the tent city and the sets, the company's operations covered twenty-four square miles.

DeMille was the General, and it was forbidden for the rank and file to speak to him—the chain of command had to be observed. Mervyn LeRoy remembered that Theodore Roberts, playing Moses, and James Neill, playing Aaron, wanted to talk to DeMille and were kept waiting for almost an hour. Finally, Roberts grabbed an assistant director and roared, "Just say that Moses and Aaron are waiting to see God."

After Moses descended from Sinai with the tablets, DeMille wanted awe and reverence from the assembled multitude, and he didn't get what he wanted. He called a break and conferred with Hezi Tate. Soon, DeMille addressed the company through his public address system. He was choking back emotion as he told the company that one of the actors had suddenly died, leaving a wife and eight children. He asked for a few moments of silence in his memory. The company had suitably reverential expressions on their faces as they considered the razor's edge that separated each of them from eternity. Meanwhile, DeMille's cameras were grinding footage of an emotionally moved population. "We had been had," was the way LeRoy put it—nobody was dead or even dying, except possibly Adolph Zukor's accountants.

Men and women slept in separate tents, and Prohibition laws were observed. "The big mess tent was open 24 hours a day," remembered Ernie Righetti, a local who worked as an extra on the film. "Pretty good food, too. I think I got $18 a day for being out there, plus $2 a day for each of the five horses I let them use in the movie. That was the biggest pay I ever got."

For recreation, there was a movie theater where films were shown, and since DeMille liked boxing, a ring was set up and Fidel La Barbara came in for a match. Pat Moore's brother Brian was chosen by DeMille to fight La Barbara, with the prize being a twenty dollar gold piece. Although La Barbara could have taken Brian apart, he allowed the kid to fight for all he was worth and earn the $20, while the professional just bobbed and weaved and made sure nobody got hurt.

Pat Moore and his mother were enjoying the location for a couple of days when DeMille invited them to watch the big scene where the Israelites walk out of Egypt. "They had these large parallels on a sand dune, about twenty feet high, maybe a thousand feet away from the entrance of Pharaoh's temple. DeMille fired a pistol, and the Israelites started coming out of the temple and from the sides, and through the gates, flocks of sheeps, goats, people carrying various things that they would possess in those days. It's a scene that I will never forget, and I knew my mother never did. They came right toward us, and the cameras, about five to seven of them, were shooting into the Exodus, and then he swung the cameras around and showed them going toward the Red Sea.

"And then the chariots came thundering out!"

DeMille had hired the 2nd Battalion of the 76th Field Artillery from the Presidio at Monterey to drive Pharaoh's chariots. The commander was Lieutenant Tony McAuliffe, who later sent the famous message of "Nuts" during the Battle of the Bulge. Unfortunately, while the men of the battalion were experienced horsemen, they had never driven chariots before, and on the first day a $10,000 team of stallions and some charioteers were injured in a collision. In a later take the small orchestra playing for the actors scattered when the horses went out of control.

When some of the drivers refused to drive the chariots down some steep sand dunes, an infuriated DeMille turned to his fifteen-year-old daughter. "Cecilia, I want you to demonstrate that it isn't dangerous. Go up to the top and ride down the slope." Cecilia did as she was asked and came down at a good clip. It wasn't quite as dangerous as it looked, at least not for Cecilia; her horse was range-bred and unusually sure-footed. When the stunt riders sheepishly followed suit, three or four chariots somersaulted over the backs of the horses that were trying to outrun them, but no animals or people were hurt.

(Cecilia's love affair with horses continued throughout her life; DeMille gave her the gorgeous black pair that drew Pharaoh's chariot in *The Ten Commandments*, and in later years she rode and showed gaited horses, still later bred and raced thoroughbreds.)

"DeMille never quit," remembered Rod La Rocque. "He worked until seven-thirty or eight o'clock and loved it, late dinner and all." Future director Henry Hathaway was working as DeMille's chair boy, and he remembered that "DeMille was an autocrat, but I guess he deserved to be. . . . He had such discipline on the set. He had a scene down in the ocean, and he was looking for a shot and he looked through his finder, and he walked towards the water. Anne Bauchens and Hezi Tate, his assistant, and all of his people—about eight of them—he walked right into the surf and all eight went with him up to his waist, and he's still looking, and they're all up to their waist, and they had not a damn thing to do with finding the shot, he was just looking. But he might put out his hand . . ."

For the parting of the Red Sea, the location was the seashore at Guadalupe, about forty feet from the water. The crew had erected two fences marking the lines where the walls of water would be matted in on either side of the Israelites. The problem was that the fence cast a shadow that would appear in the shot, so it was necessary to film the scene at high noon.

At twenty minutes before twelve, somebody came up to DeMille and said that as it now stood the bottom of the Red Sea was going to look very dry. DeMille was thunderstruck—all his thought, all his preparation, and he had completely forgotten about dressing the location with seaweed. He could postpone the shot for a day, but that would add tens of thousands of dollars to an already overburdened budget.

He began yelling for suggestions. A pump, somebody yelled. There were pumps there, and they were hooked up, and water spread, but after eight minutes the sand that had been watered down was practically the same as the dry sand.

Paint, yelled DeMille, black paint. The painter stepped up and said there wasn't enough paint in all of California, let alone on location.

There were only a few minutes left to get the shot. "Allah was kind," remembered DeMille. Just offshore was a large bed of floating kelp, and DeMille ordered the entire company to wade into the water and grab handfuls. From DeMille on down, hundreds of people launched themselves. " 'Everybody, men, women and children, get up this kelp,' and they picked up the kelp and laid it [on the sand], and at exactly 12:02 we had a nice wet bottom of the sea and we turned the camera."

As DeMille blew the whistle that signaled "Action," the musicians swung into the "Largo" movement from the New World Symphony to provide the proper emotions, and the scene was captured before the sun could cast a shadow.

After a month at Guadalupe, DeMille wrapped his location work. What to do with the set? To ship it back to Hollywood would be prohibitively expensive; to leave it out there was to invite someone to appropriate it for a knockoff that could beat *The Ten Commandments* to its premiere. Someone came up with the idea of leaving the set in a way that nobody would ever be able to use it again. A large trench was cut, and the set was bulldozed and pushed into the trench, then buried. It remains there to this day.

Back at the studio, Roy Pomeroy, the head of the special effects department, figured out how to part the Red Sea. Essentially, two large blocks of gelatin, carved with waves, sat on a huge table that was split in the center and outfitted with gas jets. As the table was cranked apart, the gas jets were lit, and the gelatin began to melt, giving an inexact but reasonable impression of moving walls of water. Run forward, the seas parted; run backward, the seas closed. The long shots of the Israelites and Egyptians crossing the seashore at Guadalupe were matted into the miniature.

For close shots, thousands of gallons of water were dumped down a U-shaped tank. There were, remembered DeMille, "two tanks holding 60,000 gallons of water each, designed to drop at the same moment onto a large curved piece of steel so that when it threw this wave into an enormous curve, the two things met at the top, and we got a wave that was enormous. The camera was almost underneath it." The result was elemental but effective—as many as fourteen exposures for the shots of the sea opening and closing—very complicated trick work for 1923.

By July, the picture was still shooting, Zukor was apoplectic, and Cecil was heartily sick of him and his complaints. He told Neil McCarthy to offer to buy the picture for $1 million. Zukor said it was a deal, and DeMille and McCarthy began working the phones. They got a pledge of $500,000 from A. P. Giannini, and $250,000 each from producer Joe Schenck and Jules Brulatour, the franchise holder for Eastman film.

On July 5, Lasky wired Zukor,

FINALLY TODAY [CECIL] CAME FROM MEETING OF HIS BANK AND ADVISED ME HE BELIEVES HE IS IN POSITION TO TAKE PICTURE OFF OUR HANDS, REIMBURSE US FOR OUR INVESTMENT AND FINANCE COMPLETION OF THE PICTURE, IN WHICH EVENT HE WOULD MAKE ARRANGEMENT WITH US TO DISTRIBUTE IT FOR [A] SMALL PERCENTAGE OF [THE] PROFITS AFTER PARTIES FINANCING PICTURE HAVE RECOUPED ITS COST.

Lasky had grown weary of being in the middle, because he suggested that Zukor give the proposal serious consideration.

The fight over *The Ten Commandments* was not an isolated occurrence but the culmination of a struggle over what the studio regarded as DeMille's profligacy. DeMille's average costs per film had remained steady in the beginning, from $15,450 in 1913 to $17,760 in 1916. But in 1918, his average costs were $59,587. Nineteen nineteen brought $144,639 and 1920 saw the figure shoot up to $258,130. A year later it was $396,271. While it's true that Zukor and Lasky had urged him to get away from the historical films that made them uncomfortable, they had also probably assumed that modern dress films would be less expensive. If so, they hadn't reckoned on their man.

For Zukor, the money Cecil was spending on *The Ten Commandments*, doubling the agreed-upon budget of $750,000, was the last straw. In a letter to Jesse Lasky, Zukor threw down the gauntlet.

As the matter now stands, we do all of the gambling while he gets his advances and guarantee. . . . I feel also that there is a tremendous expense that the Company has to bear which is not directly chargeable to his negative cost, while he is working in the present studio, and that is the increased cost of our own negatives for which he is indirectly responsible. This is a tremendous item to be considered. While I am on this subject, I wish you would work out some arrangement for Cecil to work at the Realart studio entirely separate and away from our own units. I am sure that such an arrangement would be very much to our advantage and to his as well. . . .

I can fully appreciate your personal sentiments in regard to Cecil and I certainly feel that I want to relieve you of any necessity of getting into controversies with him. . . . I more than appreciate your expression regarding your own loyalty to the Company, of which I have never been in doubt, and I know it is doubly trying on you to do justice to the Company and at the same time taking a stand against Cecil in the situation which now confronts us.

This remarkable letter reveals both how Zukor dominated Lasky as well as how Zukor cavalierly disregarded the hard fact that DeMille was far more responsible for the company's existence than Zukor. Cecil's pictures cost a lot more than the average Famous Players-Lasky production; they also grossed a lot more.

What Zukor clearly wanted was for DeMille to be broken to the status of just another director. What DeMille wanted, what DeMille expected, was the status of Most Favored Son.

Zukor backed off on selling the picture because an executive told him he thought it was a bad idea to sell something he hadn't seen. The picture was approaching completion, and the studio was out $1.5 million—this at a time when only a handful of pictures had ever grossed that much.

Zukor was beyond furious, and even complained about the fact that DeMille contractually demanded a print of each completed film for his personal archive, paid for by the company. Petty complaints about such minor costs from a man who had essentially made the company possible, who had just negotiated a settlement that kept the company's major female star a viable personality, were definitive signs that the marriage had, as they say, irretrievably broken down. But Cecil was resolute. In the midst of his own tussles with the studio, DeMille would give Jeanie Macpherson 5 percent of his share of the profits from *The Ten Command-ments*, a tacit recognition of her importance to his films and his life.

Years later, DeMille would reckon that he had some responsibility for the widening breach. "There was a time when I had to have a terrible arrogance," he would say. "There were things that needed to be changed. I had to change them. It was like a man in battle—like Eisenhower—when he told a man, 'Get those guns over there.' And the man started to mumble about, 'Well, now, I don't think they ought to . . .' Eisenhower had to say, 'Get those guns over there!' It was the only way he could win the battle. . . . But I made a lot of enemies. A lot of people hated me."

★

It was Jesse Lasky's designated role in life to calm troubled waters, and as *The Ten Commandments* neared release, he sent Cecil a letter detailing the vast preparations the company was making on the picture's—and Cecil's—behalf. On Broadway, from 43rd to 44th Street, Paramount was erecting the largest electric sign ever displayed in New York, showing a consecutive dash of Pharaoh's chariots across the front of the Putnam Building. As the chariots disappeared at 44th Street, the sign flashed "Cecil B. DeMille's *The Ten Commandments*."

Moreover, Lasky told him, "Whatever happens, you must not miss the first night opening of *The Ten Commandments* in New York. In conclusion—forget all the past difficulties and misunderstandings and concentrate on the big picture . . . and I am confident that all your problems will be ironed out to the satisfaction of everybody and without leaving a single hard feeling behind."

DeMille was growing slightly bored with the movie and thought about cutting back the Red Sea sequence, until Anne Bauchens talked him out of it. "[DeMille] said he was discouraged with the opening and closing of the Red Sea. . . . It was the first time anything like this had ever been tried and he was dissatisfied with it and not convinced of favorable audience reaction."

On October 5, 1923, an effusive Lasky wrote Zukor. "Although twenty-four hours have passed since I saw *Ten Commandments* last night, I am still under the spell of greatest motion picture that has ever been produced since very beginning of the feature photoplay. Cecil has created a masterpiece that will live long after other famous pictures are forgotten. . . . It is almost as if he were inspired, a new and much bigger Cecil DeMille. I do not believe we can measure possible earning power of *Ten Commandments*. It will make [a] new motion picture industry, make new records and show power and possibilities of the screen in a way that has never been approached."

Zukor presumably took all this with a large shaker of salt, because the movie business was in one of its periodic downturns; in a few weeks, Famous Players-Lasky would shut down for ten weeks. Lasky wired Cecil that all employees were being laid off for that period, "on account of the excessive and mounting cost of production and on account of an overproduction of pictures throughout the industry."

Cecil went along, but only up to a point. He wired Lasky that casting director Fred Goodstadt, Paul Iribe, Pev Marley, and Anne Bauchens would go on half salary for ten weeks, until he was ready to start shooting his next picture. Among those laid off completely were artist Dan Sayre Groesbeck, stillman William Mortensen, most of the wardrobe department, cameramen Bert Glennon and Archie Stout, five people who were finishing up the Technicolor work for *The Ten Commandments*, and Julia Faye.

This list gives some sense of the size of the personal staff that Cecil carried at the company's expense. Dan Groesbeck was a former artist for the Chicago *Tribune* who had been wounded in the Russian Revolution and eventually made a transition to an unusual combination of fine and concept art. Groesbeck would become DeMille's favorite artist, even to the point of the director personally collecting the artist's heroic, masculine work. Groesbeck's sole drawback was his alcoholism, and DeMille was always indulgently bailing him out of one scrape or another.

On November 21, Lasky wrote DeMille that he was going over to the Criterion Theatre to see *The Ten Commandments* for the first time with an orchestra, "but without the slightest doubt as to the verdict of the audience. . . . Now that the hatchet has been buried all around, and that the four of us, I mean of course

Zukor, [sales manager Sidney] Kent, you and myself, understand one another, I feel there is nothing in the way to our building our company to greater heights than we ever possibly dreamed of."

Kent wired Zukor after seeing the picture that

THE TEN COMMANDMENTS IS NOT A MOTION PICTURE. IT IS BIGGER THAN ALL THE MOTION PICTURES THAT HAVE BEEN MADE . . . IT WILL COMPENSATE YOU FOR ALL THE AGONY YOU WENT THROUGH THIS SUMMER. . . . IF YOU DIDN'T MAKE A DOL- LAR OUT OF IT I STILL KNOW YOU WOULDN'T EXCHANGE IT FOR ANYTHING ELSE THAT YOU HAVE HAD IN YOUR BUSINESS LIFE.

Zukor, however, was only faintly congratulatory:

I AM NOT UNMINDFUL OF THE TERRIFIC TASK SO MAGNIFICENTLY DONE BY YOU IN THE MAKING OF THIS EPOCHAL PRODUCTION,

he wired DeMille.

MY SINCERE GOOD WISHES.

DeMille's ambitions and abilities didn't stop at mounting one of the silent screen's great spectacles; for the New York premiere, DeMille was accompanied by Jeanie Macpherson *and* Julia Faye *and* Gladys Rosson.

The Ten Commandments begins beautifully, as the mists of time clear to reveal a great sphinx with one of Pharaoh's overseers in the foreground. The fifty-minute biblical prologue is a visually splendid shorthand version of the story—nine plagues have occurred before the film starts. After the sea closes over Pharaoh's men, there's a stunning shot of bodies and chariots floating underwater, and the Giv- ing of the Law is accomplished by a volcano belching out the Commandments.

The prologue fades out and we fade in to the modern story with a shot of a mother reading the Bible to her sons: a God-fearing carpenter (Richard Dix) and a mocking, corner-cutting contractor (Rod La Rocque). After studiously breaking nine of the Commandments, the contractor accidentally kills his mother when a wall made of cheaply produced cement falls on her. If that isn't punishment enough, he also contracts leprosy from his mistress.

Although the original *Ten Commandments* now seems a heavy thing, it's a luxu- rious, beautifully produced heavy thing, with great visual inventiveness: there's an ascension to the top of a construction project with a primarily first-person camera that was stolen by both Ayn Rand and King Vidor for the ending of *The Fountainhead.*

Whatever the picture's faults, the critics of the time were impressed. "The best photoplay ever made," enthused *Photoplay*. "The greatest theatrical spectacle in history. . . . It will last as long as the film on which it is recorded. . . . *The Ten Commandments* will run for years in the motion picture theaters of the world, flashing its message continuously."

The critics raved about *The Ten Commandments* and so did Cecil's peers. Tom Ince wrote "am still in a whirl of amazement over your colossal achievement which marks a decade of advance. It has outDeMilled DeMille and leaves your contemporaries still at the post." Ernst Lubitsch wired that "It is a magnificent picture." Will Hays told him that the picture "is more than a picture. It is an institution. It is magnificent."

But the tribute that moved DeMille the most came from an old friend on Christmas Eve: "I congratulate you, dear Cecil, on your wonderful achievement in *The Ten Commandments*. I'm proud of the little boy I used to bring candy to at Echo Lake, whose father was one of the most brilliant men that ever lived. . . . The DeMille family are all tucked away in my heart. Merry Christmas to you and your dear ones. David Belasco."

With a great success launched—the picture would eventually gross $4.1 million—things at Famous Players-Lasky should have been smoothed over. Certainly, Lasky was always a congenital optimist, and there is little doubt that DeMille would have been perfectly content to spend his life at the company he had helped found.

But Adolph Zukor expected even prestige filmmakers such as DeMille to be subservient to the company. In Zukor's mind, Cecil seemed more intent on celebrating DeMille and his needs than supplying reasonably priced films to Paramount.

The conflict didn't disappear, just went underground.

★

Indomitable before the world, Cecil always listened to his mother. "She talked to him about all his work," wrote his niece Agnes. "She would sit opposite him at dinner decked in the extraordinary collection of laces and beads and flowers with which she covered her beautiful gray curls and talk to him sometimes very sternly. He always listened . . . more to her than to the critics."

In mid-1923, Beatrice asked for a few hundred dollars for medical expenses. She had cancer. All the time he was on location filming *The Ten Commandments*, Cecil commuted between Guadalupe and Los Angeles while his mother underwent treatment. Beatrice refused to go to the hospital, so Cecil had a private nursing station set up at her house. Every day her hair was set, makeup was applied, and she would talk to her younger son about his movie. When production of the film moved to the studio, Theodore Roberts, DeMille's Moses, came to visit, which led Beatrice to joke, "I knew they [the Jews] would send an emissary in the end."

Beatrice died on October 8, 1923. Like her husband, Beatrice had never prepared a will, so Cecil and Bill had to divide up things themselves.

Because Cecil's father had died when Cecil was a small child, Beatrice had been by far the most important figure in his life. Just how important was revealed near the end of his own life, when Cecil's autobiography quoted a passage from one of his niece Agnes's books, and added some lines about Beatrice that were not in fact from Agnes's book, but from Cecil's heart: "At the praise or condemnation of his mother, his heart jumped. She remained critical, hard to please, and enormously proud of her extraordinary son."

The naked need indicated by this interpolation suggests that Cecil was expressing an unfilled yearning. We know that Beatrice told him how much she loved his work; perhaps there could never be enough praise.

★

Harry Carr, journalist and sometime screenwriter, left a trenchant portrait of DeMille on the set: "A DeMille set is like a royal court. Honestly, this is not of his doing; rather, it is a sincere tribute of admiration from his helpers. But anyhow, if he asks for a megaphone, a dozen people leap for it. Actors, assistant directors and writers. Along in the middle of every big scene, his necktie always gets irksome. He tears it off and throws it aside. Someone is always there to catch it. It is amusing to see them waiting for it—with jealous eyes upon each other."

Cecil's films were making a lot of money for both Paramount and Cecil. A Price, Waterhouse royalty statement for the year 1923 shows that Paramount and Cecil had renegotiated his deal. Instead of receiving 30 percent of the net on *The Affairs of Anatol* and everything he made afterward (*Saturday Night, Fool's Paradise, Manslaughter, Adam's Rib,* and *The Ten Commandments*), DeMille was receiving 20 percent of the gross up to $1 million and 25 percent of the gross above $1 million.

Under this contract, DeMille earned $234,005.24 from *The Affairs of Anatol,* and $208,284.87 from *Manslaughter,* with *Saturday Night* and *Fool's Paradise* bringing in less. His total remuneration for the five films made over three years, excluding *The Ten Commandments*—which was just entering release, and thus had not yet amassed any revenue—was $907,170.

As of July 1924, DeMille's income included $26,924 a month from Paramount as an advance against his percentages, $1,292 in monthly dividend income, and $326.40 in interest income. He was paying nearly $24,000 in salaries and miscellaneous expenses, including $800 a month to Neil McCarthy and $629.85 a month to Julia Faye.

Besides keeping an eye on his own pictures and the money they brought in, DeMille also kept up a round of screenings. When he saw an early version of Marshall Neilan's Mary Pickford vehicle *Dorothy Vernon of Haddon Hall,* he wired Neilan, "It is one of the most beautiful pictures ever made. From every standpoint

I congratulate you. Please don't think me officious if I beg you to cut a little flash of some six feet showing a soldier's legs kicking as he is being hung. The picture is so delightful and charming and breezy throughout that this one little terribly gruesome touch may do a good many thousands of dollars damage."

Neilan responded, "There is no doubt in my mind but that you are perfectly right in your criticism, as a Pickford audience generally does not like scenes of this nature in her productions. However, the young lady has grown up and I imagine her audiences have grown with her, so they may accept this this one time."

DeMille wouldn't back off and insisted the shot should be cut: "I will wager you a perfectly good bottle of Haig & Haig that I am right if you can find a means of getting a decision."

★

The pictures Cecil made right after *The Ten Commandments* were, by and large, no better than mediocre. *Triumph* introduces us to Rod La Rocque as a society wastrel who inherits a tin can factory. After a modestly interesting prologue showing how tin cans are made, DeMille gets down to the plot: Leatrice Joy loves La Rocque, but wants to be a prima donna. Victor Varconi is a politically radical foreman at the factory, who loves Leatrice and hates La Rocque. When Varconi somehow gains control of the factory, he throws the hated capitalist out. Leatrice Joy becomes a famous singer, while La Rocque stands outside pining like the mother in *Stella Dallas*. He becomes a bum.

"The making of a can—and the making of a man—are similar," intones a title that explains it all for us. "Both must have the pretty new shine pounded off, before they can be useful to humanity."

Being broke makes La Rocque a man—money corrupts, struggle strengthens. He pulls himself together and gets a job at the factory he used to own, where he works his way up to manager. Just when things are quieting down, there's a fire in a Paris hotel, and Joy loses her singing voice.

There's still one reel to go.

The setting is outlandish, the plot defies synopsis let alone rational analysis, and DeMille's filmmaking carries authority but no energy until the end, when he puts together a rousing fire sequence that looks dangerous and probably was. There's one charming in-joke—a picture of Geraldine Farrar over a fireplace. Yet the picture made money (cost of $265,012, gross of $778,526), as did the next two pictures Cecil made, *Feet of Clay* and *The Golden Bed*. Cecil had gone into slumps before, and would again, but Paramount in 1924 was the wrong time and place for a slump.

The casting for DeMille's *The Golden Bed* offers a window into the hard-nosed attitude of the producers about star salaries and the hard-nosed attitude of DeMille toward all actors. Cecil had given some thought to starring Dorothy Gish in the picture, and Jesse replied that her price would be $50,000 and her billing had to be above the title. "In our opinion these terms are out of question but unfortunately I am [in] negotiation with her manager for Lillian Gish and he is holding up negotiation until he hears from you about Dorothy. Will you kindly wire me immediately turning down Dorothy Gish suggesting the amount is too much and that you will not star any artist in your productions."

Cecil replied with a vigor that clearly represented his basic position: "It would be absolutely impossible for me to pay any sum even approaching the amount she is asking. As you know practically every artist in the business takes a great deal less salary when they work for me on account of the enormous cost of production and the value to be gained from working in it. I could not possibly pay her more than twenty five hundred dollars a week."

The cable worked; Cecil was offered Dorothy Gish for $2,500 a week, with a ten-week guarantee. DeMille thought it was still too much money and the part was strong enough to make any actress who played it—perhaps Phyllis Haver? Lasky offered up Esther Ralston, then suggested Marion Davies or Norma Shearer. They settled on the inexpensive Lillian Rich, who stayed inexpensive.

✵

While DeMille was finishing up *Feet of Clay*, Paramount announced that it had signed D. W. Griffith to a three-picture deal. Although he was already regarded as slightly over the hill, Griffith was one of the few directors whose eminence equalled DeMille's.

The Ten Commandments had grossed nearly three times its cost and proved profitable for all concerned, but Zukor was still nursing a grudge about the overhead for DeMille's unit. Griffith was to be the stick with which Zukor would enforce his demands. If DeMille didn't like Zukor's requirements, there was Griffith, ready to direct whatever specials Zukor handed him.

It is not beyond the realm of possibility that Zukor's morality might have been a contributing factor in his increasing displeasure with Cecil. Zukor, like Marcus Loew, like Nick Schenck and the other studio heads who mostly spent their time in New York, was a straight arrow who never had a whiff of scandal attached to him. Zukor would have looked askance at Cecil's mistresses, and the fact that the company was always trying to find something for Julia Faye to do. In March 1924, Sidney Kent sent out a memo to the directorial staff suggesting that Julia be used in vampire roles of the type that Nita Naldi had been playing. Dimitri Buchowetzki, James Cruze, Victor Fleming, Joe Henebery, Paul Iribe, George Melford, Frank Urson, and Wallace Worsley all got the memo. Each of them denied themselves the pleasure of Julia's presence in their pictures.

✵

On December 2, Zukor wired Lasky about a new contract with DeMille.

AFTER GOING OVER THE CECIL B. DEMILLE CONTRACT AND THE COST OF HIS
LAST THREE PRODUCTIONS . . . I HAVE COME TO THE CONCLUSION THAT WE
OUGHT TO SUGGEST A NEW PROPOSITION TO CECIL WHICH I SHOULD LIKE TO DO
THROUGH YOU . . .

CECIL TO DRAW $3500 A WEEK WHILE HE IS SHOOTING A PICTURE, THIS
AMOUNT TO BE ADDED TO COST OF NEGATIVE WHETHER BIG OR SMALL PICTURE;
COST OF PRODUCTION TO BE MUTUALLY AGREED UPON IN ADVANCE; PROFIT ON
CECIL'S PICTURES TO BE SPLIT BETWEEN US 50/50. . . .

WHILE I CONSIDER THIS A VERY LIBERAL PROPOSITION OWING TO THE FACT
THAT WE DO ALL THE FINANCING I NEVERTHELESS FEEL THAT OWING TO CECIL'S
LONG ASSOCIATION AND THE FACT THAT HE IS A MEMBER OF OUR ORGANIZATION I
WILL NOT HAVE ANY TROUBLE PUTTING IT OVER . . .

THE SUGGESTED ARRANGEMENT MUST CARRY WITH IT ALSO THE CONDITION
THAT CECIL WILL NOT RETAIN UNDER CONTRACT A NUMBER OF PEOPLE FOR WHOM
HE HAS ONLY OCCASIONAL USE AND WHOSE CONTINUOUS EMPLOYMENT MAKES
COST OF NEGATIVES PROHIBITIVE. WAYS AND MEANS MUST BE FOUND FOR A PLAN
WHICH WILL ENABLE CECIL TO WORK ECONOMICALLY AT THE STUDIO AND THE MIN-
UTE HE STOPS SHOOTING ALL OVERHEAD EXPENSE MUST CEASE.

Absolutely fascinating. Cecil's last three pictures for the studio were *The Ten Commandments*, *Triumph*, and *Feet of Clay*. (*The Golden Bed* wouldn't be released until January of 1925.) *Triumph* grossed considerably more than twice its cost ($678,526 vs. $265,012), while *Feet of Clay* grossed nearly triple its cost ($904,383 vs. $315,636). Clearly, DeMille was profitable, just not as profitable as Zukor wanted him to be. Although Zukor's proposal would have reduced the money the studio was paying for DeMille's overhead by about $150,000 a year, or $75,000 per picture, the issue was more than money. Simply, it concerned power.

Zukor regarded DeMille's large staff as a detriment psychologically as well as financially; in some way, they were a threat to Zukor's authority. As he correctly understood, their loyalty was to DeMille rather than to the company. Beyond that, DeMille always presented the possibility of going off the financial reserva-tion. Zukor wanted a stream of reliable product—singles and doubles, not Cecil's periodic swinging for the fences.

Cecil knew a cul-de-sac when he saw one, and told Neil McCarthy to look around for alternatives. McCarthy had some preliminary talks with Joe Schenck at United Artists. McCarthy told Schenck that DeMille could direct two pictures a year for about $400,000 apiece and produce other pictures for about $200,000 apiece. Schenck replied that those figures sounded fine to him and that U.A. would have no problem arranging financing.

McCarthy informed Schenck that DeMille was getting $6,750 a week to cover the expenses of himself and his staff, and that same amount would be necessary in any new deal. After some consultation with his client, McCarthy upped the budgets to $500,000 apiece for two personally directed pictures and $250,000 for six pictures DeMille would only produce.

DeMille had made plans to leave for Europe on January 10, 1925, and the studio had purchased Marie Corelli's *The Sorrows of Satan* for him—a picture he desperately wanted to make. On December 15, Cecil wrote Sidney Kent that he would be willing to make *The Sorrows of Satan* even if the two parties were unable to agree on a new deal. All he asked was 50 percent of the profits and his normal advance. Zukor politely declined this offer.

DeMille's letter to Kent was slightly conciliatory: "Mr. Zukor's proposition . . . is to my mind so far removed from my requirements that I am sending this wire to you instead of to him in the hope that by presenting it to him, you can . . . bring about an understanding between us."

Kent replied that Zukor's problem remained the "added expense caused by your separate unit from which we feel you get no return commensurate with the expense it costs us. Mr. Zukor feels that this must be taken off our backs. . . . Zukor's letter must be the general basis upon which we meet."

DeMille must have believed that the Paramount deal could be finessed, because he booked passage for Europe for a group that included his wife as well as Jeanie and Julia and their mothers in order to scout locations for *The Sorrows of Satan*. But after meeting with Zukor, Lasky, and Sidney Kent in New York, DeMille realized that the impasse could not be negotiated away.

While all this was going on, Joe Schenck passed on DeMille's prospective deal.

The final showdown with Zukor came at lunch. "I can remember standing there in the front office," said DeMille. "I had told the gentleman behind the desk [Zukor] what terms I would have to have. . . . He looked at me, his eyes were sharp as steel. I can still remember what he said as I left the office: 'Cecil, you have never been one of us. If you do this I will break you.' And his two fists came apart sharply like a man breaking a stick." DeMille would always remember this as the most bitter moment of his life.

"You have never been one of us . . ."

Superficially, Zukor was referring to the fact that he and Lasky were East Coast and financial, and Cecil was West Coast and creative. But beneath that was an acknowledgment of tribal unity that Cecil would never be able to breach. Lasky and Zukor were Jews, *landsmen*, and Cecil was only half a *landsman*, and not even that much emotionally. He could never be a full member of the firm. What made it worse was that Jesse, his best friend on earth, sat there and said nothing.

Everybody in that room knew that without DeMille, there wouldn't have been a Famous Players-Lasky company; everybody in that room knew that it didn't make any difference to Adolph Zukor, or, evidently, to Jesse Lasky . . . who sat there.

Thirty years later, DeMille would speak about this meeting with Art Arthur, who was researching his autobiography and had spoken to Zukor about that day. Zukor told Arthur that his memory really wasn't very clear about that meeting.

"I'll bet he remembers every word of it," Cecil snapped.

A little later, talking to Ann del Valle, a publicist in the DeMille unit, a brooding DeMille would say, "[Zukor] did some terribly ruthless things. First he smashed Sam Goldwyn, then me, then Lasky, then [W. W.] Hodkinson. . . . I was becoming a very important figure in the industry and he thought he could blot that out. Jesse never lifted his hand to help me."

In most respects, DeMille was not a man to hold a grudge, but he took this episode to his grave. The European trip was canceled, Griffith was assigned *The Sorrows of Satan*, and, as DeMille remembered, "I began the year of 1925 as one of the unemployed."

Cecil's east coast attorney Nathan Burkan set about arranging the terms of the divorce. DeMille would continue to draw his fixed weekly salary of $6,371 until thirty days from December 27, 1924. His percentage of all the pictures beginning with *The Affairs of Anatol* and continuing through *The Ten Commandments* was to be 12.5 percent of the gross on their continuing distribution. He was to be assigned the contracts for Leatrice Joy, Rod La Rocque, and all members of his personal staff.

Shortly before Cecil died, one of his employees started to ask him a question that began, "When you left Paramount after making *The Ten Commandments*—"

DeMille interrupted him. "When Paramount threw me out," he said.

11

In the second week of January 1925, the trade papers announced that Cecil B. DeMille was leaving Famous Players-Lasky. The financial foundation of DeMille's future was Jeremiah Milbank, a wealthy, extremely religious, and politically conservative financier.

DeMille and Milbank met in New York, but Milbank was evincing only polite interest in investing in a proposed company until DeMille mentioned that his great dream was to make a movie about the life of Christ. "The only thing that moved Jeremiah Milbank to put his resources behind me was that first mention of *The King of Kings*," remembered DeMille. This was an entirely different kind of quid pro quo than DeMille was used to. Instead of Zukor's narrow, obsessive bitching about budgets, DeMille was partnering with a man of idealism and religious conviction who was fully prepared to put his money where his mouth was.

Milbank had recently taken over a struggling distribution company organized by W. W. Hodkinson and had rechristened it the Producers Distributing Corporation—PDC. DeMille and Milbank formed a holding company called the Cinema Corporation of America, which owned the stock of Producers Distributing Corporation as well as a newly formed company called Cecil B. DeMille Pictures Corporation. PDC would distribute the movies DeMille would personally make, as well as those of other filmmakers that he was obligated to bring into the fold. Cinema Corporation of America was an equal partnership between Milbank's Realty and Securities Company and DeMille.

DeMille's primary need was for a physical plant, a studio. In January, he paid $50,000 down on a total price of $500,000 for the Thomas Ince studio in Culver City, just down the road from MGM. Ince's studio was fortuitously available because of his sudden death in November 1924. (The Ince studio was a replica of Mount Vernon and would later become the home of David O. Selznick's operation. It still stands.) DeMille took possession of the studio on March 2 with a suitably lavish ceremony at which Louis B. Mayer and Joe Schenck welcomed him to Culver City.

The trade papers bloomed with four-page ads announcing Cecil's relocation, his new trademark—an armored knight mounted on a prancing charger, holding an erect lance—and a recapitulation of his career: "*The Squaw Man*—'Effect' lighting introduced . . . *The Wild Goose Chase*—Ina Claire comes from the stage . . . *Maria Rosa*—First picture with Geraldine Farrar. Farrar contract greatest to date. Gave all motion pictures a new importance . . . *Joan the Woman*—Geraldine Farrar triumphs as Jeanne d'Arc. First successful use of color photography . . . *Don't Change Your Husband*—Thirty feet of a Sennett comedy caused Cecil B. DeMille to choose Gloria Swanson for this lead." The enumeration of several dozen successful pictures was made for an obvious reason: "History does repeat itself." The ads closed with a dignified shot of the new DeMille studio.

Besides some actors and some production people, Paramount had also agreed to give DeMille $50,000 worth of camera and lighting equipment when they parted. DeMille also asked for more prints of his pictures, a far-sighted act that accounts for so much of DeMille's output surviving. He built a stand-alone film vault on the grounds of Laughlin Park to house his film collection.

DeMille and his staff moved into their new studio. The writers and directors were on the second floor, while DeMille's suite, complete with white bearskin rug, was on the third floor, near the research department. By this time, Cecil's library had expanded to six thousand volumes, mostly nonfiction, with a special emphasis on biblical and world history. DeMille owned Bibles dating from as far back as 1690, as well as an edition measuring two feet square that had been printed for Thomas Macklin in 1800. There was shelf after shelf of reference books on costume design and art, architecture, jewelry, and ironwork. The DeMille bookplate showed a phoenix rising from chaotic mists.

From the beginning, Cecil intended that his new studio would stand for a level of display commensurate with his name. In front of the mansion stood a black doorman in full livery. When a car pulled up outside, he would run down the steps, open the car door, then run back up to the front door and hold it for the arrival.

It was a well-appointed lot with grass and flowers—calla lilies bloomed in the winter. Across from the main stage was the studio mill, and the saws were soon buzzing all day long, cutting lumber for sets.

Bill also moved to Culver City. Although the legend was that Bill's pictures were artistic but uncommercial, figures he kept show that the films he was directing for Famous Players-Lasky were generally grossing nearly three times their cost, and sometimes better than that (*Grumpy*, with Theodore Roberts, cost $92,943 and grossed $540,000). Since Bill was drawing a salary against 25 percent of the profits, he had been doing well for himself as well as for Paramount.

Bill's strengths were, as actress Bessie Love would note of his character, his "quiet, retiring dignity, classic wit and good taste"; his shortcomings were a function of his dignity and wit: "His attitude towards life always appeared to be sophisticated, urbane, in complete control, a bit cynical; he was a walking understatement. He was expert at exposing superficial, shallow human failings and foibles. But when it came to digging deep into an actor's emotional vitals and dragging out his innermost hidden thoughts, I'm sure William deMille would have been most embarrassed at the very idea."

Bill's child had been smoothly integrated into Cecil's family. Richard would come to adore Cecil for his strength, his joie de vivre, and his generosity, although he also found himself strangely drawn to Uncle Bill, who often sat across from him at family gatherings. "I was basically an idea person," said Richard, "and everybody else in the family, except William, were action people. . . . William and I were idea people."

★

Lasky and Zukor didn't meekly acquiesce to all of Cecil's requests. DeMille had guaranteed Leatrice Joy a far bigger salary than she had been getting at Paramount to come with him to his new company. She agreed to the contract, but was phoned by Lasky, who inquired why she wasn't happy at Paramount.

"I'm very happy at Paramount," she replied, "and I never wanted to leave you until Mr. DeMille told me that you had agreed to my leaving the studio with him." After talking to Lasky, Joy asked to be released from the contract with DeMille. Lasky had told her that DeMille's new company would have few theaters; all he would have was his ego. "I'm not so young anymore, Mr. DeMille," she told him. "The next three years are crucial with me." Joy told her daughter that she got down on her knees and begged DeMille to let her go, but he wouldn't budge; worse, her reluctance to accompany him to the new studio infuriated him. Joy remembered that for the next three years, the only times DeMille spoke to her were to scold or reprimand. Cecil slotted Joy into program pictures he handed to others to direct. For the rest of her long life, Leatrice Joy believed that leaving Famous Players-Lasky brought her career to a crashing halt.

★

Ramping up a studio from a standing start entails a vast amount of work and money, especially when it comes to story material. "Do you want to buy best sellers by popular authors or cheaper originals and older stories?" inquired Ella Adams. DeMille would have preferred gilt-edged properties, but there were money issues. "We are short on material for women," he wrote back. "We need eight feminine vehicles and we only have four."

Then there was the problem of stars. Lillian Gish wired DeMille to say that she had been told he was interested in her: HAVE YOU A REPRESENTATIVE HERE IN NEW YORK THAT I COULD TALK WITH OR COULD YOU WIRE ME ABOUT ANY PLANS YOU MIGHT HAVE AFFECTING MY FUTURE WHICH IS STILL UNSETTLED?

DeMille responded with a flurry of telegrams: I WOULD LIKE VERY MUCH TO HAVE YOU AS A MEMBER OF MY NEW COMPANY AS I BELIEVE I CAN DO MORE FOR YOU THAN ANYONE AT PRESENT IN THE FIELD. He told his New York man to "call upon Gish immediately, tell her I would like [to] make four pictures a year with her that I will personally supervise and in which she would be starred. Or possibly three starring pictures and have her appear in one of my personally directed productions each year. . . . If she mentions [Gish's lover, the drama critic] George Jean Nathan you can say that I have the highest regard for Mr. Nathan and would be glad to associate him in some way with her pictures. That at the same time if she is to have the benefit of my direction and supervision naturally the choice of stories and matters of that sort must be left in my hands."

DeMille's agent reported back that three or four companies were bidding for Gish's services, for what he thought was a minimum of $5,000 a week, and she wanted a definite offer. A couple of days later, he asked DeMille, "would you take Nathan if signing Gish depended on it?" The negotiations with Gish went no further; she signed with MGM.

That wasn't the only disappointment. DeMille was anxious to sign the silk hat comedian Raymond Griffith, and was willing to trade Bebe Daniels, with whom he had worked out a contract memo. But Daniels changed her mind about working for DeMille because her boyfriend was going to be working in the East and she wanted to follow him there. This left DeMille with nothing to offer of comparable value for Griffith.

What about Elinor Glyn? "I would be interested in her provided of course that her terms are right." But Glyn's contract with MGM mandated she receive one third of the profits of her pictures, with a guarantee of $40,000 per picture, not counting a salary for writing and supervising that took her compensation for each movie to about $50,000—far too rich for the DeMille studio.

DeMille managed to dodge one large bullet. Erich von Stroheim, who had just left MGM after completing *The Merry Widow*, expressed an interest in the new company. Cecil seemed to have his doubts, so he asked executive John Flinn in New York what he thought. Flinn wired back that he had just closed a deal for four pictures from Marshall Neilan and he didn't see the need for von Stroheim, thus saving the company from a fascinating production experience and premature bankruptcy.

One of the first directors DeMille went after was Ernst Lubitsch. Other available directors were Reginald Barker ($15,000 a picture), Alfred E. Green ($20,000 a picture), Victor Schertzinger ($15,000 a picture), Sam Wood, and, perhaps, Raoul Walsh. DeMille wasn't able to get any of them. Instead, he ended up with

Paul Sloane, Donald Crisp, and Alan Hale. Some good, if low-profile directors, such as William K. Howard and Tay Garnett, also came aboard.

There was an ongoing set of negotiations with a variety of other stars, among them Corinne Griffith, for whom Cecil was willing to pay as much as $100,000 a picture. But the most potentially explosive alliance was with none other than Gloria Swanson, which entailed a series of coded telegrams between DeMille and John Flinn. Marshall Neilan, who was evidently still involved with Swanson, was acting as go-between, and told DeMille that Swanson was as concerned about stories and directors as she was about money. Neilan's suggestion was that a separate combine be formed in which DeMille and Neilan would each make one Swanson picture per year, with other directors making two more per year. Swanson's attorney said that if DeMille and Neilan would each make one Swanson picture a year, and if the new company could match Famous Players-Lasky's money, she would leave her home studio. Cecil agreed to match any financial offer, but the deal fell apart anyway.

Among the actors he was successful in luring to his studio was Joseph Schildkraut, who had made a great success in the theater with Ferenc Molnár's *Liliom*, and in the movies with D. W. Griffith's *Orphans of the Storm*. DeMille wouldn't go higher than $1,000 a week for Schildkraut. "Tell him he wanted a chance and this is it and that he must make sacrifices for this opportunity with me personally," DeMille snapped.

Schildkraut would go on to a long and honorable career, although as a ladykilling character actor rather than a leading man. DeMille's daughter Cecilia once confided to a friend that Schildkraut had once kissed her hand from palm to elbow so adroitly that she never felt it.

After months of frantic negotiations for talent and stories, DeMille settled on a production policy: twenty-five program pictures in the first year exclusive of his personally directed films. One story could cost $20,000, three could cost $15,000, nine at $7,500 or less, and twelve at $5,000 or less. But DeMille would pay a whopping $25,000 for the rights to *The Road to Yesterday*, a play involving reincarnation and flashbacks to previous lives he had enjoyed when it premiered in 1906 and which would be his first independent production.

What this price structure meant in practice was that DeMille would buy the same kind of material for the studio that Famous Players-Lasky often bought for his movies: cheesy popular fiction. But the ongoing problem would be that there was nobody at the company but DeMille who could put this material over with sufficient showmanship and fire to make it saleable.

In the heady early days of the consortium, DeMille exulted that the organization would be another United Artists: "Cinema Corporation of America is not to interfere with individual brands that will unquestionably want to come in with us and release under their own trademark," he wrote Gladys Rosson. "We are planting the standard of independence around which I am confident many great artists will rally."

But the new company faced serious problems from conception, among them a lack of first-run theaters and the increasing monopolization of talent by the major studios. Then there were problems with publicity. Publicist Barrett Kiesling reported to DeMille that Famous Players-Lasky had quietly invested $100,000 in *Photoplay* magazine, just about the same time that MGM made a similar investment in Brewster Publications, the publisher of *Motion Picture* magazine. DeMille looked for a similar deal that could give his pictures pride of place in a mass-market publication, but the major outlets were already spoken for.

To a great extent, Cecil was counting on the fact that he was at the absolute pinnacle of his renown—a November 1926 poll of exhibitors in the *Motion Picture Herald* listed DeMille as the number one box office director in America.

Initially, DeMille chaired the story conferences for even the program pictures, as with a movie called *Hell's Highway*, co-directed by Paul Iribe and Frank Urson. When he liked the story suggestions of a young screenwriter named Lenore Coffee, DeMille took her to lunch, forbade discussion of the movie at hand, and quickly placed her under contract for a salary that began at $350 a week and rose to $750 a week in the third year.

Coffee loved her three years with DeMille, and even loved the demanding experience of working with him on one of his personally directed pictures, *The Volga Boatman*. She was particularly entranced by his Grand Manner. At one of their early meetings, she noticed a beautiful porcelain bowl on a teak stand. "It's a replica of the breast of Madame du Barry," DeMille informed her as he turned it upside down and she noticed that the dimple at the bottom of the bowl did indeed form a shell-pink nipple on the outside.

"What do you do with it?" asked Coffee.

"I eat crackers and milk out of it," replied DeMille.

Coffee noted Jeanie Macpherson and Julia Faye jealously swooping around each other, and sat in on casting sessions where various actresses made embarrassingly direct plays for the director, who ignored them all. Then she got to know Constance and realized that "Cecil DeMille would never have left his wife for any other woman. He had for her not only great regard but deep and lasting affection. She was an essential part of his life."

He insisted that his young writers and directors see the big pictures that were being made such as *The Big Parade* and *The Iron Horse*. Coffee noted his great admiration for movies that were completely unlike his, pictures that represented very different tastes and ideas. "I never knew a man so free of envy or so generous in praise of other producers and directors."

With his own studio, DeMille was finally able to shoot in continuity; that is, the first scene in the movie was the first scene he shot, and so forth. This was an expensive way to make movies—for one thing, each actor had to be on salary for a longer time than if their scenes were shot at one time, and every set had to remain standing until every scene on that set had been shot and approved. But it was organic—the actors grew into the emotions of their roles as they did during a stage performance, and the director could always go back and reshoot a scene because the set was still available.

For months, Cecil was functioning on a run-and-gun basis, spouting plans that had only a provisional relation to reality. On February 8, DeMille informed Gladys Rosson that the release schedule was as follows: "August 16, [Leatrice] Joy directed by [Frank] Urson and [Paul] Iribe. September 13 new star directed by new director; October 11 first La Rocque star picture director not arranged; November first DeMille Super Special Personally Directed. . . . Ask Paul Iribe if he can design me a nice trademark for the DeMille pictures . . ." and so forth.

Among the contract players was a child actor named Frank Coghlan, who was supposed to fill the role that Wesley Barry had at First National—a scrappy youngster capable of playing Tom Sawyer or Huck Finn. Coghlan noted that DeMille was friendly and good-natured between movies, but once a movie started, a personality shift took place. Once, he even snapped at Coghlan when he failed to let go of another actor when he was supposed to. "Do I have to send you an engraved invitation?" DeMille said.

Another change involved the ring on the little finger of DeMille's left hand. If his shirt was green, the ring was a jade or emerald. With a tan shirt, the ring would be topaz or a sapphire. When he wore a white shirt, which was rare, it was a two- or three-carat diamond. "His selection of finger rings must have rivaled the best that Cartier had to offer," said Coghlan.

For his leading man in *The Road to Yesterday*, DeMille chose the young dress extra from Ohio named William Boyd. A DeMille leading lady named Elinor Fair became Boyd's wife, but that marriage's quick fade didn't affect the actor's appreciation for his director. "We had a great friendship with DeMille," remembered Grace Bradley Boyd, Boyd's last wife. "We went to the house for parties. Socially, DeMille was charming, a wonderful, interesting man. He had a lot of qualities the average person never saw. At work, you only saw DeMille being DeMille, but not at home. There, he had authority and dignity, but he was a beautiful host. You couldn't be like he was at the studio twenty-four hours a day!"

DeMille began to expand the studio, then began to overexpand it. New buildings were erected; when the studio embarked on a sea picture entitled *The Yankee Clipper*, nothing would do but that the studio purchase—not rent, purchase—two ships. Since *The Bohemia* and *The Indiana* had been built in the mid-nineteenth century, they required considerable investment to become seaworthy, and were of little use after *The Yankee Clipper* was completed.

On March 4, Jesse Lasky wrote Cecil, "I had a lovely two weeks in Palm Beach and Havana and thought of you many times. You must not miss going to Havana next winter. It is the ideal place for you. I lived at the Jockey Club, which is right over the race track, and there is a large gambling casino right in the same building. I played roulette every day and found I have not lost my taste for the game. The Cubans are a charming and hospitable people. The Cuban girls are particularly attractive."

Cecil's response was suggestive of mutual understanding: "The Jockey Club and the roulette sound fascinating and I have always heard that Cuban sugar was very sweet. . . . We will endeavor to work out the cuts on *The Ten Commandments*. I should, however, be very glad of any suggestions that anyone may care to offer me as to possible cuts that can be made, for it seems to me that the modern story is pretty close to the bone as it is."

Nine months later, there was a celebration to mark the twelfth anniversary of the Lasky company. Jesse Lasky was obviously feeling guilty, for he sent a telegram to Cecil:

> I DON'T FEEL VERY GOOD ABOUT BEING PUT IN THE LIMELIGHT AND TAKING A LOT OF CREDIT THAT PROPERLY BELONGS TO YOU. YOU MAY BE SURE IF I GET A CHANCE TO TALK THAT I WON'T FORGET YOU AND WILL DO MY BEST TO PAY YOU THE TRIBUTE YOU DESERVE. I DON'T KNOW WHY I AM WIRING THIS EXCEPT THAT WHEN AN OCCASION OF THIS KIND ARISES I MISS YOUR PRESENCE MORE THAN I CAN TELL YOU. BEST REGARDS ALWAYS.

The B pictures DeMille began producing were supposed to help cover studio overhead, but B pictures have to be made within stringently observed budget parameters, and the DeMille films weren't. Harry Carr, who was supervising the films, indulged his producers. A programmer called *The Blue Danube* is instructive. It was scheduled for twenty-seven days of shooting and a budget of $242,325, but took thirty-two days and $279,838. *The Coming of Amos*, an amusing send-up of melodramas, cost $238,000 instead of $200,000, and DeMille explained that the $38,000 overage was "due to week of bad weather on location and carrying part of initial cost of opening studio."

DeMille would have a lot of trouble trying to consistently control the costs of his program pictures, perhaps because his sensibility wasn't oriented toward the bargain bin. A few years later, *Chicago*, which would later be adapted into the Bob Fosse musical, was supposed to be made in thirty-eight days and cost $236,417, but took forty-five days and $264,397, with DeMille stepping in and directing a fair amount of the picture himself.

Individually, these overruns wouldn't have been a big deal, but cumulatively, the PDC B movies tended to cost more than they earned. DeMille was part of the problem—he took $10,000 of the budget for supervision of the picture in return for writing memos about what was needed. On the upside, the DeMille program- mers are consistently the best-produced B pictures of the period—not terribly in- teresting in story, but with production values and dramatic snap that makes them far superior, as movies if not moneymakers, to the Bs produced by Paramount or MGM.

The atmosphere around the DeMille lot was pleasant, informal, and friendly. "It was like a big family," Frank Coghlan remembered. "You worked with the same prop men, the same assistant director, it was truly like a big family. I was ten years old and they called me their kid. I remember one day we were out on loca- tion on the back lot and during lunch hour [a] guy was swearing, and one of the prop men came up and grabbed him by the throat and he said, 'We don't talk like that in front of our kid!' They were protecting me; it was nice."

During lunch hour, crews would break up into baseball teams, and Coghlan would play shortstop. One day he stopped a ground ball with his mouth and de- veloped a fat lip; Coghlan's director told him to cover his mouth with a clenched fist as he watched his mother die in scenes shot the next day.

Coghlan was cast in DeMille's first independent production, *The Road to Yes- terday*. When the troupe went on location to the Grand Canyon, they stayed at the El Tovar Hotel and descended into the canyon on burros. Coghlan was playing a Cub Scout with a bow and arrow, so DeMille signed him up for two weeks of intensive work with the bow and arrow.

"He was a good director," said Coghlan. "Not like so many of them, by going out there and doing it themselves. He just sat there, in his big chair, with his legs crossed, and gave good directions, very understandable. He was very patient with kids."

As the first batch of PDC pictures reached the theaters, it became clear that the studio couldn't get sufficient first run theaters to play its films, so the films couldn't earn returns commensurate with their costs. Economies were imposed. "DEEM IT ADVISABLE YOU RETURN [to Los Angeles from New York] IMMEDIATELY FOR CONFERENCE ON MATERIAL," DeMille telegraphed Ella King Adams on November 7, 1925, "IT BEING EVIDENT WE CANNOT PURCHASE NEW YORK STAGE PLAYS ACCOUNT PRICES. BELIEVE MAGAZINES, ORIGINALS AND OLD NOVELS RATHER THAN NEW BESTSELLERS AT FANCY PRICES WILL BE SOURCE FROM WHICH WE MUST DRAW SUPPLY."

Case in point: DeMille paid a modest $9,000 for Konrad Bercovici's *The Volga Boatman*, which turned out to be a successful picture. But without the roster of Paramount stars to draw from, and with often threadbare properties, DeMille's new company had two strikes against it from the beginning.

In addition, it soon became obvious that DeMille didn't really have the in- stincts of a studio head. When Fox wanted to borrow Rod La Rocque for *What*

Price Glory, a major part in a major film that would assuredly have bolstered the actor's box office profile, DeMille turned down the deal:

UNDER NO CONDITIONS WOULD AT THIS TIME CONSIDER LOANING YOU STOP [FOX]
DESIRES TO GET AS GOOD A CLASS OF PRODUCT AS HE CAN FOR CERTAIN LARGE
NEW THEATERS THAT HE IS BUILDING AND IF HE WANTS TO PLAY ROD LA ROCQUE IN
THOSE THEATERS HE WILL HAVE THE OPPORTUNITY OF BUYING ROD LA ROCQUE IN
DEMILLE PICTURES.

Since DeMille was at the time casting La Rocque in pictures entitled *The Fighting Eagle* and *Gigolo*, turning down *What Price Glory* seems perverse.

Despite Cecil's strained circumstances, he kept an eye on old friends. Although Bebe Daniels had crossed him up on the matter of a contract, he lent her $6,000 secured by a life insurance policy. When he found out that Theodore Roberts had fallen ill and was unable to make payments on his mortgage, he wrote Jesse Lasky proposing that the two men pay off Roberts's house. Lasky replied that they "have arranged with company to continue paying Theodore Roberts same sum he now receives as long as he lives and is unable to work. Beyond this can do nothing."

Perhaps because of the studio's heavy overhead, DeMille didn't shoot a lot of film on his first independent production. On *The Road to Yesterday*, he shot only about 250 to five hundred feet of film per day, and at its premiere he was already on location shooting *The Volga Boatman*, a romance about the Russian Revolution, where three different writers were sending him suggestions for rewrites.

When Jetta Goudal's character in *The Volga Boatman* was changed from dramatic to comic, she flounced off the location and was replaced by Julia Faye. (Goudal was famously temperamental; the costume designer Adrian once collapsed after a Goudal fitting.)

The *New York Times* sent its legendarily unperceptive film critic Mordaunt Hall to California to watch DeMille in production, and his story caught the director in full indomitable flight. Hall reported that DeMille rose at 6:30 A.M. and went to bed at about 1:30 A.M. In between, there was constant dramatic tension: "Mr. DeMille's assistants literally follow every movement their chief makes on the set. If he walks three paces forward, they walk three paces forward. If he retreats, they go back too. Yet they must never be so near that they interfere with him, but they must always be within speaking distance, to hear the slightest order given in a modulated tone. While I was watching a scene that afternoon, Mr. DeMille called for Miss Macpherson, and four heads turned anxiously looking to see if Miss Macpherson were present, while only one of them called out her name. Mr. DeMille sat on a camp stool which had only a second before been placed where it was. He called for the continuity writer, and soon there was a conference on the set, as, fortunately, Miss Macpherson had been within a few yards of the stage. There was silence from all the others as the producers consulted with the two women, and when the question was settled the work continued."

DeMille remembered that the reviews for *The Road to Yesterday* weren't good. Actually, *Variety* liked the film well enough and loved William Boyd, calling the movie "lavishly made, furnished with beautiful backgrounds and settings and cast competently in every spot. To top off the generally pleasing tone of the film, DeMille has provided the greatest train wreck scene ever shot. . . . It is William Boyd . . . who takes the cake and icing away from everyone else. . . . He plays much in the old Wallace Reid manner, and what is more, looks a good deal like Reid."

But *Photoplay* did a hit-and-run: "Beautiful photography forms the background for a muddled story. . . . Involved in a train wreck [the characters] go back to a dim past where almost everything happens, entirely without visible reason. What it all means you'll have to find out from Cecil DeMille, who created it."

DeMille responded by wiring Joseph Schildkraut: I GATHER YOU HAVE BEEN PANNED BY N.Y. CRITICS. ACCEPT MY HEARTIEST CONGRATULATIONS. . . . I PERSONALLY AM LIVING IN DREAD OF RECEIVING MY FIRST GOOD N.Y. NOTICE. WARMEST REGARDS.

Far more importantly, the film's box office wasn't good (cost $477,479; gross $522,665); by the end of 1925, DeMille's new company was having money troubles. As if that weren't bad enough, Zukor and company chose this moment to pile on. Famous Players-Lasky held a sales convention, the special attraction of which was a short directed by Marshall Neilan in which comedian Ford Sterling was showing Neilan all the wonderful plans the company had for the future. The two men came to an empty chair marked "DeMille" that held a funeral wreath.

"Whatever became of him?" asked Neilan.

"Oh, he's gone down the road to yesterday," replied Sterling.

It was a classic cheap shot, and was protested by several exhibitors. Cecil's own reaction was the steely fury that constituted his authentic anger: "I am rather surprised at a vicious personal attack of this kind and assume the company's executives are ignorant of it," he wrote Sidney Kent. "This seems scarcely in keeping with the spirit of my contemplated adjustment of *The Ten Commandments* contract in which it is proposed that I voluntarily give Famous Players an amount approximating one hundred thousand dollars for no reason other than that Famous Players feels that the contract works an injustice upon them. I shall appreciate your seeing that the portion of the film alluded to above and the spoken title are removed before the film is exhibited again and I shall also appreciate a wire from you telling me that same has been done."

Ten days later, Neilan published a letter in the trade papers: "Neither Mr. Zukor, Mr. Lasky nor Mr. Kent saw the trailer before it was shown at the convention," insisted Neilan. It was, he said, "just clean kidding."

★

DeMille continued casting about for commercial help. In January 1926 he wired Sam Goldwyn in New York to find out if he might be interested in coming over to Culver City and working at the DeMille studio. Goldwyn was presently making lucrative exotic romances with Ronald Colman and Vilma Banky for United Artists. But Goldwyn, who always knew what was good for Goldwyn, wanted a profit guarantee of $150,000 per picture, essentially indemnifying him against failure—something even DeMille didn't have. Goldwyn ended up staying at U.A.; DeMille's problems continued to mount.

DeMille was finding out the truth of something he had observed about Sam Goldwyn's efforts after he left Famous Players-Lasky and went out on his own: "Mr. Goldwyn found himself without any organization at all—flat—nothing. You cannot go out and pick up an organization." The DeMille studio's start-up had been prohibitively expensive, and overhead was eating them alive.

In a February letter written by an executive to John Flinn, who handled distribution of DeMille films for PDC, the specific problem areas were outlined:

1. The merchandising of the remainder of our program for this year, including *The Volga Boatman*.

2. The production of the forty picture program for next year.

3. The merchandising of the new program.

4. The theater situation in key cities and with regard to main outlets for product.

5. The production and merchandising of the big DeMille special [the film that would become *The King of Kings*].

Other than those few problems, everything was fine.

The letter went on to admit that the sales figures "indicates that there will be some loss on a majority of these pictures. Our object should be to make our distribution so wide that we can show a substantial profit on a great many of our pictures and reduce the number of losing pictures to an absolute minimum."

Locked out from the vast Paramount theater chain, or even the far more limited but strictly A-list Loew's Inc. theaters, DeMille's pictures were limited to smaller chains and independents. There was no first-run theater playing the company's pictures in Chicago or San Francisco; they got playing time for their pictures in Cincinnati and Dayton, Buffalo and Syracuse.

After a year of independent production, the water was lapping at DeMille's chest, and he wasn't the only one; between 1925 and 1927, the net income for the Orpheum Circuit, a major vaudeville chain, would drop from $2.1 million to $1.1 million, while the B. F. Keith Corporation experienced a 10 percent drop in net income in just one year.

So it was that in a classic if you can't beat 'em, join 'em move, the Keith-Albee and Orpheum theater circuits bought a 50 percent interest in the Cinema Corporation of America, the umbrella company for Cecil's operation. On the one hand, it gave DeMille access to better theaters than he had previously had; on the other, it gave Keith-Albee and Orpheum something to play besides the jugglers and animal acts that the public was increasingly uninterested in. The amalgamation of three struggling operations into one mandated a considerable number of layoffs, thus saving on overhead, but it created a host of other problems.

If Cecil had money problems with his company's pictures, he had very few personally. A financial accounting prepared on September 1, 1926, showed that he had $107,868 worth of commercial property, including lots on Argyle, Franklin, and Highland Avenues in Hollywood, another property on the corner of Sunset and Cahuenga, and several lots on Hollywood Boulevard. He had eight cars, including a Lincoln and a Mercedes, stockholdings of $273,392, municipal bonds totaling $17,859, and even some foreign bonds.

The movies had been good to him; at the end of 1926, his assets totaled $1.92 million.

★

At the first running of *The Volga Boatman* at the house in Laughlin Park, DeMille evinced an uncharacteristically wishy-washy feeling. "I don't know what I've got here," he said. "I know what I *haven't* got, and that is a road show." As it turned out, the film was successful, costing $497,356, grossing $1.2 million.

The Volga Boatman is a surprisingly sympathetic account of the Russian Revolution. It's also a much better, if less lavish, picture than *The Road to Yesterday*, even though, according to a technical expert DeMille hired only to ignore, Volga boatmen hadn't existed for about fifty years at the time of the Russian Revolution.

The plot was nominal—revolutionary falls in love with an aristocrat's daughter and saves her from the revolution—but it features a deliciously posh silent movie moment. As the heroine is about to be shot by a firing squad, she defiantly rips her dress off her shoulder and marks an X over her heart with her lipstick. Faced with such thundering bravura, there is nothing for William Boyd to do but grab her, kiss her, and light out for the territory. Ultimately, the heroine chooses to stay with her lover in the New Russia, because "you will need the blood of the old Russia" to help form the new Russia. Julia Faye, wearing an off-the-shoulder blouse, is saucy and charming in the second female lead, one of the rare times you can see what Cecil saw in her.

Variety called it "as good as anything that Cecil B. DeMille has ever done. That is taking in a lot of territory, but in this particular instance DeMille has turned out a picture that has a lot of that quality known to the trade as 'guts.' "

★

A new addition to the lot was a young costume designer named Adrian Green-burg, who dropped his last name for the screen. Adrian was born in Connecticut in 1903 and met Mitch Leisen in New York, when he was five years out of the New York School of Fine and Applied Art and three years out of Paris. In New York, he was designing for Irving Berlin's Music Box revues.

Adrian's first movie job involved some costumes for Valentino's *The Eagle*, after which he moved on to designing the costumes for a prologue for the open-ing of Chaplin's *The Gold Rush* at Grauman's Egyptian. The prologue involved "fascinatingly pretty young women wearing astoundingly rich and beautiful gowns all blending with the Arctic atmosphere and bespeaking the moods of the barren white country."

DeMille was impressed, as was all of Hollywood; the morning after the pre-miere of the Chaplin film, Adrian had three job offers: MGM, Fox, and DeMille. Adrian chose DeMille because of the director's legendary extravagance. The only problem was that Adrian didn't know a lot about sewing, so Mitch Leisen still had to supervise the fittings.

Adrian worked for DeMille for two years, designing the clothes for *The Road to Yesterday* and *The Volga Boatman*, as well as contributing to *The King of Kings*, and designing wardrobes for more than twenty bread-and-butter movies. Adrian liked and respected DeMille, enjoyed the way he was encouraged to purchase silks and velvets, enjoyed being sent to New York with $5,000 in cash to buy gifts for Christmas and baubles for the jewelried swag the director offered female employ-ees. He loved the way DeMille would stage a preproduction fashion show with all the costumes displayed with special lighting and elaborate staging, the director watching the dresses with the eye of an experienced couturier.

"He actually was nearest to what an Eastern potentate should be," remem-bered Adrian. "He was hypnotized by beauty and demanded it with an almost vicious desire. . . . He believed in his world . . . a world of antiquity from which he actually rarely emerged."

★

DeMille's first two personal productions at the new studio amounted to a flop and a hit that canceled each other out. Cecil needed a big picture with the poten-tial to be a big hit, and his agreement with Jeremiah Milbank gave a pretty good indication as to the subject matter.

On May 26, 1926, a DeMille studio contract writer named Denison Clift wrote a memo to DeMille: "Why skirt around the one great single subject of all time and all ages—the commanding, majestic and most sublime thing that any man can ever put upon the screen: the Life, Trial, Crucifixion, Resurrection and Ascension of Christ: in other words, the LIFE OF CHRIST, with its awe-inspir-ing power, its simplicity and its unutterable tragedy. . . . The title of the picture would be:

"THE KING OF KINGS"

In retrospect, it can be seen that DeMille came to the Bible cautiously. The flashbacks to ancient times in *Male and Female* and *Manslaughter* led to the lengthy prologue of *The Ten Commandments*—by far the best thing in the picture. With those successes in back of him, and with his promise to Jeremiah Milbank hanging fire, DeMille was at last ready to embark on a full-scale venture into antiquity.

Cecil's initial thought was to reverse-engineer the Christ narrative, and focus on Judas and Mary Magdalene—a tactic used in a novel called *Thirty Pieces of Silver*. Cecil wrote to Jeanie, who was in New York and beginning to work on the script, "Upon giving considerable thought to the big idea, the thing I miss is the place where the audience will cheer. I can see the thrill, suspense, terror, beauty but I do not see the great inspiring thing that will bring the audience to its feet like the chariot charge in *The Ten Commandments*."

Jeanie replied the next day: "Dearest Chief, Do not be anxious about the cheer quality in big picture. I have no concrete idea what it will be just now but it will all come straight and part of an idea is beginning already to buzz in my mind."

Jeanie went on to tell the Chief that she would be back in Los Angeles on April 3 and was headed to Bear Valley for four or five days to work on the story. A few days later she wrote him that "It is slow, careful work, owing to the fact that we are trying to make it REAL, instead of a picture, there are a hundred unsuspected pitfalls that one can bump into—and which one easily glosses over when it is merely a 'movie' plot! You know—best of anyone—what I mean. It will come—and is coming—but it is necessarily slow work and I have to be careful not to get 'panicky' at both the magnitude of the undertaking—and at the speed necessary to get it ready."

It was no time to launch an expensive production. By August 1926, DeMille was pleading with one of his backers: "Need for working capital at DeMille studio imperative. . . . The following items must be covered: first, last year's plant improvements, equipment purchases and payments on [Ince] studio purchase contract [amounting to] one hundred thirty thousand, second this year's improvements, equipment purchases, necessary advance production work, supplies necessarily carried in stock [amounting to] three hundred thousand. Against this if the one hundred thousand [dollars] furnished last year is considered withdrawn we can only figure depreciation reserves and accounts payable, a total of about two hundred thousand. Therefore a minimum working capital of two hundred thousand is essential and should be provided at the rate of not less than ten thousand [dollars a week]."

While Cecil was preparing his magnum opus, he received a sad, touching letter from Mildred Harris, the first wife of Charlie Chaplin and the star of DeMille's 1922 film *Fool's Paradise*. "I still hope to be able to do something for you again," wrote Harris, "as I have thought so much the last two years of how much you did for me four years ago, and how well off I would have been if I had only taken your good advice. I don't wonder at all that you must have been disgusted with me."

Harris went on to talk about her new baby son, her abandonment by her second husband, and finally made her pitch. "What I really want to ask is please will you see me and, I do so want to do something really worthwhile. . . . My . . . thoughts want so much to amount to something, to do something worthwhile for the world, and to give my baby a good start in life, so that he may have all the happiness, love and success this dear world offers.

"It is so hard to go on and on not knowing from one week to the next, whether you can meet expenses. I do so want to get steady work for a while at least. . . . I don't care how little salary I start for. I just want to work for you, to show you I have really changed."

It was a typical pitch by a struggling actor fallen on hard times. One way or another, DeMille almost always responded to these letters, because he understood the desperation of the acting profession. DeMille referred Harris to the casting director at his studio, and Harris picked up a lot of work at PDC and other studios for several years, until talkies put paid to her career, and she was reduced to extra work. Her last appearance before her death was in DeMille's own *Reap the Wild Wind* in 1942.

The King of Kings was unconventionally financed by means that were probably illegal. The film was carried on the books as having cost $2.2 million, although it didn't cost anything near that. One internal document says that $500,000 was diverted from *The King of Kings* budget to "complete and equip the DeMille Studios," but the actual amount used to keep the studio running might have been more than that. Another document reveals that half of the leading actor's salary was charged to *White Gold*, an excellent William K. Howard film that was shooting at the same time on the lot.

Whether the diverted funds amounted to $500,000, $1 million, or somewhere in between, the money was used to keep the company afloat while DeMille was making good on his promise to Milbank. The money kept the studio operating, but the artificially inflated budget had the unintended effect of making *The King of Kings* look like a *flop d'estime*, when it actually made a nice profit.

Joining the production was a young artist named Anton Grot, who had worked with Wilfred Buckland on *Robin Hood* and William Cameron Menzies on *The Thief of Bagdad*. He rose to the status of co-art director on *The Road to Yesterday* and the next several films. It's clear from Grot's drawings, which make a virtue of strongly defined shadows, silhouettes, and angular perspectives, that he was a defining presence on the DeMille film.

For the part of Christ, DeMille cast H. B. Warner, who was born in London in 1876 and was thus considerably older than the part he was playing. DeMille believed—correctly—that Warner had an unusual combination of virility and sensitivity. Warner also possessed the more common combination of a drinking problem and a passion for women. He would have to be watched—the last thing DeMille could countenance was Jesus having it off with Mary Magdalene—or anybody else.

DeMille knew that the first lavish portrayal of the life of Christ was sure to be controversial as well as commercial, but he was never averse to a coup de théâter, so he once again opened negotiations with Gloria Swanson, who had left Paramount for independent production, offering her Mary Magdalene.

> AM STARTING BIG NEW PRODUCTION EARLY NEXT MONTH AND IT WILL BE MADE ON
> PROPORTIONS OF TEN COMMANDMENTS. HOW WOULD YOU LIKE TO PLAY IN IT THE
> BIGGEST AND MOST INTERESTING PART I HAVE EVER HAD TO OFFER?

Swanson replied that she had suffered a nervous breakdown five weeks earlier and would be starting another movie in mid-August. "IF I HAD NOT BEEN ILL I WOULD HAVE FINISHED MY PICTURE LONG AGO AND I MIGHT HAVE BEEN ABLE TO ACCEPT THIS PROPOSITION, HOPE SOME DAY YOU WILL ASK ME AGAIN. . . ." She must have meant it—she didn't even ask what the part was.

Two weeks later, her plans had changed and she wired him about the schedule, the money, and the name of the character. DeMille quickly replied that the part was Mary Magdalene—"THE GREATEST PART YOU WILL EVER PLAY. YOU WILL REMEMBER SHE STARTED AS THE GREATEST COURTESAN OF HER TIME WITH KINGS, PRINCES AND EMPERORS AT HER FEET AND FINISHED LIKE THAIS WITH THE DIVINE LIGHT IN HER EYES AND A GREATER THAN HUMAN LOVE IN HER HEART."

DeMille worked himself into a feverish selling rapture that sounds a lot like John Barrymore in *Twentieth Century*: "AS AN HISTORICAL AND DRAMATIC POSSIBILITY FOR YOU I BELIEVE IT EXCEEDS ANY WOMAN'S PART IN MOTION PICTURES TO DATE. . . . IT IS A PART THAT WILL ADD NEW MOMENTUM TO YOUR CAREER AS THE PICTURE WILL BE THE MOST DISCUSSED OF ANY EVER MADE." Swanson passed, deciding instead to play a different prostitute—*Sadie Thompson*.

It was announced that actors cut their salaries in order to be in the picture, with Ernest Torrence playing Peter for $300 a week, and Jacqueline Logan playing Mary Magdalene for $500 a week. This was patently untrue; as documents from the film's production show, Torrence was actually making $2,500 a week, the highest salary on the picture, more even than H. B. Warner's $1,500 a week and Joseph Schildkraut's $1,200 a week. As Judas Iscariot, Theodore Kosloff was making $1,000 a week, and even Julia Faye was on salary for $500 a week.

The young writer-director Tay Garnett watched DeMille choose every face for his movie over a week of extra calls. DeMille would stalk down the ranks and point. "You are a foot soldier. You, over there, are a soldier on horseback." Each day, the same elderly extra appeared. His collar and cuffs were frayed and each day as DeMille passed by, the old man would come to attention with his head held high. Each day DeMille ignored him. Finally, after a week, DeMille stopped before him and asked, "And what, sir, are you? A foot soldier or a soldier on horseback?"

The old man drew himself up to his full height. "I, sir, am an actor *flat on his ass!*"

DeMille grinned and said, "You're good enough for me—as an actor on foot or on horseback, and as long as this picture goes you're working."

The payroll for *King of Kings* was over $23,000 a week, just about what it cost Cecil to make an entire picture a little more than ten years before. Jeanie Macpherson was making $1,000 a week, as was art director Paul Iribe. Head cameraman Peverell Marley was only making $250 a week, and editor Anne Bauchens was on board for $100 a week—a bargain.

The crew list contains a few surprises—Willis O'Brien, later to animate *King Kong*, worked on the miniature crew for a week or so, and Jean de Limur worked as a second assistant director. Edgar Ulmer, who always said he worked on the picture, appears nowhere on the crew list.

The picture also introduced people who would work for DeMille for the rest of their lives. A young child actor named Mick Moore, the brother of Pat Moore, played the boy Mark and was still working for DeMille thirty years later, as an assistant director on the 1956 version of *The Ten Commandments*.

★

When DeMille decided to make *The King of Kings*, Jeanie bought him a Bible. Inside the cover she wrote,

> "In the beginning was the word."
> "In Him was life; and the life was the Light of men."
> "To CECIL from JEANIE"

DeMille and Macpherson used this Bible as their template for the script, and the volume is full of their emendations. One is a verse from Timothy, a citation DeMille would return to at the end of his life: "I have fought a good fight, I have finished my course, I have kept the faith."

There are multiple drafts of practically every sequence in the picture, with DeMille himself doing a lot of writing. The cumulative picture drawn from DeMille's biblical and script annotations, as well as his correspondence during this period, indicates that he saw himself as a teacher for a younger generation ignorant of its religious heritage and responsibilities. DeMille's theology drew from both the Old and New Testaments, as well as what, for lack of a better term, could be called a mystical Neoplatonism, which emphasized ideas such as mind=light=God. For DeMille, God was something above and beyond the traditional anthropomorphic conceptions through which men understand Him.

In constructing the script, DeMille stayed close to the Gospels except for one particular. He never believed the biblical account of Judas's betrayal. "Why would a man sell out someone for a mere 30 pieces of silver after he had seen him perform miracles?" he asked, not unreasonably. There had to be something else, something like . . . sex. What if Judas had had or wanted to have Mary Magdalene and was frustrated by Jesus' conversion of her?

That's motivation!

DeMille knew this particular plot point might raise ecclesiastical eyebrows, so he had researchers scour the literature for ammunition. They found similar ideas in *Mary Magdalene*, a play by Maurice Maeterlinck, in a couple of obscure poems, and *Judas Iscariot*, a novel by Leonid Andreyev, who wrote *He Who Gets Slapped*. Good enough!

Shortly before production began, he wrote Bruce Barton, one of the production's advisors, asking for suggestions about deletions. "It appears to me that we have 17 reels of picture . . . and I would like to get it as close to 12 reels as possible." Barton was clearly worried about the opening with Mary Magdalene: "Couldn't Mary's costume and her movements in the first scene be planned in such a way as to subordinate the sex suggestion as much as possible? Mary, if she was as successful at her trade as we show her, probably insisted on a good deal of respect from her admirers in public."

More usefully, Barton suggested that DeMille cast some of the disciples with younger actors: "This was largely a movement of young men. Jesus was only 29 or 30. . . . All the disciples were presumably under 50, and most of them probably in their thirties. Old men and middle aged men do not ordinarily go off after new teachers or ideas."

The final script for *The King of Kings* was a Homeric 366 pages long. It was similar to most of Cecil's scripts from the mid-1920s in that it carried his handwritten notes and interpolations on nearly every page, usually specifics about performance rather than staging. DeMille also made a series of notes for shots, or dramatic moments that could be integrated into the movie:

> Pilate writing the sign—THIS IS THE KING OF THE JEWS. . . .
>
> Drop of blood falling on the hands of the MAGDALEN—or someone else possibly—and the reception of it. . . .
>
> God's message has been given and God's messenger has been slain. . . .
>
> Blind man as a character, is healed by the Christ, and when seeing the crucifixion says—IT WERE BETTER THAT I HAD STAYED BLIND THAN BE GIVEN SIGHT TO SEE MY GOD CRUCIFIED.
>
> Handle mob with soft focus. Principals clear. . . .
>
> Sidney Olcott offers advice on Palestine.

The unforgettable introduction of Jesus as seen through the returning sight of a blind child was also outlined by DeMille: "Through the darkness comes great rays of light and in the light an indistinct figure of the CHRIST is seen, then the rays leave and as they do, the figure shapes itself into the face of CHRIST, looking with love and pity upon the blind girl. She SEES, falls at his feet, kissing the hem of his garment . . ." DeMille ties healing to the spiritual sight that characterizes faith; the audience sees Christ at the same time as the formerly blind girl.

DeMille had a staff of twelve researchers plowing through documentation on the period, and the pressures of producing an accurate biblical production sometimes nudged people into violating biblical precepts. Head researcher Bessie McGaffey wrote DeMille on July 27, less than a month before the start of production, "According to the Catholic Encyclopedia Vol. 4 and Kitto's Encyclopedia Volume 1 the Crown of Thorns was a branch of the bush *Zizyphus Spina Christi* which is noted for its long thorns. Mr. Wright, the florist, obtained two branches which I am now giving to you. He obtained it from a bush growing on a vacant lot on the corner of Broadway and Sapphire Street, Redondo Beach. . . . Would suggest that we go down and steal this bush at once."

DeMille was worried about money even before he started shooting. On August 17, he told Paul Iribe to "make the carpenter shop location right near or the same as the feeding of the FIVE THOUSAND—so as to save having to transport the people to two places." A couple of weeks later, he told Iribe to "utilize the miniature backing used on the Mary of Magdala set, which can be added to and made to be the City of Jerusalem for the background shooting away from the cross on Calvary."

For some years, Cecil had adopted the practice of telling the story of the film he was about to make to his cast and crew a day or two before shooting began—not a script reading per se, but rather a narration of the story with the emphases that DeMille believed were vital, with some idea of the staging. DeMille always had these sessions transcribed by professional court stenographers in case someone offered interesting suggestions.

On Monday, August 23, the day before production began, DeMille assembled everybody at his house and, for the next six and a half hours, told them the story. (There was a break for lunch.) He began by announcing that a recent poll of nine thousand college students showed that 16 percent did not know where Christ was born, 17 percent did not know of the Sermon on the Mount, 65 percent did not know the Golden Rule, and so forth.

"It is this class that we have to combat and to interest, this class that does not know what it is all about," DeMille told his people. "We must interest this class as well as to satisfy them and hold them interested in the story. We must interest this class and hold them, as well as the other class, born with a Bible in their hand, who will criticize and hurl curses if we change an 'if' or fail to dot an 'i.'"

"We have to protect all classes of people, especially the Jew. The purpose of the story is to treat all classes fairly and particularly the Jew, because the Jew is put in the most unfortunate place of any race in the Bible because it was not really a matter of the Jew having persecuted Jesus, it was Rome—Rome with her politics and graft. . . . The Jews are a very great race, a very sensitive race and we have no desire to hurt them, nor do we desire to hurt anyone."

The transcript provides insight into DeMille's theology, not to mention his psychology. He was insistent about the responsibility he was taking on: "The visual impression of Jesus is going to be planted in the minds of people by the man who plays Jesus in this picture, as the impression will likewise be made of the men who plotted against Him and destroyed Him."

He was equally insistent that the lessons of Jesus derive from dramatic situations. "It is said not as a platitude, but as a speech that has something to do with the lives of the people. . . . Let me get over clearly to you now, so there will be no misunderstanding, this is not a 'Man of Sorrows.' This is not a play of sorrows. It is the greatest love story ever told. It is a great and beautiful thought. Nobody is going around with their arms folded on their breast and rolling their eyes toward an imaginary heaven as though they had had a breakfast that had disagreed with them. Nobody is going to look holy."

The great Temple set is described by DeMille: "Imagine the confusion of Wall Street and Broadway, in New York. Many of you have been there. If not, imagine the crowds down here at Seventh and Broadway." He describes the atmosphere of Gethsemane as "a beautiful garden in the moonlight, clouds passing over the face of the moon and all that."

When DeMille gets to the Last Supper, he tells people to "get Leonardo Da Vinci out of your mind. It is a group of men . . . loaded with tragedy." Sometimes he captures apocalyptic images nowhere to be found in the film itself—to the film's loss. As Christ dies, and the earth begins to shake, "the graves are opened. The dead have appeared and it is a terrible scene." Other times he admits that he hasn't figured out the staging. When the risen Christ appears to his disciples, "Jesus looks at [Thomas] steadily for a moment and then comes His lovely scene with Peter. The finish I don't know as yet."

At the end, "This figure of Jesus grows greater and greater and greater . . . and the skyline of Judea and the outline of the people at His Feet grows dimmer and dimmer. As the figure grows larger, then through the skyline of Judea comes the hazy outline of the steel mills of Pittsburgh, the Eiffel Tower of Paris, the Washington [Square] arch, the skyline of London, the skyline of New York, of Paris . . . we see the Taj Mahal of India. We see a great bronze Buddha against a background of a huge Chinese pagoda. We see a suggestion of the modern world and, above it all, this great figure, with His arms outstretched embracing it. He has not moved. His arms have been outstretched since they were outstretched to the ancient world, and as it all starts to fade and grows dimmer and dimmer, through it all, in great letters we read the words, 'Lo, I am with thee always.'

"Now, do you think an audience will like that picture?"

DeMille asked for opinions about what worked and what didn't. "Were any of you bored at any time . . . let's get the cold Russian view of it. Theodore [Kosloff] were you bored?"

Lenore Coffee said that she missed the entry into Jerusalem, and DeMille said it was left out "with malice aforethought. That is one thing that I have against Jesus Christ, from the standpoint of moving pictures. He did something we cannot show on the screen, the picture of [a] heroic conquerer entering a city on a donkey."

Ernest Torrence said he didn't like showing the modern world at the end of the picture. William deMille agreed. Someone else said that if it wasn't done very well, "it is going to look like the wrapper of a package of soap."

Mainly, Cecil was worried about length. Several people missed the raising of Lazarus and DeMille responded by saying, "We have a sequence worked out for that, but unless we show the picture at three different theaters, or on three consecutive nights, I don't know how we can put that in, because we have already got about 36 reels . . . my particular interest is in taking out, rather than putting in. Bill, how do you feel about the feeding of the five thousand?"

William deMille said he'd like to lose that scene. In addition, there was too much of Caiaphas and Pilate after the Crucifixion. With unassailable logic, Bill pointed out the danger of an anticlimax after the Crucifixion. Bill also thought the Resurrection needed to be more heavily planted.

"There is that point that always used to bother me in reading the scriptures," mused Cecil. "I said to myself a hundred times, 'Well, maybe the disciples did steal Him away.' . . . I think that is a point many people have thought about."

Bill responded by saying, "That is a point some people believe and some people don't believe. I don't think I would try to prove it. They are not going to believe it anyway just because they see it on the screen."

"Yes, they are," shot back Cecil. "If you printed 75 million Bibles, their idea of the life of Jesus Christ is going to be formed by what we give them. This next generation will get its idea of Jesus Christ from this picture."

There it was, a boldfaced—and probably quite correct—assertion. It wasn't just that DeMille believed in himself, although of course he did. It was that he believed in the power of movies, in the way they colonize the audience's subconscious. To him, that belief was both a weighty responsibility and a hole card in the poker game of show business.

DeMille ended the session by telling the assembled people that they had to comport themselves with care in their private lives. "If Bill Jones gets pinched for

speeding, that doesn't make particularly good reading, but if Bill Jones, who plays
the part of the Apostle Peter, gets arrested, that is different. It will be the same
with Mary Magdalene. . . . You cannot take the great benefit that you will derive
from this picture, and believe me it will be a very great benefit, not only in your
professional work, but in your whole lives, a very great benefit, I say you cannot
take that without giving something for it. . . . I can only say, at the finish of my
talk, that the work is before us, and that the accomplishment will be well worth it.
I ask for your support. I ask for the support of all of you."

12

Production of *The King of Kings* began on August 24, 1926, and continued until January 8, 1927, using over 3.4 million feet of film. The film was made on a six-days-a-week schedule, and shot in rough script continuity. The location for Galilee and the loaves and fishes sequence was Catalina Island, where an entire village was constructed. DeMille had the idea that the cast and crew should sleep in a little colony of cabins, combining his love of moviemaking with his love of the outdoors. After the first day of shooting, he turned to an assistant and said, "This has been the happiest day of my life."

But not everybody was equally thrilled with the sleeping arrangements. One day they were shooting a scene on the Catalina shore when a luxurious yacht sailed into camera range. DeMille exploded, sending out an assistant to get rid of the yacht. The assistant reported that the yacht was for H. B. Warner; that he would be sleeping on it every night.

"And with whom was this arrangement made?" DeMille inquired in that quiet, low voice that presaged real trouble. Told that the arrangement had been made directly with Warner, DeMille said, "I thought the idea was that we're all to live and eat and sleep here, to stay in the mood of this setting which we took so much time and care to create and to let this atmosphere soak into us. If I thought Mr. Warner needed a yacht, I'd have brought my own. Just who does he think he is?"

"Jesus Christ, sir," piped up one very brave man.

After a thoughtful moment, DeMille said, "That puts me at something of a disadvantage, doesn't it?"

For the rest of the location shoot, DeMille managed to avoid looking at the arrival or departure of Warner's yacht because it spoiled his mood. After a day's shooting on Catalina, the actors and crew would eat dinner, wash the makeup off their faces, change their clothes, and troop into the recreation tent, where there would be readings from Ibsen, or a musical concert or even a Charleston contest, and then everybody would watch the rushes before falling into bed at eleven.

Other scenes were shot on DeMille's Laughlin Park grounds, because of the profusion of olive trees. Richard deMille would remember dryly, "The first time I saw Jesus I was four years old. He was standing in our garden under an olive tree. . . . While Jesus stood for a close-up, grips and prop men rushed about. Off scene, beggars and disciples were sitting on the grass, talking or playing cards, waiting to be called. Bertha and I walked among them on the Mount of Olives. Bertha was my nurse. Father didn't put either of us in the movie."

One day on the set, Micky Moore was late and DeMille began a long oration about time being money, the irresponsibility of youth, etc. When Moore showed up, his sister told DeMille that the only reason he was late was because of a mix-up about his wig. DeMille apologized to the entire company, saying the fault was that of the assistant who lost the wig, not Moore's.

Throughout the production, DeMille was frantically trying to keep the studio, and himself, afloat. On September 15, he wrote to Neil McCarthy, "I have been following your wires closely but have been working eighteen and twenty hours a day on King of Kings therefore do not take my not answering wires as lack of interest. Will you see Howard Ingels regarding fifty thousand common stock in Pacific Northwest theaters? . . . Do you consider the future financing of company definitely assured sufficiently to warrant my taking up this subscription?"

Production was complicated by a major blowup between DeMille and Paul Iribe, after which the director ordered Mitch Leisen to take over. It was Leisen who devised a way for H. B. Warner to hang on the Cross for the two weeks necessary to shoot the Crucifixion sequence. He made casts of Warner's hands, and the casts were bolted to the cross, with blood modeled down the wrists. The casts had leather pads built into the back; Warner would insert his hands into the casts and grasp the leather so that he could hang convincingly for several minutes at a time. Besides that, a bicycle seat was mounted on the Cross so that Warner's weight would be supported yet another way.

Although DeMille was clearly concerned about money, he didn't cut corners and the proprieties were observed. A curtain was dropped in front of the Golgotha set whenever Warner had to get on or off the Cross. There was no smoking, and bad language was discouraged. "Whenever DeMille started to get apoplectic about something," remembered Mitch Leisen, "I would say very quietly, 'There's a bishop right behind you.' That was my one revenge for all the hell I got from him most of the time." Poor H. B. Warner hung on the Cross for fourteen days, followed by three days of shooting on the Resurrection, followed by two days of shooting on the Ascension.

Warner's drinking problem was reactivated by the pressure. Monte Westmore was in charge of Warner's makeup, and when the actor would show up in the morning still weaving, Westmore would make him drink cod liver oil. After vomiting, Warner would be shaken but sober. Westmore continued this rough treatment for several weeks until Warner decided sobriety was preferable to cod liver oil.

Sally Rand, who would become famous for her Fan Dance in the 1933 Chicago World's Fair, played one of Mary Magdalene's slaves. Rand and Warner began an affair, which infuriated DeMille. Rand would tell friends about the day when DeMille spotted her and Warner coming to the set together. DeMille grabbed his ever-present microphone and boomed out, "Miss Rand! Leave my Jesus Christ alone! If you must screw someone, screw Pontius Pilate!"

Visiting the production was a young Jesuit from St. Louis named Daniel Lord, who would become a friend of DeMille's and an advisor on the film. Lord collapsed under the onslaught of DeMille's charm, but always managed to maintain an overall sense of objectivity about the man.

In his memoirs, Lord described DeMille as "a strange and fascinating blend of absolute monarch and charming gentleman, of excellent host and exacting taskmaster, of ruthless drive on the set and complete letdown the moment that the day's shooting had come to an end; a Renaissance prince who had the instincts of a Barnum and a magnified Belasco; frankly in love with hokum (which he liked to discuss and reduce to terms of understandable basic emotion)."

The plot invention of Judas's love affair with Mary Magdalene induced something approaching physical pain in Lord, but DeMille was adamant; he told Lord that the audience had to be won over; that they had to have a sense of luxury and beauty. "If they fall in love with Magdalene, then when she leaps into her chariot and says, 'I go to find a Carpenter,' they will go along," said DeMille.

Actually, the title uttered by the Magdalene, one of the juiciest in all of silent films, is "Go fetch my richest perfumes! Harness my zebras—gift of the Nubian king! This carpenter shall learn that He cannot hold a man from Mary Magdalene!" It is only after another character tells the Magdalene that he has observed this man healing the blind that she says, "I have blinded more men than He hath ever healed. . . . We go to call upon a carpenter!" Soon, Jesus casts out her demons: the Seven Deadly Sins.

One evening DeMille was watching rushes with Father Daniel Lord when DeMille reached over and touched Lord's hand. "He *is* great, isn't he?"

"Warner?" asked the priest.

"Jesus. He's great."

Lenore Coffee was working on the titles for the picture and noticed that there was a small miniature painting on DeMille's desk. It was of the head of Christ with the crown of thorns pressing down, an image that was in DeMille's line of vision and nobody else's. She realized that he kept the picture in front of him so that he could never forget the pain of the man on the Cross. "He was . . . a deeply religious man," she remembered.

One day Coffee found out she was pregnant. She went down to the set to tell

DeMille she had "family news." He took both her hands and said, "Not really, Lenore? Not really! Oh, I am so pleased." He took her off to the side where they sat on a big pile of rugs. "Now you're going to learn the real meaning of the word 'unselfishness.' You're going to learn what it means to care more for someone else than you do for yourself—than you do even for your own life." He told her to be sure not to overdo anything; she could work at home anytime she wanted, etc. "I've never been spoken to so kindly, so warmly, in all my life," remembered Coffee.

By September 4, Jeanie Macpherson was worried about the length of the script vs. the finished picture, and she was also worried about money. She sent a memo to DeMille specifying sequences that she thought could be cut, among them the Beatitudes, excerpts of the Sermon on the Mount, a scene between Caiaphas and Pilate, another between Caiaphas and some Roman soldiers, a sequence between Mary and the disciples after the Resurrection, and the scene where Jesus's body is put in Joseph's tomb ("This could be done with title—and everything should be done to speed up the action of story AFTER crucifixion," wrote Macpherson.)

DeMille wrote "CUT" over the scene depicting the installing of Jesus in the tomb, noted about the scene between Mary and the disciples that "this sequence is very important," and mused "could cut" about the scene between Caiaphas and Pilate. Throughout the production, noted Daniel Lord, Macpherson worked sixteen-hour days. "She had no time for anything—friendship, correspondence, hobbies or care of her health."

Daniel Lord found the "congress of nations" that assembled around such a vast undertaking fascinating. "Great character actors and actresses from Vienna and Prague and Budapest; artists from Paris and Berlin; musicians trained to interpret the masterpieces of the greatest composers." While Lord was on the set, he said Mass daily and heard confession sitting on piles of lumber.

Although DeMille was entitled to a royalty of 1.25 percent of the gross of the program pictures he was supervising, he knew that he wouldn't be able to give any more than nominal supervision to other pictures while engaged in *The King of Kings*. DeMille installed an extensive supervisor system at Producers Distributing Corp., with tough pros like screenwriter C. Gardner Sullivan riding herd on the scripts and production plans of directors such as William K. Howard, Rupert Julian, and Donald Crisp.

He was finding out that the pleasures of running a movie studio were greatly overrated. When Leatrice Joy took it upon herself to get a particularly severe haircut, DeMille was not pleased. For that matter, neither was Adrian. When Joy had a wedding scene in a picture called *Vanity*, Adrian said it was going to look as if two boys were getting married. He had to design a special headdress for Joy so that she would look appropriately feminine.

Throughout the production of *The King of Kings,* the studio was teetering. The pictures the studio was making weren't providing sufficient cash flow, yet DeMille continued to resist New York's demands for budget cuts. He fired off a message to F. C. Munroe, the president of PDC: "I can assure you no one is more interested in profits than I am but I have firm conviction there is only one way in which to get profits and that is by making good pictures. I have been through . . . years of this discussion without a losing year to my organization and with the policy of increasing the budget when I believed I had a big piece of property. There would have been no *Ten Commandments, Covered Wagon, Big Parade, Stella Dallas, Sea Beast, Behind the Front* and a dozen others I might name had a policy of sticking to a budget been adhered to when the producer saw he had a big subject and a big production in the making."

By November, capital investment had dried up and Jeremiah Milbank was keeping the studio going single-handedly. DeMille's overhead was considerable—his highest paid actor was Rod La Rocque, at $3,500 a week, but most actors were earning somewhere between $750 a week on the high end (William Boyd, Robert Armstrong, Jacqueline Logan) and $350 a week on the low end (George Duryea, a handsome juvenile who would become a cowboy star in the 1930s under the name Tom Keene, was only pulling down $125 a week).

The increasingly strapped PDC began discussing a merger with Pathé, which had a lot of assets, a production policy that focused on serials, and zero prestige. DeMille was furious. "It would be . . . impossible for my name to be attached to this type of product," he charged. On November 2, he wrote Neil McCarthy that "Pathé has stood for the cheapest brand of motion pictures for so long and the name DeMille has stood for the best brand it would be a little like combining Tiffany and Woolworth. Possibly DeMille Metropolitan Pathe might be better name. Metropolitan is a good and dignified name and stands more or less as a buffer between DeMille and Pathe. To what extent if any would the name DeMille be used in selling a new stock issue and if you all decide on the use of my name a new financing of the company must be very firmly fixed before my name is attached to it as there must be no possibility of anything but a fourteen carat proposition if it carries my name."

Six days later, his position had hardened. He wired on November 8:

I CANNOT SEE THAT PATHE WOULD BRING ANYTHING OF VALUE TO THE MERGER EXCEPTING A NAME WHICH STANDS FOR CHEAP PICTURES AND SEVEN HUNDRED THOUSAND CASH.

The possibility that the company's collapse could take down *The King of Kings* made him frantic. That same day, he suggested to Neil McCarthy that perhaps Lasky and Zukor would take over the picture and reimburse Milbank, with DeMille taking his money off the back end, as a percentage of the gross.

WILL YOU ADVISE ME IN WHAT MANNER LEGALLY I COULD WITHDRAW FROM PRES-
ENT SITUATION RETAINING THE ASSETS OF DEMILLE PICTURES CORPORATION
INCLUDING KING OF KINGS SHOULD WE SUCCEED IN MAKING SATISFACTORY AR-
RANGEMENTS WITH SOME OTHER ORGANIZATION.

On November 12, he sent a long wire to McCarthy arguing against a merger
with Pathé, which he referred to as "Pathetic". "FROM YOUR WIRES WE UNDERSTAND
THE FOLLOWING FACTS: NEW COMPANY WOULD START WITH FOLLOWING OBLIGATIONS:
PRESENT PATHETIC BONDS ONE MILLION, INTEREST EIGHTY THOUSAND; NEW DEBENTURES
FIVE MILLIONS, INTEREST FOUR HUNDRED THOUSAND; NEW COMMERCIAL LOANS TWO MIL-
LIONS, INTEREST ONE HUNDRED SIXTY THOUSAND; PRESENT PATHETIC PREFERRED ONE MIL-
LION, INTEREST EIGHTY THOUSAND; NEW CLASS A STOCK TWO HUNDRED FIFTY THOUSAND
SHARES, INTEREST ONE MILLION; CAPITAL LOANS SIX MILLIONS, INTEREST NINE HUNDRED
THOUSAND; KELLY'S NOTES ONE MILLION THREE HUNDRED THOUSAND, INTEREST EIGHTY FIVE
THOUSAND. MAKING IN ALL NEARLY THIRTY MILLION LIABILITIES WITHOUT ANY PROVISION
FOR REPAYING MY TWO HUNDRED THOUSAND CASH AND ANNUAL FIXED CHARGES OF OVER
TWO MILLION SEVEN HUNDRED. FURTHER UNDERSTAND THAT PATHETIC NET EARNINGS ESTI-
MATED EIGHT HUNDRED FIFTY THOUSAND PLUS NET EARNINGS FROM PDC SALES SEVEN HUN-
DRED THOUSAND MAKING TOTAL NET EARNINGS ONE MILLION SIX HUNDRED THOUSAND AND
LEAVING OVER ONE MILLION ONE HUNDRED THOUSAND TO BE EARNED BY SPECIALS BEFORE
THERE WOULD BE ANYTHING FOR COMMON STOCK. IS ABOVE CORRECT? . . ." DeMille went
on to point out that Pathé's earnings would be even less in the future because they
had lost Hal Roach's popular short comedies to MGM.

Ultimately, there was nothing to be done; DeMille had lashed himself to a
vessel that was heading for the rocks. He had to content himself with making the
best picture possible.

★

Katherine deMille remembered being on the set of *The King of Kings* on Christmas
Eve 1926. They were shooting the Crucifixion sequence, and the company didn't
finish until late—8:30 or 9 P.M. DeMille called a wrap, and people began moving
toward their dressing rooms so they could go home. And then DeMille's voice
rang out over the loudspeaker system.

"Ladies and gentlemen, if you'd stop for just a moment. I would like you
all to take five minutes—five minutes—for you to just think about what you have
seen tonight—and to remember that what we've seen tonight is the filming of
something that truly happened. I want you to think what it has meant to you.
I'd like you to take a few minutes of quiet. I've asked the orchestra to play some
music."

The studio orchestra began Bach's Christmas Oratorio. Many in the crowd
wept. Some doves were released, circled three times, and landed on the three

crosses. "Some got on their knees facing the cross," remembered Katherine. "In a few minutes Cecil said, 'Thank you ladies and gentlemen. Let's go home to our families, have a wonderful Christmas.' " Everyone streamed out in silence.

The doves landing on the crosses was not the only strange event that took place during production. For the final shot of the Last Supper sequence, the camera was to fade out on a shot of the Holy Grail. But one of the production's doves got loose and hopped onto the table as Pev Marley was grinding the camera. Marley told DeMille he would stop, but DeMille told him to keep shooting. The dove hopped around a bit, then settled beneath the Grail, as if seeking shelter. Telling his family about it later, DeMille said, "If I'd trained birds and tried to get it, it would never have happened. I think this picture is blessed."

An interesting memo that stands as a rebuke to the general theory that DeMille wanted only yes-men around him came in from studio general manager William Sistrom after a viewing of the rough cut. Among other things, Sistrom wrote DeMille that "The colors in the first sequence are hard. . . . There is too much film between the tremendous desire to see Jesus, which the girl's search for him arouses, and actually seeing him. . . . I believe a sequence should come out [because] I believe that the harm done by taking out any one of the sequences which it is possible to leave out will be less than the harm done by having the picture over-length. The Olive Grove or the Denial by Peter will hurt the picture least of all, in my opinion. My choice would be the Denial. . . . Please take out the kid riding on the cross . . . it shocks me when I see it and hurts when I think of it."

In March 1927, the long-dreaded merger took place: Pathé, Producers Distributing Corporation, Keith-Albee, and the Orpheum Circuit. DeMille's independence had lasted only slightly more than two years, and PDC-Pathé was officially interlocked with Keith-Albee and Orpheum in a spectacularly ungainly conglomeration of competing interests and business philosophies.

Publicly, everybody tried to put the best possible face on the hideous child; the trade papers and fan magazines featured full-page ads with pictures of the deluxe Keith-Albee-Orpheum theaters (the Palace in Cleveland, the Hill Street in Los Angeles) that were now playing the "DeMille-Metropolitan Pictures" being masterminded by Cecil B. DeMille, whose "very name . . . stands for pictures that realize the dreams of mankind. . . . His very name has come to have a magic meaning."

A month before The King of Kings was released, Adela Rogers St. Johns wrote about the film for Photoplay magazine:

It is a strangely impersonal picture, from the standpoint of actors and director. I do not know any more personal man in the motion picture industry than Cecil DeMille. He has always left his stamp all over everything he has touched. But this is different. . . .

Cecil DeMille is trying to recreate the time, the surroundings, the people, the life, and the Man. He is following the gospel narratives simply and exactly. . . . I think what he is trying above everything else to do is to show Jesus as a man, like you, like me, like our neighbors, faced with the same problem, living the same kind of life, meeting the same kind of people, faced by the same temptations.

I think that he understands that the keynote of Jesus' ministry was joy, and that the keynote of his character was strength. . . . I think he wants to make every man and woman who goes in there to see that picture feel inspired to go out and "do likewise."

It was an unusually intelligent analysis from a magazine that often threw sharp elbows at DeMille, and would continue to. (In the same issue as St. Johns's story was a gratuitous one-liner that spun off the currently popular book by Bruce Barton that referred to DeMille as "The Man Nobody No's.")

The New York premiere of *The King of Kings* took place in New York at the Gaiety Theatre on April 19. The Gaiety had to be remodeled for the occasion. An orchestra pit was built to hold thirty-six musicians, who were augmented by a backstage chorus. Fifty-two large photographs of the cast and crucial scenes from the picture were displayed in the front of the theater, and the theater itself was outfitted with one of the largest electric signs of the era, covering most of the enormous facade. DeMille brought Constance, Cecilia, Jeanie Macpherson, Anne Bauchens, and Bill Sistrom with him to New York.

The reviews were spectacular. The *New York Times* called it "The most impressive of all motion pictures," while *Variety* said that the picture was "tremendous in its lesson, in the daring of its picturization for a commercial theater, and tremendous in its biggest scene, the crucifixion of Christ." Robert Sherwood, who had lambasted DeMille for years, wrote in *Life* magazine that the film was "moving, absorbing, inspiring and everything else that Mr. DeMille intended it should be. . . . It is a masterpiece." *Photoplay* said that "DeMille has had a variegated career. He has wandered, with an eye to the box office, up bypaths into ladies boudoirs and baths, he has been accused of garishness, bad taste and a hundred and one other faults. He frequently has been false and artificial. . . . *The King of Kings*, however, reveals a shrewd, discerning and skillful technician, a director with a fine sense of drama, and, indeed, a man with an understanding of the spiritual."

The ads for the Hollywood premiere at the brand-new Grauman's Chinese left little doubt that the occasion would be impressive: "Tonight the eyes of the world are focused on Hollywood's $5,000,000 event. . . . Every world famous celebrity will be there. Mr. Fred Niblo will introduce Mr. David Wark Griffith master of ceremonies, who will present Hon. Will H. Hays, and Miss Mary Pickford will have the honor of pressing the jade button that will start the premiere performance."

The $5 million event was the result of taking $2 million as the cost of the theater and $3 million as the cost of the movie—both figures grossly exaggerated. Hollywood Boulevard between Highland and La Brea was turned into a one-way street, with traffic moving in a westerly direction only. Fifty thousand people jammed Hollywood Boulevard hoping to catch a glimpse of some of the celebrities.

Sid Grauman pulled out all the stops; the prologue, entitled "Glories of the Scriptures," depicted Bible episodes in five different locales, in six different tableaux with a lot of chorale work, and had a cast of over one hundred people. The intention was to dramatize the backstory of Christ: the manger, the coming of the Three Wise Men, the flight into Egypt, all contriving to seamlessly segue into the main title of the DeMille film.

By the time *The King of Kings* actually began, it was after 11 P.M.; by the time it was over, it was almost two in the morning. The audience—those who were left—were exhausted but pleased. DeMille was furious about the endless prologue, but when it became clear that the film was going to be an enormous critical success, he forgave Grauman for his excesses. Among the audience at Grauman's Chinese was a twelve-year-old druggist's son named Gregory Peck, who recalled the wonder and romance of the presentation: "The ushers were dressed in Chinese Mandarin garb, the carpets were a foot thick, the air was perfumed with . . . incense."

D. W. Griffith wired Cecil:

I WANT TO CONGRATULATE YOU ON YOUR MARVELOUS ACHIEVEMENT IN PRODUC-
ING *THE KING OF KINGS*. IT IS NOT ONLY AN EXQUISITELY BEAUTIFUL PRODUCTION
BUT THE VALUE TO THE MOTION PICTURE INDUSTRY ON THE WHOLE IS SO ENOR-
MOUS THAT I THINK IT IS IMPOSSIBLE TO CALCULATE.

Rabbi Edgar Magnin wired DeMille:

KNEW *THE KING OF KINGS* WOULD BE A SUCCESS. HEARTY CONGRATULATIONS TO
YOU AND MISS MACPHERSON. I BELIEVE THIS PICTURE WILL EXERCISE A SPIRITUAL
AND WHOLESOME EFFECT UPON ALL WHO WILL HAVE THE PRIVILEGE OF WITNESS-
ING IT.

Shortly after the premiere, Dorothy Cummings, who played Mary, announced that she was getting a divorce, and wrote DeMille a long explanatory letter. In the margins, DeMille scribbled a scathing reply that revealed an unfortunate identification with his main character: "My dear Miss Cummings, I am sure Judas had some similar excellent excuse."

Father Daniel Lord saw the picture and wrote DeMille that other Jesuits had told him they also disliked the opening Mary Magdalene episode. DeMille wrote him back that after watching the film with audiences in both Los Angeles and

New York he felt justified. "Everyone in the audience has come with a set idea that they are going to see something very Biblical and are in for a sanctimonious evening; and . . . the majority feel that no one can put a likeness of the Master on the screen that will satisfy everyone; and there are unquestionably many in the audience who have come to scoff—non-believers and wise-crackers.

"The first sequence gives everyone in the audience—no matter what their preconceived idea—a surprise. They forget the viewpoint with which they arrived at the theater—their idea of a religious play is all upset—and then as we gradually work into the appearance of the Christ, they are surprised into a satisfactory mental attitude toward the Figure as we presented it."

The picture ran for thirty-five weeks at the Gaiety in New York, twenty-four weeks at Grauman's Chinese in Hollywood. *The King of Kings* was a triumphant vindication for DeMille. Richard deMille asserted that *The King of Kings* would always be DeMille's favorite of his own movies—more than an important film, rather a precious accomplishment and a promise kept: "the climax of his life."

★

Cecil had always known that there was a potential for protests in replicating the Old Testament portrayal of Jews. As was indicated by his acknowledgment during the telling of the story to the cast and crew before beginning the production, he strove to ameliorate any charges of anti-Semitism. DeMille dropped the inflammatory line from Matthew 27:25: ("His blood be on us, and on our children") and inserted a (noncanonical) title for Caiaphas the High Priest during the earthquake that follows the Crucifixion: "Lord God Jehovah! Visit not Thy wrath on Thy people Israel—I alone am guilty."

On the other hand, he had cast the Jewish Rudolph and Joseph Schildkraut, father and son, as the story's heavies—Caiaphas and Judas, respectively—an action that, had he given the matter any sustained thought, certainly invited a strong reaction.

There was an immediate uproar from the Jewish community about the infamous Blood Libel and perceived anti-Semitism. The *Jewish Tribune* printed a scathing story with a subhead: "DeMille Welcomes the Jewish Protests as Publicity Stunt to Save His Film from Financial Ruin."

> He brooks no argument, no contradictions, no independence, no apologies reflecting upon him. . . . Cecil is the real son of his mother . . . an English Jewess who embraced the Christian faith early in her life. . . . Mrs. DeMille did not consider herself a Jewess, but Cecil even now likes to repeat to every handy listener how proud he is of having had a Jewish mother. On his lot, while filming *The King of Kings*, he praised those of the Jewish actors and actresses who admitted their Jewish origin and deplored the conduct of others who masqueraded as French, Russians and

what-not—never forgetting to add that he himself is not ashamed of his dear late Jewish mother. . . .

DeMille considers it of great commercial and strategic importance to boast of the Jewish blood in his veins. It is as if he were naively, yet sincerely, saying to the Jewish press and pulpit which accuse him of the betrayal of the Jewish race, "Can a man who is proud of his Jewish origins betray the Jewish race?"

The article went on to pair DeMille with Henry Ford as a notorious public anti-Semite, and claimed that the film had been a financial failure until the protests broke out, at which point, "Mr. DeMille's publicity men were very much pleased."

The *Jewish Tribune* tried to have it both ways: castigating DeMille for freely acknowledging his Jewish heritage, when they would have undoubtedly castigated him even more had he avoided the matter, then bewailing the way the Jewish media had risen to take the director's bait even as the article itself was part of the protests.

Rabbi Stephen Wise added to the protests and proclaimed that "If any Jew with the stature of a man, I do not mean a Jewish person on the payroll of the producer, but if any Jew with the stature of a man had been in Hollywood when this film was made it could not have been done as it was."

Wise was obviously referring to Rabbi Edgar Magnin, the leader of the largest temple in Los Angeles, and a friend of DeMille's. Wise went on to wonder what the Catholic Church would do if a movie company depicted Torquemada fingering his rosary beads as men, women, and children were cavalierly tossed into the flames. He called *The King of Kings* "negligible" and asserted that "there are going to be no pogroms in America by instigation of Henry Ford or at the suggestion of one of the great artists of Hollywood today. I do not believe that the picture is curable. The only way to mend it is to end it. . . . The blood of Jews will be upon the heads of the owners of this picture."

DeMille was bewildered by this criticism. From the beginning, he had vacillated about how to handle the Blood Libel. In September 1926, while the picture was being made, an executive wrote DeMille about how to get around the Bible's anti-Semitism by blaming the Romans "having overthrown the power of the Jews and practically ruling Jerusalem with their armies on the outskirts of the city."

On October 7, from the set of Herod's Temple, DeMille replied that it was an interesting suggestion but he thought it represented too great a departure from the Scriptures. Better if the emphasis was placed on "one man, Caiaphas. This particular high-up priest had worked the system of Temple graft up to a point where it was tremendously productive, and he had become enormously wealthy through it. He saw in the teachings and attitude of Christ, climaxed by the throwing of the moneychangers out of the Temple, the end of his power and destruction of his source of great wealth. . . . You can see that the dramatic possibilities of this are very great, that the Jews as a race are protected, as Caiaphas, at the rending of the Temple Veil, implores Jehovah not to visit His wrath upon the people, as he alone is to blame."

In the film, Caiaphas is introduced as "The Roman appointee Caiaphas, the High Priest, who cared more for Revenue than for Religion—and saw in Jesus a menace to his rich profits from the Temple." In another title, the center of Caiaphas's power is characterized as "The Temple . . . to the faithful of Israel, the dwelling place of Jehovah. But to the High Priest, Caiaphas, a corrupt and profitable marketplace." As a profusion of biblical scholars have noted, DeMille is repeating the medieval and Reformation caricature of the greedy, cynical Jew.

But DeMille goes out of his way to absolve the general Jewish population of any moral responsibility. When Pilate asks, "Shall I crucify your king?" it is not the crowd—as in John 19:15—but Caiaphas who replies "We have no king but Caesar," reconfiguring the blame solely upon the high priest, scapegoating a single Jew rather than an entire people. As Adele Reinhartz notes in her excellent *Jesus of Hollywood*, DeMille's portrait of Caiaphas is consonant with 1920s America, during which a modified anti-Semitism was "an almost respectable response to waves of Eastern European immigration and to labor unrest in which many Jewish workers were involved, a response fed by well-established anti-Semitic caricature."

As the picture continued to play, protests heated up. On September 28, Rabbi Magnin wrote DeMille of the pressure that was being brought to bear, and said that "an open rupture [between the Anti-Defamation League] and you could do absolutely no good to either and would likely result in harm to both. I feel that you are too fine a gentleman and that your reputation as a lover of humanity is too great to permit even the accusation on the part of thousands of people that you have done harm either willfully or innocently. . . .

"My own suggestion would be . . . both in your interest and in the interest of the cause of the Jews of the world to strike out the words 'Crucify Him' entirely. It would appear to me the action in itself is descriptive enough without the title. . . . Please give this your most careful and thoughtful consideration in the next few days and if you can possibly do so, accede to the request of the League."

Throughout the uproar, DeMille was very concerned, at one point wiring Will Hays for a transcript of a speech by Rabbi Wise. "Magnin is anxious for me to make a denial that he endorsed the picture and to make a statement that he was in frequent consultation with me during the filming and that he has the interests of his people at heart at all times. He will then make a statement to the effect that I went out of my way to see that the Jewish people were protected in the telling of the story. . . . Magnin is Okay. He realizes that Wise [is] merely seeking publicity rather than facts."

Will Hays wired DeMille, "There is nothing for either you or Magnin to do at this particular moment until we plan exactly what is to be done finally. Conferences are being held quietly today by important Protestants and also we are in touch with officers of the Bnai Brith who regret the incident very much."

DeMille prepared a statement defending his film, annotating and correcting the typescript himself:

> Jesus writes in Hebrew and is depicted as a Jew.
>
> The Roman governor sentenced Jesus and not the Jews.
>
> The entire blame for any Jewish conspiracy to bring about the crucifixion is placed upon one man, Caiaphas.
>
> The words, His blood be upon us and our children, which undoubtedly would have been the main bone of contention had they been included and also the trial before the Sanhedrin, were purposely omitted by me, and at the end of the picture, even though the Gospels do not authorize me to do so, I have Caiaphas saying that Caiaphas alone was to blame and not the Jewish people as a whole.
>
> I am positive that those who accuse me of anti-Semitism have neither studied the story of the New Testament nor the picture carefully and in an unbiased way.

Some editorials suggested that the Jews who had taken part in the film—most prominently Rudolph and Joseph Schildkraut—had sold out themselves and their people. Years later, discussing the matter for his autobiography, DeMille remembered that "[The Schildkrauts] blamed me. The old man [Rudolph] never put it in words—he came and took my hand and said, 'I understand what it means but I'm not sorry about it.' Joseph was frightened. Joseph thought his career was through; that he was done. Joseph thought he was licked and that he would never get another job and he had resentment against me, but Joseph always loved me and he could never quite put it bitterly."

By December 21, some suggested cuts were forwarded to Will Hays's office. Among them: "Eliminate all scenes of the lashing of Jesus barring the first. . . . In the scene where a Jew, in answer to the question 'What evil has He done?' shrugs his shoulders and jingles a coin, eliminate the jingling of the coin. . . . In the scene where Pilate washes his hands and puts the responsibility of the crucifixion on Caiaphas, let Caiaphas say, 'I assume the responsibility.' . . . Tone down the crucifixion scene.

"We believe a foreword is necessary and propose the following: 'The scenes of the deathless story portrayed by this picture took place nineteen centuries ago in Palestine. At that time the Jews were no longer an independent people but were under the rule of the Roman Empire."

Many of these changes were indeed made in the reduced general release version of the film, although a foreword similar to that suggested was also included on the road show version. Some subtitles were also changed. For instance, the title introducing Caiaphas in the road show version was "The High Priest CAIAPHAS—who cared more for Revenue than for Religion—and saw in Jesus a menace to his rich profits from the Temple." This was altered to "The High Priest CAIAPHAS—an appointee of the Roman government, and arch-enemy of Jesus. Upon him rests the responsibility for the world's supreme tragedy."

For the general release version, Anne Bauchens suggested taking out all the footage that had been shot on Catalina, and wanted to cut the two sequences with Caiaphas into one: "I will cut that sequence now and we can look at it and see if the difference in the two locations is noticeable." She also suggested a few other, more minor trims and concluded by asking, "Are you willing to let me go ahead and make the smaller cuts and I will carefully save every scrap and then you can run it with me and see if we miss anything?"

The King of Kings was not merely cut—by forty-two minutes—for general release, it was also reedited. The shorter, general release version moves quickly and effortlessly; it's a *Classics Illustrated* version of the Life of Christ. The original road show version is heavier as well as longer, but also carries an authentic moral weight and brooding sense of tragedy. It's one of DeMille's best films, the first of his movies that owes as much to the power and glory of grand opera as it does to cinema.

In either version, *The King of Kings* is absent DeMille's characteristic nervous energy, but its cumulative force derives from his restraint, which, the giddy opening sequence aside, limits him to largely using Scripture for the titles. The primal nature of Christ's miracles, and DeMille's belief in them, compels emotional belief. Despite his own occasional, privately expressed doubts—did the disciples steal Christ's body from the tomb, or did He rise from the dead?—DeMille understands that the power of the story can only be accessed if the miracle of Christ is not merely symbolic, but literal. DeMille was never a man to see any contradiction between sincere religious belief and a dramatic—occasionally flamboyantly dramatic—depiction of it. As the critic Glenn Erickson wrote, *The King of Kings* "is like seeing the forgotten original version of our own beliefs."

The director's eye for theatrical effect was never sharper—Satan is a suave, gliding black-cloaked figure out of Aubrey Beardsley; Pilate broods before an enormous bronze eagle that embodies all the power of Rome.

The film is surprisingly intimate; there are big sets—Pilate's throne room, the Temple, Golgotha—but DeMille doesn't linger on them and he never loses his sense of the story's proper physical scale, which is one of the primary problems with later attempts at the same material.

For DeMille, everything in life stemmed from belief—in God, in America, in DeMille. As he wrote, "I do not believe that a man can be loyal and faithful to any other man if he is not loyal and faithful to his God. And loyalty and faithfulness are now and always will be the most valuable assets of any man in business or professional life."

The film is tasteful—for our violent times probably too tasteful—and manages to get most of the big things right. It's authentically reverent, sometimes too much so. H. B. Warner's Christ may be too much of an icon, and there are times when the film is more of an illustration of the Bible than a dramatization. Jesus is usually seen standing still, which leads to a static quality partly compensated for by DeMille's studied but beautiful compositions, and by the strength and compassion of Warner's acting.

Warner always does less; the keynote of the performance is a calm serenity and sense of compassion. It's no wonder the populace panics in the Temple when Christ finally takes action. At first, he overturns the moneychangers' tables with quiet contempt, but then he warms to his task. The anger of a normally calm man can be terrifying.

With *The King of Kings*, DeMille made *the* cinematic representation of the life of Christ. Three quarters of a century later, various attempts at surpassing it, ranging from the tormented Method actor's Christ (*The Last Temptation of Christ*) to the flagellant's Christ (*The Passion of Christ*) amount only to footnotes.

Neither DeMille nor Milbank made any significant money from *The King of Kings*, signing over almost all of their percentages to make the general release version of the film widely available for perpetuity. DeMille retained only 5 percent of the picture, but the money reliably came in for the rest of his life; in 1949, for instance, he received $5,135.77 for his share. Those profits would be donated to charity and in the service of keeping the film in circulation.

It's doubtful that any silent movie has been seen so widely for so long. Part of the triumph of the film was in just getting it made, but DeMille's movie worked in 1927, and works today, seamlessly embodying all the contradictions in his extraordinary personality—the film is sacred as well as profane, broadly entertaining yet at times a genuinely moving experience.

His determination to make a picture that honored his father's teachings without compromise would cost him money and, indirectly, cost him his studio. But neither DeMille nor Milbank seems to have thought of the picture as a commercial enterprise, even though, given the state of their company, only one of the great commercial triumphs of the era could have saved it. By 1952, *The King of Kings* had grossed $3.4 million against a (probable) cost of $1.2 million, but DeMille never talked about money in relation to the picture. He proudly claimed that there were more prints of it in distribution in 1958 than there had been in 1927.

"It's not what a picture costs that makes any difference," he would say, "but what it's worth that makes a great deal of difference."

★

Because of his unconventional private life, the prevailing critical attitude toward DeMille has traditionally been that he was a cynical hypocrite who used religion as a convenient pretext for his movies.

But a thorough examination of DeMille's papers makes it obvious that he was sincerely, if unconventionally, religious. DeMille committed large portions of the Bible to memory, and assiduously studied primary theological texts. On the other hand, he seldom went to church, and when he did the church was usually empty—he found that the presence of other people tended to get in the way of direct communication.

Likewise, he selected among tenets of various religions rather than subscribing wholeheartedly to any one theology. He was personally offended by the Catholic tenet of Original Sin, saying, "I become very annoyed if someone tells me I was born in sin. I object very much. I don't think my father and mother were committing a sin. If they were, then Jesus was committing a sin by blessing the marriage. Any time you yield to the greatest physical reward that the Lord has provided us with—sexual intercourse—you are sinning? . . . I object to [that idea] very strongly."

In his archives there is a draft of a speech, written in DeMille's own hand, for radio broadcast in July 1927:

> If you are one who thinks he does not need God—or thinks that [the] philosophy of today is a better one than that of Jesus of Nazareth . . . jump yourself ahead in your mind to the end—to your last ten minutes. Alright, you are there—in ten minutes you will be through—now what have you got to take with you? The wealth you fought and slaved for, that you gave up the greater part of your life to acquire? You can't take a dollar. You say— Well, I at least have left my children comfortable—but in a few years, they will stand on the brink just as you are.
>
> Alright—then you say: I can look back on a gay life. Gosh, I had some great old times. Yes, but they are past. Do you get complete satisfaction now from the joys you had ten years ago? No, it is those of tomorrow that you are thinking about. . . .
>
> No, from the perspective of that last ten minutes, ladies and gentlemen, boys and girls, you have only what you *are* within. The degree to which you have developed that divine spark, for that spark is you and that spark is all you can take with you. . . .
>
> It is your knowledge of Truth that will make that last ten minutes a joy and an uplifting feeling of Power and triumph instead of fear, doubt and regret.

Invoking the end of life, and the end of children's lives, is not the soft-soaping method of a man out for cash, but that of a hellfire-and-brimstone preacher demanding that his message be heard.

The truth of DeMille's religious feelings can't be glossed over. "He strove to put God's word on the screen and believed that God approved of his efforts," asserted Richard deMille. "He believed that Christ had come to save sinners, and he hoped that his sins would be forgiven."

DeMille could be eloquent in describing his own frustrations with faith, for those times when sincere, even desperate prayer would bring . . . nothing. But DeMille was never after answers to demands, he was after communication—a sense of closeness with God.

"I had a little boat when I was young," he remembered as an old man. "That boat I used to row to Santa Barbara Island. You row around the pike there, then all of a sudden you come to a tremendous area with big winds that are very dangerous, and . . . I'm all alone out of the sight of the island. You go down between two of these waves. You see this gigantic thing is here and another one coming at you, and you're [helpless]—you're terrified, because if the thing hurls over on you, you're through. And that wave will pick you up and carry you to the crest. You see the whole ocean, the sky, the sun, everything, and you get a great exhilaration from it.

"I find that the spirit is just like that. You have these wavy moments. If you carry them all the time—perhaps someone can, I can't. But I don't go down as deeply in the gulley as I used to, because I found how to keep the light down in the gulley [and that knowledge] comes with experience and age."

★

The critical and commercial success of *The King of Kings* meant that DeMille reclaimed some of the territory he had lost in the eyes of critics; in April 1927, Joseph P. Kennedy invited him to speak to Harvard University's Graduate School of Business Administration. DeMille was hesitant, but Kennedy flattered him, saying that *The King of Kings* was "the greatest movie ever made" and that the president of Harvard was eager to meet him.

Cecil remained interested in new ideas that would elevate the movie business. While he was in New York opening *The King of Kings*, Douglas Fairbanks sent him a telegram: "You are no doubt familiar with the new organization we are forming called the Academy of Motion Picture Arts and Sciences to include all five branches of production. I am told you were invited to the original dinner at which this plan took shape and while you were unable to attend you expressed approval of the idea. We are now preparing for a big organization dinner and would appreciate it immensely if you will authorize the use of your name as one of the sponsors."

DeMille replied immediately: "I am much interested in the forming of the Academy of Motion Picture Arts and Sciences and gladly authorize you to use my name as one of the sponsors of it."

★

In August 1926, a young emigrée from Russia named Ayn Rand arrived in Los Angeles. She carried a letter of introduction from a Chicago distributor addressed to Cecil B. DeMille, whose films had captivated her while she was in Russia—in fact, Cecil B. DeMille had been one of her nicknames.

On September 13, she was given a courtesy interview, but was told there was nothing available. She was walking out of the front entrance when DeMille arrived. "He drives up to the gate," remembered Rand, "stops, looks at me and asks, 'Why are you looking at me?' So I told him I had just come from Russia and I am very happy to see him. So he opens the door of the car and says, 'Get in.' I didn't know where we were going. I got in and he started driving. . . . I told him that I want to be a writer and he was my favorite director. And my English was atrocious. Where he was driving was the back lot. They were shooting *The King of Kings*."

DeMille told her that if she wanted to write movies, she had to learn how movies were made. During the afternoon, he took time between setups to explain why he was doing what he was doing. Later, he wrote her out a pass: "DeMille Studios Sept. 13. Pass Miss Rand to my set good all week. C.B. DeMille."

For the next three months Rand worked as an extra on *The King of Kings*. It was on the set that she met Frank O'Connor, who was playing a soldier and would become her husband for fifty years. DeMille's nickname for Rand was "Caviar," and when the shoot was over he offered her a job as a junior screenwriter. To her own nascent ideas about the world and her place in it ("Life is achievement," she wrote in 1927, at the age of twenty-two. "Give yourself an aim, something you want to do, then go after it, breaking through everything, with nothing in mind but your aim, all will, all concentration—and get it.") was added Cecil B. DeMille— a dominating Rand hero before she began writing them.

DeMille assigned Rand to work on the screenplay for a movie called *The Skyscraper*, about two tough construction workers who fall in love with the same girl. Rand worked in both Russian and English. Midway through the job she began writing an original screenplay with the same title, about an architect named Howard Kane, whose integrity causes him to be hated by competitors and workers alike—some of the story and much of the Promethean imagery of *The Fountainhead*. (Her finale for *The Skyscraper*: "The building rises in the night as a white column, with drops of water rolling like tears on the joyously glistening walls, in the rays of spotlights. On top of the building, a man is standing, his head thrown far back—just a man looking at the sky.")

DeMille produced *The Skyscraper* in 1928 as a vehicle for William Boyd and Alan Hale, but used the original story, not Rand's original. Rand received no credit and called the result "a lousy picture."

Rand's instincts were always didactic, and she was too resistant to collaboration to be a successful screenwriter. But she would always greatly admire DeMille— she once sent a postcard to her parents that had a picture of DeMille's Laughlin Park estate on it. Rand sent DeMille autographed copies of her books for the rest of his life. In later years, Richard deMille knew Rand and happened to mention that he had a friend who was a communist. "You have *no* friend who is a Communist," she snapped in her reflexively authoritarian way—a commissar at heart.

Despite the friendship between DeMille and Rand, Richard deMille doubted that his father read her books. "She impressed him. He liked assertive, intelligent women, especially if they would debase themselves at his feet. For her, he was a commanding, romantic figure of a film director."

★

The DeMille studio was on its last legs. In February 1928, J. J. Murdock was named president of Pathé and hired none other than Joseph P. Kennedy to streamline yet another amalgamation to include Kennedy's FBO Studio. As it happened, one of Kennedy's friends was Jeremiah Milbank, who had decided to get out of the movie business.

Kennedy's main interest was the Keith-Albee-Orpheum theater chains. The earnings of PDC-Pathé had not improved since the merger, and the company's financial problems were overwhelming. Word got out that PDC-Pathé lacked capital to meet their expenditures, and the company's stock price plunged.

The widening cracks in the gimcrack consortium meant that Cecil felt it necessary to establish his commercial bona fides. On March 21, *Variety* published a complete recapitulation of DeMille's career from the standpoint of costs and box office grosses. It was, the paper said, "authentically secured," i.e., from DeMille himself. The list showed that DeMille had made fifty pictures since December 1913, costing $9.6 million; forty-seven of them had grossed nearly $22 million. The three pictures DeMille had directed since going independent were left off the list because "as these latter pictures have been released within the past two years, it is impossible to ascertain an approximate of their gross returns."

This was, of course, ridiculous, but to include the figures for *The Road to Yesterday* and even the relatively successful *The Volga Boatman* wouldn't prove the point Cecil was trying to make. Actual costs and grosses were no more common in the Hollywood of the early twentieth century than they are in the Hollywood of the early twenty-first; DeMille was telling financial tales out of school because he thought it might help save him in the coming debacle.

Variety wasn't supinely lying down for DeMille; they dropped in a nice little shot when they pointed out *The Woman God Forgot* as "the first screen appearance of Julia Faye, who has appeared in every picture DeMille since directed"—a sentence that must have caused consternation among those who didn't know why she was such an important part of the DeMille stock company.

DeMille pointed out the problems with the Pathé arrangement by printing the costs of fifteen carefully chosen program pictures that had been completed at an average cost of $192,843. "It is said that the only guaranteed revenue which the Pathe-DeMille organization has for these program pictures is through the Keith-

Orpheum houses and their associates, which brings around $60,000 a picture. Balance of the gross is calculated upon from outside bookings and the foreign market, where the DeMille name carries prestige."

But prestige doesn't pay the bills.

★

By the spring, the trickle begun by *The Jazz Singer* the previous fall had become a flood. Customers stormed theaters showing films that featured sound, anything with sound—sound effects, background music, part-talkie, all-talkie, it didn't matter. It was at this point that DeMille was spending close to three quarters of a million dollars on *The Godless Girl*—a lavish silent film without stars.

Joe Kennedy told DeMille that they must discuss a settlement of his contract. Kennedy kept to a two-pronged strategy; on the one hand, he adamantly denied being the source of a flow of trade paper stories about DeMille's profligate spending. On the other, besides leaking the stories to the press, he kept up steady internal pressure about DeMille's profligate spending. To DeMille's face, Kennedy was oleaginous; behind his back, he slagged him at every opportunity.

In truth, Cecil's overhead was high. Jeanie Macpherson was making $1,000 a week, William deMille was pulling down $2,000 a week, and Clara Beranger, Bill's new wife, was earning as much as Jeanie. Cecil was receiving $250,000 annually, plus a percentage of the gross of all the films he either directed or supervised. He could hire anybody he wanted and needed board approval only for anyone earning more than $2,500 a week. If his contract wasn't renewed, he had an option to buy the studio.

Against all those perquisites was the fact that the place was hemorrhaging money, *The King of Kings* was not going to pay off all the debts the studio had incurred, and DeMille hated doing business with the people who were now in control. It was increasingly clear that sound was a necessity, and converting his studio to talkies required a capital infusion he didn't have. Were he to get financing from someone else, he would have that much less ownership of his own company. Everywhere he looked, retrenchment seemed to be the order of the day.

On April 18, DeMille signed the papers of separation. He received $250,000 to go away, the rights to *The King of Kings*, 40 percent of the first $500,000 grossed by *The Godless Girl*, and another $200,000 as repayment for loans he had made to the company. He spent the early part of the summer editing *The Godless Girl*; after that, he'd have to find a new place to make movies.

Joe Kennedy had no particular interest in the movies beyond functioning as a quit-claim operator and sleeping with Gloria Swanson. But he had no shortage of gall. In May, a short month after shouldering DeMille out of his own company, Kennedy asked him for a favor: "Would you consider . . . directing Gloria in picture to start as soon as possible? . . . Type picture similar to what you used to do with her." Kennedy may have been thinking of DeMille taking over the reins of

Queen Kelly, although it's possible he was already looking past that obvious disaster and was thinking about commissioning DeMille to mount a follow-up rescue operation.

"I will of course do anything in my power in solving the Swanson problem," Cecil replied, and then his avid brain began running possibilities. "Have you a story in mind? It seems to me Gloria should not do another little picture at this time. The publicity angle of Gloria being with me again would in itself interest the exhibitor and public but they would expect to see a real DeMille picture with Swanson in it. If I made *The Cup* or *Silk* with Gloria for a million it would be fairly sure of two to two and one half million gross. Europe would be sure for a million and it would do not less than one half million here. It could be delivered by Christmas starting the middle of August. Let me have your view of this."

While negotiating with Kennedy, Cecil also began talking with United Artists, going so far as two separate draft contracts. The first prospective arrangement was for six pictures in four years, with Cecil drawing $3,500 a week in salary against 50 percent of the net profits. The second possibility was with Joe Schenck's Art Cinema, a United Artists subsidiary. Schenck wanted DeMille to make three or four pictures, one to star Schenck's wife, Norma Talmadge, or some other mutually acceptable player (such as Gloria Swanson, who was also at U.A.). United Artists would charge a 27.5 percent distribution fee, and the money and percentages were the same.

Neither deal went through, which was unfortunate, as DeMille would undoubtedly have had a much freer hand at United Artists than he was to have at his next port of call. On August 2, it was announced that DeMille was moving his production activities to MGM, where he would make three pictures in two years. Accompanying DeMille would be his core personnel: Jeanie Macpherson, Adrian, Mitch Leisen.

A few weeks later, Cecil's farewell to independent production opened in Los Angeles. *The Godless Girl* was a contemporary reverse image of *The King of Kings*, positing the bacillus of militant atheism spreading through America's high schools. The atheists spread their propaganda and divide the student body into two hostile factions; some of the students get sent to the reformatory, and everybody is converted by a terrible fire.

DeMille was engaged in a twofer—the film's inspiration was the viciousness of reform schools, onto which he grafted theological propaganda. Eddie Quillan, one of the actors in the film, related how DeMille researched the film by smuggling a young man into a boys reformatory and a young woman into a girls. On top of that, DeMille collected a pile of sworn affidavits attesting to varieties of brutal punishments in juvenile prisons.

The title character initially rejects God but ultimately embraces Him. Both Sally Rand and Jacqueline Logan wanted the part, but DeMille's initial casting choice was an actress named Jeanne Williams. Williams told DeMille her name was Sonia Karlov, and that she was Russian. When Williams/Karlov was introduced as the star of the picture, Lina Basquette, a former *Ziegfeld Follies* girl, recognized Williams and blurted out, "Her name is Jeanne Williams and I knew her in the Follies!"

If there was anything that DeMille couldn't stand, it was a deceitful actor. Williams was banished, and Lina Basquette was cast instead. Basquette had already had a full life by the time DeMille cast her at the age of twenty-one. A *Follies* girl at sixteen, she had married Sam Warner when she was eighteen. Sam was the brilliant middle Warner brother, and the first of her six husbands. Sam died a few days before the premiere of *The Jazz Singer,* after which sound, for which he had been the primary family advocate, swept the industry.

Lina was now a widow with a baby daughter and the object of distrust of the entire Warner family. Harry Warner negotiated a deal under which Lina received a substantial sum in return for custody of the little girl. Lina had just completed a stint as Richard Barthelmess's leading lady in *The Noose* when she went off to meet DeMille in an outfit that emphasized her youth and freshness—navy blue skirt, white blouse, and no makeup.

Basquette's telling of her first meeting with DeMille throbs with sexualized melodrama accented by DeMille's whacking a desk with a riding crop for emphasis. In Basquette's version, DeMille pointed out the deep scratches in the arms of the chair Basquette was sitting in, the results of the stark fear provoked by DeMille. "Stand back so I can get a good look at you," he said, whereupon the spotlight that was hitting her in the face changed to another light that showed her legs, presumably operated from some buttons at the side of DeMille's desk.

"My godless girl must have a beautiful body, exquisite legs, perfect form that the old masters in sculpture and Renaissance art would worship. Your body must please *this* master. There is a scene in the movie where my godless girl bathes in an arcadian pond in the nude."

"No bathtub?" innocently inquired Basquette.

"You are cheeky. So few people ever joke with me."

To investigate whether the recent mother had the requisite firm breasts the part required, DeMille supposedly thrust his hand down the front of her blouse. "You must understand when I study an applicant for a role, I have no personal interest. [In any case,] my dear, there is scarcely a woman in the world I can't take to bed." A request for Basquette to take off her blouse was refused, but she got the part anyway.

This was the more or less ridiculous version she published in her memoirs, although in interviews she gave in earlier years there was no mention of any sexual assault, which would have been wildly out of character for an extremely prudent man who had refused to respond when Gloria Swanson sat in his lap.

But Basquette's memory of DeMille's oration to her on the day she signed her contract does ring true: "You are the most important star on the lot. From now on, you are my property. All your energy must be the possession of the production and *me*. Do you understand? It is up to me to select suitable romantic interests for you, when the time is ripe. At the right time, with the right man, when it will give choice publicity to *The Godless Girl*, I'll expect you to cooperate. You will have absolutely no dates with young men in nondescript places. Stay out of that lunchroom across the street. You are a STAR. At all times, I *demand* you behave like one."

DeMille seems to have had little cause for unhappiness with Basquette, who described her character to one reporter as "the Joan of Arc of atheism." But leading man George Duryea became a target of his disdain. "Put some passion, some lust into your expression, George. Lust!" DeMille snapped during a love scene. "Duryea! I presume you have not been castrated! This is a luscious female you are holding in your arms. She has firm pointed breasts with sensitive nipples for you to kiss. . . . You should have a yard-long hard-on. Come, boy . . ."

During the shooting of the burning of the reformatory, Basquette met Constance. Typically, she found her "the essence of serenity, a gentle woman of mature calm, apparently content with the role of 'dowager queen' behind the throne. . . . Hers was an intangible beauty that depended not on perfection or arrangement of features."

Soon after the film got underway, Basquette began an affair with cameraman Peverell Marley, which angered DeMille so much he threatened to take Marley off the film. He was stopped by Constance, who told him, "How lovely, Cecil. Not since Bill Boyd and Elinor Fair have you played cupid!"

DeMille was not afraid of danger during a production; he saw no reason actors should not have the same contempt for the possibility of death he did. During the burning of the reformatory, "[the] fire and the heat were unbelievable," remembered Basquette. "DeMille kept calling for more flames and it was too much for George Duryea. He bolted, and DeMille was swearing at him and screaming at me through his megaphone, 'Stay where you are, stay where you are! Marley, get another closeup!' It was a hell of a scene—and it wasn't acting. I was truly scared for my life and really getting burned."

By the time DeMille called "cut," Basquette's eyelashes and eyebrows were singed; her eyelashes grew back, but the eyebrows never did. "The last thing I remember before I passed out was DeMille turning to Pev and saying, 'She's too good for you, Marley!' "

Despite the daffy premise, *The Godless Girl* is one of DeMille's best silent films. The man who had never been particularly interested in the moving camera as such, who preferred to tell his story through quick intercutting, suddenly goes all out with tracking and crane shots, and ramps up his editing until it approaches the Russian style. There's even a love scene set in the country that's genuinely erotic. *The Godless Girl* is a stunning exercise in style that makes you wish DeMille had done something similar with *Manslaughter* or some of the other logy pictures he had made during his later days at Paramount. Even Kevin Brownlow, no DeMille partisan, called the film "brilliantly directed."

Whether DeMille pulled out the stops as a sentimental farewell to the world of silent film is doubtful; it's more likely that he felt the cast wasn't strong enough to put over the material by themselves, so he had to step in with a dynamic directorial display.

The Godless Girl was released in Los Angeles in August, but didn't open in New York until April 1929, after Pathé grafted some talking sequences into the picture, with which DeMille had nothing to do. Silent or sound, it was a commercial disaster—a first-rate silent movie in a time when the audience was interested only in talkies. The picture cost $722,315 and grossed only $489,095. During production, advances from New York hadn't arrived in time, and so DeMille had met payroll himself.

Years later, after she left the world of movies for the world of thoroughbred Great Danes, Lina Basquette said that "DeMille didn't think sound would last. He thought it would be a drop in the bucket; DeMille was never happy later on with talkies. He didn't mind music, but he was basically a silent film man. He couldn't believe that people would give up the mystery of silent movies."

They could. They did. Sound would emphasize DeMille's weaknesses—primarily a tin ear for dialogue—just as silent movies had emphasized his strengths. Sound brought playwrights and journalists from New York, who wrote bright, slangy, up-to-the-minute dialogue, and it almost immediately rendered hundreds of silent screen veterans unemployable. Naturally, some of them turned to DeMille for work.

"In casting about in the theatrical field for talent capable of meeting this new demand of talking pictures," wrote Hampton Del Ruth, "please do not altogether overlook the 'boys' of our own 'home industry.' " Del Ruth had been supervising editor for the comedies of both Mack Sennett and William Fox, and by 1928 was writing novels and plays. He wrote DeMille with a surface bonhomie and an underlying desperation.

"It is my wish to have you disregard my former earning power, and start me in at an 'apprentice-boy's wage' as a sort of aide-de-camp director or writer of plot-plus-dialogue. It is my belief that reward will come through the opportunity I am so humbly asking for." But Cecil was about to begin his own retrenchment and in the fall of 1928 had no need for an aide-de-camp director. He sent Del Ruth his sincere regrets.

Sound brought in the banks in a big way. They financed the massive capital investment necessary to build soundproof stages containing expensive recording gear. The banks, naturally enough, wanted oversight over their investment, which meant that New York would run Hollywood far more than it previously had. As DeMille would say a few years later, "When banks came into pictures, trouble came in with them. When we operated on picture money, there was joy in the industry; when we operated on Wall Street money, there was grief in the industry."

So died an art form that had its own storytelling styles, its own acting technique, and which Cecil had mastered because he had helped create it. Of Cecil's fifty-two silent films, fully ten are superb or close to it, while another dozen or so are quite good. Few are worthless. It was a field in which he was, without false modesty, a master, as he had just demonstrated with two consecutive first-rate silent pictures.

Surveying the altered landscape, with the banks and phone companies rushing in to finance new construction, DeMille glumly told his brother, "It looks to me, Bill, very much as if we [are] all going to work for the electric companies."

And, much to Cecil B. DeMille's displeasure, they all did.

The look that signaled trouble.

PART THREE

1929–1945

"More rapture!"
–CECIL B. DEMILLE

13

With their extensive stage backgrounds, the DeMille brothers should have been sanguine about sound, but they were as confused as everybody else. In June 1928, Bill told a trade paper, "We are face to face with a marvelous opportunity or tremendous catastrophe."

As always, Bill was speaking of aesthetics, which is all well and good, but Cecil's problem was intensely practical, and his move to MGM was predicated on business considerations. He had an amicable relationship with Nicholas Schenck, chairman of Loew's Inc., the parent company of MGM, and he was also friendly with Louis B. Mayer. Mayer and DeMille, however, were very different kinds of men. DeMille was tactile, a sensualist, intoxicated by beautiful things: fabrics, jewels, women, the natural world. Mayer was uncomfortable with or uninterested in most of these things.

Once, Mayer was on the *Seaward* playing solitaire before dinner. DeMille came on deck and was transfixed by the gorgeous sunset. He mentioned it to Mayer, who continued playing solitaire. Finally, he said, "Louie, look at that sunset—you've never seen anything like it in your life."

Mayer glanced up from his cards, said, "Yeah, it's pretty," and went right back to his game. In telling the story, DeMille left the impression that he could never truly understand a man like that.

DeMille's contract with MGM was evidently arranged directly with Schenck. It stipulated that DeMille would receive a guarantee of $150,000 to $175,000 per picture in addition to a percentage of the profits. This was an extraordinarily rich deal for a company that wouldn't give percentages to any producer until later in the 1930s, and never to premier directors such as Victor Fleming, George Cukor, Clarence Brown, and King Vidor. It indicates the extent to which DeMille was regarded as much as a producer as a director, an independent nation-state within the studio walls.

After directing forty-two pictures at Paramount, Bill made four pictures for the PDC combine (*For Alimony Only, The Little Adventuress, Tenth Avenue, Craig's Wife*). When Cecil signed with MGM, Bill again joined his brother and made three pictures for MGM, starting in 1929 (*The Idle Rich, This Mad World, Passion Flower*). The reviews were not good, but less important than the mediocre response was the fact that Bill was now obviously an aquiescent caboose to Cecil's powerful locomotive. The gradual dissipation of any kind of psychological autonomy had to affect the quality of Bill's work; in very short order, there would be no more work.

MGM gave Cecil his own bungalow, designed by Mitchell Leisen in an attractive Spanish motif with beamed ceilings and whitewashed walls. The waiting room had an unpadded bench, followed by an office for a couple of secretaries with a few easy chairs, followed by DeMille's own office. *Photoplay* magazine, long a sarcastic observer of DeMille's professional and personal style, ran a still of the office with a caption calling it "The Imperial Throne Room [of] King Cecil B. DeMille's new offices" and referred to it as the area "where supplicants await their audience with the Master."

By now, Cecil was living in self-imposed isolation. Jesse and Bessie Lasky had a Santa Monica beachhouse at 609 Ocean Front, next door to Mayer. Jesse and his wife threw glistening parties on Sunday nights with guest lists that included Irene and Edie Mayer, Irving Thalberg, Douglas Fairbanks and Mary Pickford, William Randolph Hearst and Marion Davies, Norma Talmadge, Myron Selznick, Gregory La Cava, and Norma Shearer, all of them bringing their own houseguests.

Although Cecil and Jesse still regarded each other as best friends, neither Bessie nor her daughter Betty Lasky's recounting of those parties included Cecil's attendance. Cecil kept to his family in Laughlin Park, and the splendid isolation of Paradise.

The character actor Charles Bickford left behind an extended account of the pleasures of Paradise. He arrived in Los Angeles just before Christmas 1928, a few weeks before production was to begin on *Dynamite*, Cecil's first talkie and first film for MGM. DeMille found out that Bickford's birthday was January 1 and invited him for a party at Paradise over the New Year's holiday. DeMille asked him for his preferences in alcohol and, more importantly, women: "blonde, brunette or redhead?"

The ambitious Bickford replied, "Make it one of each. All I ask is that they be dainty, feminine, shapely, beautiful, intelligent and passionate." DeMille replied, "I know of only one such pearl of great price and unfortunately she's already wearing a brand."

At this point, Bickford believed DeMille was putting him on. "My impression of him was that of a ruddy stallion, pawing the earth and proclaiming himself monarch of all he surveyed."

When DeMille's chauffeur arrived at Bickford's hotel, he found three women in the back seat: a blonde, a brunette, and a redhead, each wearing a ribbon with gold letters: "C.B."

At Paradise, DeMille took Bickford into the library, where he showed him his collection of books; Bickford remembered having to feign interest in a three-volume edition of Rabelais. DeMille promptly gave it to him.

At midnight, Bickford was asked to go to DeMille's cottage. There, in a spotlight, was a blond woman dancing in a thin silk veil to Ravel's *Bolero*. The performance was greeted with applause, and afterward there was a game of dice striptease: "Very naughty but lots of fun," remembered Bickford, evidenced by howls of laughter from the men and squeals of outraged modesty from the girls as, piece by piece, the losers were forced to discard bits of clothing." Bickford kept his clothes on but ended up with the beautiful blond dancer, at which point we can assume that his clothes came off.

Among the writers on *Dynamite* was John Howard Lawson, who had a couple of theatrical successes in his past, and a role as the unquestioned communist commissar of Hollywood in his future. DeMille hired Lawson because he had seen his play *Processional* and thought that the central character of a coal miner could work as the hero of a DeMille film. The plot of the new picture involved a coal miner unjustly accused of murder. Paid off to marry a rich woman who needs a husband so she can come into her inheritance, the rough coal miner is bored and offended by the amoral rich surrounding him. He returns to the coal mines, and his wife comes after him, followed by her boyfriend. A mine explosion sorts things out.

Dynamite was Lawson's first experience in Hollywood, and a reasonable preview of coming attractions. "I had not written with any conviction," Lawson remembered, "but I had done a craftsman's job, and it seemed to insure my position in Hollywood." Lawson, who felt he was responsible for seven-eighths of the script, was furious at having to share credit with Jeanie Macpherson (she "twittered at story conferences," he insisted) and Gladys Unger.

Dynamite was a troublesome production, typical for an early talkie. Dubbing was impossible so all sound effects had to be achieved on set, during a take. Since the script involved a mine cave-in, difficulties were obvious. Shooting began on January 22, 1929, and soon ran into trouble. On January 24, production was held up while felt—to deaden the sound—was installed on a set; on January 25, valuable time was wasted while the camera booths were moved and wooden bars in a prison set were replaced with iron bars.

By the third day of shooting, the movie was one day behind schedule, with worse to come. DeMille had Mitchell Leisen fire the second lead, a young actress named Carole Lombard, because he didn't think she was taking her work seriously. On January 29, the entire day was given over to planning with "Mr. DeMille talking over action . . . rehearsing all day." This after a week of rehearsal had already taken place before the cameras turned. To compensate, the next day the company worked until midnight, with the next day's call at 10 A.M.

After a month of production, the company was six days behind schedule; after five weeks, they were ten days behind. It was DeMille's worst nightmare, a situation where his fire and drive were hobbled by production circumstances beyond his control.

"Everybody was sort of in a crouched position, ready to spring," DeMille remembered. Because the microphones picked up the sound of the gears grinding in the cameras, the cameras had to be placed in iceboxes—small, airless rooms with thick plate glass windows through which the movie was photographed, thus reducing superb lenses to mediocre ones.

"You could not pan the camera," said DeMille of those first weeks. "You could not move the camera. You rehearsed the first act of a play because everybody rushed to New York and bought plays. You rehearsed the first act of a play all the way through and then you turned the camera all the way through the first act. Everything that the silent screen had done to bring entertainment and . . . the beauty of the action, was gone. And you were back on the stage where you had to paint things."

DeMille demanded that the camera be taken out of the booth. The sound engineer walked off the set. DeMille sent to the prop room for a couple of blankets and ordered them wrapped around the camera. The sound man came back, listened, and said that he could still hear the camera but not as loudly as before. A couple more blankets were added, but the camera could still be heard. A couple of quilts were brought out, and they muffled the sound sufficiently so that a semblance of mobility could be maintained.

Douglas Shearer, the head of MGM's sound department for the simple reason that nobody knew more about sound than he did, saw what DeMille was doing and came back within a week with what amounted to a primitive camera blimp, a small box lined with blankets that fit like a sheath over the camera mechanism. This was, remembered DeMille, "my first contribution of any value to sound pictures." Several people have claimed to be the inventors of the camera blimp, but DeMille was not given to random assertions of accomplishment—quite the opposite, in fact—so there is some reason to believe that the idea was his.

Another contribution derived from the Belasco days. The climactic sequence of a mine explosion presented a serious technical problem, until Cecil remembered that on stage, thunder was simulated by bowling balls rolling down a wooden trough. A couple of hours later, the effect was tried for the microphone and found to give a reasonable simulation of a mine cave-in.

Working in a small part was a family friend, a young man named Joel McCrea. He had gone to school with Cecilia, and delivered newspapers to DeMille's house. One morning DeMille flagged him down and said, "The other kid threw it [on the lawn] in the rain—you threw it up on the porch."

"Well, you want to read it, don't you?" replied the young man. The boy had spirit—an admirable trait. At Christmas, DeMille gave the boy a silver dollar. Late in 1929, McCrea showed up at DeMille's office at MGM. He had graduated from college, had played the heavy in a silent film with Douglas Fairbanks Jr., worked with Garbo in *The Single Standard*. McCrea figured he'd see if their glancing relationship carried any weight.

"What are you doing here?" DeMille asked him. "When did I first meet you?" McCrea reminded him about the newspaper, the silver dollar, and enumerated his brief credits.

"Have you still got the silver dollar?" asked DeMille. McCrea replied in the affirmative, and DeMille assigned Mitch Leisen to make a test of the boy. McCrea ended up making $100 a week on *Dynamite* and remembered that DeMille treated him very nicely. DeMille made a mental note to keep an eye on the handsome young man. A few years later, he would pay him a lot more than $100 a week to make *Union Pacific*.

On March 4, leading lady Kay Johnson had to have emergency surgery and the company had only a few days of work they could do without her presence. The picture shut down from March 13 until March 25. By now, *Dynamite* was two weeks behind schedule, which didn't even take into account the time lost because of Johnson's health. The sound version of the picture finished on April 13, twelve days behind schedule. More than a month later, on May 28, DeMille and the company reported back to work for another seven days to shoot scenes that would be used for a silent version of *Dynamite*, for theaters that were not yet wired for sound.

By July, when *Dynamite* was released, Cecil must have been feeling slightly insecure about either the picture or MGM's attitude toward it. Louis B. Mayer wrote Cecil, "I assure you that both Irving [Thalberg] and I are sympathetic toward you, and enthusiastic in our desire to do anything possible to keep you happy and smiling. Of course, you must realize, and I know you do, that we are entrusted with the responsibility of running this institution, and therefore must look after that obligation. But I don't see why there should be any conflict between that and doing what is fine and proper for you."

Dynamite cost $658,049 (Gladys Rosson's tabulation indicates a negative cost of $511,123—the difference is probably MGM's overhead). In any case, the film grossed $1.1 million, making it reasonably profitable.

※

While Cecil was wrestling with intransigent technology, Constance was making a Grand Tour—a trip around the world with her sister Rebecca. Her letters to Cecil from the trip attest to her good eye for detail, relentless affection for her family, her natural abilities as Cecil's eyes and ears in the movie world . . . and just a whisper of worry.

"My Darling One," she wrote Cecil shortly after leaving Los Angeles. "This is a glorious day. I am thinking of my dear family. Take care of each other. I shall miss you more each day. The lilies are simply beautiful, as fresh as when you sent them; they bring you ever nearer, if that were possible."

Constance was traveling to New York on the same train as a passel of movie people: King Vidor, Laurence Stallings, Irving Thalberg, and Jesse Lasky. Jesse and Constance had dinner together, and he asked what Cecil thought about a pending Fox-MGM merger (which would fall apart due to the stock market collapse in October).

"Jesse said he didn't see why it should make any difference in the operation of the studio, and to my remark—'[William] Fox has bought a controlling interest, hasn't he?' he said, 'Yes, he bought the Loew and the Schenck stock. The Loew family made forty million and Joe and Nick Schenck ten million apiece.' (I think it was ten.)" Constance signed off: "Take care of your precious self. You are never out of my thoughts. Constance."

"The *France* is a most delightful ship," she wrote Cecil on March 19, 1929. "There is a wonderful atmosphere of making the passengers comfortable . . . It is nice to be able to order wine again . . .

"It was fine to talk to you in New York. I am so glad I know about the business situation. Suppose you are back under full steam again. Hope Kay Johnson is alright. We arrive at the Canary Isles day after tomorrow and have the day ashore. Saturday or Friday we touch at Casablanca and Sunday we arrive at Gibraltar . . ."

Three days later, she wrote after visiting the Canaries: "The country was lovely on closer inspection, quite green and much like California. I recognized many of our trees and plants even to our poppies. But the wonderful poppy which grows everywhere is brilliant red. You would adore them. The tile roofs realize all the things which Los Angeles architects strive for . . ."

Then it was on to Morocco, and it wasn't long before Constance was following in the footsteps of the director Rex Ingram by falling in love with the place. "This country seems a mixture of the Bible and the Arabian Nights." There were, however, some troubling aspects to the religion: "Everyone seems to have a good time here but the women and the donkeys. They are both beasts of burden. Neither have a soul, according to Mohamedan religion.

"You should see the motion picture ads here. Charlie Chaplin appears in pictures I never heard of. They must date back to his early days. *Ben-Hur* was in Algeria and *Wings* was to follow. We went up to the box office and I looked into the theater but decided it was only for the better class French so we are waiting to see a native evening somewhere. I think we will have to take our chauffeur along for women don't go out at night alone. I *do* want to see the Arabs see a picture."

Eventually, Constance reached Lourdes, where she gave her husband an evocative portrait of the atmosphere inside the Grotto. She arrived back in New York in June and promptly arranged a deal with Dan Sayre Groesbeck, Cecil's favorite concept artist. "He accepted a hundred and fifty a week for four weeks gladly. I was sorry I hadn't offered less but with only four weeks guarantee it seemed pretty cheap. I told him you would pay his transportation. He says to tell you he has a wife and can't leave her behind and he has no money to buy a ticket . . . He says he doesn't need any four weeks guarantee from you, he has worked for you enough to know that isn't necessary. All he wants is the opportunity."

While Constance was traveling abroad, Jeanie Macpherson was visiting relatives in Cleveland and, as usual, running short of money. "Dearest Chief," she wrote on May 12, "would you be willing to advance me one week's salary [$1,000] to Cleveland to be paid back to you one hundred dollars per week out of my salary when I go back to work."

Cecil replied the next day that he had deposited $500 that had been withheld from her MGM salary in her bank account, and his personal check for $500 was being mailed to Cleveland. "If you go to New York see the latest musical comedies as I shall probably do an operetta next," he concluded.

It was the first mention of the movie that would become *Madam Satan*, undertaken at a time when musicals were the rage, but unfortunately released when musicals had become a drag on the market. DeMille liked and appreciated music, but hadn't dabbled in it professionally since the long-ago days when he and Jesse Lasky had collaborated on operettas.

The idea was to make a lavish, modern version of the Strauss operetta *Die Fledermaus*. DeMille was clearly uneasy about the idea, but was persuaded by Mayer. "The purpose of this picture is entertainment," DeMille proclaimed at the reading of the script, which in and of itself signaled a retreat on his part, for he invariably imposed some moral or social element on his scripts. The ultimate failing of *Madam Satan*, and, by extension, his entire sojourn with MGM, was that, for one of the few times in his life, DeMille was following trends instead of starting them. On some level, his failure with independent production had shaken his faith in his own instincts.

★

In October, Cecil had investments in, among other things, an airline, some grocery stores, real estate, and even an Epsom salt mine. That month he realized that something bad was happening in the stock market. He told Gladys Rosson to sell his stocks, and she tried. But the rule of thumb at the DeMille office was to sell stocks at a half point above the market, and there were no takers at a half point above a tumbling market, so Gladys stood pat. DeMille would estimate that decision cost him around $1 million, although an inspection of his financial records indicates a loss of around $500,000 is more likely. Whatever the amount, this man who could erupt over all sorts of small things barely blinked at his huge loss. Mostly, he blamed himself for not telling Gladys to sell whatever the price.

The stock market's collapse turned America upside down shortly after sound had turned the movie industry upside down. One of the unintended consequences of sound was that it made unions inevitable, because of the profusion of journalists, sound engineers, and Broadway actors who came west in search of work. Most of them had been members of one union or another in New York or Chicago, and saw no reason why Los Angeles should be exempt from collective bargaining. Los Angeles saw it differently, as it was undoubtedly one of the most anti-union towns in America, and MGM was undoubtedly the most anti-union studio in town.

Beginning in 1929, DeMille's correspondence becomes littered with reports from various private detectives and agents who had infiltrated unions and were reporting back to him as an industry point man about union activities in Los Angeles.

Above everything else, Louis B. Mayer was a pragmatist, and more or less accepted unions when it became obvious they were inevitable, but Irving Thalberg never yielded. Reports and memos about gangsters, labor organizers, and communist infiltration of the labor movement were constantly being rushed from Thalberg's office to DeMille's and back.

The main undercover agent hired by the producers was named Jackson, who was being paid $150 a week for the dual purpose of reporting on union activities to the producers—including documents confirming his claims that there were communists among union leadership—as well as sowing confusion wherever he could. Jackson breathlessly informed DeMille that there were more than two million communists in America (!) compared to only forty thousand in Russia the day before the revolution. "They were considered a joke by the government," wrote Jackson, "just as the Communist movement here is considered at this time. . . . Unless something is done, this country will be taken over by the revolutionists in a few years."

The producers were only too glad to part with $600 a month to keep Hollywood—and America—free.

Jackson's reports were generally headlined "Strictly Confidential." Besides reports about the progress or lack of progress of unionization in Los Angeles, he also reported other tidbits. "Agent reports that he has been working for several days helping Chief of Police [James] Davis who is being framed by a bunch of niggers and prostitutes headed by John A. Quinn, a man who started a reform movement in the Motion Picture Industry a few years ago . . . In view of the fact that high-jackers and Chicago gangsters are coming to Los Angeles to unionize the Movie Industry and the Building trades, Agent thinks that the Motion Picture Producers should get back of Chief Davis . . ."

Jackson told DeMille the backstory to the growing welcome for the unions among the industry's workers, factors that DeMille would have known about all too well: "The cameramen in the union are harboring a bad feeling against the Producers and claim that they were not getting a square deal. They are worked night and day for about nine or ten months and then laid off at this time of year and usually have to go through the Christmas season on short rations."

That same day, DeMille dashed off a letter to L. B. Mayer in New York.

Dear Louis,

Greetings!

One of the cutters has just reported to me that the cutters were forced to attend a union meeting downtown, the purpose of which was to have the film cutters join the Laboratory Worker's Union.

The cutters stated that they had never heard such hatred expressed before; that the methods used seemed to be regular gangster methods of bullying them into joining the Union. One or two of them were told confidentially that it is part of a big plan to unionize Los Angeles by any means.

This substantiates the report of our agent and came to me through a source that I can't doubt—from one who personally attended the meeting. [Undoubtedly Anne Bauchens.]

The cutters were addressed by Alvin Wyckoff of the Cameraman's Union, who explained to them that the industry would soon be in the hands of Labor.

The cutters are in identically the same position as the cameraman: the good ones do not want a union, but those out of a job are forcing the union organization in order that they may place themselves on a par with the good cutters.

The gangster situation about which we have been told was corroborated.

Please try and wake up the New York Producers to this situation which is far more deadly than the stock market.

Unions had a two-pronged struggle. On the one hand, they had to fight the producers; on the other, they also had to fight the efforts of the Academy of Motion Picture Arts and Sciences, which was serving more or less as a company union. On November 8, Conrad Nagel wrote DeMille that he and Jean Hersholt, together or individually, would be happy to meet with DeMille to discuss the Academy's proposals for a new standard contract for actors, which mandated a forty-eight-hour workweek. "I would be grateful if you would send it up to Mr. Thalberg when you are through with it," wrote Nagel.

Given the sudden influx of matters relating to unionization in DeMille's papers around this time, it's possible that he was going along to get along at his new studio; that he sniffed out Thalberg's virulent dislike of unions, and became a one-man clearinghouse for information. At one point, Thalberg responded to an article DeMille forwarded to him by a pro-union journalist. "His attitude," wrote Thalberg with the icy contempt that occasionally marks his correspondence, "is still that of an Iowa tourist who has accepted as verbatim the statement issued by the radical and out of work so-called actors.

"He pictures Jetta Goudal, a temperamental young woman, who has become enraged at the producers because, as you know, they would not stand for her undisciplinary action of walking off sets leaving many actors standing around for hours and days at a time . . . and who is now using her somewhat extraordinary temper against the producers by inflaming the poor actor who is badly in need of employment . . .

"It is as ridiculous for the non-working actor—non-working because of his lack of ability, or non-working because he completely lacks the qualifications . . . and the thousands of movie struck people who call themselves 'actors,' to decide upon the fate of the working actor . . . as it is for the people of California, with the best of intentions, to decide upon the national policy of China . . ."

At the same time DeMille was disseminating anti-union information, he was keeping an eye on new technical advancements in his profession. He wrote to Theodore Kosloff, asking him to find out "How they got the shots in the French film *The Passion of Joan of Arc* made I believe by your brother-in-law [cameraman Rudolph Maté] that seem to be made with a universal focus lens which made the backgrounds in focus at the same time as the close-ups were in focus."

★

For *Madam Satan*, DeMille drove through on a much more assured basis, despite the fact that the early days of sound were still causing turbulence. MGM didn't have enough soundstages for all the movies it was making, so the studio had gone into twenty-four hour mode: each stage had three different films being made on eight-hour shifts. The first company worked eight to four, the second four till midnight, and the graveyard shift worked from midnight until eight. This meant that the sets for each film had to be erected and then struck every single day. The pressure was so intense that Mitchell Leisen had a minor nervous breakdown.

Despite the occasional delay, DeMille brought the picture in early. Scheduled for sixteen days of rehearsal and fifty-four days of production, DeMille used only fourteen days of rehearsal and forty-five days of production.

Physically, *Madam Satan* is an impressive picture that manages to look more like a DeMille picture than an MGM picture; the dirigible—in actuality a twenty-foot-long miniature—was particularly successful. DeMille's casting instincts remained strong; in December 1929, he asked Joe Kennedy about hiring Gloria Swanson for

FORTHCOMING MUSICAL PRODUCTION . . . THE PART OF MADAM SATAN IS PERHAPS THE BEST WOMAN'S PART THAT HAS EVER COME UNDER MY DIRECTION. IT IS THE TYPE OF STORY THAT I USED TO MAKE WITH GLORIA, BUT DONE WITH SOME LIGHT MUSIC STOP I AM SPENDING ONE MILLION DOLLARS ON THE PRODUCTION AND IT IS ALL CENTERED AROUND THIS ONE CHARACTER WHICH HAS THE BRILLIANCE AND DASH THAT SHE RESPONDS TO SO SPLENDIDLY AND NEEDS SO MUCH AT THE PRES-

ENT TIME STOP I SUGGEST YOU ADVISE ME BY WIRE OR PHONE WHAT THE FINANCIAL
REQUIREMENTS WOULD BE.

But Swanson was still wrestling with von Stroheim's uncompleted *Queen Kelly* as well as trying to define a talkie career of her own. Joe Kennedy wrote back explaining that "the money she might get out of picture would be so small in proportion to amount she could possibly get out of one made by herself I question whether it would be possible to get together on any terms." Although reuniting with DeMille would undoubtedly have given her career a boost—not to mention giving *Madam Satan* a boost—the reunion would have to wait until 1949, and *Sunset Boulevard*.

Madam Satan is a movie that no one but DeMille could have directed—or would have wanted to: a musical comedy/romance/drama/disaster film that touches on his marital comedies of the World War I period—the film takes a lot of shots at male egos, possibly the result of the three female writers, not to mention DeMille's own self-awareness. An unfaithful husband chafes over his wife's attitude that marriage is a school and she is the teacher. She decides to assume a more sensual identity at a masked ball held on board a dirigible. Lightning strikes, first metaphorically in the attraction between the husband and the wife he doesn't recognize, then literally as the dirigible catches fire and begins to break up.

The cast DeMille ended up with—Reginald Denny, Kay Johnson—is utterly sexless, and the film itself is dramatically overamplified and lacks charm. DeMille ladles on complications and genres indiscriminately and audaciously. It's impossible to take the film seriously, but it's equally impossible not to be entertained. Irving Thalberg watched wonderingly from a distance as DeMille exercised his contractual rights forbidding any interference from the MGM hierarchy. "It contained no semblance of reality," was Thalberg's pithy summation of the film.

DeMille was in volcanic form during the production but then, as one MGM staffer remembered, they were prepared. "His reputation in the industry was that he was a hard man to get along with," said assistant director Joseph Newman, who had begun at the studio in 1925 as Louis B. Mayer's office boy.

Lillian Roth was in the cast and had to fall through a skylight, which was made of candy glass. She was nervous and complained to DeMille. Without saying another word, he walked over to a pane of the candy glass leaning against a wall, lifted it over his head and slammed it down. The glass shattered; the skull didn't. "If it didn't hurt my old bald head," he told her, "it won't hurt your young back end."

The first assistant was Gladys Rosson's brother Richard and the second was Hezi Tate. One fine day DeMille exploded at Rosson and Tate, and they both walked off the set.

"He was very verbally abusive to many of the people on the set," said Joseph Newman. "He had used some words that I don't think you would want me to repeat right now, and this was before a hundred extras on the set." Cecil, as his niece Agnes would observe, "achieved effects not by innuendo but by command and tongue lashings and flights of baroque sarcasm."

Eventually, he would stop, climb down off the camera platform and come over to a friend or family member who had been observing the eruption. Suddenly, the topic would be politics, the weather, or that evening's dinner plans.

Richard deMille would say, "The studio explosions were a leadership technique. I don't doubt he would get angry when people didn't do the right thing, but he would act much angrier than he actually was; he would put on his 'I am the Chief' performance. It offended some people. They endured it, complained about it, and told people what a terrible man he was. And then quite a few of them came back.

"Cecil *worked* at being the great director. He had a realistic appraisal of his own capacities. It wasn't something he ever felt had been handed to him. He was always aware of the hazards of failure. He played an egomaniac, but he wasn't. It was his method of stirring up excitement."

Joe Newman was the only man left to throw into the breach.

DeMille pulled in his horns and was exceedingly pleasant to Newman for the rest of the shoot, even after Rosson and Tate returned. As Newman remembered, DeMille himself caused some of the problems on the set. He arrived thirty to forty minutes late in the mornings and "he took his time about everything; he wasn't a fast director."

Part of the underlying problem may have been, as Newman recalled, a certain unease. MGM was a communal operation, where the system took precedence over the efforts of any individual, no matter how gifted. Directors routinely stepped in to direct uncredited scenes for other directors, writers were called in to contribute lines or entire scenes for scripts predominantly written by others.

"He was used to his own studio, where he had no opposition," said Newman. "But at MGM I think he felt an outsider. I think he liked to be in control. He knew motion pictures, he was a great technician and he was a good director, except for his attitude of taking charge of everything. . . . He was the focal point of any decision that was made."

The film was originally supposed to have Technicolor sequences, but the miniature of the dirigible had to be photographed at a high speed in order to get the effect of softly floating through the air. Technicolor couldn't handle the high camera speeds, so DeMille's only fallback position was hand-tinted color. This meant, wrote DeMille, a minimum of "from eighteen to twenty splices on the Zep sequence." They decided to ignore the color option.

In the end, after several musical numbers set on the dirigible amidst Mitch Leisen's Constructivist settings, everyone parachutes to safety following the lightning strikes. A succession of quick cuts shows everybody landing, the most outlandish being a girl dressed as a six-armed Hindu goddess who falls on top of a

Harlem craps game. There's a brief foretelling of DeMille's career in broadcasting when he dubs the voice of a radio announcer.

MGM publicity head Pete Smith wrote DeMille about his reactions after a preview: "Interest in singing and dancing on the screen is at a low point as far as the public is concerned. This phase of the picture, it seems to me, should be cut to a minimum. . . . It is not a critics' picture [which] does not mean that it should not clean up at the box office." Smith went on to say that it was not a picture that could be shown at high prices or reserved seats, i.e., word of mouth would be deadly. He suggested a long list of cuts and even suggested that some of the comedy moments were "very Mack Sennetty." Smith ended by suggesting, "keep all the drama, the love and the laughs in the picture and cut down on singing, dancing and you will have a box office picture that moves right along."

Despite equivalent rumblings from Irving Thalberg, DeMille ignored most of Smith's comments, as Smith must have known he would. It was right about here that Thalberg began to scan the horizon, looking for an appropriate exit sign for DeMille.

DeMille didn't much like *Madam Satan,* and neither did MGM's accountants. The movie cost $979,933 and grossed $853,404. With advertising and publicity costs, MGM's loss came to more than $250,000. In his autobiography, DeMille noted that none of the songs "need have perturbed the dreams of the young Messrs. Gershwin, Hammerstein, Hart, Rodgers or any of the others who have delighted so many, including me, with *good* musicals."

★

Among Cecil's list of pensioners at this time was Lorna Moon, the birth mother of Richard deMille. After a brief remission, Moon's tuberculosis had returned in 1927. DeMille had been sending her money out of his personal funds on an occasional basis since Richard's birth: $3,000 in 1922–1923, $5,000 in 1928, $500 in 1929, and $1,500 in 1930. From the dates and the amounts, it appears that DeMille was supplementing her income and helping out with her medical bills at times when the disease wouldn't allow her to work. (It is possible that Cecil was being reimbursed by William, although there is no record of it; given the otherwise comprehensive nature of Cecil's financial reports, we can probably assume that he was supporting Moon on his own.)

Lorna Moon died on May 1, 1930. She left Cecil her house in Hollywood as repayment for the money he had given her. Unfortunately, the house still had $8,097 left on the mortgage, and the early 1930s were not a great time to unload real estate. Four years later, Cecil sold it at a profit and told Neil McCarthy to send the money to Lorna's daughter in England as if it were part of her estate.

Now only Cecil, William, and Constance knew the true story of yet another part of the secret history of Hollywood.

✦

The year Cecilia turned twenty-one, her father gave her twenty-one bonds, tied together with a set of seed pearls. The year before that, at the Santa Monica Beach Club, she had met Frank Calvin, the son of Edgar Eugene Calvin, retired president of the Union Pacific railroad. Frank was a few years older than his bride, amusing and amused, well liked by everybody in the family.

They were married on February 22, 1930, with Cecilia in white satin. The day was a little rainy, but otherwise the wedding went smoothly. Cecil's wedding gift to his daughter was a house just a few hundred yards from his own in Laughlin Park. When it was all over, Cecil took out a bottle of champagne he had put aside twenty-one years before, when Cecilia had been born, and opened it for the pleasure of a few special guests. The champagne had gone flat.

Cecilia's marriage lasted seven years and produced two children—Peter Calvin and Cecil's beloved granddaughter Cecilia. After the divorce, Cecil maintained an amiable but formal relationship with his ex-son-in-law.

Meanwhile, Cecil's daughter Katherine wanted to be an artist and studied for a year at the Chicago Art Institute. After that came a flirtation with writing. Finally, she settled on a career as an actress, a plan for which Cecil had no appreciation. "He thought that the impression would get around that he was forcing me on the industry because of my connection with him," remembered Katherine. Katherine's exotic beauty eventually got her a job at MGM in *Viva Villa!*—where Clark Gable relieved her of her virginity—a Mae West picture at Paramount, and Fox's *The Call of the Wild*, again with Gable.

✦

In the late summer of 1930, Cecil took off on a voyage on the *Seaward*. On August 19, he wrote Constance from Santa Cruz: "All is well. The sea is marvelous, the sky is blue, the winds are fair, the Islands beautiful—you are ever in my thoughts—I always link the beautiful and the peaceful with you—and the sea seems to strip one of all the little things of life and leave only the valuable—the petty affairs drop into their proper place and the *real* ones become the dominant factors of thought. So far the spoils have been one Marlin swordfish about 180 pounds which leaped playfully over George's bait and took mine, caught near the east end of Anna Cappa [Anacapa Island]. Give my love to all the family. . . . Discard all your fear and enjoy the love that is all about you—Cecil."

Cecil's admonition to "discard all your fear" is a clear reference to what Richard deMille would describe as "periods of tension" during which Cecil or Constance would need to get away. "Constance suffered in the bargain she had made," remembered Richard deMille. "It was a fair bargain, but Constance had gotten fat, and had to get thin, and was aware of not being [physically] competitive with Cecil's other women."

Henry Churchill deMille, from whom his younger son inherited religious devotion, a knack for the theater, and early baldness.

From his mother, Matilda Beatrice Samuel, DeMille inherited his eyes, his chin, much of his natural intelligence, and all of his immense drive. (BYU)

Cecil B. DeMille at the age of five, sporting the long curls that were the norm for children of the Victorian era, whose mothers were bewitched by *Little Lord Fauntleroy*. The future director's regal self-confidence is already apparent.

On the left, Cecil Blount DeMille, with
his brother, William. Cecil is holding
flowers, Bill is holding Homer Q. Putnam.

David Belasco, partner of Henry deMille,
spiritual father of Cecil B. DeMille, circa 1905.

The beautiful, sultry Constance Adams
as a young actress, around the time she
met DeMille. (BYU)

On far right, Dustin Farnum (holding the gun); on the far left, his wife, Winifred Kingston, the stars of *The Squaw Man*, the film that began DeMille's career.

Cecil's dynamic display of energy when directing is obvious in this snapshot taken on the back lot of the Lasky studio. Notice his hat on the corner of the director's chair.

The impatient young dynamo caught in transit in the backyard of the Lasky Barn in 1914. On the upper left are the muslin curtains that could be drawn over the stage to diffuse the sunlight.

Cecil with Dustin Farnum (right) and an unidentified man (left) auditioning rattlesnakes in 1914. In the background is the slightly elevated stage where Cecil was making his movies.

Cecil (center, wearing hat) preparing a scene at the Lasky Barn in 1914. In the background there appears to be a carpentry shop, and beyond that, the orange groves that surrounded the barn.

In the early days at the Lasky Barn, Constance DeMille was occasionally pressed into duty as an actress, as was their daughter Cecilia.

Reenacting the childhood photo: Cecil holding flowers, Bill holding a dog, in Hollywood circa 1915.

The brain trusts of the Famous Players and Lasky companies on the occasion of their merger in 1916. From the left: Jesse Lasky, Adolph Zukor, Sam Goldfish (later Goldwyn), DeMille, and Albert Kaufman.

The magnificent Geraldine Farrar was one of the few opera stars to make the transition to movie star, here in DeMille's 1915 production of *Carmen*.

Directing Raymond Hatton in *Joan the Woman* during the long, hot summer of 1916.

Julia Faye comforts Raymond Hatton in DeMille's astonishing, Zolaesque *The Whispering Chorus* (1918).

DeMille and guide returning from a successful hunt, circa 1918. In later years, he became more invested in preserving wildlife than in killing it.

Gloria Swanson, before DeMille took her in hand, and after.

DeMille coerced Swanson into allowing a lion to lie on top of her for a single, hair-raising shot in *Male and Female* (1919).

Cecil on the right with the cast of *The Affairs of Anatol* (1921): Wallace Reid is fourth from the left in the second row, while Gloria Swanson is fourth from right in the front row. Among the others: Elliott Dexter, Monte Blue, Bebe Daniels, Agnes Ayres, Polly Moran, and Julia Faye.

DeMille directing Pharaoh's army through a public address system on location in Guadalupe, California, for the 1923 version of *The Ten Commandments*.

In retrospect, it can be seen that DeMille came to epics hesitantly, in incremental steps. But given his gift for orchestrating scenes containing large sets and milling crowds, as in this mobilization of Pharaoh's chariots for *The Ten Commandments*, it was a natural progression.

Art direction as psychology: Imperial Rome dwarfs Christ in *The King of Kings* (1927).

DeMille's studied compositions for *The King of Kings* recall the painters he loved as a child.

A lunchtime conference on the set of 1929's *The Godless Girl*, with DeMille and Jeanie Macpherson flanking gossip columnist Louella Parsons.

Cecil signing his contract with MGM's Louis B. Mayer in 1929. The smiles didn't last long.

In 1932, DeMille returned to Paramount to make *The Sign of the Cross*. Here, with the camera boom on one side and costume designer/art director Mitchell Leisen on the other, DeMille directs a Colosseum sequence through the public address system, his preferred method of handling crowd scenes.

The always audacious Charles Laughton played Nero as a pouting, dissolute queen in *The Sign of the Cross*.

The devastating Claudette Colbert as the devastating *Cleopatra* in DeMille's 1934 film.

From the left: son John, wife Constance, daughter Katherine, Cecil, and son Richard deMille, circa 1932. (BYU)

The movies march on—DeMille and Emily Barrye, his longtime script girl, pose in 1934 with the modern camera used to shoot *Cleopatra*, and the old Pathé camera with which he had shot *The Squaw Man*, which always had an honored place in his office.

Cecil, Bill, and friend circa 1935, with the relaxed body language that indicates the warmth of their relationship. (BYU)

DeMille's yacht, the *Seaward*, off Catalina Island, with the Avalon Ballroom in the background. (BYU)

DeMille and Gladys Rosson, his eternally loyal secretary and managing mistress, in his cabin on board the *Seaward*.

DeMille hosted frequent nightly screenings in the house on DeMille Drive, after which he would go around the room asking people what they thought of the movie.

Although DeMille had little to do with the *Lux Radio Theatre* beyond showing up for dress rehearsals and performances, he gave the impression that he was as strenuously involved as in any of his movies.

The Money Shot Part
I: The collapse of the
temple in 1949's *Samson
and Delilah* was made
even more convincing
by matteing in terrified
crowds in the foreground
that partially obscure the
immobile figures shown in
this miniature.

DeMille's performance in *Sunset Boulevard*
captured authentic aspects of the man at
his best—gentle in his power, sensitive to
eminences of the movies' early days whose
careers had been obliterated by time and
changing tastes.

DeMille in May 1948, asking Congress to
strengthen the Taft-Hartley Act to protect
the individual's right to work.

DeMille on the front porch of Paradise, his mountain retreat (BYU).

The living room at Paradise (BYU).

Feeding some of the deer at Paradise, a task and a herd that DeMille carefully guarded for forty years. No animals could be hunted on DeMille's property (BYU).

Fearless as always, DeMille personally auditioned all the cast members of *The Greatest Show on Earth* (1952).

Riding the camera boom on location for *The Greatest Show on Earth.*

The results of careful planning and masterful composition: the apotheosis of the three-ring tent show in *The Greatest Show on Earth.*

On location in Egypt for the 1956 *The Ten Commandments,* DeMille inspects the Great Gate of Per Rameses, behind which were the picture's production headquarters, in front of which he staged the Exodus.

A week or two before his heart attack on location in Egypt, DeMille (with Charlton Heston) was already looking gray and drawn, and had lost a lot of weight due to dysentery. (BYU)

DeMille and Yul Brynner, with his ever-present 35mm cameras, during the studio shoot of *The Ten Commandments*—a relationship described by everybody who witnessed it as "father and son."

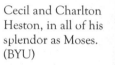

Cecil and Charlton Heston, in all of his splendor as Moses. (BYU)

The 1956 version of *The Ten Commandments* was DeMille's farewell to directing, but it was also H. B. Warner's final acting appearance. Greatly aged, unable to walk, Warner was carried through his brief but moving scene.

The Money Shot Part II: The Exodus on location in Egypt. It was during this sequence that DeMille suffered a massive coronary.

A beaming DeMille captured on a very good day during the studio shoot of *The Ten Commandments*. Favored co-workers received autographed copies of this photo.

DeMille tended to be all business on a movie set, but on his seventy-fifth birthday his charming grin was captured.

At Paramount's "DeMille Gate" with his daughter Cecilia (right) and granddaughter Cecilia Jr., or Citzie, as she was known to the family. On the left is the building that housed the DeMille unit. (BYU)

DeMille on one of his few visits to the set of the 1958 remake of *The Buccaneer* being directed by Anthony Quinn. Yul Brynner seems amused; DeMille doesn't.

DeMille at his memento-laden desk at home, shortly before his death. *The Conquest of Space* on the bookshelf behind him indicates he was in the middle of planning *Project X*, the top secret film that was to dramatize the Book of Revelation.

DeMille and Constance, whom he often called "Gretchen," very near the end of their lives, after she was already afflicted with Alzheimer's disease.

Despite the tensions over the arrangement, Constance remained protective and solicitous of him in that motherly way familiar to all husbands: "My Darling One . . ." she wrote Cecil on an undated card, "Remember you are to dine at six and go to bed at eight. I shall be missing you. All my love, Constance."

Cecil was still on close terms with Jeanie Macpherson, and the indications are that their sexual relationship had survived the arrival of Julia Faye, if not with the frequency that Macpherson would have liked. Although DeMille was paying Macpherson $1,000 a week—good money for a screenwriter in this period—she was habitually on the financial edge and always in need of a loan or advance on her salary. Cecil occasionally had to play the part of the stern parent, admonishing Jeanie about her irresponsibility: "The Bank has notified me that for nine weeks you had not made a curtailment on your note there until your recent payment of $500.00, which still leaves an overdue balance of $400.00. I must impress upon you the importance of keeping up your payments weekly. The Bank is complaining and unless these payments are kept up regularly . . . they will tie up your salary until the full amount is paid."

"HELLO CHIEF HOW ARE YOU," wrote Macpherson from San Francisco on April 30, 1930. "SHOULD LOVE TO SEE YOU WISH YOU COULD FLY OR MOTOR UP WILL SEE YOU WHEN I FLY DOWN LATER TO TALK WITH IRVING [Thalberg?] STOP HAVE SEEN THE MOST GORGEOUS SET OF CHESSMEN HALF OF THEM IN GREEN JADE AND HALF IN YELLOW JADE STOP BET YOU DIDN'T KNOW THERE WAS ANY YELLOW JADE IN THE WORLD NEITHER DID I . . . GUMP HAS THE CHESSMAN AND ASKING FOUR HUNDRED FIFTY AM TRYING TO SEE IF I CAN PAWN MY SHOES AND GET THEM YOU WOULD BE SIMPLY CRAZY OVER THEM."

DeMille replied the next day and told her he was delighted by "the happy and vigorous tone" of her letter. "The Chess men sound marvelous and I am very fond of chess, but I am very poor. The market having joined Madam Satan in her downward plunge . . ."

DeMille's comments about his impending impoverishment were slightly exaggerated; Gladys Rosson's November 1930 report of his finances showed that DeMille had cash on hand of $316,082.68, and a net worth of $2.937 million, this more than a year after the stock market crash.

∗

For the final picture on his MGM contract, DeMille threw up his hands and mounted his second remake of *The Squaw Man*, which now smelled of mothballs. Future screenwriter and playwright Leonard Spigelgass, whom Gore Vidal would immortalize as the Wise Old Hack, was then working as a reader in the script department at MGM. Spigelgass read the original play and reported that "In its hey-day . . . this was a big hit! Its hey-day seems to have passed, however, and *The Squaw Man* is a little old-fashioned. Something might be done with it, nevertheless, particularly if it is desired to make a picture that combines the outdoors with society stuff."

The changing times had brought increasing worries over the story's elements of miscegenation, now more controversial than in Edwardian times. "I think it is terribly dangerous for him to *ever* take her in his arms or touch her deliberately," Lenore Coffee wrote DeMille during the scripting process. "Any physical contact must be legitimately for a purpose—like helping her off with some wet things."

One potentially interesting development was contained in a note from Gladys Rosson to Mitch Leisen: "Clark Gabel [sic], an English actor—rather a heavy type—made a test here for Lionel Barrymore's new picture, *Never the Twain Shall Meet*. He has been suggested to Mr. DeMille for the husband in *The Squaw Man*. Will you please see this test, and if Mr. Gabel proves interesting, arrange for Mr. DeMille to look at it?" Leisen looked at the test, and evidently gave DeMille a negative report; the un-English but heavy Gable had to wait a couple of years for stardom.

In January 1931, a month before production began on *The Squaw Man*, DeMille wrote Father Daniel Lord, with whom he remained friendly. "I cannot find any inspiration at all in the type of pictures the producers want me to make. They are in a state of panic and chaos and . . . they rush for the bedspring and the lingerie the moment the phantom of empty seats rises to clutch them." DeMille told Lord that he hoped to get an organization of six to eight directors together, find some capital, and make movies that they wanted to make—the equivalent of a directorial United Artists. "Failing in this direction, or failing to find a producer who has confidence in the kind of pictures I want to make, I shall probably raise even the topsails of the *Seaward* and see how far I can sail without stopping."

On February 8, DeMille gathered Frank Borzage, Lewis Milestone, and King Vidor to form a company they called the Directors Guild, Inc. DeMille outlined the raison d'être in a manifesto: "There is a move to eliminate high salaries. With Wall Street in control, the Directors need an alliance similar to United Artists; but, with this difference: The director does better work as he grows older—the actor poorer. . . . An organization should be composed of the ten best directors to make 20 pictures a year. . . . What chain of theaters would have the poor business judgment to say NO to the product of the ten best makers of motion pictures . . . the sellers of films have been exploiting the makers of films long enough. It is the writer and director who make a picture—not the executive in his office."

DeMille took charge of finding the necessary funds and production facilities. The idea was to make movies for around $450,000 apiece, with DeMille, Borzage, Milestone, and Vidor earning $50,000 per picture and one third of the net profits.

The problems were twofold: timing, and money—the same thing, really. Nineteen thirty-one was close to the depth of the Depression, and the Directors Guild, Inc. was asking for a minimum investment of $2.5 million to fund a year's worth of pictures, until the box office returns started filtering back to the company—this in the face of a general panic in the movie business, not to mention everyplace else, about the future of capitalism.

The idea got as far as a draft contract with the increasingly moribund Fox organization, but the deal was never signed. All of DeMille's contacts at the Bank of America meant nothing when juxtaposed against a worldwide depression. The idea of a company run by directors for directors came to nothing.

★

The star of *The Squaw Man* was the perennially middle-aged Warner Baxter, who insisted on making reflexive passes at his co-star Eleanor Boardman. She didn't take Baxter seriously, and found DeMille polite to her, pompous to everybody else. (DeMille's kindness to Boardman was probably because King Vidor was Boardman's husband.) The production was enlivened by a rare scene of domestic drama. "He had a mistress for many years," remembered Boardman, "and after we'd been on location for a week or so, [Julia Faye] was with him. Mrs. DeMille appeared on this location and discovered he'd been having an affair. . . . There was a big blowup."

Since Constance had always been aware of Julia's presence in her husband's life, it's more likely that the explosion was occasioned by Constance discovering that Julia had accompanied Cecil on location; Cecil may have promised to keep his affairs away from the film sets.

The conflagration with Constance might have explained Cecil's bad temper. The child actor Dickie Moore remembered that DeMille made a move to hit him for some perceived brattishness. Luckily, the welfare worker/teacher assigned to Moore interceded and told DeMille she would immediately close down the set if he struck the child.

Even DeMille realized in retrospect that the remake of *The Squaw Man* was one trip to the well too many. As he told George Pratt, speaking of himself in the third person, "The third one is not good because it suffered from a weakness that the director doesn't generally show but he showed in this picture. He allowed the tempo to become too slow, even with a wonderful cast like [Charles] Bickford playing Cash Hawkins and Warner Baxter playing Jim, Lupe Velez giving the best of the three performances as the squaw."

DeMille was actually being overly harsh; the film is well shot on attractive locations, and the mutual seduction scene between Baxter and Velez is worthy of a better story: an isolated cabin, a woman waiting submissively in the rain, a man who invites her in to dry off before the fire. She kneels by the fire, takes off her wet dress and rests her head on his hand. They gaze into the fire. Fade out.

Beyond that, Leonard Spigelgass was right—the material was archaic. All three versions of *The Squaw Man*—only a single reel of the 1918 version survives—stick closely to Edwin Royle's original story, and they unquestioningly transmit themes common to the time: the displacement of Indian culture, the superiority of European culture, the ultimate impossibility of successful intermarriage. But, as always, DeMille apprehended the basic duality of the audience—its eagerness to vicariously experience the forbidden, while at the same time preserving a sense of respectability.

The Squaw Man was another expensive failure—a cost of $572,811, a gross of $586,163. Cecil realized the problem was not the Depression or his stars, but his pictures. " 'Depressions' " he told a trade paper, "are bad on bad pictures, but they never really affect good entertainment. In bad times people seek relaxation more energetically than in days of prosperity, but they shop more for their shows."

Irving Thalberg was delegated the job of dropping the weight. "I'm sorry, C.B., there is nothing here for you," DeMille remembered him saying. "I do not know whether MGM or I was more relieved that my contract had come to an end," DeMille said. As he packed up his bungalow to leave the studio, Cecil sent thank-you notes to production manager Joe Cohn and Doug Shearer for their courtesies to him.

For DeMille, the MGM sojourn was a washout; the only person at MGM who was sorry to see him go was the cameraman Hal Rosson, the brother of Gladys Rosson, who had shot Madam Satan and who said, "I learned more from Mr. DeMille than from any other human being I've ever known. I boast of the fact that we were very close friends."

Within eight years Cecil had been booted out by Paramount, had failed in independent production, and now at MGM—three strikes and out. Contributing to the unease was the fact that the pictures DeMille made at MGM were, on balance, weak DeMille movies, not good MGM movies. They were an unusually scattered lot, as if he were casting about for something he thought the audience might enjoy, rather than presenting something with that lordly air that had marked his previous efforts—and would mark them again in the future.

Professionally speaking, Cecil didn't have a lot of options at this point. The movie business was suffering terribly from the Depression, and there were few takers for a high-maintenance director regarded as damaged goods, one who, moreover, carried a high overhead.

Cecil contacted Jesse Lasky about the possibility of going back to Paramount with a production of The Sign of the Cross, and Jesse loyally sounded out people. The results were negative.

"While I succeeded in creating some interest," cabled Jesse on March 7, 1931, "the general opinion was that we should not consider undertaking a production of that size with a subject which, while it might succeed, it might also miss; and after a general discussion I was advised to abandon all thoughts of it for the present. . . . I am very sorry that I could not put this over, and I know you also will be disappointed. My advice is for you to buy the story, and whatever connection you make, I trust you will be able to do *The Sign of the Cross* as your next picture."

Casting about for something to occupy his attention, Cecil decided to get out of town—far out of town. In June, two months before he left for a lengthy tour of Russia, he told *Variety*, "I am not a radical, but now things are a question of right and wrong. The public has been milked and are growing tired of it. . . . There is something rotten at the core of the system. . . . There is something all wrong somewhere when a man can't invest his carefully accumulated money in the big industries of a country without having them manipulated by those at the top, with the result that his life savings and the protection for his family are wiped out."

It was going to be a lengthy, expensive trip; DeMille got a letter of credit for $65,000 from his bank. Accompanying him would be Constance and, in a return to his native country, Theodore Kosloff. Before Cecil and party embarked from New York, his niece Agnes arranged a private dance recital by her friend Martha Graham, probably in the vague hope that Cecil might see his way clear to fund some of Graham's work. Graham danced *Primitive Mysteries*, and Cecil sat there intently watching. Turning to his niece, he said, "Her hair is just the right length. Exactly the right length. Longer or shorter would have been wrong."

After the recital, Cecil graciously congratulated Graham and told her that he was glad to have lent a helping hand early in her career when she had appeared in *Male and Female*.

★

The DeMille party's first stop was London, where they saw plays featuring John Gielgud, Jack Hawkins, and Jessica Tandy. In DeMille's program of Jack Buchanan's *Stand Up and Sing*, he made a mark next to the name of Anna Neagle, and in a production of *Payment Deferred* at the St. James Theatre, he was roused to attention by a brilliant, if physically unprepossessing actor named Charles Laughton, who he thought might make a good Nero.

They moved on to the Netherlands, stopping in Haarlem to visit the church where Anthony deMil had been married in 1653. Just after they entered Russia, DeMille wrote home to Gladys Rosson, "There have been no reporters, and few people knew me. . . . Tell the family to be careful of wisecracks in their letters, as mail will probably be read before it reaches us. . . . Theodore was afraid to go in alone, but he feels that with us he will be safe. I hope he has not overestimated my influence with the Soviet."

DeMille, Constance, and Kosloff spent a month in Russia, moving about at will. Cecil's diary from the trip describes vivid, picturesque scenes, with DeMille always resonating to the sybaritic splendor of the czars. And there is a growing sense that perhaps Russia was not the glorious possibility it sometimes seemed.

The first stop was Moscow and the Hotel Metropole on August 31. He found

Lenin's tomb "thrilling." They went to a marriage and divorce registration bureau and examined documents for the district. "55% of divorces to marriages. One girl had changed her papers to make herself 18 so she could marry. Refused and cautioned not to try it again."

On Wednesday, September 2, he noted a funeral, "one old horse pulling a wagon with four white posts on the corners. The coffin tied to the body with rope. First five or six followers walking bareheaded in street . . ."

He visited a prison, "600 people three corridors radiating from center. All cell doors unlocked. Convicts all cheerful—receive 35 rubles month for their work . . . Murderer from four years to death. Some for sedition. Young man who killed his friend got two years. Greek priest for counter revolution ten years. Punishments easy. Less sullenness and more eagerness than I have ever seen in any other prison." That night they went to the Moscow Art Theater to see *Bread,* and watched Maxim Gorky on stage after the performance carrying "little satan skull cap."

Thursday, September 3: "The flow of people on the street gives the feel of a mighty river which nothing can stop. Two experiments started about the same time. Prohibition has failed and socialism succeeded. The magnificent opera house. The strange costumes of the audience. The mediocre dancing. The propaganda at the end of opera ballet, *Red Poppy.*

"They are all good actors. Worked all day on letter proposition to Mejrabpom Films."

DeMille's letters home revealed that the Russian film company wanted him to make a movie for them. DeMille would have to put up half the money in return for half the profits—an opportunity he declined. The Russians then asked for a written counterproposal, but DeMille was put off by the Stalinist love of groupthink and committees. "I do not believe I could make much of a picture that way," he wrote Gladys Rosson.

DeMille was astonished by the disparities of Russia, its splendor and poverty. "There is nothing like it in the world unless it was Rome after its fall or Paris after the revolution," he wrote Rosson. "Almost nothing that you have heard about it is true . . . it would be the most fascinating place to work, but I would probably make a better picture of it at home than here. There is more drama in one block on a street of Moscow than I have ever seen in an entire city anywhere else. . . . We have had complete freedom. I have walked into private houses, making the selection myself, and talked with the people and found drama and comedy and tragedy every foot of the way."

There was a splendidly improbable reunion when Kosloff ran into his sister selling cigarettes on the street. On September 11, the party toured the Kremlin, and DeMille was awash in jewels and ermine robes. "Emeralds, rubies, sapphires, pearls encrusted in saddles, dishes, robes, pearls embroidered on everything. The old peasant woman rubbing up the crown of Catherine the Great, polishing unconcernedly the jewel studded chair of Ivan the Terrible. Arranging the wealth of the Czars without emotion. One of the finest museums in the world. . . . Kremlin—the coaches of the Czars—the pearl embroidered robes—the church—the tomb of the child Dimitri—of Ivan the Terrible—his special throne in church . . . The great bell that wouldn't ring. The great gun that wouldn't shoot . . ."

Saturday, September 12: ". . . Russia has perhaps one face in every ten marked by smallpox . . . Left for Leningrad evening. *Very* cold—no heat in train. They turn the heat on according to dates not according to temperatures. No dining car. Samovar at end of car—porter makes tea for 20-k per glass."

Sunday, September 13: "Arrived Leningrad. Pouring rain. Very cold. Beautiful city, but of the past. Leningrad is European—Moscow Asiatic . . . Gorgeous winter palace. Private theater. Most beautiful palace in Europe. The marvelous vases of Malvelista, etc. [Malechite?] The collections of silver service."

On Tuesday, September 15, they left for Nizhni Novgorod, but before that they saw the crown jewels—"most wonderful display of jewels in the world. The crown of Alexandria, last Czarina most beautiful—hanging great thirty-fifty karat stones. The great crown of the Czars with the ruby top . . . The enormous perfect sapphires—five hundred million dollars value of whole collection. Looked through the gold and diamond and ruby field glasses given Catherine by the Sultan of Turkey 'so she could see him across the Black Sea.' The diamond design for dress. The great chain of Paul worth many millions. The ruby pin I tried to buy."

On Friday, September 18, they reached Samara—"very uninteresting town—dirty . . . In evening had three hour conversation with the Professor. He knows Lenin—Marx—and little else. Has no conception of American government. Believes the lynching of negroes, like the pogroms, is Government inspired, or at least condoned. Done by capitalists to show class hatred. Believes the shooting of political prisoners is OK but is shocked at America's having capital punishment for murder—calls it revenge."

The discussion continued a few days later. "He believes Lincoln was a capitalist president and freed the slaves to help capital. I asked if it would then be advisable to reenslave them. Stumped. No real knowledge of America—its government or ideals. Said if we found a man digging a hole under the White House to bomb it, wouldn't he be executed. When I explained only if the bomb killed someone, he was very skeptical. The gravest danger between the two countries is lack of understanding of each other's true condition and true purpose."

On to Stalingrad, as the accommodations began to radically deteriorate: "No blankets, sheets or pillows provided by railroad. No diner though on train for twenty-four hours. Food—tomatoes, watermelon, bread is bought from circles of peasants at the different stations. Grandma porter gets up kettle of boiled water and I reboil with our outfit and with cubes bought in Germany make Bullion. Stalingrad has fine new theatre and kino, but hotel is beyond words. Hygiene is what should be introduced."

On Tuesday, September 22, they were somewhere on the Steppes; "vast stretches of prairies—camels to carts like horses . . . Train going about twenty five to thirty miles per hour. Every station crowded—tomatoes and watermelons—we picnic for meals. Children begging at the railroad stations . . . poverty and sloth beyond words . . ."

On into Georgia, through small towns to Tiflis on September 24: "The sun's last rays shine on an old ruined monastery on a high hill. The town is in shadow. The Monastery just the color of the hill itself . . . Tiflis is real Orient—fought over by Persian, Greek, Turk, Arabian and Russian for centuries. It is the capitol of Georgia. Armenians, Jews added to all the above nationalities are plentiful—450,000 people. They are gay—free and well-to-do. No food scarcity. They are apparently happy under the Soviet . . ."

In Tiflis, DeMille met with Georgian filmmakers and discovered that they were still making silent movies. There were 174 theaters in Georgia and eighteen directors were making a succession of shorts and features for the local audiences. When he visited their studio, he discovered that "the studio is about the size of the Lasky studio after we had built the first two glass stages and the first laboratory. They also make animated cartoons, but had never heard of Mickey Mouse."

As the trip wound down, DeMille paused for some reflections:

Russia is a land of no liberty—of much paper money—of terrible filth—of great determination—of high ideals—and almost hopeless poverty. Russia is a land of one hundred and thirty eight million slaves and two million masters. . . . There is less freedom in Russia than in any country that I know. There are twelve million bureaucrats who cannot make a living. Their children are not given schooling—they are not given rooms, etc.

While traveling in the boat down the Volga, I brought out a box of fine cigars that I had not smoked and passed them around to all the men—there were two officers, military men, a professor from Moscow, and a couple of business men. They accepted the cigars, without a change of expression on their faces—but an indication of polite thanks. I watched them with some interest and decided that they had never smoked a cigar before. They looked the cigars all over, one tried to light his with the wrong end in his mouth—they each had a terrible time with their cigars—one could not get his lighted at all, so he just held it in his hand. The old man, about 60, who had finally gotten his lighted with the wrong end in his mouth, in a few minutes turned green, stood up for a second, and said something about being time to retire, and off he went, rather hurriedly. It was very amusing, but I'm afraid they didn't quite realize the nature of my gift.

On October 3, they arrived in Constantinople, where they visited the house of Pierre Loti, then moved on to Athens, where DeMille visited the Acropolis and realized that "the most beautiful building as to situation and design in the world is the Parthenon. It has not the mystery of the Mosque of Mahmet—but it is perfect. I sit in the chair of Marcus Aurelius in the theatre of Bacchus—the first theatre in the world." In Athens, DeMille went to the marketplace and discovered an icon, where, "after three days attempt to jew the merchant down I finally buy the bearded icon . . ."

By October 15, the party was in Alexandria, and a day later landed in Cairo, where the pyramids at Memphis "compares in thrill to the first sight of the Rocky Mountains Constance and I had from the sleeper on the way to Denver in 1904. . . . We drive home with that never to be forgotten picture of those three pyramids against the orange sky just after the sun has set and moon almost balanced on top of Cheops. I suppose for fifty five hundred years people have burst into various kinds of audible and silent appreciation of that sight, and they should for three thousand years more."

DeMille was continually intoxicated by the beauty of the scenes he witnessed along the Nile, a series of images that would impel him to personally shoot the Egyptian footage for his remake of *The Ten Commandments*.

> Village after village made of bricks of Nile mud. Always the women, always slow moving buffalo, everything moves slowly, even the Dahabia. . . . It is a land of dreams . . . I am awakened by the shrill cry of women driving off the evil spirits, then singing—then moans and screams. Throwing on a wrapper I go to the upper deck to see what's happening. A body in an open coffin is being carried on the heads of a group of men to a waiting boat to be born to the old Mohammedan cemetery on the other side of the Nile.
>
> It is like Dore's painting of Charon waiting to ferry the departed soul across the River Styx. Many women are following, moaning and always giving at intervals the high cry to keep back the evil one. The widow of the dead is being supported between the two older women. She is a young good-looking girl in the transports of grief, swaying and moaning. As the body is put into the boat she breaks away from the others—for the women do not cross with the body. She tries to throw herself into the Nile, but is caught and led away by the other women. The boat starts across the Nile. All this punctuated at regular intervals by the warning cry to the evil one.
>
> Did I say before that the most interesting countries are Russia and Egypt—the former because everything is changed—the latter because nothing has changed? . . . I see the first case of small pox, but say nothing

for fear of alarming Theodore. He also sees it but says nothing for fear
of alarming me.

The trip cemented DeMille's admiration for Kosloff; he had always admired
Kosloff's choreography, as well as his mastery of women, but to that was added
admiration for Kosloff's courage in going back to Russia. DeMille always felt that
he got to know the Russian people much better than he ever could have without
Kosloff's friendship and adept translations.

The party returned to New York on November 24. Shortly afterward, he was
greeted with the stunning news that the IRS was charging him $1,676,563 in cor-
porate back taxes, based on the government's contention that Cecil B. DeMille
Productions had been formed for the express purpose of avoiding income tax.

On top of the very expensive trip DeMille had just taken, he had no money
coming in and no prospects of any. The IRS claim had to be fought, because to
pay it would have meant something approaching financial devastation. He had
been forced to mortgage the house in Laughlin Park in order to meet the obligations of DeMille Productions. That said, he still was in far better financial condition than almost any other director in Hollywood. He had oil properties that were
proving profitable, and real estate rental that was bringing him about $50,000 a
year before taxes. Financially he was okay . . . unless the IRS won its lawsuit.

Suddenly, DeMille was more than willing to rent out the *Seaward* to other
people—Robert Montgomery negotiated a good rate for a charter group that included Douglas Fairbanks Jr., Laurence Olivier, and Edwin Knopf.

There was alteration everywhere, with the industry engaged in one of its periodic convulsions. In 1926, Paramount had paid $13 million for two thirds of
the Balaban & Katz theater chain, bringing its total number of theaters to 1,400—
more than all the other movie companies combined. A year later, Sam Katz had
told a class at Harvard Business School, "We can lose enough money in our theaters to sink the Famous Players."

Katz had been right; the Depression halved theater attendance and the studio
was stuck with expensive mortgages for 1,400 theaters that were now worth less
than what Paramount owed on them. In 1932, the studio lost a staggering $21 mil-
lion. At this point, Paramount's theaters, with a book value of $150 million, were
mortgaged for about $58 million. Adolph Zukor had gradually transformed the
company into an exhibition operation with a filmmaking appendage—in 1930,
the Paramount theaters took in $113 million, while their income from film rent-
als was $69 million. For Paramount, the theaters had become an end unto them-
selves, and in a vast depression, they nearly became *the* end.

In March 1933, the company would file for bankruptcy. For several years,
thousands of employees spread over Paramount's eighteen soundstages and
twenty-seven acres held their collective breath while teams of lawyers and trustees
argued and negotiated. Paramount would not emerge from receivership until July

1935, when a reorganization plan was finally approved, with the theaters valued at a much more realistic $61 million.

If things were bad for DeMille, they were worse for his staff, who had been laid off. On May 25, 1932, Anne Bauchens wrote, "Dear Chief, I have run across a temporary job. A private party with a lot of film on their hands that I may be able to help them with. It will possibly keep me busy four or five weeks at the most."

14

In the spring of 1932, DeMille was in New York, checking out theater. He saw *Evergreen*, *The Good Companions*, Max Reinhardt's production of Offenbach's *Die Schöne Helena*, Helen Hayes in Molnár's *The Good Fairy*, *The Warrior's Husband* with a striking young actress named Katharine Hepburn, Preston Sturges's *Child of Manhattan*, Irving Berlin's *Face the Music*, Richard Tauber in Franz Lehár's *Land of Smiles*, Ziegfeld's *Hot-Cha* with Bert Lahr, Lupe Velez, and Buddy Rogers, and *Götterdämmerung* at the Met with Lauritz Melchior. Then it was back to Los Angeles.

DeMille's politics were in the same state of flux as his career. He had supported Herbert Hoover in 1928, and made the largest contribution he ever made to a political campaign. But 1932 wasn't 1928. Aside from the worldwide Depression, there was the matter of Prohibition, which DeMille thought criminally stupid. Franklin D. Roosevelt was against Prohibition and was a man after DeMille's own heart—a warrior who was invariably the brightest light in any room, simultaneously ebullient and crafty, never admitting to difficulty let alone failure. DeMille always thought Hoover was the smartest of the five presidents he met, but it was a bookish intelligence rather than a savvy intelligence. DeMille lent Roosevelt one of his cars for a campaign swing through Los Angeles and ended up voting for him—the last time he would vote for a Democratic presidential candidate.

★

"It was a period when I couldn't get a job," remembered DeMille more than twenty years later, dictating his autobiography with a scalding awareness of his own humiliation. "I went around to all the companies—there were two or three companies that I started negotiations with—but nobody would even listen. I was through. I was dead. I was just like one of the Egyptian mummies. . . . Exactly the same amount of interest in you. You were a curiosity. You were something rather boring. You were kept waiting. Nobody said, 'Yes, Mr. DeMille, come on in.' For the years that you had done big things—nothing."

DeMille made an appointment with Sidney Kent, who was now at Fox. "He was just as cold and uninterested as anything," remembered DeMille. "Not a flicker of interest. And when he was sick, I had taken care of him. . . . I was just dead."

DeMille was apparently out of options, but he was a fighter, not to mention a gambler with a spine of cold steel. It was obvious that nobody was going to help DeMille but DeMille, and he was going to have to risk some of his fast-ebbing capital. Once again he went back through the decades to a surefire theatrical war horse of his youth. He began negotiations to buy the rights to *The Sign of the Cross* from Mary Pickford. She had bought the silent rights to the property in 1924, and was a legendarily tough negotiator. She opened by asking for $30,000, which she then raised to $50,000. For dialogue rights, DeMille had to make a separate deal with the estate of the playwright Wilson Barrett.

DeMille responded to Pickford by offering $30,000, then $35,000, basically killing time in the belief that she would come down. As was typical of Pickford, negotiations dragged on for months, until DeMille finally closed on the sale for around $38,000.

As DeMille remembered it, his return to Paramount was shepherded by B. P. Schulberg. "Lasky and Zukor were going out . . . the directors were Balaban and Katz and they were just coming in. . . . Schulberg . . . came in and said, 'You gentlemen are all crazy. You got here one of the greatest minds in the industry, grab him, take him. He built Paramount once before, maybe he can do it again . . .' Schulberg sort of manipulated them."

In truth, DeMille and Neil McCarthy approached Paramount with an unbeatable deal. Paramount was to provide the facilities and half the budget for an adaptation of *The Sign of the Cross*, while DeMille would provide the other half of the money. The total budget would be $650,000; DeMille's salary would be a minute $24,000, but only $14,322 would actually be paid in cash.

While 1932 was the deepest pit of the Depression and the studio was hemorrhaging red ink—the release slate for the first six months of the year amassed a loss of $2.5 million—a co-production with a very modest up-front investment was too good a deal to pass up, even if the director was damaged goods. Of course, if the film failed, DeMille would be finished, as well as out over $300,000. Not only that, but a lot of people thought an overtly religious play in the pit of the Depression was an abysmal idea.

Among them was screenwriter Clara Beranger—his sister-in-law. "I question if this is the time to do it," she wrote Cecil. "Just now the civilization of America is in a state of decadence resembling that of Rome before its fall, with the additional element of a financial depression such as the country has never known. . . . [The people] want entertainment, froth with no serious undercurrents. . . .

Witness the plays that have succeeded, the best sellers in books, and the type of fluffy stories published in current magazines." Cecil read her letter and filed it. He had no alternative but to follow his gut, and his gut told him that *The Sign of the Cross* was effective counterprogramming against prevailing trends.

The Sign of the Cross was essentially a rewrite of *Quo Vadis*, and would in turn be rewritten as *The Robe*—a Roman soldier falls in love with a Christian maiden, with grim but presumably ennobling consequences. Hollywood's open-armed ecumenism once again was prominent; among the screenwriters of this ardently Christian movie was Waldemar Young, a grandson of Brigham Young.

DeMille returned to a Paramount Studio that was different in both spirit and location. In 1926, the studio had bought the United Studios at Marathon and Van Ness, and demolished the old studio at Sunset and Vine, except for the barn used for *The Squaw Man*, which was moved to the new lot. In 1927, the studio had changed its name to the Paramount-Famous-Lasky Corporation, and in 1930 changed it again, to Paramount Publix.

As if walking onto the lot wasn't disconcerting enough, Cecil was about to encounter even more drastic changes. On April 25, Jesse Lasky was given his walking papers. Lasky caught a lifeline from Sidney Kent, the former Paramount executive who had cold-shouldered Cecil. At Fox, Lasky had a long list of perquisites, including his own building, but the knack for knowing what people wanted to see had disappeared. At Fox, he made some critical favorites—*The Power and the Glory*, from an innovative script by Preston Sturges, *Zoo in Budapest*, a few others—but no financial successes, which is not what the beleaguered company was hoping for.

Observing how many of his peers were falling by the wayside from a combination of factors that included talkies, changing audience tastes, and worldwide financial disaster, DeMille must have wondered if his name was shortly to be added to the list of obsolete directors that included such former signposts as Griffith, Ingram, Niblo, and Brenon.

It got worse when B. P. Schulberg was thrown out. DeMille would have to navigate a major biblical spectacular with a very modest budget and no help from the front office. Actually, he would have to hack through all manner of carefully erected obstacles and prove himself all over again. It was just like 1913, except there was much more at stake.

The man who took over the studio was Emanuel Cohen—promoted, for no rational reason, from the newsreel operation. Cohen regarded DeMille with deep suspicion. "Remember, Cecil, you are on trial with this picture" was the way he sent his new employee out to make his movie.

Adolph Zukor, who had first driven Cecil out of Paramount, then bided his time until he could get rid of Lasky as well, publicly praised DeMille, as DeMille did him, while each privately observed a wary respect for the other's borders.

How could DeMille ever trust Zukor? "Trust wasn't part of the deal," said

Richard deMille. So Zukor stayed in New York and watched Cecil make a provisional stab at reconstituting his career without giving him any help.

"There was a head cutter here named George Arthur," remembered DeMille. "For some reason he had a bitter dislike for me. I didn't know him, but he hated me. When I started to make *The Sign of the Cross* . . . they wouldn't let Annie Bauchens come and cut it. They said, 'You have to have the cutter we give [you].' The second day of shooting the cutter rushed to Cohen and said, 'For God's sake let me go anywhere, let me die, but get me away from this guy.' So Annie Bauchens came in."

Economies were necessary. DeMille had been paying Mitch Leisen $800 a week when they were at MGM, but the art director–costume designer had been working as a dress extra while DeMille toured Russia. Leisen came back as art director for $100 a week, with an additional $25 weekly thrown in for his costume designs. Cecil had Leisen plow through the costume inventory left over from *The King of Kings*, not to mention *Ben-Hur*, and found that it was in mostly bad shape but could be made usable. The sets were very carefully designed for specific camera angles, and most of the long shots involved miniatures because there wasn't enough money to build large sets.

That wasn't the worst of it; DeMille also had to submit to an unpleasant level of supervision. His contract for the picture stated that "Paramount appoints Mr. Emanuel Cohen as Supervisor of production . . . [DeMille] Productions shall accept cameramen, businessmen and other employees as assigned by Paramount, shall conform to shooting schedules established by Paramount."

DeMille began shooting *The Sign of the Cross* on July 25—the first time he had been on a soundstage in a year and a half.

After the first week of production, Emanuel Cohen sent for DeMille. Studio scuttlebutt had it that the footage was so bad it was funny. DeMille insisted that the quality of the rushes was easy enough to prove—let someone they both respected look at an assembly and judge it. DeMille suggested Al Kaufman, Zukor's brother-in-law. Kaufman loved the footage, and the shoot proceeded.

Charles Laughton, whom DeMille had seen in *Payment Deferred* in London, was perfect for Nero. There's a possibly apocryphal but nonetheless delicious story about them talking in the commissary. "Mr. DeMille," said Laughton, "I notice that all of your pictures have a religious motif. Are you yourself very religious?"

"Well," said DeMille, "I suppose there's a little bit of God in DeMille and a little bit of DeMille in God."

"How cozy," replied Laughton.

Laughton played Nero as a pouting, voluptuous queen, complete with a naked young catamite sitting next to him in the throne room—a heretofore closeted actor leaping out and streaking around a movie set, only to dart back in for the rest of his career. Although Laughton could be ferociously temperamental, he was docile with DeMille; as Karl Struss, the cameraman on the picture, said, "Nobody exhibited any tendencies with DeMille, ever." Laughton's wife, Elsa Lanchester, observed that playing Nero probably did Laughton more good than a year's worth of psychiatry.

Claudette Colbert was instantly seduced into coming aboard when DeMille leaned out a window and called down to her, "How would you like to play the wickedest woman in the world?"

"I'd been in kind of a rut playing nice, long-suffering heroines," she remembered. "I was bored with those roles, but because I happened to look like a lady, that's all they wanted me to play. Working with DeMille opened up a whole other field; they realized I could look sexy."

Colbert was a rising ingenue at this point, with only one standout production: Lubitsch's *The Smiling Lieutenant.* She was ambitious, a Paramount contractee, and didn't cost much. Although DeMille trusted his instincts, he figured he better try Colbert in a screen test, just in case. He had Mitch Leisen costume her and thought she looked magnificent. The cameras were ready, and he asked her to read a line. She did, and he promptly dismissed the camera crew; no test was necessary.

Mitchell Leisen slit Colbert's skirts up to the hip to show off her sensational legs, and Colbert wore no underwear in the picture. For the famous scene where she bathes in milk, DeMille told Leisen that he wanted the milk to barely cover her nipples. The day before the sequence was shot, Leisen had Colbert stand in the empty pool and took measurements to get the level perfect, then filled the pool with powdered milk.

In later years, Colbert usually told reporters that she was wearing a white bathing suit, but we have the testimony of cameraman Karl Struss to the contrary, as well as of our own eyes. In one shot, while the milk laps at Colbert's body, the distinct areola of a breast is revealed.

All hands agreed that it was a very unpleasant scene to shoot—hot, steamy, smelly. Mitchell Leisen had rigged up jets of compressed air to make the milk foamy, which tickled Colbert's breasts.

The compressed air and the heat from the lights made the milk thicken. Colbert later asserted that her lacquered wig began to melt. "It was really quite funny," she remembered, "but you didn't make any jokes with C.B. To him, it was important that everything be absolutely correct. He was very serious about giving the public what it wanted."

The only complication came at the end of the crucial scene. "Everybody was off the stage except the cameraman and DeMille," remembered Struss. "Julia Faye comes in with a towel and covers her up as she comes out. Over on the side, who should appear but [the head of the lab], who somehow managed to walk right past everybody. He got a nice side profile, which is more than any of us got. Oh, DeMille was mad; he really busted loose. Then, of course, he bawled Hezi Tate out for not keeping all the visitors off the set like he was supposed to. What he was really mad at was not being able to see her for himself. I was sore too!"

An equivalent problem was presented by the lions in the arena sequence, who adamantly refused to look savage. In the hopes of inciting a feeding frenzy, Mitch Leisen took a lamb carcass and costumed it, then chained it to the ground, but all the lions did was desultorily lap up blood.

This led to another DeMille explosion, but Leisen was used to the explosions and used to the man. "Everybody adored him that ever worked with him," said Leisen. "He might raise holy hell on the set, but often that was to put fear into the actor by criticizing me or the prop man. The minute we walked off the stage, he couldn't have been more charming. He'd even apologize for blowing his stack: 'There was nothing personal in that.' I'd say, 'I know, don't worry, I've been with you long enough to know that.' "

If the lions were a royal pain, DeMille was enthralled by the elephants. A scene in the arena called for the elephants to scoop up the dead, who were being played by a mixture of extras and dummies. DeMille was astonished by the gentleness with which they would pick up a live extra, "as gently as you would a piece of jewelry in a box. They'd go back to the dummy and slam it around, but they would not throw a man."

At one point, the elephants got excited and began to mill, but one female grabbed Bob Miles, her trainer, who was playing one of the dead Christians. The elephant placed Miles beneath her and resolutely stood over him, protecting him while the other elephants bumped and jostled her. She stood firm until the other elephants calmed down. "It was the most magnificent thing," DeMille remembered. "I took my hat off to her and I went over and kissed her afterwards. . . . I learned a respect for elephants that I have never lost."

Despite the stringent supervision he was being subjected to, DeMille made sure that his personal list of actors from the old days were used as extras. "A week or so ago," he wrote in a memo, "I told Joseph Sasso that he would work in the arena sequence, but he informed me tonight that he has not been called and that Mr. Weaver did not have his name on the list. Will you please see that he is called for work tomorrow?" Another note read, "Kindly make certain that every request name that I have sent through for work in the arena crowd sequence have been called and on the set tomorrow or else I will not shoot."

Cameraman Karl Struss revived a trick from the silent days and shot the entire film through a bright red gauze, which gave the images the lambent glow "of a world remembered," in Struss's words. In talkies, gauze was used for close-ups, especially for leading ladies, but Struss's gambit gave the film a luminous quality that makes the movie one of DeMille's most exquisite visual experiences.

Cecil was at his productive best. When he fell a couple of days behind schedule because of Claudette Colbert's absence, he quickly made up the time, which caused Emanuel Cohen to write, "I note on the production report today that you have caught up on your schedule. I can well appreciate what an effort this has been on your part."

Near the end of production, DeMille asked Laughton who he'd like to play next. "You," replied the actor. *The Sign of the Cross* finished shooting on September 15 and was released a little more than two months later, on November 30. The final cost was a modest $694,064, the costs kept down by DeMille's stringent planning and an economical payroll: Fredric March got $2,101 a week for eight weeks, Charles Laughton $1,250, while Claudette Colbert got a flat $15,000.

The film remains one of DeMille's most audacious creations, with a credible re-creation of ancient Rome—the streets are narrow, cramped, and well used, the homes attractively noble but quite simple—a constricted, slightly smaller-than-life environment that would be repeated a couple of years later in DeMille's *Cleopatra*, except for a sequence or two when DeMille cut loose with a stand-alone visual aria that left the impression the film was much bigger than it actually was.

The Sign of the Cross gave a gaunt young character actor his first job with DeMille, who took one look at John Carradine's face and said, "Your face is too narrow. The camera won't record anything from your face." But Carradine did a small bit anyway, and his sepulchral voice was also used for the dubbing of wild lines. Carradine was filling in gaps between acting jobs by sculpting, and DeMille commissioned the actor to do a bust of him. Carradine sketched the director on the set, then took the sketches home and worked on the bust. DeMille paid Carradine $750 for a bronze, but Carradine's landlord destroyed the clay sculpture before it could be cast. Carradine believed that his career with DeMille, if not in movies, was over, but when he told the director, DeMille simply nodded, and never even asked for his $750 back. He would use Carradine several more times over the years, most notably as Aaron in the 1956 *The Ten Commandments*.

DeMille filled *The Sign of the Cross* with a sensuality and violence that was astonishing for the period, especially a dance by Joyzelle Joyner, playing what Fredric March hilariously describes as "the most wicked and, uh, *talented* woman in Rome." She attempts to lure the Christian girl Mercia over to the debauchery of Nero's court through a paean to lesbian sex entitled "The Dance of the Naked Moon."

As she slides sinuously around Elissa Landi's Mercia, thrusting her pelvis toward her, grabbing her hair, kissing her neck, Joyner chants: "Under the naked moon, I've found you. We meet. I've seen you in my dreams. In dreams indiscreet. With tortures so sweet. I've loved you in dreams. Breathe upon me. Draw me. Gently. Touch my heart. Love will be warm. In the gold of your hair. Feed from your lips. . . . We have been two. We shall be one. Both throb . . ."

Unfortunately, the dance is interrupted by the singing of the Christians as they march to the dungeons. DeMille's basic attitude toward censors had always been indifference—he had flatly refused to make any changes in *Madam Satan* and had been backed by Irving Thalberg. "Their attitude," grumbled the Hays Office censor at the time, "is, why should any small group of people decide what the rest of the world should see?"

DeMille had submitted the script for *The Sign of the Cross* to Father Daniel Lord, his advisor on *The King of Kings*, hoping to get some help in the expected fight against the Hays Office. But amazingly, the fight never materialized. DeMille hosted Colonel Jason Joy, the head of the Production Code, who fell for everything he was told. "What I saw on the set . . . goes beyond my fondest expectations," he wrote DeMille. Joy was succeeded by a man named James Wingate, who viewed the finished film and filed some complaints. DeMille ignored him and his complaints.

"Since the director obviously used the dancing to show the conflict between paganism and Christianity, we are agreed that there is justification for its use under the Code," wrote the obtuse official censor.

The unofficial censors were considerably more savvy. *Our Sunday Visitor* and *Commonweal* thought the lesbian dance was pornography, and Martin Quigley's *Motion Picture Herald* said that the film could be recommended only to those whose "sensibilities survive the odors of Lesbos and de Sade." Daniel Lord said it smacked of "sex perversion."

Finally, Will Hays called DeMille.

"I am with Martin Quigley. What are you going to do about that dance?"

"Will, listen carefully to my words because you may want to quote them. Not a damn thing."

"Not a damn thing?"

"Not a damn thing."

Within the company, Cecil was more conciliatory. "Will make cuts you suggest if you deem it advisable," Cecil wrote George Schaeffer in Paramount's New York office, "but am personally opposed to making them. . . . As to the dance, I should only advise cutting this if you believe that it will hurt box office value. It would seem to me to have an opposite effect. Are there many people who will stay away from a theater today because of a sensational dance? It is an angle started by Father Donnelly and Martin Quigley, but was not noticeable to Bishop Dunne. . . . These same publications objected just as strongly to the modern story of *The Ten Commandments* and to the Mary Magdalene sequence in *King of Kings*, and then the Jews objected to *King of Kings*. . . . I will, however, be guided entirely by your advice, or can cut most of dance before Christian singing starts and can eliminate Amazon cutting off head of dwarf in arena. These would make sufficient cuts to enable you to make statement that objectionable parts of both have been cut out."

Paramount gave *The Sign of the Cross* deluxe treatment, releasing it as a road show complete with a souvenir program whose cover proclaimed:

1923—The Ten Commandments.

1927—The King of Kings.

1933—The Sign of the Cross.

The publicity was filled with the usual flagrant exaggeration (five hundred extras were closer to the mark than the claims of 7,500, and the arena built for the film certainly did not encompass ninety thousand square feet), and strenuous claims were made about the film's relevance to the modern viewer: "The story of the luxury and extravagance of Rome finds a striking reflection in our easy life prior to the fatal autumn of 1929."

Actually, the only place in 1932 America where you were likely to find such unrestrained sensuality was in *The Sign of the Cross.*

As the film made its way across the country, some local censor boards cut violence from the arena scenes, but the lesbian dance always stayed intact. But *The Sign of the Cross*, along with a spate of similarly sensuous and/or sleazy movies of the same period, inevitably led to a reaction.

In November 1933, Catholic officials, led by Martin Quigley, held a conference at Catholic University, where they discussed the damage the movies were inflicting on the country. Quigley and four Catholic bishops drafted a plan for the creation of the Legion of Decency, whose enforcement provision urged Catholics to boycott theaters that showed films the Legion deemed immoral. The Motion Picture Association of America, led by Will Hays, hired Joseph Breen, a professional Catholic and amateur anti-Semite from Philadelphia, to serve as chief industry censor for the next twenty years. Between Breen and the Legion, the hammer came down on screen sensuality.

When *The Sign of the Cross* was re-released in 1935, the dance scene was completely cut, along with much arena violence. The original version of *The Sign of the Cross*, along with the films of Mae West, were Exhibits A and B in the Catholic Church's war against Hollywood.

In 1944, Paramount released a "modernized" version of *The Sign of the Cross.* The new version featured an eleven-minute prologue written by Dudley Nichols and directed by DeMille showing American bombers flying over Rome, which dissolved to the Rome of two thousand years before. The lesbian dance was still missing, as was a shot of a naked girl tied to a stake about to be attacked by a gorilla. Colbert's bath, complete with a momentary glimpse of a nipple, and the murderous pygmies were retained. Luckily for film history and DeMille's reputation, the full-tilt 1932 original was preserved in his vault, and it is that print that has been used for the video restorations that have circulated since.

From its opening sequence, with Charles Laughton chanting "Burn, Rome, Burn," it's an astonishingly brazen picture, with DeMille matching Laughton perversity for perversity. In a sequence where children are tortured, and DeMille cuts to a shot of Rome's imperial eagle and a shadow of a soldier on a wall impassively standing guard, he attains a primal picture of innocence brutalized. As Charles Laughton intones, "delicious debauchery!"

Between its explosions of lasciviousness and violence, the film moves languidly, but it is those explosions that everyone remembers: an elephant stepping on the head of a man staked to the floor of the Colosseum; crocodiles crawling toward a nubile woman; an ape advancing on a woman tied to a stake; the beheading of a pygmy; another pygmy impaled on a sword and carried in triumph around the arena; and through it all the blasé reactions of the crowd, typified by a housewife nagging about her family's bad seats.

The film is a testament to DeMille's production skills—the cheapness never shows. As DeMille intended, *The Sign of the Cross* was successful—a whopping gross of $2.9 million, a net profit of $729,134. The reviews, however, were the usual. *Variety* pointed out, "Every sequence in which religion wins out is built upon lurid details . . . only one exceptional performance was registered. That's Laughton's. With utmost subtlety [!] amid a minimum of effort, he manages to get over his queer character before his first appearance is a minute old." But DeMille's old Jesuit friend Daniel Lord was repulsed by the film's "sadistic cruelty, its playing up of Roman lust and debauchery and crime." To Lord, *The Sign of the Cross* was "intolerable."

Among the intelligentsia, only the English documentarian John Grierson stood out: "Cecil B. DeMille is out of fashion among the critics. But . . . I have seen *The Sign of the Cross* twice over and am still an unrepentant admirer. There is no director to touch him in command of the medium: certainly none who strikes such awe into my professional mind. I have only to see his crowds and continuities, yes, and images, too, to think of the Milestones and Pudovkins as so many amateurs."

DeMille had gone further than ever in terms of sex and violence because his back was against the wall—whether one more failure would have finished him as an A list director or not, he seemed to believe that it would and wasn't about to take the chance. So DeMille couched sex and violence in Karl Struss's gorgeous cinematography; as one critic noted, it's one of the few films of its era to recapture the "shimmering opulence" of silent film.

Like DeMille himself, *The Sign of the Cross* is a house divided: authentic faith and belief in God mixed with a carnal zest that can only be called pagan.

★

DeMille was rarely seen to give direction to his actors, leading many to think that he was unable to talk to or was uninterested in the acting in his pictures. Actually, he was similar to Hitchcock in that he'd done all his directing by the time he got on the set. He preferred to work with actors in his office in what the staff called "office-directing." This involved reading through scenes, going over the script, reading and talking over the character. If there was a problem, a writer was called in to fix it in the office, not on the set. A movie studio, with hundreds of people standing around, was no place to discuss the reading of a line, or even the reason to cross from one side of the set to the other. DeMille believed in preparation; sets, costumes, characters, actors, and shot lists all had to be set in his mind long before he walked on the set.

Contributing to the picturesque theatricality of DeMille's style was his increasing reliance on Dan Sayre Groesbeck for concept, costume, and storyboard art. "He always knew what I wanted," remembered DeMille, "and he could capture character and drama in a few strokes of his brush, while his finished drawings, like the marvelous series he made while traveling through China, are worthy of a museum."

DeMille would pass Groesbeck's drawings around to other members of his staff as guidelines for what he wanted in terms of costume and casting, and would even use them for presentations to Paramount when outlining a new project. DeMille's office at the studio became a mini-museum of Groesbeck art from the film in preparation. When the film was over, DeMille would keep most of Groesbeck's art—a Groesbeck painting called *The Blessing of the Russian Crops* hung over the fireplace in DeMille's house—and the DeMille archives are the primary repository for the work of the artist.

It was all a trifle limiting to the other artisans on the staff. "If you look at a Groesbeck sketch," said one costumer, "it was hell to convert it into actual three-dimensional materials. It looked great the way he drew it, but if you can't tell how it is going to be cut or draped, you're not going to get what's in the picture."

Groesbeck was an amiable man who always smoked while he worked, and painted loosely, almost impressionistically. He was a gifted illustrator, and seems to have known it, for he was modest and usually self-deprecatory. Groesbeck was also admired by William Cameron Menzies, who used him as a concept artist on *Gone With the Wind* and *For Whom the Bell Tolls*.

The end result of DeMille's increasing reliance on Groesbeck was that the nervous energy of his earlier films gradually subsumed into a more staid reliance on compositions within the frame. Beautiful, painterly, but, as with the work of Rex Ingram, there was a loss of energy that, combined with DeMille's shaky ear for dialogue, meant that many of his middle period films could seem stagy or archaic.

★

Micky Moore, who had played Mark in *King of Kings*, had seen his acting career plummet when he hit puberty. In 1932, he was working on a fishing boat and his wife was expecting a baby. He called DeMille's office and asked for an interview.

When Moore showed up at the office, he told DeMille he wanted to get back in the business. "Micky, what do you want to do?" asked DeMille.

"I could have said anything—camera, grips, but I said, 'I would like to be a prop man, Mr. DeMille.' Two weeks later I was working as a prop man and kept going with DeMille for all the time I was at Paramount, until I changed over into an assistant director."

Working for DeMille on props was no less demanding than working for DeMille as an actor. "If you had a sack of grain on the set, there had to be grain in that sack," remembered Moore. "When an extra or a bit player had to walk across the street, there had to be a reason for him to walk across the street and go to that wagon."

Moore became part of DeMille's extended filmmaking family and would be invited to the house to watch movies. After one screening, Moore and his wife left the house, to find that their car had been burglarized. He went back into DeMille's house and asked to use the phone because his car had been broken into.

DeMille stared at him, dumbfounded. "Micky, it couldn't have been broken into. It was in front of my house!"

"It took me a while to convince him that somebody would break into one of his guest's cars," remembered Moore. "His reaction always kind of tickled me."

★

With the great success of *The Sign of the Cross*, DeMille and Paramount negotiated a new contract, guaranteeing him 50 percent of the net profits of his films. While DeMille was reconstituting his career, Neil McCarthy was fighting the IRS for him. Ultimately, a judge found that a company formed more than ten years earlier, a company that had been beset with a full measure of squabbles and whose accumulated surplus had been amassed for the purpose of going into independent production, could hardly have done so to avoid taxes, most of which hadn't even been in existence at the time of the company's formation. The case would drag on until shortly before World War II, but DeMille would ultimately be found not guilty, largely because of the minutes of company meetings and depositions that emphasized the contributions and expertise of Constance—the corporation's vice president.

★

DeMille was still affectionate toward Jeanie Macpherson. "Why not telephone an impatient lad?" he wrote her in January 1933, signing it "Tyfib." But their relationship was increasingly a thing of the past, despite Jeanie's attempts at arranging trysts. DEAR CHIEF WHAT ARE PROSPECTS OF YOUR COMING HERE PRESENT WEEK OR NEXT, she wired from the Claridge Hotel in New York on March 1. AM ANXIOUS TO SEE YOU HERE AND WILL MAKE MY OWN PLANS ACCORDINGLY. DO HOPE YOU WILL COME.

That same day, DeMille wrote back without committing himself, saying that the following week was a possibility. On March 6, Macpherson was still cooling her heels at the Claridge and wired again. IF YOU ARE NOT COMING WILL RETURN HOME END OF THIS WEEK BUT WOULD WAIT FOR YOU IF YOU ARE COMING SOON AS DON'T WANT TO MISS YOU LOVE. Four days later, DeMille finally popped her balloon. PICTURE SITUATION HERE TOO SERIOUS TO LEAVE. CANNOT TELL WHEN. AFFECTIONATELY. C.B.

By late 1934, he was furiously snapping at her in interoffice memos: "Dear Jeanie. If there isn't sufficient work to keep you in your office, there certainly isn't sufficient [work] to keep you on the payroll. I have been trying to get in touch with you this morning without success. Cecil B. DeMille." Despite the 5 percent of the profits she had from the 1923 *The Ten Commandments*, and the fifteen years of being a well-paid screenwriter, Macpherson was still scraping by, with numerous small loans—$800, $250, $200, $2,700—made to her from either DeMille or the Bank of America. The general impression left by her correspondence and banking records indicates that it wasn't easy being Jeanie Macpherson. It was going to get even harder.

★

In 1933, Grace Bradley went in to interview with DeMille for a part. She had been warned not to put on any nail polish—DeMille didn't like it. "The part was, he said, a virgin, and only a virgin could play a virgin. I walked in and sat down and he looked at me and said, 'No, I can't see you in the part. You don't look like a virgin.' Now, my mother was outside waiting for me! 'I see you on a long couch,' he said, 'with leopard skin, and two nubian slaves with feather fans on both sides of you.' I just sat there with my mouth open."

For the film called *This Day and Age*, DeMille cast Frank Coghlan, his juvenile at the DeMille studios, now a teenager, for one of the supporting parts. DeMille must have had a soft spot for Coghlan—one day on location, the young actor was late. He just walked in and took his place, which would usually earn a burst of excoriation about courtesy and professionalism. Instead, DeMille said nothing.

The child star Diana Serra, the former Baby Peggy, witnessed DeMille at his worst, after he had been nursing a grudge against leading lady Judith Allen. "Judith Allen [real name Mari Coleman] was promoted as this pristine little ingenue," remembered Serra, "but it came out that she was married to a wrestler [named Gus Sonnenberg]. Then they tried making her a socialite who had married down, but it didn't take. She had kept her marriage quiet and DeMille felt deceived. Then she got a divorce, and he got *really* angry.

"When it came time for her to do this scene, she was green, and she had trouble, and he laced into her. The F-word was just for openers, and those words were not in common usage at that time.

"I'm sure that he thought he would make her cry, and he did, but it became a deluge; she got hysterical. Richard Cromwell, who was only about twenty-three, was gay—I think most people on the set knew—and he was the only man on that set who had the guts to say, 'Mr. DeMille, if you don't let up on this girl, I'll deck you.' And DeMille looked at him and saw real was real and he quit. And Cromwell picked her up—she was *completely* hysterical—and took her home." (Richard Cromwell later became Angela Lansbury's first husband. After his acting career petered out, he became a successful artist, selling exquisite ceramic screens weighing four and five hundred pounds to many in Hollywood.)

"The thing about DeMille," continued Serra, "yes, he was a good father and a good director, but he was also a tyrant. He was of that era—a mogul with his own unit, and nobody ever told him 'No!'; nobody ever called him on the carpet."

★

This Day and Age belongs firmly to the Social Breakdown genre of the early days of the Depression, along with William Wellman's *Wild Boys of the Road* and so forth. And on the surface, it's also part of an exceedingly disturbing crypto-fascist grouping that includes *Gabriel over the White House* and *The President Vanishes*.

The films of the left—King Vidor's *Our Daily Bread*, Chaplin's *Modern Times*—proposed that the social chaos could be ameliorated through everybody pulling together for a common goal of survival. The films of the right proposed that everybody pull together for the common goal of ignoring the law, although DeMille is careful to characterize the power structure as not just absent, but apathetic and corrupt. As one character says, the law can't beat "a million dollar a year mouthpiece." In the absence of law and order, the idealistic young take charge.

The story of *This Day and Age* is simple: a group of teenagers are appalled when a gangster who has murdered a friend of theirs eludes a murder charge through the machinations of his lawyer. They kidnap him, torture him, and come close to lynching him until he confesses and is led away by the newly awakened police.

The film begins with a snappy, frenetic montage of modern life—cities, dirigibles, surging crowds. Throughout, DeMille directs in a much more current style than in his costume pictures; he directs for speed, with a nervous editing rhythm. (In many respects, the film is a counterpart to *The Godless Girl*, although not as successful.)

DeMille burdens himself with actors who are either colorless (Richard Cromwell, Judith Allen) or bizarre (Fuzzy Knight and Billy Gilbert play gangsters). But DeMille also moves beyond the clichés he's handling. The Jewish tailor who is murdered, thus generating the plot, begins as a stereotype out of *Abie's Irish Rose*, but as he clings to his independence he becomes individual and admirable.

The critic and screenwriter Andrew Bergman called the film a bizarre amalgam of Joseph Goebbels and Corliss Archer, although the film provides an example of fairly advanced racial politics. One of the high school students is a young black man named George, who is enlisted in a plot to kidnap the gangster. "Do you shine shoes?" one of the kids asks him.

"I shine my own," he replies.

During the kidnapping, the black student plays the part of a shambling Stepin Fetchit. When the gangster is bound and stuffed into the car, a passerby asks "What was that?"

"That's a high school fraternity initiation! Yes, ma'am," the character says, as he tosses the the dialect aside.

This Day and Age captures DeMille at a moment when he, like most of America, was enraged by a void in authority that had led to the stock market crash and a worldwide depression. "We haven't got time for any rules of evidence," yells the leader of the teenage vigilantes. DeMille understood authority as only an autocrat can, and he was voicing dangerously Democratic sympathies—"I am not a radical, but now things are a question of right and wrong," he said. "The public has been milked and are growing tired of it. It is not [financial] speculation alone. There is something rotten at the core of our system."

The climax is an uncomfortable sequence where the gangster (Charles Bickford) is trussed up and lowered into a pit full of rats. It's a fairly obvious variation on the climax of Fritz Lang's M, and was pointed out as such by several critics. When the police arrive, they decide to support the kids, and a local judge is woken up and convenes a new trial that will certainly find the gangster guilty. Shot in a little more than four weeks for a cost of $279,811, *This Day and Age* was released in August 1933, and grossed $668,375, eking out a profit of $21,712.

A month later, DeMille was already shooting his next picture, *Four Frightened People*. DeMille made plans to go to Hawaii to film at a time of exceptional turmoil in the movie industry. The International Alliance of Theatrical Stage Employees (IATSE) was battling over the rights to organize the soundmen. A general strike was called for the summer of 1933, which would have made the DeMille film a runaway production and the people working on it scabs. Cameraman Karl Struss was getting a lot of calls at home demanding that he go out on strike, but he was resolute in planning to make the picture.

At this point, DeMille was known around the Paramount lot as "a terror on the set," remembered Joe Youngerman, who began working for him as a prop man and rose to be an assistant director. Youngerman earned DeMille's respect when the director noticed that Youngerman came to the studio on his day off to check the props for *The Sign of the Cross*. Youngerman believed that DeMille liked him because he was the only prop man who had the same guts as DeMille. DeMille walked into the lion-filled arena set of *The Sign of the Cross* armed with only a whip and a chair. Youngerman did it too, but was terrified and couldn't sleep for the next two nights.

Youngerman found that DeMille was not above enjoying a crack at his own expense. One day Youngerman told his boss that his pictures would be better if DeMille limited himself to the long shots and Ernst Lubitsch did the close-ups. DeMille smiled, said, "Maybe that's so," and laughed.

Preparing *Four Frightened People*, DeMille told Youngerman that he expected him to come on location. "I can't go," Youngerman said. "We're on strike."

"Well, you know unions never win a strike," said DeMille.

Youngerman held firm. To get out of the line of fire, he took his family to the World's Fair in Chicago.

Youngerman was always a strong union man—he was the executive secretary of the Directors Guild for twenty-seven years—and the cameramen's strike was added evidence that DeMille wasn't. As it happened, the strike was settled by September, when *Four Frightened People* actually began shooting, but DeMille's willingness to shoot his film and the unions be damned began to earn him his reputation as a reactionary. DeMille wanted no third party interference on his set, and his antipathy toward unions probably stemmed at least as much from issues of control as it did political philosophy. "He was very wonderful to socialize with and very horrible to work for," is the way Youngerman summed up the experience.

DeMille's funny line about *Four Frightened People* was that after he saw it there were five frightened people. He needn't have been embarrassed. It's a nimble, amusing, unclassifiable movie that's part screwball comedy, part survival melodrama, all of it hurtling forward from the opening scene: a group of passengers on a tramp steamer piling into a lifeboat because of an outbreak of plague, later washing up on an island shore. Claudette Colbert plays a mousy schoolteacher who becomes more ravishing the more disheveled she gets, Leo Carillo plays a native named Montague. The formidable Mary Boland plays a society reformer determined to introduce birth control to the South Sea natives.

Actually, the movie is a variation on *Male and Female*, with Herbert Marshall's society wastrel gradually assuming a leadership role and William Gargan's bloviating reporter growing increasingly hysterical, while the schoolteacher becomes a knowing siren. DeMille's casting saddled him with some problems, foremost among them having to work overtime to disguise Herbert Marshall's artificial leg, mainly by having him wear heavy furs around his waist while co-stars William Gargan and Leo Carillo walk around in cutoffs.

More seriously, Colbert was recovering from what she once described as "an emergency appendectomy," but which almost certainly was the abortion she told her friend Arnold Scaasi she underwent during her marriage to Norman Foster— Colbert was afraid a baby would sidetrack her career. "The first day I arrived on location," remembered Colbert, "with the nurse from the Good Samaritan Hospital, [DeMille] put me in a swamp up to my shoulders. A real swamp. The nurse yelled, and he said, 'I've waited for her 10 days already.' "

Two days later, Colbert was very sick with a 104-degree fever and DeMille was extremely apologetic. "It's just an act," he explained. "People expect that of me. I'm not really like that underneath." At that point, Colbert couldn't have cared less what DeMille was really like, but, as she would say, "I liked the old boy. I think I was the only woman who ever talked to him as an equal."

Four Frightened People cost $509,006, and lost $261,365. Despite the fact that it's made with playful panache, and, with the exception of only a few studio shots, is beautifully shot on location, the critics howled; Mordaunt Hall in the *New York Times* called it "an extravagant mixture of comedy and melodrama, and the terror in some of the scenes stirred up almost as much mirth from an audience yesterday as did the levity in others."

DeMille's own estimation of the picture was that it was "a light comedy. . . . I didn't want *Four Frightened People* to be taken that seriously." But light comedy was not what people wanted from C. B. DeMille. Much later in his life, he said that perhaps he should "leave whimsical stories to directors like Preston Sturges or Leo McCarey or Billy Wilder who are so good at that type of picture."

With two exceptions, DeMille shied away from contemporary stories for the rest of his life; his taste for slightly archaic dialogue increasingly nudged him toward costume pictures, and a DeMille picture gradually became a synonym for a rejection of almost any kind of modernity except technical. The elaborate machinery DeMille constructed could be animated only by primal matters—religion, war, patriotism. Costume pictures could easily contain all of those things.

On some level, he decided that he would never again paint a miniature; instead, he set himself on a course that would make him cinema's premier painter of vast historical and religious frescoes.

15

In contrast to his rock-solid certitude with actors and staff, DeMille's status at Paramount remained uncertain for financial reasons. *Four Frightened People, This Day and Age,* and *Cleopatra* would be cross-collateralized; that is to say that rather than each picture being treated as a separate financial entity, losses were charged against the profits any of the pictures made, seriously limiting DeMille's profit participation.

Ultimately, this worked to the studio's advantage; as of October 1955, *This Day and Age* had a profit of $21,712, *Cleopatra* had a profit of $394,010, but *Four Frightened People* had a loss of $261,365. There was an aggregate net of $154,984 for the three pictures.

DeMille's return to ancient times was in the works while he was still in Hawaii wrestling with *Four Frightened People*. For *Cleopatra*, DeMille again wanted Claudette Colbert, but she was angry over her Paramount salary. DeMille had a long talk with Colbert before they left the Hawaiian location and told her that "she was making a serious mistake to her career to allow money to be the main influence at this point . . . that even if she had to play for another year at less money, it would be a far better financial interest to her to play the part of Cleopatra at less money than to play just a picture at $50,000 per picture, which she claims she has been offered."

Colbert and the studio compromised; she received $47,000 for *Cleopatra*, and DeMille didn't have to pay overhead charges on the $21,000 of Colbert's salary that Paramount added to her contracted amount.

As he was casting *Cleopatra*, Mary Anita Loos, Anita Loos's niece, wrote DeMille and said she was interested in becoming an actress. DeMille called her in for an interview.

"Are you a virgin?" he asked.

Loos told him the truth. "Yes," she said.

"The last actress who said yes to that question was secretly married to a wrestler," DeMille noted glumly. He cast Loos as one of Colbert's ladies-in-waiting, but the star had casting approval and Loos's dark, sultry looks collided with the star's. "She's too young and too dark," she told DeMille. A blonde, Colbert said, would be much better.

Loos was furious, and DeMille was irked, but he knew how to get around leading ladies' vanity. "Don't worry, baby," he told Loos. "You'll be in every shot I can put you in."

"I thought he was fantastic," remembered Loos. "I was terribly impressed. If he didn't like somebody or something, it was 'Away with them,' but it was part of his act of importance. Underneath the act, he was actually a very nice man. And he never made a pass at me."

DeMille put up with Colbert's affectations because she was a good actress, extremely sexy, and—most of the time—a pro. "She wanted to do something different with Cleopatra," he remembered in 1956, "not make her lofty or fussy or superstitious, nothing like that. She set out to give her humor and humanity, and she stamped her own personality on the role. She emerged from it most vividly, I thought."

For Antony, DeMille hired a comparative unknown named Henry Wilcoxon, late of the Birmingham Rep. Wilcoxon had a chiseled face and physique and was completely fearless. "I've decided Antony would keep dogs," DeMille told the actor. "I'm sending you out to Pasadena to a kennel that has a pair of Great Danes I like. They should live with you while we prepare. I want them to follow you wherever you go on the set."

Those who believed that DeMille's aggression was merely verbal had their horizons broadened one day during a battle scene when DeMille was trying to get a shot of Antony, back against a tree, fending off an enemy advance. Wilcoxon and the stuntmen were using metal swords, metal shields, and real spears, which might have been the reason they were a bit cautious.

After a couple of insufficiently combative takes, DeMille stormed over to Wilcoxon, grabbed a spear and a shield from an extra, and, with a cry of "Guard yourself, Harry! And the rest of you, watch!" began hacking away at Wilcoxon. "For the next two or three minutes I fought like a madman," remembered Wilcoxon. "Back and forth, lunge, parry, wrack, until I'd hacked his shield to pieces and he cut my costume to ribbons and I thought: This is crazy! How am I going to get *out* of this?"

Finally, Wilcoxon sidestepped a thrust and cut the head of the spear off with his sword. "All right!" yelled DeMille. "Anyone who doesn't want to fight like that can leave right now!"

"There was an immediate rapport between us, and our relationship was more than director and star," Wilcoxon remembered. "I loved the old buzzard. You either hated him or you loved him, there was no half-way measure at all." Wilcoxon was transfixed by the control DeMille exerted over his cast and crew, the way he demanded specificity of his extras. "I don't want any extras on my set," he told them. "I only want actors and actresses. During the making of this picture, if I come up to you, and I say, 'What are you doing, and where are you going?' and you can't tell me, either you or the assistant director who is responsible for your segment will be fired. I want you to *think*, and act. When you're crossing the square, I want you to be able to tell me that you're crossing the street to the sandal maker's to get your sandal repaired. Or I want to know if you are going to pick up your little son."

As part of his attempt to humanize his characters, DeMille thought that Adolphe Menjou might make a good Caesar, or perhaps John Gilbert. The idea that an actor with a racy or slightly disreputable quality might make Caesar more accessible is an indication of the way DeMille's mind worked—bending history to time, character to star, broadening things so that the dullest members of the audience would get the point. DeMille ended up casting Warren William, who was playing suave cads at Warners.

Agnes deMille was struggling in London to make ends meet when Cecil hired her for six weeks at $250 a week to create the dances for *Cleopatra*. It ended badly, but then it was always going to; both Agnes and Cecil were authoritarians in their work, unable and unwilling to cede primacy to anybody else.

In a letter to Agnes, Cecil told her what he was looking for. "Antony had seen all the regular dancers in the world, so they could not interest him. Cleopatra would not have made the mistake of just staging a dance, therefore, when the first course, which was clams, is to be served, she has a net dragged over the side of the ship dripping with water and seaweed and dragged by slaves before the table and couch of Cleopatra and Antony, and then the net is opened and with the kelp wrapped around them, beautiful girls come to life, their hair still dripping with the sea water. . . . Again, later, when Antony tries to free himself from the spell being cast over him, I see a bull led before him, on the back of which lies a beautiful dancer, whose costume suggests, perhaps, the mate of the bull. Perhaps her headgear are horns, and her shoes are hoofs, like Edmund Dulac's "Europa and the Bull."

Cecil's concept of a dance whose centerpiece was a live bull with a writhing, nearly naked woman on top was amusingly over-the-top, a clear successor to the lesbian dance in *The Sign of the Cross*, as well as rather dicey material to try to slip by the new Production Code. This wild series of overheated tableaux indicates the extent of the misalliance between Cecil and Agnes. Nevertheless, she needed the job, so she tried to give her uncle what he wanted.

At first, all was rapture. Agnes stayed at the house at Laughlin Park and her uncle called her "Baby." Agnes wrote her sister a few days after she arrived: "Uncle Ce keeps a killing schedule. Up at 6:30 a.m. he has breakfast at 7 with Aunt Con in her beautiful east bedroom, the sun pouring through the climbing roses . . . he drives through the Paramount gate at 8:10 . . . lunches at 12:30 in the commissary . . . his table is in the center and on a raised platform and all his staff sits with him.

"Back on the set at 1:30. . . . He does everything (sets every camera angle. . . . His cameramen, although the best, take instructions from him.) He breaks at 7:00. Rushes . . . office conferences, and business decisions until 10:30. Home alone at 11 p.m.—dinner—(kept hot by Aunt Con in double boilers) . . . conversation with her until 1 a.m. . . . He personally locks up the whole house, speaks to the night watchman [and then reads the Bible in bed]. He never smokes, and he takes only a little wine. . . . He is on his feet all day . . . a general in full battle. . . . [He has] the unflagging zeal, the undivided strength of the prophet, the fanatic—or, alternately, the absolute monarch."

But she also noted his strange contradictions. "C.B. trusts no one and does not seem to take the deciding voice with expedition and certainty," she wrote her mother. "Yet he insists on okaying every single item from hairpins to the still photographs that are released for my personal publicity, also all estimates of cost. You can imagine the entailed amount of waiting."

For Agnes's audition, she devised a more aestheticized version of what DeMille wanted to a Rachmaninoff and Rimsky-Korsakov medley. When Agnes was finished, Cecil frowned and shook his head. "Oh no, oh no . . . I am so disappointed. . . . It has no excitement, no thrill, no suspense, no sex." DeMille turned to the censor, there to make sure that the dance fell within the strictures of the Production Code.

"Would that rouse you?" asked Cecil.

"It sure wouldn't," the censor replied.

"It wouldn't rouse me," said Cecil, "nor any man."

Agnes was off the picture. The next day she left the DeMille house. Her failure was bad but what was worse for the insecure Agnes was her uncle's pronouncement that it "wouldn't rouse anybody." Years later, she told the legendarily cruel and manipulative David Merrick, "Mr. Merrick, I worked for my uncle, Cecil B. DeMille, and nothing you can do to me can be worse than what he did."

★

Claudette Colbert's only memories of Warren William were that he raised wire-haired terriers and was terrified of their director, "but then DeMille frightened almost all his actors." He didn't terrify Colbert. During one missed day that cost the production $10,000, DeMille grumbled, "She always was a bitch."

Colbert's diva-ish habits were beginning to drive him to something approaching distraction. She thought nothing of taking time off for her period, or generalized vapors. As DeMille wrote Emanuel Cohen after his leading lady had gone missing for several days, "She may be sick, but I'm the one that's dying."

This was a genuine breach of ethics as far as DeMille was concerned, and even after Colbert was working on another picture he was angry. "I have just learned that last week Colbert had a cold and was not shooting [*Imitation of Life*] at Universal," he wrote Cohen a few months later. "I suggest you . . . cover in some way the fact that she is sick in every picture she has made. Agreeing, perhaps, to give her a week for sickness in the middle of the picture, but if she is sick at any other time than this allowed week, that would be deducted from her salary."

Colbert's third film with DeMille left her with much the same feeling as many DeMille actors—it was enjoyable, often a lot of fun, but not something to be taken entirely seriously. "In one scene he wanted Caesar to drop rose petals on my feet. . . . I said, 'He can touch my foot, he can even bite it, but if he drops rose petals on it, I'll just burst out laughing.' He finally agreed; it was one of the few times I ever won an argument with him.

"To us, a lot of his ideas were corny, but I don't think you can call him phony. He really believed in what he was doing. When we did the scene in *The Sign of the Cross* with the Christians being eaten by lions, he really suffered. . . . DeMille's films were special: somehow, when he put everything together, there was a special kind of glamour and sincerity."

For his part, DeMille appreciated Colbert as a psychiatrist appreciates a favorite client. He knew that she didn't like the idea of handling snakes, even so small a snake as the creature that was playing the part of the asp with which Cleopatra commits suicide. DeMille solved the problem by walking onto the set holding a five-foot-long California king snake, ominous-looking but harmless. Colbert was appalled. "Oh, Mr. DeMille, I couldn't touch that snake! I couldn't possibly. Please don't ask me to."

At that point, DeMille handed off the king snake and brought out the small snake, "Oh, that one?" exclaimed Colbert. "Why, that's just a baby!" Cleopatra's death scene was quickly and easily made.

✳

DeMille immediately serves notice that his version of *Cleopatra* is going to be different from Shakespeare's and Shaw's when he shows a nude woman under the main titles. All of DeMille's historical films are fantasias on a theme, and *Cleopatra* is about a woman with power—political power deriving from sexual power.

Warren William seems a giddy idea as Caesar, but, liberated from the sleazy parts Warner Bros. habitually gave him, he's a bitter, imperious ruler.

"Together we could conquer the world," Cleopatra tells Caesar.

"Nice of you to include me," he replies. Later, Caesar muses about Antony, "I don't know what the young man means, but he means it violently."

Wilcoxon's Antony is a bit of a thunderstruck lummox, but you can't really blame him—Colbert's endless eyelashes and a succession of alluring Travis Banton outfits that barely cover her perfect body could have brought on the Production Code all by themselves.

It's an energetic tab version of the story—100 minutes!—whose centerpiece is the barge sequence, in which Cleopatra enlists a cast of thousands to seduce one angry man—history defined as erotic conflagration. The entertainment that Cleopatra puts on for Antony is built around the idea of female subservience—the dance with the bull that got Agnes fired lasts perhaps thirty seconds. There's more dancing involving whips, girls in leopard costumes, and flaming hoops. Antony's Great Danes are startled, as well they should be.

"Women should be but toys for the great," says Cleopatra. "It becomes them both." As the couple draws together, slaves lift a satin shield so that the coupling can proceed in privacy. Rose petals rain down, and the camera slowly pulls back, back, back as the affair is consummated, past the rowers propelling Cleopatra's barge through the water, past the hortator pounding out the rhythm of the rowers'—and Antony's—stroke. The effect is somewhere between amusement and amazement—grandiose, but also rhapsodic.

Throughout the picture, Victor Milner's Oscar-winning photography glows, illuminating the characters from inside, while the dialogue illuminates them from outside. As Joseph Schildkraut's Herod says, "All major emotions are greedy."

Later, Antony sees servants carrying a body out of the palace and has a slow, dawning realization that the queen doesn't do long-term relationships. "What's this?" he asks. "The queen is testing poisons," is the reply. DeMille cuts together a splendid battle montage, aided by some clips from *The Ten Commandments*, and ends the picture.

DeMille called in the great art director William Cameron Menzies to design the montages. DeMille had known Menzies for twelve years, although this was the only time they worked together. The experience must have been pleasant; DeMille wrote Menzies both a thank-you note ("I appreciate your fine work and cooperation") and a letter of reference ("He is an artist of unquestioned standing and ability and has, to the best of my knowledge, an excellent character").

Cleopatra is enlivened by Claudette Colbert's rare ability to mix emotion, sex, and irony along with the light touch of an expert comedienne. As Gary Allen Smith noted, the story and the treatment of DeMille's film may be synopsized as deriving one part from Shaw, one part from Shakespeare, and two parts DeMille. But by ramming the narrative through, and holding the sermons, DeMille tells the same story in less than half the time as Joseph L. Mankiewicz's lamentable 1963 version.

Visually, it's a splendid re-creation of the romantic images of Victorian painters who specialized in ancient times: Alma-Tadema, Lord Leighton. DeMille fought Travis Banton's request for a sole credit for the costumes because, he wrote, "He only is designing thirteen costumes out of 3,000. I presume his credit should read 'Miss Colbert's costumes designed by Travis Banton.' "

Once again, DeMille was working economically; although a dozen barges were seen on screen in the sea battle, the Paramount special effects department built only two miniatures, one of which was the miniature for the royal barge seduction scene redressed as a war galley. Split screen work was used to give a far more lavish effect. The catapults were also miniatures. Besides the shots from the 1923 *The Ten Commandments*, other random shots came from *The Sign of the Cross* and Raoul Walsh's silent film *The Wanderer*.

The reviews were nearly as entertaining as the film. Rob Wagner wrote that "When C.B. DeMille is at his best, he's the grandest pageanteer of them all. And this picture tops anything he has done. . . . What better motivation for throwing away an empire than Claudette Colbert?"

Just before *Cleopatra* premiered in August 1934, Constance was back in East Orange, recuperating from an unspecified illness. "I am in fine shape, spending this week at John's. The nurse still comes every morning but I hope to be through with her this week. I don't feel at all weak and am reveling in my new slimness. Tell Katherine that with my clothes on I only weigh 135 pounds. . . . I am very happy to think of you off on the *Seaward* this week. I hope you have no business associate with you and that you are sleeping twelve hours a day. . . . All my love to the family and more for yourself."

The mention of "no business associate" is one of the few (veiled) references Constance would ever permit herself to make about Cecil's mistresses, a small glimpse into the psychic costs of Constance's life.

DeMille shot *Cleopatra* in a brisk seven weeks, from March 12 to May 2. It was released in August. His control over his production was so tight that the difference between the preview version and the release version was precisely 108 feet of film. *Cleopatra* cost $842,908, grossed $2.287 million. The net profit was $217,410.

★

After her humiliating rejection, Agnes went back to New York. "At last my family, my powerful world-renowned family, had offered practical help and then thrown me away as trash," she wrote years later, the experience still a burning poker against her skin. She spent the rest of her long, distinguished life attempting to mediate her feelings about her "Uncle Ce"—open admiration for his ambition, drive, and ability to manage his life and career, open contempt for his aesthetics.

"Cecil's pronouncements were given with total certainty," she remembered. "Kipling's 'If' was the greatest poem in the English language, the best composers were Wagner and Tchaikovsky; Alma-Tadema was one of the finest painters, although he also liked Rubens. He stated the evaluations with less hesitancy than I have ever heard from professors, critics, or historians, his aplomb unmarred by any wide exposure to the spectrum of achievement. Differing views were unthought of at his table."

Agnes was a case study in ambivalence—on the one hand, she embodied lofty cultural standards; on the other, she was possessed by a strong emotional need to compete in the entertainment marketplace, where the primary arbiter is worldly success. She wanted to do her father's work and receive her uncle's rewards.

As far as Cecil was concerned, he undoubtedly felt he was doing an altruistic good deed, offering a chance to a niece who had gained little notice for her choreography as yet. It would be a few years until Agnes broke through as a choreographer with her work in *Oklahoma!*, *Carousel*, and *Brigadoon*—putting dance at the dramatic center of musical comedy, always integrating it with the story—as well as such ballets as *Rodeo* and *Fall River Legend*. But the abortive dance for *Cleopatra* caused a breach between uncle and niece that would never be completely healed.

William deMille couldn't exactly take up the cudgel for his daughter because he needed Cecil desperately. Bill's problems stemmed from his divorce. Under California's community property laws, half of William C. deMille Productions belonged to his first wife, Anna. When they separated in 1926, she wouldn't accept stock in the corporation, so the corporation loaned Bill about $200,000 to pay off Anna, the money deriving from a mortgage taken out on a piece of property owned by the company. Bill made some payments on the mortgage of between $10,000 and $15,000 a year for a number of years, but some bad investments, coupled with the stock market crash in 1929, ruined Bill's finances.

The IRS disallowed the methods by which Bill had paid for his divorce and asked for $92,158 for 1924 to 1928 inclusive. There was also slightly more than $1,000 owed in property taxes that were about to become delinquent. As of December 31, 1934, Bill had $215 in the bank, plus some real estate.

In what must have been excruciating letters to write, Bill asked for his brother's help. First, he asked Cecil to come to an objective appraisal of his assets and debts. "I really am busted, have not got a fortune buried anywhere and have been foolishly honest in keeping such property as I had vulnerable rather than try to play any legal tricks," wrote Bill. "I hate to ask you to bother yourself with my affairs when I know you are starting a major production [*The Crusades*] but after all you are the only man that I can trust intimately."

Gladys Rosson had William's balance sheet appraised and told Cecil that his brother's assets totaled $41,516.66, while he owed $54,557—not counting the IRS obligation. Bill also had life insurance worth $30,000 on which every dollar had been borrowed. Bill's gross income for 1934 had been $5,391.22, while his net was $856.84. The movie business seemed to be done with Bill, and he was making his living by selling an occasional piece to *Liberty* magazine, and lecturing.

In short, Bill was in serious trouble.

For immediate living expenses, Cecil made $5,000 available to his brother, to go along with $17,500 that Clara, Bill's second wife, had raised from her own savings for a settlement with the government. Bill wrote his brother a long letter that began, "I thought I had parted with human emotion forever, but I found that your wire touched me. Thanks."

A later letter from Bill asked Cecil for legal help, because he did not feel he could trust anybody else in Los Angeles. It made typically restrained note of his overall situation: "I am not downhearted about the future, but am not quite used to having no money whatever after the good old days." Bill wanted to deed over to Clara four lots and two houses, as well as all the property within them, as collateral for the $17,500 she was giving him. Bill wanted Neil McCarthy to handle all this, as he felt he had been the recipient of bad advice by his own attorneys—as indeed he had. "It will be of the greatest help to me if you will take personal charge in my behalf. And please remember that the element of time in this situation is most important."

Cecil told McCarthy to take care of the matter, and to bill him directly.

In the midst of Bill's financial distress, Cecil also tried to promote a prospective William deMille version of *Pagliacci* with Paramount. The studio said that raising the money for the film was the problem. Cecil countered by saying that he would arrange Bill's half of the financing with the Bank of America, presumably guaranteeing the loan himself, if Paramount would hold off on taking first monies; in other words, let the bank recoup their investment before Paramount.

On May 4, Bill wrote his younger brother. "I have heard no direct reports from *Cleopatra*, but hope everything is progressing as well as you could wish. Very sorry you and Agnes could not see eye to eye. Of course there is no artist as positive as a young artist, unless perhaps it is an old artist. I am sorry for I had hoped she could be of real help."

Cecil replied that he hadn't seen the test that Bill had made for *Pagliacci* because Paramount president John Otterson, who had no interest in opera films, hadn't shown it to him. He would, however, do what he could by running interference with Zukor and Emanuel Cohen.

"I was amused by your comments relative to Agnes, but I must confess that I was not greatly amused by Agnes. Apparently in her mind, motion picture companies are just great big foster-fathers created for the purpose of furnishing little girls with funds gratis. I was particularly sorry because of the relative angle which, of course, put me in a rather foolish light with the Company."

He closed by suggesting that there were better ways for Bill to get exercise than tennis, which doctors had told Bill to minimize. "Get your exercise in a more homely and pleasant manner. . . . There are a number of ways that I could suggest that have been tried successfully for centuries. You may remember the method of reviving David in his last hours."

The boulevardier aspects of the relationship hardly need elaboration, and indicate the commonalities between the two men beneath their differing aesthetic and political tastes. Richard deMille—who still had no idea of his true parentage—took note of the fascinating differences between the brothers. "Cecil envied William his intellectual standing and he said so. You would never know whether William envied anybody anything. William was simply not an open person. He wasn't cold, but he only showed what he wanted to show. It was nice to be around him, he was comfortable as a person, but he wasn't telling you very much about himself. He'd tell you how the world worked, he'd tell you how to fix it, he'd talk about schemes to produce paradise on earth, but about himself—not much.

"William was a nineteenth-century liberal reformer, a social reformer, who was committed to utopian schemes like Henry George's. The single tax was to make business moral, to make governments moral, to make everything the way God wanted it."

Besides his brother, in this period Bill was supported by his wife, Clara Beranger. "She was very devoted to him," remembered her daughter, Frances Triest. "When he was disturbed, it affected her. I was crazy about him, and it was a very good marriage; they were devoted to each other."

Over the next few years, Cecil continued to help Bill out with small loans— there is a note from Bill to Gladys Rosson as late as May 1938 asking for "the other $500"—as well as some writing work. William never paid back any of the loans. In October 1938, Cecil wrote off William's indebtedness to the tune of $5,505.28. Agnes deMille gave no inkling of Cecil's assistance to his brother in this terrible period in any of her memoirs, and it's entirely possible her father never told her about it. She would write, "Cecil had always been generous to Father with his yacht, with his car, with his tennis court, with tickets for all Hollywood functions, for racetracks, for tournaments, for benefits, for whatever big spectacle was afoot, but he would not share business opportunities. Father was a grown man and he should be able to take care of himself."

Frances Triest, William's stepdaughter, implied that Agnes's judgments were merely her opinions. "Cecil and William were devoted," Triest said. "Cecil once told me, 'If only I had William's brains, there's nowhere I couldn't have gone.' I used to go to the house quite a bit, and he invited me up to the ranch in Paradise. I was terribly shy, tall, and he used to call me 'the tall girl with eyes.' He was very kind."

In 1935, casting about for something that would raise some money, Clara Beranger wrote Cecil to thank him for some recent help, presumably financial. She mentioned a newspaper story she had seen about someone writing a biography of him, and thought about the possibility of writing a magazine story about her brother-in-law.

A few months later, she proposed a full-scale, serialized biography, and gingerly asked Cecil if he had any plans of his own in this regard. He replied by saying that it would be all right with him, but she needed to make up her mind, "as soon as possible as [journalist] Idwal Jones is also desirous of immortalizing me."

A month later, Clara replied that she had decided it was best for somebody outside the family to do the job. "If by chance you disagreed with my conclusions there might be a little personal feeling, which I want most particularly to avoid.

In other words, I am turning down the possibility of earning a large amount of money in order to keep the *entente cordial* of the family." Besides that, Bill was beginning work on a series of reminiscences for *The Saturday Evening Post* that would be collected as *Hollywood Saga* in 1939, and the idea of dueling books was something Clara wished to avoid.

In 1941, Clara Beranger deMille helped get her husband a job as founding head of the USC Department of Drama, a job at which he excelled and which gave him both a sense of purpose and a sense of security.

As for Agnes, success and the responsibility for an entire theatrical production would gradually increase her respect for her uncle. As she put it, "When I began to direct I recognized what went into these spectacular displays of endurance."

As a person, Agnes was defensive, spiky, authoritarian, brilliant. Like many homely women, she became more attractive as she aged, her character, accomplishments, and dignity giving her a distinguished cast she had never had in youth. In her emotional fierceness, she was far more like her Uncle Cecil than her father.

★

With the movie business still struggling from the effects of the Depression, much of Cecil's energy was occupied with keeping his own head above water. In 1934, John Herz offered Cecil B. DeMille Productions the opportunity to buy Paramount pictures. The stock was selling for around $2 a share and DeMille looked at the deal carefully, in spite of his professed lack of interest in ever running a studio again. But DeMille Productions didn't have the cash—it was $600,000 short of what would have been necessary to take over the studio, and Cecil didn't want to be saddled with debt, assuming, of course, that he could have obtained a loan. He let the deal pass, and, in fact, gave up some small monies that were due him from the 1923 *The Ten Commandments* in order to get his share of the earnings from *The Sign of the Cross*.

Although Cecil was back at Paramount, he was not entirely comfortable. It would take nearly ten years before he felt secure. His unease was amplified by the studio's cross-collateralizing his pictures, and punishing him for a commercial failure by nudging him gently but persistently toward projects it regarded as more commercial. Cecil's privileges were tentatively granted and he knew it.

★

For *The Crusades*, DeMille surrounded himself with some pretty fair writers: Dudley Nichols, Charles Brackett, Harold Lamb, Waldemar Young, and Howard Higgin, in addition to Jeanie Macpherson. Not only that, he sounded out Leopold Stokowski about writing the musical score, so long as the cost wouldn't be prohibitive. He wanted Stokowski to write "seven or eight songs . . . including Crusader Song, and production will start the middle of November, at which time perhaps one or two of [the] songs should be available." Production didn't start until January, but Stokowski was too busy to take on the project.

By the end of 1934, Dan Groesbeck was working on a series of spectacularly heroic images that DeMille would more or less reproduce. As always when word got out that DeMille was heading into production, he received dozens of letters from actors from the silent days asking for a spot in the picture. He had a "preferred list" of various old-timers including such once hallowed names as William Farnum, Clara Kimball Young, Charles Ray, Grace Cunard, and Florence Lawrence, who always got first call for any bits or extra work. Added to the list of actors for *The Crusades* was Hobart Bosworth. "I am looking forward with unusual joy and some trepidation to the making of *The Crusades*," wrote DeMille to the old actor. "It is probably the biggest yet undertaken, and I have put your name down at once to see where I can fit you in. It will be a pleasure to have you with me once again." DeMille paid Bosworth $1,000 for ten days work, good money for an actor whose best days had been twenty years before.

But Cecil couldn't employ everybody left stranded by changing times. There were hundreds of actors and dozens of writers from the old days who had been knocked out by the double punch of sound and the Depression. Sada Cowan, a screenwriter who had credits on twenty-six pictures from 1921 to 1928—including Cecil's *Fool's Paradise*—first saw work dry up, then, after the coming of sound, disappear entirely. In the decade of the 1930s, she earned precisely three screen credits. In late 1934, in the hope of avoiding foreclosure on her house, she wrote Cecil offering the house at a bargain price.

Cecil didn't need another house, but he had Cowan come to the studio and told her he'd put in a word for her with Paramount. Nothing happened, and she responded by offering to manage his apartments, feed the chickens at Paradise—anything, anything at all.

"Dear Deanie," he wrote her, "I have an idea that might work into something which I will try and bring to a head shortly. . . . Keep your memory green before me. As always."

"You say 'Keep your memory green before me,'" replied Cowan, who had moved to an apartment and given up her car. "Not knowing what your plan is, or if it may take a week, a month or a year to evolve, I do not know if you wish that reminder weekly or monthly . . . so if I overdo it forgive me." By the end of the year, Cowan was thanking DeMille for the beautiful Christmas present of employment.

★

The Crusades illustrates DeMille's technique of compressing history, as it telescopes several different crusades spread over several centuries. Mainly, the film focuses on the Third Crusade of 1189–1192, which involved the marquee personalities of Richard, King of England, and Saladin, sultan of Syria and Egypt. Yet DeMille introduces Peter, a wandering holy man based on Peter the Hermit, a fanatical preacher from Amiens in France, who led the first wave of the First Crusade to defeat in 1096. The real Peter committed atrocities against Jews and many others, but DeMille's Peter is a saintly man, a transplanted Old Testament prophet.

Both Richard and Saladin undergo conversion experiences. Richard begins as a gruff, warlike man who is ultimately humbled and who makes peace with Saladin so that all Christian pilgrims can visit Christ's tomb—except for Richard. Led by Berengaria's wisdom, Richard becomes an agent of peace, while Saladin evolves until he is the chivalrous and magnanimous leader depicted by his admiring Arab biographers.

In historical fact, Richard did no such thing. He vowed to continue the war against Saladin until Jerusalem was back in Christian hands. Overall, it's an unusually peace-loving movie for a man whose reputation—and many of whose movies—were nothing if not combative. But in *The Crusades*, the female lead goads the men into making peace, helped by the obvious sexual attraction between her and Saladin:

Berengaria: "Oh, what if we call him Allah or God, shall men fight because they travel different roads to him? There's only one God. His cross is burned deep into our hearts. It's here, and we must carry it with us wherever we go. Oh don't you see, Richard, there's only one way. Peace. Make peace between Christian and Saracen."

Richard: "You ask me to lay down my sword?"

Berengaria: "If you love me."

Richard is played as a stalwart Robin Hood surrounded by Merry Men. Henry Wilcoxon's Richard is often glimpsed with a hawk on his hand, or resting his hand on his sword, the better to indicate ferocious masculinity. Wilcoxon was a splendid-looking man, and a decent actor, but he lacked star quality, as DeMille and Paramount would find out to their mutual distress.

The film has a sense of heraldry that makes it a pure product of the Champion Driver—three armored men on horseback announce "A Cecil B. DeMille Production." (All DeMille characters wear armor, at least metaphorically.) There is one deliciously bad line ("The Christians are coming!") but the battle of Acre is beautifully realized, and is an obvious influence on Eisenstein's handling of a similar scene in *Alexander Nevsky*. The vast sets are by Hans Dreier and Roland Anderson, and DeMille pulls off an emotionally moving scene after the battle when Richard finds the body of the old man who made his sword. Exhausted, Richard looks to heaven and says simply, "If You are there, receive this old man's soul." Introducing the element of spiritual ambivalence into Richard's mind is a strange and moving admission for DeMille, who usually insisted that his characters reflect his own certainty.

The Crusades is a picture to gladden the heart of anybody who ever thrilled to the art of N. C. Wyeth or Howard Pyle, a heady combination of Old Testament and New, but mainly it's DeMille at his most vigorous, orchestrating a vast pageant with exceptional brio, lifting episodes from the literature of the past—the duel of wits between the two men in which Saladin triumphs by slicing a piece of silk with his scimitar derives from Sir Walter Scott's *The Talisman*, as do some other plot elements. As *Time* magazine said, "As a picture it is historically worthless, didactically treacherous, artistically absurd. None of these defects impairs its entertainment value."

Modern critics have been harsher, as with the screenwriter George MacDonald Fraser, who hilariously wrote of *The Crusades* that "There is much horseplay, hearty chorus work (mostly by Alan Hale as a dreadful Blondel), a tolerable assault on the walls of Acre, and some real comic-strip nonsense in which Saladin falls in love with Berengaria and Richard, if I was not deceived, becomes a convinced Christian." Fraser closed his broadside with, "Mischa Auer plays a monk."

Reminiscing for his memoirs, DeMille was, for the most part, modest about his films and accomplishments, but he did bluntly assert that "I saved the technique of silent pictures, instead of entirely eliminating all the technique which the others did." He probably meant that he placed the primary emphasis on the visual and used a strong, forceful, and basically unambiguous narrative line.

It's an oversimplification—John Ford and a few others also made sure that the image maintained primacy over the word—but not by much. Most audiences judged DeMille by his dialogue, which generally was the kind of writing used as titles for silent films—acceptable for reading, but spoken at the actor's peril. But in *The Crusades* and many of his other talkies, DeMille tosses off shots and radiantly crowded compositions that never could have happened in life. For DeMille, movies were not like life, nor were they supposed to be. They were intrinsically bigger and better than life itself can ever be.

The Crusades finished eighteen days behind schedule and cost $1.42 million—$336,000 over budget, with much of the overage paid for by Cecil B. DeMille Productions. DeMille shipped off an angry memo saying that none of it was his fault.

"The estimated cost of *The Crusades*, as given to me by Paramount, was $1,350,149. The approved budget on this picture was $1,041,899. This approved budget . . . included an overhead charge of 25%. In determining the cost of the picture completed, the overhead was computed at 32%, which is an item of approximately $91,000. This increase in studio overhead was caused by the fact that production at the studio at this time was almost at a standstill, and that aside from *The Crusades*, there were very few pictures being made at the studio during this period. . . .

"I told Mr. Emanuel Cohen, who was at that time in charge of the studio and of production . . . that it could not be produced for less than $1.2 million and that it could not be made for the approved budget. . . . Mr. Cohen started to nevertheless proceed with the picture and that he would take it up later with New

York and that if it was a big success—and we were both confident that it would be—that the cost would be forgotten."

But *The Crusades* was not a success, not even close. It was, in fact, a flat-out financial flop, losing $795,000 in its initial release. (A later reissue cut the loss in half.) Unlike other DeMille flops, such as *Four Frightened People*, which became the butt of jokes for the director, he always believed—correctly—that *The Crusades* was a good picture, and never understood its financial failure.

Unhappily for Henry Wilcoxon, the picture essentially ended his career as a Hollywood leading man; unhappily for DeMille, Paramount once again began making rumbling noises signifying dissatisfaction. DeMille responded with fury; for a time, he remembered, "I again deliberated breaking away from the Paramount organization. The studio was reorganizing its personnel. The executives and I could not agree on the subject I was to make next."

He had bulled sixty pictures into existence and he believed that most of them were to his credit. The name of DeMille would have been a distinguished part of show business for fifty years. But after some reflection, DeMille realized that he could not be happy tending to investments, not be happy doing anything but riding a camera crane, radiant with command.

Because of the commercial death of *The Crusades*, the cumulative loss on his pictures since he returned to Paramount in 1932 was $358,000. *The Crusades* had been the first picture of a two-picture deal, with *Samson and Delilah* scheduled to be the second, perhaps with Wilcoxon and Miriam Hopkins. But Paramount wanted nothing to do with the story or—especially—the cast. Not only that, Paramount's management was going through one of its periodic convulsions. During the production of *The Crusades*, Emanuel Cohen had been removed as production chief, and Ernst Lubitsch was installed, the only time a world-class director has been placed in charge of a movie studio.

DeMille courted Lubitsch's good opinion. He forwarded some laudatory comments about *The Crusades* from theater managers and critics. Lubitsch responded, "Please accept my heartiest congratulations at the magnificent reception your picture received."

"Lubitsch was very funny," remembered DeMille. "When I used to go in to talk to him, you would see him turn red all over. Lubitsch and I knew each other very well on our values; we had been the two top men in the industry. For me to come in and ask Lubitsch permission to do something—he nearly died. Embarrassed. He tried to do the job but he was not right for that any more than I was. I was not right for the DeMille studio and he wasn't right for [Paramount]. We could make our own pictures but we didn't have interest in somebody else's pictures."

When DeMille was shooting *The Crusades*, Lubitsch would take a break from his executive duties and go down to the set and watch. One day DeMille came over and complimented Lubitsch on *Trouble in Paradise*, saying it was like "a present from Cartier's with the tissue paper just removed." When DeMille asked what Lubitsch found so interesting about his set, Lubitsch replied, "I'm *hypnotized.* There isn't a cocktail shaker or tuxedo in sight."

As a studio head, Lubitsch made some good pictures, but he had trouble controlling costs. Not surprisingly, his tenure as studio head lasted only a year, and he was pleased to go back to directing. After a failed attempt to lure Irving Thalberg away from MGM, Paramount installed the experienced showman William LeBaron as production head. LeBaron, of course, had worked as a writer with Cecil and Jesse Lasky in their theater days, and the two men were friendly. Cecil was also on good terms with Barney Balaban, the Chicago exhibitor who became Paramount's president. Balaban ran Paramount from 1936 to 1964, approving only "prudent" expenditures, while leaving most creative decisions to Y. Frank Freeman, who supervised studio operations from 1938 to 1959.

After a number of years where his corporate overseers had been unsympathetic, Cecil would again begin connecting, both in the corporate and commercial senses. Although Paramount had an extraordinary roster of prestige directors—Josef von Sternberg, Leo McCarey, King Vidor, Rouben Mamoulian, and Ernst Lubitsch were all sharing production space with Cecil in the mid-1930s—it was Cecil who maintained pride of place, largely because from 1935 until 1957, every single one of his films earned a place in the top grossers of that year.

★

DeMille never stayed too long at the fair; if a picture in a particular vein failed, he would quickly retool and launch himself into another genre. He knew that the merry-go-round always comes around again. Just as two consecutive modern pictures (*This Day and Age* and *Four Frightened People*) had been disappointments and led him back to spectacle, now the failure of *The Crusades* sent him hurtling into a different epoch, one he hadn't dabbled in since the early days of the Lasky company—the western. *Samson and Delilah* was tabled, but DeMille's resolve could only be postponed, never vanquished.

The western subject was to be Wild Bill Hickok, the star was Gary Cooper, and the early plans mandated that the movie cost no more than $600,000, exclusive of Cooper's salary. In fact, including Cooper's salary *The Plainsman* cost $974,000, $400,000 less than *The Crusades.* Playing opposite Cooper as a very ahistorical Calamity Jane was Jean Arthur. DeMille demanded that Arthur learn to crack a bullwhip, and wouldn't let her wrap the business end of the whip around an extra's wrist before she had done it to him. The lash marks were on DeMille's wrist for days, but, as always, he wouldn't ask anybody to take a risk that he wouldn't take himself.

A young actor named Anthony Quinn was in Ensenada, Mexico, about to ship out on a Japanese fishing boat when he got word that DeMille was looking for an Indian who was the same size as Gary Cooper. Quinn's mother was Mexican, his long-gone father Irish, so Quinn wasn't an Indian, but he was six foot two. Encouraged by his brother, Quinn hopped a freight train to San Diego, then hopped another train to Los Angeles.

Quinn remembered that DeMille walked all around him like a man looking at a horse he was considering for purchase. "He would ponder everything and make it look like Moses," said Quinn. The actor pretended he didn't understand English, and uttered some gibberish that was meant to be and was accepted as an Indian language. DeMille fell for it and hired him for $75 a day.

During a lunch break, Quinn saw Katherine DeMille on the set and told her she should read Thomas Wolfe.

"Why?" she asked.

"Because if you like Thomas Wolfe, you'll like me."

There have been far worse pickup lines, and Quinn managed to back it up, especially when Katherine found Thomas Wolfe interesting. He took her to East Los Angeles, introduced her to his mother, brought her to Aimee Semple McPherson's temple, introduced her to a world she had never experienced. "There was no courtship, really," Quinn would write in his memoirs. "From the first, it was clear where our relationship was headed, although the reasons for its course were unclear."

Quinn's need for a family and a father were the keynotes of his obsessively masculine personality, and the fact that the prospective family was rich and powerful would not have been a disadvantage. Katherine was swept away by Quinn's masculinity . . . and, one suspects, by his inappropriateness in her father's eyes.

Quinn was talented, ambitious, and insecure. He was hyperconscious of what he called "the tremendous anti-Latin feeling" of California and Los Angeles. There had been Latin movie stars in the silent era—Ramon Novarro, Antonio Moreno—but none in the talkies. "There was no place for a Latin," grumbled Quinn. "I used to play Hawaiians, Indians, bandits, gangsters and just generally the heavy."

Quinn had fallen in with the wild roisterers surrounding the declining John Barrymore. They consoled Quinn as he struggled through a courtship that was not exactly encouraged by DeMille, but was never actively opposed either. Eventually, Quinn was invited to the house in Laughlin Park. He didn't have a suitable outfit, but bought one. Quinn was impressed by the house—"I didn't think people lived like that," he said—and managed to get through dinner. Constance, as always, went out of her way to make the nervous young man feel welcome and was the soul of graciousness.

When coffee was served, Quinn took a plate that he thought was sugar and dropped in two spoonfuls. Actually, it was the salt. He drank it anyway. DeMille smiled at Katherine as if to say "OK, he's got character. You can marry him."

DeMille and Quinn developed a good relationship, but the actor knew that that didn't necessarily mean Cecil thought Quinn was an appropriate match for his daughter. "Surely DeMille would have preferred a man of better means, and more pretentious beginnings for his lovely daughter," remembered Quinn, "but he never said anything. I could read his disappointment in his grudging acknowledgment and patronizing tone, but he respected his daughter too much to openly oppose her."

They were married on October 5, 1937. Cecil gave his daughter away, and Quinn claimed that neither his mother, his sister, nor any of his friends were invited to the wedding. Other family members claimed his family was invited, but Quinn didn't want them there.

Quinn would spend the rest of his life angry about his need for a father, and angrier still that DeMille could never quite bring himself to be that father. The fact that, as Quinn would remember, "I was never truly happy with Katherine, and if she was ever truly happy with me, I cannot imagine it was for very long," might have had something to do with his dissatisfaction.

Quinn never felt that DeMille made him feel a part of the family, but he also said that DeMille never made anybody but Cecilia feel a part of the family. "He had two adopted sons, John and Richard, and I don't think they ever felt part of the family. I don't think Katherine was quite part of the family ever." (In fact, Quinn's imputations of emotional estrangement were diametrically opposed to the recollections of Richard deMille as well as Katherine.)

Cecil presented the newlyweds with a house located on a plot of land below his own house, which caused John Barrymore to tell Quinn, "Every night, Tony, your father-in-law will step out on his balcony, and urinate upon you—a golden stream in the moonlight."

The lasting breach came a little later, when Quinn and Katherine went to DeMille for a loan for another house. DeMille asked about collateral. Quinn was furious and stayed furious. Thirty years later, he was still angry. "Grandfather would have done that for several reasons," remembered his granddaughter Cecilia. "To keep Tony's pride intact mainly; Grandfather never loaned money without a pledge of return. But Tony didn't see it that way; he thought Grandfather should loan the money on faith and he felt insulted. I suppose it was a clash in cultures. Tony never got over it.

"Grandfather thought him a brilliant actor and when they were together they seemed to laugh and have fun, but anybody who knew either of them could see the strain. It was a love/hate relationship."

"DeMille and I did not understand each other," remembered Quinn. "As a result, he lost a son and I lost a father. Constance was a wonderful, wonderful woman who accepted me in the family from the word go. She was a lovely, quiet lady who took a back seat to him. And he was a very nice host in his home, a wonderful host, but he was also kind of untouchable, the image that he built around himself—the puttees, the riding breeches. He could quote the Bible like nobody else I've ever known. He knew chapter, verse, everything. I admired that in him. But in a way I think that his best reference to life was the Bible. . . .

"I found him not easy to be around. He was very mannered in his gracious- ness. The house seemed to belong to royalty rather than a motion picture director. To his daughter Cecilia, he was a wonderful father. There was nothing she wanted that she couldn't get."

In years to come, the relationship was to be further clouded because of DeMille's affection for Katherine—by all accounts the most universally beloved member of the family—and by the fact that Quinn tried to bed every attractive woman he met and often succeeded. He treated Katherine badly, and DeMille would certainly have known about it. Yet, given the other women in DeMille's life, there wasn't a lot he could say.

★

The Plainsman is an enjoyable picture, if only because DeMille combines the pur- est romanticism with massive amounts of period authenticity and some splendid staging; as George MacDonald Fraser noted, "DeMille can make a production out of such a simple thing as a steamboat casting off, or find genuine beauty in a long shot of a wounded scout slumped in his saddle under a leafless tree; his crowd scenes are like Remington pictures come to life."

In 1937, westerns had not yet been reborn and were largely the province of B pictures made for rural audiences. Although John Ford has always been given the credit for reviving the genre with *Stagecoach* in 1939, DeMille deserves some of that credit by establishing the genre as a fit subject for major directors two years earlier.

The Plainsman marked the beginning of DeMille's reliance on second unit di- rectors for his big action sequences. For *The Plainsman*, only four days of DeMille's forty-six-day shooting schedule were on location. Most of the action footage was done by Art Rosson on location in Wyoming and Montana.

DeMille didn't go any easier on Rosson than on any other of his employees.

THE CAVALRY CHARGE HAS NO THRILL WHATEVER STOP IT APPEARS TO BE CRANKED NORMAL FOR MOST OF THE CHARGE IT IS IMPOSSIBLE TO TELL WHETHER THEY ARE INDIANS OR CAVALRY STOP IT IS IMPOSSIBLE TO GET A THRILL FROM A CHARGE COM- ING DIRECTLY AT CAMERA STOP APPROACH SHOULD BE DIAGONAL SO THAT WE CAN SEE MEN ARE GALLOPING. . . . THE EFFECT OF THIS SCENE MUST BE FAST SPEED AND THUNDERING HORSES NOT LITTLE TOY PUPPETS TWO OR THREE MILES AWAY. . . . LOCATION OF CHARGE IS NOT GOOD STOP SHOT WITH TREE IS BEST. USE SOME- THING TO BREAK THE FOREGROUND. . . . LET ME SEE SOMETHING THAT WILL MAKE AN AUDIENCE GET UP AND CHEER INSTEAD OF THE SLEEPY HOLLOW SCENE THAT YOU SENT DOWN. REGARDS.

The Crusades and *The Plainsman* were cross-collateralized. As of 1954, the loss on *The Crusades* was $374,916, which was charged against a profit of $1.2 million on *The Plainsman*.

★

By now, DeMille's style was codified, and he was essentially making movies about what Martin Scorsese referred to as the "solidity of the frame." DeMille's early preference for a theatrically accented naturalism had drifted toward an aesthetic that had about as much to do with the real world as *Aida*.

After the coming of sound, and especially after World War II, American movies drifted inexorably toward naturalism. DeMille's style—thin characters set amidst titanic productions with an overlay of narrative didacticism—struck most critics, especially in later years, as willfully perverse or antediluvian, even as audiences continued to be entranced by the show DeMille put into show business.

But DeMille's primary goals for his films were for elemental conflicts of dominance and submission, worlds in collision without any excess of talk. His films were not about camera movement; they weren't even about the characters. They were about staging and framing and texture—the atmosphere of the sets and costumes and the extras, especially the extras.

"He was able to deal with crowds in the frame," said Martin Scorsese. "He was able to deal with the positioning of crowds in the frame, and the movement of people [so well] that it's something we began to take for granted. Today, the [only] one who can handle crowds like that is Spielberg. Just look at *Empire of the Sun* and the Japanese invasion of Shanghai."

Many critics snickered at the sexuality and violence with which his tales of Christian redemption are imbued. Catholics are traditionally given a certain license to emphasize these things because of the sensuality of the ceremonies of the Catholic liturgy, but DeMille went far beyond that, and John Grierson thought he knew why.

"He is the only Jewish director," wrote Grierson, "who is not afraid of being his Jewish self; and the thin and squeamish Western mind may not therefore be fit judge of his Oriental opulence. He is our only Oriental director. Not a picture of his but comes slap out of the Old Testament . . . the fiestas in Gomorrah, the celebrations before the calf of gold, the Amami nights in the palace of Solomon; the living, pulsing, luxuriating aspect of the Hebrew life, which the parsons, Hebrew and otherwise, have suppressed."

"A lot of the human condition is sexuality and passion," Martin Scorsese told Kevin Brownlow, "and he takes that and ups it to a certain extent, commercially seeing how much he can get away with."

DeMille's gusto in the depiction of those things is part of the frankly sensual tone that makes his pictures so pleasurable. Scorsese points to the scene in *The Sign of the Cross* where a wife berates her husband for not being able to get them better seats in the Colosseum as key to the way DeMille could make the witnessing of human anguish "dangerously accessible—to put yourself as part of the audience—and with a great sense of humor."

As one professional appraising another, Scorsese was frankly awestruck at DeMille's skill. "It's a mammoth job to do what he did on camera, and to put those elements in the frame, a mammoth job. To deal with your main actors is one thing, but it's the people around the main actors, it's the people in the crowd scenes, in the foreground, three in the back, five on the sides, they have to be given specific directions, they've got to behave in a certain way, they've got to be great actors, and the director has to have an eye on every one of them in the frame. . . . He had an extraordinary skill with crowds, for the truth of what the crowd was about. . . . You really believed that they were taking Jerusalem or worshipping the Golden Calf. This is why the name 'DeMille' meant that I was going to see a real movie."

16

Whatever dissatisfaction DeMille might have had about his situation at Paramount was ameliorated by being hired to host a radio show. Not just any radio show, but the *Lux Radio Theatre*, which would become the most lucrative and prestigious job in its field. Much as TV would make Alfred Hitchcock a household name, radio transformed DeMille from a movie director into a national media celebrity.

Initially, DeMille was part of a rescue operation. The *Lux Radio Theatre* had begun in 1934, and within a year the show was facing cancellation. Danny Danker, an executive with the J. Walter Thompson advertising agency, was assigned the task of saving the show. Danker recommended moving the show to Hollywood and making it an extravagant, star-laden production.

Beginning June 1, 1936, DeMille signed a twenty-one-week contract with ten options of thirteen weeks each. For the first year he was to be paid $1,350 a week, rising to $1,800 a week by the third year.

DeMille's opening phrase became famous: "Greetings . . . *from Hollywood!*" intoned in his most stentorian tones, which, as one magazine noted, sounded like "This is God, speaking from heaven." The show paid well for everyone, especially actors. A top star could earn $5,000 for an appearance, but it was a five-day commitment.

The broadcasts involved at least fifty people—twenty-five musicians, twenty or so speaking parts, plus technicians. The first rehearsal was a Thursday table reading, with serious rehearsals beginning on Friday—a two-hour session at noon, a lunch break, and more rehearsing in the afternoon. On Saturday, the actors worked with the sound effects, on Sunday the orchestra would rehearse its cues and two dress rehearsals were scheduled for Monday, the first at 10 A.M., which was recorded so the director could judge its effects. The final dress rehearsal was at 7:30 P.M. and the broadcast went out that night at nine.

For nearly ten years (June 1, 1936, to January 22, 1945), DeMille was the host of what John Dunning called "the most important dramatic show in radio. It had the biggest stars, the highest budgets, the most acclaim." Before DeMille took the show over, it had mostly adapted Broadway plays; afterward, it was all movie adaptations. When a star got a part on the *Lux Radio Theatre*, shooting schedules were shifted to accommodate the broadcast. A movie company could stand idle while a star rushed off for a rehearsal, because an adaptation on the *Lux Radio Theatre* could result in a box office boost for the movie in question.

The network did everything possible to make it easy for DeMille to do the show—it was broadcast from the thousand-seat Music Box Theatre near the old Hollywood Brown Derby—minutes from both Paramount and DeMille's house.

DeMille was billed as "managing director," but he had nothing to do with the show's writing and production. "He was a figurehead more than anything else," said George Wells, who scripted the show for a number of years. "I worked in probably six Lux Radio Theaters," said Frank Coghlan. "C.B. never showed up until the dress rehearsal, when we had already been working on the show for three days. He got credit for directing, but didn't." DeMille's "sides" were typed on heavy cardboard, to avoid rattling paper, but he gave attention to the words written for him—the scripts are often cut and rewritten in his own hand.

The fact that it was a live broadcast, going out to an audience of something like 30 million people, translated to some major cases of stage fright for actors accustomed to retakes until they got it right. Joan Crawford's hands shook so badly she couldn't hold her script; Lily Pons was so distraught that her husband, André Kostelanetz, had to fly in from New York to lead the orchestra for the broadcast and lend his calming presence to his wife.

Mostly, Cecil was all business during the broadcasts, but writer George Wells remembered one time when he got a glimpse into his competitive nature. "One time we had his brother on because C.B. was sick; his brother William deMille stepped in for two weeks. Well, he only lasted one week because C.B. didn't like his brother being the head man so he arrived in a hospital bed—came wheeled in on a gurney. . . . He did the show from the bed and from the gurney."

The show offered some very interesting pairings of star and story that in some cases could have been more interesting than the movies that were being adapted: Theda Bara supporting William Powell and Myrna Loy in *The Thin Man* (6-8-36), Jack Benny in *Brewster's Millions* (2-15-37), Walter Winchell in *The Front Page* (6-28-37), Clark Gable in *Cimarron* (9-27-37), Spencer Tracy in *Arrowsmith* (10-25-37), Laurence Olivier in *Goodbye, Mr. Chips* (11-20-39), Ronald Colman in *Rebecca* (2-3-41), William Powell in *Shadow of a Doubt* (1-3-44), Judy Garland in both *Morning Glory* (10-12-42) and *A Star Is Born* (12-28-42).

The radio show was a commitment that took up about forty-five weeks a year—there was a break during part of July and all of August—and it became a contributing factor in DeMille's decision to stay close to Hollywood and delegate much of the action footage of the next ten years to second unit directors.

The *Lux Radio Theatre* encouraged DeMille's exhibitionistic tendencies—if he was comfortable with anything, it was fame, and now he had his own FDR-style fireside chats to spread that fame even further. DeMille had made a few appearances in newsreels and trailers over the years, and even a scene in MGM's Buster Keaton vehicle *Free and Easy*, but it's no accident that beginning in the mid-1930s he ramped up his appearances. In shorts like *Hollywood Extra Girl* (1935) and *Gretchen Comes Across* (1938), and in features like *Star Spangled Rhythm, Variety Girl, My Favorite Brunette*, and, of course, *Sunset Boulevard*, DeMille is seen very much as DeMille—kind but driven, and capable of turning on a dime toward impatience.

What's interesting is that DeMille understood that whitewashing his personality into blandness was not a good idea. The turbulent personality in the pictures DeMille appeared in was effective promotion for the turbulent pictures DeMille was directing, and the *Lux Radio Theatre* made DeMille a familiar name even to people who didn't go to the movies.

While DeMille was engaged in expanding his influence beyond Hollywood to the world, he was also involved in the nascent Screen Directors Guild. The Guild had attracted only about ninety members since its founding in February 1936, with A list talent such as John Ford, Frank Capra, and King Vidor in at the creation. The Supreme Court's upholding of the Wagner Act made it possible for the Hollywood unions to achieve some leverage.

It wasn't long before the Directors Guild membership was up to 550 members. DeMille joined, but he, along with a conservative faction within the Guild, objected to an alliance with the Screen Actors Guild because of SAG's affiliation with the American Federation of Labor. As if all this wasn't enough, he also served as a delegate to the 1936 Republican convention in Cleveland. DeMille was an active supporter of Alf Landon, and one visitor to his suite at the Statler Hotel reported that it was filled with "smoke and politicians."

DeMille's finances, after the rocky period of the late 1920s and early 1930s, had stabilized. Each month Gladys Rosson prepared a complete financial summary that broke down income, expenses, disbursements, and loans to the last penny. To take one month at random, in August 1936 income totaled $5,147.75, while expenses totaled $4,445.42, for a net profit of $702.33. That month, DeMille had cash on hand of $35,587.47.

DeMille's expenses were varied. Julia Faye was receiving $300 a month, while Cecilia was receiving $175 a month. He had a weakness for custom-made shirts, and spent several hundred dollars a month on liquor for Paradise and the *Seaward*. He was always looking for books or theatrical memorabilia relating to his father or himself, as in July 1936, when he spent $1.00 for a theater program for *The Warrens of Virginia*. He made donations to organizations as varied as the reelection campaign for Los Angeles district attorney Buron Fitts, and the Widows and Orphans Fund of the Motorcycle Officers of California.

For his next picture, DeMille tried to sell Paramount a story that had fascinated him since he was a playwright in New York—an ambitious Cossack who masqueraded as Dimitri, the son of Ivan the Terrible. DeMille wanted to eliminate the epic scale and battle scenes and concentrate on the intrinsic drama of the situation. Moreover, he wanted to make the movie without a big star, except for Peter Lorre as Boris Godunov, who murdered the real Dimitri. Adolph Zukor was doubtful; selling "a piece of Russian history that nobody knows about" wouldn't be easy, he said.

DeMille finally settled on something a little closer to home: the loose assemblage of five thousand soldiers and militiamen from Tennessee and Kentucky, free blacks and Creole aristocrats, Acadians, gunboat sailors and pirates, who confronted twice their number of British soldiers at the Battle of New Orleans in 1815. Beyond New Orleans, at stake was the entire Mississippi River basin—the heartland of a young nation. Leading the Americans was Andrew Jackson, a backwoods general, backed up by Jean Lafitte, a privateer and smuggler headquartered on Grande Terre island, forty miles south of New Orleans, who rejected a British bribe of around $30,000. Instead, he became an American ally for nothing.

In sum, it was ready-made historical truth that read like extravagant historical fiction.

For the script of *The Buccaneer*, DeMille tried out a young writer named Preston Sturges, who had recently had a hit with Mitchell Leisen's *Easy Living*. The relationship didn't last because Sturges wrote a scene that had Napoleon mistaking Louisiana for Lithuania, while behind him a wall map kept rolling up like a recalcitrant window shade. "He's made a comedian out of Napoleon!" exclaimed DeMille, but he followed through on Sturges's suggestion of casting Akim Tamiroff as Lafitte's second in command.

A more comfortable fit was Jesse Lasky Jr., who would last for twenty years on the staff and leave behind a revealing, very funny memoir that devoted more space to DeMille than to his own father. Said Jesse Jr.'s wife, "DeMille was more of a surrogate ogre than a surrogate father. Jesse was always quite deferential to DeMille. For instance, he always called him 'Mr. DeMille,' never 'C.B.' He had been a child around DeMille, who was his father's partner. He always absolutely adored writing the DeMille films, even though he was never paid much for them. He could make more money at other studios, but he felt that the work was important and significant and would last longer. It always stuck in his craw that the one later DeMille film he didn't work on, the circus picture [*The Greatest Show on Earth*] got the Oscar. He was always furious about that.

"Jesse was of an older school. His mother was a mystical creature, a poet, and he was like her in some ways. He was totally unassertive, always reluctant to put himself forward."

Although he wasn't credited on *The Buccaneer*, Lasky Jr. made a suggestion about a line of dialogue that DeMille had liked. In gratitude, he sent the young man a case of champagne—Bollinger 1928. The newcomer noted with some amusement Jeanie Macpherson's habit of wearing only one color at a time and "haunting his corridors like a ghost of paradise lost, hoping for occasional invitations to be present at meetings." DeMille's attitude toward Macpherson by this time was a mix of exasperation and condescension. "If that woman doesn't drive you screaming, raving insane—if you can keep from strangling her with your bare hands—she occasionally comes up with something usable," he said.

In time, all writers ran into the wall of DeMille's perceptions of their congenital inadequacy. "He used writers like a general who counted no costs and spared no feelings," remembered Lasky Jr. "Casualties were generally high in wounds of the ego." If the withering sarcasm drew blood and a writer began to respond in kind, DeMille would draw himself up and snap, "Don't you dare get mad at me! *I'm* the only one who gets mad on a DeMille picture!" That generally brought an end to the heated part of the conversation with something resembling a smile.

DeMille worked differently from other producers and directors, who usually sent a writer off to work for several weeks before going over his pages. DeMille had his writers in the bungalow and worked with them on a weekly, if not daily basis, driving, driving. A scene submitted for DeMille's approval could be returned with handwritten criticisms such as "What I've crossed out I don't like. What I haven't crossed out I am dissatisfied with." If he really disliked the material, he would scribble things like "This is baloney," "This isn't the way we talked about it," or simply a stentorian "NO!"

A lot of script meetings were taken down by stenographers. Sometimes he would read his writers chapter and verse from the Bible story they were adapting, with long DeMillean interpolations after every sentence. When DeMille began planning *Samson and Delilah* years before he actually shot it, he had a script session that sent him off in a reverie about the plans for the picture itself: " 'And he found a new jawbone of an ass, and put forth his hand and took it, and slew a thousand men therewith.'

"Probably the fight has grown," he observed. "He probably killed three people and by the time it had got to the tribe of Levi it was ten thousand. Now, I want to tell you this. . . . This picture doesn't need crowds; they are of no value to it. The ruins are little bits of places. I'm going to get a lot of the effects with [matte] painting, a lot of shooting outdoors, and up at my ranch without even any transportation charges. The magnificence of costumes. Yes, the magnificence of drapes because that's the setting of the jewel. There's only one big set that I see and that's the temple scene at the end."

Other times the transcripts of the story meetings provide intimate glimpses of DeMille knocking heads over a perceived insufficiency in a love scene. "Her body is against him, her cheek against him," he orates to one writer. "He's having a helluva time and she's in seventh heaven with him in her arms. He should say, 'I'll have none of you. I know you, you little bitch. I know what you're here for. You've come to try and get me, haven't you? . . .'

"They should make a pair that are flint and steel, whereas you have a pair that are rubber gloves . . . you don't get the power of these two characters. . . . Up to now I think we have tried to write this scene a little from the grand opera standpoint rather than from two people. You have got to get it down where I believe it. Joe and Mabel down behind the cotton mill by the Los Angeles River. When you get it on that basis, it will be true." DeMille was incapable of approving anything that he had not personally decimated, then restructured to his own specifications.

For DeMille, Jesse Jr. became his house Hebrew, even though he had grown up in a completely secular household and had never even been bar mitzvah. Lasky's heritage was Jewish, therefore he was a Jew. It took a while for Jesse to get the hang of the DeMille process. Four writers working together, each one working on different areas, or scenes, with the other writers going over the work to assure uniformity of style.

Jesse's main ally in the DeMille circle was Anthony Quinn, who respected the fact that Jesse had published poetry as a teenager and was well read. Quinn would come over to Lasky's house and ask, "Tell me what I should be reading." He'd leave with ten books and return with them a week later, leaving with ten more.

The Buccaneer was a saga of buckle and swash, custom-made for Cecil's interests and audience. But despite DeMille's well-earned reputation for extravagance, he was willing to cut corners, so long as it was never obvious. Anne Bauchens thought there might be some costumes left over from James Cruze's silent Old Ironsides that could be used, and she went through the Paramount film library looking for scenes of pirates or beaches that could be used for stock shots or process backgrounds. She sent a memo to Cecil that there were six reels of material from Old Ironsides that he should look at, three reels from Lazy River, some background shots of bayous shot for a never-made movie called Old Don, and a series of beach scenes taken in Panama for Swing High, Swing Low.

All of DeMille's successive historical epics are very much of a piece, although the visual swag of The Buccaneer, deriving as it does from equal parts N. C. Wyeth and Douglas Fairbanks's The Black Pirate, puts it very near the top of the roster. The storytelling is forceful and at all times linear, the narrative and characters powerful and vivid. There are complications, but no real complexity.

Perhaps because DeMille's audience was underwhelmed by the prospect of Fredric March in a pirate movie, The Buccaneer underperformed. At a negative cost just under $1.4 million, it carried a net loss of $162,505 as late as 1952. The audience missed a good picture. The fun begins with the credits, as a group of picturesque pirates tramp up a beach toward the camera, then dig up some buried treasure. As the top of the treasure chest opens, "A Cecil B. DeMille Production" appears, and the unrolling of a scroll on the top of the chest offers the main title.

As is typical with DeMille, he begins with historical characters for exposition and credibility, in this case James and Dolley Madison, then segues into a fictional story hung on the bare bones of historical incident. Fredric March was a talented performer, but there was always something reedy and actorish about him in costume pictures, and here he's a contender for the Dick Van Dyke Worst Movie Accent Hall of Fame. But March also had a sense of irony that was rare for a DeMille leading man, so his Lafitte is basically a big, overgrown kid playing a pirate.

The Buccaneer is a splendidly picturesque anthology of pirate tropes, with costumes that were a collaboration between Natalie Visart and Dwight Franklin; the latter had also designed the costumes for *The Black Pirate.* It looks great, although DeMille is obviously hoping no one notices that March is a hopeless action hero and has to be heavily doubled. The director even offers a couple of chorale sections of pirates singing as they move through the bayous, including one sequence tinted a beautiful deep green. The genuflection toward the silent days continues with one shot masqued to an iris.

It's rousing fun, and even reasonably faithful to the vague historical record.

★

The early preparation of *Union Pacific* marked the first of DeMille's health crises. At the end of March 1938, the director underwent emergency prostate surgery. DeMille would characterize the operation as a "major prostatectomy, one of the worst operations there is. All your functions are gone, they have to put tubes up and all that so that you urinate with a drip all the time. It's horrible."

Worse, there was an ensuing low-grade infection, which, in those days before widely available antibiotics, meant a long period of discomfort. If the infection wasn't stopped, the doctor told him, it would inevitably kill him. DeMille told his son Richard that he owed his life to streptomycin.

DeMille took the entire month of April off to recuperate, and didn't go back to the studio until May 5. As *Union Pacific* got underway in November, he was still fighting the infection. His face gray and gaunt, his crotch packed in ice, he was strapped onto the camera boom. He directed even though he was in pain. "If ever a man deserved a medal for courage," remembered Jesse Lasky Jr., "it was DeMille as he directed from his mobile bed of pain."

The nature of the operation, and DeMille's own understandable vanity, makes ascertaining the severity of the prostate surgery impossible at this late date. For a time, Cecil was given to quiet complaints about his dysfunctional mechanics. After a time, the complaints leveled off, then ceased. Some in the family tend to the view that the surgery was the end of his functioning sexuality, while others noted his continuing strong relationship with Gladys Rosson, although that relationship could have been maintained without sex.

By this time, Richard deMille remembered that "Julia Faye was a lush. She wasn't the young woman that he started with, she was older and there was more of her. She wore a strong perfume which I liked, and she was very warm and very nice. Gladys was a pert, businesslike, Scottish type, and not much to look at—short, stocky, well-built, no glamour doll or seductress. She was madly in love with him."

If DeMille was having trouble with his own equipment, he felt it his duty as a father to make sure that Richard's was functioning. When John and Richard became old enough, Cecil himself gave them a talk about sex, complete with a frank explanation of the value of contraception. A few years later, the sixteen-year-old Richard was startled when Cecil suddenly asked him, "Have you been with a woman?"

"Uh, no," replied the embarrassed boy.

"You should be with a woman," said DeMille thoughtfully. Shortly afterward, Richard was with Cecil and his associate producer Bill Pine at the racetrack when he was introduced to an attractive Jewish girl who had done some extra work for Cecil. Shortly after that, the same group found themselves together again at Paradise. Bill Pine leaned over at dinner and asked Richard, "Like her?"

"Yes," replied the startled boy, who was beginning to realize that the fix was in.

"Well, you can romance her a little."

As Richard deMille would dryly remember nearly seventy years later, "I wasn't sure what that meant, but I found out. Cecil was a very practical person."

Cecil was always concerned that Richard make the right choices in life, although he tended to speak in metaphors. "He once told me, apparently in all seriousness," remembered Richard, 'Love God, honor the Queen, shoot straight and keep clean.' And I have always done that, but that isn't the way most people were teaching in those days."

Cecil told Richard that he shouldn't marry the first girl he found, but should wait for the right one. "I could have married a girl whose father owned a box factory," explained Cecil, "and I could have been head of that box factory, and I would have had a fine job making boxes, but that would not have been the right thing to do."

★

For *Union Pacific*, DeMille felt he needed someone new and unusual to illuminate the dramatics, so on September 13, 1938, he offered the female lead to a young actress named Vivien Leigh. He was more generous than was his wont with young actors, offering $2,000 a week with a seven-week guarantee and a four-picture option, with appropriate raises.

But Leigh, whose primary film appearances at this time included *Fire Over England*, *Dark Journey*, and *A Yank at Oxford*, had already set her sights on the part of Scarlett O'Hara and didn't care all that much about DeMille; she counteroffered with a demand for $20,000 for six weeks and an option for one picture.

DeMille retreated in stony silence, and decided to go with the tried-and-true—Barbara Stanwyck.

It worked out well; in spite of a dubious Irish accent she assumed for the movie, Stanwyck the pro admired DeMille the pro: "You certainly knew where his pictures were going [and] why they were made," remembered Stanwyck in 1981. "I loved DeMille and he loved me. We only made *Union Pacific* together, but we did lots of radio. We got along great. If there were 500 people up on a mountain, he knew who the hell each one was. He could hear the train long before he could hear the whistle."

Opposite Stanwyck, DeMille went to Joel McCrea, who had recently asked for his release from Sam Goldwyn when the producer signed Gary Cooper to a contract. When McCrea mentioned to DeMille how difficult his relationship with Goldwyn had been, DeMille sighed philosophically. "Everybody has a little trouble with Sam," he said. "What do you think Jesse and I went through?" McCrea told DeMille that he would probably have a more successful picture with Gary Cooper, and DeMille agreed. "I can't get him," he said. "I wanted to because I love Cooper. But I talked to his agent and he's committed at Warner Bros. and at Goldwyn. He can't do it. So would you like to do it?"

On the first day of production, DeMille rose to address the cast and crew and proudly introduced McCrea as his former newspaper boy. "What a showman!" McCrea told Pat McGilligan. "Right away it set me up. It set me up with all the people who said, 'Who the hell is McCrea? . . . He isn't very well known.' " (Actually, McCrea had already made, among others, *Bird of Paradise* for King Vidor, *Dead End* for William Wyler, and *Wells Fargo* for Frank Lloyd, so he was not an unknown quantity.)

McCrea adored DeMille. "Everyone thought he was a big, cold guy . . . but he had sensitivity. He was great with a lot of people. He could handle them and make it look right. As people say, he was kind of hammy, but I think it was showmanship; I think it was like P. T. Barnum and the circus, you know? He was a showman, a showman on the set, and a showman with the picture."

Drawing a diametrically opposed picture was a young actor that DeMille hired to play Stanwyck's weakly villainous brother. "He was no director," Robert Preston would remember. "For over two weeks of shooting [on *Union Pacific*] Stanwyck and I were alone in a boxcar, and because there were no crowd scenes, no special effects, just two people acting, you'd never have known the old man was on the set. He didn't know what to do with it, except just roll and print. He didn't know what to tell us. Also, he was not a nice person, politically or any other way."

The studio devised a rolling series of premieres involving the cast and crew steaming into towns on a train. The studio rented a dieselized electric train that towed an old steam locomotive behind it. When they got a couple of miles out of town, they'd travel the last leg on the old train.

The first night out of Los Angeles, DeMille called Preston into his private car and told him that, while he was supposed to act as the MC at the rolling premieres, he didn't really know anything about Preston. What, he wanted to know, had Preston done before? There had been three small movies before *Union Pacific*, but DeMille wasn't going to acknowledge those. DeMille asked what he had done before that, and Preston replied "Theater."

"I mean work," replied DeMille.

"The only thing I've done that you'd call work was when I was at the Pasadena Playhouse and I was on the cleaning crew in the morning and parked cars at Santa Anita Race Track in the afternoon."

A press agent's dream! For the next several weeks, DeMille introduced Preston as a boy he found parking cars at Santa Anita. Soon afterward, when DeMille handed him the script for *North West Mounted Police* and asked him how he liked it, Preston retorted that "It's the same part I played for you last year. I'll change costumes and play it again."

"You ungrateful son of a bitch," said DeMille. "If it weren't for me, you'd still be parking cars at Santa Anita!"

"And he meant it!" said Preston nearly forty years later.

Preston would be one of the few stars with nothing good to say about DeMille, although, like everyone else, he was fond of Constance. "C.B. wasn't a king, but she really was a queen. She was a marvelous woman. I don't know how she . . . Well, I guess she didn't see much of him!"

Union Pacific is essentially a remake of John Ford's *The Iron Horse*, with different figures in the foreground, and made mostly on a soundstage instead of on location in Nevada. There are a lot of stage Irish accents, and DeMille injects colorful pieces of business—Robert Preston blows smoke into a small box, then taps the box to make the smoke emerge in small puffs. He also drops in a cute in-joke, as a telegraph operator is named "Mr. Calvin," a tribute to Cecilia's father-in-law, Edgar Eugene Calvin.

Paramount had kept a young assistant director named Arthur Jacobson away from DeMille's films because, as Jacobson remembered, "they wouldn't allow him to break my spirit." But on *Union Pacific*, the studio was caught short and Jacobson was assigned to direct a short scene where gold is discovered and a bar empties out as the inhabitants rush to the fields.

"I read the script and I was thrilled because I knew I could do good things with it. I went to see him to find out what he wanted, because I wanted to direct it the way he would direct it.

"Well, I went three nights running, and I couldn't get in to see him. One night, Lynne Overman, a good actor who was a friend of mine and had worked for DeMille, said, 'Oh, for Chrissakes, come on.' He took me over to DeMille and said, 'Pop, listen to this guy, he needs to talk to you.'

"So DeMille and I talked, and for the next two or three nights I shot the scene. I went to the [screening room] to see the rushes and the production manager asked what I was doing there. I told him I was there to see the rushes, and he shook his head and said, 'He'll eat you alive, he'll tear you to pieces.'

"I sat in the projection room and a slate comes on with my name on it. [After a while] I heard that great voice of his calling out, 'Is the young man here who shot this stuff?'

" 'Here I am.'

" 'Excellent, young man, excellent!'

"And from that time on, the world could kiss my ass."

Union Pacific is longer than it needs to be and more enjoyable than it ought to be. What puts it over is the chemistry between the excitable Stanwyck and the calm, unflappable McCrea, some spectacular second unit work by Art Rosson and some equally spectacular miniature work by the special effects department. Unusually for DeMille, the plot mechanism involves capitalist chicanery on the part of railroad entrepreneurs.

DeMille's westerns are all good fun, but he didn't have the same feeling for them that he did for other genres. The best westerns feature the land as a character and have a sense of leisure about them. Despite his own feeling for nature, DeMille would never have shot a scene in which a man leans back in his chair and spends ten seconds balancing on a post, as John Ford did in *My Darling Clementine*, because DeMille didn't trust any scene that didn't advance the story. A director like Griffith or Ford would use spectacle as a representation of the obstacles faced by their characters, but DeMille was interested in spectacle for its own sake.

Union Pacific went eleven days over its eighty-two-day schedule and $161,139 over its $1.2 million budget, but it was a hit, grossing $3.2 million, for a net profit of $296,576. It was obvious that both Paramount and DeMille could have made a lot more money if he had managed to control his occasional penchant for going over budget, but he had a horror of cheating the picture, or the audience. As he would say, "If you have a $500,000 picture that looks like $1 million, then you have a million dollar picture; but if you have a million dollar picture that looks like $500,000, then you have a $500,000 picture."

★

In late 1938, Will Hays asked DeMille to take on the assignment of supervising the American movie industry's contribution to the 1939 New York World's Fair. *Land of Liberty* was a large-scale compilation film that told the story of America through film clips. The budget was only $25,000, but DeMille assumed the costs of putting Jeanie Macpherson and Jesse Lasky Jr. on the project.

DeMille was initially at a loss as to how to create a sense of audience involvement, and worried about making "a lengthy and perhaps dull education feature with very little mass appeal." DeMille shot some footage of a typical American family "reviewing American history," but he didn't think it worked and decided to go strictly with film clips with voice overs by Gayne Whitman and DeMille himself.

DeMille used scenes from his own films—*The Plainsman*, *The Buccaneer*, *Union Pacific*. Other films plundered for material included *Old Ironsides*, *So Red the Rose*, *Wells Fargo*, *Of Human Hearts*, *San Francisco*, *In Old Chicago*, and dozens of newsreels.

Although it wasn't intended as a profit-making venture, *Land of Liberty* was very well received, and overflow audiences at the World's Fair and the Golden Gate International Exposition in San Francisco meant that DeMille was asked to shorten the film from its 137-minute running time so as to get in more shows per day.

"I am opposed to cutting a success," he wrote in response, "even to permit one more show a day . . . never tamper with success, because you never really know just what made it a success." The film was picked up for distribution by MGM in 1941, and $150,000 in profits was donated to war relief charities in America and Europe.

★

Like any director, Cecil put in much time and effort on projects that didn't get made. An aborted western called *Rurales* cost him and the studio over $300,000, and he was also heavily invested in a project unfortunately called *Queen of Queens*, the story of the Virgin Mary. He even put Bill on the script for a time, and seems to have treated him just as badly as he did other writers. DeMille genuinely wanted to make the picture, but could never win over the Legion of Decency and other Catholic representatives, among them Father Daniel Lord and Bishop Fulton J. Sheen, who regarded the whole project as verging on blasphemy because of the impossibility of depicting any kind of normal marital relationship between Mary and Joseph.

To get away from an overwhelming aura of becalmed piety, DeMille introduced an affair between Judas and Salome, complete with the dance of the seven veils. "It was completely dreadful," wrote Daniel Lord in his memoirs. More to the point, William deMille knew it. "[William] knew the scenario was a hash and a hazard and though he submitted it to me with objective justice and some show of enthusiasm, the moment I began to take it apart he was entirely in agreement."

Probably the most interesting of the lost projects was an adaptation of Ernest Hemingway's *For Whom the Bell Tolls*, which was published in 1940 to vast acclaim and equally vast sales, and with a male part that was perfect for Gary Cooper. Paramount paid a whopping $100,000 for the rights. For that kind of money, even the truculently anti-Hollywood Hemingway was not averse to a personal appearance, so he came to the studio and was photographed with DeMille. Everybody was happy.

Then DeMille read the book.

"[The book was] really in a communist cause," DeMille would say. "I bought it without reading the book, on the basis of Gary Cooper's intent." But mindful of his public image, and not eager to appear any more reactionary than absolutely necessary, in his memoirs DeMille said that he abandoned the picture because John Hay Whitney asked him to consider a movie on Latin American themes.

Cooper stayed interested—a good part is a good part, especially if it's written by a pal, even if he is left-wing—and played the part of Robert Jordan, but it was Sam Wood, DeMille's old assistant director and fanatical anticommunist, who ended up directing the picture.

For DeMille's immediate future, it was back to the past.

Although the credits announced that North West Mounted Police is an original screenplay by the interesting triumvirate of Alan LeMay (*The Searchers*), Jesse Lasky Jr., and C. Gardner Sullivan, a great screenwriter whose credits extended back to William S. Hart in the silent days, the film was actually loosely based on *The Royal Mounted*, a play that Cecil co-wrote with William in 1908.

The film, unlike the play, centered on the Riel Rebellion of 1885, in which a mixed-race schoolteacher led an uprising against the Canadian government. Louis Riel had one or two early victories because the Mounties were too thinly stretched, but an attempt to incite the Indians to join the uprising failed. Riel was captured and hanged in November 1885. The colonialist bias of the story fit in nicely with DeMille's previous westerns, which emphasized themes of Manifest Destiny, appropriate at a time when the British Empire was still supreme. (Today, Riel is regarded as a premature victim of the fight for Indian rights, and there is a heroic statue of him on the grounds of the Manitoba legislature.)

Cecil added a strand borrowed from *The Squaw Man*: an Indian woman desperately in love with a white man. "I see a tough son of a bitch," he said in a story meeting, "who is a half animal, and a magnificent one, crafty as hell, beautiful as hell, and unconsciously a terrible destroyer."

DeMille always saw an overtly sexual female as someone to be dominated and tamed, and the character of Louvette would be an early version of mixed-race wanton sexuality that would reach its parodic height in David O. Selznick's *Duel in the Sun*. DeMille cast Paulette Goddard in the part.

North West Mounted Police marked DeMille's first picture in Technicolor, but it was otherwise business as usual. Contractually, DeMille received an advance of $100,000 against 50 percent of the net profits. In return, DeMille Productions had to put up 15 percent of the production budget. DeMille initially wanted Joel McCrea for the male lead, but Gary Cooper suddenly became available when a picture fell through, and DeMille felt he had to go with the bigger star. (Cooper was the one actor for whom DeMille always expressed enthusiasm.) An abashed DeMille offered McCrea the second lead, but McCrea knew a thankless part when he saw it and passed with no hard feelings.

DeMille sent Gladys Rosson to make the loan arrangements with the Bank of America, and she wrote a memo to her boss laying out the proceedings:

> Mr. [J. H.] Rosenberg was cordial as always. He thought your subject and cast and color splendid. He asked the cost. I quoted $1,576,000 as the budget and that you and Mr. LeBaron expected to get it down to $1,400,000 or $1,450,000, he said, "Whew—that's a lot of money—but you can have whatever you want—you know that." He asked how much we were allowing for color. I said $300,000. . . . He said, "Are you paying Cooper $150,000?" and I assented. . . .
>
> He said that you were their oldest picture account, and that "with all due regard for our other accounts," they felt pretty close to you and valued your business, the way you did business and the cooperation you never hesitated to give the bank. . . .
>
> We set $217,500—15% of $1,450,000, as the probable amount we would borrow. . . . He said "You have about the sweetest deal in pictures—you can't lose the way you are set up."
>
> He asked what the radio was bringing you in, and I said $80,250 last year. He shook his head as if to say, "marvelous."

Less than two months after the film was released in the fall of 1940, DeMille Productions had paid off the loan from the Bank of America.

The production of a DeMille film was now as much industrial as aesthetic. Even simple scenes—Madeleine Carroll bandaging the foot of a child—were undertaken with stand-ins for the stars and a dummy for the child. DeMille would direct the camera crew with his microphone to his mouth, so that his breathing was magnified through the speakers on the soundstage. At the end of a half hour of searching for the right camera angle, the crew finally heard, "I shouldn't be surprised if this would do. Yes, very well indeed. The stand-ins will retire. Call Miss Carroll, please, and Mr. Cooper, and the child . . ."

North West Mounted Police came in $80,000 under budget and seven days under schedule, costing under $1.5 million—a modest figure for an adventure movie in Technicolor—of which $332,816 went for the cast. The picture began shooting on March 7, 1940, finished on May 13, and was released on November 22, a remarkably efficient schedule that DeMille would have reason to feel nostalgic about in years to come.

Art Rosson's second unit footage provided effective bursts of action. One stunt, in which Gary Cooper's double ropes a Gatling gun and yanks it downhill behind him while on horseback looks—and probably was—dangerous.

From its jaunty Victor Young score to its improbable casting—Akim Tamiroff as a French Canadian—to the major plot point of the rebels getting their hands on a Gatling gun, thus causing a lot of picturesque head wounds, North West Mounted Police embodies a zest that would become rare in DeMille's films of the 1940s, and only infrequently recaptured thereafter. Once again Robert Preston is cast as the charming but irresponsible scapegrace, once again Gary Cooper is the handsome and stalwart hero, this time a Texas Ranger named Dusty Rivers. The second lead is played by Preston Foster, who's better than he has any right to be, considering the dialogue he's given: "Never trust a blue-eyed squaw," he snaps.

The film moves well, and DeMille feels secure enough in his material that Gary Cooper doesn't get the girl, just his prisoner. North West Mounted Police returned nearly $6 million, with a net profit of $1.4 million as of 1952.

DeMille always placed his faith in spectacle, the pleasures of linear narrative, and, beginning with North West Mounted Police, florid splashes of Technicolor. But in Natalie Kalmus, the ferocious ex-wife of Technicolor founder Herbert Kalmus and guardian of what would and would not be allowed, DeMille ran up against a will as imperious as his own. Kalmus had her own Ten Commandments of Technicolor, and prominent among them was "Thou Shalt Not Use Red and Orange in the same scene." DeMille, whose taste in colors would prove as delirious as his taste in dialogue, fumed about this restriction, then yelled, "Well, it's too bad the good Lord up in heaven didn't have a Technicolor consultant when he made apples and oranges!"

DeMille was quite taken with Paulette Goddard, as well he should have been. The common-law wife of Charlie Chaplin was delicious-looking, witty, and frankly acquisitive. She became one of the few actresses invited to Paradise, and remembered that DeMille told her, "Bring your most glamorous clothes." Unfortunately, DeMille's penchant for flambéing the food meant that there were sparks flying around that could incinerate said clothes. "Not only was everything flambéed during the dinner," she remembered, "but at the end there was cherries jubilee to top it off. DeMille would hand me a gun as I went down to my cabin, and he'd say, 'In case of wild animals.' And I said, 'The only wild animal I'm leaving is up here.' He thought I was quite amusing."

Goddard loved the organization, the Russian silk blouses. She also loved the caviar that DeMille served her and no one else. "It was as though we were living in Roman times. Before the fall. It was fabulous at his place. I thought I was in a movie while I was living."

But Goddard was a temperamental actress, and DeMille was a temperamental director. He grew particularly irritated about a leather skirt that his wardrobe people could never get to his satisfaction. One day Goddard came bouncing into the office and announced she had modeled the skirt for Chaplin, who promptly told her the problem was the fringe at the bottom of the skirt. Lose the fringe, Chaplin said, and use a simple rough leather for the hem. DeMille was finally pleased.

DeMille's affection for Goddard even led him to extend an invitation to

Charlie Chaplin to Paradise for Thanksgiving weekend in 1941, but Chaplin replied that he "had made arrangements to go to Sun Valley for Thanksgiving, but will accept a rain check any time after. As ever . . ." Thus ended an opportunity for some interesting political discussions.

The period immediately leading up to *North West Mounted Police* marked the reentry of Julia Faye into DeMille's life. For a couple of years, she had attempted to establish a life outside his orbit. There had been a flirtation with an opera career that didn't get far, then a nervous breakdown. Faye recovered, married, but the marriage failed. There seemed to be no alternative; better to exist in the reflected light of Cecil's powerful sun than languish in the shade.

After her return to the fold, Julia continued to be demanding, and DeMille continued to find her charming. In October 1938, just before the start of production on *Union Pacific*, Gladys sent DeMille a note to the effect that "Julia phoned about her check this morning, and said that her salary from *Union Pacific* will be used to pay off the $300 note that comes due on December 12th. There is $200 due on November 1st, that she will bring in for you to renew; and the $600 note will not be due until Jan. 3rd."

A month later, Julia telephoned to say that she owed $1,265 for clothing and could settle for less than half the total amount. If she could get four weeks' work at $150 a week, she could take care of the debts and apply the leftover amount to one of her notes.

Cecil's general attitude toward Julia seemed to be indulgent and fondly amused. "Your Thursday morning letter bespattered with tear-drops has arrived on the Seaward," he wrote her in August 1938, "and I hasten to mingle my own tears with yours as I enclose the endorsed note for $200. Also, I am enclosing a little check to provide food and to keep you round and rosy until my return to the studio next Friday—but not enough to make you fat.

"I only expect to be in town Friday and Saturday, and perhaps Monday morning, so probably Saturday afternoon would be the best time for you to see me. However, I suggest that you phone on Friday.

"In the meantime, be [a] good sweet maid and let who will be clever. The Old Man of the Sea."

For the rest of Cecil's life, Julia would be featured in small parts in DeMille movies. As she once explained to Ann del Valle, one of the publicists in the DeMille unit, being the second woman in Cecil DeMille's life was better than being the first in any other man's. "She really loved him," remembered del Valle.

*

DeMille hadn't kept talent under personal contract since the days of Rod La Rocque and Leatrice Joy, but in the fall of 1937 he signed up a young girl from Georgia named Evelyn Keyes, who was escorted into his office by Jeanie Macpherson and encountered "a bald man in his fifties, quite grandfatherly, except for eyes like electric drills."

"Lift your skirt, so he can see your legs," said Macpherson, but DeMille immediately snapped, "Don't you dare! That's not what I want!"

"I stood there stunned," remembered Keyes, "and he asked me where I came from, I answered, and then I'll never forget. He said to Macpherson, 'I think I will sign her.' And then he pointed right at me, the finger was this near, 'But that accent has to go. You don't want to play Southern girls all your life, do you?' "

Keyes was besotted. "Anything. I was his. A wonderful man. Frightened? There was no way to be frightened; he was bigger than life, that's all. Whatever he said to me to do, I did, whatever he said not to do, I didn't do. He was in total charge and I was happiness itself."

DeMille closed by telling her to have her agent call him, then told her, "Glad to see you don't wear that vulgar red stuff on your nails," by way of dismissal.

So began several years of diction and acting lessons, and parts in *The Buccaneer* and Paramount Bs such as *Sudden Money*. She did test scenes with Anthony Quinn, and there were a few offstage scenes with Quinn as well.

When he cast her in *The Buccaneer*, and a makeup person moved to refresh her lipstick, DeMille thundered out over the loudspeaker system, "You *need* to think about your *acting, not* the way you *look*. You'll *never get anywhere* that way." Fredric March patted her hand and told her, "Don't worry. He does that to *everybody*."

Keyes had another taste of his temper when she witnessed Anne Bauchens bringing him the wrong reel of film. DeMille yanked the reel out of the can and left an unspooled mess all over the floor.

In late 1938, DeMille sent Keyes over to the Selznick studio to audition for a part in *Gone With the Wind*, where her vanquished Georgia accent had to be recultivated. "If you don't get the part in *Gone With the Wind*, with your Southern accent, I'll have to shoot you at sunrise," he told her, leaving her little choice. She got the part of Suellen, Scarlett O'Hara's sister.

★

After Cecilia's marriage to Frank Calvin failed, she fell in love with a family friend, a businessman named Joseph W. Harper. Her second marriage took place on January 21, 1938, in Kansas City—because *The Buccaneer* had been premiered there that night. Cecilia's daughter, also named Cecilia, had been born shortly before the divorce from Frank Calvin. Everybody liked and respected Joe Harper, including his father-in-law, perhaps because the one time DeMille accidentally introduced him as "Frank Calvin," Joe Harper smiled and seamlessly thanked "Mr. Goldwyn."

"Grandfather adored him," remembered Cecilia Jr. "Joe was the one real male friend he had. Grandfather could confide in him and did; he even told him things he didn't tell mother. Since mother always lived down the hill from grandfather, I could divide myself between the two houses and spend the night in either place. Both grandfather and mother liked it that way, and so did I. We never dined at our house, though; we always had dinner at the big house, with grandfather and grandmother."

Other children were more troublesome. Even though he was barely out of his teens, John had developed a drinking problem and signed a series of pledges that he would refrain from drinking hard liquor (beer and light wine were permitted in moderation). If John hewed to the straight and narrow path, DeMille agreed to pay him $500 a year, an amount that was gradually raised to $1,000.

★

Reap the Wild Wind, DeMille's next saga of fanciful Americana, was one of his more swaggeringly entertaining pictures. "I want to smell the brine and hear the creak of rigging," DeMille ordered his writers. "I want to feel the bite of hurricanes. I want the birth of America's lifeline on the seas—and to see it threatened by the toughest tribe of murdering pirate wreckers that ever gutted a ship to steal a cargo! . . . I want to see the teeth of a reef bite through a ship's bottom—photographed from underwater!"

The story of pirate shipwreckers in the Florida Keys in the 1840s had everything necessary for a DeMille movie, including a beautiful re-creation of nineteenth-century Key West, complete with widow's walks on top of the houses. It had, in fact, everything except a climax. "I [keep] asking myself the question," Cecil muttered to Jesse Lasky Jr. in a burst of hyperbole that would have left Belasco breathless, "What, in *Reap the Wild Wind*, would galvanize headhunters in an Amazon River jungle? What would fascinate Eskimos in the igloos, harness harassed housewives, rivet restless children? What can we offer to match the opening of the Red Sea in my silent picture *The Ten Commandments*? Because until we've got that, gentlemen, we just haven't got a moving picture."

The crisis was averted when screenwriter Charles Bennett had a brainstorm in the bathtub and shared his inspiration. "The first instant that the [two men] start to hack at each other [underwater] you see behind them—rising out of the belly of the dead ship, one great long red tentacle—and then another. . . . Then, faster than a striking cobra, it sweeps around the body of one of the men. It heaves him up, light as a doll in the fist of a giant—for giant it is. A giant squid!" Bennett acted out the scene, first taking one actor's part, then the other, finally taking the giant squid's part.

DeMille was transfixed, gazing off into the middle distance, visualizing the scene. "*And in Technicolor!*" he muttered. The special effects department constructed a thirty-eight-foot-long squid with tentacles of sponge rubber covering a forest of wires and hydraulic pistons that controlled everything from the movements of the tentacles to the position of the eyes.

DeMille's original casting for the leading part was Joel McCrea, but he had committed to Preston Sturges for *Sullivan's Travels*. "He's some writer," argued DeMille. "The picture will be forgotten. But a picture with me . . ." McCrea replied that might very well be the case, but "I'm not getting a percentage of your picture; I'm just working for a salary. And this fellow has a great script."

DeMille hired John Wayne, only a few years past John Ford's *Stagecoach*, to play the weak second lead to Ray Milland. The director and Wayne had a history, although DeMille may have preferred not to acknowledge it. During the preparations for *The Plainsman*, Wayne's agent got his client an interview with DeMille for the part of Wild Bill Hickok. Wayne was on time for his interview, but DeMille was late, and when he finally emerged from his office he told Wayne he was going to lunch. Reminded of the interview, he asked the actor to come into his office.

"He said to me, 'You were in *The Big Trail*, weren't you?' " remembered Wayne. " 'I saw it and you did just fine. But a lot of water has gone under the bridge since then.' That was DeMille's way of turning me down. To him I was now just a minor star of mere B westerns."

But that had been five years before, and Wayne now had heat. Besides *Stagecoach*, Wayne had recently made *The Long Voyage Home*, again for Ford, *Dark Command* for Raoul Walsh, and *The Shepherd of the Hills* for Henry Hathaway—completely different types of pictures for respected, tough directors, and Wayne had held the screen in all of them.

DeMille sent Wayne the script for *Reap the Wild Wind*. The actor stayed up all night reading it, then dictated his reaction before he left on a trip the next morning. "I was disappointed in the lack of color and character in Jack," Wayne wrote. "However, I recalled the picture . . . that Mr. DeMille painted for us in his office, so I disregarded the play of the character as painted by the writers. . . . At the entrance of Steve [the Ray Milland character] into the story Jack becomes negative in all scenes that include the three principals. I think there is a possibility of developing him into a great character without distracting from Steve or Loxi [Paulette Goddard] and will add color to the script as a whole and will make Loxi's part more believable. This can be done simply by making him an individualist played boldly and impulsively instead of being played as a plodding dullard.

"Steve is the suave, eloquent, and mental type written with care. Jack should be brusque and sure of himself in all physical situations because of the station of life that he has reached at a youthful age. He doesn't need to be a mental giant—maybe a little short on logic, but must not be dull—must possess a definite sense of humor to help him through two or three melodramatic situations that arise."

DeMille walked into the conference room where Jesse Lasky Jr. Alan LeMay, and Charles Bennett were working and read Wayne's letter out loud. They waited for him to explode and vow never to hire the arrogant young pup as long as he lived. Instead he looked at his writers and said, "If an actor can see what's wrong and work it out, why couldn't you?" It was the beginning of a close relationship between Wayne and DeMille.

The script encored the central dynamic that DeMille had used on *Union Pacific* and *North West Mounted Police*: a stalwart hero (who in this case does origami), and a lusty, semi-heroic figure who, through a single weakness of character, turns bad but atones by dying nobly (Robert Preston in the earlier films, Wayne in the new one). Paramount also used this mechanism in such other films of the period as *Spawn of the North* and *Men with Wings*, but nobody lovingly mounted dramatic clichés like DeMille . . . and in Technicolor!

At the end of the picture, the giant squid is staked through the eye, and the explosion of ink envelops the divers. Simultaneously, on the surface of the ocean, a tsunami hits.

For DeMille, too much was never enough.

For most of its running time, *Reap the Wild Wind* has energy, and there are times when it's downright exhilarating. Although Wayne was playing the second lead, DeMille assured him that he had taken good care of Preston Foster in *North West Mounted Police*, despite the fact that the star of the picture was Gary Cooper. He promised that he would never put Wayne in a position on screen where he would lose his dignity, to which Wayne replied that getting "beat up by Ray Milland would lose anybody's dignity."

As a conciliatory gesture, DeMille allowed Wayne to select his own costume, including a show-stopping orange scarf. Another thing binding them together was their shared conservatism. "Wayne was one of the few actors DeMille never yelled at," remembered Jesse Lasky Jr. "DeMille liked Wayne so much that he invited him to join him for lunch every day, which was an honor for any actor." When a group of exhibitors was touring the set the day a shipboard donnybrook was to be filmed, DeMille interrupted the rehearsal. "John, I want you to show them how to play this scene," he announced over the microphone.

Wayne demonstrated for the visitors how actors threw and took punches, then placed the actors and stuntmen and choreographed the fight scene. DeMille liked what he saw and called "Action!"

In August 1941, Sid Grauman asked DeMille to come to the Chinese Theatre and place his hand and footprints in the forecourt in honor of his sixtieth birthday. Since DeMille was in the middle of shooting and didn't want to take an afternoon off, Muhammad came to the Paramount mountain. On August 7, the cement for the slab was mixed on the soundstage and, supported by Grauman and actress Martha O'Driscoll, DeMille went through the ceremony in a few minutes between setups, then went back to work. In his memoirs, DeMille foretold a day when tourists would inspect the tablet "in the forecourt of the Chinese Theatre for generations to come, and ask each other, 'Cecil B. DeMille? Who was he?' "

Once again, DeMille filled the cast with old-timers from his and the movies' youth: Victor Varconi, Raymond Hatton, Julia Faye, bits for Monte Blue, George Melford, Mildred Harris, Claire McDowell, Elmo Lincoln, Dorothy Sebastian, Max Davidson, and Maurice Costello. And once again, DeMille sent out Art

Rosson to shoot the second unit footage. He handed him a painting by Roland Anderson of a ship at dock and told him he wanted it copied exactly on film. Rosson looked but couldn't find a pier in California that was long enough or wide enough but did the best he could at a lumberyard near San Pedro, even though it meant that the top of the masts and the bow would have to be cut off.

When DeMille saw the footage he yelled for Rosson and held up the painting. "What happened to the rest of the ship and the masts that are in Roland's painting?"

Rosson explained the situation but DeMille told him to go back and get what he had asked for in the first place. At the same time, the studio was alarmed by the overages and asked Rosson to stall. When the budget got to the point where DeMille would have had to personally pay for the retake, he decided to live with Rosson's original footage.

Working as an assistant to Roland Anderson was Henry Bumstead, who would become the legendary art director of Hitchcock's *Vertigo* and many Clint Eastwood films. "I started at Paramount in 1937," Bumstead remembered, "and I worked on some DeMille pictures as a draftsman drawing sets. But then Roland Anderson took me under his wing, and working with Roland, I got to know DeMille quite well. I was more or less an assistant art director on *Union Pacific*. I liked DeMille. He was tough, very demanding, and didn't stand for any foolishness. He demanded the very best from everybody; he was the sort of man it's good to encounter when you're young, because they can whip you into shape. He was a stickler for detail; he researched everything to the finest point. And he created lots of jobs. He was good for the industry and very good for Paramount."

From watching Anderson work with DeMille, Bumstead learned how a good art director can make life much easier for a director. The laying out of the set, the positioning of the lights, make it possible for the director to come in and do his job with the actors expeditiously. Emphasizing that approach was the system established by Paramount's chief art director Hans Dreier. "Dreier had come over with Lubitsch from UFA," remembered Bumstead. "He was ramrod straight, a Prussian officer, and he was tough but fair. He taught me that sets had to look like the characters would actually live in them. Dreier wouldn't allow you to put a scribble on a piece of paper to indicate a wall; you had to be specific. Hans would come around twice a day to see how things were, and he would call you into his office if he didn't like what he saw. He wouldn't raise his voice, but you knew he was unhappy."

Reap the Wild Wind came in a whopping $313,210 over its $1.725 million budget. The overage was at least partially caused by the $172,103 that went for special effects, i.e., the squid battle. The costs of the second unit alone came to $310,156 on a forty-seven-day schedule, just about the amount of time and only a little less money than Paramount was spending on many of its A movies.

Shortly before production began on *Reap the Wild Wind,* tragedy struck the DeMille family. On March 15, 1941, Tony and Katherine Quinn's two-and-a-half-year-old son, Christopher, wandered away from his house, across the street, and over to a shallow fish pond on the lawn of 2015 DeMille Drive, which was being rented by W. C. Fields. Christopher's eye had apparently been caught by a toy sailboat that was bobbing on the water.

A nurse noticed that the baby was missing and called the police. DeMille was notified that Christopher was nowhere to be found and came home. Then a gardener saw the child floating on the surface of the pond. DeMille stood off to one side, tears streaming down his face, while the fire department vainly tried to revive the boy. When Quinn arrived, he went into emotional hibernation. "Everything stopped moving," he remembered. "My entire world was frozen. All around me was commotion and grieving, but I could not notice."

Neither of his parents went to Christopher Quinn's funeral, but his grandfather was there. Anthony Quinn never visited the grave near the DeMille family plot in Hollywood Memorial Cemetery—now Hollywood Forever—for that would have meant he had to concede the fact of his child's death.

"The worst thing that ever happened to me in my life was losing the child," remembered Anthony Quinn. "The worst. I've never really acknowledged his loss. To me, he's an architect and he's in Japan designing buildings.

"It's not the sort of thing that can be dealt with. People who say they deal with the death of a child are wrong—nothing else in life comes near it. The marriage went on, we made four children after that, but my wife and I, we never dealt with the realities of it."

Aside from the emotional difficulties, Quinn was having financial problems. Before Christopher's death, he had borrowed $350 from DeMille; afterward, he borrowed another $2,500, both loans at 5 percent interest. He needed the second loan for, among other things, the child's burial expenses. The loan was repaid in full on August 8, 1941.

Bearing the grief of her son's death sent Katherine into a lifelong study of religion and the afterlife. "It was very hard on her," remembered Richard deMille. "She dedicated her life to being a wife and a mother. She never got over Christopher's death; she looked for evangelistic inspiration and even went through a spiritualist phase where she tried to communicate with Christopher. [Cecil] never criticized her. Everybody felt sorry for her. She had no enemies and no critics."

Christopher Quinn's death impelled DeMille to become even closer to his other grandchildren, especially Cecilia Jr., who was five at the time of her cousin's death, and was practically adopted by her grandfather. But Katherine's spiritualism gradually alienated her husband, and left him feeling outside of the marriage.

★

During the scripting of *Reap the Wild Wind*, DeMille grew fond of the screenwriter Charles Bennett, who had written some of Hitchcock's best films, including *The 39 Steps*, *Blackmail*, and *Foreign Correspondent*. Bennett spent most of the next decade working for DeMille, who regularly invited him to Paradise. The first time Bennett visited, he was transfixed by the sight of two or three hundred deer gathered on the front lawn, as if awaiting DeMille's arrival. When Bennett asked about it, DeMille replied, "I'll tell you, Charles, it's hunting season. And the deer know it, and every year during hunting season they come and stay on the front lawn of my house. I know many of them year after year. Look at that old one there, he's a great friend of mine." Bennett noticed that DeMille had cowboys patrolling his land to protect the deer from hunters.

"And this was the 'great bully,' " snorted Bennett. "He wasn't a bully at all. He was a terribly nice man. I would say DeMille was in every way as literate [as Hitchcock], in many ways as sophisticated, but in most ways kinder. I adored DeMille. He was a very, very kind man . . . the kindest, gentlest person I knew. I loved him dearly."

By this time, DeMille's affection for animals had achieved Disneyesque proportions; he told Bennett that every morning as he went down for his skinny-dip in the pool at Paradise, he would pass the same tarantula. DeMille would always say "Good Morning," and he insisted that the tarantula waved some of its legs in greeting. He named the tarantula Charlemagne.

Bennett noted that DeMille had a hierarchical mind in all things, especially writers. Jesse Lasky Jr. made around a third of Bennett's salary, for instance, so if a scene fell short, DeMille took it out on Lasky, not Bennett. For another, DeMille "seldom worked with actors at all. He trusted immensely Gary Cooper or Raymond Massey or whatever actors he hired. He assumed they knew their job. . . . The great screen was what he was thinking of," said Bennett. "He wasn't thinking of individual performances."

Bennett found that the only drawback to working for DeMille was the director's propensity for injecting terrible dialogue into the script. In story conferences, a stenographer took everything down. When DeMille devised Belasco-era dialogue that he would instruct the reporter to circle in red, a mortified Bennett and Alan LeMay would delete the lines. When the finished script landed on his desk, DeMille would read it and invariably notice that his favorite dialogue was missing. It wasn't missing for long. "DeMille was not a writer," sighed Bennett. "And not a constructionist." That said, for Bennett, "DeMille was a genius, in spite of the fact that he couldn't control actors, or didn't want to."

On March 7, 1942, a year ahead of the actual anniversary, Paramount hosted a lunch at the old Lasky Barn, which had been moved to the Marathon lot, to mark DeMille's thirtieth year in movies. Many of the old stalwarts had died (Dustin Farnum, Thomas Meighan, Agnes Ayres, Theodore Roberts, Elliott Dexter, Milton Sills) but there were a lot of the old-timers still around. Gloria Swanson, Winifred Kingston, Leatrice Joy, Vera Reynolds, and many of the more current DeMille stars saluted their director.

A few weeks later, Paramount threw a lunch in New York for DeMille and five hundred of his closest friends at the Waldorf, as *Reap the Wild Wind* was opening across town. Cecil made his entrance in a spotlight in the otherwise darkened room. In his speech, he focused not on a retrospective of his career, but on the responsibility of the movie industry in a time of national peril. Liberty, he said, was a woman—"a beautiful, desirable and very jealous woman . . . [and] no woman likes to be taken for granted." The industry, he said, had to "get mad, forget hours and profits, roll up its sleeves, spit on its hands and go to work. . . . The stupidity of partisanship is treason in these times, whether it be partisanship of capital, labor or government. The job of motion pictures is to help bring home a full realization of this crisis and of the deadly peril that lurks in internal squabbling. . . .

"Ours is the task of holding high and ever visible the values that everyone is fighting for. I don't mean flag-waving, but giving the embattled world sharp glimpses of the way of life that we've got to hang on to in spite of everything."

Reap the Wild Wind was an enormous hit, Paramount's biggest all-time grosser until Leo McCarey's *Going My Way*. Against a cost of just over $2 million, there was a worldwide gross of almost $7 million, with a net profit of $1.7 million (these figures include a 1950 reissue).

Before Pearl Harbor, DeMille's feelings about peace-at-any-price groups such as America First were a steely contempt for what he termed "the sob stuff. . . . Let other people's sons be killed to preserve democracy, but oh, not ours." After Pearl Harbor, he had few serious complaints about Franklin Roosevelt's conduct of the war. At this point, his politics could be characterized as Churchillian conservative. "In foreign policy, when Franklin D. Roosevelt looked at Hitler and Mussolini, he saw straight and true from the start," according to DeMille. Which is not to say that he had any sympathy for the New Deal. "In domestic policies," he would say with what he undoubtedly felt was considerable understatement, "I felt that the New Deal had done a certain amount of good and a great amount of harm."

Shortly after war broke out in Europe, DeMille's office became the meeting place for a group of British expatriates whose goal was nudging America out of its isolationist stance. Since the Neutrality Act made any kind of pro-war agitation illegal, the meetings were secret. The key members included Boris Karloff—his brother, John Pratt, worked for MI6—Reginald Gardiner, Charles Bennett, and directors Robert Stevenson and Victor Saville. The group's activities resulted in, among other things, the RKO propaganda film *Forever and a Day*.

DeMille's alignment with President Roosevelt would seem an odd pairing for an intrinsically conservative man, but many of the people who were preaching isolationism at this point were communists supporting the Hitler-Stalin nonaggression pact, as well as the usual paleoconservative America Firsters.

DeMille's efforts became more aggressive six days after Pearl Harbor, when Neil McCarthy contacted James Roosevelt and told him that DeMille wanted to organize and head an ancillary FBI unit based in Hollywood and would finance it himself if necessary. DeMille asked J. Edgar Hoover for his permission, stating that he would happily work for both the Washington and Los Angeles offices. Hoover replied that "I appreciate deeply the very generous and patriotic offer made by DeMille but at the present time it does not seem necessary for us to avail ourselves of it as we have the situation well in hand."

Still, DeMille was a very important man and, as the saying goes, he knew a lot of people. Hoover asked the agent in charge of the Los Angeles office to confer with DeMille "in order that the appropriate contact is established and that we utilize any of DeMille's services or contacts that may be necessary in any future developments of the present emergency. . . . Handle the situation tactfully. . . . I do not wish to offend DeMille and would like to have him feel that we will call on him in the event his offer can be utilized."

A few days later, R. B. Hood, head of the FBI's Los Angeles office, met with DeMille and a loose arrangement was set up "identical to that followed by the Bureau in handling informants in any national defense industry." Hoover told Hood, "I wish to emphatically point out that this is a most important contact and every effort must be expended by you to formulate a workable plan wherein the services and facilities of Mr. DeMille will be fully developed and exploited."

For the next seven or eight years, DeMille was a point man in the loose surveillance of various people in the movie industry. He gave the FBI a list of the heads of the various departments at Paramount, as well as the names of some people he felt were responsible and could become confidential informants.

Hood wanted DeMille to check on a woman named Lucy Ludmilla Chereokova. DeMille had her contacted by an employee at the studio and personally interviewed her under the guise of an audition for a part in one of his films. When the Bureau asked about possible fascist sympathies of the pianist José Iturbi, DeMille replied that Iturbi used to be his next-door neighbor and was indeed a Franco supporter but not necessarily a fascist. DeMille personally supplied information about the screenwriter John Howard Lawson and the King brothers. When the Bureau became interested in Fritz Lang, DeMille, as an FBI document of March 19, 1943, attested, "was able to have an informant work with LANG in the production of a current motion picture, and to advise us fully of LANG'S activities while on the road making the picture. He furnished valuable information concerning outside contacts of LANG, about whom we would have had no information at all.

"He was later able to obtain the picture immediately upon its completion and had a private showing of it for me and the interested Agents in the case, and it was very enlightening, inasmuch as the influence of other Communist associates of LANG can be very clearly seen in the picture, the title of which is 'Hangmen Also Die.' " The Lang movie was co-written by Bertolt Brecht.

DeMille also investigated the actor Ludwig Stössel, who was given a part in Paramount's *Miss Susie Slagle's* so that he could be interviewed and some of his political sympathies ascertained. Surprisingly, DeMille also investigated John Wayne, Wayne's business manager Bo Roos, and Esperanza Bauer, the Mexican actress who would become Wayne's second wife. With someone named Jacob Heimann, who was under investigation because of a requested security clearance, DeMille personally visited Heimann's home under the pretext of seeing whether his art collection might be useful for some set decorations in a DeMille film. DeMille then submitted a ten-page report about Heimann.

In Hood's estimation, DeMille was "much more stable than the average person engaged in motion picture work, and in view of his integrity and intimate knowledge of the industry, he is regarded as the most all-around valuable contact in this field."

Also being drawn into the FBI's surveillance work was Charles Bennett. "I would get a call from DeMille's secretary," Bennett told Patrick McGilligan, " 'Mr. Bennett, Mr. DeMille would like you to come across to his office.' I would say to Alan LeMay, 'Excuse me, but Mr. DeMille wants to see me.' I would go across the hall, and there would be Richard B. Hood of the FBI, the head of Naval Intelligence, people like that. And I would be asked to do certain jobs . . . very few people in the world knew that DeMille was mixed up in the Secret Service."

Some of this work was anti-Nazi, which was fine with Bennett, but a lot of it was also anti-Soviet, which Bennett thought was odd because the Soviets had become America's allies. Nevertheless, he went along; for one thing, he was on DeMille's payroll for $1,500 a week; for another there was a war on, and Bennett felt guilty about not doing anything concrete to help out England—eventually, in early 1944, he went back home and worked for the British Ministry of Information.

By August 1942, the FBI called DeMille "one of the best Special Service Contacts the Bureau has. He is very frequently used by the Los Angeles office." Shortly after the war, DeMille would be given the Bureau's Special Service Award.

★

The war mandated rationing and sacrifice—four gallons of gas a week, dim-out restrictions, high taxes. To do his part for the war effort, DeMille became the air raid warden for Laughlin Park, walking around at night looking for any untoward displays of lights. One night in 1942, an offender was, of all people, W. C. Fields. DeMille knocked on his door and told him to darken down. Although Fields might have been more obstreperous had it been anybody else, Christopher Quinn had been dead for only a year and a half.

The next day, Fields wrote DeMille a meek letter of apology: "Dear Mr. DeMille: It was very kind of you to inform me about my lights last evening. I wish to apologize for putting you to the inconvenience of having to come over and apprise me of my remissness. I assure you I shall be more careful in the future. Again my thanks and my best wishes always and appreciation. Sincerely, Bill Fields."

★

On April 28, 1942, DeMille was listening to one of FDR's fireside chats when the president talked about Dr. Corydon Wassell, a former medical missionary who evacuated a group of wounded Americans from the interior of Java under the noses of the Japanese army, eventually getting the men to safety in Australia, in spite of the fact that he had been ordered to abandon his patients to the advancing enemy.

DeMille instantly thought that this had the makings of a great contribution to the war effort. He called Secretary of the Navy Frank Knox. "I want Dr. Wassell and the United States Navy."

"You can have Dr. Wassell," replied Knox, "but the Navy is rather busy nowadays. There is a war on, you know."

Radio had made DeMille as big a star as any of his actors, and the production of *The Story of Dr. Wassell* accommodated that fact. There were bleachers set up in the studio so visitors, especially visiting military people, could watch the movie being made. DeMille naturally enjoyed having an audience and seems to have regarded it as a way to spread good word of mouth for his movie.

DeMille compared his story to a military version of *Goodbye, Mr. Chips*—a main character who is a good shepherd for all seasons. "The reason the story is great and different [is that] while it is war, it isn't a question of killing; it's a story of life saving rather than life taking."

DeMille took a lot of time with the casting of the young sailors that Wassell moves out of harm's way. Contract players such as Yvonne De Carlo and Elliott Reid performed scenes from the script on a stage at Paramount that was separated from the audience by glass, behind which DeMille and his entourage would sit and comment. After the sailors were cast, they finally met their director. "He was gracious," remembered Elliott Reid, "like the village squire visiting the tenants. Very nice, courteous, generous."

But Reid tested DeMille's patience one day when he overslept. "I forgot to push in the thing on the Westclox alarm clock to make it ring. And I overslept, by quite a bit. And I was awakened by the phone. It was an assistant director, who said, 'Where are you? *Mr. DeMille is waiting!*' "

A petrified Reid stumbled into the studio, then stumbled into makeup, then stumbled onto the stage, which was bathed in a sepulchral silence; DeMille had refused to move on to another scene and had been sitting and stewing, waiting for the young actor.

There was nothing for Reid to do but fall on his sword. "DeMille was sitting under the lens of the camera. I had to do the death march from the door of the stage down to him, and nobody was moving. 'Why are you late?' he asked me in this sort of flat New England accent he had. And I made no attempt to excuse myself, which saved me. 'I have no excuse, Mr. DeMille. The alarm didn't wake me, and I am deeply embarrassed. I apologize to you and everybody else here for delaying everything.' He stared at me and didn't say anything. And then he said, 'All right, let's get to work.'

"Here is how I know that he forgave me. When they called lunch, I was in bed with my arms all bandaged for the scene, and I was slow to get up; I was still semi-paralyzed by embarrassment. DeMille lagged behind everybody else and came over to me on the bed. And this is what he said: 'You know, you remind me of myself when I was young. Except you're a better actor.' That was his way of saying 'I forgive you.' He was so warm, so nice. He was a gentleman, an old-school actor/gentleman, so flattering and so gracious."

There were two areas of discontent on *Dr. Wassell*. The first was an actor named Renny McEvoy, who was playing what DeMille intended as comic relief except nobody had bothered to give McEvoy anything funny to do. "Why aren't you funny?" DeMille asked him one day in front of everybody. "This part is a funny part, you're supposed to be funny." McEvoy stood there and took it. As Elliott Reid would observe, "That's why actors die young."

The other explosion was at a greensman, one of the people who take care of plants on a movie set. The greensman was told to stand in a small pond, but he was nervous about nearby arc lights and the possibility of being electrocuted. DeMille was infuriated. "I hate a man who's a quitter. You're afraid that something is going to happen. Do you want to quit? Do you want to go?"

"Mr. DeMille, it's risky."

"*We've all had risks! Don't talk to me about risks!*" DeMille finally gave the greensman permission to stand someplace else.

A movie set takes its emotional temperature from its director and its star, and helping to keep the production on an even keel was Gary Cooper, whom Reid remembered as "the nicest, most simple man, delightful, just the same as he had been the first day he went before a movie camera—a lovely, humorous man."

DeMille drove the picture through under schedule—eighty-one days instead of the planned eighty-seven, and a modest $40,805 over the $2.7 million budget. Once again, most of the action footage was in the hands of Art Rosson, who directed thirty-seven days of a second unit that cost $362,282.

DeMille's budgets were rising. For one thing, he was spending more on writers—$112,666 on *The Story of Dr. Wassell* compared to $54,257 on *North West Mounted Police*. The industry has always thrown the blame for rising costs on actors and labor unions, but the studio was lining its pockets as well. Part of the expansion of the budgets between *North West Mounted Police* and *The Story of Dr. Wassell* only four years later was the fact that Paramount increased the studio overhead from 24 percent to 26 percent.

Yet 1944 was still a spectacularly successful year for DeMille. *The Story of Dr. Wassell* grossed $6.4 million against costs of $2.7 million. Net profits were only $230,294, because DeMille and Paramount donated $157,484 to Navy Relief, and the budget was burdened by $154,948 for half of the costs incurred by the abandoned *Rurales* (the other half of the costs would be appended to the budget of *Unconquered*).

That same year, the reissue of *The Sign of the Cross*, which had cost $118,061 for the new prologue and the editing necessary to meet Production Code standards, grossed $1.2 million, returning $494,227 in net profit.

The Story of Dr. Wassell premiered at Constitution Hall in Washington and DeMille was invited to the White House to meet FDR. DeMille came bearing gifts—some rare Dutch stamps for the president's collection, as well as one of the DeMille half-dollars he had minted as a special gift for employees who went above and beyond the call of duty. The opportunity was too great to pass without a touch of the needle, so DeMille also brought along a small clay tablet from his collection of antiquities. It was, he told Roosevelt, an ancient tax receipt—clear evidence that the Democratic Party was four thousand years old. Roosevelt threw back his head in his characteristic boisterous laugh.

Unfortunately, *The Story of Dr. Wassell* is one of DeMille's worst pictures. Told straight, it could have been a good adventure movie, but by this time lavishness and narrative elaboration had become DeMille's weakness, and he overwhelmed the story with irrelevant, interminable flashbacks—to Arkansas, to China—and an unconvincing love story with a nurse. DeMille couldn't see that the story's strength lay in its simplicity and straight narrative line; his style had reached a point where he could no longer depict real life, and the story of Dr. Wassell demanded only that. Even though the movie is based on truth it feels false.

★

The war affected the DeMille unit only marginally; Jeanie Macpherson spent her free time, of which she had a great deal, writing bad hortatory poetry about the conflict. DeMille continued to do his patriotic duty—during the Fourth War Loan

Drive, he personally bought $11,000 worth of bonds, and Cecil B. DeMille Productions bought $35,000 more.

DeMille's old assistant Cullen "Hezi" Tate was pulling heavy duty in the South Pacific with the 1st Marine Division as they cleaned out Peleliu, and wrote a long series of letters to his old "skipper." Tate was an overaged fifty, and used the letters to blow off steam. One letter was headed

PELELIU ISLAND GARDENS

Pelau Estates
Coral Strands Acres.
We Now Have Our Own Air Strip.
Acreage Lately Acquired Available.
Hunting the Year Round. Live Game.
Bring Your Own Tommy Gun.
Bask in the Breezes of the South Pacific.

Tate sent DeMille a Japanese flag taken "from enemy officer that doesn't live here anymore," as well as a box of Japanese chocolates. Tate was suffering from heat prostration, body sores, impetigo, and an ulcerated tooth, but he was alive. "If you should have words with Mr. Forrestal," wrote Tate, "you may tell him for one Marine he's got the greatest team that ever bathed in salt water, and from a Marine that's praise indeed."

In return, DeMille wrote Tate a chatty, unusually informal series of letters: "You and the other Marines really do things in a big way. They tell me the fighting on Peleliu was the toughest of the lot, so that flag with the setting sun right in the middle of it really sent a thrill of pride down the middle of my spine. From his picture, the owner was quite good looking for a Jap. Do you suppose he's a distant (now very distant) cousin of our star in *The Cheat?* . . .

"I haven't dared to try the two little boxes of Japanese chocolates. Do they ever have poison booby traps?

"*The Story of Dr. Wassell* continues to do big business and we have already sent Navy Relief our first check for $50,000—I suppose the Marines get their proportionate share. Had a fine letter from Admiral Richardson thanking DeMille and Paramount for the contribution. In another month I think we'll have another $50,000 for Navy Relief; not bad for a sea horse opera."

In other letters, DeMille told Tate the good news about the successful reissue of *The Sign of the Cross.* He canceled *Rurales,* he said, "because I was a little afraid of repercussions below the Rio Grande, and as the picture would have cost three million dollars, we could not take the risk, even though we had $300,000 in it. I have set it aside and will probably turn once more to United States history for my subject.

"I can't wish you a Happy New Year because there are too many terrible things going on in the world to make that possible, but I wish you a successful New Year and a free one." While Tate was in the South Pacific, DeMille paid his bills.

☆

By this time, the critics had DeMille pegged, and each film was greeted pretty much like the last: condescension, if not contempt. DeMille returned the favor. "There are four classes of critic," he would snarl. "The agnostic, the communist, the smart boy and the religious ignoramus. . . . There are few critics throughout the country, in fact, I think, throughout the world, that have followed my work with real interest, with constructive interest. . . . It couldn't be any good because I wore boots, which is the stand taken by most critics. 'It can't possibly be any good because he wears his hat backwards.' Nobody ever took the trouble to find out why a director wore his hat backwards—because with it forward you can't look into the camera finder—the brim stops him. When he wears it backwards, he can look into the camera, follow the action and rehearse. I rehearse through a camera. . . . But nobody ever takes the trouble to find that out—it must be a pose! . . . [I wear boots] for the same reason the army wears boots—because you can stand up for 14 hours in a pair of boots and you can't stand up for over three in a pair of shoes."

Within the industry, there was more of a divide. At Paramount, Preston Sturges took delight in tweaking DeMille's leanings toward pomp. One day Sturges asked a friend to measure the chair DeMille habitually sat in at his table in the commissary. Sturges then ordered that *his* chair in the commissary be wider, higher, grander than DeMille's. Since Sturges's table was directly opposite DeMille's, C.B. could hardly have failed to notice.

DeMille and Paramount tolerated the Peck's Bad Boy antics because Sturges was the wunderkind of the studio, adored by studio chief Y. Frank Freeman. Freeman was a gray-haired, quiet Georgia businessman. He had a southern drawl, a gentlemanly manner, a passion for Coca-Cola, and racial attitudes that dated to Jefferson Davis. Liberals like George Stevens would refer to him as "Why Frank Freeman?" but he was known for being fair with labor and having an open-door policy regarding his employees. As a political conservative, Freeman was also close to DeMille.

DeMille's old art director and costume designer Mitchell Leisen was now a successful director (*Midnight, Hold Back the Dawn*) at Paramount, and he knew the proper scale of DeMille's gift. In a piece in *American Theater*, Leisen paid tribute to those directors who he believed to be authentic artists, the equivalent of great painters. After mentioning John Ford and Frank Lloyd—for his use of the sea in *Mutiny on the Bounty*—Leisen said that DeMille was the equivalent of Michelangelo and singled out *The King of Kings*. "I think particularly of his interpretation of the Crucifixion," wrote Leisen. "But virtually every scene in that production is art.

That it is moving, emotional, satisfying creative art will be attested by millions upon millions of people who have seen it."

As the *Lux Radio Theatre* went on, DeMille worked with many people that he would probably never have run into in the daily course of his life and career. Orson Welles starred in *Jane Eyre* and returned a few weeks later with Rita Hayworth, for *Break of Hearts*. Despite the vast differences in their age and aesthetics, Welles quickly grew fond of DeMille. "He was very nice to me," he told Peter Bogdanovich. "I liked him. A fascinating old showman, you know, in his way . . . plus a wonderful sense of his own persona. As a director on the set he had the greatest act that's ever been seen."

Now, in his fourth decade of making movies, DeMille smoothly incarnated the character of a titanic impresario he had sculpted, partly out of his authentic personality, partly out of amber-colored memories of David Belasco. A frequent visitor to DeMille's sets was his granddaughter. Cecilia described herself as "a lot rat. His sets were the most exciting place to be in the world, an electric atmosphere. People were so thrilled to be there; they were energized. When he walked into a room, he lit it up, even if it was an enormous soundstage. Five feet ten, a barrel of energy."

After attending Columbia and USC, Richard deMille had joined the Army Air Corps, then worked at Fort Roach in Culver City. He was regarded by everybody who met him as spiky but brilliant, apparently coldly ironic, but actually a covertly warm person. "He hoped I'd stay out [of the industry]," remembered Richard. "He really did not want any more DeMilles being in the movies because there had been enough. He never said this, but I think that's what he felt. . . . He never said to me, 'What are you going to do in life?' I didn't have the foggiest notion what I was going to do in life, so I just bumbled along going through school. There was very little control of any of the children—a total lack of manipulation. We were allowed to be ourselves."

But DeMille and his son-in-law came to an uneasy standoff. "I don't feel Tony was ever in the family, not really," Richard deMille would say. "Of course, Tony loved Constance—she made no demands. But it was always a contest between him and the Old Man. Tony would usually sit at one end of the room with the younger women gathered around him, while Cecil would sit at the other end with the older women gathered around him."

During one family gathering, Tony was expounding about the beauty of Japanese art and culture, and ended the disquisition by saying that perhaps it might be better if Admiral Tojo was in the White House rather than Roosevelt. "Cecil didn't blow up," remembered Richard deMille. "He recognized Tony for what he was and it didn't surprise him. He was very stoic about other people's failings."

An associate of Cecil B. DeMille's once remarked that the key to understanding him was realizing that he was a totally different man in his house than he was outside the house. "Inside the house, he was everything you could want in a human being." Outside the house, the actor took over.

His office at the studio was in total disarray during production. Sketches, books, scale models of sets, statues, all manner of printed material filled up the chairs, couch, and his own desk. He didn't like handling old money, so secretaries would have to go to the bank for uncirculated currency. In his wallet he kept a small cardboard disc that had embossed on it GOOD FOR 1 QUART OF MILK—a remnant of the days when he and Constance were itinerant actors.

His office at home was likewise a fascinating collection of artifacts. The sword of Richard the Lionheart from *The Crusades* was hanging on the wall. Next to it was a table with three shrunken heads in glass bells. Richard deMille remembered that "shrunken heads have a very unpleasant expression on their face. I think it's resentment." There were books, awards, and on his desk was the camera that had photographed *The Squaw Man.*

He preferred to dress for dinner, and regarded anything else as a signpost of cultural barbarism. Along with the decorous manners went a decorous personality—when he was home. At such times, he carried around with him a benevolent warmth that could convince whoever he came into contact with that they were by far the most affectionately regarded person DeMille had seen all day long. He was always polite in conversation before women in social situations; he thought Hemingway and D. H. Lawrence were salacious, but he had a habit of slipping Frank Harris–style erotica into his fine leather-bound editions. He was, in short, the model of an Edwardian gentleman.

"He was much more domestic at home," said Richard. "He wasn't being the tribal chief so much. He was the king of the house, but he wasn't commanding everybody to do things. He was the center of attention in every room. You could feel that Father was home or not home by the vibrations in the house."

He believed that children should be heard as well as seen, but there were strict rules of behavior—no matter the age, the female should be a lady, and the male a gentleman. "He got along very well with children, actually," said Richard deMille. "Although he wasn't the good father of the twentieth or twenty-first century, he was the good father of the nineteenth century. He had a very winning way; it was fun to be around him and he told wonderful stories, had a very beatific smile. He was a comfortable father."

"He never scolded, never," said his granddaughter. "His demeanor was to get a point across with a story, always about somebody else, usually famous. I remember him telling me stories about Napoleon and Josephine. At home, he was in total subservience to the women in his life, including the cook and the maid. If he was told to go to dinner, he went to dinner. His family was the most important thing in the world to him. He was lenient and delightful. Nobody was actually disciplined, you were just expected to behave. It was a house where a stray anything was welcome, a very pleasant house. And if you weren't pleasant, somebody asked you to leave the room."

His attitude toward adults was not dissimilar. While he freely served liquor in his house, guests were expected to know their limitations. If someone became drunk they would never be invited again. "It was a formal house," said Richard, "with an old-fashioned formal Victorian culture, one where the husband and wife just happened to get into the theater business. The point of view was that of the aristocracy."

When Richard went off to college at Columbia, he initially wrote long letters home, and Cecil responded: "Your letter was very welcome. And the heading from Columbia University took me back many years—to the days when I watched the dome of the library being built, stone by stone or concrete by concrete. I can't remember of which it is made . . . I'm glad you like the 'scenes of my childhood.' It's quite a Burg when you get to know it—which takes some time . . . Be sure you visit the N.Y. Museum of Natural History before I reach New York, or I'll take you there, and that will be tough on us both . . .

"Your list of studies sound like quite a formidable array. They look to me as though they will produce a writer . . . All goes well here, and you are much in our conversation. . . . With love from the Old Man."

As Richard's social circle widened, and he felt more comfortable in his new environment, he forgot to stay in touch with his parents, as young people have since time immemorial. But most of those children hadn't grown up with Cecil B. DeMille.

"Having had no word from you for several weeks," DeMille wrote in a telegram, "I suggest that if you are living you notify your mother, and if you are dead you notify the coroner. Affectionately, Your father."

His daughter Cecilia would remember that "we were raised on research, and to us the Bible was a divinely-inspired history book . . . However, religion was never rammed down our throats. Instead, it was introduced to us as something in which any normal person should be greatly interested, to which they should turn for guidance."

Richard deMille's estimation of Cecil's relationship with God was that "He was not a completely conventional Christian. He didn't take direction from popes and prelates. He was more of a Protestant man of the Book. He did read the Bible and believed the things he read. It meant a lot to him. I never found him being accused of insincerity by any person who was religious. Those who accused him of not being truly religious don't understand the religious experience, don't understand how varied it is, and may have been doing it for some political purpose, to denigrate him."

When the children were small, they would do their homework in the dining room so they would get a chance to spend some time with him if he came home late, as he did when he was in production. DeMille's inveterate habit of amassing collections seemed delightful to the children—there were selections of everything from ancient firearms to seashells. As usually the case with people who like to acquire, he disliked throwing things away, and his daughter could only remember one time when he got rid of old clothes—a clothing drive during World War II.

When the children were young, he or Constance kept in close touch with daily telegrams and letters. Years later, nothing much had changed, except the letters tended to be about their granddaughter Cecilia. In September 1940, Constance went to New York to visit Richard at Columbia. "Dearest Madam," Cecil wrote to Constance on September 14, 1940, "Your granddaughter has just finished breakfasting with me and has left the usual amount of toast crushed and bleeding on the floor under the table.

"I told her that you had sent her your love and asked if she had any message to send you. She said, 'Yes, I got my love from Grandmommy.' I then asked her, 'Don't you want to send your love to her?' and she replied in a rather disgusted tone, 'That's what I just told you,'—so you can work it out to suit yourself . . .

"This morning little Cecilia wanted to know why I had a footstand to use when lacing my shoes. I explained that bending over was a little hard on my back as I was getting old, to which she replied brightly, 'Yes, I guess you'll soon be in heaven.'

"Tell Richard that I think his magazine, *The Nation*, is pretty red. . . ."

A week later, Cecil was writing from Paradise, "with about thirty deer around, regarding the human element as somewhat of an intrusion upon their home. There are four magnificent bucks, ten or twelve spikes, and numerous mammas and brats . . .

"Last Wednesday, I was summoned to board the [Presidential candidate Wendell] Willkie train at Santa Ana and ride with him to San Diego, which I did, and found him to be a strong and capable personality. His speeches, I believe, are improving, though I suggested to his staff that I thought a little less abuse of the President would gain him more votes . . . Give much of my love to Rebecca and keep the remainder for yourself."

Between pictures, DeMille had screenings at the house nearly every night. Because of his friendship with William Boyd, he made a habit of watching all of the Hopalong Cassidy movies. Part of DeMille's creative process was to watch movies that dealt with the same milieu he would be covering. Thus, in the latter part of 1934, when he was preparing *The Crusades*, he looked at Douglas Fairbanks's *Robin Hood* twice, with the screenings a month apart. At the same time, he watched W. C. Fields's *The Old Fashioned Way* and his own *Joan the Woman*. When he was preparing *The Greatest Show on Earth*, he watched circus movies: Lon Chaney's *Laugh, Clown, Laugh* and Griffith's *Sally of the Sawdust*.

The screenings were useful for casting as well. Watching *Now and Forever* stimulated him to say that "Carole Lombard might be worth giving some thought to."

He thought Myrna Loy's diction was bad. A test of a young actress named Elizabeth Fraser evidently aroused erotic impulses: "Fit for ruin, rape and sorrow—but
the girl can act."

And sometimes he would be struck by a bizarre casting idea that would thank-
fully waft away like a summer zephyr, as when he watched *Small Town Girl* while
preparing *The Plainsman* and noted that "James Stewart might make a good Buffalo Bill." On other occasions, he'd have a spectacular idea that would be subma-
rined by events beyond his control. For the same picture, he wanted W. C. Fields
for the part of the fabulist pulp writer Ned Buntline, but William LeBaron told
him that Fields's health was terrible at that point.

On occasion he would watch one of his own movies. His granddaughter Cecilia had a particular affection for *The Plainsman* and he would have it run for her
every few years. Cecilia saw *Cleopatra*, *The Sign of the Cross*, and most of the talkies,
although *Madam Satan* and *Four Frightened People* never made an appearance, nor
did any of her grandfather's silent films.

Invitations to the 9 P.M. screenings were informally offered, but amounted to
command performances. If one of his staff begged off because of exhaustion or
prior engagement, they were sure to be prodded about it soon afterward. "Didn't
that actor give a good performance? What did you think of the dialogue? You
weren't there? Oh. . . . How sad that you despise the filmmakers's art to preserve
yourself from the possibility of usefulness to our project." It was easier to go, and
smart to bring along your wife, because DeMille adored women and always made
sure the mood was light and charming when they were around.

At dinnertime, Cecil made sure to include the children in the conversation.
School, politics—movie politics, national politics, labor politics—constituted the
bulk of the flow. "I never heard a word about Hollywood scandals in my entire
youth," remembered Richard deMille. "It wasn't the sort of thing that belonged
in our home. Mother didn't run that kind of house; it was a very dignified New
England establishment."

DeMille remained naturally indulgent of animals. There were always a couple
of house dogs, as well as a German shepherd that belonged to the night watchman. And there was a cat named Petunia that he adored. But one cat implies
others, and, as one employee remembered it, "Leaving for the studio one morning, cats scampering here and yon underfoot, he got irritated and made a mighty
sweep of one arm and intoned fiercely, 'I want every one of those cats gone by the
time I come home tonight.' "

To which little Cecilia responded, "And Petunia too?"

The cats stayed.

Cecil voluntarily kept William informed of his son's progress in Cecil's
house. "They talked on the telephone all the time," remembered Richard, "and
Cecil had a very strong feeling of treating his brother with respect and fairness.
They had made this bargain, and William was allowed to know things about me,

he just wasn't allowed to announce himself as my father or be around too much. Clara didn't know about my parentage, neither did Agnes."

DeMille had a habit of bestowing nicknames on employees, which was not a function of affection but derived from the fact that he had a terrible memory for names. As Richard deMille would remember, "He could easily list the twelve apostles, but not the fifty technicians." The music editor would always be addressed as "Mr. Music," while a minor actress was always referred to as "Dottie Coughdrop." "Get Dottie Coughdrop," he would tell Joe Egli, the casting director, and Egli would have to match a face to the vague name.

His demeanor around the younger women on his staff was rigorously professional and fatherly. When a gorgeous Iowa girl named Mary Bennett came to work in his office, he offered her a screen test and acting training if she wanted it. She didn't and later regretted her decision, but all her life idolized DeMille as an ideal father figure.

Professionally, he agonized over major decisions, especially subject and casting. "DeMille always had a hell of a time [making] decisions, about anything," remembered Henry Noerdlinger, his highly regarded head of research. "[But] once he had made a decision then there was no deviation from it."

"He was a very *exacting* person," said A. C. Lyles. "If you went to him for something, he would want to know *exactly* what the subject was and wanted to know *exactly* the answers when he asked you what they were. And you couldn't con him. He knew the business. He *made* the business. I always found him to be very friendly, cordial, very open to suggestions, very willing to help people who wanted to be helped."

Mitchell Leisen would assert that "He had very positive ideas of what he wanted and he wasn't satisfied until he got it. . . . I owe him everything I ever learned about making pictures. The most important thing of all is the power of concentrating, never deviating from your objective. Once he started on a project, he concentrated on that and thought of nothing else."

On the set of a picture, he was everywhere, even directing the taking of the stills. Robert Parrish, who worked for him as an extra, said that "he often seemed to spend as much time and energy on the still as he did on the actual scenes." For stills, he would get in front of the company and do what he never did during the picture itself: act out the scene. As the actors mimicked him, he would wait for the expression he wanted, then yell "STILL!" and everyone would freeze. If anyone moved and spoiled the shot, he would become irate.

One day, Parrish witnessed an episode that would grow into a legend, as two men in the back of the crowd began talking while DeMille was launching into an oration about a full day's work for a full day's pay. DeMille stopped and asked what the men were talking about. One of them refused to say. He was promptly sent home.

The other fellow was called up to the camera platform. "There are four hundred people waiting for lunch because of you. Will you kindly tell them what you had to say that was so important?"

The extra, Eddie Boyle, took the proffered microphone and said, "I said, 'I wonder when he's going to call lunch.' " The crowd erupted into applause. DeMille's response was a trace of a smile. The assistant promptly called "Lunch. One hour." Parrish asserted that the response that became the stuff of a hundred Hollywood anthologies—"I wonder when that bald headed old son of a bitch is going to call lunch"—was strictly a myth. "Eddie Boyle was tough and seasoned," Parrish wrote, "but he was not as tough and seasoned as all that, though some of us at the time wished he had been."

Parrish also witnessed a moment when DeMille's chair boy accidentally nudged his script binder so that dozens of script pages fell out. There was a wind machine cranking away right behind the director, and the pink, blue, and white pages went sailing out over the set. DeMille lashed out and smacked the chair boy on the buttocks. For men like DeMille, telling actors where to stand and cameramen where to put the camera was only directing a movie; to order people around, to intimidate them, was to direct life itself.

Several times during production, he would seize his microphone and launch into a condemnation of chatter on the set. "WHAT I WANT IS QUIET! QUIET BEHIND THE CAMERA AND INTELLIGENCE IN FRONT OF IT. I KNOW I CAN'T HAVE BOTH AT THE SAME TIME BUT LET'S SEE IF I CAN GET ONE OR THE OTHER."

DeMille would almost never criticize a star on the set. It just wasn't good sense to unnerve someone the public was paying to see. But he often worked on the star through other luckless people. If an actress was late to the set, he would grab the microphone and lay into the hairdresser, and the point would be made. With few exceptions, his rages were calculated for effect; DeMille was the Sun Tzu of filmmaking, employing the Art of War to achieve the Art of DeMille.

DeMille despised limp, halfhearted acting. For that matter, he despised limp, halfhearted anything. He wanted projection, he wanted dynamism, and he wanted it from stars and extras alike. He would also excoriate extras that failed to give him the level of excitement he needed. "You hear bugles and drums in the distance and you know you're going to be saved," he told one group one day. "Do you understand? You're going to be saved! You and your kids and your loved ones. So WHAT DO YOU DO? YOU JUMP UP AND DOWN, YOU CHEER, YOU GRAB SOMEONE AND DANCE, YOU GO CRAZY WITH JOY. Have you given me that reaction? From the way you're acting I merely assumed you have just read the market reports and your favorite stock has gone up a couple of points. . . . GODDAMN IT, I'M GIVING YOU THE CHANCE OF A LIFETIME TO ACT IN A DEMILLE PICTURE. I WANT EVERYTHING YOU'VE GOT!"

"He would spare no effort," remembered the composer Elmer Bernstein. "Whatever it took—yelling, shouting, sometimes cajoling—he would spare no effort in what he considered to be his endless search for perfection. He was, by the way, as unsparing of his own efforts as everybody else's. I have vivid memories of him looking at dailies and saying he hated it, it wasn't good enough. He was as unsparing of himself as anybody else, which of course made all of us feel better."

In spite of the reliable explosions on the set, his crew stayed with him for decades; to work on a DeMille picture was a plum assignment, and that emphatically included Eddie Salven, DeMille's favorite assistant director, who would be the target of some abuse during every picture. But one day DeMille came on a little too strong, roasting Salven for his perceived shortcomings in ever-increasing volume and variety until the AD could take it no longer.

"I'm no mind reader," snapped Salven. "Tell me what you want and I'll do it. What in hell would you like to have?"

DeMille took a few seconds, looked from Salven to other members of his crew, then said in a quiet voice, "I'd like to have an assistant director who won't bawl me out in public."

DeMille had great enthusiasm for the work of directors who were his diametric opposites: the exquisite Fabergé miniatures of Lubitsch, the poeticized emotionalism of Capra. He liked their pictures and felt no envy because, while he realized that he couldn't do what they could do, the reverse was also the case.

DeMille had a realistic appraisal of his own gifts. "He thought he was very good," said his granddaughter. "He thought he was an innovator; he could look back and see the things he had done. That's the reason he saved everything—because he thought it would be important." Nor was he burdened by false modesty. For the 1938 Academy Awards, he voted for himself as Best Director for *The Plainsman*, followed by his second choice of Sidney Franklin for *The Good Earth*, then Victor Fleming for *Captains Courageous*, then Leo McCarey for *The Awful Truth*.

"He worked at being the great director," said Richard deMille. "It wasn't something he felt had been handed to him. He was always aware of the hazards of failure. He never had it made. Does anybody feel that? Nobody doing things out in the world, contending in a risky business, feels that way. He *played* the egomaniac, but he wasn't actually; it was part of the process of stirring up excitement."

Similarly, he cared about the critics far more than he let on. Nobody is completely indifferent to having the work of years denigrated or ridiculed, but Cecil also realized that in a business like the movies, if you can't have both critics and audiences, hope for the audience.

17

In many respects, Cecil B. DeMille lived a custom life. Around 1938, he began stocking two perfumes, compounded strictly for him, that he presented to women who earned his goodwill or admiration. Julia Faye got them, of course, as did Gladys Rosson and Richard deMille's girlfriend Olive Grismer, who was Joe Harper's half-sister. One smelled of ocean spray and was named "Seaward"; the other smelled of sweet blossoms and was named "Paradise." Richard remembered that "Paradise" was romantic, but "Seaward" was preferable because it was provocative.

In the morning Cecil would shave with murky brown water bottled in gallon jugs at San Pedro Harbor, which he preferred to tap water because the San Pedro water was soft. He lathered his face with an old-fashioned brush and a large lather cup, then shaved with a modern safety razor.

The first day of a DeMille picture was always marked by an unchanging ritual. Constance DeMille would arrive on the set and everybody would stop what they were doing and gather around. She would pin a rose on her husband's lapel, hug him and wish him well, and the picture could begin shooting.

All the children adored Cecil unreservedly, but they had a hard time feeling the same way about the highly reserved Constance. "She was a sweet, kind person," said Katherine DeMille, "but she didn't know how to make you feel her love. . . . I liked her, but I can't remember ever having any deep communication with her. I'm not sure if she even knew how."

It was Constance who took charge of the contributions to charities, most of them having to do with children: the Los Angeles Orphan's Home, the Children's Protective Association, the Boys and Girls Aid Society, the Tuberculosis Association, the VFW. Constance also regularly helped out less affluent relatives, with Cecil's knowledge. Funding all this charity was Cecil's rapidly growing fortune—by 1946, it would be overestimated at $8 million.

DeMille's taste in magazines was mainstream—he subscribed to *Life, Coronet, National Geographic, Story, Box Office Digest, The Hollywood Reporter*, and *Film Daily.*

He collected rare editions. In 1937, he bought volumes 156–61 of the *Illustrated London News* and bound volumes of *Harper's* magazine from before the Civil War.

Unusually for his time and place, DeMille put a high value on taking care of his body; he kept himself trim and toned, and he was as disciplined with food and alcohol as he was with everything else—an ounce of bourbon in an old-fashioned, which he made himself every night, with bitters, sugar, and a big seltzer bottle. He had enjoyed an occasional cigar as a young man, but in his maturity his smoking was limited to a pipe every night after dinner. Likewise, he took care of his own suits and clothes, until the last seven or eight years of his life, when Cecilia made him get a valet.

If there was a movie to be screened, he would sit in his large red leather chair and toss the matches and pipe ashes into an oversized brass bowl on the floor in front of him. The grandchildren were all fond of the bowl; when it wasn't being used they would sit on top of it and Cecil or someone else would spin it—and them—around.

The kindness and consideration he could evince often seemed surprising to those who only knew him on the set. Donald Hayne, one of Cecil's assistants, remembered a time just after World War II, when the two men were on a train on the way to a speech. Hayne took an afternoon nap, which stretched into the early evening. He awoke to find DeMille sitting quietly in the dark. He had been afraid that if he put on the light or even closed the door between their adjoining bedrooms, Hayne might wake up. DeMille had a terrible head cold and was feeling blue; as the two men sat down to dinner, DeMille mumbled to himself, "I wonder why people in Hollywood don't like me."

As far as his partial Jewish heritage was concerned, Richard deMille said that Cecil had "mixed feelings about individual Jews," but "had a very strong attachment to the Jewishness of the Old Testament. He never rejected the Jewishness of his mother; he was proud to be a cousin of Sir Herbert Louis Samuel." Yet DeMille's public emphasis on his Episcopalian half, along with his staunchly conservative politics, which at the time were virtually synonymous with anti-Semitism, led many to feel he was one with many of his political friends.

★

The DeMille unit was housed directly behind the famous wrought iron Paramount gates, in the building on the left as you stood looking at the gates from Marathon Street. This was why the gate was generally called "The DeMille Gate." There were two floors, and a large reception room, with three secretaries. Behind them was a long hall of nearly one hundred feet leading to DeMille's office at the end. On the walls of the hallway were large framed sepia prints of scenes from his greatest pictures, beginning with *The Squaw Man*. Off the hallway were offices for his associate producer, the writers, publicists, and so forth, with a conference room.

"Everything that was important moved [toward DeMille's office]" observed Phil Koury, DeMille's executive assistant for a number of years, "and we were wont to gauge the importance of a visitor by the degree of his penetration down the corridor."

DeMille continued to keep an inquiring eye on the competition, both on the Paramount lot and off. He liked Billy Wilder's movies a great deal, and he was fond of Rouben Mamoulian's as well. "He always wanted to see other people's movies," said Richard deMille. " 'What are they doing? What are they doing that I can steal?' He did a lot of technical things in his films, so he didn't want people to get ahead of him. And it was a way of gauging the audience, to see what was selling. He wasn't isolated from the filmmaking community, not at all. He never felt secure; he always felt he was being tested."

Although movies have always been an intrinsically mutable business, shape shifting to keep up with cultural fashion, DeMille movies almost never resembled anything but DeMille movies. Yet many younger producers like David O. Selznick seem to have had only admiration for the older man. "My father had incredible respect for him," said Daniel Selznick. "Not politically—DeMille was to the right of everybody, even Grandpa [Louis B. Mayer]. But my father almost had a sense of awe about DeMille. Not only could DeMille conceive of these vast movies, but he could cast them, get them mounted and then he went so far as to direct them himself as well. He was a one-man operation."

At the office, everybody seemed to operate on a slightly submissive level around DeMille, even those who had been his most devoted acolytes, as with poor Jeanie Macpherson, who no longer commanded a four-figure salary and whose correspondence from this period verges on the obsequious:

Dear "Chief"

Would you be willing to lend me $65 and let me pay you back . . . $5.00 per week? I pay $100 per week out of my salary *each week* (through the studio's deducting it) to keep up my income tax and so—with deductions for bonds etc, some weeks are pretty "tight sledding"! I need this $65 to pay up dues for "Screen Writer's Guild."

I should greatly appreciate the help. With love, "Jinny."

There was a clear demarcation between the staff at 2100 DeMille Drive, and the staff at the studio. The house staff, led by Gladys Rosson, made policy regarding both movies and investments; the studio staff carried them out. The house staff addressed the office staff by their first names; the studio staff addressed most of the house staff as "Mr." and "Miss."

Hollywood has always been a small town, so some aspects of DeMille's unconventional domestic arrangements were known, or at least intuited. It was widely assumed that DeMille's marriage was little more than a business relationship. It seemed that a publicly religious man with several mistresses was the essence of hypocrisy, which fit in nicely with DeMille's self-created image as a domineering autocrat with a large ego.

Yet there are many different kinds of marriage, and there is no doubt that Constance and DeMille maintained an emotional devotion that bordered on the absolute.

On holidays and on their anniversary, Cecil would always give her lilies of the valley, the symbol of their engagement, with accompanying notes. Their content was always slightly different, but with the same underlying meaning. Constance saved the notes all her life:

> "My true, sweet, dear bully [?] Mrs. McGucken. It's perfect. Cizzle."
>
> "A Happy New Year to the two funny ones and all the love in the world from Da."
>
> "Dearest Little Mother Here's another Easter and you're a dearer pal than ever—"
>
> "Christmas 1910 Once again Little Mother and Da is sure grateful for the help you are and have always been no matter what the luck. God bless you."
>
> "This is the twelfth bunch of Christmas lillies and yet they are as fresh as the first In which is contained a deep moral Marry Gretchen. With all the love in the world Da."
>
> "Gretchen—twenty six years is a long time—but not long enough C—"
>
> "To Gretchen with the compound love of twenty nine years—Cecil"
>
> "This is the 29th Basket—each carrying more love—and admiration of your endurance. Cecil—"
>
> "Only a saint could stand 30 years—with a Saytre—all my love C."
>
> "As of old—"

★

In line with the emphasis on decorum, the house on DeMille Drive had a living room that contained a Steinway, a Gramophone, sofas, a rocking chair for Cecil, a Velázquez copy, and a Rubens that Agnes deMille thought was probably a copy but a good one. There was silver everywhere, always immaculately polished. There was little color in the drapes or furniture, but accents were supplied by the plethora of fresh flowers on tables and the piano.

Cecil's office had things that were often remarked on—suits of armor, Doré prints, an 1878 edition of George Catlin's Indian paintings. But perhaps the most remarkable thing was that in the afternoon, the room would glow from the light coming through the small-paned windows and fall on the bowl of stunning ruby red roses that were placed on his desk every day and arranged by Gladys Rosson.

Outside in the yard, between the barn and the tennis court, there were gardens of pansies and carnations and two rose gardens, a white one for Constance, and a red one for Cecil. Constance's roses were pale and delicate, while Cecil's were dark and passionate.

DeMille's bedroom was plain—a queen-sized bed, a desk at one end with the usual voluminous number of books and scripts. A dresser, a mirror, a chaise longue. The closets in the Laughlin Park house tended toward the small, so he used an anteroom for his wardrobe. Beside the dresser was a door that led to an outside porch, where he exercised and sunbathed. In the bathroom, he first took a hot bath, then an immediate cold shower. (He would claim that "I never turn the hot water on in a shower.") At Paradise, he swam in an unheated pool that left most people numb and then claimed that after that he took a cold shower to warm up.

The atmosphere around the house was genteel, polite, and formal. Sons- and daughters-in-law always called him "Mr. DeMille," never "Father," never "C.B." Richard deMille said that he never hugged Cecil in his life, only shook hands. The preferred social hierarchy was Cecil at the top dispensing largesse to those beneath. "He did not mingle socially where he could not dominate," wrote his niece Agnes.

His personal generosity remained largely hidden. "He supported a lot of people," said his granddaughter Cecilia. "Between twenty and thirty. And he didn't talk about it. I know at Christmastime, I would come in and see him putting money in envelopes. I said, 'Grandfather, don't you realize most of these are scams?' And he would say, 'Pet, if one out of 100 are authentic, it's worth it.' "

Cecil's Republicanism was increasingly veering toward the dramatic, which is why in time he would favor Douglas MacArthur over Dwight Eisenhower. "He liked a strong leader who could state things simply, as in the movies," said Richard deMille. "He went through different stages. At the beginning, he was sucked in by Roosevelt's false promises, but then he proceeded to a very systematic socialist program and DeMille turned against him. And then he became impressed by him again, when Roosevelt cooperated with him during the war on *Land of Liberty*. He was subject to the blandishments of great men."

DeMille's granddaughter Cecilia would say, "Increasingly, he made a distinction between a good American and a liberal. He hated communism with such a passion, thought it was a godless tyranny; he thought anyone who was a fellow traveler was a traitor. But he liked Roosevelt very much personally."

He contradicted himself? Very well then, he contradicted himself.

If he wanted to spend time on his yacht, the *Seaward*, DeMille would drive down to San Pedro in his Ford convertible, top down, never doing less than fifty, and usually more. There was always a loaded gun in the glove compartment because, DeMille said, it was well known that he liked to carry a lot of money around with him.

Some of Richard deMille's most cherished memories revolved around the *Seaward*, which he described as "108 feet of beauty and 115 feet of mast." Richard remembered "marvelous excursions to the Channel Islands. Once he and I got down into a rowboat and rowed into a cave—he did the rowing—and in this cave I thought I saw a white seal. Rudyard Kipling would have been proud of me. Whether I did or not, that white seal is always in my memory as the discovery I made with father in the cave on the island."

DeMille had a diving suit on the *Seaward*, and he liked to go over the side and walk around on the bottom of the ocean and view the sights while somebody on board manually pumped air down to him. Richard remembered him going down on the floor of the ocean for as long as twenty minutes. It was, said Richard, "a little bit like sitting in the church all by himself—DeMille meditating on the great mystery of existence."

DeMille would donate the *Seaward* to the merchant marine for service during World War II. After the war, she was handed back stripped of her brass fittings and beautiful paneling. Henry Wilcoxon inspected the boat and told DeMille it would take a fortune to get her back into shape. DeMille said to let it go, and never saw her again. He never bought another boat.

When he wasn't in production on a picture, DeMille would get up around nine in the morning, take a late breakfast on one of the porches, and leave for the studio each day around 11:30. The distance was only a couple of miles, and would take somewhere between five and ten minutes. As DeMille's car left the house, a call was placed to the studio: "Mr. DeMille is on his way." This enabled people to assume their positions. The door from the studio street to the bungalow was propped open, and an assistant was standing by at the garage entrance so that he could take DeMille's briefcase as he stepped from the car. People could be summoned from the commissary or the stage; if DeMille had sent word that he wished to see someone "this morning," that meant immediately upon arrival, so the person would station himself outside the inner sanctum, with DeMille nodding as he strode past.

Around 1 or 1:30, DeMille would lead the dozen members of his staff to the commissary for lunch. There were frequent guests of a clerical nature—Rabbi Edgar Magnin and, later, Billy Graham—and a Bible at either end of the table, just in case a citation needed checking.

DeMille always set the conversational parameters; the only topic that was off-limits was the movie business. Favorite subjects were history or the Bible or comparative religions, occasionally writers and composers. The tone was set by DeMille; the staff was expected to be happy when he was happy, angry when he was angry, concerned when he was concerned.

"You were a courtier at that table," said Elmer Bernstein, "and there was no question he was the grandee." Yet he would bridle if he felt someone was overtly fawning. "If you said, 'Yes, it's wonderful Mr. DeMille,' " remembered

Bernstein, "you had better have a good reason, because the next question was, 'Why?' You had to know his tempers very well. He was an artist and he had an artist's sensibilities."

In return for his staff's devotion, he was often solicitous, and sometimes devoted. Bessie McGaffey, a DeMille researcher, remembered how her Christmas present one year was a registered nurse to help her get well after surgery.

The studio that DeMille, Lasky, and Zukor had built was one of the friendliest, low-key places in Hollywood. "It was . . . the difference between a lovely, warm friendly village, which was Paramount, as against a factory city, which was MGM," remembered Angela Lansbury. "We used to call MGM the factory. It was all very sterile at MGM. But Paramount, on the other hand, was a much friendlier, warm, family sort of place, and everybody used to run in and out of their dressing rooms and in the evening, after shooting, they would all get together in one or the other dressing rooms and have a drink before they went home. They knew one another and they fraternized with each other."

DeMille delegated correspondence—a reply had to be prompt, could not begin with "I," and could not use clichéd pleasantries. He delegated all sorts of things, but when it came to his movies, their production and physical presentation, he delegated nothing. He sat with the sound mixers, he supervised the color on the release prints. He made no apologies for his temperament, for his insistence of nailing down the last detail of any given production.

All this conspired to give the impression that the making of a DeMille movie transcended the usual meager Hollywood concerns of profit and loss, or even good reviews, and was somehow crucial to the continuation of Western Civilization.

Likewise, he never seemed to think that he should earn any accolades for having a predominantly female staff, from Anne Bauchens to Jeanie Macpherson to Gladys Rosson. There was some disagreement about Gladys's true personality—Richard deMille thought she was physically unattractive but admired her as a person, while DeMille's granddaughter said she was "rigid, almost prissy." But there was no disagreement about DeMille's dependence on her. The actress and writer Lisa Mitchell, who worked for DeMille, said Gladys was "officially a secretary, but she was truly . . . the vice president, his aide-de-camp, she was his right hand literally; she knew what he was going to do before he thought of it, and he relied on her utterly, utterly, utterly."

It was Gladys who decided who would accompany DeMille on business trips; it was Gladys who decided his wardrobe while on the road, and would set out the clothes, including the ring that matched his tie. It was Gladys whose sole object in life was to make sure DeMille never had to lift a finger unless he wanted to.

DeMille's explanation for this reliance on women was simple: "I had a mother that won my admiration, and I have liked women ever since. We seem to strike a note of understanding. And I like fighting with them and enjoy their reactions."

"DeMille loved women, truly loved them, liked them, appreciated them," said

Lisa Mitchell. "DeMille *got* women, he understood that the most interesting, attractive thing about a woman is her brain, and the women he surrounded himself with were very, very smart."

This comfort with women had resulted in a succession of strong roles for strong actresses in his movies. From the early marital comedies with Gloria Swanson and Bebe Daniels to Barbara Stanwyck in *Union Pacific* and the later biblical films, it was the women characters who took charge, who instigated change.

But in later years, his on-screen women basically fell into two camps: fighting-mad vixens and wily beauties. Humor and companionability were not on display. "This was very strange," observed Agnes deMille, "because the women in Cecil's own family life—his mother, his wife, his daughters, his step-mother-in-law, and his sister-in-law—were strong, humorous, dedicated, loyal, and enchanting people, of considerable wit and presence. Obviously he longed for another kind."

DeMille had labored long and hard to establish his position at Paramount, and he intended to keep it that way—other Paramount pictures could be pillaged for stock footage, but DeMille's footage and outtakes were off-limits for anybody but DeMille.

Likewise, he paid attention to his place in movie history. His private film library entailed a fair amount of work. In May 1940, Gladys Rosson noted that twelve of DeMille's movies were still missing from the vault (*The Arab, The Captive, Chimmie Fadden, The Devil-Stone, The Dream Girl, The Golden Chance, Kindling, The Man from Home, Temptation, The Unafraid, We Can't Have Everything,* and *The Wild Goose Chase*). Some of the holes were being filled as late as 1952, when DeMille received copies of *The Golden Chance, Kindling,* and *The Unafraid.*

DeMille's prescience in taking the responsibility for preserving his own life's work was both extremely rare and extremely wise; of 1,014 silent feature films produced by Paramount and its predecessor companies, precisely thirty-seven were preserved by the company itself.

Others too were conscious of DeMille's place in film history. When Alfred Hitchcock came to America in 1939, he was asked to name his ten favorite films of all time. He responded with a list of nine silent movies, and only one talkie—*I Am a Fugitive from a Chain Gang.* The silents included Chaplin's *The Gold Rush,* Rex Ingram's *Scaramouche,* E. A. Dupont's *Variety,* von Sternberg's *The Last Command,* Maurice Tourneur's *The Isle of Lost Ships,* John Robertson's *Sentimental Tommy,* the same director's *The Enchanted Cottage,* and two movies by DeMille: *Saturday Night* and *Forbidden Fruit.*

★

DeMille loved doing the *Lux Radio Theatre;* in 1938, he said that "I wouldn't take a million dollars for the experience I've had in radio."

He was to forfeit the experience for much less.

DeMille had joined the American Federation of Radio Artists in 1939 and would assert in his memoirs, "I do believe in the necessity of unions. I remember well the low wages, long hours and atrocious working conditions which were all too prevalent in American industry when I was a boy and young man. When Mrs. DeMille and I were touring in plays, we sometimes saw from the window of our train little children, carrying their lunch pails, going to work at dawn."

On August 16, 1944, DeMille received a letter from the American Federation of Radio Artists: "By action of the Board of Directors of AFRA, each member has been assessed $1.00 to finance the campaign in opposition to No. 12 or the mistitled 'Right of Employment Amendment' to be submitted on the State Ballot in November. . . . Immediate payment of assessment is required. It must be paid on or before September 1st, 1944. Failure to pay will result in suspension."

The union's 2,300 members were being assessed $1 apiece—on top of their $100 yearly dues—to fight Proposition 12. If Prop. 12 passed, it would mean that membership in a union would no longer be a requisite for employment on radio. In other words, where radio was concerned, California would become an open shop.

Naturally, the union wanted the proposition defeated. Naturally, the conservative DeMille favored it and felt outraged that he was being assessed $1 to fight something he believed in. Moreover, the union's bylaws contained no mention of the right to assess for any purpose, and, furthermore, the members had never been called for a vote to be asked whether they agreed with the assessment. The union wasn't asking for voluntary contributions, it was *demanding* a dollar on threat of suspension.

DeMille's flamboyant displays of anger were purely for show; his real anger was deadly quiet and ice-cold. As he read the letter, he began to grow genuinely angry. He believed that the union "was demanding, in a word, that I cancel my vote with my dollar. . . . Did my union, did any organization, have the right to impose a compulsory political assessment upon any citizen, under the pain of the loss of his right to work?"

Both Y. Frank Freeman, the head of Paramount, and Bill Jeffers, the president of the Union Pacific railroad, encouraged DeMille to make a stand for an individual's right not to be in lockstep with his union. Others counseled differently: pay the dollar, take his munificent radio salary, and use some or all of it to support Prop. 12.

DeMille went to Neil McCarthy to find out what he thought the cost of a lawsuit to fight the assessment would be. "This will take us three or four years to run through the courts," said McCarthy. "We will probably lose, and you will be giving up $125,000 a year. I will consider myself privileged to devote my time to it, and I will do so without any compensation."

It was not the answer DeMille wanted to hear, but he was curious. Why did McCarthy think they would lose?

McCarthy explained that constitutional law was not an exact science and that judicial decisions were often a matter of individual psychology and social viewpoint on the part of judges; given the pro-union drift of the government and the population of the time, it was doubtful that they could find a court to uphold their position.

McCarthy would remember that there were several meetings with the union—"in the friendliest atmosphere" according to the lawyer—to see if some compromise could be effected. The union went so far as to offer to have someone else pay the dollar for DeMille, but DeMille said that the principle was the same—the amount of the assessment was irrelevant, and so was the identity of the person who paid it. He could, he said, no longer respect himself if that principle was compromised.

DeMille refused to pay the dollar. The union refused to cancel the assessment.

After much thought, DeMille came to believe that the silencing of his voice from the *Lux Radio Theatre* would hurt the union. In his memoirs, he wrote that he had "no wish to hurt my union," but, since the union was doing its best to hurt him, that statement can be taken with a shakerful of salt.

It's likely that he believed that the entire affair could be turned into effective anti-union propaganda, that the 20 to 30 million people who listened to *Lux Radio Theatre* every week would want to know why this nice grandfatherly man was being yanked off the air.

The *Lux* show involved far more than just $125,000 a year. There was the positive collateral impact on DeMille's movies, of course, but beyond that, there was the authentic sense of intimacy it gave him with the American public. "It meant families in Maine and Kansas and Idaho finishing the dishes or the schoolwork or the evening chores in time to gather around the radios," he would remember. "It meant people, not in the mass but individuals, who did me the honor of inviting me into their homes; people to whom I was no longer a name filtered through the wordage of imaginative press agents, but a person whom they knew."

He announced that he would give up broadcasting rather than pay the $1. "Such grave issues are involved that I consider it a duty to forego, if compelled to, the sum of money which I have been receiving weekly for broadcasting rather than pay one single dollar in a political tribute which acknowledges that I am no longer a free man. . . . If any organization can assess one dollar, it can assess $1000 for any political or other purposes. It could assess Communists for the support of the Republican party.

"Surely a situation is unsound that denies an individual the right to work unless he contributes financially to the support of political views to which he may be opposed."

DeMille may have been extrapolating an apocalyptic conclusion from a modest premise, but drama was what he did for a living. But there was no doubt that the union's position was ethically questionable, while DeMille's baseline position was solid—even a union man could see the principled logic of his argument.

That said, he seemed to be aware that he had a tiger by the tail. "Bill, can you get me out of this mess?" he said wearily to William Pine, his publicity man. Pine suggested that he, Pine, should pay the dollar. "That's out," said DeMille. "It would make no difference *who* paid it. I will never pay the dollar and no one will ever pay it *for* me."

What made it all worse was that Prop. 12 was defeated in the November election. And DeMille still owed the dollar. The union extended the payment deadline to December 1. On November 30, DeMille sat down with Constance. What should he do?

There was really only one answer. "She told me," he related to a staffer, " 'You have no choice.' That if I paid the dollar I would be telling the world I placed money above principle. Besides, she said she was a partner in the firm and would not pay her half of the dollar."

DeMille made his last broadcast for the *Lux Radio Theatre* on January 22, 1945. He sued the union for reinstatement and lost. He appealed up to the California Supreme Court and lost.

When AFRA was broadened to AFTRA, to include television, the ban's range was broadened, and DeMille was effectively forbidden from appearing on television. He formed the DeMille Foundation for Political Freedom, with offices in the Merritt Building on West Eighth Street in downtown Los Angeles, to campaign for right to work legislation throughout the country, and he began a series of speaking engagements that took him around the country for the next several years.

In an address to the American Legion delivered on the steps of Federal Hall in New York in September 1945, after first paying tribute to his ancestor Anthony deMil, who was buried nearby in Trinity churchyard, to John Peter Zenger and to George Washington, who was inaugurated on the same spot, DeMille launched into his primary points:

> This is not a question of unionism or non-unionism. It is not a question of closed shop or open shop. It is not a question of capitalism versus socialism. You will find good Americans on both sides of all these questions. But you will not find any dispute among good Americans on the one fundamental question: do an American's rights as a citizen belong to him or are they a trinket to be bartered away by some boss, whether in a union or anywhere else? . . .
>
> Here and now I am speaking for the thousands of individual workers who have had no voice but who were faced with the same hard, un-American choice—either to pay political tribute or to lose their right to earn a living.
>
> When one man or group has the power to decide who shall work and who shall not, that is a national cancer—a cancer that must be

cut out before it render our country too weak to resist the poisons of totalitarianism.

From focused attacks on closed shops, DeMille gradually broadened his pamphleteering to include unions and communism. In a later speech, he quoted William Z. Foster, the head of the American Communist Party ("The general strike is no toy. It is a revolutionary weapon of the first order"), then pointed out that the year before France had been crippled by a series of nationwide communist-inspired strikes.

> Communist controlled unions nearly wrecked France. Communist controlled unions can wreck America unless we take the same measures France took, or stronger measures, to protect the right to work. Even if we were not at war, it would be insane to leave in the hands of any half-dozen men the power to paralyze and cripple this whole country. Today, it is worse than insane. It is criminal.
>
> I am not saying that all of the powerful union leaders in this country are communist sympathizers or communists. I am saying that even if they were angels from heaven, no country should hand the keys of its industries, its communications, and its transportation, to any organized private group controlled by half a dozen men. . . .
>
> Our enemy has done his work of deceit and confusion well when the courts declare it libel to call a man a communist but do not declare it treason to vote for one.

The subtext to DeMille's understanding of unions and politics was power—power being removed from the hands of the few people that controlled America's industries and transferred to the few people that controlled America's unions.

DeMille would always claim that he was by no means anti-union, that he belonged to several unions himself. On the one hand, this was true—his true antipathy was never toward the rank and file but toward union leaders such as Walter Reuther and Harry Bridges, whom he regarded as tinpot dictators.

But on the deepest emotional level, this claim was an evasion. Remember the 1929 letter to L. B. Mayer about an organizing meeting in Los Angeles for a film editor's union that ended, "please try and wake up the New York producers to this situation which is far more deadly than the stock market."

Underlining the union struggles were issues of control and allegiance, not to mention the perceived betrayal of old employees like Alvin Wyckoff. DeMille's identification would always be with the moguls who controlled the purse strings of the industry. On a primal level, Louis B. Mayer felt that MGM was his personal creation; similarly, DeMille felt that Hollywood owed its existence as the world's center for movie production to him and men like him. Hadn't he always taken good care of his people, fighting the studio to keep them on salary between pictures? What right had a union to tell him what he should pay Anne Bauchens, or what issues he could support with his checkbook?

If the courts failed him, perhaps the people would eventually see the validity of his argument, which he backed up with a quote from Thomas Jefferson: "To compel a man to furnish contribution of money for the propagation of opinions which he disbelieves and abhors is sinful and tyrannical."

After his defeats in the lower courts, the U. S. Supreme Court declined to review DeMille's lawsuit. The position of the appeals courts had essentially been that while the union may have taken his dollar to fight against the measure, DeMille could still vote for it, meaning neither DeMille's suffrage nor his speech had been limited.

Just because he had lost his case was no reason to stop working for what he believed. DeMille appeared before the committee considering the Taft-Hartley bill, and his testimony helped lead to a clause that outlawed the closed shop in interstate commercial relations. The Taft-Hartley Act of 1947 forbade denying anyone the right to work for refusing to pay a political assessment, but the law wasn't retroactive. The ban on DeMille appearing on radio and television except for the express purpose of publicizing a movie remained in effect for the rest of his life.

The end result of the entire imbroglio was that DeMille became a heroic figure to the right, and a figure of anathema to the left—not merely for his anti-communism, a stance many liberals shared, but for a position widely regarded as anti-union. It was a posture that would only deepen in the years to come, which ultimately resulted in actions that had catastrophic consequences for his standing within the industry.

Not that he cared. On some level he was emboldened by the entire experience. For the first time in decades, Cecil B. DeMille had an authentic cause.

A difficult day during production of *The Ten Commandments*.

PART FOUR

1946–1959

"Never give money to a woman.
Make her borrow it. Never settle for one woman.
Never be humbled by anyone."

–Cecil B. DeMille

18

Around Paramount, DeMille was regarded as a remote figure, a studio within the studio—beyond criticism, beyond advice. Costume designer Edith Head, one of the other great careerist powers at the studio, seemed irritated by his fetish for physical authenticity, and by a perfectionism she regarded as pedantic: the finished costume had to be identical to the sketch. "He never showed enthusiasm," she complained. "No 'Wonderful!' No 'Beautiful!' No 'Good, Edith.' Once I said to him, 'Mr. DeMille, in all these years we've worked together, you've never told me a costume was good. The most you say is, 'That will do.' He almost smiled. 'If I say it will do, it's good.' "

Nineteen forty-five brought the usual parade of business obligations; he co-signed a loan for Jeanie Macpherson for $371, but this time the money was for an ominous purpose: hospital bills. William Boyd offered DeMille the opportunity of producing and/or financing a new series of Hopalong Cassidy movies. Boyd had bought out the producer Harry Sherman, and was going to produce the pictures himself, but offered DeMille first refusal. DeMille investigated the possibilities for a couple of weeks, but finally told Gladys Rosson that "the profit seems to me in these very strenuous times, with another strike pending, not to be sufficient to off-set the risk." Boyd produced twelve Cassidy pictures to indifferent results before suspending production, but would benefit from windfall profits when he leased the pictures to television, making him wealthy very quickly.

The year also brought a full ration of political activities that were taking up an increasing amount of DeMille's time. In February, Representative Karl Mundt of South Dakota sent a letter to a handful of movie people—Walt Disney, James Cagney, Louis B. Mayer, Darryl F. Zanuck, Harry Warner, and Will Hays. Mundt was heading the House Committee on Un-American Activities, and asked these eminent Americans to give the committee their opinions about the proper scope of activities that should engage the attention of the committee.

DeMille's response was blisteringly specific:

The task of the new House Committee on un-American Activities is to expose to the public for whatever corrective action is necessary, any activity of any agency or organization which menaces the Constitution of the United States or destroys the liberty and rights of the citizens guaranteed him by the Constitution. . . . No agency or organization, be it State, Federal, executive, legislative, judicial or unofficial, should be beyond the scope of the Committee.

Right now an un-American activity which surely should be investigated and brought to the attention of the public, the Congress and the legislatures for correction by law is the encroachment by certain Unions upon the guaranteed rights and liberties of the American citizen.

When a Union can literally shackle a citizen by forbidding and actually preventing him from working at his trade, because he refuses to pay a political assessment to support a cause on the ballot to which he is opposed, a situation is created which is un-American and unendurable, and the people of the United States are in the grip of a tyranny as all-out as Fascism or Nazism or Communism.

★

Wilfred Buckland's son Bill had long been bedeviled by major emotional problems complicated by alcoholism. The young man had been in the California State Mental Hospital at Camarillo, and DeMille had tried to help out by giving the young man a job. Wilfred Buckland hadn't worked regularly in the movies since 1927, and was surviving by remortgaging his house. Complicating matters was the death of his beloved wife, Veda, from cancer.

DeMille put Buckland on the payroll for the picture that would become *Unconquered*. In June and July of 1945, Buckland was sending DeMille research notes on everything from the use of charcoal in smelting iron to Indian war dances. His last contribution was suggesting the spectacular climax of *Unconquered*—a canoe going over the falls—and, spinning off the Cave of the Winds at Niagara Falls, a way for DeMille's hero and heroine to hide behind a waterfall from pursuing Indians.

In August, Buckland wrote DeMille a letter telling him he had gotten a job at MGM and Billy was starting a job at Columbia. "I can never tell you my appreciation of the splendid way you helped me through the valley of despair. Gratefully, Wilfred."

Buckland's personal and professional stability didn't last. On July 18, 1946, he shot and killed his son while he slept, then committed suicide. He was eighty years old. When DeMille was told, he seemed to physically shrink, and then recovered and went on, with very little verbalization of his emotions. "That was a typical Cecil reaction to things," said Richard deMille. "He felt deeply things that he did not express openly."

Buckland's murder-suicide was bad enough, but things got worse for DeMille. In the spring of 1946, Jeanie Macpherson had called the office to say she was ill and couldn't make it to the studio for a story conference. That night she was taken to the hospital; DeMille rushed over to be with her. Jeanie hadn't been feeling well for a year or two, and a full examination revealed cancer. The doctors tried surgery, followed by radiation, but nothing worked. As her strength began failing, DeMille tried to spend at least a part of each day with her. The last time he saw her he held her hand and told her he knew they would meet in the next world. She quietly said that she believed that as well. Her death on August 24, 1946, marked the end of what DeMille probably regarded as the best years of his life.

DeMille offered to support Macpherson's mother, but Jeanie's sister in Cleveland took care of the older woman, and she lived comfortably in her apartment until her own death on Christmas Day 1949. As she lay dying in the hospital, Jeanie Macpherson told Gladys Rosson that she never would have been happy anywhere but as a member of Cecil B. DeMille's staff.

★

Unconquered continued the theme of the glories of Manifest Destiny that had also been a prominent feature of *The Plainsman* and *Union Pacific*. Gary Cooper was back on board, after he meekly listened to a DeMille lecture about some of the mistakes he had been making in his recent pictures; DeMille took particular umbrage at the comedy western *Along Came Jones*. "You shouldn't do that sort of thing," he told the actor. "Playing a man on the screen who can't shoot. You are the guy who is supposed to know how to do such things. . . . Never play anything that lets the public down, your public. If you kid a western, if you kid a hero, you are doing yourself damage. . . . You can let down your public once, Gary, and be forgiven. But don't try it a second time."

Unconquered is a physically splendid but slow show, colorful but only mildly entertaining—the mixture as before, with the director clearly falling back on formula. DeMille's historical details are far more interesting than the ostensible dramatic narrative—how irons worked in colonial times (they were hollow and you filled them with hot charcoal), the construction of counterweighted drawbridges, the operation of flintlock pistols.

Howard Hawks supposedly asked his friend Cooper how he could get his mouth around some of the dialogue DeMille insisted on. "Well," he replied, "when DeMille finishes talking to you, they don't seem so bad. But when you see the picture, then you kind of hang your head."

But the critics were, in their way, swayed. James Agee wrote in *Time*, "The movie is . . . to be sure . . . a huge, colored chunk of hokum; but the most old-fashioned thing about it is its exuberance . . . which Director DeMille preserves almost single-handed from the old days. . . . Mixed with all the nineteenth century theatricalism, the early twentieth-century talent for making movies move, and the overall impression of utter falsity, *Unconquered* has some authentic flavor of the period."

But when *Unconquered* was released in October of 1947, it was a surprising financial failure, costing $4.3 million, losing $1.1 million. Part of the problem was the sky-high budget; there was also the traditional audience resistance to movies about the Revolutionary period.

As with most of Hollywood in this period, rising costs were a problem. The cast costs for *Unconquered* came to a whopping $715,452. DeMille's script costs had spiked to $146,666 and he went over schedule, shooting for ninety-five days instead of the scheduled eighty-six, accounting for the $394,053 the picture went over budget. The cost analysis reveals that DeMille had a tiered pay scale for writers. Jesse Lasky Jr. was paid only $500 weekly, but writers with more prestigious pedigrees, such as the uncredited Norman Reilly Raine ($2,500 a week) and the credited Charles Bennett ($1,500 a week), got money that the old reliables could only dream about.

DeMille paid his actors the going rate, and then some. Aside from Gary Cooper's $300,000, Paulette Goddard got $111,923 and Boris Karloff $25,000. Friends from the early days got more than their going rate—Robert Warwick was paid $750 for a week's work, while Raymond Hatton got $1,000 for a scene that could only have taken a day or two. And DeMille took very good care of his extended family—Katherine was paid $500 a week for more than nine weeks, in spite of the fact she had a very small part, while Julia Faye was paid $300 a week for 116 pro-rated days, longer than the picture actually took to make.

Unconquered brought DeMille's ongoing flirtation with Paulette Goddard to an end. He was always willing to put an actor in a modest amount of jeopardy if it would help sell the shot, but Goddard flatly refused to stand still while flaming arrows dropped around her. DeMille lost his temper and yelled at her in front of the crew. Although she began to cry, she still wouldn't do the shot. Goddard's double was enlisted. In spite of the fact that the double's wig caught fire, thereby proving Goddard's point, the bloom was off the rose. "Mr. DeMille wouldn't speak to me for years and years," she said.

As late as December 1957, *Unconquered* was still $885,648 in the red. DeMille took the lessons of the film to heart. His next couple of pictures would cost much less and gross much more.

✶

Most of DeMille's staff was off-limits to any other producer at Paramount, but because of the increasing time between his pictures, Anne Bauchens would occasionally cut a picture directed by someone else. Among the interesting movies she edited over the years were William Dieterle's *Love Letters*, Charles Brabin's *The*

Beast of the City, Victor Fleming's *The Wet Parade*, and John Farrow's *Commandos Strike at Dawn*.

A new addition to the staff was Henry Noerdlinger, a Swiss who had been an assistant researcher at MGM and would become DeMille's head of research. Noerdlinger had several interviews with DeMille, who had trouble making up his mind. Finally, DeMille gazed at Noerdlinger over his glasses and said, "Mr. Noerdlinger, do you know they call me a son of a bitch in Hollywood?" Noerdlinger immediately replied, "Mr. DeMille, if you are a son of a bitch or not, I'll find out if I work for you."

He was hired.

Noerdlinger was a moderate Democrat, who viewed with trepidation the picture of J. Edgar Hoover on DeMille's wall, and the monthly visits of FBI agent Richard Hood. Noerdlinger noted DeMille's utter reliance on Gladys Rosson, and grew to appreciate her intelligence. Among the writers, he respected Aeneas MacKenzie and Barré Lyndon. "Frederick Frank and Jesse Lasky Jr. were both weak personalities. Jesse Jr. in particular was a sort of whipping boy. . . . [Frank and Lasky] really were sort of just, if you will allow the expression, DeMille writers."

Noerdlinger was frequently invited to screenings at DeMille's house. "In his house, DeMille was very urbane, very polite. . . . After the film was shown he wanted everybody's opinion. Did you like it, did you not like it, what didn't you like? Who do you think played the best part and so on. And he was always very polite and would not interrupt you. He would let you have your say and he would not give his opinion. But he was quite a different man than when he was wanting information or when he was in the middle of a story conference or when he was on the set."

★

As the inevitable diminishments of age began to add up, DeMille had the small consolation of knowing that the company to which he had devoted the majority of his life was on top of its profession. In 1946, Paramount's net profits rose to $39.2 million on revenues of $170.40 million—a profit twice that of second-place 20th Century Fox. Not only that, but that same year Paramount attained debt-free status—neither Paramount nor any of its subsidiaries had any interest-bearing obligations whatsoever. No other movie company was anywhere near as healthy as Paramount.

DeMille's relationship with the FBI seemed to have cooled slightly. He and Hoover were always trying to arrange a meeting, but the difficulty of reconciling their schedules was a problem. In February 1947, DeMille testified in favor of right to work legislation in Washington, then traveled to New York. He asked if someone from the Bureau could meet him at the train station. "I told him this could be done," wrote agent L. B. Nichols to Clyde Tolson, "and suggested that he wait on the train ramp near the stairway for an Agent to contact him. With

the DeMille touch he stated he would wear a black coat, blue hat and gray gloves."
Once again, Hoover extended an invitation to visit him at the Bureau, and once
again there was a schedule conflict.

After more than ten years of Americana, the flop of *Unconquered* would spur
DeMille to go back to the Bible. In July 1946, DeMille reactivated *Samson and
Delilah* and began story conferences. He hadn't made a biblical story since *The
King of Kings*, or even anything with an overtly religious theme since *The Crusades*,
so it was something of a struggle to convince Paramount that the story had com-
mercial potential. To sway the executives, he showed them a concept painting by
Dan Sayre Groesbeck of a muscular man in a loincloth and a beautiful woman in
an abbreviated costume.

Sold!

Groesbeck made several different sketches for Samson, one almost a Cro-
Magnon man, another a vaguely Tartarish prince. DeMille's initial impulse was to
cast an imposing physical specimen as Samson, perhaps even a bodybuilder, which
necessitated a very big star as Delilah. He mulled over Alida Valli ("bad legs," he
noted after screening one of her movies), Maureen O'Hara, Gene Tierney, Rita
Hayworth, Hedy Lamarr, Rhonda Fleming, Jean Simmons, and Lizabeth Scott.

The list didn't stop there; at one time or another, DeMille considered everybody except Maria Ouspenskaya. There was Lana Turner, Lucille Ball, Susan Hay-
ward, Linda Darnell, Ann Sheridan, Gail Russell, Joan Fontaine, Jennifer Jones,
Jane Russell, Ava Gardner ("she whispers" he muttered after screening *Singapore*),
Jane Greer, Vivian Blaine, and Diana Lynn.

Finally, it came down to either Hedy Lamarr or Jean Simmons, and he chose
Lamarr. Lamarr received $100,000 for ten weeks of work, with $10,000 a week
afterward on a pro-rated basis. Paramount also agreed to a drama coach for Lamarr, at a salary not to exceed $350 a week, plus her usual hairdresser and ward-
robe girl—"It being understood that the coach, hairdresser and wardrobe girl shall
abide by the directions of Mr. C.B. DeMille."

For Samson, DeMille considered Robert Taylor, Glenn Langan, Robert Mit-
chum, Errol Flynn, Rory Calhoun, and Robert Ryan. In the unknown category
were William Hopper, the son of gossip columnist Hedda Hopper and later the
co-star of TV's *Perry Mason*, or John Bromfield.

A strong possibility was the young bodybuilder Steve Reeves. DeMille wanted
Reeves to lose weight, which was easily managed, but he also wanted Reeves to
learn to act, which was another thing entirely. Reeves was handed off to a drama
coach and began eating lunch with DeMille daily.

"Once a week I would have to do a skit for him," remembered Reeves. "I
would study it, and they'd give me other actors to work with. I was on a stage
where they had a glass window between the seats and me, and I couldn't see him.
I did this on and off, I guess, for about three months. Then [DeMille] called me
into his office and said, 'Some days your skits are really good, and some days

they're terrible. It looks like you're preoccupied with something. I'm going to start the picture a month from now, and I'm going to have to use Victor Mature. He's not ideal for it, but he's an experienced actor, and I can depend on him." Later, a dubbed Steve Reeves would become a star in *Hercules* and dozens of other peplum epics made in Italy.

Before DeMille committed to Mature, Henry Wilcoxon made a strong pitch for Burt Lancaster, but DeMille was uneasy about Lancaster's liberal politics. Mature didn't have politics. The political litmus test was extended to most of the actors; when Jesse Lasky Jr. proposed Olive Deering for the part of Miriam, DeMille asked, "What about politics? Where does she stand? In the Kremlin?"

DeMille decided on Mature mostly because of his excellent performance in *Kiss of Death*. As with casting, DeMille was always toying with genuine innovation before retreating to the conventional. For the music score, he attempted to get the rights to Saint-Saëns *Samson et Dalila*, but the publishers refused to license the composition. After that, he went after Aram Khachaturian for five minutes of music to be entitled "Philistines' Bacchanal." That too came to nothing, and DeMille finally commissioned an attractively sultry score from the graceful and reliable Victor Young.

Despite the failure of *Unconquered*, DeMille would no longer have to cross-collateralize his pictures. Beginning with *Samson and Delilah*, Paramount treated each picture as a separate financial entity. Also, as a recognition of more than thirty years of service, DeMille cut in Neil McCarthy for 20 percent of Cecil's 50 percent of the profits. The percentage payments to McCarthy were the beginning of a series of beau gestes that would enrich hundreds of people who worked on DeMille's pictures.

By now, the entire family had grown fond of McCarthy. In 1953, McCarthy would take Cecilia Jr. on a trip to Ireland, and when she wasn't dodging his fast hands, he regaled her with hilarious stories about the early days of Hollywood. When Cecilia told her grandfather about McCarthy's grabby tendencies, he just laughed.

Always specific and attentive when it came to matters of business, in November 1949, DeMille proposed to sell Paramount 37.5 percent of his 50 percent of the profits of his older pictures. Y. Frank Freeman said that he'd immediately cut a check for $2.4 million for that 37.5 percent. DeMille curtly replied that if that was what Freeman thought the pictures were worth, they couldn't do any business. Thus began a long period of bargaining.

Freeman said that there was no point in worrying about the money DeMille might make from television, as he didn't think movies would succeed on television. "If you were putting our *Samson and Delilah* [on television] and Selznick was putting *Gone With the Wind* on television at the same time, you'd have tough opposition," said Freeman.

"Don't brush off television," DeMille replied.

DeMille asked Freeman to tell him personally, i.e., as a friend not an executive, what he thought about the prospective deal. Freeman said that it was very much to the studio's advantage to get that 37.5 percent back, that he had told DeMille a year earlier that most of his pictures would go on and on. The discussion was tabled.

★

Nothing disturbed DeMille's long-standing rituals with Constance. In 1947, she responded to his annual bouquet of lilies of the valley with a note: "My Darling One, The dear lilies of the valley carried me back to that night in Boston when we watched the century come in. For forty-five of those years we have been married. It has been a thrilling, exciting, adventurous life. You have brought me great happiness. Whether through sunshine or occasional shadow my love has grown stronger. Today is a day for presents, but I can only give you again what I gave you many years ago and which has been the strongest thing in my life—All my love. Constance."

A year later, she wrote, "My Darling One, Forty-six years ago I hitched my wagon to a star. Sometimes it was a shooting star, but always one that burned brightly. I watched it and loved it. Its light is my life and always will be. Constance."

It was the last time Constance would write a brief but eloquent testimonial of love for the bumptious young man who had won her heart. Writing itself, and most communication, would soon be impossible.

★

In 1949, DeMille and fifty or so old-timers got together for the opening of a bank on the corner of Selma and Vine, the original site of the Lasky Barn. Jesse Lasky was there, and Mack Sennett, Francis X. Bushman, Elmo Lincoln, William Farnum, and Ramon Novarro. The women included Blanche Sweet, Mae Murray, Arline Pretty, and Theda Bara.

DeMille ordinarily didn't participate in publicity functions for non-DeMille projects, but he was amused by the fact that a bank had opened on the site of his old studio. "I was even in doubt then if there'd be a bank in Hollywood," he said. "We used to cash our checks in those days at Hall's grocery store on Hollywood Boulevard. You might say that the California Bank has replaced Hall's grocery store."

Back at work, DeMille had his staff come up to the house for a screening of George Fitzmaurice's 1926 silent movie *The Son of the Sheik*—Valentino's last picture, in which the woman he loves betrays him to his enemies, who whip and humiliate him. In one scene, the young Sheik unbends a sword that his father (Valentino played both parts) has bent. DeMille replicated that moment, as well as modeling the brawl at the wedding feast after the older picture's tavern fight—the protagonists using tables as shields and hurling lighted lamps at their enemies.

Samson and Delilah began shooting on October 4, 1948, and DeMille soon had cause to regret casting Victor Mature. The actor had lost some weight for the part, but his muscles had no definition so he looked slightly flabby. Mature was an amiable, funny, easygoing lug who refused to do anything risky at all, let alone fight a lion, no matter how tame. DeMille had to stage the scene with Mature's double, Kay Bell, with Mature stepping in to wrestle a stuffed animal, which made DeMille agonizingly uncomfortable and resulted in an awkward, obviously fake scene. The set was closed to insure that no onlookers could report on the ludicrous display.

"I've never known an actor so happily aware of his limitations," Richard Burton would say of Mature. "He rejoiced in them. He liked to joke that he was no actor and he said he had 60 films to prove it. But against him I looked like an amateur." Indeed, whenever Mature got a chance with a good script or director, as with *My Darling Clementine* or *Kiss of Death*, he delivered.

DeMille didn't hate Mature—it was impossible to hate him. He just thought that Mature lacked courage. "The man is the greatest coward ever born," he would snarl. "I've never seen a man or a child as afraid as he." DeMille became uneasy about the entire production; as he wrote in a note, "I have to believe it myself," and all the creative cutting in the world couldn't disguise the cardboard theatrics.

Angela Lansbury won the part of Semadar by knowing how to display herself. "DeMille loved all the color and the trappings and the characters who took attitudes. They were vessels to be filled. He cast you by your feet, not your profile; if you had good feet, you were in. He insisted that everyone wear sandals. You weren't told in so many words, but Edith Head, the costume designer, explained that I'd have to walk around barefoot in his office one day. I wasn't to feel too badly about it; he'd just like to be sure. He'd take a quick look as you walked by and give her a nod if all went well."

For actors of a younger generation, DeMille was a curious figure, an exotic throwback to a world they had never known. As Lansbury would remember, "He really was considered an icon of the business. . . . He thought of himself as a very special kind of person and demanded special treatment and was prepared to play the role of the great Hollywood director to the hilt."

He was also fully prepared to play the role of the genial elder statesman capable of bestowing papal indulgences. "I found him to be a very nice man, actually," remembered Lansbury. "He was a warm and interested person, and he would sit and chat [with] you when you weren't on the set. He wasn't a cold person who didn't wish to be spoken to. He had a kind of very congenial way of dealing with people and younger actresses, and he would talk about the past, as those gentlemen loved to do. He was very approachable, much more so than you would think, but nevertheless you felt you were in The Presence."

Although DeMille was now nearly seventy, his dynamic strength was undiminished. Joe Egli, the Paramount casting director, was epileptic, and when he felt a seizure coming on, he would grab the nearest man in a dangerously strong grip. Many people moved away when Egli went into a seizure, but DeMille always endured the onslaught and held tightly on to the man while others tried to put something in his mouth so he wouldn't bite through his tongue.

Hedy Lamarr never brought much expression to her movies, but she brought something else—that lithe body, that perfect, if frozen, face. Cecilia Jr. witnessed her impact on men, who were often struck dumb by her presence. Yet Lamarr was a pleasant, unaffected woman and Cecilia Jr. liked her a great deal, although DeMille seems to have initially intimidated the actress. Once, he complimented her after she had finished a scene, and she burst into tears, saying, "Why do you always say such terrible things to me?" DeMille was confused, then figured that she must have been concentrating on his body language more than the actual content of what he said, which she seemed to translate into her native German, garbling things in the process. After that incident, he always spoke to Lamarr slowly, with a smile or a fatherly look of concern, and everything went well. Near the end of her life, Lamarr remembered DeMille as "the most delightful man. He let me do what I wanted. I thought he was charming and kind."

DeMille claimed that he walked around Paradise picking up peacock feathers for Delilah's cape. Edith Head denied it, saying "of course he didn't go out and gather dirty bird feathers. My own staff helped collect them and bring them in. We sorted by size, color and brilliance. It took days."

Head fretted for the rest of her life about that peacock cape. "I doubt very much that there were any peacocks around or nearby in the days of Samson and Delilah. Nor would anyone, even Delilah, have worn the kind of cape that I designed—or any of the other costumes for that matter. I supposed only scholars would know that the costumes were not historically correct, but it bothered me terribly." In DeMille's mind, the peacock was his, the feathers were his, it was his concept to use the peacock feathers for Delilah's costume—therefore, the actual labor must also have been his.

The Champion Driver could still emerge at a moment's notice. Russ Tamblyn, cast as the young Saul, had a scene where he was to rush up to Samson in the Temple and tell him he would help Samson fight his way out. In the first take, Tamblyn put his hand in front of his face. "No, no," said DeMille as he came up to him, "put your hand behind your ear."

But on the next take, Tamblyn again put his hand in front of his face. DeMille came up and grabbed the boy's wrist. "*Don't* put your *hand* in front of your *face*," he said, first banging the boy's hand on his own forehead, "put it *behind* your *ear*!" then banging Tamblyn's hand behind his own ear. Since DeMille's mike man had the microphone in front of his face, the directions and the sounds of Tamblyn's hand hitting his head were broadcast throughout the soundstage. "When DeMille walked away, I kind of lost it," Tamblyn remembered. "I started to blubber a little. I was only ten years old—he couldn't do that today."

Lansbury thought that DeMille's outbursts were a combination of impatience, an inability to suffer fools—even nervous ten-year-olds—and not wanting the crew to drift, to focus them on the matter at hand. "He wanted excitement, he wanted drama and he got it."

Henry Wilcoxon, who was playing a part as well as functioning as associate producer, took everything seriously, while Lansbury and George Sanders were off giggling in corners. Sanders kept the mood light by devising filthy limericks, and Victor Mature endeared himself to everybody except Lamarr and DeMille.

DeMille's energy and enthusiasm were infectious and permeated the set, where almost all the film was made—except for some brief second unit footage, the film is rather stagebound. "His calling card," said Angela Lansbury, "was his absolute belief in what he was doing, and the importance of what he was doing. He loved every minute of making those epic pieces, he really loved them. He loved the material, he loved what he was." And the script offers one prime piece of DeMille's own pantheistic belief system when Samson says about God, "He's everywhere. In the wind . . . the sea . . . in the fire."

On January 21, 1949, DeMille wrote to Katherine, in Chicago with Anthony Quinn, who was playing Stanley Kowalski in the road company of A Streetcar Named Desire. January 21 was the last day of shooting on Samson and Delilah and he gave the epistolary equivalent of a philosophical sigh for the good old days: "It is more and more difficult to make a picture today. The different unions require so many people to do one man's work, that no one man can get anywhere near the work to do it, with consequent result of chaos on their part and not too good temper on mine.

"Samson and Delilah looks as though it [has] great beauty, but I haven't seen it altogether yet, so I can't vouch for its drama, although I believe it will be a great picture. It has some big scenes in it. Victor hated Hedy all the way through it, and Hedy returned his emotions in kind. . . . I keep hearing very good things about Tony and wish him the world's best. Embrace my two delightful granddaughters for me . . . and for you, my love always . . ."

Another correspondent around this time included his old aspiring screenwriter Ayn Rand, who had written the script for her novel The Fountainhead. DeMille screened the picture at home and promptly wrote her. "Need I tell you that I liked the philosophy of it? Gary Cooper's final speech at the trial was a summing-up of what we are fighting for in the world today. I might question whether the picture will be a tremendous financial success, but it is pure-blooded and has the sterling qualities that mark all your work."

Rand wrote back, thanking DeMille because "your opinion will always mean a great deal to me, as it did in the days when I first met you." She also told DeMille that the film was doing well at the box office—not strictly true—and that audiences everywhere were breaking into applause at the end of Roark's speech, which she took as an indication of political sympathy rather than commiseration with Gary Cooper for getting through it.

★

Samson and Delilah starts out as another of the series of disappointing pictures DeMille had been making during and after World War II, but something begins to click two thirds of the way through. The theme of sexual abandon leading to physical and emotional subjugation brings the film to life, and Mature delivers a believable performance of guilty masochism and glorious suicide—the ceremony of sex leading to the ceremony of humiliation leading to the ceremony of revenge and suicidal atonement, all experienced by an eyeless man in Gaza.

The special effects were in the hands of Gordon Jennings, who DeMille said was the best technical man he was ever privileged to work with. The bottom third of the Philistine temple was built full-scale. There was also a huge model, thirty-seven feet high. The squat, froglike god Dagon was seventeen feet tall—both statue and model designed to look as if they were over a hundred feet tall. The miniature temple was populated with little puppets about two feet high that were obscured by live action figures matted into the foreground as the temple collapses.

This was the money sequence, and DeMille and Jennings's planning and execution—the temple had to be destroyed three times in order to get enough angles—took a year and $150,000. Paramount showed off a new motion repeater system, an early piece of pre-computer technology that enabled the camera to repeat exactly all pans and tilts when photographing either the miniature or the full-sized set. This technology made it possible to match full-scale and miniature action with great accuracy in the final composites.

DeMille masterfully introduces the temple sequence—the camera first tracks back, then lifts slightly to show girls dancing in front of the base of the temple. Then, slowly, the camera tilts up to reveal the entire vast structure, the miniature joined with the full-size set, first teasing, then revealing—the director proudly holding the shot and daring you to guess how it was done.

Samson is led out, where dwarfs reenact his capture by jabbing at his legs with pitchforks—the ceremony of humiliation. Delilah leads him to the pillars, promises she'll save herself, but stays behind, a few feet away, eager to join him in his destruction. As he struggles and strains against the stone, the music stops at the first crack, as does the laughter of the crowd. For the rest of the sequence, DeMille uses no music, only natural sounds and screams. As the statue of Dagon falls, the temple crumbles, obliterating the hated Philistines as well as Samson and Delilah.

The final destruction is so massive, so desired by the lovers themselves, that it constitutes a happy ending—a very Wagnerian triumph achieved through death. The climax redeems everything wrong with the film—its wordiness, the coarseness of some of the conception and execution, with the Philistines celebrating at the wedding "like cowhands on payday," as one critic scoffed.

At the end, DeMille has Victor Mature lit and made up to resemble a ravaged, semi-muscular Christ, except this is a Christ without doubt—he has sinned, knows it, and is willing to pay the price. As George MacDonald Fraser wrote, "This . . . was one of Hollywood's great moments—two minutes twenty seconds, to be exact, from the time the first tiny crack came at the foot of the pillar . . . and then the eerie silence, another crack, and the whole colossal structure coming down in awful ponderous ruin. We had visualized, from childhood, a sort of roofed cathedral; DeMille, with authority, gave us a huge open temple, the great god Dagon with a fire in his belly toppling on the Philistine mob. It was sublime and worth whatever it cost." And then Fraser summed up the entire latter part of DeMille's career with open appreciation: "It may not have been great art, but we had seen Samson and Delilah."

The reviews were, to use the most generous term, mixed. On the upside, *Esquire* said that "This, friends, is an epic; a tremendous, stupendous Cecil B. DeMille production with no holds barred." Others were put off by the broadness, but were gradually won over: "The Technicolor is brilliant and beautiful," wrote one critic, "the sets are stupendous, the costumes (there were 5 costumers) fabulous, the battle scenes awesome, the love scenes tantalizing and the religious message as delicate as a sledge hammer." *Variety*, usually a DeMille supporter, noted that "It's a fantastic picture for this era in its size, in its lavishness, in the corniness of its storytelling and in its old-fashioned technique. But it adds up to first-class entertainment."

A particularly discerning review came from the highbrow *Hudson Review*, whose critic, George Barbarow, admired "the constant use of drastic visual contrast throughout the picture [that is] thoroughly appropriate to the representation of conflicts that are in themselves merciless and barbaric. . . . What is significant about this eye-blasting contrast is its harmony with the spirit of the Old Testament, pregnant with wrath, and saturated with blood."

Samson and Delilah was a smash hit, grossing $11.3 million against a cost of $3.09 million—$1.5 million less than was spent on *Unconquered*. The economies were effected largely in two areas—script, where DeMille spent only $112,865, nearly a third less than he had spent on *Unconquered*, and the cast, where the costs came to $463,005, $200,000 less than on *Unconquered*. Factoring in a seventy-two-day shooting schedule, the picture was made very economically. This was part of the reason that, as of June 1958, there was a net profit of $3.9 million to be split between the studio and DeMille.

★

On July 27, 1948, DeMille had attended the funeral of the largely forgotten, alcoholic D. W. Griffith. Lillian Gish remembered that only six people came to the funeral home the night before the funeral; one was DeMille, another was John Ford. For the funeral itself, where there were sure to be cameras, there was a crowd.

Sitting there, DeMille must have thought about the meaning of Griffith's life, and the circumstances of his death, about roads not taken, and why he, alone of all the directors of his generation, maintained a preeminent position in the industry.

DeMille's reputation as a man who remembered and honored his peers was reinforced in October 1950, when he received a panicked letter from Erich von Stroheim. The actor-director reported that his U.S. citizenship was on the verge of being revoked because of a technicality in the law stating that naturalized citizens could have their citizenship revoked if they resided in another country for five continuous years.

"I beg of you to take cognizance of my case for justice' sake," wrote von Stroheim, "and do whatever you can to have section 404 of the Nationality Act of 1940 repealed as quickly as possible during the next session of Congress." Von Stroheim went on to explain that he had moved to France in order to make a living because "through the advent of sound in films and on account of my accent it became more and more difficult for me to secure employment as director and actor in Hollywood." He moved to France in 1936, where there were plentiful acting offers, returned to America when the war broke out in 1939, and went back to Europe when the war was over, with the exception of a few months in Italy and, from March until August 1949, the shooting of *Sunset Boulevard*.

Von Stroheim went on to call the law un-American, un-democratic and un-constitutional because "it differentiates between a born citizen and a naturalized one." In a handwritten P.S. at the bottom of the letter, von Stroheim added: "If you would want to be exceedingly kind you could let your secretary make three copies of the enclosed proposed letter and have one copy sent to the Chairman of the Committee on the Judiciary, House of Representatives, Wash. D.C. . . . and one to your Senator and the third to your Congressman. Thanks!"

Although it's possible that DeMille had never met von Stroheim—they have no scenes together in *Sunset Boulevard*—he took up the cudgel and wrote several letters. The first one, in October, seemed to have an almost immediate effect—the State Department indefinitely extended von Stroheim's passport in November. The second letter was written in January 1951, after INS inspectors made some further inquiries about von Stroheim and DeMille's support of him.

"I have known Mr. von Stroheim for many years as a fine artist in his profession of acting and directing," wrote DeMille on January 8. "I was happy to say a good word for him to various members of congress. . . . I felt that there were special circumstances in Mr. von Stroheim's case which might justify an exemption from the rigid application of the general law, if such an exemption were possible. . . . I am very glad to add to my previous efforts this word of recommendation that Mr. von Stroheim be given every possible consideration; in view of his good record in his profession, the services to his country rendered by him through his motion picture portrayals in the period of World War I and by his two sons through their military service in the period of World War II, and the special circumstances which make it necessary for him to remain abroad in order to earn his living."

The matter was soon closed; von Stroheim retained his American citizenship to the end of his life.

But by then, DeMille was engaged in a battle that, appropriately enough, was full of Old Testament overtones.

19

There is almost nothing about politics in DeMille's correspondence of the 1910s, and little more in the 1920s. Even in the 1930s, when he went to Russia and the world was plunged into a depression, his allegiance to the Republican Party was nominal, as was proven when he voted for Roosevelt in 1932, although by 1937 he was sharing information about communist rallies with the local Chamber of Commerce, especially if it involved studio labor.

But his fight with the American Federation of Radio Artists during World War II pushed DeMille further to the right, and there are various notes in DeMille's handwriting that indicate just how far he swerved:

"At the time of election the voter should take a loyalty oath at the same time he receives his ballot."

"The happiest man in the world to see a continuance of the Truman regime would be Joseph Stalin."

Before the AFRA blowup, DeMille had never avoided hiring left-wing writers. As late as 1942, he had both John Howard Lawson and Albert Maltz working on the script for *Rurales*. Both men would be among the Hollywood Ten, the writers blacklisted during the postwar Red Scare, and Lawson was the leader of the Hollywood communists, as DeMille surely would have known. But after the AFRA matter, for a number of years potential DeMille writers as well as actors were thoroughly vetted for untoward political sympathies.

DeMille's attitude toward his employees was always, as his assistant Donald Hayne would put it, "outmoded paternalism." Employer-employee relations for DeMille had been codified by the Ludlum steel works in his New Jersey boyhood. Old Mr. Ludlum owned and managed the mill, lived in the same town as his employees, knew each and every one of them by name, and worshipped alongside them in Christ Church every Sunday. As far as DeMille was concerned, unions were necessary only because there weren't enough owners like Mr. Ludlum.

Similarly, Hayne believed that while DeMille had seamlessly transitioned to glorious Technicolor in his work, his mind remained a black and white instrument. "Communism," Hayne wrote, "is black. Therefore, any kind of anti-Communism is white—except Socialism, since Socialism and Communism are both 'left,' and 'left' is bad. Since 'left' is bad, 'right' must be good; which explains some of the political affinities of a man whose heart, I suspect, would find more in common with some of those whom he has mentally labelled as 'left.' . . . Partly, the simple vigor of DeMille's convictions, right or wrong, stems from a deep need in his nature: He must succeed."

On February 7, 1944, the leading edge of right-wing politics in Hollywood was created when the Motion Picture Alliance for the Preservation of American Ideals was organized in the ballroom at the Beverly Wilshire Hotel. Sam Wood was elected president; other initial members were Morrie Ryskind, Walt Disney, Ward Bond, Donald Crisp, Gary Cooper, King Vidor, George Marshall, Leo McCarey, Michael Curtiz, Victor Fleming, Ginger Rogers, Barbara Stanwyck, John Ford, John Lee Mahin, Pat O'Brien, Robert Taylor, Irene Dunne, John Wayne, Robert Montgomery, Adolphe Menjou, Roy Brewer, Hedda Hopper, Dimitri Tiomkin, and DeMille. Ford would eventually have his name removed from alliance stationery, but seems to have maintained a loose association, if only through old friends Ward Bond and John Wayne.

The alliance became heavily involved in the 1944 presidential election. Hollywood's political left was mostly headquartered at Warner Bros., while the right was predominantly at MGM. Industry Republicans mounted a rally for their candidate, Thomas Dewey, staged by DeMille at the 100,000 seat Los Angeles Memorial Coliseum. Ginger Rogers, Hollywood vice chair for Dewey, called it "a mobilization against the New Deal."

Roosevelt won reelection by three million votes. A small group from the Motion Picture Alliance met afterward to assess the damage. Walt Disney, Sam Wood, Clark Gable, and Gary Cooper believed that if the electorate wouldn't cooperate, then Washington would have to do the job. The House Committee on Un-American Activities would be solicited to ferret out communists.

By July 1945, Democratic congressman John Rankin of Mississippi was quoted in the Congressional Record as saying, "I want to say . . . that these appeals [for a congressional investigation] are coming to us from the best people in California, some of the best producers in California are very much disturbed because they are having to take responsibility for some of the loathsome, filthy, insinuating, un-American currents that are running through the various pictures sent throughout the country to be shown to the children of the nation."

DeMille was not one of those agitating for a government investigation; as he explained to anybody that would listen, there were communists in the steel industry, the publishing industry, and in every business you could think of. Why single out the movies?

No matter. The movies were about to be singled out in a spectacular fashion.

★

The forces of reaction had been kept more or less at bay by Franklin Roosevelt's immense popularity, but his death in April 1945 began a cascading series of events that led to the blacklist era. By September of 1946, the *Hollywood Reporter* carried an approving story headlined HOLLYWOOD STARS ARE BLASTED AS 'RED' BY AFL OFFICIAL, wherein a vice president of the American Federation of Labor threatened the movie industry with a nationwide picketing of stars he branded as communists: Edward G. Robinson, Myrna Loy, Burgess Meredith, and James Cagney.

At the same time, the Hollywood unions began engaging in political wars of their own. The right-wing IATSE (International Alliance of Theatrical Stage Employees and Moving Picture Operators) was violently opposed to the leftist CSU (Conference of Studio Unions). In 1946, the CSU called a strike that came close to bringing Hollywood to a standstill. The strike focused on Disney and Warner Bros. and hardened an already divisive situation. It was essentially a jurisdictional strike between two unions that didn't really involve management, but strike leaders were determined to close the studios and halt production.

Most of Paramount was deserted, but DeMille crossed the picket lines and hunkered down at the studio with his staff, sleeping on cots in the office. From his vantage point, DeMille could only say I told you so. "We had to struggle [to get] people into our plant to get them to work," he said wearily. "It was like a besieged army."

DeMille's feelings about communism were synopsized in a speech he gave in June 1947 in New York City:

> We have let abuses of freedom grow up in our own midst—and perhaps the worst abuse of all was letting ourselves be taken in by the bait of selling freedom for supposed security. We started toward the precipice when we began to look on America as a land of security instead of as a land of opportunity; when we began to think that being safe was better than being free. . . .
>
> We shall be accused of being "red-baiters." Good. That is a designation we can wear proudly. Knowing the reds for what they are—the servile lackeys of a brutal conspiracy against freedom—I do not know any more useful or patriotic occupation than red-baiting.. . . .
>
> The great majority of our union members are not communists by any means. . . . In my profession, I work and talk and eat with my fellow union members every day. They aren't strange foreign creatures. They are fine Americans, most of them. They want their homes and their children and their country to be American. . . .
>
> [But] when the communists have captured his union—as they have

many unions—the individual union member, regardless of his own fine Americanism, has become a pawn in the game of Soviet power.

DeMille's anger had led him to a closed loop of illogic—to be against the open shop was to be in potential thrall to communism, to be against DeMille was to be in mortal combat with the American ideal. The squabble with AFRA had awakened the political warrior in DeMille and it would lead directly to the epic fight for the heart and mind of the Directors Guild in 1950.

★

In 1947, the conservative Ohio Republican senator Robert Taft drafted the Taft-Hartley Act, which outlawed several key tactics that had been used successfully by unions in and out of Hollywood over the previous fifteen years. The act mandated loyalty oaths for all federal employees and union officers, and forbade communists from serving in labor management. President Harry Truman called Taft-Hartley the "Slave-Labor Act," but it passed over his veto.

That same year saw the House Committee on Un-American Activities first sojourn into Hollywood and the Hollywood Ten blacklist—the beginning of a world of secrecy, guilt by association, the prevailing assumption that a citizen under suspicion was disloyal until proven loyal. Ultimately, it led to the denial of employment to people found on any list for any reason, including error or vendetta—this in a town where the FBI's roster of possible communists never totaled more than 324 out of a workforce of 34,000.

By this time, DeMille's influence had gone beyond his patriarchal presence as the man who had founded Hollywood. Because of his seniority, and the cliquishness of the founding generation of Hollywood elders, he had a great deal of influence within the Directors Guild as well as industrial America.

The list of initial contributors to the DeMille Foundation ranged from General Motors ($20,000) and Chrysler ($10,000) to smaller contributions from General Mills; Allis-Chalmers; the Los Angeles Times; the Atchison, Topeka & Santa Fe Railway, as well as individual conservatives such as Frederick Crawford, Leonard Firestone, and Richard K. Mellon. (DeMille's personal donations were minor—seed money of $1,000 in 1945, and another $1,000 in 1955, with some smaller donations in between.)

The contributors' list clearly shows that the motivating forces behind the foundation were conservative activists and corporations with a vested interest in fighting unions.

Although DeMille, of all people, knew full well that no mere screenwriter or actor could inject radical politics into a script because of the close supervision endemic to the studio system, the right wing nevertheless worked overtime to create the impression that hundreds, if not thousands of people on Moscow's payroll were poisoning the minds of Americans with unwarranted attacks, in turn provoking the termite danger—communists, assiduously working for decades in Hollywood and elsewhere, were undermining the foundational structure of America.

When Joseph L. Mankiewicz was elected president of the Directors Guild in 1950—after having been nominated by none other than Cecil B. DeMille—he signed the loyalty oath mandated by Taft-Hartley. He was, however, adamantly against a mandatory loyalty oath for the rank and file, which was not required under Taft-Hartley or any other law. DeMille began agitating for the mandatory oath, and, moreover, suggested that directors file reports on the politics of their employees that could be kept on file for prospective employers.

Hedda Hopper, the Madame Defarge of the Red Scare, backed DeMille and also endorsed an industrywide loyalty oath, adding that "Those who aren't loyal should be put in concentration camps before it's too late."

At Paramount, as at most other studios, the hierarchy was uneasy; political beliefs were in conflict with atavistic impulses for fair play. "I don't think it's OK," Barney Balaban told his daughter about the blacklisting. "There's something about it that's OK, but there's something about it that's terrible, and I don't quite understand it yet."

Joe Mankiewicz's first inkling that something was being fomented at the Directors Guild came courtesy of George Seaton, who was sitting in the office of Y. Frank Freeman when DeMille came through the door. "Mr. Mankiewicz was very eloquent last night, and I was very eloquent in return," announced DeMille, referring to a preliminary meeting about a Guild-wide loyalty oath. "I think I'll straighten out our young president. He's a good boy, so I think he'll see the error of his ways. He's just feeling his oats a bit."

"Look, C.B.," said Freeman, "I know Joe Mankiewicz. He used to work here. He's no more a Communist than you are."

"Frank, I know he's not a Communist. But I know that his father, a professor, campaigned for Morris Hilquit, a Socialist, in the New York mayoralty campaign of 1914, and those tendencies are very often inherited."

That year DeMille hosted Wisconsin senator Joseph McCarthy at his table in the commissary. When DeMille, his entourage, and McCarthy entered the commissary at 12:30, they found it nearly deserted. Writers were at a café, across the street, actors were in their dressing rooms, and crews had brown-bagged it. "Mr. McCarthy made it clear," remembered Henry Wilcoxon, "that this simply confirmed his view that Hollywood had a great deal to hide."

As the lunch went on, it was suggested that perhaps Wilcoxon could do a little light reconnaissance for McCarthy while at Guild and social functions, because anybody who was not for McCarthy was obviously against America. Later, DeMille would even suggest that Wilcoxon should have McCarthy to dinner at his house, but Wilcoxon's wife refused.

As the year wore on, meetings cascaded into more meetings. At one, Frank Freeman announced that he would sign a loyalty oath offered by anyone. "Even the Ku Klux Klan?" asked Dore Schary. As Schary proceeded to enumerate his reasons against a loyalty oath, DeMille took notes.

All this was the preliminary. The main event was about to get underway.

★

Power at the Directors Guild of that time resided not with the membership, or even with the president—a largely ceremonial position—but with the fifteen-member board of directors, which was described by one historian as "self-perpetuating." The board ran the Guild, and the board was a gentleman's club with little accountability. As a powerful member of the board, DeMille had sponsored Mankiewicz's installation in early 1950, possibly because the younger man, while nominally a Republican, had no interest in political activism.

DeMille's proposal for a mandatory loyalty oath was defeated by a vote not of the general membership, but of the board: Seymour Berns, Claude Binyon, Frank Borzage, Clarence Brown, David Butler, Merian Cooper, DeMille, Harvey Dwight, John Ford, Tay Garnett, Walter Lang, Frank McDonald, John F. Murphy, Mark Robson, William Seiter, Richard Wallace, and John Waters. At that point, DeMille should have let the matter lie, because, with a few exceptions, it was a conservative board, including some men—Merian Cooper, Clarence Brown—who were every bit as conservative as DeMille.

At the meeting, John Ford announced that he had asked Cooper, his partner in Argosy Productions and a brigadier general in the Air Force, about the mandatory loyalty oath. Cooper said it was a blacklist. That was good enough for Ford. If Merian Cooper said it was a blacklist, then "it's a goddamn blacklist," and Ford was against it.

But DeMille was determined that the Directors Guild would be the first craft union to institute a loyalty oath. Partly, this may have been because Frank Freeman told DeMille that he thought this would have a steamroller effect—that if the Directors Guild instituted an oath, all the other guilds in Hollywood would fall in line as well.

It seems never to have occurred to DeMille, who had given up over $100,000 a year to fight for the right to work, that he was promulgating a platform that said in effect that anybody who didn't agree with him would inevitably lose their right to work.

The internal dynamics of the Guild were split. Beneath Joe Mankiewicz were Al Rogell and Lesley Selander as, respectively, first and second vice presidents, with Vernon Keays as secretary. All three were conservative and on DeMille's side in the matter of the loyalty oath. Many of the men who would line up in back of DeMille were marginal directors of B movies, and it's certainly possible that there was an element of careerist toadying in their willingness to serve DeMille.

DeMille's plan was to put the question of a loyalty oath up to the general membership. It was to be an open ballot, so DeMille and his people would know where everyone stood: for or against, up or down. To implement their plan, they decided to wait until Joe Mankiewicz was on vacation in Europe. Although DeMille had supported Mankiewicz when he ran for president, he obviously felt that the younger man would ignore him, otherwise he would have waited a couple of weeks until Mankiewicz was back in town.

The loyalty oath was headed "Affidavit of Noncommunist Guild Member." It went on to assert that the signer was a member of the Directors Guild and was not a member of the Communist Party, or affiliated with such a party: "I do not believe in and I am not a member of nor do I support any organization that believes in or teaches the overthrow of the United States Government by force or by any illegal or unconstitutional methods."

In August 1950, Mankiewicz left the country, and DeMille mobilized the board, mailing out numbered open ballots—so tabs could be kept on how each individual voted—with boxes to be checked "Yes" or "No" underneath the proposed oath. The results, unsurprisingly, were 547 in favor of the loyalty oath, 14 against, with 57 abstentions.

Mankiewicz returned from vacation and was outraged to discover what had happened in his absence, expressing his fury to anyone who asked and many who didn't, invoking the term "blacklist." DeMille replied that what he was proposing would not in fact constitute a blacklist; people who refused to sign the oath would simply be regarded as "not in good standing," a designation usually limited to DG members who didn't pay their dues. They would, he insisted, still be able to work at any studio that wanted to hire them.

Mankiewicz didn't buy it. "This guy's un-American, but you can hire him— that's a blacklist," he protested at an angry board meeting on October 9. "It seems to me that kind of thing only happens in Moscow." At a lunchtime conversation, DeMille explained his position to his staff: "My purpose . . . is to tell the President of the United States that the Screen Directors Guild is 98½% American and willing to sign a statement of loyalty; that 1 and ½% are not. Should I include the Guild's president in that 1½%?"

During an October meeting of the board, DeMille pointed out to Mankiewicz that only fourteen members had voted against the loyalty oath. "Are you going to be on the side of the 14?" he asked.

"I'm on the side of all the members," replied Mankiewicz. "They didn't have a chance to discuss this."

"Now is the time," said DeMille, "for good Americans to stand up and be counted."

"Very true," said Mankiewicz, "but who appointed you to do the counting?" Mankiewicz went on to say that DeMille's plan to send the names of those who wouldn't sign the loyalty oath to the studio heads was a blacklist. "And your open ballot. That's not right. It's un-American."

Mankiewicz was adamant. DeMille's faction then attempted a recall petition to negate Mankiewicz's presidency. As the DeMille faction wrote in a law-suit, "Mr. Mankiewicz has . . . pitted himself against the legal governing body of the Guild, its Board of Directors. He repudiates the democratic vote of its membership. . . . The issue is whether Mr. Mankiewicz is to rule the Guild." Bringing the lawsuit were DeMille, Clarence Brown, David Butler, Frank Capra, Tay Garnett, Henry King, George Marshall, Leo McCarey, Frank McDonald, Al-bert Rogell, William Seiter, Lesley Selander, Andrew Stone, Richard Wallace, and John Waters.

The recall needed a 60 percent vote to pass. The DeMille faction sent out telegrams announcing the recall on October 13, explaining that, according to the bylaws, the vice president was empowered to act in the absence of the president, and Mankiewicz had, after all, been out of the country when this pressing matter that couldn't be tabled came up. The recall ballots were quickly mimeographed; they read "This is a ballot to recall Joe Mankiewicz. Sign here—yes." There was no space for a "no" vote. Once again each ballot was numbered so the voters could be identified.

Fifty-five members of the Guild were scratched off the list because it was felt that they were Mankiewicz partisans. Motorcycle messengers were dispatched on the night of October 12 to distribute the recall ballots, while DeMille partisans worked the phones to sway those who might be in doubt. Andrew Stone told one director that he "had a son in Korea with the army, and we all feel that Joe Mankiewicz is not only destroying the Guild but sticking a knife in the backs of all our boys who are over there fighting for us in Korea."

Mankiewicz was in a screening room at Fox when his brother Herman walked in. "What do you have in common with Andrew Johnson?" Herman inquired rhetorically, then answered his own question. "You're being impeached, my boy."

A quick response was necessary, and word of a counter-petition must have reached the DeMille faction because the offices of the Guild were unaccountably closed the next day, in a stalling tactic. As Robert Parrish remembered, "The peti-tion [to recall the recall petition] had to be signed, notarized and turned in to the executive secretary of the Guild before the DeMille recall votes were counted or all was lost."

Under the bylaws, a petition had to be circulated calling for a special meet-ing of the full membership to consider the recall of the DeMille petition. "It was a Friday," remembered Joseph Losey, "and we had to get [twenty-five] sig-natures by midnight to head [DeMille] off. I remember it was a warm day and Fred Zinnemann, John Huston and I and various people decided to get together a group of directors at Chasen's at seven that night and we spent the afternoon rounding up others. The meeting occurred and Mankiewicz insisted on bringing [attorney] Martin Gang. When we gathered we found we had twenty-three or twenty-one, not twenty-five."

Throughout Beverly Hills and Bel-Air, homes, restaurants, and gin mills were scoured for directors willing to sign the petition to save Joe Mankiewicz's presidency. The men who finally signed included John Huston, Michael Gordon, Andrew Marton, George Seaton, Mark Robson, Richard Brooks, John Sturges, Robert Wise, Robert Parrish, Richard Fleischer, Fred Zinnemann, Joseph Losey, William Wyler, Jean Negulesco, Nicholas Ray, Billy Wilder, Don Hartman, Charles Vidor, and John Farrow. (One of the most interesting aspects of this entire brawl is its generational nature; the most conservative members of the Guild tended to be the industry pioneers, while the centrists or liberals were twenty to thirty years younger.)

That wasn't all. Mankiewicz proposed that "If we're going to fight this vicious thing we've got to be clean ourselves, and I suggest that we jointly declare that we are not members of the Communist party." It was a classic Catch-22—Mankiewicz couldn't be saved without twenty-five people acquiescing to the very thing to which they were adamantly opposed.

This threw everybody into an uproar; people were against having to do what the DeMille faction was demanding in order to fight the DeMille faction. Martin Gang leaned over to Joe Losey and said, "I don't know whether you're in the [Communist Party] or not but you're not under oath so it won't be perjury—sign it!" Eventually, everyone came around and signed the non-communist oath.

"You can't imagine the emotions," remembered Richard Brooks, who was at Chasen's that night. "Some men were weeping. That's how scared they were."

Everyone seems to have known that the resolution of the conflict would not be through the courts, but through direct confrontation. The counterpetition was notarized and filed in time. The special meeting of the entire membership of the Directors Guild was set for Sunday night, October 22, 1950, at 8 P.M. in the Crystal Room of the Beverly Hills Hotel.

The week before the meeting, DeMille called Mankiewicz to his office and told him that his group had rethought its position. They were willing to resubmit the loyalty oath on a closed ballot. In return, they wanted Mankiewicz to sign a statement of what DeMille called "contrition." Mankiewicz responded with some choice words and stormed out.

Rumors swept through town that DeMille might resign from the board. The day before the meeting, on October 21, George Sidney called DeMille's office and left a message that resigning would be a sign of weakness and he hoped that nobody on the board would do it. Donald Hayne told Sidney that DeMille had no intention of resigning.

Before the October 22 meeting, DeMille was regarded as a principled conservative; afterward, he was regarded as an antidemocratic ideologue and quite possibly a bigot. The destructive echoes of the October 22 meeting have echoed down into the succeeding century, damaging DeMille's reputation. Joe Mankiewicz walked into the meeting convinced that he was going to be deposed. DeMille's faction had the momentum, he believed, and he suspected that they also had the votes.

In later years, Mankiewicz would tell his son Tom that he believed the entire affair was the result of a misapprehension on DeMille's part. The two men had an amicable social relationship, and DeMille knew Mankiewicz was a registered Republican. Therefore DeMille believed that Mankiewicz would support the efforts of the Republican majority on the board. What DeMille didn't know was that Mankiewicz was a liberal Republican—what would come to be known as a Rockefeller Republican. (Later in life, Mankiewicz would change his registration to Democrat, and become a notably liberal one at that.)

In keeping with the practice of the Guild for the previous several years, no official transcript was made of the meeting, which meant that reports of the meeting have tended heavily toward the anecdotal—accurate only in the broadest, emotional sense. But there was indeed a stenographer present, and the transcript has survived in a private archive.

✶

Joe Mankiewicz made the opening statement: "This meeting can become very easily the most important in our history. It is entirely up to us whether we shall remember this night with satisfaction and pride or whether it shall be remembered as the night we lost the Guild."

After a thorough and largely impartial recitation of the events that had led up to the meeting, Mankiewicz turned the floor over to DeMille.

"Mr. President," he began, "I first want to compliment the President on his splendid presentation of events that have led to an unfortunate but not an irreparable situation. . . . I have come before you neither to praise Caesar or to bury him, and I have only one interest at heart in this, and that is the interest of the Guild. There is nothing I want from the Guild. There is nothing the Guild can give me. I do not seek any office, nor would I accept any office . . . my race is nearing its end. It is at the last lap, so that I have nothing to gain but the welfare of this body."

DeMille had obviously taken the temperature of the room and hadn't liked the results. He was rather more conciliatory than was his custom. "It has never been the Board's intention to create a blacklist. The only purpose of the oath is to give assurance to the men who join this Guild that they are joining a clean organization, to give assurance to the industry and to the country that the men who directed their picture are not . . . ashamed to declare their loyalty to the United States. Is that too much to ask? . . . I would be happy to take that oath once a week.

"No one has accused Mr. Mankiewicz of being a Communist. When I nominated him for President of this Guild, I thought he was a good American and I still think he is a good American. As an individual member of this Guild, he has every right to oppose this by-law, and he had every right to refuse to take the oath, but he had no right to use his office as President to obstruct the will of the Guild and to cast forth damaging accusations at its Board of Directors and its members. That and that alone was the reason for the move to recall Mr. Mankiewicz."

So far DeMille was on reasonably solid ground, and was arguing his case cogently and well. And then he made his fatal mistake.

"Who are some of these gentlemen [signing the petition in support of Mankiewicz]? One of them was Chairman of a testimonial dinner for the Hollywood 'Ten.' Five of them were on the Committee for the First Amendment. One of them was on the Board of the Actor's Lab. Two of them were on the Committee of Arts, Sciences and Professions and another on its predecessor, the Hollywood Democratic Committee. One was a sponsor of the Hollywood League for Democratic Action. The Freedom from Fear Committee was represented. So was the old league of American Writers' School. Troubled waters attract strange specimens sometimes. I am making no accusations against anybody, least of all Mr. Mankiewicz."

Among others, DeMille was referring to John Huston, chairman of a testimonial dinner for the Hollywood Ten; George Seaton, who had served on the Committee for the First Amendment, as had Billy Wilder and William Wyler. George Seaton was also on the executive board of the Screen Writers Guild, while Michael Gordon had been on the executive board of the Actor's Lab, Richard Brooks had been a member of the Committee for the First Amendment and had sponsored a benefit rally for the Ten. Lastly, Mark Robson had served as Orson Welles's film cutter, aside from contributing in 1948 to an unnamed communist front organization.

It was around this point that many who were present would, in later years, claim that DeMille read out the names of the men who had signed the petition to call the meeting, emphasizing, in many cases, their foreign origins—"Villiam Vyler," "Joseph Mankievitch," etc.

The implication of a Jewish cabal behind Mankiewicz has been Exhibit A in the case against DeMille as an anti-Semite. But the transcript of the meeting contains no such occurrence, nor does anybody else in the meeting refer to such a moment. In fact, at one point DeMille explicitly states that he has named no names, named only the dubious (in his mind) associations of some of the petitioners, which is confirmed by a statement Vincent Sherman made later in the meeting.

In all of the extensive literature devoted to the meeting, nobody ever claimed that DeMille had done any such thing until 1984, when Fred Zinnemann published his memoirs—and Fred Zinnemann was not at the meeting. It's only after 1984 that Mankiewicz and other men who were there take up the story.

There are several possibilities:

1. DeMille did in fact mention names and the stenographer missed it. This seems highly unlikely.

2. DeMille had done such a thing at an earlier meeting not involving the full membership and word leaked out.

3. It's an urban legend.

What is certain is that the story is the linchpin for DeMille's ascribed anti-Semitism, even though the transcript made by a professional court reporter contains no such record. Given the increasingly violent tenor of the meeting, a blatant racial slur would have provoked outrage, if not an outright melee. Much later in the meeting, Rouben Mamoulian stood up to say how awful it was that he felt he had to apologize for having an accent. It's probable that, decades later, Mamoulian's remark about his accent in the face of DeMille's thundering, 100 percent Americanism and naming of possible communist front associations was converted by time and the trick of memory into an actual speech that strongly implied anti-Semitism.

What actually turned the tide against DeMille was his tactic of guilt by association. In the margins of the surviving transcript, someone has written "booing starts" after DeMille's speech. DeMille forged ahead. "Is it their object to split this Guild wide open so that the Daily Worker and Pravda can gloat over the spectacle? Do they want to widen the breach between the President and the Board of Directors until members of the Board will resign and leave the door open for these repudiated elements to return to power?"

DeMille offered a resolution—that the balloting to recall Mankiewicz be closed and that all the ballots be destroyed. In effect, he was backing down, not to the extent of banishing the issue of the loyalty oath, but in letting Mankiewicz stay on.

As DeMille ended his speech, Robert Wise was very nervous. "DeMille was a very articulate guy," he remembered. The question of who would carry the day was very much in doubt.

At this point, the meeting was thrown open to the membership for debate. For the next four hours, famous and powerful men stood up and expressed bafflement, rage, hostility, and sorrow that things had come to such a terrible pass. John Cromwell said that he was "astounded at the acrimonious accusations, the unfounded accusations of Mr. DeMille." Don Hartman said that he resented "paper hat patriots who stand up and holler 'I am an American' and that no one else is."

An openly contemptuous John Huston asked DeMille, "In your tabulations of the 25 [petitioners] how many men were in uniform? How many were in uniform when you were wrapping yourself in the flag?" Delmer Daves stood up and said, "I am a Republican too, Mr. DeMille. My children are fourth-generation Californians, and I resent beyond belief the things that you said as you summarized the 25 men. . . . I think it was disgraceful."

Leo McCarey, who had signed the petition to recall Mankiewicz, used a particularly unfortunate metaphor when he said, "it was a fire, and maybe we used the wrong nozzle." Joe Mankiewicz retorted that, "as far as using the wrong nozzle is concerned, I am the only one who got wet."

And Rouben Mamoulian announced that he was "a little nervous standing up here tonight . . . it is my accent. I have an accent. . . . I don't remember any time when a fellow director had to get up and before expressing what he had to say he had to declare himself to be an honest, reputable man. He has to mention how far back he goes of any generations to be born in this country. That leaves me hanging in the air, because I was not born in this country. I came here and I am a naturalized citizen. . . . I wanted to be an American, and I would not want anyone challenging my being a good American so I will forget the embarrassing feeling or being shy about my accent.

"I have known Mr. DeMille for a long time, not very well. He has always been most cordial to me. . . . Tomorrow it is I who may be the subject of your remarks. I think it is wrong for a member of the Guild within the family to accuse anyone even anonymously without actual data or actual direct knowledge, because it is that that suddenly sows seeds of a terrific mistrust, fear and anxiety and suspicion."

George Seaton stood up and reminded DeMille of his meeting with Frank Freeman, who told him "C.B., Joe Mankiewicz is no more a Communist than you are."

That opened up yet another point of anger at DeMille—he had served as a mole for powerful producers—the bête noir of the Directors Guild. Seaton's story prompted William Wellman to stand up. "I don't like to go to dinner, the very few times I go to dinner, and hear producers and actors and their wives talk about a subject that concerns the Directors Guild, and they knew a great deal more about it than I did. Where they got it, I don't know. . . . Let Mr. Mankiewicz stay as President. He is a good guy. He is very capable."

George Stevens, a man of integrity respected by left and right alike, stood up and gave a background briefing about the recall petition. "Mr. Mankiewicz' recall was done in such a manner that no Board member that wasn't part of it could find out anything about it. It was rigged, and it was organized, and it was supposed to work. And, gentleman, it hasn't." Stevens then made the perfectly valid point that the board had ventured far outside its mandate; that it was more focused on communism than on defending the rights of directors.

With DeMille's offer to take back the recall petition still hanging in the air, Don Hartman asked if DeMille would be willing to rescind the guilt-by-association charges he had made against the signers of the petition, "which were just as unfounded, which were made without any investigation, which were done by insinuation and association, which is the method of rabble-rousers."

DeMille obstinately refused. "The organizations to which they belong . . .

[are] a matter of record in the Capitol," he responded. "This is not guess-work or hearsay. And the members seem to have admitted membership in these organizations . . . one of those organizations is listed as subversive by the Attorney General of the United States. One is declared to be in the Kenney Report the Voice of the Communist Party, etc. So these violent attacks that have been going on against me, I don't know whether they are a smoke-screen to cover the issue or not. . . . I am a little astounded that the attack has turned so completely against me, but I have taken attacks before, and I will have to take this one, I presume. I cannot retract it, because my statement is fact."

By repeating his charges, instead of retracting them, DeMille enraged those who had only been angry. Don Hartman stood up and asked for DeMille's resignation from the board. John Cromwell seconded. William Wyler stood up and said, "I am one of the 25. . . . [According to DeMille] I am a 'Commie' although I tell you that I am not, and I have signed two oaths to that effect. . . . I am sick and tired of having people question my loyalty to my country. The next time I hear somebody do it, I am going to kick the hell out of him. I don't care how old he is or how big.

"I have seen guys that have jobs that are conservative Republicans—good Americans—and they are scared today, because they are not quite as conservative as they are asked to be by the group that is trying to run this Guild. . . . How was this fear spread? Why is it? I think it is absolutely appalling."

With the introduction of threatened violence, it was past time for a cool head to make an appearance. It was about one in the morning when Joe Mankiewicz said, "John Ford has to be heard." Ford, one of the Guild's founders, universally respected because of his pictures and his distinguished service during World War II, rose to speak.

"I am a director of westerns," began Ford. "I am one of the founders of this Guild. I must rise to protect the Board of Directors in some of the accusations made here tonight. Before I continue, I would like to state that I have been on Mr. Mankiewicz' side of the fight all through it. . . . I have been sick and tired and ashamed of the whole goddamn thing . . . if they intend to break up the Guild, goddamn it, they have pretty well done it tonight. . . .

"I don't agree with C.B. DeMille. I admire him. I don't like him, but I admire him. Everything he said tonight he had a right to say. You know, when you get the two blackest Republicans I know, Joseph Mankiewicz and Cecil B. DeMille, and they start a fight over Communism, it is getting laughable to me. I know Joe is an ardent Republican. I happen to be a state of Maine Republican.

"I think Joe has been vilified, and I think he needs an apology. . . . I admire C.B.'s guts and courage even if I don't agree with him. [And] if Mr. DeMille is recalled, your Guild is busted up."

Mankiewicz was stunned. He didn't really know Ford very well; within the younger membership, Ford was regarded as right-wing, although not part of

DeMille's cabal. For the first time, Mankiewicz began to believe he might win, because Ford was the only man in the room, and the only other member of the board, with both the force of personality and the moral authority to stand against DeMille.

Throughout Ford's speech, DeMille stared straight ahead, refusing to look at him. At this point, Ford made a brilliant tactical leap to forestall further damage to the Guild. "I believe there is only one alternative, and that is for the [entire] Board of Directors to resign and elect a new Board of Directors. They are under enough fire tonight. It appears they haven't got the support of the men that elected them. I think that there is only one alternative, and that is for us to resign. . . . I don't see any other course."

The motion was quickly voted and quickly carried. The entire board was deposed, obliterating DeMille's influence and allowing Mankiewicz to continue his stewardship without having to worry about watching his back. The meeting, which began at 7:30 P.M., finally broke up at 2:20 A.M., just after giving the twenty-five signers of the petition a vote of confidence.

A devastated Cecil B. DeMille went home to Laughlin Park. The next day at lunch DeMille was quiet, munching potato chips as his eyes circled the staff. Finally, he said, "If you don't think our country is in danger you should have been at last night's meeting." He would tell Henry Wilcoxon, "Nobody is my friend today, Harry. Nobody wants to know me. Last night was one of the worst nights of my entire life."

On October 23, DeMille sent a cable to Clarence Brown in Rome:

SUNDAY NIGHT MEETING MEMBERSHIP ASKED BOARD TO RESIGN WHICH WE DID. THE "BOYS" NOW IN COMPLETE CONTROL. ATTACK UPON BOARD AND ME LED BY HUSTON, HARTMAN, WYLER, CROMWELL, STEVENS, POTTER, ET CETERA. REGRETS AND REGARDS.

That same day, John Ford sent a note to DeMille. "I wish to have it formally recorded on paper, with my signature attached that from the so-called membership meeting of the Screen Director's of America, Sunday evening October 22, 1950 you emerged as a very great gentleman. Yours very respectfully . . ."

Ford followed up his note with a phone call. "That meeting Sunday night was a disgusting thing to see—not a wolf pack, but a mice pack attacking you," said Ford, according to DeMille's notes. "That was your greatest performance. I just wish you could have seen yourself—a magnificent figure so far above that goddamn pack of rats. I have recommended men for courage in battle, but I have never seen courage such as you displayed Sunday night. God bless you, you're a great man. I have talked to many men in Hollywood in the last two days including Joseph Mankiewicz, and all agree you will emerge from this greater than ever."

What to make of this extraordinary exchange?

For one thing, it needs to be pointed out that, rather than some Manichaean clash of titans, which is how the evening has usually been portrayed, Ford and DeMille were social friends. Ford had invited DeMille to fund-raisers for his Field Photo Farm—a clubhouse for veterans of Ford's unit during World War II—in both 1948 and 1949, addressing him as "Dear Cecil" and signing the letters "Jack." DeMille attended both events, something he rarely did unless he supported both the man and his charity. Moreover, the two men regularly sent each other their new films for viewing.

There's an impression that Ford, besides trying to pour oil on troubled waters, was enacting the old joke that ends with the punch line, "Who are you going to believe, me or your lying eyes?" He was, after all, the man who had first told DeMille that he was far out of line, then proposed that the entire board resign, eliminating DeMille and his influence on the Directors Guild.

Nevertheless, DeMille responded graciously, writing, "Thank you for your friendly expression. Attack I am used to, kindness moves me very deeply. Sincerely . . ."

And then came another stunning reversal. The victorious Mankiewicz put his name to an open letter that urged all Guild members to sign the loyalty oath "as a voluntary act in affirmation of confidence in your guild." The voluntary oath was signed by every member of the Directors Guild but one: Charlie Chaplin.

Tom Mankiewicz, Joe's son, explains that after the meeting, his father "came under tremendous pressure from the Guild's center and the center-right to heal the wounds. They said he had to make some kind of unifying gesture. He thought about it and decided that he'd go so far as to say that the loyalty oath could be voluntary; those who wanted to could sign the oath if they wished, and those that didn't wish to, didn't have to. That was the olive branch."

So the Directors Guild circulated the first loyalty oath in Hollywood. As a result, the Guild's attempt to head off a blacklist has to be considered an utter failure. Under the leadership of Ronald Reagan, the Screen Actors Guild implemented a separate loyalty oath that same year, and the blacklist remained in force for another ten years.

That evening proved the profound truth of Dalton Trumbo's observation that the blacklist era resulted in mass victimization of left, right, and center. Only John Ford's unexpected display of courage, political savvy, and theatricality redounded to his benefit.

The long night sealed DeMille's reputation as a reactionary. The entire affair was traumatic for Joe Mankiewicz; he came to the conclusion that he didn't want to be the president of the Directors Guild anymore, and years later he told his son that if he had to do it all over again, "maybe I'd keep my mouth shut."

"To the end of his life, Dad harbored a certain animosity toward DeMille for what he'd been put through," said Tom. "He never really forgave him."

The reverberations of this episode would echo through Hollywood for decades. In a sense, they still do. Certainly, it was an unseemly overreaching on DeMille's part, one that caused obvious discomfort among people who loved him more than a half century later.

Typically, DeMille believed that his actions were justified and never apologized. Equally as revealingly, he didn't mention the night of the Guild meeting in his memoirs.

Soon after the meeting, the FBI requested that DeMille "make available information concerning the controversy which took place in the Screen Director's Guild over the installation of a loyalty oath for members of that organization. . . . Through his position as an Executive Board member [DeMille] was able to furnish complete information to this office concerning the individuals who opposed this loyalty oath and the tactics employed by them."

For the next several years, even though he had been deposed from the board, DeMille continued funneling information to the Bureau "concerning the activities of Guild members whom he believes may be Communist Party members or Communist Party sympathizers."

2 0

American critics had written DeMille off around the mid-1920s and *Samson and Delilah* didn't rouse them to reconsider. A lot of people in Hollywood didn't think much more highly of him than the critics; King Vidor told Kevin Brownlow that "When I saw one of his pictures, I wanted to quit the business."

But in France there began to be a cautious appreciation and reappraisal. Jacques Doniol-Valcroze wrote a piece for *Cahiers du Cinéma* in 1951 that saw DeMille's embrace of capitalism as critical to his moral, religious, and aesthetic convictions. Doniol-Valcroze compared DeMille's Delilah to Salammbô and defended the director from those who didn't take him seriously as an artist.

> We too easily overlook what the history of filmmaking owes to DeMille. . . . He was indeed one of the pillars of the Hollywood temple, and so he remains; he incarnates the best of it and the worst of it. . . . The durability of this success is absolutely unique in the history of the American film industry, a great devourer of personalities. Whereas Griffith, Ince, Seastrom, Stiller and Stroheim quit making films, the wheel of fortune continued to turn in DeMille's favor. . . .
>
> DeMille is certainly a poet and a romantic in his own way, but [his] only resemblance to [Victor] Hugo is in the abundance of his production. Frankly, the two are very different. The only thing they have in common is that both have been victims—Hugo, victim of the myth of the white beard . . . DeMille, victim of a continuous commercial success that has deprived him of that [aura] of failure which allows one to assess the films of Stroheim, for example.
>
> The man has his faults . . . but it appears to me that his outstanding quality, spanning the whole length of an abundant career, is an almost total unity of style, a constant fidelity to one perspective, and a conception of history of the plastic arts and literature, a conception he did not

originate on the screen, but of which he was perhaps the most important and talented popularizer.

I think DeMille is absolutely indifferent to questions of fashion and is totally resistant to influences. He is one of the rare Hollywood figures left wholly unmoved by the flashing emergence of a Welles or by the phenomenon of Italian neo-realism. . . . It seems to me that he makes films largely for the pleasure of it—he is one who breathes movies instead of air.

Doniol-Valcroze may have patronized DeMille—French intellectuals always tend to regard American artists as inspired primitives—and he was considerably oversimplifying DeMille's career, for the director's style shifted radically during the first fifteen years. But in his tribute to DeMille's vision (which could be debated) and his passion (which couldn't) he was on to something.

☆

The fight with AFRA and the imbroglio at the Directors Guild convinced DeMille that communist forces had singled him out for elimination from American public life. There was a resultant wariness that verged on paranoia.

When *Samson and Delilah* got a bad review in *The New Yorker*, he exploded. "Do you think for a moment the *New Yorker* crowd cares whether *Samson and Delilah* is good or bad! This is a political attack against me, against my beliefs. It has nothing to do with the picture!" He set his staff to gather information about the political leanings of various leading critics.

When the Democrat James Roosevelt ran for the governorship of California in 1950 against the Republican Earl Warren, DeMille issued a warning to his staff: "Anybody in this office who votes for Roosevelt can pack his bag and head for the door."

In 1952, DeMille would contribute $200 to Joe McCarthy's senatorial campaign, and enclose a check from Frank Freeman for $100. (The members of the Hollywood for McCarthy Committee included DeMille, Rupert Hughes, John Wayne, Ward Bond, Morrie Ryskind, Harold Lloyd, Louis B. Mayer, Adolphe Menjou, Ray Milland, Dennis Morgan, George Murphy, Leo McCarey, Pat O'Brien, Dick Powell, and Randolph Scott.)

DeMille's very public support of McCarthy drew some angry letters from the public, which were answered with the same dispatch as every piece of correspondence that flowed into the office. "Dear Mr. Blum," went one response. "I have received your postcard, condemning me for supporting the re-election of Senator McCarthy. You say that you are going to boycott my pictures and urge other Americans to do the same.

"Honest and loyal Americans differ in their opinions of Senator McCarthy. I think he is a brave man, fighting for America and against Communism. You do not like him. The voters of Wisconsin have decided between your opinion and mine.

"But I cannot imagine what this difference of political opinion has to do with my pictures. I would not stop trading at your store or buying your products simply because we differ politically. I am certainly not asking you to go and see my pictures if you do not like them—but America would be a poorer place to live if we all followed your policy of doing business only with people who happened to agree with us politically."

The letter was copied to Senator McCarthy.

"DeMille became more DeMille as he grew older," summed up Richard deMille. "He became more dedicated to the few clear ideas he had about things."

In every respect besides politics, DeMille remained remarkably forward-thinking, adamant in his interest in and support of pay TV at a time when it was a very distant speck on the horizon. "In 1898," he wrote, "I told my college roommate that he was wasting his time with such an absurdity as the horseless carriage. Since then I have tried to remember that time and the inventive mind of man march on."

If DeMille was giving some signs of being an artery-hardened reactionary, he was a financially cautious one. He would invest only a nominal $120 in the start-up of William F. Buckley's *National Review*. Jeremiah Milbank, who had financed *The King of Kings*, tossed in $10,000.

★

While Cecil went from triumph to triumph in his profession, Bill slowly receded. Agnes deMille wrote of a "rivalry [that] was profound and lasting. . . . Father, the thoughtful and subtle one; Cecil, the adventurer. The contest strengthened Cecil; I think in some ways it broke my father."

If it was a rivalry, it was unstated. The two men remained emotionally bound all their lives, and their deeply divergent political beliefs never seemed to put a strain on their relationship. Agnes deMille asserted that Cecil would call his brother to complain about members of the USC theater faculty that he believed were communists; Bill would refuse to fire them and that would be that.

Bill had thrown himself into his teaching. His tastes as head of the Drama Department ran to plays like *State of the Union*, *Watch on the Rhine*, *The Little Foxes*— strong construction, few shades of gray. Shakespeare wasn't performed often, and Bill didn't like William Saroyan or Tennessee Williams at all. He believed that the actor's job was to carefully, incrementally communicate the intentions of the playwright.

Clara Beranger deMille was a regal presence who taught screenwriting at the same school, although she wasn't held in the same high regard as Bill. "It tended to be all about writing [silent movie] titles," remembered the actor Marvin Kaplan, who was one of her students. "Dialogue was her weak point."

In other respects, Bill adopted some of the demeanor of his brother, using sarcasm to control his unruly charges. "[William] deMille was very caustic, very sarcastic and incredibly witty," said one of his students. "He would select someone who was not of great consequence to him and destroy them to show everybody else that he could do that, and then everybody else would shape up right away so they wouldn't be the next one." One of Bill's prize pupils was an erudite young man named Jack Gariss, whose expansive knowledge of literature and the theater would be put to use when Cecil hired him as one of the writers for his remake of *The Ten Commandments.*

Bill had his eccentricities; he was well known for collecting all sorts of odd things—empty egg cartons, toilet paper rolls—on the off chance they could be used in set construction. One of his joys was his vast collection of 78 rpm classical records. His students remember him as a first-rate teacher, and a true original. "He was the only man I ever knew who could drink martinis *and* play tennis," remembered Fess Parker, who took a seminar from William in 1950–1951, just a few years before Parker would become a baby boomer icon on television as Davy Crockett. "Every Saturday morning, he would come into the Hollywood Sports Club, go directly to the bar and have two martinis. And then he would go out and play tennis. He didn't move; if the ball was within arm's reach, he would smack it. Otherwise, he let it go."

Parker's final examination for Bill's course consisted of a scene from *Of Mice and Men* in which he played Lenny. When the class was over, Parker approached his professor and told him that he was thinking of going into the movie business and asked deMille if he had any possibility of success as an actor.

Bill looked at him and said, "I have no idea."

"He was dead honest," remembered Parker, "but he didn't say, 'For God's sake, you're mindless up there, don't even think about it,' which was all the encouragement I needed. He was a good teacher. He taught what he called the Truth of the Unreal. He would describe it this way: if someone is truly grief-stricken, crying and out of control, in life people can back off from that extreme emotion. But in drama, all an actress has to do is loose one tear and the audience begins reaching for their Kleenex."

A young man named Syd Kronenthal, a friend of John Ford's, grew to know William when his sister served as his teaching assistant. Kronenthal thought William "the most gifted person. He was a very creative educator. He loved to analyze talent. He would say, 'That person is a natural for the stage,' even though that person had never been on stage in their life. He was a very good teacher and a meticulous director. He had the air of an academician, although he could loosen up and carry a conversation if he chose.

"He didn't speak about his brother. Once someone said to him, 'You're Cecil B. DeMille's brother!' And all he said was, 'No. I'm William deMille.' "

Bill no longer competed in the world that Cecil had made his own. Once a year he would go to New York to see plays, but mostly, "he felt he was no longer part of the business," remembered Marvin Kaplan. "He was slightly ashamed, I think. Disillusioned. Academic life was a come-down for him. William was a very shy man, you see. He believed the bedrock of the theater was the playwright; he bent most of his efforts to telling actors how to get the writer's ideas across. He didn't believe in the Method. 'Say the lines, hit your mark, give a performance whether you feel it or not,' was the way he put it.

"Mr. deMille was a magnificent teacher, and all of his productions were excellent. He wouldn't give line readings, but he would direct an actor by showing them what he wanted physically. That's Original Sin for a director, but at the time I didn't mind it at all. He had one problem: he couldn't face an audience; I think he was afraid he might be perceived as a has-been. When he opened his production of *Androcles and the Lion* with Joe Flynn as Androcles, he wouldn't sit out front; he sat in the wings and drank."

Actually, it seems that William drank quite a bit. Usually he held it rather well, but sometimes at lunch he'd have a large martini in a milkshake glass, and as a result he could be a trifle foggy in the afternoon.

"It was impossible not to be fond of those guys," remembered William's student Rory Guy. "They had such a Broadway/Hollywood aristocratic aura—crusty old men, but knowledgeable and capable of great affection. I always think of FDR when I think of William. You always felt that you were in The Presence."

Clara, as well as William's friend Frank Reicher, would always come to his openings, but not Cecil. Bill went on walks with Reicher, smoked his Cuban cigars, played his limited tennis, drank his martinis, and seemed to his family to be notably kinder than he had been as a younger man. Underlying much of this was a vague sense of diminishment.

For all this, his daughter blamed her stepmother. Agnes believed Clara Beranger was unworthy of her father, while her own mother had been a harrowing burr under his saddle. Beyond that, there was Bill's own delicate internal mechanism that had grown sick of losing.

"Father simply withdrew," Agnes wrote, "and held himself aloof. . . . He was not a success as Cecil was, a fact he acknowledged readily. . . . But I think he got used to conceding. He began to accept failure on his own terms. . . . He stepped aside from his own standards, and this was a tragedy. He lost his nerve. . . . He never again achieved his possibility."

But it was more than that. Time revealed character, as it always does. As Richard deMille would note, "Cecil was an adventurer, William was a philosopher. Cecil was fearless, William was cautious. Cecil fared forth every day girded for mortal or business combat; William preferred to rise above the fray." William had been tested by failure, as every artist eventually is, and his lack of defiance had placed him on the sidelines.

What made it worse was that his daughter had inherited, not her father's professorial mien, but the warrior temperament of her uncle. Elia Kazan, who worked with her on Broadway's *One Touch of Venus*, said that Agnes "was the most dominating personality I ever worked with, so dominating in fact that I was reduced to a kind of stage manager . . . and arranged the lights and stage space to her bidding."

"It was her pride that [Agnes] outdid [her father], and it was her sorrow," noted Richard deMille. "She became the hero she had wanted him to be."

In 1951, both brothers were taken aback when Agnes sent them the manuscript of her memoir *Dance to the Piper*. In his response, William wrote his daughter that she had portrayed him as the "villain" of the book for insufficiently supporting her early attempts at dancing and for divorcing her mother. "The picture of my being fired from the studios makes me an object of pity—and to say I later joined the university where I made a reputation as a 'lecturer and coach' is a bit rough. When I take charge of a stage and put on a whole production, I am still a director, my dear, not a 'coach.' " He also strenuously objected to Agnes's referring to Clara as the "current" wife, "as if she were one of a constantly changing series." Clara deMille could speak for herself and did, telling Agnes "you have both by commission and omission been unfair, disloyal and in some places dishonest."

As for Cecil, the long-festering wounds from Agnes's abrupt dismissal from *Cleopatra* were at last allowed to burst. In 1944, flush from the success of *Oklahoma!*, she had given an interview to *Collier's* in which she depicted Cecil as a pompous vulgarian. When the article appeared, she claimed she had been misquoted; he sent three dozen red roses to the opening of her new show with a note that said, "Colliers come, Colliers go, We go on forever. Luck and love. Uncle Ce."

Seven years later, nothing had changed except the venue. Cecil took umbrage at her mention of his wardrobe, what she called three-hundred-odd English shirts and nearly as many neckties.

"I have never counted my shirts," he responded, explaining that when they got old, "my excellent shirt maker cuts the tails off to make new collars and cuffs. When the replaced collars and cuffs become too badly frayed, the family sends them to what is termed the 'shirt morgue' at my ranch where they work out their last days in rough work of tree surgery, wood chopping, clearing fire trails, etc."

As for his ties, they "were acquired over some fifty odd years—many of them Christmas and birthday gifts, yet unworn, and many of them knitted by some gentle souls . . . as a sincere expression of appreciation of some of my work."

He took particular exception to her statement that money was a ruling force in his life: "Your paragraphs on my attitude toward religion and mankind that follow so closely your above expression on the subject of money being a God in your Aunt Constance's house tend to present me to the public as a charlatan. . . . If that is your opinion, I presume you have a right to state it. . . . [It was] a bit difficult for me to be sympathetic to having the private lives of our families laid on the public operating table, but if you feel that the public will better understand your struggles, failures and successes, I shall try to accustom myself to this trend and wish you all success."

Agnes made some token deletions in her book, but after Cecil died everything she had originally written found its way into print.

★

In late 1949, Bill had been diagnosed with cancer. He beat it back, but in 1952 it returned. Cecil wrote his brother a loving letter, and Bill replied from Catalina Island.

I was greatly touched by your warm and affectionate letter of August 9th. It showed me that the steady bond between us has not been affected through these many years by certain superficial differences of opinion or by those who have so frequently tried to put us in opposition to each other because of our differences of opinion.

I feel more than ever that you and I are working for the same end; a free and secure America where every individual will have as much freedom of ideas, speech and property as can be achieved without trespassing on the proper rights and freedoms of other citizens. We both realize that the right of every man to swing his arms stops where the next man's nose begins. If we take slightly different roads towards this goal, who cares! Certainly not I.

The rest over here has done me much good, tho' following doctor's orders I have done nothing but rest. No fishing this trip, for the first time in 35 years. We are returning next Thursday, the 28th, and I'll be on the job at U.S.C. on Sept. 2.

But, again by Doctor's orders, I'm going to lighten my load a bit this year by giving up the direction of plays. . . . I'm going to put in a younger man to do the heavy work, and I will supervise. I hate to do this but I am forced to realize that Cancer is a tricky enemy. We licked him 2½ years ago and I think we've got him stopped again, for a while, but if I lighten my work load a little, I'll be able to enjoy my work and not pay too much physically.

The point is that your fraternal ties mean much to me and I am grateful that time and circumstances have been powerless to change them. . . .

Hope to see you soon.

Love from us both.

Bill retired from the USC Drama Department in 1953, when he was seventy-five years old. The occasion was marked with a party at which the surprise guest was Cecil, who responded with a warmly emotional speech. He talked about the four pictures of Bill in his bedroom, one from 1888 featuring their dog Homer Q. Putnam, the second taken in Hollywood, the third showing the two men in white pants standing on the deck of the *Seaward*, and the last from only a few years earlier, as Cecil received an honorary degree with Bill.

Cecil recalled the beautiful call of their favorite Pompton bird. "Bill reminded me of the chewink-chewee one Christmas only a year or two ago—and it brought back our whole boyhood—the swimming club, fishing with bent pins in Strubel's brook, the stories of Bert Terhune—all the wonder and fun and glory of being a boy, in that one word, chewink-chewee. I pity any boy or man who hasn't a che-wink-chewee—his own personal chewink-chewee—somewhere in his boyhood. . . .

"We used to watch the chewink-chewee—building its nest on a bank on the way to Strubel's brook—then courting its fluffy little mate and watching them mothering their brood—and finally sending out a whole new family of chewink-chewees on the wing—with the world before them."

He talked about the time Bill had covered for him for four weeks in the tour of *Lord Chumley* when Cecil came down with the measles, then lent him money to keep the tour going; he talked about their primary personality difference: "Bill had the brains. I had the bash. Bill with his gentle razor-edged wit would slice his way through any problem where I would have to butt through like a bull."

Cecil was equally solicitous with family members at the beginnings of their lives. Jody Harper sent his grandfather a letter from Lake Arrowhead in which he told him about lunch, swimming in the pool, and a prospective speedboat ride. Cecil responded by telling Jody that he had just returned from Paradise, "where the fox had dinner with me both Thursday and Friday night—sharing the remains of my charcoal broiled steak one night and the carcass of a roast duck the next. He carried most of it off to his madam and the children, who I think live under the porch of the stone house.

"It was so hot the deer all sounded like the bellows on the old blacksmith's forge when I was a boy."

By this time, DeMille had trained not only the deer at Paradise, but a number of birds. He would break off pieces of bread and put them on the railing and then watch. "I bet you that little guy grabs the first piece," he would say, and a small bluebird would swoop down and get a piece, only to be overtaken by a much bigger bluebird, who would take the bread right out of the smaller bird's mouth.

"Goddammit, isn't that just like life?" DeMille said.

2 1

In mid-1949, before *Samson and Delilah* was even released, DeMille began preliminary work on what he always referred to as "the circus picture." He traveled with the Ringling Bros. circus throughout several states, observing the vast harmonies of manpower and mechanics that enabled a traveling tent show to function. Gladys Rosson accompanied DeMille, and her notebook of 135 pages attests to the thoroughness with which he observed the scenes in front of him—circus slang, and vignettes of domestic life amidst large mammals.

Outfitted in breeches, boots, and open shirt, he climbed up rope ladders to the aerialist's platforms, walked among the lion tamers and through clown alley, all in search of camera angles and story ideas. During the circus parade, he lay in the bottom of one of the wagons and checked out possible shots with a viewfinder. Generally speaking, he gave a very good impression of an overage Toby Tyler. In Eau Claire, he got a cherry picker to lift him up to the top of the tent, forty feet higher than the trapeze artists. He came down to tell Art Concello, general manager of Ringling Bros., that it was 101 degrees up there and the circus should open at least one slit in the tent for air.

At night, he was exhausted—his years were just beginning to catch up to him—but he never showed fatigue in public. Sometimes he would fall asleep at dinner, and Gladys Rosson would have to hold his head to keep it from slamming into the dishes. But with five or six hours of sleep, DeMille in the mornings could give a reasonable impression of a vigorous thirty-five-year-old.

DeMille was set afire by the drama of the circus, the camaraderie, the rapid procession of images. "You see 2,800 eggs fried at the same time," he enthused. "I wanted to get a shot of that so much. I haven't room for half of what I have. . . . There are 28 languages spoken under that big top. Like a League of Nations in operation. . . . These people—I saw them in blow downs—I saw them when these terrible storms that ripped the thing to pieces, when the flyers were up—the audience panicked and the wonderful flyers didn't come down. . . . There were a thousand wonderful shots in fifteen minutes."

DeMille was accompanied by a sketch artist, and lots of times DeMille would look over his shoulder while he was drawing. "That man is cross-eyed," he'd say, and the artist would look up from his pad and sure enough, he was.

The most thrilling moment for DeMille was accompanying the man whose job it was to release the last rope holding the circus tent to the main pole. This ritual was called the "main fall"; when the pin was pulled, the sixty-foot-high canvas roof plummeted thirty feet until the air caught it and the tent slowly settled down as the air was forced out of the sides. The seconds of the tent rushing down struck DeMille as something out of a nightmare, and he was disappointed that he couldn't figure out a way to photograph the scene.

Fredric Frank was put on the payroll by mid-November for $500 a week to begin the long, arduous process of a script, and he was joined by Theodore St. John and Barré Lyndon, among others. DeMille's script meetings with the writers were more specific than usual because of the time he had spent on the road with the circus. His instructions to his writers were curt: "The first of you gentlemen that mentions the words 'circus' or 'big top' is fired. I don't want that at all. Tell me a story about people, a very basic story, which could be dropped into a fish cannery, a studio . . . or a circus. First I want the plumbing in this house and a strong foundation. Don't write me a lot of beautiful trimmings. Don't start putting curtains up before the windows are built."

Later, as they got deeper into the writing, he wanted specific shots: "We fill the departure of the circus with wonderful stuff. Some little clown who's left something, some midget falls and someone picks him up. . . . Someone says, 'Look out, your elephant's got his trunk out!' 'Well, he's starting to travel, isn't he?' . . . All those people. The fat woman? How about her? How the hell does she get through the door? Does she have to go into the elephant car? The living skeleton—does he help the fat lady? Is there a romance between them? The bearded lady is terrified of everything—that I know. She's the most timid. She has beautiful feet and legs and lovely breasts, well dressed, a lovely feminine person with a terrific black beard."

DeMille felt something extra was needed for the script, so he went further afield than normal. Ben Hecht worked on the picture for a while, in spite of the fact that, as he remembered, "I never liked [DeMille's] pictures very much. They seemed to be made with horses and for horses chiefly, but he himself was a man of great potency and wild imagination."

Also joining the writing staff was Stephen Longstreet, who had been in Paris in the 1920s, and written novels such as *Stallion Road*. Longstreet was hot because he had written the screenplay for *The Jolson Story*, and DeMille brought him in to polish the dialogue, in spite of the fact that Longstreet was not entirely free of political taint. DeMille felt compelled to show Longstreet the file that the FBI was keeping on him. The most damning content was an observation that Longstreet had lunch with the Hollywood Ten's Albert Maltz one day at Paramount.

"He showed me *Samson and Delilah* and asked me what I thought of the dialogue," remembered Longstreet. "He was still tied to the other picture, and very proud of the fact that 'in my picture, nobody says "thee and thou." ' "

"I found him to be a wonderful phony. Practically everybody in Hollywood was a phony, but DeMille was *theatrical*. I had been blacklisted because I gave money to Loyalist Spain, and DeMille pulled my FBI file out of his desk. 'Don't worry,' he said, 'I can handle the FBI.'

"You'd have to march into the dining room and wait for Mr. DeMille to enter. His chair was on blocks so it was a foot higher. I ordered a hamburger, and I was told, 'No, Mr. DeMille always orders first.' At the time, he wasn't eating anything but hard-boiled eggs, in order to lose some weight, so everybody else on his staff was eating hard-boiled eggs. I didn't order hard-boiled eggs, but I was freelance so he forgave me. He had a bunch of refugee writers, Germans, who did a lot of his research. He called them 'wily Orientals.' "

One day DeMille was ruminating about his career to Longstreet and sighed, "Well, a forty-year run is about as permanent as anything is these days."

In December of 1949, Paramount signed John Ringling North and Ringling Bros. Circus to a ten-year agreement. The studio committed to paying Ringling $25,000 each year for the next ten, in addition to which the circus received $75,000 as an advance against royalties of 10 percent of the film's gross. The royalties kicked in when the film earned back 1.9 times its negative cost if in black and white, and two times negative cost if color.

For the circus, the deal was a godsend; Ringling Bros. was still reeling from the after-effects of a catastrophic circus fire in Hartford, Connecticut, in July 1944, in which 168 people died, and both the money and the prestige were needed. For DeMille, the deal, steep as it was, gave him absolute access to the Ringling Bros. operation—one great entertainment name allied with another.

As *The Son of the Sheik* had given him some ideas for *Samson and Delilah*, he again turned to silent movies for angles about the circus picture. E. A. Dupont's *Variety* became his touchstone, although he didn't steal the primary dramatic situation of a trapeze catcher who knows that his partner is sleeping with his wife.

John Jensen, an infantry veteran of the Battle of the Bulge, was hired as an artist. After a preliminary interview with Henry Wilcoxon, Jensen was brought in to meet DeMille. "Did you draw this horse?" asked the director. "Draw another one."

"He watched me draw another one," remembered Jensen, "he nodded and I was hired. Then he told me to go travel with the circus. 'Draw anything you think looks interesting.' They were still writing the script. They gave me a room in the circus train, and I went around with a sketchbook and made quick sketches. How they raised the big top, for instance; I could understand that and break it down because I was an engineer."

When Jensen came back to the lot with his 18 x 24 drawings, DeMille and he went over each one, with the director asking him to explain what he was after and what each drawing represented. As Jensen talked, DeMille would rock back and forth in his chair and consider what Jensen was saying. DeMille was particularly appreciative of the fact that Jensen could tell him how much time elapsed between one sketch and another. The opening sequence of *The Greatest Show on Earth* and the fascinating montages that document a vanished era of entertainment essentially derive from Jensen's drawings of the mechanical infrastructure of the circus. DeMille's meticulous reliance on concept art for big scenes had now evolved to where he was essentially pioneering yet again, this time in the use of what would come to be known as storyboards.

"Everything that was in the script, he wanted visualized," remembered Jensen. "He liked to show big crowds, then move in with the camera. I designed a lot of master shots for him, then he could see how he could move in with the boom and pick up the sequence of shots. We got along great; I didn't know a thing about the movie business, but he taught me all about it.

"In a lot of ways, he was like a father. Sometimes he'd reminisce about how he started in the business and show me this little Saturday Night Special, a nickel-plated pistol he had—a .32, I think. An early film of his [*The Squaw Man*] had been sabotaged, so he stayed with it carrying this pistol. He watched them develop the film and stayed awake for two days and nights standing guard over his film with the pistol."

For the rest of DeMille's life, Jensen worked on the storyboards for big special effects sequences—the train wreck in the circus picture, the parting of the Red Sea in *The Ten Commandments*. Jensen also worked on costuming; he designed much of the men's wardrobe for *The Ten Commandments* and *The Buccaneer*.

★

DeMille rehired Henry Wilcoxon for the circus picture as associate producer. Welcoming Wilcoxon back into the fold would be the last piece of the puzzle of the DeMille unit. In Henry, Cecil had a steadfast associate who could absorb the gaff and wouldn't wear down. It also completed a psychological circle.

"Henry was rejected by his father and had the most god-awful childhood out of a Dickens novel," said his friend and biographer Katherine Orrison. "And DeMille looked exactly like Henry's father. Henry had to earn his father's love, and he was so bright and instinctive I'm certain he could feel he could do that. DeMille's own father had died young, and he had not been the favorite, but the second son. And DeMille was looking for a surrogate son all his life. One man looking for a father, another man looking for a son."

Wilcoxon would come to be regarded by many members of the DeMille unit as a good and honorable man, but slightly ineffectual. As Henry Noerdlinger would say, "DeMille could never admit failure. He had brought this guy over from England, tried to make a star of him, did not succeed, so finally he made an associate producer out of him. That didn't work too well and finally he made a producer of him and that didn't work either."

The story of DeMille and Wilcoxon is the story of a man who made Wilcoxon, unmade him, then made him again . . . but not quite. One of the reasons Wilcoxon was admirable in DeMille's eyes was because he always had women on the side, sometimes three or four of them. He was discreet and never talked about it, but he had a diary written in code that indicates he didn't spend many nights alone.

★

The casting process for the circus picture was arduous because of the large number of people required, and DeMille took pains over even small parts. He interviewed an actress named Vicki Bakken and learned she had worked in the circus riding elephants. "Weren't you afraid of being on that great big animal?" he asked.

"No, elephants are wonderful creatures, sir. Dignified, intelligent and capable of great love and affection. I love them very much."

DeMille held up a photo of one of the Ringling Bros. lead elephants and asked if Bakken knew which elephant it was.

"Big Ruth," she replied. "She's the best one to use when doing publicity photos."

Bakken was hired and given the gospel according to DeMille: "There are no extras in my movies. I only hire actors. I tell everyone the story we're making—the story of the scene they're in; the who, what and why of their character." Bakken played one of the circus performers and was Gloria Grahame's stand-in.

DeMille often said that casting was between 50 percent and 75 percent of the performance. If an actor was correctly cast, the director shouldn't have to talk to him all that much; conversely, if an actor was miscast, all the directing in the world couldn't salvage the performance. DeMille's always dilatory casting process was complicated in the late 1940s by his insistence on consulting *Red Channels*, the political scandal sheet that was printing names of everyone who was supposedly a communist.

When Henry Wilcoxon again put forth Burt Lancaster as the obvious choice for the part of Sebastian in *The Greatest Show on Earth*, DeMille hemmed and hawed. Lancaster was big, handsome, sexy and had been a trapeze artist; he wouldn't have to be doubled except for a couple of shots, contributing greatly to the verisimilitude of the film. He was dream casting, but DeMille couldn't warm to the idea, preferring Robert Stack or—to the astonishment of his staff—Michael Wilding.

Wilcoxon persisted with his pitch for Lancaster when suddenly DeMille turned on him. "Look, Harry! I am well aware that Paul Robeson is your friend and I *try* to be tolerant, but I've had just about enough on this subject. I don't want to hear any more from you about this Lancaster fella. Do I make myself clear?"

Whoever was being cast, DeMille's dictum about actors' salaries was "Cut the price in half, then argue like hell." Didn't they understand what a DeMille picture could do for their careers? Why quibble over a few dollars when the rewards would be so munificent? DeMille's first choice for the part of the circus manager was Kirk Douglas, but his price was $150,000 and not a penny less. DeMille believed in putting the money on the screen, not in an actor's pocket. Gary Cooper was one thing, Kirk Douglas quite another. DeMille kept looking.

Wilcoxon suggested Charlton Heston, a young actor with one film under his belt. After screening *Dark City*, DeMille said, "He's not quite right for our picture. He has a sinister quality. He's sincere—you believe him—he has some power, but he's not attractive in this. Find out if he has any humor. Everything I've seen him in, he's dour."

Soon thereafter, Heston was driving off the lot in his convertible and passed the DeMille bungalow where the director was standing by the door. Heston waved in a friendly, cavalier fashion, and DeMille asked "Who was that?" "That's Charlton Heston," said Gladys Rosson. "He just did a picture for Hal Wallis, *Dark City*. You ran it last week and you said you didn't like it."

"I liked the way he waved just now."

DeMille screened David Bradley's production of *Julius Caesar* in which Heston played Antony, which began to convince him. There were more screenings of *Dark City* for a couple of months and several meetings in the office before DeMille would commit to the young actor.

Heston would remember the anomalous DeMille audition process with some wonder. Basically, the pretext was a discussion of the character of the part and the film, with DeMille sizing up the actor in front of him. "He would never say, 'I'm considering you for this part' or 'I'm told that you might be good in this, and possibly it may work out,' " remembered Heston. "He certainly would never have you *read* for a part. He would merely *talk* about it, which left you at a loss for a response. You couldn't say, 'Well, I think I could do that,' because the question had never come up. I never did figure out the proper tone to strike there. Through half a dozen interviews for the circus picture, and maybe the same number for Moses, all I could say was, 'Certainly is interesting. Sounds like it would make a fine film.' He would describe a scene or the climax and show you the sketches and you'd say, 'Certainly sounds like it should work.' What else could you say?" If DeMille decided to hire the actor, he would never tell the actor, but rather would call the actor's agent.

Paulette Goddard was lobbying hard for the part of the aerialist, even though she was slightly old for the part. She accidentally on purpose ran into DeMille one night at the circus. The freeze that had come down after their disagreement on *Unconquered* was officially broken, and he invited her to sit in his box. Soon afterward, she sent him a note: "Dear C.B. I'm sorry I missed saying goodbye to you after my thrilling evening with you at the circus. I do hope and pray that I get 'The Part' in your coming film. I will be a good, good girl. In the meantime I shall be working hard in summer stock. Yours, Paulette. P.S. You can get me from Paramount. I have pretty feet, too. Love, P.G."

DeMille's response was curt: "Yes, your feet are beautiful. What bothers me is that those same lovely feet might be tempted to walk off the set a second time." Goddard refused to be put off. "Hope all those rumors about my going into The Greatest Show on Earth are true. I'm returning Monday to sign the contract."

But DeMille signed Betty Hutton for the part of the trapeze artist, whereupon Goddard let it be known that she would also accept the part of the elephant trainer. When DeMille chose Gloria Grahame, Goddard had been passed over for two parts in the same film for two younger actresses. It was an incontrovertible sign that her days as a major star were over.

Although James Stewart had just broken through with a percentage agreement at Universal, he accepted the part of a clown for a straight $50,000—25 percent of his usual fee. As Stewart would remember, "I had always loved the circus, and when I heard that DeMille was making a circus film, I sent a wire and asked if I could be in it and play a clown. You see, everyone wanted to do this picture. We all had our dreams about running away and joining the circus. Making this film was a joyous time for everybody, much more than just a movie." Stewart's ardor for the part caused DeMille to wonder if he could have gotten Stewart's price down even further.

DeMille's key decision on *The Greatest Show on Earth* was to film a lot of the movie on the road, where the circus lived. This in turn meant that he was uneasy about delegating so much footage to a second unit director. Because he was no longer tied down to Hollywood ten months a year by a radio show, he decided that most of the location footage would be DeMille footage, shot by DeMille, following the Ringling Bros. operation on tour.

As they moved closer to production, John Jensen found that DeMille's temper got closer to the surface. "His pet peeve was anybody that told him they could do something and then couldn't do it. Then he could dress you down like a first sergeant, although I never heard him use foul language. But when it was over, it was over—no grudges. I would tell him right out if something was very difficult, because I was used to that during the war. I got along very well with him because I was always honest with him. Films are really a lot like a military operation: Get in position, shoot, get the hell out."

Imbued with the spirit of the enterprise, Betty Hutton went through two months of trapeze training on Paramount's Stage 3, thrilling DeMille with her fearlessness. In terms of the costuming, DeMille was particularly interested in the hat Heston was to wear. "The hat is very important," he said. "It's much more important than any other piece of wardrobe you wear." DeMille had wardrobe bring over about fifty hats of various sizes and colors and Heston put on about twenty-five of them, each one invariably drawing a "No" from DeMille, until the magic hat was reached and DeMille said "That one will do." The hat, and a beat-up brown leather jacket, were the touchstones for Heston's character, just as the identical hat and leather jacket would be for Indiana Jones years later.

Sarasota, Florida, had been the Ringlings' winter quarters since 1927, where John Ringling had bought and converted an old fairground. It was more than a storage facility; tourists came by the thousands and provided considerable income during the off-season. Production began in Sarasota on February 5, 1951, and from the beginning DeMille was delighted with Charlton Heston, despite an awkward start.

Heston's first shot called for him to drive a jeep into the shot, jump out, and read Betty Hutton the riot act. He drove up, jumped out, tripped over a ring post, and fell flat on his face.

"I think we had better do another take on that, Chuck," said DeMille. "It can only get better from here."

Although Heston was only twenty-seven years old, he handled himself with aplomb, grace, and humor. Heston remembered that, contrary to DeMille's reputation, "I didn't find him a tyrant. He wanted what he wanted when he wanted it, and he was determined to get a shot made the way he wanted it, and he would stay with it until he did. He was demanding. He might have been a martinet in his early days but that had mellowed a bit. He was extraordinarily courteous with the actors, but he would use assistant directors and prop men as whipping boys."

That courtesy with actors extended even to actors who weren't cutting it. Heston was in a scene with a day player who, Heston insisted, blew his line on twenty-seven consecutive takes spanning two full hours. (The line was "Hey, Brad, Holly's spinnin' like a weather vane in a Kansas twister!" so it wasn't all the actor's fault.) Heston remembered that DeMille "never spoke sharply to the man; he was infinitely patient." After two hours, DeMille replaced him, but with an attitude of regret rather than rage.

Cornel Wilde, who had been cast as the aerialist when DeMille refused to consider Burt Lancaster, was a different issue entirely. It turned out he had a terrible fear of heights, which he had somehow neglected to tell DeMille. Wilde had trained on a trapeze a few feet off the ground, and had been able to easily climb a rope hand over hand with his legs held horizontally, but in the big top, sixty feet in the air, he froze. At night, he had terrible nightmares about falling. The safety net was about seven feet off the ground, and, from his vantage point, Wilde could see right through it. It was as if the net wasn't there at all.

Since DeMille interpreted most fear as a failure of will, as far as he was concerned it was Victor Mature all over again. "If I'd gone with Lancaster I wouldn't have these problems," DeMille muttered to Wilcoxon, who could only stare at him in amazement. DeMille would occasionally make unflattering comments about Wilde. One day, the actor was riding a horse in a white silk outfit he had to wear for the film, and DeMille pointed him out to some visitors, saying, just loudly enough so that Wilde could hear him, "There you see a typical Hollywood cowboy." Other times he would call Wilde "son," but the actor remembered him as "the sort of man you had to stand up to."

The trapeze was lowered a few feet, which seemed to help, and when the trainer who was working with Wilde put burlap bags over the surface of the net, so Wilde could see it clearly, that helped even more. Eventually, Wilde got to the point where he could work about forty feet in the air.

"DeMille was sixty-nine years old when we started on the circus picture," remembered John Jensen, "and he showed Cornel Wilde how to hang upside down on a trapeze. He wasn't far off the ground, but there he was, upside down. Cornel had complained that his knees were hurting, and I told Mr. DeMille it wasn't his fault. The trapeze he was working on wasn't right for a catcher; those trapezes are custom-taped, for the catcher's legs to absorb the shock, and his wasn't. But DeMille thought he was just being a sissy."

DeMille hired a batch of Ringling Bros. performers to work on the picture, paying them slightly elevated salaries—for six weeks of work, the performers earned more than eight weeks of their circus salaries. Jackie Le Claire began working at Ringling's in 1944, mostly as a clown, although he had also done time as a flyer. Because of their similar builds, he was chosen to double for Cornel Wilde on the trapeze.

"Cornel was the nicest man in the world," remembered Le Claire, "but he was terrified of heights. He got the job at the last minute." Le Claire's hair was thin, so he had to wear a wig, and the tights weren't standard circus wear—the Paramount costume department had made them out of wool with sequin decorations. After Le Claire did the shot where the Great Sebastian aims his body through a circle of paper ribbons, the loudspeaker boomed out "Mr. DeMille wants to see you." DeMille asked him if he could do the trick one more time.

"The circus is rough," said Le Claire. "Mostly, they'll just tell you, 'Get up there and do it again, you son of a bitch.' But the secret of DeMille was that he treated the circus people with the greatest respect and dignity. He always addressed us as 'Mr.' or 'Miss.' So I did it again, and he thanked me. Every time we did something, he always thanked us. He was a very appreciative man, a very nice man, a delight. Well, the circus people fell in love with him. When he spoke, my God, we'd do anything for him. One of us, Lola Dobritch, named her son DeMille. Now, he would get mad at the crew, although he never used bad language. With them, he was tough. Very firm. He didn't kid, he didn't joke."

The dangerous stunt of Sebastian's fall to the ground—actually a net hidden by a ring carpet—was shot in Sarasota. "It was the severest I saw DeMille," said Jackie Le Claire. "Art Concello did the fall. He said, 'If anybody's gonna get hurt, it'll be me.'

" 'Now we only want to do this once,' DeMille said. 'This is dangerous.' He really laid them out, and I'll be damned, they did get it on the first take."

Julia Faye came on location and became friendly with Le Claire. "She told me that the best theatrical name you can have was two first names. That's why she used Julia Faye." Jimmy Stewart never came on location, so Ted Mapes doubled for him in clown makeup. Le Claire said that Betty Hutton "was a movie star, so everybody laughed like hell at her smallest joke. She thought she was lowering herself to the circus, and she ended up lowering herself way below my level in demeanor and language. I told her that I'd seen her in *Annie Get Your Gun*, and that I'd also seen Mary Martin in the road company of the show.

" 'She was too fucking dainty,' Betty said. I lost all respect for her. And as the film wore on, she got very temperamental as well."

She wasn't the only one. After two weeks of locations in Sarasota, people longed for the controlled conditions of the studio. Berenice Mosk noted in her diary that "everybody is so tired, edgy and groggy and everything this day kept going wrong. We need a vacation—from each other." A few days later, Mosk wrote, "The gals are at it again—Hutton and Lamour. Each claims she's never been so insulted." For reasons lost in the mists of time, Hutton also developed a dislike for Cornel Wilde.

DeMille's manner with the actors was old-school. If Betty Hutton was late on the set, as she was once or twice early in the picture, he would greet her cordially and proceed to ream out her hair, wardrobe, and makeup people. "Don't you people realize that Miss Hutton has an important scene to do with us this morning? We've been waiting for twenty minutes. You had two hours to make her ready on time and you failed. I can't tolerate that. I won't tolerate that, believe me ladies and gentlemen . . ."

"She got the message," remembered Charlton Heston. "Working for him . . . was a marvelous basic course in professionalism."

One day, DeMille got caught between the camera boom going forward and a jeep that was in the shot driving toward the boom. Although there was contact between DeMille and the jeep, he insisted he wasn't hurt and ordered another take. The driver was apologetic but said that he was torn between spoiling the scene or killing the director.

"Always kill the director," replied DeMille.

Once an actor, always an actor.

After five weeks on location in Sarasota, the production moved back to Hollywood. Shooting the aftermath of the train wreck sequence took a week, with DeMille ramrodding the proceedings with the fire of a man thirty years younger, as a transcript proves: "Hey! What have you done with your hands?

There are three men here and I see only two pairs of hands . . . DO YOU HEAR ME? WHAT HAVE YOU DONE WITH YOUR HANDS? DAMN IT! LISTEN TO ME, WHAT HAVE YOU . . . There, that's better . . . There were only two men when I rehearsed it . . . The elephant was much farther forward. THE ELE-PHANT WAS MUCH FARTHER FORWARD! Will someone in this vast assem-blage of talented assistants listen to me? We've only been at this three days now. Not a bad record you know. If we keep going at this speed we may finish the pic-ture by 1963. GET THAT ELEPHANT BACK! He keeps edging forward all the time . . ."

It was during one of these explosive, microphoned monologues that an el-ephant dropped a load of manure, whereupon assistant director Eddie Salven yelled out, "Shovel Man!" breaking everybody up, including DeMille. (DeMille would tell Henry Wilcoxon that he thought the sexiest women in the world were elephant riders; the pelvic undulations made while straddling the giant animal entranced him.)

After eight weeks of studio work in Hollywood, DeMille and a small crew went back on the road, following the circus to Washington and Philadelphia for a week, then back to the studio for a couple of days of pickup shots. The total time spent was seventy-eight days of production at a cost of $3.8 million.

All things considered, the shoot went smoothly, and DeMille felt he had a good picture. William Boyd's beau geste in making a guest appearance in the picture pleased DeMille enormously, and he gave Boyd an autographed picture of the two men in his dressing room. They're each hoisting one of Boyd's Colt .45 Peacemakers, and are beaming at each other with undisguised love.

"To Bill," the inscription reads. "Father and Son—C.B. DeMille."

DeMille carefully oversaw Anne Bauchens's work in assembling the picture, and sent her a stream of handwritten notes: "Annie—Isn't there a take where the elephant moves its head?" "Parade—try low band music with the narration in." "Parade shorter."

DeMille was stunned when the Catholic Legion of Decency gave the film a B rating: "morally objectionable in part for all persons," because of the character of the clown, who has killed his fatally ill wife rather than see her suffer. "With these Catholics a little euthanasia goes a long way," DeMille said.

Helping out with the publicity for the picture was a young man named David Friedman, who was hired because he was one of the few movie publicists with a circus background. Friedman suggested a tie-in with Oldsmobile, naming it "The Greatest Car on Earth."

"I love it," said DeMille, who proceeded to hire Friedman for the duration of the picture's release.

Friedman noted how Cecilia was her father's right arm. "Joe [Harper] would sit on the side and tell war stories, but Cecilia really ran her father's business and she ran it with an iron hand." DeMille genuinely liked Harper, giving him—and, of course, Cecilia—2.275 percent of the proceeds from *The King of Kings, Samson and Delilah*, and *The Greatest Show on Earth*.

Friedman noted that DeMille's energies had to be carefully husbanded; although the wonderful actor still gave an impression of boundless vitality, he could fade very fast after a long day.

Billy Wilder and DeMille remained friendly, so DeMille invited him to a studio screening of the new film. Wilder was in the process of writing *Stalag 17*, so he went with the screenwriter Edwin Blum. Wilder squirmed uncomfortably through the entire running time, and Blum wondered what Wilder was going to say to DeMille afterward.

As the lights came up, Wilder leapt to his feat with his usual energy, then bowed. "Cecil," he said, "you have made *The Greatest Show on Earth*."

DeMille, believing that Wilder had told him he had made "the greatest show on earth," was very pleased.

The Greatest Show on Earth was another smash; released in January 1952, it was in profit by September, netting, as of 1962, revenue of $15.79 million. After Ringling Bros. took its 10 percent and Paramount deducted its distribution fee, there were profits of $6.6 million to be divided between Paramount and DeMille. The profits just kept coming; as of the end of 1969, there was another $900,000 to split.

Most importantly, *The Greatest Show on Earth* gave the industry the opportunity to acknowledge DeMille's immense historical importance when it gave him the Best Picture award for 1952, in addition to the coveted Thalberg Award for a distinguished career in production. With two consecutive worldwide successes at an age when most directors were retired, and at a time of rampant box office retrenchment, Cecil now symbolized not just Hollywood, but the commercial supremacy of the American film industry.

DeMille's acceptance speech at the Oscars reflected a touch of asperity about the long wait: "I wish to thank you all for the great patience you have shown me over the years. It was exceeded only by my patience with you!"

There are newsreels showing DeMille entering his offices the day after the Oscar ceremony. He is clutching his awards, receiving the congratulations of his staff, and beaming like a child on Christmas morning. Finally, Cecil had gotten the pony that David Belasco had promised.

The Best Picture award was indeed a gift, considering that *The Greatest Show on Earth* was competing against *The Quiet Man* and *High Noon*, but the picture was better than *Ivanhoe* or *Moulin Rouge*, the other nominees. If it was an early example of a Lifetime Achievement Award, it also served as a clear signal that the recent unpleasantness at the Directors Guild was, if not forgotten, at least forgiven.

The Greatest Show on Earth is an overstuffed box of Cracker Jack—there's corn, there's nuts, there are some delightful surprises, among them guest appearances from Bob Hope and Bing Crosby, William Boyd as Hopalong Cassidy, not to mention the great clown Emmett Kelly. It's magnificent corn, punched over with energy and panache.

DeMille's narration continuously hypes the physical and emotional perils of the circus. Certainly, the circus of the 1950s was an endangered institution, as many of the tent shows were folding or consolidating. The narration posits the ceaselessly moving circus as an army waging war on its natural enemies—weather, carelessness, exhaustion—with only raw strength and eternal vigilance holding it together. The dynamic is something DeMille understood from the inside: a man functioning as both field marshal and father figure, risking his and everybody else's lives to put on a colossal show—a lot like the making of a DeMille film.

As for the issue of authenticity, Jackie Le Claire says that "I love the picture, but there's one thing wrong with it. When they're playing cards in one of the railroad cars, and sleeping in the bunks on the train—nothing that spacious ever existed in the history of the circus. Way too much room. And the story is idiotic. A clown who sleeps in his makeup? That's the first guy the cops would look for!

"But the camaraderie that DeMille portrays is *exact*. My mother had MS, and every year, when the circus came to town, the performers would take up a collection for her. One year, they put $50 together and got her a wheelchair. Circus people take care of their own.

"DeMille captured our way of life."

★

A memo from Gladys Rosson to a new butler at the house showed how strictly DeMille's life was ordered.

WHILE MR. DEMILLE IS WORKING ON A PICTURE:
Go into Mr. DeM's bedroom at exactly 7 am and draw back the curtains and put up the Venetian blinds. This will awaken Mr. DeMille. Every night, Mr. DeM puts the clothes he has worn in the dressing room for you to take and clean, press and polish.

Every night Mr. DeM lays out the clothes he will wear in the morning. He will put the coat of the suit—and then you match the coat from the closet with the trousers.

You will learn what hat, gloves and overcoat Mr. DeM wears with the different type suit. But at first, Mr. DeM will have to tell you.

The tray with breakfast is left down in the kitchen . . . and after you take the tray upstairs and Mr. DeMille is eating his breakfast—then you go to the garage at #2010 and bring Mr. DeM's car out to the front of our office. . . .

While Mr. DeMille is shaving, bring up the first part of his breakfast (fruit and toast).

After Mr. DeMille puts on his shirt and necktie, then have his heavy blue cashmere dressing gown ready for him to put on. He wears this during breakfast and puts on his trousers afterwards.

When Mr. DeMille wears a gray or blue suit, he uses the silver chain attached to his keys; when he wears brown, he uses the gold chain—so put his keys on whichever one he will use. . . .

Then, when Mr. DeM is ready to leave his bedroom, always take his briefcase, hat, gloves and overcoat (if he wants one) over to the office at #2010 and down to his car when he is ready to leave the office. . . .

We have a gasoline tank in the lower garage and you will keep the DeSoto Suburban filled, marking down on the chart the date and amount of gasoline taken. . . . Mr. DeMille never likes his cars to have less than ¾ full. And Mr. DeM always leaves the keys in his cars. . . .

Mr. DeMille alternates in the use of his 2 cars: the Chrysler and the DeSoto—so every morning give him the one that was not used the day before. In this way, Mr. DeM's car is always fresh to start off with [in the] morning. He likes his cars well polished and perfectly clean inside and out. . . .

Mr. DeM has a lot of watches on his bureau. He winds them at night but he likes you to wind some of them in the morning. Ask him for instructions about this. . . .

The revolvers in Mr. DeM's bedroom closet are loaded, so use care when you handle or move them. And the guns in the gun case at the ranch are loaded."

★

Cecil was now living a life evenly divided between the accomplishments of the past, and his plans for the future. *The King of Kings* remained his favorite of his own films, and over the years he occasionally rented the Pantages Theatre on Hollywood Boulevard to show the film for free. When a former GI named John Hampton opened the Silent Movie Theatre on Fairfax Avenue after the war, he made it a point to run *The King of Kings* every Christmas, to reliably good business. But in 1952, Hampton decided to give the picture a rest and run something else. Phone calls and complaints flooded in, and the movie's absence was even covered by the newspapers. The following year, Hampton again scheduled the film at Christmas, and DeMille sent over a basket of two dozen mums accompanied by a handwritten note: "To John Hampton and the Old Time Movie Theater: Again you mark the Christmas season with the reminder that it is the birthday of the King of Kings which we celebrate. My warmest greetings and God's blessings upon you and your audience. Cecil B. DeMille."

It was around this time that Richard deMille learned about Cecil's unusual domestic arrangements, and the true status of Gladys Rosson. He was thunder-struck. "I knew all those women. I knew they accompanied him on trips and such, but it never occurred to me that they were *doing* anything. I remember I was astonished when I found out that Gladys Rosson was one of them. She was a rather plain and uninteresting secretary, and my idea of a mistress was Gina Lollobrigida."

But beneath the increasing financial success and the overdue industry accla-mation, DeMille's life was struck by an incremental tragedy, as Constance began to show signs of mental deterioration. Henry Wilcoxon accompanied her to the Golden Globe Awards for 1952 and returned home to tell his wife that something was very wrong with Mrs. DeMille. She repeated herself constantly, seeming to have a short-term memory of no more than five to ten minutes.

Domestic arrangements had to be altered. Cecil and Constance had always had adjoining bedrooms with a shared bathroom. Constance's illness mandated her own bathroom, as well as round-the-clock care. In time, the nurses became virtual family members, as with Kay Travers, who had the day shift and regularly ate lunch with Constance, Cecilia Sr. and Jr., as well as Cecil. Kay would take Cecil's great-grandson to Europe and South America, leading him to name his own son Travers.

Constance's slow retreat from the center of Cecil's emotional and business life forced him to depend on others, predominantly his daughter Cecilia. In most respects, Cecilia was the sort of person who would have gotten his back up, but she was Constance's daughter, and that was enough.

"She was so much like him, just as tough," remembered Cecilia Jr. "She'd actually go after him. He would tell me, 'No iron rod exists as strong as the one up your mother's back.' But their underlying love was undeniable. That's why he took me in when her first marriage broke up—he got to raise her all over again.

"The dynamic among the children was interesting," continued his grand-daughter. "He loved Richard—Richard was his brother's child and he loved his brother. He adored Katherine; she was as beautiful inside as she was out. John was . . . different. But my mother devoted her life to her father."

★

Always alert for something new and innovative, always a sucker for visual splen-dor, DeMille was not above expressing ingenuous pleasure to a fellow director, as in a letter he wrote to Michael Powell and Emeric Pressburger early in 1952:

> Recently I had the belated pleasure of seeing your picture "Tales of Hoff-man." Perhaps you will not mind my writing you a fan letter about it.
>
> From my earliest theater going days I have been a lover of Grand Opera. The physical drawbacks of the average operatic presentation have often bothered me—in fact it is hard for me to remember a production

which did not make heavy demands on the imagination. The only satisfactory frame of mind to bring to the theatre was to say to oneself, "Well—you can't have everything."

Your production of "Tales of Hoffman" has proven that you *can* have everything. For the first time in my life I was treated to Grand Opera where the beauty, power, and scope of the music was equally matched by the visual presentation.

I thank you for your outstanding courage and artistry in bringing to us Grand Opera as it existed until now, only in the minds of those who created it.

Powell was thrilled. "Cecil B. DeMille!" he wrote in his memoirs. "The great C.B.! . . . The greatest showman of them all, whose productions were a legend. . . . We had revered him since we were schoolboys and now he was addressing us as colleagues." Powell and Pressburger had the letter framed and hung on their office wall.

In the fall of 1952, with Powell and Pressburger having trouble setting up a production of *Die Fledermaus*—*Tales of Hoffman* broke even, but no more—they wrote DeMille to ask for his help in arranging financing with Paramount. Pressburger's diary for October 20 carries the notation: "Letter from Cecil B. DeMille. Very nice, he'll recommend the head of Paramount get in touch with us." Paramount agreed to finance the picture, but the casting was wrong—the icy Mel Ferrer was used because Powell hoped to be able to get Audrey Hepburn, Ferrer's wife, for a future film of *Ondine*. Inauspiciously retitled *Oh . . . Rosalinda!!*, it was a fast flop, as movies with two exclamation points invariably are.

Also earning a measure of DeMille's appreciation was Tony Quinn, who had carved out a major career as a character actor, earning—and deserving—an Academy Award for going mano a mano with Brando in *Viva Zapata!* But it was another picture that truly opened DeMille's eyes to his son-in-law's gifts. "After the first Academy Award, he started to change, but it was too late by then," remembered Quinn. "But the thing that changed him the most was when I made *La Strada*. He was blown away by *La Strada*. 'My God,' he told me, 'no costumes, no jewelry, and they made a picture about those people.' He was floored by the effect of the picture."

When Quinn was out of the room, it was another story: "Why make a movie about a man's faults?" he asked his granddaughter. "The picture made me want to take a bath."

⋆

DeMille had been thinking about writing his autobiography for some time, but finally began organizing the project in late 1952. Negotiations with publishers were slow—since DeMille was used to getting 50 percent of the profits of his movies, he was perfectly willing to let a publisher share in his profits, rather than the other way around. His original plan for the book was to intersperse his reminiscences with material by others. He thought Neil McCarthy could write a chapter about DeMille's contributions to the aviation industry, Bill or Cecilia could write about him from the family angle, Chet Huntley or some other "non-communist liberal" could write about his politics. Other contributors might include people "who might even hate the sight of him." DeMille thought that one of the people who could write about his movies was Bosley Crowther of the *New York Times*, who DeMille noted with rueful pride, "gave me two favorable notices in thirty years."

A contract with Prentice Hall was finally signed in August of 1953, with publication scheduled for 1955. The advance was a modest $10,000, but DeMille got a remarkable 17 percent royalty on the first 15,000 copies, and 21 percent thereafter. Art Arthur began an extensive series of interviews with DeMille, and prepared some sample chapters, as did Donald Hayne, whom DeMille said was "closer to the deepest places of my mind" than anybody who had ever worked with him.

Hayne had come to work for DeMille as a speechwriter in the wake of the AFRA mess. He was a former priest who had married and had children although many people believed him to be bisexual. In any case, Hayne never seemed to have a philosophical problem with the Catholic Church. Hayne was tall, extraordinarily intelligent, and a physical mess, with terrible teeth. In fact, DeMille insisted that he get his teeth fixed as a condition of employment. "Grandfather found him honest and trustworthy, not always common qualities in Hollywood," said Cecilia Jr., "and he was easy and enlightening to work with. Certainly, DeMille changed him socially, which was needed."

One of the reasons that DeMille kept Hayne around was because he was interesting. DeMille had little patience with dull people; his eyes would glaze over, a surreptitious signal would be given, and a secretary would usher the offending party out. Some people in the DeMille organization, as well as some people in the DeMille family, became jealous of Hayne's ability to fascinate DeMille with his discourses on philosophy and religion. Hayne would write most of the memoir, for the director's attention was increasingly monopolized by the biggest picture of his career—indeed, the biggest picture of anybody's career.

DeMille's initial impulse for his remake of *The Ten Commandments* was to structure a film much like the 1923 version—a biblical prologue followed by a modern story, perhaps a tale of civic corruption. But DeMille felt that the prologue of the original film dated much less than the modern story because of the timelessness of its moral lessons. Once the decision was made to go with an entirely biblical narrative, there was some thought given to illustrating each of the Ten Commandments through the personal stories of some of the people involved in the Exodus. But once again, DeMille decided to let the Bible story speak for itself.

The proposed budget was nonexistent—DeMille knew that the special effects would have to go far beyond what anybody had done before, so estimating what they would cost would be impossible. Certainly, it would cost more than anybody had ever spent on a movie.

Paramount was understandably nervous, but Adolph Zukor, for what seems to have been the first and only time, reminded everybody that DeMille was responsible for the very existence of the movie studio and was the most consistently bankable director in the business. "I find it embarrassing and deplorable that it takes a Gentile like Cecil here to consistently remind us Jews of our heritage! . . . What kind of men are you? What kind of Jews are you? I, for one, think it's a good idea, not a stupid idea."

After DeMille made some vague rumblings about doing the picture elsewhere if Paramount lacked the backbone, the board acquiesced. When Frank Freeman looked over the figures DeMille presented him with, he said, "You know, C.B., these figures won't give your company . . . as big a percentage of returns as you got from *The Greatest Show on Earth* or *Samson and Delilah*."

DeMille explained that he was ceding a great deal of his profit percentage because of the risk Paramount was undertaking. "I can't tell you what *The Ten Commandments* will cost, except that it will be over $8,000,000. I don't know how much over."

As soon as the deal was done, the studio's anxiety was transferred to Cecil. "I didn't sleep," he would say about this period, "I worried day and night. I wouldn't have lost a dollar, but it would have killed me; I wouldn't have come out of it alive if I had ruined Paramount. It would have meant a hell of a lot more than the fact that I didn't [make] any money."

By 1953, plans were well underway. DeMille believed that credibility was the key to the miracles of the story, with at least a semblance of what amounted to science. For the parting of the Red Sea, he examined the work of government hurricane experts and decided that the event could most convincingly be dramatized through two gathering storms approaching the center of the frame, colliding and discharging their fury downward into the sea, blowing apart the waters so the Jews could pass through.

While the picture was still in the planning stages, DeMille welcomed James Card of the Eastman House, who wanted DeMille's movies for his museum's collection. DeMille wasn't interested in donating his prints—he worried about writers stealing his plots, as if the plots were what made his movies special—but he liked Card and welcomed him back to the office several times.

Card remembered that DeMille enjoyed talking about how he evaded censorship, pointing to a still of Claudette Colbert from *Cleopatra*. Colbert was in the background, while a harpist was in the foreground, the strings covering most of the frame. "Do you see what the harpist's fingers are doing to the body of Cleopatra lying there in the background?"

Several times Card and DeMille were interrupted by Henry Wilcoxon with some problem relating to the new film. Card noted with amazement that Wilcoxon backed out of the room after his questions had been answered.

For *The Ten Commandments*, DeMille agreed to use VistaVision, Paramount's designated widescreen process. It was the clearest of the widescreen films. VistaVision was photographed with 35mm film running not vertically but horizontally—exactly like a 35mm still camera. The negative area was thus considerably larger than conventional 35mm negative, which meant that when it was printed, it featured a remarkable focus that reduced grain. When Technicolor printed the film from its ultra-fine-grained three-strip matrices to release prints, the result was a picture of unparalleled clarity and stunningly saturated color. As widescreen historian Martin Hart explains, "Technicolor [VistaVision] yielded almost 3-D looking prints." VistaVision was also modern in that it could be exhibited in any widescreen ratio from 1:66 to 1 (the preferred ratio) to 2:1—very close to the way most neighborhood theaters showed CinemaScope, which had started the whole widescreen revolution in 1952 and 1953.

There was only one problem—VistaVision had no provisions for stereophonic sound. Stereo greatly impressed DeMille when he saw the film version of *The King and I* made under the musical direction of Alfred Newman at 20th Century Fox, one of the most advanced studios in town. DeMille badly wanted *The Ten Com-*

mandments to have an equivalent sonic grandeur, but Frank Freeman explained that the hierarchy at Paramount didn't believe that anybody bought tickets to movies because of their sound. Having gone through the 1927–1930 era, DeMille strongly disagreed, but Freeman refused to upgrade, greatly upsetting the director.

★

The Bible drops Moses after he is discovered in the bulrushes, then picks him up again at the age of thirty. DeMille and his writers had to devise a story for the intervening years, which is where Henry Noerdlinger proved invaluable. Noerdlinger sat in on every writers' conference, guiding the narrative possibilities. DeMille needed documentation, even if it was fanciful, so that the script would not be dogged by criticism from one religious group or another. Noerdlinger kept track of the books and files he consulted, as well as a list of the libraries and museums he drew on. The tally came to 1,644 publications, which was used as evidence for the painstaking quality of the research. The research in turn became one of the selling points of the film.

The sources for the script included the Midrash Rabbah, an ancient compilation of rabbinic commentaries, the Qur'an, Philo's *Life of Moses*, and the writings of Josephus and Eusebius. These texts were written centuries after the Exodus, and Noerdlinger carefully referred to them as "traditions" rather than "histories," but he argued that they still constituted valid evidence for the story of the film's first act: that Moses was in fact a prince of Egypt who had conducted a successful campaign against Ethiopia and had been cast out by court intrigues—an idea drawn largely from Josephus and Eusebius.

This backstory added a revenge motif to the biblical story, and was avidly seized on by DeMille, who set up Moses and Rameses as rival princes. This approach had been used by a writer named Dorothy Clarke Wilson for a novel entitled *Prince of Egypt* in 1949, but Noerdlinger convinced DeMille that basing his script on ancient texts, however dubious, gave him more veracity than adapting a modern historical novel.

Eventually, the film's research was published by the University of California as *Moses and Egypt: The Documentation to the Motion Picture The Ten Commandments.* DeMille paid for the book's publication. The book would be criticized as an example of "pseudo-history" because Noerdlinger gathered every possible source, canonical or not, without any attempt to authenticate one over the other or to reconcile contradictions. But Noerdlinger pointed out that *Moses and Egypt* was not supposed "to give full justice to any given subject, but rather to point out what we did in the picture and with what justification."

So the story devolved into that old DeMille standby—two men vying for the same woman. Upping the ante was that each of them is also after the same throne—Moses through humane slave driving, Rameses through inhumane slave driving. On this spine DeMille could hang enough drama until the biblical narrative kicked in, with its flamboyant miracles and dramatic traction of Moses's transformation into the spokesman for universal freedom.

Casting proceeded in the usual stop-and-start DeMille manner. His first choice for Moses was Charlton Heston, but he teased people with the left-field possibility of William Boyd. DeMille called Boyd for lunch, after which they disappeared into DeMille's office. Boyd didn't need money—Hopalong Cassidy had made him very wealthy—and he was unsure he was the right actor for the part. Not only that, he didn't share DeMille's belief that the audience would overlook his identification with Hopalong Cassidy. But DeMille wasn't serious; the casting of Boyd would have necessitated a thorough overhaul of DeMille's dramatic structure, losing the early section where Moses is in his late twenties or early thirties. Boyd was 59 years old in 1954.

DeMille decided on Charlton Heston when Henry Wilcoxon pointed out that a bearded Heston looked just like Michelangelo's statue of Moses. "If he's good enough for Michelangelo, he's good enough for me," DeMille announced. Since *The Greatest Show on Earth*, Heston had been marking time with a series of programmers: *Arrowhead*, *Secret of the Incas*, *The Naked Jungle*, *Ruby Gentry*, and so forth. Heston signed on to play Moses for the bargain rate of a flat $50,000. But *The Ten Commandments* would transform the actor's career and permanently elevate him into a Hollywood icon.

DeMille wanted Audrey Hepburn for the part of Nefretiri, and while her face was perfect for the wigs and makeup, the artists and costume designers could never devise an Egyptian dress that looked good on her slender figure. The role of Joshua went to John Derek even though, as DeMille noted sourly, "He knows nothing about the Bible." For Rameses, DeMille ran past Anthony Dexter, Stewart Granger, William Holden, and Michael Rennie. Holden even came in for an interview in the fall of 1952. But on February 26, 1953, DeMille, accompanied by his granddaughter Cecilia, Gladys Rosson, and Donald Hayne, saw Yul Brynner in *The King and I* on Broadway. "After the first act grandfather and I went backstage and met Yul," remembered Cecilia. "[Grandfather] said 'Good Evening' to him, and the second thing Grandfather said was, 'How would you like to play the most powerful man on earth?' There was an extra step in Yul's performance, I think, after that."

It was an invitation no actor could resist, but Brynner was tied up with the show. DeMille agreed to hold off production until Brynner was free in 1954 and agreed to pay him considerably more than Heston: Brynner was to get $7,500 a week for ten weeks, with the next two weeks free, with everything over that payable at $2,000 a week. As it turned out, DeMille was so happy with Brynner's performance that he waived the two free weeks and paid him the extra $15,000—an unheard-of gesture from DeMille toward an actor.

For Bithiah, DeMille wanted Jayne Meadows, but she didn't want to leave her husband, Steve Allen, and their children for the necessary length of time. Henry Wilcoxon suggested Nina Foch, with whom he had just worked in *Scaramouche*.

For the part of Dathan, DeMille made an offer to Raymond Massey, then thought better of it and decided on Jack Palance. Then Palance's agent stole a copy of the script to give to his client. A furious DeMille needed an alternative. Jesse Lasky Jr. suggested that Edward G. Robinson was perfect: "Jewish, a great villain, and had a strong screen presence but . . . too bad about what *Red Channels* had to say." (Robinson had been graylisted for his unexceptional liberal politics.) DeMille decided he had paid too much attention to *Red Channels* and signed Robinson.

"No more conservative or patriarchal figure existed in Hollywood," wrote Robinson in his memoirs, "no one more opposed to communism or any permutation or combination thereof. And no fairer one, no man with a greater sense of decency and justice. . . . Cecil B. DeMille returned me to films. Cecil B. DeMille restored my self-respect."

For Lilia, DeMille wanted Pier Angeli, but MGM wouldn't loan her out, so he hired Debra Paget without an interview. John Carradine was working at Paramount on a Bob Hope picture called *Casanova's Big Night* when he ran into DeMille in the commissary. DeMille hugged him and asked, "Are you going to be with me?" and Carradine was abruptly cast for the role of Aaron.

Mostly, DeMille paid below market value for talent. Yvonne De Carlo worked for $25,000, while Henry Wilcoxon got $500 a week during preproduction and postproduction, and $1,000 a week during production for both associate-producing and acting. It didn't matter; as Vincent Price remembered, "You couldn't call yourself a star unless you had been in a DeMille picture!"

When word broke that DeMille was making an epic about the Bible, other studios quickly got into the ancient act. Fox made *The Egyptian*, Warners made *Land of the Pharaohs* and *Helen of Troy*, all of which reached the theaters before *The Ten Commandments*. DeMille and the staff would troop in to look at these movies, prepared to change anything in their script that had been inadvertently—or purposely—stolen. DeMille's primary response to *The Egyptian* was to shudder at the presence of Victor Mature: "Worst actor I ever worked with. Never want to see him again as long as I live."

By now, Pat Moore, the child actor who had played the child Pharaoh in the first version of *The Ten Commandments*, was working as a sound editor at Paramount. Moore's mother had recently died, and one day DeMille saw Moore on the lot and took him aside. "Pat, this is something that is going to affect you for the rest of your life. When my mother passed away, it meant a great deal to me, it hit me very seriously. Your mother was a very sweet woman."

Moore was struck by the gentle, fatherly gesture of the personal DeMille, and how it differed from the professional DeMille he had grown used to seeing on the set—strict, analytical, tempestuous.

★

In the early summer of 1953, while preparations for *The Ten Commandments* were gathering momentum, Gladys Rosson was diagnosed with cancer. In a letter to a mutual friend of theirs, DeMille wrote, "Gladdy is a brave little girl. You may wonder that I say little girl, but to me she has been just that for nearly forty years. She is, has been, and always will be so much a part of my life that she has a place in my heart that nothing else can ever fill."

Once again, DeMille had to face losing someone he loved to cancer. Specialists were called in, but none could offer any hope. Henry Noerdlinger went to visit Gladys at her house and brought some gifts. Gladys was already bedridden, and Noerdlinger noticed that her house was done in gentle pastels.

By way of conversation he said, "Isn't it nice to hear the birds singing?"

"Now, I can hear them too," she replied. Noerdlinger realized that she had never really had time for things like birdsong until her failing health mandated rest.

When Gladys had to go back into the hospital, DeMille was afflicted with a quiet anguish over what to say to this woman who had shared his professional and personal life for nearly forty years. Finally, he decided to rely upon the first chapter of the Gospel of St. John. When Gladys died on June 14, 1953, DeMille was devastated. "I would have given . . . a million dollars to save her life," he stated flatly in his autobiography. "All I could give Gladys Rosson, the last time I saw her, was the first 14 verses of the Gospel according to St. John; Gladys was one who knew their meaning and their worth."

"Gladys Rosson was a person that he couldn't do without," remembered Henry Noerdlinger. "When she died he was really depressed. It was a tremendous loss to him." When Gladys's estate was probated, it was revealed that DeMille had taken very good care of her; she left $127,887, a considerable amount for an executive secretary in 1953.

A few years later, he would say of Gladys, "I liked her better than any woman I've ever worked with. . . . Plain, tough . . . terribly sensitive, but stubborn for virtue. It had to be done right; it had to be done this way." DeMille could have been speaking of DeMille, of course, which is why he and Gladys were so simpatico.

Gladys had been so comprehensively competent that it took three people to replace her: Doris Turner took over her duties as a production secretary; Cecil's daughter Cecilia took over his private finances, and Florence Cole ran the day-to-day office duties. And just because Cecilia was his daughter didn't mean Cecil cut her any more slack than he did anybody else. "Cecilia," her father wrote her one day, "you do not keep me sufficiently well advised as to the best sellers in books each month. It is important for me to know."

★

As the hiring of Edward G. Robinson indicated, DeMille was beginning to show signs of softening his political fervor. He would never be anything but a conservative anticommunist, but a January 1954 letter that he wrote to L. W. Douglas, a banker and good friend of Spencer Tracy's, shows his growing respect for Eisenhower in spite of the fact that the president lacked the fire-breathing theatricality of Douglas MacArthur, or the rigid isolationist politics of Robert Taft, the men who had been Eisenhower's competition for the 1952 Republican nomination. In his autobiography, DeMille asserted that he was a Taft man, and called him "one of the most misunderstood men of American history," but his archives contain a fair amount of MacArthur campaign material as well.

"I not only like Ike," wrote DeMille, "I like the way he has gone about his job slowly, thoughtfully, not rushing in with a lot of hasty 'must' legislation. I think his particular recommendations all have to be considered against the background of his deep convictions on the Constitutional separation of powers in our government. He has restored Congress to its place as the body that initiates legislation."

★

In the fall of 1953, a survey party flew to Egypt. Cameramen Loyal Griggs and Peverell Marley scouted locations on both sides of the Nile, and the special effects cameramen John Warren and Wallace Kelley looked for a location for the parting of the Red Sea. Eventually, a dry lake bed with a high promontory rock was discovered near Abu Rudeis. With water matted in, the site would be completely convincing; multiple photographs were taken so the promontory could be duplicated back at the studio on the blue screen stage, where much of the special effects would be shot.

When he had made up his mind to make the film, DeMille had opened negotiations with King Farouk for permission to film in Egypt. Farouk agreed, but he was deposed in mid-1952. His successor was General Muhammad Naguib, but after eighteen months he too was forced out, by Colonel Gamal Abdel Nasser. In early and mid-1954, DeMille had to engage in furious renegotiations, because the location work was scheduled to begin that fall.

"DeMille was telling [Nasser and Hakim Amer, Nasser's minister of war] why the picture was good and why it was wonderful, and they started to laugh," remembered his granddaughter Cecilia. "He got hold of himself and started again, and they started to laugh again, and he stopped and looked at them and Hakim Amer said, 'Mr. DeMille, we grew up on your film *The Crusades*, and we saw how you treated us and our religion. Our country is your country.' "

Preparation for a DeMille movie was always painstaking, but *The Ten Commandments* was unusually complex. Instead of having the studio confect costume jewelry for the film, DeMille ordered exact reproductions of ancient Egyptian jewelry that used real gold and precious stones. DeMille's customary fetish for physical authenticity caused some problems. Anne Baxter, who was hired to play Nefretiri and costumed to resemble Claudette Colbert in *Cleopatra* as much as was possible, remembered that she did costume fittings for eight months. "I made two other pictures in between fittings," she asserted.

The finished script carried this opening manifesto: "All these things are as I have found them in the Holy Scriptures, the Glorious Koran, the ancient Hebrew writing, and in the annals of modern discovery. CBDM." In DeMille's mind, he was not interpreting the life of Moses; rather, he was filming the definitive historical account.

From the beginning, it was clear that this was no ordinary production. DeMille took his daughter Cecilia, Cecilia Jr., and Donald Hayne with him on the voyage to Egypt, and on the first or second night at sea, as they left the dining room they were stopped by a waiter who offered his hand. "I know you, but from where?" asked DeMille. "I'm Schwartzman," replied the waiter. Cecilia Jr. stepped between the two men, for she recognized Schwartzman as a stalker who had threatened to kill DeMille a few years earlier because the director wouldn't produce his movie script.

DeMille realized that it was going to be a long voyage, and he couldn't avoid Schwartzman for ten days, so he agreed to meet with him in his stateroom. Behind one door was the ship's captain, holding a gun, while behind another was Cecilia's husband and Donald Hayne, with no gun at all. Cecilia Jr. remembered thinking that Hayne was a useless appendage, for he was no man of action. As it happened, DeMille turned on the charm and defused Schwartzman's ire, while the captain and crew kept an eye on him for the rest of the voyage. DeMille went so far as to find Schwartzman a job in Germany after the voyage.

Initially, DeMille was quietly jubilant on board the ship, enjoying the champagne (Mailly Rosé Brut 1947) that Barney Balaban had ordered served to his party for the entire ocean voyage, and falling in love with the candied ginger that the *Queen Elizabeth* served as an appetizer. But the mood didn't last; the letters home of the production secretary Joan Brooskin provide an invaluable record of a shoot that started out as difficult, soon became exhausting, and finally life-threatening.

When he got to Egypt, DeMille inspected the Gates of Rameses and the Avenue of the Sphinxes that had been erected at Beni Youssef, about fifteen miles from Cairo, three miles from the Pyramids. The Gates were 107 feet high, in front of which stretched an Avenue of Sphinxes that was nearly a quarter mile long.

DeMille took it all in and pronounced himself pleased. Prop master Bob Goodstein took a jeep ride with DeMille through the acres and acres of props that Goodstein had bought and built. When DeMille saw one wagon that looked too much like another, he told Goodstein to use one or the other, but not both.

The cameras began turning on October 14, 1954. By October 22, Joe Harper was asking anybody who would listen whether they had been gone two years or two and a half years. DeMille had already lost weight—he would eventually drop over twenty pounds—and was brown from the sun.

On October 28, the entire party came to the set to watch DeMille shoot Yul Brynner leading Pharaoh's chariots past the Avenue of the Sphinxes. DeMille noticed that Brynner was nervous about driving a chariot in front of the Egyptian army. "Don't worry," said DeMille. "It's safe. Here, I'll show you." DeMille got into the chariot, raced the horses around in a circle, and stopped right on the spot where he had taken the reins.

The shot completed, Brynner took off for Acapulco, leaving behind his friend, the film's doctor: Max Jacobson. Jacobson would become known as the quintessential Dr. Feelgood dispensing his specially concocted brand of pick-me-ups to dozens of celebrity patients, among them DeMille, John F. Kennedy, Alan Jay Lerner, and Tennessee Williams. DeMille had been seeing Jacobson occasionally since January 1952.

No one seemed to know or care what Jacobson was prescribing, only that it banished fatigue and made sleep optional. Jacobson's manner and thriving medical practice gave him an aura of omnipotence that wasn't to be found in the usual dispensers of pep pills that were pandemic in Hollywood in the 1940s. In fact, Jacobson was injecting customized doses of methedrine, which raises blood pressure, relieves fatigue, and induces a touch of euphoria.

Jacobson was described by Christopher Plummer as "a cross between Conrad Veidt and Martin Bormann," and Tennessee Williams would write that the doctor had "a magical atmosphere of understanding and compassion. . . . I don't think he even took my pulse or blood pressure or had me fill out a questionnaire about my medical history. He just looked at me . . . then started concocting the shot, drawing a bit of fluid from one bottle and another and another as my suspense and my alarm increased." But the aftermath of the injection was almost miraculous: "I felt as if a concrete sarcophagus about me had sprung open and I was released as a bird on the wing." Williams's response was not unusual; one female patient described the effects of the injections as resembling an orgasm.

Jacobson's method was to give two injections, one in the arm, one in the buttocks. "He had a basic formula, and he would vary it according to your size," remembered Eddie Fisher. "He was like Rasputin; he could make you believe anything. He was from Berlin and had a German accent. He could be warm or he could be a tyrant, but he had a tremendous sense of humor with a great grasp of the English language. You were under his spell; he believed he had found the answer to Eternal Youth. He may have meant well in the beginning, but as he saw what power he had, he became more destructive and took a lot of chances. A lot of people OD'd because he'd give them too much. I became as addicted to him as I did to the drugs."

Richard deMille smelled a rat. "Max Jacobson was what we would now call a guru. He was slightly mysterious, and always had the latest medical information and spoke in a technical language that had a grand sound to it. He was a total charlatan."

Henry Noerdlinger, who was more sophisticated than most of the people on DeMille's staff, was on to Jacobson fairly quickly. Noerdlinger remembered going into a tent in Egypt with Jacobson one day, and without a word, the doctor said, "Don't tell me, I know what's wrong with you," whereupon he produced a syringe, had Noerdlinger drop his pants, and gave him a shot.

"He was a most peculiar doctor," Noerdlinger would say with commendable European understatement. When Joan Brooskin came down with dengue fever, Jacobson gave her a couple of shots and told her that not only would she get over the fever, she would never have migraines or menstrual cramps again!

"When DeMille's energy lagged, he would pick himself up with a shot of Dr. Feelgood's juice," remembered Anthony Quinn. "He was hooked and so was Katherine. She even started taking the children to see Dr. Feelgood." Quinn too began seeing Jacobson for pick-me-ups.

DeMille's increasing dependency on the quack, attested to by the unquestioned respect in his correspondence to Jacobson, would be the most obvious manifestation of a naïveté that Donald Hayne had observed: "The latest glib expert to come along can make an impression on DeMille, at least if he claims expertness in a field with which DeMille is not fully familiar." Hayne believed that this curious Achilles' heel in an otherwise strong-minded man derived from DeMille's ego and need for success: "If he has invested time and initial confidence in a man, the man must make good, and DeMille will continue to swear by him as long as there is any chance that he might [make good]; and sometimes, unfortunately, longer."

It is unclear whether DeMille's California doctors knew about Jacobson's "treatments," but Cecil's medical problems didn't begin and end with one quack. His cholesterol around this time was a sky-high 400. In a note to himself, Cecil noted that "normal [was] 150–200." Jacobson would attend DeMille off and on until DeMille's death, and the doctor's "treatments" undoubtedly shortened his life. As Anthony Quinn remembered, there were times when "DeMille never knew if he was up or down. He was prone to tremendous mood swings. His energy came and went. It was sometimes difficult for him to talk." Jacobson's medical license would be revoked in 1975.

★

The Mitchell camera company had built four custom VistaVision cameras specially for DeMille, and they worked splendidly. But in other respects, the production was assaulted by the elements. Most days, the temperature was past 90 degrees Fahrenheit by 7 A.M. Yet, by November 1, DeMille was almost four days ahead of schedule and was making shots that were originally intended to be done back in

Hollywood. But there were gathering pressures—some overcast weather angered him, and he grew snappish. After a particularly hard day, Brooskin broke down in tears, writing her husband, "You can't win—he misses Miss Rosson so much."

One day early in production, a black car pulled up and a man in a white linen suit got out. It was William Boyd, come a very long way to wish his old boss godspeed. Boyd asked if he could "play through" the sand trap. DeMille was overwhelmed at the graciousness of this arduous gesture and tears rolled down his cheeks. It was the happiest he would be during the Egyptian shoot.

As on their previous picture together, DeMille liked Charlton Heston's intense seriousness. DeMille took a page from his experience working with H. B. Warner on *The King of Kings* and instructed Heston that when he was in costume, he should never sit down on the set, never be seen reading a newspaper, having a cup of coffee, or talking on the phone. When he was in wardrobe for Moses, he was to act as Moses. The result was that the Arab extras would never take their eyes off Heston, and would murmur "Moussa! Moussa!" as he walked past. An aura of charismatic reverence was created that DeMille hoped would seep into the film. Before Heston had a big scene, he would go off by himself in costume for fifteen minutes and walk up and down preparing himself for the scene. DeMille never asked what he was thinking about, but whatever it was, it worked.

When DeMille and a skeleton crew reached the base of Mount Sinai to shoot Moses's climb up the mountain, there were no roads of any kind. There were about sixty people, plus porters, traveling in a fleet of Plymouths that also held provisions for the troupe. The entire party had to walk the last mile up the mountain. DeMille was at the head of the column, head down and panting but setting a good pace.

Shooting on Sinai itself took three days. These scenes in the Holy Land would endanger and ultimately shorten DeMille's life, but to him they were worth it—Mount Sinai, the desert, and the Exodus, the primary scenes shot in Egypt, would validate the rest of the film, give it the scent of the real.

The base for the scenes on Mount Sinai was the monastery of Saint Catherine, one of the three or four oldest monasteries in Christendom. There were a dozen monks left in what had once been a flourishing community, and only one of them spoke English. DeMille was given the room usually reserved for the Archbishop of Sinai. There was a tall wood-burning stove in the bedroom, and on the desk a silver canister of black sand did the job of blotting paper. DeMille was amused by the gleaming modern tub in the bathroom.

The next morning, a group of monks appeared at DeMille's door, carrying holy water. They recited prayers and sprinkled water, while asking the blessings of God upon DeMille's work. From the monastery, it was a two-hour camel ride to the top of Sinai. The cameras had to be taken apart and reassembled at the location. The days were brutally hot and the nights were chilly.

One night, Henry Wilcoxon took DeMille up a long flight of stairs to the roof of the monastery to soak in the beautiful isolation and look at the stars. Wilcoxon noticed that DeMille was laboring. His color was bad, he was gasping for breath, but he refused Wilcoxon's offer of a hand up. He was a seventy-three-year-old man a long way from serious medical care.

In a series of letters from the location, publicist Rufus Blair kept Art Arthur back in Hollywood informed about what was going on. Heston earned the respect of everybody for his uncomplaining work ethic in the scenes where he had to stumble through the parched wilderness, "which is as much broken stones as sand," according to Blair. "Every time he stumbled and fell, he had to land on these sharp, three cornered stones. His legs, thighs, arms and chest are a welter of bruises, and yet the man goes at it, under this gruesome sun, as if it was something good and cold to eat." On top of that, Heston earned the gratitude of the prop men when, after a take, he wiped his own footprints from the sand with his robe before the next take.

It took DeMille and the company an entire day to get these shots that would be edited together for a montage. One day, there was no water for five long hours, as someone forgot to completely turn off the tap on the ten-gallon water can on the back of the prop truck. Another day, a group of Bedouins passed behind the cameras, and the braying of their camels meant that DeMille had to shoot without sound.

The land was not only savagely hot, it was uneven, so most of the shots were made on a tripod, but head grip Dominic Seminerio somehow laid forty feet of track on Mount Sinai so DeMille could get a dolly shot of Moses going up the mountain to receive the Commandments, and eighty feet of track for another dolly shot over a riverbed. These tracking shots gave some movement to the sequence of Moses's exile in the wilderness, and DeMille regarded them as both physical and engineering feats.

With the Sinai scenes done, the monks rang all the monastery bells in farewell, and the Bedouins who had worked as extras and porters staged for the company *The Wolf and the Sheep*, a little drama of group action foiling marauding wolves that the Bedouins had enacted for thousands of years. DeMille was thrilled to realize that Moses might have seen the same play performed on the same spot. DeMille had organized and mobilized his crew so well that the scheduled twelve days of Sinai locations were completed in nine days.

The Egyptian government proved as good as its word, and the assistance promised DeMille all showed up: men, horses, and nine airplanes for use as wind machines. All this activity was facilitated by John Fulton, who had taken over the special effects department at Paramount after Gordon Jennings died of a heart attack on the golf course in 1953. Fulton worked closely with Griggs and DeMille in selecting desert sites that would accommodate miniatures, matte paintings, and blue screen photography. Sketches by Albert Nozaki and John Jensen were used as lineup clips in the cameraman's finder, enabling him to see how the concept would look against the reality, as well as saving a lot of headaches for the optical department months later.

Because the sun went down early, DeMille and company rose at 4:30 A.M. so as to start shooting by 6:30 or seven. A couple of mornings began with DeMille and Heston swimming in the Red Sea, until they were told that it was full of sharks. The production day lasted until 4:30 P.M., then DeMille went over the next day's complicated schedule with the technicians, rarely getting to bed before eleven. As if the sun and the work itself weren't bad enough, dysentery hit everybody at one time or another, usually for around three days, and people began to visibly lose weight.

After the Sinai location, the crew returned to Cairo to shoot the Exodus. Behind Pharaoh's gates was the company production headquarters: offices, storage sheds, medical tent, horse and sheep corrals and parking for the fleets of cars, a commissary large enough to feed thousands of extras, water for hundreds of livestock, corrals for the dozens of horses that pulled Pharaoh's chariots. The structures were wood, and some had awnings out front so people could take advantage of whatever breezes were to be had. None of the buildings was air-conditioned. (At Abu Rudeis, the site of the Red Sea crossing, DeMille's accommodations consisted of a simple trailer with an awning—again, no air-conditioning.) The set and headquarters encompassed sixty acres in all, and *Time* magazine called the re-creation of the Gates of Rameses the biggest piece of Egyptian construction since the Suez Canal.

On November 7, it was time to stage the Exodus sequence. Unit production manager Don Robb—who would spend three days short of a year on the location—had realized that trucks couldn't supply enough water for the location, so had had wells drilled to draw water for the thousands of people and animals that would be in the Exodus sequence. Robb's unit was responsible for pumping around 200,000 gallons a day just to stay even with demand.

Buses began running the night before, seventeen of them ferrying extras out from Cairo beginning at 10 P.M. The buses shuttled back and forth all night long, spilling extras out on the sand, after which they were fed, given water, and costumed. Bob Goodstein's prop department had been on site for six months buying and building every wagon, every bundle, every animal to be used in the sequence. The lowest estimate for the number of extras used was eight thousand, although assistant director Chico Day thought that for some shots there may have been as many as twelve thousand to fourteen thousand. The prop departments also had charge of the animals, and used five thousand camels, five thousand water buffalo, about four thousand oxen, two thousand geese, and two thousand ducks.

Since all of the extras and most of the forty-five assistant directors—every fifty or so people had a designated leader—were Egyptians, communication was crucial. Henry Wilcoxon learned twenty-four basic sentences in Arabic. The signals included trumpets played over loudspeakers and the firing of blank cartridges, while DeMille used a little gold whistle that penetrated for several hundred yards. As DeMille would give directions, an interpreter by his side would translate, and the assistants in the crowd would make sure the instructions filtered down to their specific charges.

The set was vast, so binoculars were standard issue for the production personnel, and all departments of the production were identified by various colored streamers worn on their hats. Assistant directors wore red, props wore green, wardrobe wore white.

All of the four VistaVision cameras were deployed for the Exodus sequence—DeMille rode the A camera mounted on a boom in front of Heston and the multitude, while the other three cameras, mounted on specially designed cars, were initially hidden behind sphinxes for close shots.

Charlton Heston said at the time that "The outstanding ingredient in Mr. DeMille's talent as a filmmaker is his absolutely insatiable capacity for an infinity of detail and his relentless determination to get what he wants."

Generally an admirable quality, although Heston had a few moments on November 7 when he wondered what he had gotten himself into.

"When the shot was finally ready, you or I or I believe almost any director in the history of pictures would be so overcome by the magnitude of what he had wrought that he would just be inclined to say 'Roll 'Em! Print! My God, that's wonderful!' To sit there and fiddle with it once you'd gotten them out there—it is a frightening thing to have the courage to do."

While Heston stood in full costume and makeup in the broiling Egyptian sun, DeMille began rearranging people in the crowd. "The woman with the blue shawl between the feet of the third collosi from the back; I don't want her there, no, no, the third collosi, that's the woman, I want her down on the sand."

Dear God, thought Heston, is he going to do this with eight thousand people? "And he very nearly did it with 8,000 people. And you think, this is ridiculous, we will never, never turn a camera. But finally he got what he wanted and that's when he shot. And it is this kind of determination that is required to make a film like this."

There were three takes of the Exodus, with DeMille signaling action by firing a .45 pistol. After each take, a hundred laborers spread out to collect all the debris that had been created by the eight thousand extras, then the sand in front of the set was watered down so there would be no obscuring dust kicked up by the vast crowd.

Each take lasted for ten minutes, one entire reel of negative film, and then came two hours of reassembling the multitude back at the starting point. The first take was done early in the morning, the second around noon, and another late in the afternoon.

On the third take, there was a problem with the camera on top of the Gates of Rameses, the one that was supposed to shoot a reverse angle of the Exodus, with Heston a tiny dot in front of the thronging thousands behind him. DeMille was halfway up the 107 foot height with Henry Wilcoxon right behind him when he suddenly stopped and began to sway. DeMille hooked his elbow around a rung to keep his balance as Wilcoxon came up behind him. DeMille looked old and desperate, his face contorted in pain. He was panting.

Wilcoxon held him by the legs and told him he wouldn't let him fall. DeMille didn't think he could climb down, and Wilcoxon didn't think he could carry him down, so the two men inched their way up the rest of the ladder to the top of the gates. By the time they got DeMille underneath an umbrella, he was "an odd shade of gray and shiny with sweat," according to makeup man Frank Westmore.

"What happened out there?" DeMille asked Westmore. Westmore told him that some of the Arabs had run off, but DeMille waved that off. "That's all right, Frank. I got the shot."

Wilcoxon moved to loosen DeMille's collar and told him that he'd better not try to climb down, but DeMille slapped his hand away, then slapped him away. "Who the hell do you think you are? Nobody tells me what to do! What choice do I have?" Wilcoxon said they could rig a bosun's chair on a pulley to get him down, but DeMille's response was curt: "Shut up, Harry." A camp doctor was brought up to the top of the set and ordered complete rest while DeMille stayed under the umbrella and Wilcoxon got the rest of the shots they needed. DeMille remained adamant. He would walk or he would die. Soon after dark, he slowly descended the ladder and was rushed to the hospital in Cairo.

Attending him were Dr. Hussein Ibrahim, the brother of the owner of the luxurious apartment where DeMille was living, and Max Jacobson. Both doctors told DeMille that he had suffered a major heart attack, but that if he rested in bed with oxygen for four weeks, he would recover.

"Forget it, gentlemen," he said, "I'm going to the set in the morning." Henry Wilcoxon said that it wasn't necessary, that the shots had all been rehearsed and he could direct them while DeMille got some much needed rest. DeMille shook his head; it was his picture—he would be there in the morning.

DeMille was livid at his faltering body and took it out on Wilcoxon, "Right now, Harry, shut up or you're fired."

"I don't care if I am fired, you can't go out there tomorrow."

Cecilia DeMille came over and put her hand on Wilcoxon's arm. "*I'm* telling you to shut up, Harry. If my father wants to kill himself, let him do it."

Cecilia understood. There was a film to be made, a film that he believed in, a film that Henry deMille would be proud of. Paramount had given him their money as well as their trust. If word got out about the coronary, it would be a disaster for the film and, especially, for Paramount. People were depending on him. Neither his age nor his heart were relevant. He *had* to be there.

So DeMille and Jacobson worked out a plan for him to continue directing the picture while enduring as little physical stress as possible.

At 7:20 the next morning, DeMille's limousine pulled up to the set and he stepped out, ready to work. He was gray and weak, but he was there. Chico Day remembered that "He was amazing that day." He made it through most of the day, but it was evident that he was relying on his crew to a great extent: Wilcoxon stepped up, Loyal Griggs stepped up, Eddie Salven stepped up, and everybody went to Cecilia for major decisions. Frank Westmore was particularly invaluable, regularly getting up at four in the morning, doing his own job as well as taking care of DeMille as if he were his father. Westmore even directed a couple of scenes, as did Cecilia.

With the concept art drilled into everybody's head, with Wilcoxon and Salven implicitly knowing how DeMille wanted scenes staged, the production continued to move ahead smoothly. Strangely, DeMille seemed less concerned than the few people who knew the medical facts. For the remaining weeks of the location shoot, the old man spared himself only the exertion that he gauged would kill him outright. He had always been good at calculating; now he was engaged in the riskiest calculation of his life, up to and including deceiving the studio.

DeMille wrote Y. Frank Freeman back in Hollywood. "Heston is doing fine work and is an impressive Moses. . . . When I got back to Cairo I had lost 21 pounds and weigh at present 151 pounds which was my weight when I was married 52 years ago.

"Most of us have suffered from dysentery, which we did not seem to be able to cure, so I sent for Dr. Max Jacobson to come on from New York. He flew out here with Yul Brynner. I did not mention to the New York office or anyone why I was sending for him. He has been here now for four days and we are all in much better shape. As you know, he is one of the best doctors in America, and I felt the situation was sufficiently important to bring him on at my personal expense, which I did."

DeMille was attempting to pass off his heart attack and weight loss as dysentery, and he was paying for Jacobson out of his own pocket to avoid studio oversight and the corporate panic that would have resulted from a seventy-three-year-old director making the most expensive movie in history with a location coronary. Joan Brooskin knew the truth and wrote her husband, "Don't mention it to anyone except as indigestion, but it is more serious than that." It's entirely possible that Frank Freeman and Barney Balaban were never fully informed of DeMille's condition.

It was decided to leave some scenes set in the Valley of the Kings to Wilcoxon and Arthur Rosson. After forty-four days of production in Egypt, DeMille's unit finished shooting on December 3, 1954, and Cecil was home two weeks before Christmas.

★

Soon after Cecil was back in California, it became clear that Bill's health was every bit as imperiled as his brother's. Cecil read an article in the *Journal of the American Medical Association* about a promising new cancer treatment and called it to the attention of Clara deMille. She responded with a somewhat curt letter that made it clear she had no intention of allowing Bill to be a medical guinea pig.

Clara wrote that her brother—a doctor—Bill's throat specialist, and his radiologist all agreed that the new treatments "would be much too violent a treatment for William both because of his age and his medical history." By this time, Bill had endured two bouts of cancer, a nasty case of lumbar pneumonia, as well as a recent small stroke, which had combined to take a heavy toll on his vitality.

"I must say I cannot see putting him through severe treatments, the results of which are at best problematical. At the moment, he is cheerful and serene, and I want to keep him that way. . . . Thank you just the same for your effort in his behalf."

Since Clara deMille said nothing about Cecil's own condition, it's clear that, like most people in Hollywood, she didn't know about it.

As if DeMille didn't have enough problems, Eddie Salven began disappearing. Salven had been an alcoholic for years, but he had never started drinking until the end of the day. This was something different. DeMille was very concerned, both for Salven and because, now more than ever, he needed his assistant director.

DeMille told Wilcoxon that he would pay whatever it would cost to get Salven back. He instructed second assistant Chico Day to have all the bills sent directly to him—"medicines, doctors, hotels, automobiles, clothes, whatever." But Salven had been divorced twice, had remarried, and was trying to support three women and children on an AD's salary. It couldn't be done. Wilcoxon found Salven in the gutter with pneumonia. He was admitted to Good Samaritan Hospital, but died on January 22, 1955.

Shortly after Salven's death, it was found that Bill's cancer had spread to his throat and lungs. Agnes deMille said that Cecil went to visit his brother in his long dying only twice, and compared that to his attentiveness to Jeanie Macpherson and Gladys Rosson in their dying. Yet Bill's stepdaughter Frances denied the implication of neglect. "Cecil often called William and William loved his calls. I was there. [Agnes] was not. At William's funeral Frank Reicher said it was amazing how devoted these two men were to each other when they were so different."

Cecil urged Richard, who still had not been told the truth about his parentage, to go see his Uncle Bill while he could, and Richard did. Shortly afterward, Richard became engaged to Margaret Belgrano. Cecil told her that Richard was "a real deMille," although he didn't explain just what that meant. William wanted to meet Margaret. He looked the couple over carefully and seemed to approve. He was warm and charming, "made some kindly wise old comments," according to Richard, and the meeting was over.

A couple of days before Bill died, Cecil came to say goodbye. It was late afternoon, and Bill was very weak. Clara worried that Bill was getting too tired, and Cecil stood up to go, but Bill stopped him. "Let him stay till the sun sets," he told his wife.

Finally, on March 5, 1955, Clara called Cecil and told him his brother was dying. Cecil came to Bill's bedside. When he came out of the bedroom, he began to cry, sobbing into his hands like a child. The last thing William deMille was heard to say was, "They tell me it's a nice day."

Cecil asked Richard if he wanted to accompany him to the funeral, but the young man demurred, because he hadn't been all that close to William. Richard would carry his guilt for that refusal for the rest of his life. "I wasn't thinking of father [Cecil]," he would write. "He had lost his only brother, the companion and teacher of his youth, the comrade of his pioneer days. He wanted me to come with him and pay my respects and be seen to pay them. He was right, and I was wrong. He didn't say I was wrong, and he didn't hold it against me."

At the funeral home, Cecil was among such friends as Jesse Lasky, and Bill's friends Joe Mankiewicz and Frank Reicher. He stood beside the coffin for long minutes, abandoning himself to grief. Bill's ashes were placed in the DeMille plot in the Hollywood Cemetery. (Cecil had bought the plot of land in 1944, and it's probable that he had consulted with Gladys Rosson about a likely area, as the spot DeMille settled on was close by Gladys's family plot, as well as the grave of his grandson Christopher.)

In some ways, Agnes's loss was greater than Cecil's. Cecil knew Bill had loved him and had depended on him in crisis, but Agnes was never entirely sure. With bitterness disguised as blunt truth, Agnes wrote one of Bill's students after his death that "All the fatherly love and attention which he found himself unable to give us during our growing up and my early professional struggles, he was free to lavish on his students."

Other than Constance, Cecil never had a relationship as intimate as the one with his brother. "He loved beauty," Cecil remembered in his autobiography. "In our more than seventy years together we had watched together many times the infinitely varied splendor of the setting sun; and one day, together, we shall see it rise again."

★

Now Cecil had to keep his promise to Bill and tell Richard the truth about his paternity. A couple of weeks after Bill died, Richard found Cecil sitting at his desk in the west wing of the house. "Stay a moment. I want to tell you about your parents. Before you were born, your Uncle William and I agreed that whichever of us died first, the other would tell you about your parents. Your father was your Uncle William. Your mother was a writer. This is a book she wrote." He handed Richard a small black volume entitled *Doorways in Drumorty*. There was an inscription inside the front cover: "To my friend William deMille, very tenderly, Lorna Moon."

"Being told was like being hit with a very large wave," remembered Richard. "You're still standing, but you don't really know how you managed to stay upright. You say to yourself, 'Well, I managed to live through that, what's next?' I accepted it, but I didn't deal with it. I was too busy living my life and I had other things to do. It was only later in life that I began thinking about what had really happened here.

"It had always been fairly obvious in our family that Cecilia, his natural daughter, had a higher status than anybody else among the children. That was never made explicit—she knew it, everybody knew it, nobody mentioned it. I always felt as though I were something of a guest in a house where the father figure was a really great guy that I liked a lot. When I was told that Uncle William was my father I felt, not more of an outsider, but suddenly more included. Uncle William was part of the family, and I wasn't something they had found in a car or walking down the street, so that actually improved my status in the family."

✶

Construction for the studio portion of *The Ten Commandments* dominated everything on the lot; of Paramount's eighteen soundstages, twelve were taken up with sets for the DeMille picture. There were twenty more weeks of principal photography to go, then another year of special effects work. The parting of the Red Sea presented a particular problem because there wasn't a pool big enough to create the illusion. The studio began demolishing the buildings that separated Paramount from RKO, then used the newly created space for a 200,000 cubic foot pool. Production restarted on March 28, 1955.

Annie Bauchens began editing as the film flowed into her cutting room. DeMille arrived on the set early and wouldn't get into the projection room to look at his rushes until early evening. "They would discuss it all every day," remembered DeMille's granddaughter Cecilia. "Annie was very much a part of the process."

DeMille invited Charlton Heston to the studio to look at a rough assembly of the Exodus sequence. Heston thought it looked marvelous, but tried to commiserate with DeMille about his heart attack, implying that the risk entailed in continuing with the Egyptian location work hadn't been worth it. "No, no," DeMille said brusquely. "I *had* to finish, there and then. We couldn't have made these shots anywhere else."

For the rest of the studio shoot, Chico Day's technique of short-circuiting a DeMille tirade was to give back as good as he got, which generally resulted in a steely request from DeMille to solve the problem as quickly as possible. When Day came up with a piece of business for the Exodus—a father handing down belongings from the second floor to his son on the ground, a metaphor for the passing of generations—DeMille immediately expressed appreciation and told Day to direct the shot himself.

"I have nothing but praise to offer about the wonderful old man," remembered Day. "But I call him the old man affectionately, because he had a heart this big. There was nothing small about this man." Day was walking with DeMille through the studio when an extra stopped them and inquired as to when he would be called for his scenes. "In about 30 days," replied DeMille. The extra said nothing, but DeMille saw the same frayed, downcast look he had himself carried through innumerable stock company tours. DeMille peeled off $100 and pressed it into the man's hand. "You can pay me back when you start working," he said as he walked away.

"That was the man that everybody called such an s.o.b.," said Day. "I knew him very differently."

Production ground on endlessly, with the Golden Calf sequence being a particular trial. The sequence inspired one of the legendary stories about Hollywood, when one of the extra girls walked up to an assistant director and inquired, "Who do I have to fuck to get off this picture?" (Charlton Heston insisted it actually happened.) The assembled multitude had to indicate debauchery and lasciviousness without actually showing anything because the film was intended for all ages.

"What's wrong with you people?" yelled DeMille one day. "I have never been so disappointed with any display of acting on my set as I am today. Why am I wasting film on this? Why have we rehearsed till we thought it was right? Why is Paramount ten million in the hole? Don't any of you realize how important this work is? Our whole movie has built up to this scene. Moses bringing the tablets down at the end of this orgy is the climax of our picture—and everyone looks like they're going on a Sunday school social!"

DeMille's solution was to reshoot the entire sequence as if it were a silent film. Professional exotic dancers were called in and real music was played on the set, as it had been thirty years earlier.

Among the figures in the throng was a young man named Robert Vaughn, who would go on to become a well-known actor in films and television. "DeMille was like God," he remembered. "The assistant directors mostly handled us. We never approached the Eminence ourselves. Not even close." Also lurking about was an extra named Robert Fuller, who would become a star of TV westerns. "I remember C.B. walking up and down in his jodhpurs, carrying a riding crop, which he used to point with. He was pretty scary. I stood two feet away from him many times. We were never told not to speak to him, but I didn't open my mouth. I can't imagine anybody that would."

DeMille came home one day complaining about the performance of Edward G. Robinson. The actor, he told his granddaughter Cecilia, wasn't giving him what he wanted. "Why don't you tell him what you want?" she asked.

DeMille seemed surprised. "How could I dare say anything to so talented and respected an actor?" He waited for Robinson's performance to develop and was ultimately delighted with the actor's sardonic humor.

Oddly, the slight intimidation DeMille felt about Robinson wasn't present when he was directing Sir Cedric Hardwicke as the aged Pharaoh. "Of all the directors I have met," remembered Hardwicke, "[DeMille] was the only one who really knew what he wanted—he and Olivier. In his seventies, DeMille's energy was unbelievable."

Because DeMille spent such a long time in preproduction, his time on the set was focused. He always got his master shot first and wasn't afraid to play an entire scene in the master if it was strong enough. Before deciding the next setup, he would check out the sketches. He would take a little more time in rehearsal so he could spend less time shooting. Even complicated scenes went fairly smoothly; Charlton Heston remembered that DeMille rarely shot more than six takes. At the end of the day, he would hold his core crew (cameraman, camera operator, sound mixer, script supervisor, and the assistant director) on the set while he picked the first shot for the next morning. The following day's work could thus get off to a flying start, setting the pace.

Vincent Price was entranced by the entire experience. "DeMille was a wonderful director to work with, unlike any other in the business. He was one hundred percent visually minded. Really, his [scripts] were very thin, but the visual effects he pulled off were marvelous. . . . What he was interested in was what was on the screen—the use of crowds particularly."

Price told a story of acting against a blue screen, having to react to a spectacular combination of matte, miniature, and live action shot in Egypt that combined to show the erecting of Pharaoh's obelisk.

"You're not reading that line with much conviction," DeMille pointed out.

"That's because I haven't the slightest idea what I'm talking about," said Price.

"You're right!" said DeMille. "Let's go into the projection room and I'll show you." Price watched what he correctly said was "one of the most impressive scenes ever photographed. After seeing it, I changed my reading."

Particularly difficult was shooting the crossing of the Red Sea against the hot lights of the blue screen process, with extras carrying tons of belongings while DeMille and John Fulton worked to match studio shots with Egyptian footage.

One day Charlton Heston thought he'd be witty. Just before DeMille called action, Heston raised his staff and asked, "What's my motivation, Mr. DeMille?"

There was a long silence. DeMille stood with the microphone for a few beats, then quietly said, "Are we ready? Action!"

Heston noted that DeMille no longer felt compelled to live up to his reputation. "He was very good with actors, a very courteous man, and extremely nice to extras at a time when it was not fashionable to do that. If DeMille had big scenes, as most of his pictures did, with a lot of extras in them, he'd try to schedule those scenes between Thanksgiving and Christmas so they could get a lot of work in during the holidays."

The special effects for the California shoot were predominantly done live on the set. Turning the Nile to blood was done by head prop man Bill Sapp handling a garden hose timed to coincide with Moses's staff touching the water. The hail fire was popcorn with flames and sound effects added in postproduction. The pestilential death spreading over the land at Passover was hot oil in a conventional fogger with green vegetable dye for color. Getting it to go in the desired direction was done with blowers. The set was built with gullies in the middle of the street; the fog was heavier than the air and stayed at the approximate level of the lowest point on the set.

All the air-conditioning on the set had to be turned off, and getting the fog to move as it had to was very difficult. "Open the doors!"—the order to disperse the fog—became the synonym for "Cut!" One day, during a take that was going perfectly, a prop man suddenly yelled out, "Open the doors!"

DeMille was livid. "I want to know who said that—if they have the guts to come forward!"

The prop man came forward and DeMille demanded to know why he had interrupted the take. "The props are all wrong for this scene, Mr. DeMille."

"Why?"

"I just goofed, is all."

A pause. "Okay. Have it right tomorrow."

"We all learned something," said actor Donald Curtis, who witnessed the exchange. "Face the music and survive. Stand up for yourself, but never make excuses."

There was one plague that was planned but never used, a plague of frogs. Anne Baxter appeared in a test that involved her screaming as hundreds of rubber frogs hopped up and down in her bedroom and onto her bed. Since frogs are not generally perceived as terrifying, her reaction seemed comic, so the scene was jettisoned.

As production continued, Henry Wilcoxon was a frequent target of DeMille's displeasure. "Everything [Wilcoxon] did had to be perfect," remembered actress Vicki Bakken. "If something was wrong, it was Henry's fault." But a half hour later, everything was fine. As Pat Moore noted, DeMille didn't hold grudges against anybody except, perhaps, Victor Mature.

Eugene Mazzola, the six-year-old chosen to play Pharaoh's son, would sit on DeMille's lap. DeMille would hand him his microphone and whisper instructions in his ear.

"Tell them 'Quiet on the set.'"

"Quiet on the set, please."

"Tell them to take their places."

"Places everyone."

"Call 'Action.' "

"ACTION!"

Edward G. Robinson was elected to approach DeMille and tell DeMille that the actors were disconcerted to be given orders by a child; it was inappropriate for such a serious film.

DeMille's expression never changed. "Mr. Robinson, believe me, no one knows like I do what a serious film we're making here. Tell them 'Places,' Eugene."

DeMille handled the child very carefully, never losing his famous temper, always asking, never demanding, that the boy try something: "Can you try to be more surprised?" With actors he liked or respected, he would invariably say, "Please do this for me," rather than just demand it, which he would do with an actor that he felt was failing him or failing his own talent.

DeMille cast Heston's newborn son Fraser as the infant Moses. What amazed Heston was that, following his son's birth at three in the morning, the first wire he got came two hours later, from DeMille. "Congratulations!" it said. "He's got the part!" "He must have had his people planted in the hospital," Heston said wonderingly years later.

The sense of cosseted detail on a DeMille set was remarkable and particularly comforting to the actresses. Anne Baxter found that the beautiful enameled collars she wore as Nefretiri were carefully warmed by the wardrobe girl before they were fastened around her neck so that she wouldn't have even a moment of discomfort from the cold necklace.

The set was electrified on the day the great H. B. Warner shot his scene. Warner had gone on to a distinguished career after *The King of Kings*—in particular, his turn as the alcoholic pharmacist in Frank Capra's *It's a Wonderful Life* proved he could still summon a devastating mixture of anger and pathos.

By 1955, Warner was already in a nursing home, and it was thought he had only months to live (he would in fact live until 1958). DeMille believed it was important for the old actor to go out with his boots on. An ambulance brought Warner to the set, and he lay on a stretcher while he went through costume and makeup. "It was clear H.B. couldn't walk—could barely breathe," remembered actor Donald Curtis. DeMille told the burly Curtis to pick up Warner and carry him through his scene. Warner didn't want to be carried, but Curtis told him he was there to help. "Mr. DeMille is ready for you," Curtis told him. Those magical words quieted the actor, and Warner allowed himself to be carried.

Curtis picked up Warner—"He had the weight of a child"—and carried him over to Nina Foch's sedan chair. Warner's speech was taken from Psalm 22: "I am poured out like water, and all my bones are out of joint; my heart is like wax. . . . My strength is dried up like a potsherd; and my tongue cleaveth to my jaws; and thou has brought me into the dust of death."

There were more words than Warner could manage, and DeMille told him to say whatever he wanted. "I am poured out like water," Warner said. "My strength is dried up to the dust of death." And so H. B. Warner made his last, immeasurably moving appearance in a motion picture.

Yul Brynner had been a CBS TV director until his acting career took off. A smart, sophisticated man, his friend Sidney Lumet chided him about going out to Hollywood "to do that crap."

"Sidney," replied Brynner, "they ain't seen crap until they have seen me out there." And he meant it.

Somewhere along the way, Brynner stopped feeling superior and became enthralled. Soon, he and DeMille formed a mutual admiration society, a relationship described by everybody who witnessed it as "father and son." Part of the bond was that DeMille and Brynner were both intrinsically imperious personalities who could get away with things lesser men would never have attempted. Anne Baxter remembered how Brynner, "expressionlessly arrogant," would thrust out an arm with his first and second fingers in a victory sign, into which his gofer would slide an already lit cigarette. Brynner would never even look around to catch the servant's eye, just expect that he would be there. "This used to really impress DeMille," remembered Baxter, but then DeMille had been doing the same thing for forty years with his chair and microphone boys.

"DeMille was his father figure," said Brynner's daughter Victoria. "DeMille brought something into my father's life he didn't have; when you have such a strong persona, people come to you, admire you, look up to you, and it was nice for my father to have someone else to look up to and admire. To the end of his life, he talked about DeMille a lot."

If Yul Brynner became a surrogate son, then Brynner's son Rock became a surrogate grandson, and Rock observed the two alpha males' frank enjoyment of each other. "In my father's mind, DeMille was the founder of world cinema. Yul could accept those at the top of their sphere, and since DeMille was forty years older and they weren't in competition with each other, my father wasn't driven to compete.

"By the time my father worked with DeMille, he'd studied photography, he'd directed one or two hundred TV shows. He wasn't slumming in the movies, he knew the craft and he put it all together and he had the right questions for DeMille. He earned DeMille's respect.

"I liked DeMille then more than now," Rock Brynner remembered. "That's probably because of his politics and my own perspective about willfulness. DeMille had a thing about Christmas presents. He'd always have a large room full of presents, and he was meticulous about unwrapping each one. He would save the paper, and coil the ribbon. It took days! And he loved Paradise and the deer that ate out of his hand. There's no question that there were very endearing things about him, but in retrospect, he was an autocrat verging on a martinet."

One of the people working in the film was the immensely dignified black actor Woody Strode, who would go on to be a member of John Ford's stock company. Strode actually appeared in several parts in *The Ten Commandments*, because DeMille took a liking to him and wanted Strode to work as much as possible.

Not all of the cast basked in a similar approval. DeMille took particular umbrage at Debra Paget, a beautiful woman but an actress whose dramatic efforts continually failed to please him. "Now Miss Paget!" he growled at her one day. "We will have to do that again; not that you show *any* signs of doing it *any* better, but maybe the fates will *smile* on us yet."

A fifteen-year-old girl named Lisa Mitchell went in to try out for the part of one of Jethro's daughters. "DeMille came over and sat down beside me on a little couch and talked to me for about a half hour, and told me what he hoped to do with this movie, how important it was to him. This was a movie that my grandchildren would see, and every part was important to him, and that the part that I would be playing was important because it was something teenagers could identify with.

"He said, 'Now if I give you this part you have to make a bargain with me, you are inexperienced; you have never acted before, and not only have you never been in a movie before, you have never seen how I work before. If I give you the part I want you to come on the set every day during rehearsal and after rehearsal.'

"Every day after I finished rehearsal [of the dance sequence] I was obliged to go on the set and watch him, to get used to his way. And he also said I had to agree to allow him to yell at me if he needed to, and I agreed, and he had me shake hands with him. It was a gentleman's agreement.

"He was very wonderful to talk to because he did not talk down to me, he treated me with respect. It was really a business deal."

In Mitchell's first scene, stage fright rendered her voice a whisper. "I can't hear you," DeMille said, and after another take, he repeated "I can't hear you. What are we going to do? We have to get somebody else because you can't say your lines. What are we going to do? What are *you* going to do about it?"

Mitchell got mad at being called out in front of hundreds of people and said "I'll yell!" and he said "Good."

"I yelled, he could hear me, and from that time on he was just as sweet as pie to me."

There were some brief time-outs for humor. A. C. Lyles had risen from Adolph Zukor's office boy to become a producer on the Paramount lot. He had always wanted to have the job of DeMille's chair boy, but DeMille refused to give it to him. "Sometimes on the set I get mean. I like you and I wouldn't want you to see me that way."

But one day DeMille sent for Lyles and told him, "A.C., for thirty years you have wanted to be my chair boy. This is your chance." Lyles grabbed the director's chair and followed DeMille around. When DeMille would stop and stoop, Lyles would put the chair down, then DeMille would rise and start walking again. This went on for some time, with the crew enjoying the spectacle. Fifty years later, Lyles would recount the story and proudly say, "I was Cecil B. DeMille's chair boy. That's got to be a highlight of my whole career."

DeMille was responsible for one of the great Hollywood musical careers when he hired a young man named Elmer Bernstein to supply some incidental dance music. Victor Young, who had been DeMille's first choice to score every one of his films since *North West Mounted Police*, was in New York wrestling with a musical version of *Seventh Heaven* starring Gloria DeHaven and Ricardo Montalban. Young was a master melodist who had composed some of the most luscious songs of the era ("Love Letters," "Stella by Starlight," "My Foolish Heart"). DeMille liked Young because of his broad melodic lines. Young . . . well, Young didn't really like DeMille, whom he found excessively demanding.

"Every picture Victor said, 'I'll never do another picture with him again. Never!' " remembered Paramount music editor June Edgerton. "But of course he always did." With Young stuck in New York, Bernstein got a one-week contract for *The Ten Commandments*. "I was taken over to meet him," said Bernstein, "and he was very courtly. I was always 'Mr. Bernstein' even though he was old enough to be my grandfather. He said, 'Mr. Bernstein, do you think you could do for ancient Egyptian music what Puccini did for Japanese music in *Madame Butterfly*?' That was his first question to me. I thought about that, and God was good; I think I gave him the only answer that would have kept me on the film. I said, 'I really don't know, but I would sure like to try.' And I think that was precisely the right answer for him. I think if I had said, 'Oh, yes, of course . . .' I would have been out of there very quickly."

In a week's time, Bernstein wrote his Egyptian dance and played the recording for DeMille with great trepidation; the head of the Paramount music department had heard it and said that DeMille would hate it because "it has a lot of high woodwinds and he doesn't like high woodwinds."

DeMille sat quietly and listened to the piece, then asked to hear it again. After it was over, he got up and headed for the door, pausing just before he left to turn and say, "Fine. Thank you very much." After that, Bernstein got a succession of weekly contracts writing chants, fanfares, and other incidental music. DeMille liked everything Bernstein wrote except for one piece. He lacerated Bernstein for his failure, got up and stalked out of the room.

Bernstein turned to Henry Wilcoxon and said, "I guess I'm fired." "Don't be silly," said Wilcoxon. "He was making love to you now compared to what he can do when he's really angry." That night, Bernstein ran into DeMille as they were both leaving, and no reference was made to the earlier incident. Rather, DeMille complimented "my young friend, Mr. Bernstein" on becoming a father.

Bernstein stayed on the picture until the end of principal photography, at which point Victor Young was to return from New York and begin composing the score. But *Seventh Heaven* flopped, and when Young came back to the West Coast it was clear that he was in no condition to write anything, was, in fact, in failing health. (He would die in Palm Springs in November 1956 at the age of fifty-six.) "If you have any way of getting to do this film, don't worry about me," Young told Bernstein, but the younger composer didn't think he had a chance.

The head of the music department put the possibility to DeMille, who replied by asking him if he thought Bernstein "could be another Wagner?" That led to DeMille asking Bernstein to write some major themes for the score. A few weeks later, DeMille came in to listen to Bernstein play his themes on the piano. DeMille called out the names of the characters, and Bernstein responded by playing the music for that character. "Let me hear the theme for Moses," he asked. Bernstein complied. "How would you play that when he was a baby in the bulrushes?" asked DeMille. Bernstein had prepared nothing for that sequence, but he improvised.

Bernstein went through his themes for a half hour, then DeMille turned to his secretaries and asked, "What do you think?" The ladies applauded, and DeMille turned to the composer and asked, "Mr. Bernstein, do you think you could stand me for another six months?" And that was how the temporary employment became permanent. Soon afterward, "Mr. Bernstein" became "Elmer."

DeMille wanted to hear Bernstein's work as it was completed. Bernstein had been a concert pianist, so he could play things in a florid manner, but DeMille would stop him and ask for a stripped-down, almost one-finger rendition, so he could judge the effectiveness of the themes without musical frills. "He was basically supportive, he was very clear about what he wanted," remembered Bernstein. "I think we probably rewrote about 25 percent of the score for one reason or another, things that didn't work for him, but he was never cruel about things that he rejected, he was always positive."

While he was working on the film, Bernstein was identified in one of the anticommunist publications as a member of the Communist Party. DeMille called the composer into his office. "I'm going to ask you a question I have no constitutional right to ask you. But I'm going to ask it anyway. Are you a member of the Communist party?"

"No, I'm not," said Bernstein. "He looked at me for a while, sort of made up his mind about me, whether I was telling the truth or not telling the truth. He then gave me a long speech about the dangers of being associated with such people, who, as he told me, were only users and were using the people that they ensnared, and that was the end of it as far as he was concerned."

It was DeMille who gave Bernstein what he remembered as "the single greatest lesson of my life in scoring films." For the scene of the Exodus, Bernstein had written a quasi-Hebraic anthem that duplicated the pace at which the Jews were marching out of Egypt. DeMille hated it.

"What's wrong with it?" asked Bernstein.

"It's too slow."

"Well, I'm just mirroring what I am seeing on the screen. I mean, these people are moving slowly, they are burdened, they are carrying their life's possessions with them."

"No, no, no. It's too slow. You must trust me on this: *If you write something that is moving faster than what you are seeing on the screen, it will make it all seem more lively and fast, and it will work!*" DeMille suggested something with the same tempo as "Onward Christian Soldiers," which Bernstein found amusing.

Bernstein said he would try it, and it worked. "It was the greatest lesson I learned in my life, and it did me great service in films later on, particularly in films like *The Magnificent Seven*, which was a film that was essentially slow, but I remembered what DeMille had said, and moved it on with the music. So finally we got the Exodus right."

Bernstein loved watching DeMille and Anne Bauchens spar. "They used to chide each other if they thought there was any hearing loss, or any sign of old age, they would get into a fight about it, like people who had known each other, as they had, for all their lives. It was kind of fun to watch."

Bernstein noted that DeMille took his cues for behavior from other people; that is, "if you thought DeMille was your friend and you treated him in this kind of way, then he was your friend. If you thought he was terrifying, he would be terrifying. He assumed a role which he thought was suitable for the particular individual, so basically you called the shots, you decided what part he should act. I was never terrified of him, I admired him, I enjoyed being in his presence, I thought he was just an amazing man, so I never had any personal difficulty with him at all.

"Cecil DeMille probably knew more about what the function of film music was than probably anybody of his time. . . . He had a great feeling for opera, which suited his dramatic sensibilities, in particular Wagner and Puccini."

★

By the end of May 1955, DeMille had suffered a major heart attack, the deaths of his brother and most trusted assistant director, yet *The Ten Commandments* was only five days behind schedule, a remarkable feat considering the size of the picture. More importantly, he was happy with his rushes, terming them "magnificent." He was writing Max Jacobson regularly about what the director referred to as "the magic fluid. I have been taking the morning and night ampules and I think they are very good indeed, but unfortunately, they have the same effect on me that Egypt had, and I have to stop them every two or three days to let my system get a fresh start in life."

In another letter six weeks later, DeMille asked about "the 'injection' medicine, which I will call the 'wonder' drug. I have just noticed that this should be kept under refrigeration, and I have not so kept it up to now, but I presume there will be no ill effects on that account." DeMille went on to say that he was feeling the wear and tear of the production, but had had only one angina attack, a week before in the middle of the night. "The pain was not violent, but it was a definite pain." There was five or six weeks left of principal photography, wrote DeMille, and he was working hard to complete his job. "I think probably you are as much responsible for that completion as I will be."

As long as he was in principal photography on *The Ten Commandments*, DeMille's staff would communicate with him by brief typewritten notes on small white sheets of paper: "Dr. Bettenbaugh at Olive View Sanitarium called to ask your permission to hunt deer with a bow and arrow on your ranch." Below the question was the answer: "Mr. DeMille emphatically said NO."

John Carradine remembered how they finished the picture. It was a shot of extras moving through the desert, and DeMille decided he needed a shot from the top of a studio hill. As he marched up the hill with Loyal Griggs, he suddenly grabbed Griggs's arm and collapsed. DeMille's face turned pale, and people rushed for a doctor. After some time, DeMille looked at Griggs and said, "Let's go. I want to finish this goddamn shot."

"For me," said Carradine, "that moment summed up DeMille. He finished what he started. That day was the last time I saw him, and it's the way I always want to remember him."

On August 13, after 161 days of production, DeMille wrapped principal photography on *The Ten Commandments*. Ahead lay more than a year of special effects work. Still, there was time for a breather, and DeMille finally had more time to attend to personal matters. On September 15, he wrote to his granddaughter Cecilia, newly married to Abbas El Boughdadly, whom she had met when he played the captain of the Pharaoh's chariots during the Egyptian shooting, "Your grandmother and I get a great deal of joy from hearing of your happiness, your well being and your activities. One or two of those activities slightly puzzle us—for instance, you allude to Abbas going [into] business, but we do not know what business. . . .

"I understand you are taking up polo. That is a hair-raising contemplation! Taking your horses over the high hurdles here contributed to the loss of my hair, but if you start polo I will soon look like Yul Brynner. . . .

"I am also in the throes of cutting. At present the picture is about 25,000 feet in length, which means that I have about 5,000 feet to cut—this is not bad for a picture of this length. . . . I see Abbas every day on the screen, but I miss seeing you, but every evening before I retire, your picture is close to me and I pray God's blessing upon you, and upon Abbas, and upon the happy union of your marriage."

DeMille brought Cecilia Jr. up to date on the rest of the family. "Your grandmother continues in good health. Her memory is not as sharp as it was once for all things, but she always remembers you both and whenever she has misplaced anything and cannot find it, whether it is a bag, her gloves, her glasses, or her shoes, she says, 'Well, Cecilia asked me for those and I gave them to her to take to Egypt.' This is a daily routine with some article, but she is peaceful, calm of mind and physically well.

"As to me, I miss you more than I can say. . . . That is all the news that comes to my mind at the moment. I am leaving tonight for two days at Paradise, and as [servants] Joseph and Margaret are on their vacation, I am taking up my meals from here and will be in a virtual state of camping out—and also of bliss!

"I hope that you both are enjoying the blessings and beauty of an understanding love . . . and you, my little baby, are learning the good things of life, and learning tolerance, kindness and understanding.

"My love is yours. God bless you both . . ."

Three months later, Cecilia Jr. was pregnant and DeMille responded: "I am not quite sure whether to kiss you or spank you—but either way, I am thrilled with the wonderful news your letter contains. Though nineteen years of age is still a little girl to me, seventy five years is about right to become a great-grandfather. . . .

"Nothing equals my delight than to know that I may have you in my arms again in April. I miss you terribly for you have always been very dear to me. In fact, yesterday I was looking at a little snapshot that I keep in the mirror in the dresser in my bedroom—a picture of a tiny little girl sitting beside me in a big chair on the lawn at Paradise with three deer and a peacock looking her over curiously. Now before long you will be snapping the picture and I will have another little girl or boy sitting beside me watching the deer. Time certainly marches on.

"*The Ten Commandments* is really beginning to take great form. I am shooting the closing of the Red Sea now, dumping 10,000 gallons of water from 24 tanks into a specially built tank at the same minute—and flooding a little bit of Hollywood every time we do it! But I think the effect is going to be very good. . . .

"This will be the first Christmas without you, and I shall hang a special star and burn a special candle on the tree just for you and Abbas and the very little unnamed one, who will be the blending of you both, and whom I am sure will bring good into the world, for the world certainly needs it right now. My blessings on you both. My thoughts and my love are always with you. . . ."

★

Of the numerous special effects scenes in *The Ten Commandments*, the most crucial was the parting of the Red Sea, "the single greatest special effect in movie history," according to Steven Spielberg. John Fulton accomplished it by constructing, in the middle of the Paramount parking lot, a giant tank with twelve smaller tanks on either side that sequentially released a total of 360,000 gallons of water. Filmed in slow motion, with footage from both the Red Sea and the outcropping at Abu Rudeis, the shots were used for the opening of the sea. The parallel walls of water between which the Israelites pass were created by mounting cameras shooting straight down at water that was being agitated at the bottom of an eighty-foot

ramp to create the effect of churn. The walls of water were shot separately in segments and combined using soft-edged mattes.

The most difficult shot in the entire film was, of course, the money shot: the
extreme long shot of the sea parting, with hundreds of extras gathered around
Heston in the foreground. The blue screen behind the actors was twenty-five by
eighty feet, and when DeMille was composing his shot through the viewfinder,
he realized that he needed extras beyond the parameters of the blue screen. The
special effects technicians painted a moving silhouette matte around the extras
and composited it with the blue screen matte. By the time they were through with
the shot, it involved thirty-four original negatives.

Just printing the final composite of a single shot could take three or more
fifteen-hour days, after which everything was shipped to Technicolor for the inevitable color corrections. Paul Lerpae, the optical supervisor for the film, remembered that "I worked on that picture 16 hours a day for nearly a year and a
half. . . . We had to rephotograph each frame many times, working to tolerances
of one-ten thousandth of an inch. Any discrepancy larger than that would have
resulted in an area of four or five inches on the wide screen."

While the technicians worked, James Card was back for another attempt at
convincing DeMille to donate his movies to the Eastman House. DeMille was
simultaneously editing his film, trying to get the special effects right, and working
on getting Yul Brynner back for some retakes. Yet he seemed serenely confident
that it would all come together. "The [front] office is worried," he commented to
Card. "They're trying to put a ceiling of $14 million on the picture, but it may run
to $17 million." Card was amazed—he had no great affection for DeMille's sound
films, but he realized that this was a man working far beyond the realm of money.

While Anne Bauchens worked on the editing, Elmer Bernstein was moon-
lighting by quickly writing his seminal jazz score for Otto Preminger's film *The
Man with the Golden Arm*. Months later, as the special effects shots were being
spliced into the picture, DeMille told his composer, "I ran *The Man with the Golden
Arm* last night. I really thought what you did was fine in that film. But don't do
anything like that in *The Ten Commandments*."

The Ten Commandments was the most complicated special effects movie of its
time. The film's dynamic opening shots showed slaves pulling a large statue with
ropes. The statue was a miniature, the sky was a painting, and the foreground
action was a series of traveling mattes. (The shot, along with many other DeMille
images, would later be imitated in the DreamWorks animated feature *The Prince
of Egypt*.)

Together, DeMille and Fulton devised shots that still haven't been equaled.
The perfectly realized scene of Pharaoh's city involved foreground action shot in
Egypt, a background miniature for the city itself, a matte painting that tied the
two elements together, with some live action matted in on the top of the miniature to give a sense of movement. The sequence's culminating tour de force, the

raising of the Obelisk, was a miniature tower blue-screened against a background of the completed composite city.

One of the problems DeMille faced was photographing details that historians had only a vague knowledge of. For instance: the tablets of the Ten Commandments. What script should be used? How to arrange the Commandments on the tablets? What should the tablets look like? For DeMille, nothing would do but the red granite of Mount Sinai. Paramount's prop department made three sets of tablets out of fiberglass; the granite master set kept in DeMille's office was too heavy to hold—strongly suggesting that, among Moses's gifts, perhaps the most valuable next to his remarkably long-lived natural force was his spectacular physical strength.

The fiberglass duplicates were speckled to resemble the red granite; since they were to be carved by God's firebolts, the tablets were made irregularly, with chips, craters, and dings. The proportions of twenty-four inches tall by twelve inches wide approximated the "six handbreadths" dimensions that were noted in ancient Midrashic descriptions of the tablets.

Henry Noerdlinger's research suggested that the Commandments were inscribed four on one side—dealing with man's relationship with God—and six on the other—man's relationship with other men. The writing DeMille chose was an early Canaanite script used in the thirteenth century B.C.—Moses's approximate era. During the Giving of the Law sequence, the Commandments were pre-carved on the wall of the set, and the letters were filled with magnesium, which was set off on cue.

Charlton Heston worked against a blue screen for weeks at a time, with the backgrounds and special effects matted in later. "DeMille would explain it as we went along," remembered Heston. "For the parting of the sea, we had some discussion as to how fast I should point. That was synchronized to the effects scenes months later. Blue screen shots are not very interesting in themselves, and they're very hard to act in. At the same time, we were working in a very high key. God, it was hot!"

In the writing of the script, DeMille had the brilliant idea of using cloud formations as indicators of impending Divine acts. The script specifies the visual dynamics of the parting of the sea: "As the thunderheads grapple in the darkened sky, Moses raises his staff and turns to the turbulent sea. He stretches his rod above the water, the voice of God speaking through him. 'Behold his mighty hand!' . . . From the darkening sky comes the rumbling howl of a hurricane that strains the robe against Moses' body. A second seething rush of air screams over the surface of the waters. The two cloudbanks collide with a thundercrash in a titanic impact that fuses them for instants before detonating downward in a maelstrom's swirl."

The clouds—imitated by Spielberg in *Raiders of the Lost Ark*—were formed by white smoke filmed against translucent sky backings with the colors optically added later. Tracking the progression of the clouds was so difficult—magenta as

the Egyptian chariots speed after the Jews, then an apocalyptic green for the parting of the waters—that they basically involved a special unit.

Then there were the sound effects. For the finger of fire that writes the Commandments, Gene Garvin recorded gas jets at high speed and mixed that sound
with a barrage of rockets fired from a Navy ship, while the rumble of the Red Sea
closing over the Egyptians was recorded during an atom bomb test in Nevada.

Shepherding all this was an old man with a bad heart engaged in unceasing
labor on the biggest picture anybody had ever attempted.

Bringing a much needed touch of levity to the proceedings were some of
the younger actors around Paramount. In the commissary, on the wall behind
DeMille's chair, was Norman Rockwell's impressive life-sized portrait of Victor Mature pushing the pillars apart at the end of *Samson and Delilah*. One day
DeMille arrived for lunch to find an equivalently sized painting of Jerry Lewis,
dressed as Samson, sporting tennis shoes, trying unsuccessfully to push the pillars
apart.

During production, publicist Ann del Valle joined the DeMille unit as executive assistant in charge of public relations to liase between the studio and
churches. "At our first meeting, DeMille asked me one question: 'What do you
think this picture has to say?' I said that I thought it was a great picture to promote
brotherhood. And he said, 'Besides that . . . ' and then he started talking."

Del Valle found him "an absolutely fabulous man to work for. Once he knew
that you knew what you were doing, he'd leave you alone. There was never any
second-guessing. Nothing was too much trouble for him. . . . When I would bring
people on the set, the custom was that I'd send him a note in advance, telling him
who I had with me. I never went near him; when he had a break, he'd come over
to me. During that time, the few minutes that he spent with anyone, he gave them
his total attention. They may have only had five minutes with him, but they left
feeling it had been an hour."

DeMille remained driven, but the obvious manifestations of ego, the emotional display for its own sake, had been burned away by age and intimations of
mortality. "I once told him I thought he had been arrogant," said del Valle. And
he said, 'There was a time I was. I thought that was the way I should be.' But as he
lived, he grew wise. I saw no arrogance in him."

The burning edge about politics was gone as well. Del Valle was a Democrat,
but DeMille left it alone. "He didn't presume that of an employee. He might twit
me a bit if a Democrat got licked in an election, but that was all. He had lived a
long time. He had made a lot of mistakes that he knew were mistakes. One of the
mistakes he had made was that he had been too authoritarian. When I knew him,
he had wisdom, and one of the things he had learned was to let people go their
own way. The people that worked for him loved him and protected him."

★

As 1955 became 1956, the time squeeze became a problem. "It wasn't unusual for Anne Bauchens to work around the clock," said Ann del Valle. "She was a nice little grandmother, as sharp as a tack. She had a gentle, sweet voice, and you would never think of her as someone with authority. But DeMille would listen to her absolutely."

The film was locked into premiering in November 1956, and by summer of that year DeMille and his crew began to sweat. The director okayed some composites that should have gone through the printer a few more times, but postponing the holiday season premiere would have been unthinkable. Specifically, the Writing of the Tablets and the Pillar of Fire, originally planned as matte fire effects, were accomplished by the less elaborate alternative of cel animation because of the time squeeze. John Fulton was never happy with those sequences.

DeMille was demanding shots that were stunningly complex for the optical technology of the time. People have pointed out the existence of the occasional matte line in the finished picture—the amazing thing is that there aren't more.

Throughout the production, Henry Wilcoxon functioned as the smoothing agent who kept feathers from getting too ruffled. He was more conventionally religious than DeMille; when Elmer Bernstein told Wilcoxon that he was having understandable trouble writing a musical theme for God, Wilcoxon said, "Don't do anything about it."

"What do you mean?" asked Bernstein.

"Trust God," replied Wilcoxon.

"It was a great thing to say, actually," remembered Bernstein, "because there was a sense of relief that I didn't have to try, that it would somehow happen, and somehow it did. But that was quintessential Henry.

"DeMille was a man of power. I think that he probably felt connected without the need for intercessors with God. Curiously enough, that is a very Hebraic attitude, and I think, curiously enough, that his faith in God seemed always to be more Hebraic than Christian. I don't know if he would have seen it that way, but it seemed that way to me."

★

In February 1956, DeMille took time out from postproduction to be honored by the Screen Producers Guild Milestone dinner. The president of the Producers Guild was a rising young man named Walter Mirisch, who would become the leading producer of the 1960s with his collaborations with Billy Wilder (*Some Like It Hot, The Apartment*), John Sturges (*The Magnificent Seven, The Great Escape*), and Norman Jewison (*The Russians Are Coming . . . , The Thomas Crown Affair*). Mirisch was not thrilled with the idea of honoring DeMille and went into it holding his nose. "I thought at the time that his movies were corny, with horrible overacting. And I hated his ultraconservative politics. I couldn't believe how successful he was."

The only problem was, that after a meeting or two Mirisch was completely won over. "I became very fond of him. He was a very warm man, and if he set out to charm you, believe me, you *were* going to be charmed. He wanted to win me over and he did, and I ended up bending over backwards for him. DeMille's secret was that he was an actor, and he never got over being an actor."

Mirisch was repeating the process begun by so many younger men, who met DeMille expecting the fire-breathing dragon of the Directors Guild confrontation, only to encounter a gentle grandfather. "Chuck Heston just loved him, and, his politics aside, Chuck was a good, decent, highly intelligent man. I would talk to Billy Wilder about him a lot. Billy had anticipated trouble with him on *Sunset Boulevard*, but all DeMille asked him was, 'What do you want?' Wilder told him what he wanted and DeMille gave it to him."

In his address to the Producers Guild, DeMille cut loose about condescension toward silent movies: "The great classics of the screen deserve better treatment. They remain, not second-rate, but first-rate specimens of the motion picture art. And I include among them a number of the old silent pictures—which, for pure motion picture art, have not been surpassed. . . . The industry will not come of age until it makes a determined effort to keep its own great classics alive—and to present them regularly to the public in a manner worthy of their merit." He railed against calling the occasional theatrical release of an old movie a reissue. "We do not say the next time you go to the Louvre you see a re-issue of the Mona Lisa."

He also commented on censorship, saying that if the self-appointed arbiters of the screen "had their way they would repeal the very definition of art as a mirror held up to nature. . . . Neither motion pictures nor any other art has the right to corrupt morals, but it has the right to be judged as an art and by judges who know what they are talking about."

Back at Paramount, postproduction dragged on. Casting the voice of God presented understandable problems. "We tried everything suggested by anyone," remembered DeMille. They tried individual actors, they tried a chorale. They tried voices underwater, they tried voices amplified in canyons. There was even some thought about using mechanical means, as with an organ, with the sound department organizing the tones into words. "We tried everything, and everything was wrong," said DeMille.

Finally, the project was broken down into different voices for different segments. The voice heard by Charlton Heston at the Burning Bush is actually Heston's slowed down. As DeMille put it, "God spoke to Moses through his mind, so it was natural it would be his own voice." Moreover, a biblical text said that at the Burning Bush, God spoke to Moses in the voice of Moses's father, so as not to frighten him.

One day Henry Wilcoxon heard a burst of florid profanity emanating from the sound department and stuck his head in.

Was something the matter?

"Oh, it's nothing, really," said sound editor Gene Garvin. "It's just the voice of God is all fucked up again!"

The voice of God on Mount Sinai was a different matter entirely. Many believed it was actually the resonant voice of Donald Hayne, who certainly dubbed a version of the Commandments as a note from Florence Cole attests: "Anne has reserved the theater at 2:15 today for re-running the pestilence and the Ten Commandments with D. Hayne voice."

Edmund Penney, a writer attached to the unit who supervised the dubbing of the picture, asserted it was a combination of Heston, DeMille, and a couple of other people. But as the historian James D'Arc discovered, neither Hayne nor DeMille dubbed the voice of God. It was actually a small-part actor with a bass voice named Delos Jewkes. (If you want to hear Jewkes's voice without technical trickery, he has a part in *The Music Man*, where his voice is recognizable.)

Getting the voice right, getting the special effects right, was a painstaking process and time began to run out. In addition, Paramount, having spent more money than anybody had ever spent on a movie, was very nervous. When New York made inquiries about wrapping up the picture, DeMille had his response ready: "Tell them we can stop right now and call it The Five Commandments."

Despite the squeeze, despite his age and health, DeMille hand-crafted the picture. He had Arnold Friberg paint a new Paramount logo expressly for the opening frames. The traditional Paramount logo derives from the Matterhorn, but Friberg gave it a more dramatic lighting that indicated Mount Sinai. Friberg also designed a new typography for the credits.

A few weeks before the premiere, DeMille shot an unprecedented introduction for the film, parting gold curtains and striding toward a microphone that rose from the floor to address the audience. The introduction put the film in the context of freedom vs. slavery, God vs. godlessness, democracy vs. communism. Historically, this was an extremely shaky premise—the Egyptians, after all, were very religious—but DeMille was speaking to a world that was about to witness the brutal suppression of the Hungarian uprising. The introduction also openly explained that it had been necessary to "fill in" the areas of the life of Moses that the Bible omitted. On the one hand, the emphasis on ancient texts defused potential protests; on the other, for anybody that was paying attention, the nature of said texts also made the audience aware that parts of the narrative were, shall we say, conjectural.

On September 18, there was a celebratory lunch in honor of Anne Bauchens at the studio. DeMille invited Charlton Heston, and after lunch there was a screening of the picture—Heston's first look at *The Ten Commandments*. "The whole picture is so much more than the sum of its parts that I feel only the smallest responsibility for what's on the screen," Heston wrote in his diary. "Everyone at the lunch, from Grover Whalen to Louis B. Mayer, seemed impressed with it. I guess I'll stand or fall on this one."

There would be many more screenings in the next few months, and Heston's considered take would always be tempered: "Unique and inimitable it certainly is, and often magnificent as well. I'm afraid it's also shot through with flaws, but maybe the man who could've avoided the flaws wouldn't have captured the magnificence. As for my own work, it could be better."

The film's sole public preview was in Salt Lake City. The print DeMille and his entourage brought to town ran three hours and forty-five minutes. A reporter for the *Deseret News* was present and wrote that "moviegoers sat in awe . . . completely spellbound . . . other times they applauded."

Copious notes were taken during the screening of the audience reaction, and the preview cards were overwhelmingly positive. David McKay, the president of the Church of Jesus Christ of Latter-day Saints, called the movie "exacting" and "a real experience." Preview cards used words like "noble" and "stupendous." DeMille must have been satisfied; only six minutes would be cut from the preview version.

As the prints were shipped across the country, DeMille wrote a letter to accompany the exhibitor's manual that Paramount sent out with every print: "After five years of work THE TEN COMMANDMENTS is completed and is ready to be handed over to you to present to the public. Your help in following the suggestions contained in this folder will insure a standard of presentation worthy of the great subject of this motion picture. My sincere thanks."

The exhibitor's manual mandated a sound level two decibels above normal—the sound helped to sell the spectacle—and carefully outlined every moment of the presentation: "The opening scene of the DEMILLE INTRODUCTION begins on closed curtains, with Cecil B. DeMille making his appearance about 12 seconds after the projected image is first visible. . . . After the intermission title fades out, close the scrim and wait 5 seconds before bringing up the house lights. Part I ends on a highly spiritual and emotional scene, and suddenly flooding the theater with light would be most unwelcome to the audience. . . . The End Title of THE TEN COMMANDMENTS carries a nine-word message, and the scrim should not be closed until this title has completely faded out, otherwise the title could not be easily read. After the scrim is closed, wait 5 seconds before raising the house lights."

For the film's first studio screening, DeMille carefully escorted Constance into the projection room. "He treated her as if she was a queen," said Ann del Valle. "Not only did he treat her as a queen, he spoke of her like that as well. She had Alzheimer's, and I must have looked like someone she had disliked in her past; when we were introduced, she looked at me with genuine dislike."

Beginning September 29, DeMille began a grueling six-week advance publicity tour for the film. A week in New York, a day in Philadelphia, then another week in New York. After that it was one or two days apiece in Boston, Baltimore, Washington, Buffalo, Niagara Falls, Toronto, Chicago, Detroit, Cleveland, Cincinnati, back to New York for the premiere, to Washington on November 9 and home three days later.

The Ten Commandments premiered at the Criterion Theatre in New York on November 8, 1956. The reviews were quite good, and business was spectacular. A week later, on the 14th, the film premiered in Los Angeles at the Stanley Warner Theatre to the same response.

For the next six months, DeMille embarked on what can only be described as a victory tour, flying around the world with the movie as it rolled out. In Italy he was received and blessed by Pope Pius XII; in France, he received the Legion of Honor; in Germany, he had long talks with Konrad Adenauer and Willy Brandt. "They seemed to like my pictures," remembered DeMille wonderingly. "They seemed to like me."

Once again, David Friedman was brought on board for publicity, and traveled with DeMille, Cecilia, and Joe Harper. "Cecilia ran things for her Dad," remembered Friedman. "I would give her a schedule of where we would be, and she would say, 'This is too much; cancel this, cancel that.' His energy was not what it had been, and she was protecting him.

"DeMille was always very kind. Anytime I did something he liked, he would send me a thank-you note. Always very courteous in an old-world way, although he did not have a lot of time for small talk—sell the picture! Anne Bauchens and Florence Cole were also in the entourage, and Florence would have the daily box office reports from all over the world.

"DeMille was seriously religious. I never even heard him say, 'Darn!' He was dedicated to making pictures, did not suffer fools gladly, but knew what he wanted, demanded it, and got it. And boy, could he charm people! He was just a fabulous old gentleman."

The Ten Commandments was the greatest financial success since *Gone With the Wind.* Against its final cost of $13.2 million were initial receipts of $64 million. Because the cost was so high, DeMille's profit percentage was on a sliding scale that topped out at 20 percent of the gross instead of the 50 percent of the net he had been earning. DeMille knew that the picture could never have been completed without the strenuous labor of his staff and crew. He took 10 percent of his profits from the film and began doling it out to his staff and crew. "There had to be 100 people," remembered his granddaughter Cecilia. "I wrote checks twice a year for fifty years." Over the years, each of these stipends amounted to tens of thousands of dollars—a pension courtesy of C. B. DeMille. As Chico Day, the assistant director who took over after Eddie Salven died, said "Even if it was only one buck, it's still one buck more than anybody else in show business ever gave [their crew.]"

The Ten Commandments was nominated for Oscars in seven categories; including Best Picture but only won for Special Effects. DeMille was wounded—he knew the film represented the summation of his career—and he also knew that it had, as a later generation would say, pushed the envelope in art direction, sound, and costuming, among others.

After the picture was released, DeMille called Elmer Bernstein into his office. There, scattered around the room, were forty or fifty paintings by Dan Sayre Groesbeck, some painted as concept art, some just Groesbeck paintings. DeMille asked him which one he liked best.

Bernstein pointed to a painting of a Chinese scribe. DeMille wanted to know why Bernstein liked that one.

"It has a tremendous sense of repose," replied the composer. "A kind of peaceful feeling, and it gives me that same feeling." DeMille nodded and sent Bernstein on his way. When Bernstein got home that evening, the painting of the scribe was waiting for him, beautifully framed. Bernstein kept it in his Santa Barbara house for the rest of his life.

"*The Ten Commandments* was something more than a film," said Elmer Bernstein. "And DeMille was much more than a director."

The success of *The Ten Commandments* confirmed DeMille's beliefs about the nature of movies, and of how filmmakers forget showmanship and emotional and physical size at their peril. "You're not going to wipe out theaters with home television or anything else," he snapped. "*The Ten Commandments* on a 46-foot screen is a completely different thing from the same film on a 24-inch screen. You put Rosa Bonheur's "The Horse Fair" on a postage stamp and you'll not be able to see even the horses."

DeMille was flooded with letters from viewers who loved the film, and, as with all of his correspondence, it was carefully catalogued and filed. One thought ran through many of them: "This picture has made God real to me."

It was precisely the response he had been hoping for. The letters made him think of his father reading the Old Testament to him, of the struggles of itinerant acting, of E. H. Sothern and Belasco, of the nearly fifty years of moviemaking, all of which Constance had shared, all of which was now lost to her. The letters, he would say, were recompense for the years spent making the movie, for the years spent making all the movies.

In spite of vast changes in special effects technology and film style, *The Ten Commandments* has continued to be a part of the social fabric of the world for more than half a century. Along with *It's a Wonderful Life*, it's the last of the great movie warhorses still trotted out on American network television on a yearly basis.

The spectacle scenes of *The Ten Commandments* speak for themselves, but the theatrical splendor of the interiors is often overlooked. DeMille's tableaux compositions resemble classical paintings: actors emoting to each other, moving very little. Dialogue is largely expositional, positioning characters by speech rather than deed. It's old theater, but *great* old theater, sometimes ridiculous, always impressive.

The picture's first half is slow, although there's a tantalizing hint of what used to be called miscegenation in Moses's first scene at court, as he and a Nubian princess eye each other appreciatively. Confronted with large amounts of exposition, DeMille remains confident in his command of both his material and his audience. There are wonders ahead: turning water into blood, the first Passover, the Exodus, the parting of the Red Sea, the giving of the Commandments. DeMille knows that his trump card is his story, its primal embedding in our race memories, and his willingness to confront it *literally*, without glib irony.

Yul Brynner is almost like a statue in some scenes, but the statue radiates a glowering power, and Edward G. Robinson and Vincent Price are both sly and subversive—in and out of character at the same time. (Oddly, although Cedric Hardwicke is playing a Pharaoh who's working the children of Israel to death, his character is written and played with great sympathy.)

At times, the film owes a lot to Griffith, especially in DeMille's use of animals—the little donkey that doesn't want to leave Egypt, a link to an agrarian world that DeMille knew from his childhood and from Paradise. Charlton Heston has to make only a few minor adjustments from his last performance for DeMille to play Moses; in both cases, his character is tasked with keeping the show on the road.

The film is obviously made by a devout man with a split personality—reverence hand in hand with lust. But there's a modern, neurotic edge to some of the proceedings as well: Yul Brynner's Pharaoh only wants to possess Nefretiri because he knows she's in love with Moses. And in Moses, DeMille, as David Thomson notes, creates the hero of the age: "a man of action and conscience in a cynical world."

And the color! Everybody wears a different shawl or robe, and the saturated rainbow cascades over the viewer. One commentator noted "a certain cheapness to his moral vision—he's always looking out for the sex and the legs and the crowd appeal—but it's a marvelous film by a very good director." Beyond that, the film rises with assurance to its peak moments: the Exodus and the parting of the Red Sea. If those scenes don't deliver sequential bursts of energy and grandeur, the film would have failed, but they do and it succeeded. It still does.

To see *The Ten Commandments* as a child is to be marked for life—images like the Angel of Death descending on Egypt as the splayed fingers of a skeletal green hand are brilliant metaphors given physical life.

"It's *the* traditional literal re-telling of the Bible stories," says Martin Scorsese, "and his vision of the parting of the Red Sea, it's almost like a story that we've heard many times and we want to hear it again. Charlton Heston's acting is very, very deliberate, and it has that style with no apologies. It grabs the audience. The

Passover dinner and all the violence that's going on outside, it's all done with the soundtrack. This is very, very powerful. I don't care what year it was made, whether you believe in the Bible or not, that story, that scene, the way he directed it, was strong and valid.

"Elmer [Bernstein's] music doesn't decorate the film, it sort of permeates the film. It's there every second, it's like color, it's like design, it's big and strong and powerful. The film is still kind of popular and I think it's because of the level of production. There was an extraordinary amount of care and an extraordinary amount of detail that went into each frame, and *The Ten Commandments* was his final statement on that style."

Throughout the film, DeMille and Anne Bauchens use an interesting cross-dissolve to link sections of the film. When a humiliated Rameses returns to his palace after the closing of the Red Sea wipes out his army, he and Nefretiri sit side by side in glowering silence. Finally, Rameses says, "His God *is* God." As DeMille holds on the shot, the background of the palace dissolves out as Mount Sinai appears in the background, overwhelming the supposed ruler in the foreground, then Rameses and Nefretiri slowly fade out.

Beyond the film's style, DeMille inserts fascinating bits of drama that verge on the covertly liberal—during the first Passover, a band of black attendants is quietly included in the privileged group of survivors inside, while the firstborn of Egypt die outside.

In many respects, *The Ten Commandments* is a reversion to the theater of DeMille's childhood—a pageant with stage settings, colored gels for lighting accents, compositions and stand-and-deliver acting whose dramatics owe a lot more to the dramatic literature of 1900 than to the Hollywood of 1956. It is only in the innovative special effects sequences that remained state-of-the-art for nearly twenty-five years that the film was of its time. DeMille's never faltering mastery of physical scale and command of the chugging engine of plot distinguish him.

Cumulatively, it's the sort of last movie that is seldom vouchsafed to directors—a summing up as well as an example of his interest in technical innovation. There are no loose ends in the episodic plot. Every character and situation ultimately pays off. One reason why the movie never seems boring despite the nearly four-hour running time is the elegant narrative cross-stitching, which is rarely noticed because of the clunky dialogue: "Oh, Moses, Moses, you stubborn, splendid, adorable fool."

But there are more moments when DeMille transcends the theatrical and creates moments that seem to be really happening—the pylon being raised in Pharaoh's city, the spectacular long shots of the Exodus, thousands of people setting off into the desert, moving toward the Promised Land. At moments such as these, DeMille does what most historical movies try for and seldom accomplish: he re-creates a legend, permanently setting it in the mind of the beholder.

It took another great showman to understand what made DeMille DeMille, even if this showman did like *The Greatest Show on Earth* more than *The Ten Commandments*. For Louis B. Mayer, DeMille was about display and pomp, but only up to a point. "The circus picture was his greatest achievement," said Mayer only a few months before he died. "*The Ten Commandments* had quite a bit of story. But to take the circus—a two reel subject—[and] create one of the greatest pictures ever seen, that's when he showed how great a showman [he was]. When you take an *ordinary* subject—again the clowns, again the trapeze artists—and get a great picture; he took nothing and made something.

"*It's all a question of story. He goes for story.* If it calls for spectacle he'll give it. But first story. . . . If Al Woods did it, it was 10-20-30. If Belasco did it, it had a quality. When [DeMille] gets through, it's like *Belasco*" (italics added).

The Ten Commandments was one of his few starring pictures that Yul Brynner loved (another was *The Magnificent Seven*). Rock Brynner says that his father regarded the DeMille film more as a great behemoth than a great work of art. "It was a giant, circus-like thing, but he was proud of his performance, and very proud of being in the film. He regarded it as the biggest film ever made, forever."

2 3

With his greatest risk converted to his greatest success, DeMille relaxed, and, for a time, basked. He nudged the Paramount publicity department to pay for granite monoliths of the Ten Commandments to be installed on courthouse lawns, city halls, and public squares wherever the film played. Sure, it was good publicity, but he also thought the moral lessons embodied in the Commandments ought to be front and center in American life. More than four thousand monuments were installed, and one of them, in Austin, Texas, became the basis for the Supreme Court decision of 2005 that allowed the monuments on public property but banned them from courtrooms.

At family gatherings, he remained attentive, especially to the young. "Children liked him a lot because they felt that when he looked at them he was really looking at them and appreciating them," remembered Richard deMille. "My stepson was a little boy who was very enthusiastic about all kinds of things, and especially Grandfather DeMille. He was about ten years old or so, and he said he was going to make a movie. And Cecil said, 'Well, what is the title of your movie?' and my stepson, whose name is Tony, said, *The Spears of the King*. Cecil said, 'Good title.' That was the way he treated children."

Ann del Valle had been accepted as a member of DeMille's extended family, and was frequently invited to the house. "Most of the social things he did revolved around family. We used to go to their Christmas party, which was always in the afternoon. There were two steps down from the entrance hall into the living room, and there was always a child falling down them. Every year it was a new kid; it wasn't Christmas until a child fell down those stairs."

Constance now exhibited primarily a sweet vagueness: she wouldn't always recognize her children, but was happy to spend time with them. DeMille's attitude toward her illness was far advanced for the day. He never tried to hide it, never acted ashamed of it, and was endlessly kind and patient with her.

For some members of his filmmaking family, his bottomless compassion toward Constance revealed qualities of forbearance they hadn't known he possessed.

By 1956, Constance's disease had progressed to the point where she no longer dined with the family, but Cecil made a point of spending time in her room every night, talking to her even if she no longer understood what he was saying. Sometimes at night, Constance would grow restless, and Cecil would walk with her in the corridor that connected the two houses until she grew calm and could go back to bed.

★

At the end of 1956, Cecil was contemplating a sound remake of *The King of Kings* and asked Jeremiah Milbank what he thought of the idea. Not much, as it turned out. Milbank pointed out that pleasing all the various religious denominations and sects would be impossible: "I am of this opinion because of . . . the changes which we have been urged to make in the film, even though the narrative related in the picture was in nearly complete accord with the New Testament. I knew if we made one change, many more would be pressed upon us, and I was, and still am unwilling to depart from the actual gospel written by disciples."

Cecil put the idea aside.

That same year, in December, the old barn where it had all begun forty-three years earlier was declared a state historic landmark. The barn had been moved onto the Paramount lot in 1926, then converted into the studio gymnasium in 1929, and served that function even after it was incorporated into the studio's standing western set. At the December 27 dedication, Jesse Lasky, Sam Goldwyn, and Adolph Zukor listened as DeMille spoke: "Streams of celluloid that have flowed from here have encircled the world. . . . The barn is a symbol of Hollywood. . . . It is not only a landmark of the State of California, it is a landmark for the entire world."

DeMille finally turned serious attention to his autobiography. He was leery of tape recorders, finding them intimidating, but he agreed to Art Arthur's suggestion of a hidden machine. The Paramount sound department installed the system in February of 1957. Whenever Arthur would enter DeMille's office, Florence Cole would turn on the tape recorder, and as DeMille began reminiscing, Arthur would flip a switch to activate the machine. At the end of a session, whether ten minutes or an hour, the reel-to-reel tape would be transcribed, then cross-filed by topic.

"He never seemed conscious of being recorded," Arthur told James D'Arc. "Except one time when we were talking of what he would like to do for his next picture. He began to tell the story of Esther from the Bible, in a way that made it not just a Bible story but a warm human drama, and he told it in a way that was utterly spellbinding. When he finished, he looked at me as I got up to leave and he asked, 'Is that on tape?' I replied that it was and he ordered a copy of it for his further elaboration into story form. As it turned out, he found the tape recorder a valuable first draft for projects."

Arthur also interviewed various DeMille alumni, including actors, technicians, and executives. Arthur began to write sample chapters, which would be passed on to DeMille for notes and comments in his favored editorial medium of red pencil. The annotated draft then went to Donald Hayne for a final polish. Most of the taping was completed by December 1957, when Art Arthur left for a job in television, and Hayne continued the writing alone.

Despite his affection for Arthur, DeMille hated his first draft, saying of himself as he came across in the draft, "I think this fellow is an SOB. I want no part or parcel of this guy because he's a phony, a boaster, a guy who likes to strut, who doesn't recognize that anybody else had anything to do with making pictures. Nobody else had anything to do with making *The Squaw Man*, this SOB did it all. It says ego, ego, ego all the way through on every page. . . . In other words, a great hero is writing the story of a great hero. If I have a boastful side, it has to be handled with humor. . . . Now I think that it shows a drive, a directness of purpose that is very good, but I hope it's not me. If it is me, then I'm going up to Paradise and stay, because I'm no good."

He pointed out that the brashness reflected in the first draft wasn't at all the way he had felt in the early days of his movie career: "I had a frightful responsibility on my shoulders." And he particularly objected to the disparaging treatment of Oscar Apfel, terming it "condescending. He was a real motion picture director."

As Donald Hayne immersed himself in the book, DeMille paused briefly to give some triumphant interviews regarding the immense success of *The Ten Commandments*. "Actually, I feel closer to my picture *The King of Kings* than I do to *The Ten Commandments*. These two and my picture *The Sign of the Cross* make up a trilogy. . . . *The Ten Commandments* is about the giving of the law, *The King of Kings* is about the interpretation of the law, and *Sign of the Cross* is concerned with its preservation."

He concluded by saying that he would never retire and borrowed a phrase from General Douglas MacArthur: "I would rather wear out than rust out. Right now I am trying to select one of four stories I have in hand for my next picture. One of them is Biblical. Whether I'll be permitted to do any of them is, of course, in bigger hands than mine."

Old friends stayed in touch; Ayn Rand sent him an autographed copy of *Atlas Shrugged*. If it wasn't to DeMille's taste as reading material he nevertheless put his bookplate in it and added it to his library. He was deluged with various awards from civic and religious organizations, and a junior high school in Long Beach was named after him.

At Paramount, he was now as much of a monument as the Marathon Gate. At lunch, young stars such as Sophia Loren would be brought to him for a brief welcoming meeting that amounted to a sort of public benediction. It was felt that with DeMille's smiling approval, the young star would have a place at the studio.

As an elderly man with a compromised heart, mortality was much on his mind. One day in 1957, he sat down and wrote out several pages of notes in which he tried to comprehend the meaning of his life: " 'The Lord giveth and the Lord taketh away. Blessed be the name of the Lord.' It can only be a short time, a few years at most, until those words—the first in the Episcopal funeral service—are spoken over me.

"I should like to begin my story then after those words are spoken. What am I? Let me disassociate myself from my body and see what I am, for I am only what I have accomplished. How much good have I spread? How much evil have I spread? For whatever I am a moment after death—a spirit, a soul, a bodiless mind—I shall have to look back and forward, for I have to take with me both."

★

The Ten Commandments was the greatest triumph of DeMille's life, but it was also the most debilitating experience. He had wagered high, and when the odds were heavily against him he had doubled down. He won, but at a terrible cost, and he knew it. Age had muted the daring Champion Driver; in his place was a man all too conscious of downside risk.

"I was not frightened at my first picture," he said while reminiscing one day for the autobiography, "but I was terrified at my last picture. You can neither eat nor sleep for about four weeks before you start. You think about all the things that can go wrong, and try to outguess the mistakes that are going to be made. . . . That is what you are thinking of constantly. To try to outguess these mistakes—and then someone says, 'You're not in a very good mood today, are you?' "

In July 1957, DeMille was visited by an emissary from the Cinémathèque Française, which was looking for costumes and artifacts for its museum, a "Louvre of the Cinema," according to its founder, Henri Langlois. DeMille was reserved, but the temperature was soon raised, in line with Langlois's instructions: "Tell him how much we admire him, how much we would like to host a tribute to him in Paris. Remind him that we already wrote about him for the [fortieth] anniversary, remind him that he replied to us that he was busy preparing *The Ten Commandments* but was prepared to lend us all the material for a grand exhibition about him. . . .

"Flatter, flatter, flatter. He's a man who is so accustomed to flattery that if by misfortune one doesn't flatter him enormously, he will imagine, like Matisse, that one doesn't admire him."

The flattery worked, and DeMille agreed to donate material and to arrange for films to be sent to Paris for a retrospective. Langlois was exultant: "If we can pull off this program, it would be such a slap in the face to the imbeciles and such a revelation to all those who are unaware of the immense artistic importance of DeMille that I dance with joy and I sacrifice to C. B. DeMille the dates I had reserved for Charlie Chaplin."

Langlois's ambitions were always far in excess of his organizational abilities, so the retrospective did not take place until June 1959—five months after DeMille was dead.

In October 1957, Cecil left for Europe and some final openings for *The Ten Commandments*. On October 31, he met with Winston Churchill at his London residence, 28 Hyde Park Gate. Churchill was receiving guests in bed that day, with his pet parrot in attendance. DeMille related some anecdotes about the location shooting in Egypt, and then told Churchill that he thought there were similarities between him and Moses. "I mean historically. No people could have been in a worse plight than when Moses stepped up and led them from Egypt—and the same with England when Sir Winston led them to victory."

At this, Churchill's eyes got shiny. When they shook hands to say goodbye, DeMille said he'd rather shake Churchill's hand than any man in the twentieth century or before.

"Oh, well, then let's shake hands again," exclaimed Churchill.

★

The Buccaneer was born out of the mutual enchantment between DeMille and Yul Brynner, and the new film was planned as Brynner's directorial debut.

In the early stages of discussion, it was supposed to be a drama with music. Serious planning got underway in April of 1956. By the end of the year, there was a first draft script, for which DeMille made notes. In the margins next to a description of the aftermath of the Battle of New Orleans, he wrote "costly—unneccesary." At this point, Brynner was still supposed to direct, but two months later he had dropped out, and DeMille and Wilcoxon were discussing potential directorial replacements.

Wilcoxon's preferred choice was John Sturges, but also in the mix were Robert Parrish, Frank Lloyd, Tay Garnett, Frank Capra, John Ford, Edward Dmytryk, Robert Mulligan, Fred Zinnemann, and Mark Robson. There was even the offbeat suggestion of Mel Ferrer, in order to get his wife, Audrey Hepburn, to star opposite Brynner. DeMille wasn't sure about Robson; he placed a question mark after his name on one internal document, possibly because of Robson's anti-DeMille political stand during the Directors Guild fight years earlier.

One day at lunch, DeMille pressed Wilcoxon for his choice of a director. For some inexplicable reason, Wilcoxon said, "Budd Boetticher." DeMille wasn't familiar with his work and called over his son-in-law Anthony Quinn, who was eating in the commissary and had worked with Boetticher on *The Magnificent Matador*. Quinn gave a withering estimation of Boetticher's abilities and said that he could do a better job directing than Boetticher could.

"Is that so, Tony? Well, how would you like to direct *The Buccaneer?*" Quinn's own memory of the episode was that DeMille called him over to compliment him and Anna Magnani on their performances in the rushes of *Wild Is the Wind*, and then moved the conversation around to the fact that Brynner was backing out of his promise to direct a picture, whereupon he tendered the offer to Quinn. "You're not gonna say no to me too, are you? You're not gonna turn coward on me?" The overt challenge to Quinn's masculine pride certainly sounds like DeMille.

Quinn remembered that he went home and complained to Katherine about the way DeMille had couched the offer. "You always wanted to direct a picture," countered Katherine. "Direct it."

"But it's not my picture," said Quinn. "It's his picture he wants."

Quinn was signed to direct in January 1957, for a salary of $45,000—good money for a man with no experience. The bet was hedged by having John Jensen do a complete set of storyboards for the film. For Quinn, at long last, the sword had fallen on his shoulder.

By this time, Quinn's great success as an actor had, as his brother-in-law Richard deMille would write, turned him into "a carnivorous egotist." "I was wild about Katherine," remembered Richard deMille. "She was extremely lovable and beautiful, a terrific combination. Was she ill-used by Quinn? Absolutely, but not in a way that she resented. She was always in love with him. Cecil had respected Constance and always treated her fairly; I don't think Quinn treated Katherine fairly."

Quinn went to work with another writer to write a straight, dramatic version of *The Buccaneer*, which DeMille hated. That led to Jesse Lasky Jr. writing a third version, which incorporated some of Quinn's ideas into a revision of the 1938 original, which in turn led to a fourth version incorporating some of DeMille's new ideas. The result, as Henry Wilcoxon remembered it, was that "Yul hated Tony's version. Tony hated Yul's and DeMille's. DeMille hated Tony's and Yul's. DeMille hated Jesse's."

Three strong-willed men were struggling to control the picture, but there was only one who actually had power. Jesse Lasky Jr. would come to believe that in some perverse way, DeMille wanted Wilcoxon and Quinn to create a disaster; that he wanted to make sure that nobody but DeMille could make a DeMille film.

Many in the DeMille unit thought the picture was a bad idea, and many in the family agreed. DeMille's daughter Cecilia thought that, given her father's age and health, the only possible motivation he could have for embarking on still more movies was his desire to continue to employ his staff.

But only Henry Noerdlinger voiced his opinion. "When you first expressed your intention of remaking *The Buccaneer* under your banner," wrote Noerdlinger in a confidential memo in July 1957, "I stated that if the 1937 version of this picture was good enough to be remade, it was good enough to be re-released. . . . Since that time considerable amounts of money have been invested in the re-writing of the script, the designing of sets and costumes, the contracting of players and other accounts. Knowing all this full well, I take the liberty once again to express my conviction that it would be far more profitable to rerelease the 1937 picture than to invest a minimum of from three to $3,500,000 in the remaking of it . . . if the 1937 version of this film were released again, it would at least recover the expenses so far incurred in the preparation of the new version."

DeMille's response was curt but fascinating: "I agree with Henry."

Despite the presentiments of disaster, plans for the remake moved forward, possibly because DeMille felt indebted to Henry Wilcoxon, possibly because he felt that pulling the plug would damage Katherine's marriage, possibly because a problematic film was better than no film.

DeMille's notes on the scripts are muted, almost as if he had given up on the picture before it started. On the September 10 draft, he writes, "pretty tame entrance & stuff." A fight scene draws the comment, "sounds like the usual."

DeMille was still friendly with Yul Brynner and invited him and his mistress Claire Bloom to Paradise. "It was a big, beautiful place," remembered Bloom. "Julia Faye was living there at the time. She was very charming and elderly. She seemed older than DeMille. She had been extremely pretty, and he obviously doted on her. Actually, he was very courtly to all women, in a Victorian manner. Very formal and very nice." What Bloom did not know was that DeMille's breathing was becoming a problem; oxygen was being installed at his beloved Paradise.

DeMille appeared at most of the casting sessions for *The Buccaneer*, but appeared on the set only once, at the beginning of production. "It was kind of a royal procession," remembered Claire Bloom. "We all bowed and curtseyed and fell to the floor, and then he left. His involvement was strictly behind the scenes."

Charlton Heston was playing Andrew Jackson, more or less as a personal favor, and he received an invitation to a private lunch with DeMille. Afterward, DeMille poured Heston a drink of Madeira from a bottle dated 1815. "That's the year Jackson fought at New Orleans," DeMille said. "Along the Old Chalmette Road. You know all that, you do your research."

DeMille went on to talk a little shop, mentioning that he had heard that Heston was up for the part of Ben-Hur for William Wyler. True, said Heston, but

Wyler couldn't decide which part Heston should play. The hero and the villain, Messala, were both possibilities.

"Well, Ben-Hur's the part, of course," said DeMille. "You can always get good actors to play bad men. Heroes are harder. Ramon Novarro was wrong for it in the silent version. Dead wrong. You can do that part. I'd call up Mr. Wyler and tell him, but—directors like to make their own choices. . . . Yes, that'll make quite a picture. High time someone did it. Get it right this time. If I were you, I wouldn't worry." DeMille called Wyler and recommended Heston anyway.

Heston thought that DeMille seemed greatly aged since he'd last seen him. He no longer nervously paced in his office, re-creating the entire arc of a movie with sweeping narrative brilliance. Now, he seemed perfectly content to sit behind his desk, or the chair in the commissary. The banked fires sprang to life only when he mentioned the possibilities of *Ben-Hur*. Then his eyes lit up and Heston could sense the old man's flare of engagement—his desire to make a great spectacle, just one more time.

On the set of *The Buccaneer*, things began breaking down very quickly. On top of Brynner's affair with Claire Bloom, Anthony Quinn was having an affair with Inger Stevens. Brynner stopped taking direction from Quinn. When a young movie aficionado named Mark Haggard visited the set, he saw Quinn on his knees in front of Brynner, begging the star to cooperate. No dice.

"A couple of times Brynner didn't show up when he was supposed to," remembered the actor Kenny Miller. "He was still playing the part of the King in *The King and I*, even when he wasn't acting." There was always a goblet of water covered with a napkin nearby, in case Brynner got thirsty. DeMille had finally found an actor whose affectations were worthy of the great Belasco—or DeMille.

The crew was split down the middle; everybody knew the script wasn't good, and it was clear from the rushes that the picture wasn't working. Ann del Valle was doing publicity on the picture and enjoyed watching Quinn direct. "He was fascinating and entertaining. He played every role, including a little old lady selling flowers. He was marvelous to watch, but it didn't come over in the picture."

DeMille looked at the rushes, saw that Quinn was giving line readings to the actors and went berserk. "I never in my entire life ever told an actor how to read a line! That's *their* job—to act. *Mine* is to direct!" Looking at multiple takes that Quinn had shot with the venerable actor Robert Warwick, DeMille exploded at the nearest available target, who happened to be Henry Wilcoxon. "I've *never* seen Warwick need more than two or three takes for any scene. All this money going down the drain and for what? This is an outrage! I couldn't teach you how to produce a DeMille movie if I had the next 25 years to do it! You should be ashamed to take home your paycheck every week. It's grand theft, that's what it is!"

DeMille fired off a memo to Wilcoxon: "The point to get over to Tony is that he should . . . bring out what is in the actor. Do not put into the actor what is in the director. He robs each actor of his own personality by trying to get him to imitate the director. The director's job is to take what the actor has to give and bring that up to the point he wants. You can't do that by showing them how to act."

John Jensen remembered that part of the problem was Quinn's indecision. "I'd be drawing stuff for one end of the set, and he'd change his mind overnight and start on the other end. Quinn was used to smaller pictures, where you don't have to rely on assistant directors. He would have been a good director working closely with actors, but a big DeMille production was a different thing. For that, you have to have control and timing; you can't change your mind when there are five hundred extras waiting."

One day Elmer Bernstein was in the projection room looking at an assembly of footage when DeMille was excoriating Wilcoxon and Quinn. He finally stopped and turned to Bernstein. "Elmer," he said, "you'll have to save this scene."

For Wilcoxon, all this was mortifying, and there was no way out. He couldn't fire the director because the director was DeMille's son-in-law. There was nothing to do but take it. "When DeMille shouted at me, you could hear him through the door, down the hall, and out in the street. And when he shouted, it was heart-stopping. And what was I going to do? I knew he was dying. I knew it was only drugs keeping him going, too. I wasn't going to shout back at a sick old man."

DeMille kept looking at the rushes. On January 20, 1958, his notes included observations that Yul Brynner and Charlton Heston were both looking the wrong way in their close-ups, and that a scene with Brynner and Inger Stevens couldn't be used because extras were "standing like statues in the background. Will have to do over or use Annette angle."

Jesse Lasky Jr. would note that DeMille "had become moody, resenting the creeping limitations of his years. He was, except for rare flashes, a rather bitter old man." Lasky might not have known about the disastrous treatments of Max Jacobson and the resultant mood swings, which were only exacerbating DeMille's anger at a misbegotten pirate movie.

By February 1958, Y. Frank Freeman had sent a memo informing Henry Wilcoxon that his salary was being cut from $1,000 a week to $500. *The Buccaneer*, Freeman said, was a whopping $700,000 over budget; Wilcoxon had already earned $73,000 for producing what had started out as a moderately budgeted movie, and the studio was blowing the whistle.

DeMille's name was on the picture, so he didn't want it to fail. "I think the best way to sell *Buccaneer*," he told Wilcoxon, "is as a children's picture. It's a little bit of American history. It has pirates with plumed hats and a colorful president and soldiers at a fancy dress ball. There's no objectionable sex or excessive blood-shed. . . . In other words, nothing to interest an adult, but a lot of things that look different to youngsters. Let's play up its wholesomeness, its old-fashioned qualities."

As soon as shooting was completed, Quinn was gone from the movie. As he remembered, "I walked away thinking I had been done a horrible injustice, when really all that had happened was just business as usual. . . . We exchanged words . . . but it was mostly a worthless discussion, filled with more than twenty years worth of venom and frustration. He was a dying man, facing down his up-pity son-in-law; I was a misunderstood artist, beating back authority."

Quinn would later claim that the picture he shot was considerably better than the picture that was released, and that DeMille reedited the picture behind his back. Claire Bloom denied that, saying "the film is a fair representation of what was shot."

On April 9, Quinn broke his silence and sent his father-in-law a letter to thank him for the opportunity. He had, he explained, been terribly busy, had gone from acting in one picture to acting in another picture—one for the money, one as an antidote to his directorial experience. "In some ways it was a painful one, but in other ways it was wonderful."

In any case, lessons had been learned and he was, he said, grateful. He quoted the line of Dominique You to Jean Lafitte: "The one man in the world I never wanted to disappoint was you," and said that he hoped that DeMille was not too disappointed and that his faith in Quinn had been at least slightly justified.

The letter stops just short of groveling. For a very proud man, the humiliation had been nearly total; Quinn never directed another picture.

For the last time, DeMille filled a film with names and faces from the silent days: Fred Kohler, Julia Faye, and Madame Sul-Te-Wan, a veteran of *The Birth of a Nation*. In DeMille's original production of *The Buccaneer*, Lafitte had been played lightly, tongue-in-cheek, but Yul Brynner lacked irony and had to dominate every scene. Mainly, the remake is dull, and because of the landlocked studio produc-tion and the stagy roistering, a lot of it feels like an eerie forerunner of *Pirates of the Caribbean*—the ride, not the movie, although, to be fair, the big battle scene is picturesque and the main character achieves a certain corsair's nobility as he moves toward the ending.

The Buccaneer cost $4.7 million and earned world receipts of $7 million—not a disaster, more of a disappointment. Most of the money came from overseas, where the film was quite popular—American rentals totaled only $2.8 million. DeMille's company was in for 13 percent of the profits that kicked in after receipts totaled $8.2 million, i.e., breakeven.

"Look, DeMille was old," summed up Elmer Bernstein. "The basic reason he didn't direct the movie himself was that he wasn't physically able anymore. It was a very painful experience not just for Quinn, but for Henry Wilcoxon, who was a very nice and gentle man.

"A few months ago I was in Seattle with nothing to do, so I put on the television. *The Buccaneer* was on. I couldn't make it all the way through."

★

On January 13, 1958, Jesse Lasky collapsed and died of a heart attack. On the day of Lasky's interment, Cecil remained behind at the crypt at Hollywood Memorial Cemetery after everybody else went home, stayed until nearly dark, giving himself over to a full and merciless appraisal of their shared lives.

On some level, DeMille must have felt he hadn't done enough for his old friend and partner. With his own mortality no longer a distant issue but an immediate concern, DeMille undertook perhaps the last generous act of his life. Jesse had died not merely broke, but deeply in debt to the IRS over a disallowed claim from a capital gains deduction he had taken on the profits from *Sergeant York*. The IRS had put a lien on the Lasky house at 235 North Saltair in Los Angeles and was threatening to take possession of it as partial judgment of Jesse's debts, throwing Bessie Lasky out of her house.

DeMille made some inquiries, and it was ascertained that the IRS would accept $45,000 to settle the debt. DeMille began calling around town. He would, he told people, put in a large amount of money, but he thought it incumbent upon some other people who had benefited from Jesse's talents to help out as well. Sol Lesser contributed $5,000, financier Louis Lurie contributed $5,000, Spyros Skouras $2,500, Gilbert Miller $10,000. Even the studios got into the act—Paramount and Warner Bros. both cut small checks.

Finally, DeMille called Sam Goldwyn. For more than forty years, Goldwyn had brooded about his former brother-in-law choosing Adolph Zukor over him and throwing him out of Famous Players-Lasky. Sam listened to Cecil's explanation of the situation and request for funds. When DeMille was finished, Goldwyn sighed, paused, and said he'd think about it. When he called back, it was to contribute $10,000.

With DeMille's own contribution of $11,500, the IRS got its money. The contributors took the deed on the house and Bessie Lasky lived there for the rest of her life. When she died, the profit from the sale of her house went to her estate.

★

In February 1958, DeMille received a letter from William F. Buckley inviting all the West Coast stockholders of *National Review* to a meeting at Morrie Ryskind's house. "Am I a stockholder in this?" he scribbled on the letter. "What was their review on 10 Commandments?" Conservative principles were one thing, but not as important as good reviews.

While DeMille was wrestling with *The Buccaneer*, he was also struggling with his autobiography. The creative problem of the book's early pages stemmed from the fact that DeMille had devoted paragraphs to his father's family, but couldn't figure out how to introduce his mother's Jewish origins. Donald Hayne wrote a memo in which he said that the pages as DeMille had left them were an attempt at concealment, and that if Beatrice's family was to be ignored, then Henry's had to be as well.

Ultimately, DeMille decided to give his mother's maiden name in full and let it go at that. DeMille had been living with nineteenth-century attitudes about his bloodlines—the same attitudes that had compelled David Belasco to wear a clerical collar—for seventy-six years. He had spent a lifetime painstakingly constructing a patrician persona that didn't have much room in it for Jewish secondhand silver merchants from Liverpool. He had always believed that in some way his mother's heritage, perhaps even her life, began only when she converted to her husband's religion, and he wasn't about to change his opinion now.

Max Jacobson was still lurking about, and his patient list extended past DeMille to his office staff. When DeMille had visited New York between February 15 and February 25, 1957, one of the secretaries who accompanied him wrote Jacobson, "Get the needles ready! . . . Incidentally, I never received any kind of a bill from you—so hit me with it when I get to New York—okay?"

In February 1958, Paramount sold its pre-1948 library of over seven hundred films to the MCA talent agency. The price was $50 million, payable over twelve years. It was an insanely bad deal for Paramount, indicative only of aging management, and a windfall for MCA, which probably recouped its money within six or eight years. The Paramount deal quickly gave MCA one of the most valuable film libraries in the country.

For his 50 percent of the net profits of all the pictures he made between *The Sign of the Cross* and *Unconquered*, DeMille received what his granddaughter remembered as $4 million. It seemed like a good deal for an aging man in increasingly poor health, partly because so many of his pictures of this period were cross-collateralized, to DeMille's disadvantage. A successful picture like *Union Pacific*—$323,711 in profits as of 1957—was bracketed with the 1938 version of *The Buccaneer*, which was still $133,638 in the red by the same date. The net profit of the two pictures combined was $190,072, so DeMille's half was only $95,036. Since he had taken advances of $100,000 against his percentage for each picture, he hadn't seen any additional money from either picture since they were released.

Money continued to come in from the Technicolor period of *North West Mounted Police* and *Reap the Wild Wind*, but *Unconquered*, the last of his films to be included in the sale, had been a flop. It was a very good price. Not only that, the buyout would have been categorized as capital gains, hence taxed at a much lower rate than regular income.

On April 21, DeMille sat for his last in-depth interview, with George Pratt of the Eastman House. It was a recapitulation of the things he had been feeling and thinking about the movies for the last forty years. He paid generous and eloquent tribute to D. W. Griffith, said that he thought *The Birth of a Nation*, *Broken Blossoms*, and *Orphans of the Storm* were his best pictures, then noted that he also liked the early one- and two-reelers, including *The Battle at Elderbush Gulch*—"I ran it not long ago. But I'm a Griffith fan. . . . He was the first one—and the one who taught us all—to photograph thought, that is, to bring a camera close enough to photograph the expression of the eyes. . . . And Griffith is my Number One director."

He admitted that "every honest director finds something that he doesn't like in every picture that he's made. And generally something that he likes in every bad picture that he's made." At the end of his life, DeMille's favorite DeMille pictures were *Joan the Woman*, *The Cheat*, *Male and Female*, *The Whispering Chorus*, the first *The Ten Commandments*, *Forbidden Fruit*, *The King of Kings*, *Dynamite*, *The Plainsman*, *Union Pacific*, *Reap the Wild Wind*, *Samson and Delilah*, *The Greatest Show on Earth*, and the second *The Ten Commandments*.

Of those, he said that the second *The Ten Commandments*, *The King of Kings*, and *The Sign of the Cross* "are the three really important films in my career, that have had the most effect upon the world. . . . Those three pictures, because people can cling to them—they show the way out, those who have a spark of the soul left in them, a soul that knows that there is God."

★

On May 13, DeMille wrote to an old friend who had attended the Pompton School for Girls. "I have the advantage of not having seen you all through the years, so that the recollection of our youth together is still so clear in my mind—and it is a pleasant recollection. I even remember how your gray uniform with the dark red bolero fitted, and your . . . dimples were not unnoticed.

"Do you know if Meta Wachenhut is still with us in this world? She has been angry with me for the past fifty years for being a jealous, hot-tempered boor, which I unquestionably was. But fifty years is long enough for her to be angry with me, and I wish she would write if she is still living.

"Constance, my wife, I deeply regret to tell you, is not at all well. She has lost the power of speech, and is under nursing care twenty-four hours a day.

"But you and I seem to be like Tennyson's brook and go babbling on forever—and you babble most charmingly."

Constance's condition weighed heavily on him; when he informed one friend that Constance was now an invalid, he continued, "We've been married 55 years and we were engaged two years. Fifty-seven years. I never heard her say an unkind word about any human being in that time. Several times she should have said [an unkind word] about me."

In May, he scribbled some thoughts in response to a questionnaire. He saw pay television as a "positive and constructive" development; he thought the most important component of a movie's success was story ("What great star is in *Snow White?*").

On June 7, DeMille left Los Angeles for the East Coast. In New York he stayed at the Plaza and saw Max Jacobson every night he was in town. On June 12, he traveled to Philadelphia to receive an honorary doctor of law degree from Temple University. On Monday, June 16, he testified in Washington before a subcommittee on Labor-Management Relations of the House Committee on Education and Labor.

It was a spirited exchange; one congressman offered the insulting opinion that Cecil had never been poor enough to offer an opinion about labor laws. DeMille promptly mentioned that he used to walk seventy-two blocks home from the theater every night in order to save a nickel so he could buy milk for Cecilia.

He returned home on June 17. Two days later, DeMille suffered a mild heart attack, but three days after that he was hit by a far more serious coronary. He was in Cedars of Lebanon hospital until July 20, and his recovery was slow; Hedy Lamarr remembered that she personally made up a bouquet of flowers for DeMille and left it for him. Cecil's daughter called the next day and gave Hedy his love. "He said to tell me that in my case, forget-me-nots were superfluous," Lamarr remembered.

On July 2, the sets that Sam Goldwyn had built for his film of *Porgy and Bess* went up in flames. In his hospital room, DeMille roused himself to send his old friend a message: "The phoenix arose from the ashes of a great fire and so will you with your great strength." Touched, Goldwyn replied, "Dear Cecil, your message was very sweet and it is just like you to always want to help. You remember the experience we had on *The Squaw Man*. That was even worse and we can take it better now than we could then."

In fact, DeMille could not take much more. He had lost a great deal of weight and stairs were now a problem: while he was still in the hospital an elevator was installed at the Laughlin Park house to enable him to get up and down from his bedroom.

By August 1, DeMille was taking short walks in his garden and was able to dictate some correspondence, but back at Paramount there was a good deal of concern. Some days he could barely get out of his bed, other days he felt reasonably well.

On August 6, an FBI agent came to Laughlin Park for a brief visit, and he reported back to Hoover that "While Mr. DeMille weighed considerably less than he did prior to his recent illness, he is alert and vigorous." DeMille planned to go to Paradise that weekend and hoped to spend his seventy-seventh birthday on August 12 at the studio. On August 8, Hoover sent an early birthday letter and hope for a speedy recovery.

On August 12, DeMille was able to get to the studio for a birthday lunch in his honor, but after this he could make it to the studio only for an hour or two every day. As sick as he was, as old as he was, he couldn't stop thinking about making another movie. He started giving some thought to doing the story of Barabbas, the thief who is set free by the Romans while Jesus is tortured.

DeMille was invited to attend a reception in Los Angeles for J. Edgar Hoover on August 26, but had to send his regrets due to doctor's orders—a tacit admission of the seriousness of his condition, for nothing short of imminent death could have kept him from sitting on a dais with Hoover.

He took care of his business, but as an absent eminence who communicated via handwritten notes to Russel Treacy of his office staff: "Treacy—please order me 2 cases of 10 year old 3 Dagger Rum—Joseph can take to Paradise next time I go up."

"Treacy—please give Cecilia (little) check for $350 her birthday present—she will call for it."

"Treacy—I have read these and signed them. The Egyptian writings on the Temple of Karnak are easier reading than a U.S. income tax form."

*

On November 7, Cecil wrote a letter to his daughter: "Dear Cecilia, I am leaving for the ranch and I wanted to give you a day to think before we dine together Sunday night.

"I have made a commitment with Frank Freeman for two pictures; one to be produced by me as a 'DeMille picture,' this one will be the boy scout picture with David Niven as Lord Baden-Powell; the second picture will be REVELATION to be produced and directed by me.

"I will start work upon the Baden-Powell picture immediately.

"Think over what if any interest Motion Picture Associates wish to take on this first picture and/or the second picture, which at present is in nebulous form. The above is not known so please do not discuss it with anyone but Joe.

"I have told Frank Freeman I would cover both of these agreements with him by letter Monday."

It was signed, not "Father," but "Cecil B. DeMille."

In his mind, *Revelation* was the more important of the two projects; he knew there was no time to do both, and was expecting that Henry Wilcoxon would direct the Baden-Powell movie, so he could spend his remaining time on *Revelation.*

Wilcoxon had known David Niven before either of them got into the movies, so he was able to persuade the actor to come to California from New York for a face-to-face meeting without telling him anything more specific other than that DeMille wanted to hire him.

Niven arrived early in the morning, and Wilcoxon took him to his hotel, then up to DeMille Drive for breakfast. DeMille took his time, made some small talk, and complimented Niven on his pictures—"he was almost Oriental," remembered Wilcoxon. Niven was writhing in anticipation, and finally DeMille revealed his plans. "When you play this part, not that this would make you scared, I promise that you will be knighted by the crowned heads of [England]. The part, David, is that . . . of . . . Lord Baden-Powell, of Gilwell."

Niven, the descendant of two generations of soldiers—his father had been killed at the Dardanelles, and Niven himself was a veteran of the Highland Light Infantry—was overwhelmed and began to cry. "Do you know, Mr. DeMille, that Baden-Powell has always been my great hero, all my life? My God, what a part—I'll do it for nothing."

Had DeMille been in better shape, he might very well have tried to hold him to his offer, but Niven's gesture would remain untested.

Revelation was to be based on the books of Daniel and Revelation. Essentially, it concerned the struggle of mankind to find God and it would end with the Second Coming and the beginning of the thousand years of peace on earth.

Henry Noerdlinger was leery of the subject; the profoundly philosophical Book of Revelation has always presented problems to clergy and scholars and it probably always will. Noerdlinger thought that the picture couldn't be made in the traditional DeMille style, and he believed that the director was far too old and set in his ways to adopt another style better suited to the subject.

Nevertheless, DeMille moved ahead, reading C. S. Lewis's books *The Screwtape Letters*, *Miracles*, and *Mere Christianity*. DeMille agreed to hire Jack Gariss at $350 a week to work on the story, with a raise to $600 when work on the screenplay began. But Gariss got another job and begged off, a clear signal that he felt the film's prospects were iffy.

On November 11, DeMille dragged himself to the studio and had a conversation about *Revelation* over lunch. "The brain is the wire, the message that comes through is the mind," he said. "The control of mind over physical objects—this goes back to the prophets. The complete great mind in tune with the Divine Mind will give you the parting of the Red Sea. . . . The theory I hope to prove in this picture is that the mind is this tremendous force with which any man can draw at will from it what he wants. Good or evil. Jeremiah bears this out. . . . He can do the things that you want. It isn't his worrying about you; you have to worry about it. . . . All knowledge is there if you can take it."

The conversation moved toward atheism, about which DeMille was surprisingly benign: "The atheist jumps and runs at the name of God but in reality is probably closer to that force than the so-called believer. We brand the Russians, etc. as Godless people. They may be much better than any of us. Russia has made their own religion. God knows very little about religion."

DeMille was still groping toward a story that could encompass his ideas and his imagery, which was startling: "The Four Horsemen in the end with the new horsemen with chromium heads and jet bodies that scream into the sky for untold distances." The problem was the story, and DeMille's desire to show the duality of human nature: "Everyone has in them the essence of good and the essence of evil. Some develop one and some the other. . . . Take Revelation and rewrite it as you would today. Instead you are talking about the church in the body in each individual. It is that potentiality in both. It was in Adam—in Christ. . . . This is the first hint of how to do the story."

In a handwritten note from this period, DeMille scribbles a reminder to himself: "Henry [Noerdlinger] says science and Religion are not after the same things—the truth of science is always impersonal; the truth of Religion can never be impersonal."

★

DeMille had a preliminary conversation with Jesse Lasky Jr. about writing *On My Honor*, the Baden-Powell film, and John Jensen was put to work designing the picture. The script covered Baden-Powell's entire life, from his time as a young cavalry officer in India to different military campaigns, then Africa, the Boer War, and Mafeking.

But it was becoming increasingly obvious that DeMille's ambitious plans were the triumph of optimism over reality. A few months before the premiere of *The Buccaneer*, Ann del Valle helped guide DeMille through shooting the trailer, which was photographed by Hal Rosson. "I had to stand there and tell him if his voice was weak or strong. It was hard for him to do it because his voice was shaky, and it was hard for me because I had to tell him he'd have to do it over." Del Valle had come to adore the man, and at the end of her own life she would say of DeMille with admiration and some wonder that "he wasn't perfect, but at 77 he was still trying to be better."

Against doctor's orders, in December Cecil traveled east to promote *The Buccaneer*. Max Jacobson was along for part of the trip. They were in Louisiana on December 11 for the world premiere a day later, and spent Christmas week in New York. He was attended by a nurse from December 20 to December 23, and there were also visits to Jacobson's office on December 15 and 20.

While DeMille was in New York, he was at long last honored by the American Academy of Dramatic Arts, from which he had graduated nearly sixty years before. "I noticed that you allowed the full 58 years to elapse before giving me an award," said DeMille in some extemporaneous remarks, "and I think the Academy, in that as in all things, showed great judgment.

"The Academy has done great things. Its place in the world is much greater than the little building which it occupied when I first went to it and where my father also taught. There were great names that shone over it. I do not know whether anyone here ever had dinner with Edwin Booth—but I did. My father took me to dinner with Edwin Booth when I was a little boy. . . . You speak about Mr. [Charles] Jehlinger, who is probably the only man in the world I was ever frightened of. . . .

"I want to thank you for your graciousness in this award. I shall not go on further—I talk too much. It is a very lovely thing for you to do—I shall keep it close beside me for the few years I have left. . . . It is very beautiful—Steuben glass is the finest in the world, and even more beautiful than its classic design is your thought-fulness and your recognition to an old man of 77 that he has not wasted his life."

A Paramount executive named Leonard Allen was accompanying DeMille on the trip and remembered that "We were all afraid he would die then." DeMille was gray and exhausted. A recording of a radio show he did in New Orleans reveals him sounding elderly and tentative, his diction mushy, his voice lacking his traditional booming vitality. "There wasn't much there there," he responded to a question about the Hollywood of 1913. "Lots of lemons." He was still clear-headed and capable of wit ("Let me ask you a blunt question . . ." asks the host, only to be interrupted, "My middle name is Blount"), but it was obvious that the Champion Driver was played out.

He attended the premiere of *The Buccaneer* in Santa Barbara, and met with Donald Curtis, who had quit acting and become a minister. "I must tell you, Donald, how much I admire you," DeMille told him. "I can see you take your life's work very seriously to have walked away from an acting career and devoted yourself to the service of God."

DeMille and Curtis took Paramount's limousine and drove to the minis-ter's house overlooking the ocean. The two men sat watching the sunset over the Pacific.

"I know I'm made fun of," DeMille told him. "I know they call *The Ten Commandments* the *Sexodus* and what have you. . . . But my ministry was mak-ing religious movies and getting more people to read the Bible than anyone else ever has."

★

"When he came back to the studio there was no doubt in my mind that he was dying," remembered Ann del Valle. "He was the color of wax. I kept up the illusion. We all did. We told everybody that we were sending everything up to the house, or that he'd been in the office for a half hour. Our goal was to make sure that he didn't pick up the paper and see a headline: 'DeMille Is Dying.' "

He continued to tend to those people he loved, as well as those who had earned his loyalty. Vera Reynolds, the leading lady of *The Road to Yesterday* and a lot of programmers during Cecil's time in independent production, was in financial distress. DeMille sent her a personal check for $100 and wrote her, "The Trustees of the DeMille Trust will discuss the matter among themselves and [Joe] Harper will call on you again in the near future to see how best to be of further service.

"It has been many years since I have had the pleasure of seeing you, but I remember you as a sparkling-eyed young lady and a very good actress. Your picture hangs on the wall of a long hall leading to my office, which, because of the many photographs on both sides of the wall, has come to be known as the 'Hall of Fame.' "

On December 17, he held a conference about *On My Honor* and talked about a reissue of *Samson and Delilah*, possibly with a new introduction by himself, or a new prologue. (A 1954–1955 reissue of *Reap the Wild Wind* had returned domestic rentals of $1 million.) DeMille estimated the budget for *On My Honor* as $6 or $7 million and realized that sounded quite high for anyone who didn't know the full scope of Baden-Powell's life. "Do you think they are going to give me several million dollars to rub sticks together and make camp fires? . . . It isn't what you think it is going to be." In DeMille's mind, the picture would be a combination of *The Covered Wagon*; *Goodbye, Mr. Chips*; *The Lives of a Bengal Lancer*; and *Cavalcade*.

Jim Voorhees, who had delivered the mail to the DeMille unit for years, came by and gave DeMille his Christmas present: one of the new transistor radios, complete with ear plug, just like Voorhees's radio that DeMille had admired a few weeks earlier. "He was very frail and sweet and let me take over in my usual brash way. A copy of *On My Honor* was sitting on the desk, and he patted it, saying, 'In the New Year, I promise to find a part for you, Jim, either on the crew or as one of my actors. Until then, have a Merry Christmas!' "

On Christmas Eve, he handed out bonus checks to the staff, and offered anybody who dropped by his office a glass of wine. Special friends received a Christmas gift from beneath the tree in his office. When it was nearly six o'clock, DeMille buzzed Berenice Mosk into the inner sanctum. He gave her a check, a gift, and a hug. As she embraced him, she felt his shrunken arms and shuddered; the muscular vibrance that had always been the essence of his personality was completely absent. As he walked out that night, he told her, "Well, sweetie, we have a lot of work to do in the next three years!"

Tony Quinn, who was leaving for Europe to make *The Savage Innnocents*, thought it was probably necessary to make peace with the father figure whose approval he had never quite been able to earn. They sat in the courtyard between the office and the main house. DeMille was in his bathrobe and slippers, and Quinn realized that the old man's stentorian voice was gone. In its place was an old man's whisper.

"We never really knew each other, Tony," DeMille said. Quinn was touched by how honestly sad DeMille seemed, and by his shyness. Illness had stripped him of his prideful bearing, the omnipresent aura of success that he had always wielded and that had a way of making most other people feel like failures.

"No, sir, we didn't."

"I'm sorry."

"I'm sorry, too."

The two men sat there for a while, talking about their lives and missed opportunities—the one for a father, the other for a son in his own image. "I knew it was the last time I would see him," Quinn would remember. "I was sincerely sorry. We both could have learned so much from each other. As I got up to leave, afraid he was growing tired, I said: 'You know in Europe I learned a very nice thing! . . . Men hug each other on saying goodbye.'

"I took the frail man in my arms. He made a feeble attempt to hug me. In that minute out of twenty-odd years we became father and son . . . [and] I still love him deeply for that minute when he was in my arms."

After New Year's, DeMille went to the studio on a few days, but it was hard for him to get any work done. After January 9, he could no longer leave the house, but he still got dressed, looked at movies, talked about the scripts for the films he must have known he would not be able to make.

"He never really recovered from the heart attack," said his granddaughter Cecilia. "His attitude was an impatience with his body. He fought back, just as Agnes [deMille] would after she had her stroke years later; his brain remained sharp, but his body would not cooperate. What gave him some solace was his belief that he would see his beloveds again, in Beulah Land."

"He was *enduring* death," said Richard deMille. "He wasn't afraid of it. He *endured* it. He would have liked to be struck down in battle, but that didn't happen. But even at the end he was still fearless, physically and emotionally—one of the least fearful men I've ever known. A daredevil."

Because he could no longer use salt, Cecil complained about the tasteless food he was compelled to eat. He wanted large pillows at the foot of the bed on either side of his feet so that the blankets wouldn't press down on his feet, which were extremely sensitive. He read his Bible, underlining things that particularly spoke to him, as with David's cry: "Be not thou far from me, O Lord, for trouble is near, and there is none to help." In his New Testament, he referred to some of the pages Jeanie Macpherson and he had marked when preparing *The King of Kings*: "I have fought a good fight, I have finished my course. I have finished the work which thou gavest me to do."

He could no longer access the strength and comfort that Constance had always given him. As he struggled through each day, he considered roads not taken and reflected unease with the way he had typed himself. "If I had to do it over again," he said toward the end, "I would have made twice as many movies. I let too much time go in between them. I wish I had made more. I tried to follow the policy of making a big picture and then following it with one not so big instead of trying to find something . . . better than the one before. You can find some subjects that are beautiful little miniatures that don't cost much to make or take too long. Like Leo McCarey."

About ten days before DeMille died, Henry Wilcoxon came over for a lunch meeting. DeMille was in his pajamas, sitting behind his desk. The kitchen had made up bite-sized hors d'oeuvres for his lunch, but he just pushed them around the plate, managing to nibble on one. "They're really quite good," he said, "I just don't seem to be hungry today."

He continued to look at movies: In the last weeks of 1958 he had seen *Black Orchid; The Lives of a Bengal Lancer; Gigi; Bell, Book and Candle*; and *Beau Geste*. In the first ten days of 1959 he saw *Tonka, I Want to Live!, Torpedo Run, The Trap, The Old Man and the Sea, The Barbarian and the Geisha*, and *The Restless Years*. The last movie he saw was on January 12, a British picture called *The Silent Enemy* with Laurence Harvey. A few days after that, there was yet another coronary episode, which left him too weak to walk from his bedroom to the screening room at the other end of the house.

He still insisted on locking up the house. "Let me do this for you, Mr. DeMille" said Joe Harper. "I've done this for forty years," he replied. "I can do it tonight."

But he couldn't, and Cecilia began to cry. Finally, the doctors made him realize that he had to go to bed or he might die right there. He seemed surprised, almost astonished, and obeyed.

On January 20, the last full day of DeMille's life, his granddaughter visited. Cecil did most of the talking. The subjects included the family, *Revelation*, and God—"the mind of the universe," as DeMille described Him. He told Cecilia Jr. that he had been reading some of Einstein's lectures at Princeton, and he was pleased that Einstein had described himself as a pantheist. DeMille had always believed that God could be found in nature far more often than in church, so he was pleased to find agreement from such an eminent man. His mind was clear, but, as with H. B. Warner in *The Ten Commandments*, he was poured out like water.

Very early the next morning, his bed was empty. The staff went rushing through the house looking for him, and found him in Constance's bedroom, sitting quietly beside his wife, holding her hand.

He was led back to bed, where he died at five past five in the morning of January 21, 1959.

For the first time in seventy-seven years, the air around Cecil Blount DeMille was quiet.

Joe Harper called Richard deMille, who came over to the house and found a nurse tying Cecil's feet together. When the hearse came, Richard followed the three men who carried the dead man down the stairs. A reporter from the *Los Angeles Times* arrived and asked Richard what DeMille's favorite possession had been. "His children," Richard replied. The reporter did not think that piece of information newsworthy and it never got into print.

★

"I have been here a long time," said the producer A. C. Lyles, "and I've seen a lot of joyful times, and a lot of sorrowful times, and one of the most sorrowful, if not the most sorrowful, was when Cecil B. DeMille died. The whole Paramount lot went in mourning, Hollywood went in mourning."

One of the first telegrams to arrive at the house was from J. Edgar Hoover: "I was deeply saddened by the news of your father's passing, and I want to offer my heartfelt sympathy to you and your family. . . . All of his friends in the FBI share your grief at this trying time, and we urge you to let us know if we can be of any help. I hope you can find some comfort in the knowledge that he was loved by all and that his many unparalleled accomplishments will not be forgotten by the American people."

Charlton Heston was returning from shooting *Ben-Hur* in Rome when his wife told him DeMille was dead. "The death of a man of 77 can hardly be surprising," wrote Heston in his diary, "but it shook me. Still, if ever a man died at his moment, he did. He achieved all he wanted or could've hoped for. I radioed and was sorry to get a reply that the funeral will be Friday, before we land."

Heston remembered their final lunch, when he had been just about to start his cameo in *The Buccaneer* and they had shared a glass of nineteenth-century Madeira. He had thanked DeMille for lunch, but he suddenly realized that "I should have thanked him for my career."

The family asked that no flowers be sent but that contributions be made to the American Cancer Society, the Hollywood Studio Club, and the Children's Hospital. It was decided that anyone that would have been welcomed into his office would be welcomed at his funeral. The service was held on January 23 at St. Stephen's Episcopal Church on Yucca Street in Hollywood. Four hundred people were inside the church, five hundred gathered outside. The list of mourners was a Hollywood Who's Who: Bob Hope, Alfred Hitchcock, Joel McCrea, Sam Goldwyn, among others.

Ann del Valle and other members of the staff stood at different entrances, watching for those who would be allowed in. Del Valle was touched and saddened when Woody Strode showed up, not at the church's front door, but at the back door. The church wasn't segregated, but Strode thought it might be. He was duly ushered in.

Sam Goldwyn, the last survivor of the Jesse L. Lasky Feature Play Company, arrived an hour before the services began and sat quietly in the narthex watching the other mourners arrive. When the polished mahogany casket was brought into the narthex, Goldwyn gazed at the royal velvet covering the coffin for a few long moments, then walked into the nave of the church.

Passages from the Bible that had been marked by DeMille on his deathbed were read: "I will lift up mine eyes unto the hills; from whence cometh my help? My help cometh even from the Lord, who hath made heaven and earth." There were the 91st and 121st Psalms, the Epistle to the Romans, and the Gospel According to St. John. The Book of Common Prayer that Father Harry Owings read from had been given to DeMille by his parents, and it carried the inscription, "Cecil Blount DeMille on his 11th birthday, August 12, 1892, with the love of Papa and Mama."

The lectern from which the service was held had been a gift from DeMille in memory of his parents, while the pulpit had been given by him in memory of Gladys Rosson. The only flowers in the chapel were DeMille's beloved red roses on the altar, and a separate vase of long-stemmed red roses nearby. The pallbearers were Adolph Zukor, Sam Goldwyn, Neil McCarthy, Russel Treacy, Donald Hayne, Henry Wilcoxon, and Henry Noerdlinger.

Donald Hayne spoke, and said of DeMille that he "had faults, irritating smallnesses, blind spots, vanities—and a prince's grandeur, and astonishing humilities. Famous in every corner of the world, he was unknown to most, misunderstood by many, cordially disliked by some, beloved by those who knew him best. . . . He was a man of unquenchable faith and hope and a courageous heart. . . . He was a man of vision. Now he sees."

Cecil Blount DeMille was buried in the family tomb, a spot carefully chosen so he would be in clear sight of the movie studio that would never have existed without him. At the cemetery, remembered A. C. Lyles, "There were a lot of people at the service, hundreds of people. We had big, big baskets, big bouquets of flowers that people all over the world had sent—Kings, Queens, Presidents. A grip from Paramount showed up in his work clothes. Clutched in his hand was a bouquet of flowers picked from a garden in front of the DeMille Building at Paramount. The bouquet had a rubber band around it, and the grip put that down amidst the expensive, elaborate floral arrangements.

"I thought that represented more than anything the feeling that all of us at Paramount, the employees of Paramount, our family, the Paramount family, had about Cecil B. DeMille—that grip's little bouquet of flowers."

*

The night after DeMille's funeral, Ann del Valle hosted a gathering for members of the DeMille unit. Anne Bauchens was there and told a story of how DeMille had spotted someone lighting a cigarette as they passed through the Gates of Rameses during the Exodus in the final print of the second version of *The Ten*

Commandments. Bauchens believed that if DeMille saw it, it had to be there, so she ran the footage for two days straight, over and over again. She never found the offending shot—nobody ever has—but she had been worrying about that phantom cigarette for the last three years and would for the rest of her life.

Then she began to cry.

On the portico of the Laughlin Park house.

EPILOGUE

"I once asked him how many Oscars he had won.
'Eleven,' he answered, 'but they only gave me three.'"

—ART ARTHUR

The obituaries gave DeMille his due as a pioneer. *The Hollywood Reporter* said, "He was—and this perhaps more than anything else was responsible for his stature and his success—a true showman." Bosley Crowther in the *New York Times* wrote that "He was the undeniable image of propriety and absolute aplomb in a community loaded with yahoos and cheap self-seekers of the most conspicuous sort. . . . Yet he, in his brilliantly clever and quietly professional way, was as keen and frank a self-promoter as anybody there. . . . The trademark 'DeMille' on a picture endowed it with his magnified prestige. It was, in its engineering, one of the greatest promotional feats of all time."

A more generous salute took up the back page of the *Journal of the Screen Producers Guild* for March 1959. It featured a photograph of a beaming DeMille, on the occasion of his acceptance of the Milestone Award in 1956. Beneath the photograph were two sentences: "No one man has given more to his industry, or to his audiences which have totaled twice the population of the earth. IN HUMBLE MEMORIAM TO CECIL B. DEMILLE."

All this praise would have been met by DeMille with a curt nod in recognition of what he knew to be true. The highest recognition would undoubtedly have been the fact that by August 1959, after nearly three years of continual release, *The Ten Commandments* had been seen by an estimated 98.5 million people.

★

505

DeMille's will, which he signed in a firm hand on June 21, 1958, was simultaneously a surprisingly emotional document and a masterpiece of legal vagueness, with a clear line drawn between Cecilia and the other children: "My wife and I have no issue other than one daughter the issue of our marriage, namely CECILIA deMILLE HARPER. We have three adopted children, namely, KATHERINE deMILLE QUINN, JOHN BLOUNT deMILLE and RICHARD deMILLE.

"My wife, Constance Adams deMille, has been my loyal, devoted and able helpmate during our marriage and has adequate provision to care for her needs. It is for this reason that I make no monetary or material provision for her under this will. My love and respect and my admiration for her are deep and profound, but inadequate when measured by the devotion, loyalty and cooperation she has always given me and the great material contribution she has made to our success."

There were numerous small bequests to the household staff and some of the members of the DeMille unit. Julia Faye was left $10,000, Florence Cole and Russel Treacy $5,000 apiece.

Four trusts were established: one for Peter deMille Calvin, one for Cecilia Jr., one for Joe Harper Jr., and one in which Katherine, Richard, and John had equal shares. The estate inventory revealed that Cecil had savings accounts worth $123,592 at the Bank of America, $132,298 at the California Bank, and $116,744 at Security First National. He owned two cars, a 1955 Chrysler Town and Country station wagon and a 1955 Plymouth Suburban station wagon. There were generous holdings of mid-twentieth-century blue chips: Transamerica; AT&T; Bank of America; American Airlines; American Tobacco; R. J. Reynolds; U.S. Steel; Norfolk & Western; the Atchison; Topeka & Santa Fe; Union Pacific; du Pont; Goodyear; Southern Pacific . . . and Paramount Pictures.

In addition, there was a lot of real estate; besides Paradise and the house in Laughlin Park, there were nearly ten other properties, including property known as Kagel Canyon and a citrus operation known as the Wyckoff Ranch. The funeral expenses came to $5,908, and DeMille's debts—mostly real estate—came to $375,148.

Cecilia was first among nonequals, inheriting what Richard deMille remembered as 95 percent of the estate, including all the real estate, except for Paradise, which was left to the DeMille trust. DeMille's will left no doubt as to his priorities: "with the hope that the Trust will make such . . . disposition of the property that the birds and supposedly wild animals thereon, including deer and foxes, which have become largely domesticated and permit me to feed them, will, if possible, be preserved and not molested or killed."

Cecilia was given first crack at the personal property as well, up to an appraised value of $5,000, and half of all her father's securities, with the other half to go into the trust. It was a hard realization for the other children, and a confusing one. Although Cecil certainly differentiated in his treatment of Cecilia in his will, he hadn't in life. "One reason the will was sort of a shock was that he hadn't ever acted that way in person," said Richard deMille. "Sometimes he acted like he thought I was better than Cecilia. I was somewhat regretful about it, but I've always been stoic and philosophical. He had a basis for what he did."

The autobiography was essentially completed by the time DeMille died, and was published in November 1959. Art Arthur's chapters, the story of DeMille's life until 1915, were excerpted in *Life* magazine. The critical response was largely adulatory, as it should have been, for the book is vigorous, enthralling, and, within certain obvious limits, honest. Robert Kirsch wrote in the *Los Angeles Times* that it was "a fascinating and compelling volume"; the *Chicago Tribune* said that it was "The best and most important autobiography that has ever come out of Hollywood," while the *New York Times* called it "a document of American history."

Constance never knew that the kindly old gentleman who visited her so often and who would quietly hold her hand had died. A little over a year later, on July 17, 1960, Constance Adams DeMille died in her house at the age of eighty-seven and was laid to rest next to her husband at the Hollywood Cemetery. Just as Cecil had prophesied on that Boston curb on December 31, 1900, they saw the next century in side by side.

Clara Beranger had died just a few years after her beloved Bill, in 1957. Anne Bauchens died at the Motion Picture Home in May 1967, at the age of eighty-five.

For a time, Cecilia kept Henry Wilcoxon and Jesse Lasky Jr. on salary for rewrites of *On My Honor*. Jesse's widow would remember the script as "Very heavy and very long, although it was only a first draft. In today's market, it would have to be tightened up." But the lukewarm response to *The Buccaneer* and the stories about the backstage difficulties of its production did not inspire confidence in Wilcoxon's ability to bring a picture of this scale in on budget; over the next several years, the project slowly came to a standstill. Until his own death in 1984, Wilcoxon always used the present tense in speaking of DeMille.

Among Cecilia's new responsibilities was Julia Faye. "Well, Cecilia, I guess you've inherited me too," said Julia. Cecilia did as her father expected and took care of Julia. Early in 1963, Cecilia bought Julia's two-story Spanish house in Pacific Palisades for $40,000, and Julia and a couple of relatives lived rent-free until her death in April 1966. Following in the footsteps of Gladys Rosson, whose will left Cecilia Jr. jewelry and some money, Julia willed Cecilia Jr. a white ermine coat. After Julia's death, "800 selected items" that had belonged to her were auctioned off by the Ames Art Galleries on Wilshire Boulevard. There was no mention in the newspaper ads that most of the jewelry had been chosen by Cecil B. DeMille.

The DeMille family donated Paradise to the Hathaway Foundation in 1963, where it became a residential treatment center for emotionally disturbed children. Paradise housed several hundred children referred by the courts and social service agencies—hard-core kids who walked through the heavy iron gates made for *King of Kings* and lived on the three hundred acres for anywhere from one to ten years.

The Lasky Barn was moved off the Paramount lot in 1979; as a state landmark, it had to be in a more accessible location. After a couple of temporary moves, it found a permanent home in the parking lot of the Hollywood Bowl on Highland Avenue, where it serves as a museum perpetuating both early DeMille and early Hollywood.

The house on DeMille Drive was impeccably maintained and held by the family for nearly thirty years after Constance's death. Nothing was changed. The color scheme remained cream, the gardens and vines were carefully tended. Behind the heavy oak front door with a large pane of frosted glass, the heavy burgundy drapes still shielded the living room from the harsh California sun.

Each morning, Florence Cole placed a red rose in the bud vase on DeMille's desk in his beautiful Gothic office with its leaded windows, as if he were about to come down from breakfast and begin transacting business. Scattered about the room were the tablets from *The Ten Commandments*, and the family Bible from which Henry deMille had read while Cecil and Bill took turns rubbing his head. On the desk was the camera that had photographed *The Squaw Man*, with "C.B. DeMille" stenciled on the side.

On the left side of the desk were pictures of his parents, at the center of the desk was a collection of jade pieces—a Buddha, a letter opener. Inside the desk drawers were hundreds of snapshots of DeMille with family and friends, dozens of matchbooks, and a freshly filled tobacco pouch. There was a small address book, the leather cover falling away from the binding, which held pencil entries: "Gary Cooper Arizona 31321"; "Ernst Lubitsch 268 Bel Air Road." The only modern feature on the desk was a push-button phone that had replaced the black rotary-style model.

Awards cluttered the walls and dressers, hall tables and mantels. Two Academy Awards shared space with a plaque from the Northridge Pony Baseball League. On the bookshelves were such volumes as Lou Tellegen's *Women Have Been Kind*—DeMille disliked the book because Tellegen paraded his conquests but he kept it anyway—Mary Pickford's *Sunshine and Shadow* inscribed "With love, Your little sister 'Betty Warren' Sometimes known as Mary Pickford," and *We the Living*, inscribed "To Cecil B. DeMille from a little Russian immigrant to whom he gave her first chance at writing—gratefully Ayn Rand ('Caviar') 4-2-36."

DeMille's own bedroom still contained his simple bed, two small Victorian rocking chairs, and the old wooden desk. The circa 1950 black and white TV with its round and fuzzy picture, which DeMille knew instinctively didn't constitute any competition for him, also maintained its place.

People who went through the house were always startled by its lack of ostentation. Condé Nast executive Leo Lerman arrived for a photo shoot in 1985 and noted "the contrast between his grandiose, opulent films and this almost colorless austerity. 'Mrs. DeMille liked only pink flowers in the house,' said the 85 year old housekeeper. 'She didn't like to see them being cut or carried in. She just liked them to be there.' A Cherry Orchard feeling in the dusty velour and endless memorabilia."

In the film vault, where DeMille had carefully stockpiled the content of his working life, the reels of nitrate film were regularly inspected and rewound. Eventually, Cecilia shipped them to the Eastman House, where preservation copies were made.

Finally, in 1988, the decision was made to sell the property. None of the heirs wanted to live there, and zoning restrictions prevented the house from being converted into a museum or study center. The house and grounds brought $2 million.

A few months later, more than three hundred items from the house and the DeMille estate went on auction at Christie's in Manhattan. A gold money clip, estimated as being worth between $100 and $200, sold for nearly $2,000; a turquoise and gold necklace worn by Anne Baxter in *The Ten Commandments* had been estimated to be worth $2,000 to $3,000, but it brought $27,500. Norman Rockwell's portrait of Victor Mature as Samson bringing down the temple brought $82,500. The single most valuable item proved to be DeMille's oak Gothic Revival desk, which brought $121,000. In total, the auction earned $710,919, around $300,000 more than the values listed by the Christie's catalogue.

In 2009, the house on DeMille Drive—six bedrooms, ten baths, nearly eleven thousand square feet, now overhauled, brightened, and more or less thoroughly unrecognizable, except for the kitchen, which was as DeMille had left it—was for sale for $23.9 million.

★

The DeMille movie died with DeMille. Before budget constrictions made them impossible, movies like *Spartacus, Ben-Hur,* and *The Fall of the Roman Empire* attempted to have it both ways—spectacle with a literate script, even though the literate script had a way of dragging down the spectacle. Even Joe Mankiewicz came to realize that when it came to spectacle, DeMille knew what he was doing. Caught in the quicksand of the ridiculous *Cleopatra* in 1962, making a terrible, flaccid movie and destroying his self-confidence in the process, Mankiewicz raged to anyone who would listen about how terrible his crowd scenes were and how impossible it was to shoot thousands of extras any way other than the way DeMille had done it. "DeMille knew how to do it, and I have never been able to shoot a big scene like this the way I want to, because nobody will ever listen to me."

Nobody will ever listen to me—a sentence that had never been uttered by Cecil B. DeMille.

The times continued to work against DeMille's reputation. After his relationships with Jeanie Macpherson, Julia Faye, and Gladys Rosson became public, the charge of hypocrisy was commonly leveled at him. Jesse Lasky Jr. said that "I prefer to call DeMille a great actor and a great showman rather than a hypocrite. He had the capacity to absolutely believe what he was doing and saying while he was doing and saying it. If he happened to be talking about the virtue of the American home, he'd believe it at the moment, although he was violating it in his personal life. . . .

"There was a dichotomy in his moral code, a comfortable yet somehow sincere dichotomy. . . . DeMille tried to be all things to all men, including himself. He . . . was very loyal. He took care of his worn-out actresses and hangers-on. He always took care of his people; he had that quality of *noblesse oblige*."

On top of the charge of hypocrisy was the frequent accusation that DeMille was enslaved by commercial tastes, always operating with one or both eyes on the box office. It would be far more accurate to say that he was a slave to his own vast, self-created myth, which demanded commercial validation. That's why he never cared overmuch about chasing contemporary tastes. DeMille's thematic concerns were established in the first ten years of his career. His style would broaden and amplify, but his interests would never be altered in their essentials. DeMille's movies were a pure expression of DeMille, defiant throwbacks to another century's beliefs and styles, yet too audaciously conceived and executed ever to be entirely dismissed.

Carefully modeling himself after David Belasco, he played the part of a megalomaniac so convincingly that he managed to persuade everybody that was what he was. Sometimes he even persuaded himself.

His movies, which had been the essence of modernity before and during World War I, slowly retreated until they were frozen in cultural amber, demonstrating that he was a child of Barnum and Belasco. DeMille's concern was with the past, his outlook primarily Edwardian, but his personality was so dynamic, his showmanship so vivid, that he sustained a primarily nineteenth-century vision into the middle of the twentieth.

He was never afflicted with the typically short-term, expedient attitude that afflicts show business. He kept copies of his films; he maintained his papers. He respected his own accomplishments, and he respected the art and the industry he did so much to establish. His character was built on the solid foundation of his religious confidence, embodying equivalent amounts of exaggeration and modesty. His nature was such that he never attempted to reconcile the extremes and come to some happy medium. Sensuality happily coexisted with spirituality—all part of his humanity, all part of what made DeMille DeMille.

His niece Agnes asserted, "Cecil B. DeMille lived at an ideal time for himself. . . . Had he been born earlier, his gifts for storytelling and drama would not have found their proper expression, for he was not a good writer. His ear was poor, but his eye and sense of dynamics were supremely fine. He needed, therefore, a visual medium. The motion picture was invented just in time for him. . . . The extraordinary phenomenon Cecil presented was enormous craft combined with secondhand subject matter and an amazing lack of sophistication."

Pat . . . slap . . . pat . . . slap. Agnes's backhanded compliments, her passive-aggressive anger at her uncle for being more focused, more successful than her father never abated.

Adolph Zukor once characterized DeMille as "the greatest showman of them all," a sentiment that would probably garner something close to universal approval. Certainly, his true inheritor is not the oft-cited Steven Spielberg, but James Cameron—another director with a gift for apocalyptic imagery whose visual eloquence dwarfs the bad dialogue and dramatic contrivances for which he has a weakness.

Beyond that, DeMille's achievement and legacies remain firm: he was instrumental in the founding and development of a primary movie studio and also a city, an art form, an industry. He was the most famous director of his generation and the most powerful religious propagandist of that generation as well.

As a director, he wasn't interested in a single performance so much as an overall tidal effect. In his mind, he was a director who directed thousands, not a couple of stars. He emphasized the validity of jaw-dropping special effects as ends unto themselves, but he painstakingly husbanded them, built up to them. He took endless pains.

Charlton Heston, with some of the clarity of the Old Testament patriarch that he played for DeMille, said simply that "He was a great man." Elmer Bernstein went into more detail: "He was more than a director, he was an institution, a monument. He was a man in complete control of every aspect of his film. He knew what he wanted, his vision was clear, it was grand, he was willing to take risks. . . . He was a man of terrific concept, of terrific authority, he was a man who believed in himself as no other director I have ever worked with."

Anthony Quinn—one great egotist summing up another—said that DeMille's great weakness was his strength. DeMille, said Quinn, was so determined to be strong, to be dominant in nearly every situation that he could never allow himself to be vulnerable. Following that line of reasoning, being Cecil B. DeMille would have been a lonely enterprise, but he seemed endlessly invigorated by the struggle. And that was why, during their last meeting, when DeMille allowed Quinn to see him as an old, sick man, the moment was so revelatory that the younger man remembered it the rest of his life.

As with the other men who forged an empire of dreams out of a drowsy resort town, it will not do to sentimentalize Cecil B. DeMille. "Forget the beautiful obituaries," said Jesse Lasky Jr., "and think of these men as cold, tough, ruthless men who would do anything to achieve what they did achieve and perhaps this is why they did achieve it. I suppose without them there wouldn't have been any great American film industry."

That same indomitability attracted those in need. "He could be the hardest and most terrifying man I have ever met," said his niece Agnes, "yet he sat beside many a deathbed, because in the last moments his voice, his strength, and his faith were needed for comfort. People called to him when they were dying. This is a fact, and it is unanswerable."

By the time of DeMille's last film, the competition for public and critical favor included such accepted and very modern masterpieces as *The Searchers* and *The Bridge on the River Kwai*—strong, corrosive movies with adult themes and a corresponding adult treatment. By comparison, DeMille's customary compilation of sin, spectacle, and reverence injected into the presentational context of nineteenth-century theater should have been archaic. But the critics always overlooked—and continue to overlook—the incantatory strength of DeMille's own conviction in his beliefs, in his worldview. He crafted movies that believed in themselves, and the way he unified theme with treatment gave his work the internal coherence of a parallel universe.

Beyond that, he was also a great innovator both artistically and commercially; certainly, no other filmmaker in history has had such a consistent knack for giving the public what it wanted before it knew what it wanted. Jim Tully wrote that he was a "cultivated Barnum," but he was more than that.

For a time, DeMille was a great director—in the early days, nobody's films were as dazzlingly lit, as innovatively daring. After that, with a few exceptions, he settled for being a great showman, and the name "DeMille" became a synonym for spectacular entertainment that never let an audience down. To this day, whenever a spectacle is released that combines panache and visual wonder, his is the name invoked as a comparison. Cumulatively, he did size, scope, and the delineation of details within a heaving, moving mass better than anybody else in movie history.

He glorified the Bible, but beyond that, he praised the general richness of American culture. Lincoln Kirstein once wrote that the American style was defined as "a leanness, a visual ascetism, a candor, even an awkwardness, which is in itself elegant, shared also by some of our finest Colonial silver, the thin carving on New England grave slabs and the quicksilver of Emily Dickinson's unrhymed quatrains."

That's an intellectual's idea of the American aesthetic. There is another one: abundance—abundance of design, abundance of effort, abundance of material— and that was incarnated by DeMille. DeMille could demonstrate a potent eroticism, but what was often eroticized was not sex, but material goods.

In this, and in so many other ways, he was completely and profoundly in the American grain. Beyond giving the world Hollywood as a production center, he incarnated the world's *idea* of Hollywood: gleefully dramatic, willfully unsophisticated, exuberantly, joyously excessive. He transcended his individual identity to become the living embodiment of the movie director and, beyond that, the embodiment of Hollywood itself.

Martin Scorsese once wrote that what moved him about DeMille was his sense of wonder. "DeMille presented such a sumptuous fantasy that if you saw his movies as a child, they stuck with you for life. The marvelous superseded the sacred. What I remember most are the tableaux vivants, the colors, the dreamlike quality of the imagery, and of course the special effects. . . .

"DeMille's legacy is . . . putting on a giant show for people who were working class people, who don't have much money to go and see a film in a theater. They are told it's a spectacle and they really do see a spectacle. He wouldn't let the audience down at all, and it always paid off in that beautiful flow of poetic and dream-like images."

Alone among the survivors of a bygone era, DeMille persisted in constructing vast pieces of silent music: Pre-Raphaelite, pre-Freudian images that rendered dialogue irrelevant. His silent films have maintained DeMille's reputation as a great director by those lucky enough to see them, and the enormous spectacles have kept his name alive for audiences more than fifty years after his death.

★

Years after DeMille's death, Gloria Swanson visited Palm Springs, where William Holden was living. Holden was in Africa, so Swanson left a note for him on a toilet seat.

"Dear Joe," [his character's name in *Sunset Boulevard*] I'm leaving this note where I know you'll find it.

"Where is Max? Where is DeMille? Where is Hedda? Where has everybody gone?

"Love, Norma Desmond."

★

Once, when DeMille's granddaughter Cecilia was a little girl, she asked him what he did for a living. He thought about it for a moment, then smiled.

"I tell stories," he said.

ACKNOWLEDGMENTS

The problem with most books about the movies is that they're too much like the movies, too much about heroes and villains, too seldom about the complexities of human beings as we actually experience them—the mingled motives and ambitious missteps that make people so endlessly fascinating. As one author wrote in another context, the task of biography is "to provide . . . the vivid sensation of lived life. . . . Set the dead in motion and make them speak: I am not a stick figure in a textbook; I was once alive, emotionally complex, beset with fears and daydreams, just as you are now."

My ambition was to create a three-dimensional portrait of a man who was capable of heroism and loyalty, as well as grievous wrongheadedness, but always in the grand manner. Cecil B. DeMille was many things, but he was never small.

In the general sense, this book began nearly fifty years ago, when I saw the 1956 version of *The Ten Commandments* for the first time. In the specific sense, it began at the Giornate del Cinema Muto in Pordenone, Italy, in 1991, when all the surviving silent films of the DeMille brothers were shown. That experience permanently altered my perceptions of both of them. In the clinical sense, the book began in 1998, when Richard deMille and Cecilia deMille Presley agreed to let me write the authorized biography of Cecil B. DeMille.

A quarter century before that, I had begun collecting string for this book by interviewing Karl Struss and John Carradine, and I continued talking to veterans of DeMille pictures whenever the opportunity presented itself, long before I actually embarked on the project.

None of what has resulted would have been possible without the faith and trust shown by Richard and Cecilia, who gave me complete access to Cecil B. DeMille's archives, as well as to some private material still held by family members, without asking for approvals or controls of any sort. Richard's sole request was simple: "Just be fair to the Old Man."

My greatest regret is that Richard died before he could read the book he wanted me to write. Without Richard's honesty, humor, and wisdom, there would be no *Empire of Dreams*.

Through my half dozen research trips to the Harold B. Lee Library at Brigham Young University in Provo, Utah, James D'Arc and his associate Norm Gillespie gave me the keys to the kingdom: the DeMille collection, two thousand boxes strong. More importantly, Jim gave me the benefit of his own voluminous insights and research into DeMille, which are salted throughout this book.

At the DeMille office in Burbank, California, Helen Cohen turned her attention to whatever I needed with endless good cheer and quiet competence. The best thing you could say about Helen was that she could have worked for DeMille himself.

At the Museum of Modern Art in New York, Charles Silver and Ron Magliozzi helped out with alacrity, and Pat McGilligan was always ready to supply me with material from his own archives.

DeMille's granddaughter remembered that whenever he spoke of his mother, a woman many people found difficult, he had a faint smile on his face. I found the same thing to be true when most people spoke of DeMille. But not always. Whether they liked him or loathed him, I hope I've been true to the perceptions of the people who talked with me: Elmer Bernstein, Grace Bradley Boyd, Irving Brecher, Rock Brynner, Victoria Brynner, Henry Bumstead, David Carradine, John Carradine, Diana Serra Cary, Frank Coghlan, Ann del Valle, Eddie Fisher, Richard Fleischer, Dan Ford, Leatrice Gilbert Fountain, David Friedman, Robert Fuller, Rory Guy, Mark Haggard, Charlton Heston, Arthur Jacobson, John Jensen, Marvin Kaplan, Syd Kronenthal, Hedy Lamarr, Betty Lasky, Pat Silver Lasky, Jackie Le Claire, Stephen Longstreet, Mary Anita Loos, A. C. Lyles, Tom Mankiewicz, Diane Disney Miller, Kenny Miller, Walter Mirisch, Lisa Mitchell, Joseph Newman, Fess Parker, Robert Parrish, Anthony Quinn, Elliott Reid, Arnold Scaasi, Karl Struss, Russ Tamblyn, Frances Triest, Robert Vaughn, Billy Wilder, Robert Wise, Joseph Youngerman.

A special bow of gratitude to Robert Wagner, my once and future literary collaborator and friend, whose humor and total recall continue to illuminate the byways of the studio system of which he was a part.

Bob Bender leapt in where other editors feared to tread and bought this book, thereby fulfilling my fondest biographical dream. His associate Johanna Li is both an editor and a writer's best friend, and the team at Simon & Schuster, my publishers for more than fifteen years, are unparalleled: Victoria Meyer, the magnificent Leah Wasiliewski, and my darling Gypsy da Silva and her team—Fred Chase, Bill Molesky, and Anthony Newfield.

As he has for decades, Kevin Brownlow gave me access to the interviews he did for his great book *The Parade's Gone By*, as well as those done for his and Patrick Stanbury's excellent documentary about DeMille. Kevin and Patrick also read the manuscript and saved me from numerous mistakes of fact and emphasis.

Dave Kehr helped at a couple of crucial moments, both with critical insights and his experience with DVDs. Dave's friend Dennis Delrogh assisted a perfect stranger and earned his gratitude.

Jeff Heise has been doing research for me for a quarter century, and he's never failed me yet. Care to sign up for another twenty-five, old friend?

I owe a special debt to Betty Lawson of the American Academy of Dramatic Arts, who rummaged around in their files and came up with the unbelievable rarity of DeMille's audition report from the year 1900, as well as his heartfelt speech to the academy fifty-eight years later.

My agent, Fran Collin, sold this book the same way she has sold all of my books—with total belief in her author and bulldog tenacity. She will always have my deep gratitude.

James Curtis has held my hand through a half dozen books, giving me sage advice, contact information, and a lot of laughs, nearly all of it at his expense. I trust him implicitly, and I'm proud to call him my friend.

Dennis and Amy Doros of Milestone Films have been holding my hand even longer, and Adam Doros is already demonstrating the talents of a great researcher. Sign this kid up!

At the *Palm Beach Post*, Jan Tuckwood keeps the faith—in newspapers, and in me.

Finally, my enduring gratitude to my wife, Lynn—my love, the meaning of my work and my life.

And now, at long last: So let it be written; so let it be done.

Scott Eyman

Paris, Los Angeles, New York, Provo, Sonoma, Palm Beach

March 2004–May 2010

NOTES

ABBREVIATIONS

AADA   American Academy of Dramatic Art
AMPAS   Academy of Motion Picture Arts and Sciences
Autobiography   Cecil B. DeMille. *The Autobiography of Cecil B. DeMille.*
             Englewood Cliffs, N.J.: Prentice Hall, 1959.
BYU   Brigham Young University
MOMA   Museum of Modern Art, New York City
S.E.   Scott Eyman

Prologue

Page

1   *His first scripted line:* DeMille's script material for *Sunset Boulevard* is at Brigham Young University (hereafter BYU), *Sunset Boulevard* files, box 418, f. 19 and f. 3.

2   *"It was wonderful":* Staggs, p. 109.

2   *"Very good, my boy":* Ibid., p. 105.

2   *"I was an actor once":* Goodman, p. 201.

3   *"The thoughtful side":* Wilcoxon, p. 178.

3   *"DeMille was very good":* Wilder to S.E.

3   *"In his compassionate regard":* Staggs, p. 103.

4   *DeMille's remuneration:* BYU, DeMille to Paramount, 10-29-49, box 418, f. 19.

4   *DeMille was five foot ten and a half:* Height and weight derived from his gun permit, in BYU, box 65, f. 25.

4   *"His name":* Lyles to S.E.

5   *In Kevin Brownlow's: Parade's,* 180.

6   *"DeMille simply vulgarized":* Photoplay Productions, Sidney Lumet interview.

6   *"[He was] terribly unfashionable":* Raymond, p. 22.

7   *Although he eventually:* This point derives from Ringgold and Bodeen, p. 5.

7   *DeMille's personality:* This point derives from the writings of and conversations with Dave Kehr.

8   *Neither Gregg Toland:* Roud, p. 266.

9   *"coercion, aggression and deceit":* DeMille Legacy, p. 20.

519

9   *"He seemed to have"*: Orrison, p. 138.
9   *"He appeared to be"*: *Photoplay*, Angela Lansbury interview.
10   *ferbissana*: Brecher to S.E.
10   *"I remember you"*: *Photoplay*, A. C. Lyles interview.
10   *"He had more fun"*: Ibid.
10   *"We had stars"*: Ibid.

PART ONE

Chapter 1

Page
13   *"The old Belasco plays"*: BYU, autobiography clips, box 10, f. 24. DeMille was a genealogy buff, and I have taken most of this from his *Autobiography*, after checking it with documents at BYU.
15   *That same year*: *Autobiography*, p. 10.
16   *"it made it a little hard"*: Henry deMille's diary/autobiography is at BYU, box 6, f. 5, p. 21.
16   *When Henry asked his mother*: *Autobiography*, p. 11.
16   *in his diary*: BYU, Henry deMille diary, box 6, f. 5, pp. 3–4.
17   *"I used to meet Beatrice"*: Ibid., p. 25.
17   *"Our marriage"*: Ibid.
17   *"She loved Henry"*: *Photoplay*, Richard deMille interview.
17   *"In evening"*: BYU, Henry deMille diary, box 6, f. 5.
17   *"after a day"*: Ibid.
17   *In the autumn*: Edwards, p. 18.
18   *"August 12 my little boy"*: BYU, Henry deMille diary, box 6, f. 5, p. 30.
18   *Born in 1853*: Edwards, p. 19.
18   *"Baby Cecil's"*: scrapbook, BYU, box 6, f. 5.
18   *"Many pleasing traits"*: BYU, Henry deMille diary, box 6, f. 5, p. 32.
19   *For the rest of his life*: BYU, del Valle to Hayne, 2-5, no year, box 12.
19   *"receiving excellent"*: BYU, Henry deMille's diary/autobiography, box 6, f. 5.
19   *Money was tight*: BYU, box 6, f. 3.
19   *"I had to get along"*: Ibid.
19   *"At the French"*: Ibid.
20   *"My Darling Loved One"*: BYU, Henry to Beatrice, undated, box 1010, f. 1.
20   *"We were successful"*: Koury, p. 68.
20   *"My condition was desperate"*: BYU, Henry deMille diary, p. 57.
21   *"slender young man"*: *Autobiography*, p. 21.
21   *Henry liked to have his head rubbed*: *Autobiography*, p. 31.
22   *"It was a bitter experience"*: Ibid., p. 23.
22   *"Its fate was for some nights"*: BYU, Henry deMille diary, box 6, f. 5, p. 57.
23   *Henry renamed*: Ibid., p. 58.
23   *Henry's projects*: I am greatly indebted to Betty Lawson of the American Academy of Dramatic Arts for this information and for much else besides.
23   *"Dear Sweety"*: Cecil to Beatrice, 6-22, no year, but about 1888, Richard deMille collection.
24   *"I love you"*: BYU, box 1010, f. 1.
24   *"Poor Little M"*: BYU, Henry to Beatrice, undated, box 1010, f. 1.

24   *William remembered:* William deMille, *Hollywood Saga*, pp. 49–50.
25   *My Hunting Story:* Richard deMille, *My Secret Mother*, pp. 25–26.
25   *"He would sit writing":* BYU, biography notes, 5-27-57, box 30, f. 3.

Chapter 2

Page
27   *"I was elected":* BYU, Henry deMille diary, box 6, f. 5, p. 59.
27   *Cecil would remember:* DeMille speech to AADA, 12-16-58, courtesy of Betty Lawson.
27   *On the other hand:* Higashi, p. 46.
27   *William was with them:* BYU, Henry deMille diary, box 6, f. 5, p. 60.
28   *The house was finished:* BYU, box 6, f. 12.
28   *Another neighbor:* Autobiography, p. 38.
28   *Cecil's first crush:* BYU, del Valle to Donald Hayne, 2-5, no year, box 12.
28   *It was around this time:* Cecil outlines the beginnings of the Champion Driver in the Autobiography, p. 39.
28   *Henry deMille's politely veiled:* BYU, Henry deMille diary, box 6, f. 5, p. 60.
29   *In a spectacular example:* BYU, Henry deMille to Henry George, 7-19-1892, box 38, f. 9.
29   *At the end of 1892.* Autobiography, p. 32.
29   *"The boys decorated":* BYU, Henry deMille's diary/autobiography, box 6, f. 5.
29   *"Attended second":* Ibid.
29   *About February 1:* Ibid.
29   *"He sent for me":* Koury, pp. 51–52.
30   *The obituaries:* BYU, undated and unsourced, box 1266, f. 1.
30   *"a domineering and aggressive":* Agnes deMille, *Portrait Gallery*, p. 161.
31   *"Don't use the bat":* Autobiography, p. 34.
31   *"Just one year":* BYU, diary/autobiography, box 6, f. 5.
31   *An ad:* Edwards, p. 30.
31   *She made them kiss:* Agnes deMille, *Wings*, p. 54.
31   *Although he would eventually:* Ibid.
31   *After her death:* BYU, box 1010, f. 2.
32   *"quivering pink poppy":* Kotsilibas-Davis, *Great Times*, p. 483.
34   *Cecil's audition report:* I'm indebted to Betty Lawson of the AADA for this.
35   *"the only man in the world":* DeMille speech to AADA, 12-16-58, courtesy of Betty Lawson.
36   *Wellington Putnam:* Autobiography, p. 47.
36   *a notation in the playbill:* BYU, box 10, f. 4.

Chapter 3

Page
37   *By then the two:* This account of Cecil and Constance's courtship is largely taken from BYU, DeMille reminiscence, 7-24-33, box 305, f. 13.
38   *"This is the woman's age":* Edwards, p. 32.
38   *Beatrice developed:* Autobiography, p. 63.
38   *As he remembered:* Lowrey, p. 46.
39   *Agnes deMille:* Agnes deMille, *Portrait Gallery*, p. 178.
39   *As Anne Edwards noted:* Edwards, p. 34.
40   *Once something went wrong:* Autobiography, p. 52. Some of Cecil's touring memories are

contained in the *Autobiography*, p. 54, while other stories were told to his granddaughter Cecilia deMille Presley, who related them to S.E.

41   *"You're not an actor if you do"*: BYU, Donald Hayne, "You Don't Know DeMille," unpublished article, box 9, f. 17.

41   *Constance's memories*: Talmey, pp. 143–44.

42   *"She was always for anything new"*: BYU, autobiography transcripts, 5-23-57, box 30, f. 1.

42   *A close friend*: BYU, Jesse Lasky transcript, box 30, f. 1.

42   *DeMille remembered*: BYU, reminiscences, 7-24-33, box 305, f. 13.

42   *"Constance was quietly dismayed"*: Richard deMille, *My Secret Mother*, p. 18.

43   *"Cecil B. DeMille was capital"*: Louvish, p. 24.

43   *It was a standard boilerplate contract*: BYU, box 838, f. 10.

43   *He borrowed $1,000*: All of the loan agreements are at BYU, box 150, f. 7.

43   *Pickford recorded*: Pickford, p. 98.

44   *in his production of* Madame Butterfly: Wilmeth and Bigsby, vol. 3, p. 518.

45   *"The reason most*: BYU, box 8, f. 3.

45   *DeMille's own copy*: BYU, box 235, f. 8.

45   *"I do not for a moment"*: Autobiography, p. 61.

47   *"He thereafter"*: Agnes deMille, *Portrait Gallery*, p. 164.

47   *"Belasco surrounded himself"*: Autobiography, p. 62.

47   *"He was a journeyman"*: Agnes deMille, *Wings*, p. 57.

48   *"Oh, by the way"*: Edwards, p. 228.

48   *In April, he formed*: BYU, box 235, f. 2.

48   *A few months later*: Ibid.

48   *His list, carefully annotated*: BYU, DeMille to Morehouse, 6-20-34, box 314, f. 2.

49   *"A great actor"*: Autobiography, p. 219.

Chapter 4

Page

50   *"In retrospect"*: Betty Lasky to S.E.

50   *his brother-in-law would remember*: Johnston, p. 39.

50   *The Folies Bergère failed*: Ramsaye, p. 623.

51   *"Cecil and I surveyed"*: Lasky, pp. 188–89.

51   *Cecil and Jesse signed*: BYU, box 235, f. 2.

51   *"He and Mr. DeMille"*: Betty Lasky to S.E.

51   *That same month*: All theatrical comings and goings in this period are detailed in BYU, box 235, f. 12.

52   *"these mild adventures"*: Lasky, p. 91.

52   *"We were in Claridge's Grill"*: BYU, DeMille oral history with Columbia University, 6-9-58, box 221, f. 6.

52   *Just like that*: Most of this account derives from Jesse Lasky, p. 92, which jibes with DeMille's own memories.

52   *"Jesse was not too"*: BYU, Goldwyn interview, box 17, f. 35

52   *In Ramsaye's telling*: Ramsaye, pp. 622–24.

53   *"Bess, we are going"*: Bessie Lasky, p. 40.

54   *"Do what you think right"*: Autobiography, p. 69.

54   *Goldfish made an appointment*: Berg, *Goldwyn*, p. 35.

54   *"I thought he would stay"*: BYU, Goldwyn interview, 3-20-57, box 17, f. 35.

55   *Farnum's contract*: Birchard, p. 5.

55   *"The name we bore"*: William deMille, *Hollywood Saga*, p. 46.
55   *I was quite disturbed*: The letter is quoted both in *DeMille Legacy*, p. 124, and in Easton, p. 20.
56   *"Sam put up $5,000"*: BYU, autobiography files, 5-21-57, box 30, f. 1.
56   *Beatrice sold Pamlico*: BYU, box 6, f. 12.
56   *in the thirteen years*: Internet Broadway Database, Cecil B. DeMille credits on Broadway.
57   *"The present conditions"*: Birchard, p. 1.
57   *William Haddock*: Rosenberg and Silverstein, p. 326.
57   *"had a proven ability"*: BYU, Cecil B. DeMille's Hollywood, *Evening News*, 1-5-37.
58   *the Lasky company*: *Moving Picture World*, 7-11-14, author's collection.
58   *"I can make a picture"*: BYU, biography notes, 6-3-57, box 30, f. 1.
58   *"Apfel knew a great deal"*: Autobiography, p. 77.
58   *"When we got off the train"*: BYU, reminiscences, 7-24-33, box 305, f. 13.
59   *"Actually, to tell"*: Wilcoxon, p. 13.
59   *"Dearest Gretchen"*: Richard deMille, *Secret Mother*, pp. 20–21.
62   *"It was a barn"*: Autobiography, p. 79.
62   *On December 22*: Gene Fernett, "The Historic Film Studios," *Classic Images*, no. 136, October 1986, p. 46.
62   *The price for lab services*: Birchard, p. 6.
63   *By 1912*: Jura and Bardin, p. 12.
63   *By 1913*: Ibid., p. 28.

PART TWO

Chapter 5

Page

67   *"a country town"*: Agnes deMille, Kevin Brownlow interview.
67   *"There was a little bank"*: BYU, Reminscences, 7-24-33, box 305, f. 13.
68   *"well-known in film circles"*: Higashi, p. 13.
68   *"Oscar Apfel"*: BYU, conference notes, 6-3, no year, box 30, f. 1.
68   *Stella Stray remembered*: BYU, Stella Stray interview, 3-19-56, box 225, f. 8.
69   *As the film historian Marc Wanamaker*: *DeMille Legacy*, p. 292.
70   *"When [Stern] watered"*: MOMA, DeMille file, "Hollywood Discovered—And Gold!", undated, but 1950.
70   *The muslin gave the bright California*: Dan Kamin generously shared his experiences working on location for Richard Attenborough's *Chaplin*, which featured authentic lighting and stage sets of the period.
70   *"It was like San Francisco"*: BYU, Reminiscences, 7-24-33, box 305, f. 13.
70   *"At first"*: BYU, conference notes, 6-3, no year but probably 1957, box 30, f. 1.
70   *"When you see the picture"*: BYU, biography notes, 6-3-57, box 30, f. 1.
71   *"That would have finished us"*: BYU, biography notes, 6-3-57, box 30, f. 1.
71   *"When the shot was fired"*: BYU, biography notes, 6-3-57, box 30, f. 1.
71   *"We were shooting the scenes"*: DeMille heritage, p. 206.
71   *"It was a new feeling"*: Ibid.
72   *"The cutting paraphernalia"*: BYU, biography notes, 6-3-57, box 30, f. 1.
72   RAN SQUAW MAN COMPLETE: BYU, undated, but January 1914, club files, box 9.
73   *"I couldn't believe"*: BYU, biography notes, 6-3-57, box 30, f. 1.
73   *"I would say"*: BYU, biography notes, 6-3-57, box 30, f. 1.

73   CAN WE PROCURE: BYU, DeMille to Brulatour, undated but January 1914, club files, box 9.

74   CAN'T ARRANGE PERFORATION: Birchard, p. 10.

76   JUST RETURNED FROM SEEING: BYU, Beatrice to DeMille, 2-16-14, box 38, f. 9.

76   *The* New York Dramatic Mirror: Ringgold and Bodeen, p. 24.

77   "The success of The Squaw Man": A Man with the Back On," *Moving Picture World,* quoted in program for *The Squaw Man's* 75th anniversary, Hollywood Heritage.

Chapter 6

Page

78   *"might easily have led to gunplay":* BYU, "Cecil B. DeMille's Hollywood," *Evening News,* 1-6-37.

79   *"Why don't you learn something":* Ibid.

79   *she had appeared:* Usai, Griffith Project, vol. 11, p. 291.

79   *love letters she had written:* Beauchamp, *Lying Down,* p. 74.

79   *"After Constance":* Cecilia deMille Presley to S.E.

80   *both Jesse Lasky and William deMille:* Edwards, p. 68.

80   *"I don't believe":* Picture Play, August 1918, p. 252, author's collection.

81   *"Buckland is a man":* Higashi, p. 15.

81   *"I will challenge":* Birchard, p. 22.

82   *"The dominant characteristic":* Ringgold and Bodeen, p. 29.

82   *"I have bought the laboratory":* BYU, DeMille to Goldfish, 2-21-14, club files, box 9.

82   *"One thing I have always admired":* William deMille, *Hollywood Saga,* p. 237.

83   *"I did not and do not":* Autobiography, p. 111.

83   *"Tickled to death":* BYU, DeMille to Goldfish, 9-17-14, club files, box 9.

84   *"He had bronzed and hardened":* William deMille, *Hollywood Saga,* p. 71.

84   *"Hollywood itself":* USAI, *DeMille Legacy,* p. 134.

84   *"a few scratches & bruises":* Ibid., p. 138.

86   *"These pictures are full":* BYU, DeMille to Goldfish, 9-30-14, club files, box 9.

86   *"There is one scene":* BYU, DeMille to Goldfish, 10-21-14, club files, box 9.

86   *"is best he has done for us":* BYU, DeMille to Goldfish, 11-27-14, club files, box 9.

87   *"I saw the picture":* BYU, DeMille to Blanche Goldfish, 8-20-14, club files, box 9.

87   *"some of your creditors":* Edwards, p. 56.

88   *"She spent money":* Easton, p. 42.

88   *You will note that my end:* BYU, DeMille to Goldfish, 9-9-14, club files, box 9.

89   *"Many companies":* DeMille Legacy, p. 140.

91   *Last night Hobart Bosworth:* BYU, DeMille to Goldfish, 4-14-14, club files, box 9.

92   *she organized the secretarial department:* MOMA, obituary for Anne Bauchens, *Variety,* 5-17-67.

92   *"I hung onto the brake":* BYU, biography notes, 6-3-57, box 20, f. 12.

93   *"I was trying to get composition":* Higashi, p. 54.

93   *"confined and shallow":* Lea Jacobs, "Belasco, DeMille and the Development of Lasky Lighting, *Film History,*" vol. 5, 1993, p. 408.

95   *he directed thirteen:* Birchard, p. 41.

95   *But Peters put his foot down:* Peters Jr., p. 20.

96   *"You know, sex and love":* Agnes deMille, *Portrait Gallery,* p. 182.

96   *"Jesse's affairs":* Betty Lasky to S.E.

96   *"an extremely sensitive nature":* Koury, p. 83.

97   *"She wrote like a plumber":* Koury, pp. 79–80.

97   *"an exceptional collaborator"*: Scott, p. 70.
97   *"Nothing could be"*: Sweet to Brownlow, Kevin Brownlow archives.
98   *"I do not hesitate"*: Ringgold and Bodeen, p. 85.
99   *"John didn't fit"*: Richard deMille to S.E.
101   *"Exterior, Federal Trenches"*: BYU, box 1260, f. 3.
102   *"your Broadway Jew"*: Easton, p. 85.
102   *"Every salad"*: BYU, DeMille/Rasbach interview, 4-28-58, box 20, f. 12.
102   *"They are colored"*: Ann del Valle to S.E.
102   *"I can understand being bored"*: Ibid.
103   *"There was a film"*: Edwards, p. 92.

Chapter 7

Page
104   *"You're still that damned"*: Walsh, p. 127.
105   *Her welcoming gift*: Bessie Lasky, pp. 56–57.
105   *One tough pro*: Ibid., p. 58.
105   *"The decoration"*: Ibid., p. 60.
105   *Blanche Sweet got into the habit*: Bodeen, *From Hollywood*, p. 54.
106   *Although contemporary trade journal*: Altman, p. 369.
106   *Her retinas*: Farrar, p. 168.
106   *"The cosmetics applied"*: Ibid., p. 167.
106   *"I thought DeMille"*: Brownlow, *Parade's*, p. 368.
107   *"the furnace heat"*: Slide, *Selected, 1912–1920*, pp. 42–43.
107   *"Cecil is feeling very fit"*: BYU, Lasky to Goldfish, 10-12-15, club files, box 9.
108   *Jesse wrote Sam*: BYU, Lasky to Goldfish, 10-25-15, club files, box 9.
109   *"The odor"*: This description of the early days of the Lasky studio is largely derived from
       Bessie Lasky, pp. 44–46.
110   *"I saw him directing"*: Agnes deMille interview, Kevin Brownlow archives.
111   *"We thought pictures"*: William deMille, *Hollywood Saga*, p. 115.
111   *"There was great excitement"*: Agnes deMille interview, Kevin Brownlow archives.
112   *"I was a little leery"*: BYU, box 20, f. 12.
112   *"Scene dyed Red"*: Higashi, p. 101.
112   *The script doesn't mention*: BYU, box 1222, f. 17.
112   *"the lighting is advanced"*: Deutelbaum, *Image*, p. 118.
113   *"knew the psychology"*: Sessue Hayakawa, 1959 oral history with Columbia University,
       courtesy of Dennis Doros.
113   *"pictures like this"*: Slide, *Selected, 1912–1920*, p. 45.
113   *"as a work of art"*: Slide and Wagenknecht, p. 39.
114   *"Let our aspiring"*: Brownlow, *Behind*, p. 349.
115   *"Each scene"*: Louvish, p. 148.
115   *"This is without doubt"*: BYU, Cecilia DeMille Harper, "Behind the Scenes with Cecil B.
       DeMille," unpublished article, box 9, f. 2.
116   *"I am just in receipt"*: BYU, Lasky to Goldfish, 11-2-15, club files, box 9.
116   *"we are having trouble"*: BYU, Lasky to Goldfish, 11-19-15, club files, box 9.
116   *The company advanced*: BYU, Lasky to Goldfish, 11-29-15, club files, box 9.
116   *Lasky suggested*: Autobiography, pp. 147–48.
117   *"practically the highest ground"*: Wanamaker, *DeMille Legacy*, p. 298.
118   *While the room was large*: Knight and Elisofon, pp. 40–41.
118   *"Two DeMilles at once"*: BYU, Beatrice to Cecil, 11-1-15, box 239, f. 1.

118   *"I find . . . no hope"*: BYU, Friend to DeMille, 10-28-15, box 239, f. 1.

118   *"I appreciate your imploring"*: Cecil to Beatrice, 11-8-15, box 239, f. 1.

119   *"I need not say"*: BYU, DeMille to Higgins, 1-24-16, box 239, f. 1.

119   *"We played that game"*: BYU, biography notes, 1-31-57, box 20, f. 12.

119   *"She was not so lovable"*: BYU, DeMille to Rasbach, 4-28-58, box 20, f. 12. The actual word "lovable" is obliterated in the transcript by the tender mercies of one of DeMille's watchful secretaries, but DeMille's usage is clear from the context of the sentence and the preceding question.

119   *"to suggest a bargain"*: William deMille, *Hollywood Saga*, p. 194.

120   *"Residents dressed in white"*: Bessie Lasky, p. 50.

122   *the operating profit*: BYU, box 241, f. 27.

122   *"for months"*: Sumiko Higashi, "Legitimating Feature Films as Art," *Film History*, vol. 4, 1990, p. 195.

122   *"Famous Players was making"*: Lasky, *Horn*, p. 122.

123   *"He was a creator"*: Zukor, p. 124.

123   *"every hour on the hour"*: Ibid., pp. 177–78.

125   *"When I left the company"*: BYU, Goldwyn interview, undated, box 17, f. 35.

125   *In 1916, Cecil was earning*: BYU, précis of income and debts, 1917–1919, box 32, f. 4.

125   *he lent Wallace Reid*: BYU, box 32, f. 13.

126   *"Mr. DeMille is thinking"*: Henry King to Brownlow, Kevin Brownlow archives.

126   *Her two-story bungalow*: Scott, p. 9.

126   *"very calm"*: Scott, p. 10.

127   *"the most moving"*: George Pratt, "Forty-five Years of Picture Making: An Interview with Cecil B. DeMille," *Film History*, vol. 3, 1989.

127   WIRE ME STRAIGHT MESSAGE: BYU, DeMille to Kley, 5-18-16, club files, box 9.

128   *"a thrilling experience"*: Farrar, pp. 174–75.

129   *"Well, he was so nice"*: Brownlow, *Parade's*, p. 368.

129   *"like many another"*: Autobiography, p. 125.

129   *"When the history"*: Ibid., p. 126.

131   *"It's completely surrounded"*: Ibid., p. 164.

132   *Cecil grew especially fond*: Scott, pp. 103–4.

132   *"There were no wives"*: Claire Bloom to S.E.

133   *DeMille would toss in a ruby*: Koury, pp. 45–46.

133   *"Paradise wasn't San Simeon"*: Agnes deMille, *Portrait Gallery*, p. 181.

133   *Constance stepped back*: BYU, autobiography transcripts, 5-23-57, box 30, f. 1.

133   *"Wonder why"*: Los Angeles Herald, 12-8-20, quoted in Long, p. 165.

134   *"I have no desire"*: Pickford, p. 180.

135   *"I was quite honored"*: Spears, p. 175.

136   *"He was filled"*: Bogdanovich, *Who the Devil*, p. 355; quote slightly rearranged.

137   *"Everything about The Little American"*: Brownlow, *Mary Pickford*, p. 134.

137   ARTCRAFT PICTURES: Birchard, p. 111.

138   *"While there is no question"*: Autobiography, p. 212.

138   *"Tellegen chose"*: Farrar, p. 179.

139   *"The company must realize"*: BYU, Buckland to DeMille, 11-30-16.

139   *"Uncle Cecil's attitude"*: Agnes deMille, *Dance to the Piper*, pp. 31–33.

141   *"I am taking"*: BYU, DeMille to Lasky, 10-16-18, box 240, f. 13.

141   *He became a volunteer*: McCandless et al., p. 47.

142   *Lasky looked at the piece of paper*: Autobiography, p. 147.

Chapter 8

Page
144   *the cameraman Karl Brown*: Brown, p. 237.
144   *"It was just after lunch"*: BYU, Julia Faye, "Flicker Faces," undated, but mid-1940s, pp. 49–60, box 12.
146   *"Julia was the most"*: Richard deMille to S.E.
146   *reproduce Fokine's dances*: Morris, p. 47.
146   *Kosloff would eventually*: Debra Levine, "Theodore Kosloff Cut a Fouette Figure," *Los Angeles Times*, 4-5-09.
147   *"write something typically American"*: Autobiography, p. 212.
147   *"At last, I should say"*: BYU, Rosa Sovell to DeMille, undated, box 239, f. 1.
147   *Joseph Henabery*: Henabery, p. 154.
147   *"To see him"*: Ibid., p. 156.
149   *"He was of the Belasco"*: Gloria Swanson tapes, University of Texas, Austin; courtesy of Dennis Doros.
150   *"I liked the way"*: BYU, box 305, f. 13.
150   *that paid her*: BYU, DeMille to Lasky, 12-23-18, box 240, f. 13.
150   *"She was so excited"*: Adela Rogers St. Johns to Brownlow, Kevin Brownlow archives.
150   *"He had such a powerful way"*: Swanson tapes, University of Texas, Austin.
151   *"There was no other director"*: Gloria Swanson to Brownlow, Kevin Brownlow archives.
151   *"he turned"*: Basinger, pp. 208–9.
152   *"The little things"*: Pratt, "Forty-Five Years of Filmmaking: An Interview with Cecil B. DeMille, *Film History*, vol. 3, 1989.
152   *Between 1880*: May, p. 201.
152   *"an internal domestic"*: Ibid., p. 209.
153   *"They were sought"*: Jacobs, p. 338.
154   *"Prolong it!"*: Eoooe and Lee, p. 66.
154   *"I remembered"*: BYU, biography notes, 5-27-57, box 30, f. 2.
155   *"the most valid"*: Card, *Seductive Cinema*, p. 226.
155   *His true subject*: My analysis of the marital comedies owes much to Carlos Clarens in Roud, p. 267.
156   *it was Thomas Meighan*: Photoplay, October 1919, p. 112, author's collection.
156   *When Lasky hesitantly*: Autobiography, p. 222.
157   *as critic David Thomson*: Thomson, *Have You Seen*, p. 512.
159   *"I have gone into this matter"*: BYU, DeMille to Lasky, 12-27-18, box 240, f. 13.
159   *"Despite all this praise"*: BYU, Neilan to DeMille, 2-6-19, box 240, f. 21.
159   *"Your words of praise"*: BYU, DeMille to Neilan, 2-21-19, box 240, f. 21.
160   *"There were only two"*: Autobiography, p. 194.
160   *Locally, they used*: Ibid., p. 198.
161   *The engine restarted*: Jesse Lasky, p. 111.
161   *"The worst thing you could do"*: BYU, Zukor interview, box 19, f. 2.
161   *The airline's*: BYU, box 32, f. 3.
161   *Including moguls*: Bonadio, pp. 113–234.
162   *She then asserted*: BYU, Cecilia DeMille Harper, "Behind the Scenes with Cecil B. DeMille," unpublished manuscript, box 9, f. 2.
163   *"There is not the smallest"*: BYU, DeMille to Zukor, 2-26-20, box 241, f. 8.
164   *"From my observation"*: Semenov and Winter, p. 133.
165   *"He was having a quiet"*: Chierichetti, *Leisen*, p. 22.

165   *"Alvin, who's that?"*: Deutelbaum, p. 225.
166   *"It was on the corner"*: Eyman, *Five*, p. 64.
166   *After some unpleasantness*: McCandless et al., p. 37.
166   *"I remember"*: James Wong Howe to S.E.
167   *Charles Rosher told*: Brownlow, *Parades's*, p. 227.
167   *"The photography was independent"*: Eyman, *Five*, p. 4.
168   *"I had a star"*: Edwards, p. 86.
168   *"I use her"*: Swanson tapes, University of Texas, Austin.
169   *"was thoroughly detested"*: "American Epic," a documentary by Kevin Brownlow and Patrick Stanbury.
170   *are "really about only"*: Basinger, p. 216.
171   *"your poor person"*: Wakeman, p. 213.
171   *"I think he was filming"*: Agnes deMille to Brownlow, Kevin Brownlow archives.

Chapter 9

Page
173   *"Dearest"*: Richard deMille collection.
173   *The women paid*: Architectural Digest, 11-08, pp. 118–24.
174   *"DeMille respected"*: Arnold Gillespie to Brownlow, Kevin Brownlow archives.
174   *her baby boy's celebration with a poem*: BYU, Beatrice deMille to DeMille, 8-12-21, box 38, f. 9.
175   *"He buys other women"*: Scott, p. 138.
175   *"We rehearsed a bit"*: Lois Wilson to Brownlow, Kevin Brownlow archives.
175   *"In my opinion"*: Usai and Codelli, *DeMille Legacy*, p. 18.
175   *"The only thing"*: Edwards, p. 81.
175   *"It was interesting"*: Scott, pp. 128–29.
176   *"how can you raise"*: Edwards, p. 81.
177   *"The key to the entire"*: Richard deMille to S.E.
177   *"When a man has been married"*: Agnes deMille, *Portrait Gallery*, p. 184.
177   *"Look out for"*: Frances Triest to S.E.
178   *"Mother could have"*: Agnes deMille, *Wings*, p. 263.
178   *DeMille received 30 percent*: BYU, box 241, f. 10.
178   *"We have been able"*: BYU, Lasky to DeMille, 5-21-21, box 241, f. 20.
180   *"Having seen"*: BYU, DeMille to Lasky, 9-17-21, box 241, f. 8.
180   *"DeMille was very theatrical"*: Betty Lasky to Kevin Brownlow, *Photoplay*.
181   *the reports she turned in*: BYU, Faye story reports 1922, box 241, f. 32.
181   *"Dear—These are the pine"*: BYU, Faye to DeMille, undated, box 65, f. 38.
182   *"Don't think of your"*: Agnes deMille, *Portrait Gallery*, p. 171.
182   *Cecil paid Bill*: BYU, Day to DeMille, 4-9-25, box 38, f. 7.
182   *"Cecil was interested"*: Richard deMille to S.E.
182   *"How can you work"*: Fountain, p. 76.
184   *When Boyd broke his ankle*: Boyd and Cochran, p. 47.
184   *DeMille told the story*: Richard deMille to S.E.
185   *"When are you going"*: Drew, p. 72.
186   *"DeMille didn't want her having sex"*: Leatrice Fountain to S.E.
186   *"He makes me think"*: Sadoul, p. 60.
186   *"DeMille looks"*: Talmey, pp. 139, 146.
187   *Hays had accumulated*: McCartney, pp. 42, 226.
187   *"used language"*: Ibid., p. 227.

187   *"We all gathered"*: Hart, p. 313.
188   *Davenport told two*: Mark Lynn Anderson, "Shooting Star: Understanding Wallace Reid and His Public," in McLean and Cook.
188   *it was widely assumed*: Ibid.
188   *"Too long"*: BYU, report from Robert Blair, 2-5-23, box 244.
188   *Another New York critic*: Jacobs, p. 339.
189   *"Censorship, whatever its"*: Bruce Long, pp. 155, 185.
189   *"we had lovers' quarrels"*: Swanson tapes, University of Texas, Austin.
190   HAVE HAD LONG TALK: BYU, DeMille to Lasky, 2-17-23, box 244.
191   LET THERE BE NOT: BYU, Hays to DeMille, 2-18-23, box 244.
191   MATTER WILL BE ADJUSTED: BYU, DeMille to Lasky, 3-6-23, box 244.
192   *"affiant has had"*: BYU, Somborn affidavit, 3-22-23, box 244.
192   *The last clause*: BYU, contract, Swanson with Famous Players, 3-22-23, box 244.
192   *"This was quite"*: Swanson tapes, University of Texas, Austin.
192   *"unwavering allegiance"*: Ann del Valle to James D'Arc, BYU interview.
193   *"When I first came"*: Edwards, pp. 75–76.
194   *DeMille enjoyed Richard's*: Richard deMille to S.E.
194   *"He has no assets"*: Berg, p. 115.
194   *"It was natural to Sam"*: BYU, autobiography files, 8-57, box 20, f. 12.

Chapter 10

Page
195   *"would jump on a train"*: Autobiography, p. 247.
196   CECIL'S PRODUCTION WILL: Higashi, p. 187.
197   *Even the cast*: Rosenberg and Silverstein, p. 245.
197   *"He was elegant"*: Drew, p. 78.
197   *"Being a small boy"*: Moore to Brownlow, Kevin Brownlow Archives.
197   *The young Mervyn LeRoy*: Stevens Jr., p. 147.
198   *The extras lined up*: Photoplay, September 1923, p. 38, author's collection.
198   *"Just say that"*: William deMille, p. 241.
198   *"We had been had"*: LeRoy, p. 59.
198   *"The big mess tent"*: Peter Brosnan, "The Lost City of Pharaoh DeMille," California Living, 12-15-85.
198   *Although La Barbara*: Pat Moore interview, Photoplay.
199   *Cecilia did as she was asked*: BYU, Cecilia DeMille Harper, "Behind the Scenes with Cecil B. DeMille," unpublished story, box 9, f. 2.
199   *"DeMille never quit"*: Rosenberg and Silverstein, p. 244.
199   *"DeMille was an autocrat"*: Henry Hathaway to Brownlow, Kevin Brownlow archives.
200   *"Allah was kind"*: DeMille, "Motion Picture Directing," Harvard University Graduate School of Business, 4-26-27.
200   *"two tanks holding"*: Ibid.
201   FINALLY TODAY: Birchard, p. 184.
202   *DeMille would give Jeanie*: BYU, box 60, f. 5.
203   *"[DeMille] said he was discouraged"*: Bauchens to Zeitlin, undated, but 1957, box 20, f. 12.
203   *"Although twenty-four hours have passed"*: Birchard, pp. 187–88.
203   *"Now that the hatchet"*: BYU, Lasky to DeMille, 11-21-23, box 244.
204   *DeMille was accompanied*: BYU, box 244, f. 14.
205   *"I congratulate you"*: Autobiography, p. 260.
206   *Beatrice had never prepared*: BYU, box 38, f. 6.

206   *His total remuneration:* BYU, "Royalty Statement for period ending Dec. 29, 1923," dated July 21, 1924, box 244, f. 24.

206   *As of July 1924:* BYU, Cecil B. DeMille Productions receipts and disbursements July 1924, box 60, f. 16.

210   *"I can remember":* Koury, p. 108.

211   *Nathan Burkan set about arranging the terms:* BYU, Burkan to Lasky, 1-8-25, box 258, f. 4, 7, 8, 14.

211   *"When you left Paramount":* BYU, biography notes, 5-27-57, box 30, f. 3.

Chapter 11

Page

212   *politically conservative financier:* Phillips-Fein, p. 81.

213   *The trade papers bloomed:* MOMA, "Cecil B. DeMille—An Open Record," undated trade paper ads.

213   *It was a well-appointed lot:* Beauchamp, *Adventures,* p. 167.

213   *figures he kept:* BYU, William deMille to DeMille, 7-26-28, box 270, f. 12.

214   *"His attitude towards life":* Love, pp. 120, 121–22.

214   *"I was basically":* Richard deMille to S.E.

214   *"I'm not so young":* DeWitt Bodeen, "Leatrice Joy," *Films in Review,* April 1977.

214   *Joy told her daughter:* Leatrice Fountain to S.E.

214   *"Do you want to buy":* BYU, Ella Adams to DeMille, 1-14-25, box 258, f. 2.

214   *"We are short":* BYU, DeMille to Ella Adams, 2-26-25, box 258, f. 2.

215   I WOULD LIKE VERY MUCH: BYU, DeMille to Beahan, 4-7-25, box 261, f. 12.

215   *But Daniels changed her mind:* BYU, DeMille to Nathan Burkan, 4-3-25, box 258, folders 4, 7, 8, 14.

215   *Glyn's contract with MGM:* BYU, Burkan to DeMille, 4-3-25, box 258, folders 4, 7, 8, 14.

215   *Other available directors:* BYU, Rosson to DeMille, 1-30-25, box 258, folders 4, 7, 8, 14.

216   *Cecilia once confided:* Scott, p. 154.

216   *One story:* BYU, DeMille to Adams, 10-30-25, box 258, f. 4.

216   *"Cinema Corporation":* BYU, DeMille to Rosson, 2-5-25, box 258, folders 4, 7, 8, 14.

217   *Publicist Barrett:* BYU, Kiesling to DeMille, 6-12-26, box 265, f. 10.

217   *When he liked:* Coffee, p. 138.

217   *"It's a replica":* Ibid., p. 141.

218   *On February 8:* BYU, 2-8-25, box 258, folders 4, 7, 8, 14.

218   *"His selection of finger rings":* Frank Coghlan, "C.B. and Me," *Classic Images,* November 1992, p. 16.

218   *"We had a great friendship":* Grace Bradley Boyd to S.E.

219   I DON'T FEEL VERY GOOD: *Autobiography,* p. 270.

219   *"due to week":* Birchard, p. 207.

220   *"It was like a big":* Coghlan to Brownlow, *Photoplay* Productions.

221   *"have arranged":* Birchard, p. 207.

221   *DeMille didn't shoot a lot of film:* BYU, box 261, f. 2.

221   *"Mr. DeMille's assistants":* Hall, "DeMille Is Director as Disciplinarian," *New York Times,* 7-19-25.

222   I GATHER YOU HAVE BEEN PANNED: BYU, DeMille to Joseph Schildkraut, 12-1-25, box 261, f. 6.

223   *he wired Sam Goldwyn:* BYU, DeMille to Goldwyn, 1-12-26, box 264, f. 1 and 2.

223   *Goldwyn ended up:* BYU, DeMille to Murdock, 1-14-26, box 265, f. 19.

223   *There was no first-run theater:* BYU, Monroe to Flinn, 2-10-26, box 264, f. 1 and 2.

223   *between 1925 and 1927*: Wertheim, pp. 252, 253.
224   *The movies had been good*: BYU, Cecil B. DeMille trial balance, 9-1-26, box 43, f. 9.
225   *"He actually was nearest"*: Gutner, p. 22.
225   *"Why skirt around"*: Birchard, p. 217.
226   *"Need for working capital"*: Birchard, p. 218.
227   *One internal document*: BYU, Schedule of Costs and Gross Receipts, 1-31-31, box 62, f. 18.
227   *half of the leading actor's salary*: BYU, box 279, f. 2.
228   *Torrence was actually making*: BYU, cast list, 9-10-26, box 282, f. 6.
229   *"You're good enough for me"*: Garnett and Balling, p. 85.
230   *"It appears to me"*: BYU, DeMille to Barton, 8-12-26, box 282, f. 1.
230   *"This was largely"*: Barton to DeMille, 8-12-26, box 282, f. 1.
231   *"Through the darkness"*: BYU, "Memos from Mr. DeMille's note-pads," 8-12-26, box 282, f. 6.
231   *"utilize the miniature"*: Birchard, p. 223.
232   *The transcript provides*: BYU, 8-23-26, box 282, f. 11.

Chapter 12

Page
235   *"This has been the happiest"*: Coffee, p. 158.
235   *"That puts me at something"*: Ibid., p. 160.
236   *"The first time"*: Richard deMille to S.E.
236   *DeMille apologized*: Michael Moore interview, *Photoplay*.
236   *"Whenever DeMille"*: Chierichetti, *Leisen*, p. 37.
236   *Poor H. B. Warner*: BYU, shooting schedule, part 2, box 282, f. 6.
237   *"Miss Rund"*: Barry Paris, "The Godless Girl," *New Yorker*, 2-13-89, p. 59.
237   *"a strange and fascinating blend"*: quoted in Birchard, p. 223.
237   *One evening*: Koury, p. 123.
237   *Lenore Coffee*: Coffee, p. 158.
238   *"This could be done"*: BYU, Macpherson to DeMille, 9-4-26, box 282, f. 1.
238   *DeMille was entitled*: BYU, "Pathé Exchange Account with Cecil B. DeMille Productions Inc., July 13, 1929," box 838, f. 1.
239   *"I can assure you"*: Autobiography, p. 274.
239   *his highest paid*: BYU, undated DeMille studio "Contracts in Force," box 259, f. 6.
241   *"If I'd trained"*: Richard deMille to S.E.
241   *whose "very name"*: For instance, the March 1927 issue of *Photoplay*, p. 95, and the April issue, p. 11, where the ad copy quoted here originates.
241   *"It is a strangely impersonal"*: Adela Rogers St. Johns, "Will the Screen Bring Christ Back to Us," *Photoplay*, March 1927, p. 94.
243   *Sid Grauman pulled out*: Endres and Cushman, p. 36.
243   *"The ushers were dressed"*: Haney, p. 53.
243   *Rabbi Edgar Magnin*: BYU, Magnin to DeMille, 4-24-27, box 282, f. 9.
243   *DeMille scribbled*: BYU, DeMille to Cummings, box 270, f. 4.
244   *"Everyone in the audience"*: BYU, DeMille to Lord, 5-7-27, box 284, f. 4 and 5.
244   *"He brooks no argument"*: Undated clipping in the author's collection.
245   *"If any Jew"*: BYU, box 282, f. 9.
245   *In September 1926*: Both sides of the issue are discussed in BYU, Murdock to DeMille, 9-15-26, DeMille to Murdock, 10-7-26, box 265, f. 13.
246   *"an almost respectable response"*: Reinhartz, pp. 239–40.

246   *"an open rupture"*: BYU, Magnin to DeMille, 9-28-27, box 284, f. 5.

246   *"Magnin is anxious"*: BYU, DeMille to Hays, 12-5-27, box 282, f. 9.

247   *"Jesus writes in Hebrew"*: BYU, manuscript "HOLD—Under Rabbi Magnin," box 282, f. 9.

247   *"Eliminate all scenes"*: BYU, unsigned letter to Carl Milliken, 12-21-27, box 282, f. 9.

248   *"I will cut that"*: Bauchens to deMille, 11-22-27, box 282, f. 1.

248   As the critic Glenn Erickson wrote: DVD Savant, posted 2-5-05.

249   in 1949: BYU, box 947, f. 1.

250   If you are one: BYU, "KNX," handwritten draft and typescript, dated 7-11-27, box 282, f. 6.

250   *"He strove"*: Richard deMille, p. 291.

251   *"I had a little boat"*: BYU, DeMille/Rasbach interview, 4-28-58, box 20, f. 12.

252   *"He drives up"*: Britting, p. 35.

252   *"Life is achievement"*: Rand, p. 3.

252   *"The building rises"*: Rand, p. 10.

253   *"She impressed him"*: Richard deMille to S.E.

253   *"It is said"*: "DeMille's Costs-Grosses," *Variety*, 3-21-28, p. 5.

254   Joe Kennedy told: Beauchamp, *Kennedy*, p. 151.

254   It was increasingly clear: An overview of DeMille's financial travails is in BYU, box 282, f. 6.

254   He received $250,000: Beauchamp, *Kennedy*, p. 157.

255   United Artists would charge: BYU, box 37, f. 17.

256   Williams was banished: Samuel Marx, p. 81.

256   In Basquette's version: Basquette, pp. 109–10.

257   *"the essence of serenity"*: Ibid., pp. 129–30.

257   *"The last thing"*: Barry Paris, "The Godless Girl," *New Yorker*, 2-13-89, p. 61.

258   *"DeMille didn't think"*: Lina Basquette to S.E.

258   *"In casting about"*: BYU, Del Ruth to DeMille, 8-22-28, box 48, f. 5.

258   *"When banks came into"*: Autobiography, p. 289.

259   *"It looks to me"*: William deMille, p. 275.

PART THREE

Chapter 13

Page
263   Mayer glanced up: BYU, biography notes, 4-16-57, box 30, f. 3.

264   *"The Imperial Throne Room"*: Photoplay, May 1929, p. 83.

264   Charles Bickford left behind: Edwards, pp. 111–12.

265   *"I had not written"*: Norman, p. 161.

265   and Gladys Unger: Ceplair and Englund, p. 61.

265   a young actress: Swindell, p. 80.

266   *"You could not pan the camera"*: This account of the early days of sound derives from George Pratt, "Forty-five Years of Picture Making: An Interview with Cecil B. DeMille," *Film History*, vol. 3, 1989, and the *Autobiography*, p. 293.

266   Another contribution: Rosenberg and Silverstein, p. 184.

266   *"The other kid"*: McGilligan, *Film Crazy*, pp. 104–5.

267   On March 4: Daily production reports, UCLA.

268   *"Jesse said"*: BYU, Constance to Cecil, box 50, f. 1.

269   *DeMille was clearly uneasy*: BYU, box 20, f. 22.

269   *"The purpose of this picture"*: BYU, box 298, f. 1.

270   *Beginning in 1929*: BYU, box 295, f. 1.

272   *The pressure was so intense*: Chierichetti, *Leisen*, p. 39.

272   *DeMille brought the picture in early*: Madam Satan daily production reports, USC.

272   FORTHCOMING MUSICAL PRODUCTION: BYU, telegram to Joe Kennedy, 12-5-29, box 294, f. 29.

272   THE PART OF MADAM SATAN: Birchard, p. 245.

273   *"the money she might"*: Ibid., p. 244.

273   *"It contained"*: Samuel Marx, p. 132.

273   *"His reputation"*: *Photoplay*, Joseph Newman interview.

274   *"The studio explosions"*: Richard deMille to S.E.

274   *"he took his time"*: Joseph Newman to S.E.

275   *"need have perturbed"*: Autobiography, p. 301.

275   *Unfortunately, the house*: BYU, box 814, f. 9.

276   *The year Cecilia*: Scott, p. 202.

276   *"He thought"*: Edwards, p. 137.

276   *"All is well"*: Cecil to Constance, 8-19-30, Richard deMille collection.

276   *"Constance suffered"*: Richard deMille to S.E.

277   *"My Darling One"*: BYU, box 305, f. 13.

277   *"In its hey-day"*: Squaw Man script notes, 5-13-30, USC.

278   *"Clark Gabel"*: BYU, Rosson to Leisen, 7-15-30, box 295, f. 18.

278   *"There is a move to eliminate"*: The Directors Guild documents are at BYU, box 62, f. 18.

279   *"He had a mistress"*: Drew, p. 53.

279   *The child actor Dickie Moore*: Raymond, p. 95.

279   *As he told George Pratt*: George Pratt, "Forty-five Years of Picture Making: An Interview with Cecil B. DeMille," *Film History*, vol. 3, 1989.

280   *"I'm sorry, C.B."*: BYU, box 10, f. 24.

280   *Cecil sent thank-you notes*: BYU, DeMille to Cohn, DeMille to Shearer, 6-5-31, box 296, f. 25.

280   *"I learned more"*: Maltin, *Art*, p. 101.

281   *DeMille got a letter*: BYU, box 57, f. 3.

281   *"Her hair is just the right"*: Agnes deMille, *Martha*, pp. 186–87.

281   *In DeMille's program*: Autobiography, p. 307.

281   *"There have been no reporters"*: Ibid., p. 308.

286   *the IRS was charging him*: Autobiography, p. 316.

286   *Robert Montgomery negotiated*: Fairbanks Jr., pp. 180–81.

286   *Sam Katz had told*: *Fortune*, March 1937, which contains most of the facts and figures cited in this section.

286   *Paramount would not emerge*: Gomery, p. 32.

287   *"Dear Chief"*: Birchard, p. 250.

Chapter 14

Page

288   *the last time he would vote*: Wanamaker, *DeMille Legacy*, p. 302.

288   *"It was a period"*: BYU, autobiography files, box 30, f. 5.

289   *"Lasky and Zukor were going out"*: BYU, autobiography notes, 3-20-57, box 30, f. 3.

290   *"Trust wasn't part"*: Richard deMille to S.E.

291 *"How cozy"*: Dave Friedman to S.E.
292 *"It was really quite funny"*: MOMA, "Claudette Colbert Still Tells DeMille Stories," *New York Times*, 11-16-79.
292 *"Everybody was off the stage"*: Eyman, *Five*, p. 15.
293 *a lamb carcass*: Chierichetti, *Leisen*, p. 43.
293 *"Everybody adored him"*: Ibid., p. 23.
293 *"It was the most magnificent"*: BYU, DeMille to Art Arthur, autobiography transcripts.
293 *"of a world remembered"*: Higham, *Hollywood Cameramen*, p. 128.
294 *Near the end of production*: Callow, *Laughton*, p. 52.
294 *"Your face is too narrow"*: John Carradine and David Carradine to S.E.
295 *"Their attitude"*: Vieira, *Sin*, p. 26.
295 *DeMille ignored him*: Barrios, p. 91.
295 *"Since the director"*: Vieira, *Sin*, p. 107.
295 *"Not a damn thing"*: Ibid.
296 *In November 1933*: Haberski, pp. 24–25.
297 *"Every sequence in which"*: Slide, *Selected, 1931–1940*, pp. 232, 234.
297 *"Cecil B. DeMille is out of fashion"*: Bowser, *Film Notes*, p. 86.
297 *"shimmering opulence"*: Barrios, p. 83.
298 *DeMille believed in preparation*: Wilcoxon, p. 15.
298 *"He always knew what"*: *Destined for Hollywood*, Whittemore, p. 34.
298 *modest and usually self-deprecatory*: Ibid., p. 40.
299 *"I could have said anything"*: *Photoplay*, Michael Moore interview.
299 *"Why not telephone"*: BYU, DeMille to Macpherson, 3-1-33, box 307, f. 3.
300 IF YOU ARE NOT COMING: BYU, Macpherson to DeMille, 3-6-33, box 307, f. 3.
300 *"Dear Jeanie"*: BYU, DeMille to Macpherson, 9-8-34, box 314, f. 2.
300 *"The part was, he said"*: Grace Bradley Boyd to S.E.
300 *He just walked in*: *Photoplay*, Frank Coghlan interview.
300 *"Judith Allen"*: Cary to S.E.
301 *The critic and screenwriter Andrew Bergman called*: Bergman, pp. 112–13.
302 *"I am not a radical"*: Doherty, p. 65.
303 *Youngerman held firm*: Youngerman, p. 24.
303 *More seriously*: Arnold Scaasi to S.E.
303 *"The first day I arrived"*: Quirk, *Claudette*, p. 62.
304 *"a light comedy"*: AMPAS, DeMille file, 1-28-34.
304 *"leave whimsical"*: Autobiography, p. 330.

Chapter 15

Page
305 *There was an aggregate*: BYU, box 751, f. 3.
305 *"Are you a virgin?"*: Mary Anita Loos to S.E.
306 *"She wanted to"*: Quirk, *Claudette*, p. 68.
306 *"I've decided"*: Wilcoxon, p. 13.
306 *"I loved the old buzzard"*: Maltin, *Hollywood*, p. 123.
307 *"I don't want any extras"*: Ibid., p. 126.
307 *"Antony had seen"*: Birchard, p. 281.
307 *Agnes wrote her sister*: Edwards, pp. 133, 136.
308 *"C.B. trusts no one"*: Gottlieb, p. 842.
308 *"Oh no, oh no"*: Edwards, p. 136.
308 *"Mr. Merrick"*: Easton, p. 393.

308   *"She always was"*: Gottlieb, p. 844.
309   *"In one scene"*: MOMA, "Claudette Colbert Still Tells DeMille Stories," *New York Times*, 11-16-79.
310   *DeMille wrote Menzies*: BYU, DeMille to Menzies, 6-13-34 and 6-19-34, box 314, f. 2.
311   *Besides the shots*: Gordon Jennings, "Special Effects for Cleopatra," *American Cinematographer*, December 1934.
311   *Rob Wagner wrote*: Slide, *Selected, 1931–1940*, pp. 51–52.
311   *"I am in fine shape"*: Constance to Cecil, 7-24-34, Richard deMille collection.
311   *"Cecil's pronouncements"*: Long, p. 54.
312   *"I really am busted"*: BYU, William deMille to DeMille, 2-2-35, box 68, f. 18.
312   *"I thought I had parted"*: BYU, William deMille to DeMille, 2-2-35, box 68, f. 18.
313   *"I am not downhearted"*: BYU, William deMille to DeMille, 5-27-35, box 68, f. 18.
313   *Cecil countered*: BYU, DeMille to William deMille, 3-31-34, box 65, f. 32.
313   *"Cecil envied"*: Richard deMille to S.E.
314   *"She was very devoted"*: Frances Triest to S.E.
314   *In October 1938*: BYU, box 77, f. 17.
314   *"Cecil had always been generous"*: Agnes deMille, *Portrait Gallery*, pp. 183–84.
314   *"Cecil and William were"*: Frances Triest to S.E.
315   *"When I began to direct"*: Edwards, p. 189.
316   *"I am looking forward"*: Birchard, p. 289.
317   *In historical fact*: All this derives from Aberth, pp. 86–89.
318   *"There is much horseplay"*: Fraser, p. 44.
318   *"I saved the technique"*: BYU, autobiography files, 5-16-57, box 30, f. 2.
319   *"I again deliberated"*: BYU, "Cecil B. DeMille's Story of Hollywood," *Boston Globe*, undated, but January 1937.
319   *"Lubitsch was very funny"*: BYU, biography notes, 3-20-57, box 30, f. 3.
320   *"I'm hypnotized"*: Eyman, *Lubitsch*, p. 232.
320   *Balaban ran Paramount*: Gomery, pp. 35–36.
320   *The lash marks*: Oller, p. 94.
321   *"From the first"*: Quinn, p. 134.
322   *"Surely DeMille"*: Ibid., p. 136.
322   *"He had two adopted"*: Turner Classic Movies transcript, courtesy of Patrick McGilligan.
322   *"Every night, Tony"*: Kotsilibas-Davis, *Barrymores*, p. 193.
322   *"Grandfather would"*: Cecilia deMille Presley to S.E.
322   *"DeMille and I"*: Anthony Quinn to S.E.
323   *"DeMille can make"*: Fraser, p. 198.
324   *The Crusades and The Plainsman*: BYU, box 751, f. 5.
325   *"It's a mammoth job"*: *Photoplay*, Martin Scorsese interview.

Chapter 16

Page
326   *Beginning June 1*: BYU, box 1055, f. 5.
327   *"the most important dramatic"*: Dunning, p. 416.
327   *"I worked in"*: *Photoplay*, Frank Coghlan interview.
327   *the scripts are often cut*: BYU, box 1055, f. 6.
329   *"a piece of Russian"*: Youngkin, p. 139.
329   *"He's made a comedian"*: Curtis, *Between Flops*, p. 113.
329   *"DeMille was more of a surrogate"*: Pat Silver Lasky to S.E.
330   *"haunting his corridors"*: Lasky Jr., p. 151.

330   *"He used writers"*: Lasky Jr., p. 156.

330   *"Probably the fight"*: Koury, p. 217.

330   *"Her body is against him"*: Ibid., pp. 231, 233.

331   *He'd leave with ten books*: Pat Silver Lasky to S.E.

332   *"major prostatectomy"*: BYU, autobiography files, 8-14-57, box 12, f. 9.

332   *If the infection*: BYU, autobiography files, box 30, f. 5.

332   *Some in the family*: Richard deMille wasn't sure about DeMille's impotence, but thought it was a distinct possibility.

333   *"Have you been with a woman?"*: Richard deMille to S.E.

334   *"You certainly knew"*: Bernard Drew, "Stanwyck Speaks," *Film Comment*, March–April 1981, p. 45.

334   *"Everybody has a little"*: Berg, p. 334.

334   *"What a showman!"*: McGilligan, *Film Crazy*, p. 105.

334   *Drawing a diametrically*: "Robert Preston," *Films in Review*, August–September 1982.

335   *"I read the script"*: Arthur Jacobson to S.E.

336   *In late 1938*: Allen W. Palmer, "Cecil B. DeMille Writes America's History for the 1939 World's Fair," *Film History*, vol. 5, 1993.

337   *"[William] knew"*: Koury, p. 226.

338   *"I bought it without"*: BYU, autobiography files, 6-13-57, box 30, f. 4.

338   *"I see a tough"*: Marubbio, p. 89.

339   *Mr. [J. H.] Rosenberg*: Birchard, pp. 314–15.

339   *"I shouldn't be surprised"*: MOMA, Idwal Jones, "DeMille Discovers the Mounties," *New York Times*, 4-28-40.

340   *"Well, it's too bad"*: Chierichetti, *Hollywood*, p. 64.

340   *"Not only was everything"*: Gilbert, pp. 273–75.

341   *"had made arrangements"*: BYU, Chaplin to DeMille, 11-15-41, box 92, f. 7.

341   *Faye recovered*: BYU, box 29, f. 10.

341   *Gladys sent DeMille a note*: Rosson to DeMille, 10-27-38, box 77, f. 1.

341   *If she could get*: BYU, Rosson to DeMille, 11-18-38, box 77, f. 1.

341   *"Your Thursday morning"*: BYU, DeMille to Faye, 8-13-38, box 77, f. 1.

341   *"She really"*: del Valle to S.E.

342   *"a bald man"*: Keyes, p. 21.

342   *DeMille thundered*: Zollo, pp. 130–31.

342   *Keyes had another*: Photoplay, Evelyn Keyes interview.

342   *"Grandfather adored him"*: Cecilia deMille Presley to S.E.

343   *signed a series of pledges*: BYU, John deMille to DeMille, 9-17-38, box 77, f. 7.

343   *"I [keep] asking myself"*: Lasky Jr., p. 219.

343   *"The first instant"*: Server, p. 29.

344   *"He's some writer"*: McGilligan, *Film Crazy*, p. 113.

344   *"He said to me"*: Munn, p. 50.

344   *"I was disappointed"*: Davis, *Words into Images*, pp. 97–98.

344   *"If an actor"*: Munn, p. 78.

345   *"Wayne was one of"*: Ibid., p. 79.

345   *In August 1941*: Endres and Cushman, p. 156.

346   *He handed him a painting*: Coleman, p. 77.

346   *"I started at Paramount"*: Henry Bumstead to S.E.

347   *"Everything stopped moving"*: Curtis, *W. C. Fields*, pp. 434–35.

347   *"The worst thing"*: Anthony Quinn to S.E.

347   *He needed the second loan*: BYU, box 93, f. 19.

347   *"It was very hard"*: Richard deMille to S.E.
348   *"I'll tell you, Charles"*: Davis, *Words into Images*, p. 10.
348   *"And this was"*: This paragraph combines quotes from Server, p. 26, and McGilligan, *Backstory*, p. 41.
348   *DeMille would always say*: Server, p. 26.
348   *Bennett noted*: Davis, *Words into Images*, p. 10.
348   *"DeMille was not a writer"*: Server, p. 28.
348   *"DeMille was a genius"*: Davis, *Words into Images*, p. 13.
349   *"a beautiful, desirable"*: MOMA, "DeMille Honored by Film Industry," *New York Times*, undated, but March 1942.
349   *"the sob stuff"*: BYU, box 875, f. 38.
349   *"In foreign policy"*: *Autobiography*, p. 370.
349   *Shortly after war*: McGilligan, *Hitchcock*, p. 257.
350   *"I appreciate deeply"*: All of the material relating to DeMille's FBI activities and J. Edgar Hoover derives from DeMille's FBI file, FOIPA No. 1014090-000, and a précis within it dated 10-10-45.
351   *"much more stable"*: Hood to Hoover, 3-19-43, DeMille FBI file.
351   *"I would get a call"*: McGilligan, *Backstory*, pp. 38–39.
352   *"Dear Mr. DeMille"*: Fields, p. 195.
352   *DeMille naturally enjoyed*: George Mitchell to S.E.
352   *"The reason the story"*: Meyers, p. 190.
352   *"He was gracious"*: Elliott Reid to S.E.
353   *"Why aren't you funny?"*: Elliott Reid to S.E.
354   *DeMille came bearing gifts*: *Autobiography*, p. 382.
354   *Jeanie Macpherson spent*: BYU, box 384, f. 4.
354   *during the Fourth War Loan*: BYU, box 384, f. 6.
355   *One letter was headed*: BYU, Tate to DeMille, 9-23-44, box 393, f. 11.
356   *"There are four classes"*: BYU, autobiography transcripts, 4-16-57, box 30, f. 1 and 3.
356   *One day Sturges*: Jacobs, p. 226.
356   *He had a southern drawl*: Diane, Jacobs, p. 170.
356   *"I think particularly"*: MOMA, Mitchell Leisen, "Painting in Motion," *American Theater*, March 1940.
357   *"He was very nice"*: Welles and Bogdanovich, p. 147.
357   *"a lot rat"*: Cecilia deMille Presley to S.E.
357   *"I don't feel"*: Richard deMille to S.E.
358   *"Inside the house"*: Katherine Orrison to S.E.
358   *In his wallet*: Koury, p. 178.
358   *"He was much more domestic"*: Richard deMille to S.E.
358   *"He never scolded"*: Cecilia deMille Presley to S.E.
359   *"He was not a completely"*: Richard deMille to S.E.
361   *"James Stewart might"*: BYU, screening books, pp. 176–78.
361   *For the same picture*: BYU, DeMille to LeBaron, 2-28-36, box 326, f. 10.
361   *"Didn't that actor"*: Lasky Jr., p. 164.
361   *"I never heard a word"*: Richard deMille to S.E.
362   *"He could easily"*: Richard deMille to S.E.
362   *"He was a very"*: Zollo, pp. 117–18.
362   *"He had very positive"*: Chierichetti, *Leisen*, pp. 23–24.
363   *"Eddie Boyle was tough"*: Parrish, p. 92.
363   *"You hear bugles and drums"*: Koury, p. 142.
363   *"He would spare no effort"*: *Photoplay*, Elmer Bernstein interview.

364   *"He thought he was very"*: Cecilia deMille Presley to S.E.
364   *"He worked at being"*: Richard deMille to S.E.

Chapter 17

Page
365   *The first day*: Photoplay, A. C. Lyles interview.
365   *"She was a sweet"*: Richard deMille, p. 13.
365   *Funding all this*: MOMA, "Cecil B. DeMille Is Dead on Coast," *New York Times*, 1-22-59.
366   *In 1937*: BYU, box 858, f. 82.
366   *he took care of his own*: Cecilia deMille Presley to S.E.
366   *Donald Hayne*: BYU, Donald Hayne, "You Don't Know DeMille," unpublished article, box 9, f. 17.
366   *"had a very strong attachment"*: Richard deMille to S.E.
367   *"Everything that was important"*: Koury, p. 16.
367   *"He always wanted"*: Richard deMille to S.E.
367   *"My father"*: Daniel Selznick to S.E.
367   *Dear "Chief"*: BYU, Macpherson to DeMille, 9-25-43, box 378, f. 7.
369   *"I never turn the hot water on"*: BYU, biography notes, 5-27-57, box 30, f. 2.
369   *"He did not mingle"*: Agnes deMille, *Portrait Gallery*, p. 172.
369   *"He supported"*: Cecilia deMille Presley to S.E.
369   *"He liked a strong"*: Richard deMille to S.E.
370   *There were frequent guests*: Photoplay, Elmer Bernstein interview.
371   *"It was . . . the difference"*: Photoplay, Angela Lansbury interview.
371   *"officially a secretary"*: Lisa Mitchell to S.E.
371   *"I had a mother"*: Koury, p. 31.
372   *"This was very strange"*: Agnes deMille, *Portrait Gallery*, p. 186.
372   *In May 1940*: BYU, Rosson memo, 5-3-40, box 220, f. 9.
373   *"I do believe"*: Autobiography, p. 367.
373   *"By action of the Board"*: Quoted in DeMille speech of 3-17-45, in DeMille FBI file.
373   *"This will take us"*: BYU, McCarthy, "History of Labor Suit," box 19, f. 6.
374   *"It meant"*: Autobiography, p. 347.
374   *"Such grave issues"*: BYU, undated clipping, box 1168, f. 2.
375   *"Bill, can you"*: Koury, p. 295.
375   *"She told me"*: Ibid., p. 294.
375   *This is not a question*: DeMille speech, 9-25-45, DeMille FBI file.
376   *Communist controlled unions*: DeMille speech, 4-19-48, DeMille FBI file.
377   *"To compel a man"*: Koury, p. 295.

PART FOUR

Chapter 18

Page
379   *"Never give money"*: Edwards, p. 214.
381   *"He never showed"*: Rivkin and Kerr, p. 317.
381   *William Boyd offered*: BYU, DeMille to Rosson, 11-29-45, box 393.
382   *The task of the new*: BYU, DeMille to Mundt, 2-6-45, box 392, f. 1.
383   *The last time he saw her*: Richard deMille, p. 23.
383   *"You shouldn't do that"*: Meyers, p. 195.

383   *Howard Hawks supposedly*: Ibid., p. 201.

383   *"The movie is"*: Bojarski and Beals, p. 203.

384   *"Mr. DeMille wouldn't"*: Gilbert, p. 310.

385   *Noerdlinger noted*: BYU, Noerdlinger-James D'Arc interview.

385   *In 1946*: Gomery, p. 38.

385   *"I told him"*: Nichols to Tolson, 2-15-47, DeMille FBI file.

386   *Hoover extended an invitation*: Hoover to DeMille, 2-17-47, DeMille FBI file, DeMille to Hoover, 3-1-47, DeMille FBI file.

386   *"Once a week"*: Perfect Vision interview, Steve Reeves, undated.

387   *When Cecilia told her grandfather*: Cecilia deMille Presley to S.E.

388   *"My Darling One"*: Constance to Cecil, 8-16-47, 8-16-48, Richard deMille collection.

388   *"I was even in doubt"*: Goodman, p. 368.

389   *The set was closed*: Koury, p. 163.

389   *"I've never known"*: Munn, pp. 79–80.

389   *"The man is the greatest"*: BYU, box 30, f. 4.

389   *"I have to believe it"*: BYU, box 150, f. 1.

389   *"DeMille loved all the color"*: Edelman and Kupferberg, p. 64.

390   *Joe Egli*: Lasky Jr., p. 259.

390   *"Why do you always say"*: Cecilia deMille Presley to S.E.

390   *"the most delightful"*: Hedy Lamarr to S.E.

390   *Russ Tamblyn*: Russ Tamblyn to S.E.

391   *"His calling card"*: Photoplay, Angela Lansbury interview.

391   *"It is more and more difficult"*: BYU, DeMille to Katherine deMille Quinn, 1-21-49, box 418, f. 2.

391   *"Need I tell you"*: BYU, DeMille to Rand, 7-29-49; Rand's response is dated 8-27-49, and is in box 418, f. 19.

392   *This was the money sequence*: Barsacq, pp. 188–89.

392   *Paramount showed off*: Turner, p. 67.

393   *"This . . . was one of Hollywood's"*: Fraser, p. 9.

393   *"This, friends"*: Slide, Selected, 1941–1950, p. 203.

394   *"I beg of you"*: Both ends of the Stroheim–DeMille correspondence are in BYU, von Stroheim to DeMille, 10-17-50, DeMille to District Director of Immigration and Naturalization, 1-8-51, box 432, f. 18.

Chapter 19

Page

396   *sharing information about communist rallies*: Horne, pp. 137–38.

396   *various notes*: Among others, they are in BYU, box 939, f. 27, and box 50, f. 1.

396   *"outmoded paternalism"*: BYU, Donald Hayne, "You Don't Know DeMille," unpublished story, box 9, f. 17.

397   *Industry Republicans*: Sperber and Lax, p. 279.

397   *"I want to say"*: Dmytryk, Odd Man Out, p. 34.

398   *DeMille crossed the picket lines*: Autobiography, p. 397.

398   *"We had to struggle"*: Horne, p. 138.

398   *We have let abuses*: DeMille speech, 6-12-47, FBI file.

399   *The act mandated*: Sito, p. 217.

399   *The list of initial contributors*: BYU, box 1137, f. 11.

400   *"I don't think it's OK"*: Norman, p. 309.

400   *Joe Mankiewicz's first*: Geist, p. 176.

400   *As the lunch went on:* Wilcoxon, p. 197.

400   *At one, Frank Freeman:* Schary, p. 241.

401   *Power at the Directors:* James Ulmer, "A Guild Divided," *DGA Quarterly,* Winter 2006.

401   *DeMille was determined:* MOMA, Greg Mitchell, "Winning a Battle but Losing the War over the Blacklist," *New York Times,* 1-25-98.

402   *The loyalty oath:* BYU, box 1240, f. 10.

402   *The results:* Geist, p. 177.

402   *"This guy's un-American":* James Ulmer, "A Guild Divided," *DGA Quarterly,* Winter 2006, p. 94.

402   *At a lunchtime conversation:* BYU, DeMille notes, 9-5-50, box 1210, f. 10.

403   *Andrew Stone told:* Geist, p. 185.

403   *"It was a Friday":* Navasky, p. 180.

404   *Martin Gang leaned over:* Ibid., p. 181.

404   *"You can't imagine":* Michael Cieply, "The Night They Dumped DeMille," *Los Angeles Times,* 6-4-87.

404   *The week before the meeting:* Kazan, *A Life,* p. 390.

404   *Donald Hayne told Sidney:* BYU, Donald Hayne note, 10-21-50, box 1240, f. 10.

405   *Mankiewicz would tell his son Tom:* Tom Mankiewicz to S.E.

405   *"This meeting":* All of the quotations from the Screen Directors Guild meeting derive from a court reporter's transcript in the author's collection.

407   *"DeMille was a very articulate":* Robert Wise to S.E.

410   *The next day:* Koury, p. 303.

410   SUNDAY NIGHT MEETING: BYU, DeMille to Brown, 10-23-50, box 1210, f. 10.

411   *Ford had invited:* For instance, BYU, Ford to DeMille, 1-17-49, box 931, f. 28.

411   *Tom Mankiewicz:* Tom Mankiewicz to S.E.

411   *"To the end of his life":* Tom Mankiewicz to S.E.

412   *Soon after the meeting:* FBI file, special service contact information, 11-25-50.

412   *For the next several:* FBI files, special service contacts, 9-17-51.

Chapter 20

Page

413   *"When I saw":* Brownlow, *Parade's,* p. 187.

414   *"Do you think":* Koury, p. 288.

414   *"Anybody in this":* Ibid., p. 299.

414   *In 1952:* BYU, box 1168, f. 4.

414   *The members of the Hollywood:* BYU, Hollywood Committee for Senator Joseph R. McCarthy, box 1168, f. 4.

414   *"Dear Mr. Blum":* BYU, DeMille to Blum, 9-11-52, BYU, box 1168, f. 4.

415   *"DeMille became more":* Richard deMille to S.E.

415   *In every respect:* BYU, letter to FCC, 5-11-55, box 1168, f. 6.

415   *"In 1898":* BYU, DeMille to McDonald, 4-17-50, box 1168, f. 8.

415   *"rivalry [that] was profound":* Agnes deMille, *Portrait Gallery,* p. 159.

415   *"It tended":* Marvin Kaplan to S.E.

416   *"deMille was very caustic":* Weddle, p. 83.

416   *"He was the only":* Fess Parker to S.E.

416   *"the most gifted":* Syd Kronenthal to S.E.

417   *sometimes at lunch:* Rory Guy to S.E.

417   *"Father simply withdrew":* Agnes deMille, *Portrait Gallery,* p. 189.

418   *"the most dominating":* Kazan, *Directing,* p. 140.

418	*"It was her pride"*: Richard deMille, p. 195.
418	*"The picture"*: Easton, p. 303.
418	*"I have never counted"*: Ibid., p. 305.
419	*I was greatly touched*: William deMille to DeMille, dated 8-9-52, but written later than that, Richard deMille collection.
420	*"Bill reminded me"*: BYU, DeMille speech, 5-24-53, box 445, f. 11.
420	*"where the fox"*: BYU, DeMille to Harper, 7-13-53, box 445, f. 6.
420	*"Goddammit"*: Richard deMille to S.E.

Chapter 21

Page

421	*Sometimes he would fall*: Koury, p. 258.
421	*"You see 2,800"*: AMPAS, Hedda Hopper Collection, 12-10-51.
422	*"The first of you"*: Essoe and Lee, p. 270.
422	*"We fill the departure"*: Koury, p. 252.
423	*"He showed me"*: Stephen Longstreet to S.E.
423	*"He watched me draw"*: John Jensen to S.E.
424	*"Henry was rejected"*: Katherine Orrison to S.E.
425	*"DeMille could never"*: BYU, Henry Noerdlinger transcript, p. 29.
425	*"There are no extras"*: Orrison, p. 139.
426	*"Look, Harry!"*: Wilcoxon, p. 199.
426	*"Cut the price"*: Koury, p. 168.
426	*"He would never say"*: Essoe and Lee, p. 256.
427	*"Yes, your feet"*: Gilbert, p. 322.
427	*"I had always loved"*: Lamour, p. 183.
427	*"His pet peeve"*: John Jensen to S.E.
428	*"The hat is very"*: Photoplay, Charlton Heston interview.
428	*It was more than a storage*: Apps, p. 210.
428	*"I didn't find him"*: Heston to S.E.
428	*Heston remembered*: Essoe and Lee, p. 254.
428	*Wilde had trained*: AMPAS, "Survival, Cornel Wilde," *Films and Filming*, vol. 17, no. 1.
429	*"If I'd gone"*: Wilcoxon, p. 218.
429	*"DeMille was sixty-nine"*: John Jensen to S.E.
429	*"Cornel was the nicest"*: Jackie Le Claire to S.E.
430	*"everybody is so tired"*: Koury, p. 35.
430	*"She got the message"*: Heston, *Arena*, p. 109.
430	*"Hey!"*: Koury, pp. 163–64.
431	*"Annie"*: BYU, box 150, f. 1.
431	*Friedman noted*: David Friedman to S.E.
431	*giving him*: BYU, box 193, f. 5.
432	*The profits just kept*: BYU, box 752, f. 4.
432	*There are newsreels*: In DeMille's film archive is a reel of miscellaneous outtakes and lighting tests that often give glimpses of an emotional and physical intimacy missing from his oral histories and autobiography. There is a startling shot of DeMille and the young Gloria Swanson wrapped up in a large coat, hugging each other with genuine pleasure. Ditto a lovely shot of Cecil and William on some stairs, their knees touching, each smoking a pipe and enjoying each other's company in brotherly companionship, while spotlights are shifted around them. For comic relief, there's a Julia Faye screen test for a Robert Z. Leonard film that conclusively shows why she never became a star,

and a shot of Fanny Ward accidentally falling off a bridge into a pond, with the crew immediately hurtling toward her to make sure their star is OK.

433   *"I love the picture"*: Jackie Le Claire to S.E.

433   *A memo from*: BYU, Gladys Rosson memo, 4-28-51, box 947, f. 23.

435   *"I knew all those"*: Richard deMille to S.E.

435   *Kay would take*: Cecilia deMille Presley to S.E.

435   *"She was so much"*: Ibid.

435   *Recently I had the belated*: Macdonald, p. 329.

436   *Powell was thrilled*: Powell, p. 139.

436   *"After the first"*: Anthony Quinn to S.E.

436   *DeMille had been thinking*: James V. D'Arc, "So Let It Be Written . . . ," *Literature/Film Quarterly*, vol. 14, no. 1, 1986.

437   *The advance was*: BYU, box 10, f. 17.

437   *"Grandfather found him"*: Cecilia deMille Presley to S.E.

Chapter 22

Page

438   *"I find it embarrassing"*: Wilcoxon, p. 228.

438   *"I can't tell you"*: Autobiography, p. 414.

439   *"I didn't sleep"*: BYU, biography notes, 6-3-57, box 20, f. 12.

439   *Card noted*: Card, *Seductive Cinema*, p. 213.

439   *The negative area*: Coe, p. 150.

439   *Martin Hart explains*: E-mail to S.E., 11-1-05.

440   *DeMille needed documentation*: Eldridge, p. 147.

440   *These texts were written*: Ibid., p. 149.

440   *DeMille paid*: Ibid., p. 148.

441   *the casting of Boyd*: Orrison, p. 47.

441   *DeMille was so happy*: Birchard, p. 354.

442   *"No more conservative"*: Robinson, p. 272.

442   *"You couldn't call yourself"*: Price, p. 174.

442   *Moore was struck*: Photoplay, Pat Moore interview.

443   *"Gladdy is a brave"*: BYU, DeMille to Bowman, 5-27-53, box 445, f. 6.

443   *"I would have given"*: Autobiography, p. 296.

443   *she left*: BYU, box 193, f. 5.

443   *"I liked her better"*: BYU, autobiography files, box 30, f. 4.

443   *"Cecilia, you do not"*: BYU, undated, box 939, f. 2.

444   *a fair amount of MacArthur*: BYU, box 130, f. 15.

444   *"I not only like Ike"*: University of Arizona Library Special Collections, DeMille to L. W. Douglas, 1-21-54, Douglas papers, courtesy of James Curtis.

444   *"DeMille was telling"*: Cecilia deMille Presley to S.E.

445   *"I'm Schwartzman"*: Cecilia deMille Presley to S.E.

446   *"Don't worry"*: Bob Thomas, p. 197.

446   *DeMille had been seeing*: BYU, box 130, f. 19.

446   *Jacobson was described*: Plummer, p. 233.

446   *Tennessee Williams would write*: Williams, pp. 208–9.

446   *"He had a basic formula"*: Eddie Fisher to S.E.

446   *"Max Jacobson was"*: Richard deMille to S.E.

447   *"He was a most peculiar"*: BYU, Noerdlinger transcript, p. 45.

447   *"When DeMille's energy lagged"*: Quinn, p. 281.

447   *"The latest glib expert"*: BYU, Donald Hayne, "You Don't Know DeMille," unpublished article, box 9, f. 17.

447   *His cholesterol*: BYU, box 50, f. 1.

448   *"You can't win"*: All of Brooskin's letters are at BYU, box 1266, f. 1.

448   *DeMille took a page*: Charlton Heston to S.E.

451   *"When the shot was finally"*: All this background of the shooting of the Exodus is in BYU, box 989, f. 20.

451   *The first take*: Orrison, p. 77.

452   *"an odd shade of gray"*: Edwards, p. 214.

452   *"Who the hell"*: Wilcoxon, pp. 289–93.

452   *Cecilia DeMille*: Essoe and Lee, p. 274.

453   *"Heston is doing fine"*: Birchard, p. 357.

453   *"Don't mention it to anyone"*: BYU, 11-8-54, box 1266, f. 1.

454   *"I must say"*: BYU, Clara deMille to DeMille, 12-29-54, box 954, f. 18.

454   *He instructed*: Shorris and Bundy, p. 129.

454   *"Cecil often called"*: Richard deMille, p. 192.

455   *"made some kindly wise"*: Richard deMille to S.E.

455   *When he came out of the bedroom*: Agnes deMille, *Portrait Gallery*, p. 190.

455   *"I wasn't thinking"*: Richard deMille, p. 53.

455   *"All the fatherly love"*: Easton, p. 347.

455   *"He loved beauty"*: Autobiography, p. 410.

456   *"Being told"*: Richard deMille to S.E.

456   *"They would discuss"*: Cecilia deMille Presley to S.E.

456   *"No, no"*: Heston, *Arena*, p. 136.

457   *"I have nothing"*: Shorris and Bundy, p. 129.

457   *"What's wrong with you"*: Wilcoxon, p. 315.

457   *Professional exotic*: Orrison, p. 106.

457   *"DeMille was like God"*: Robert Vaughn to S.E.

457   *"I remember C.B."*: Robert Fuller to S.E.

458   *"Of all the directors"*: Hardwicke, p. 283.

458   *"You're not reading that line"*: Price, pp. 174–75.

459   *The special effects*: Orrison, p. 74.

459   *Since frogs*: Orrison, p. 76.

459   *Eugene Mazzola*: Orrison, p. 120.

460   *"It was clear H.B."*: Orrison, p. 106.

461   *"DeMille was his father"*: Victoria Brynner to S.E.

461   *"In my father's mind"*: Rock Brynner to S.E.

462   *"DeMille came over"*: Photoplay, Lisa Mitchell interview.

463   *"I was Cecil B. DeMille's"*: Photoplay, A. C. Lyles interview.

463   *"Every picture"*: Marmorstein, p. 184.

463   *"I was taken over"*: Essoe and Lee, p. 281.

464   *DeMille wanted to hear Bernstein's*: Elmer Bernstein's recollections of working for DeMille are a combination of my interview with him and *Photoplay*'s.

465   *He was writing Max Jacobson*: BYU, DeMille to Jacobson, 5-27-55, box 461, f. 5.

465   *In another letter*: BYU, DeMille to Jacobson, 7-8-55, box 461, f. 5.

466   *"Dr. Bettenbaugh"*: BYU, 8-31-55, box 461, f. 1.

466   *John Carradine remembered*: John Carradine to S.E.

466   *"Your grandmother and I"*: BYU, DeMille to Cecilia deMille Presley, 9-15-55, box 461, f. 5.

467   *"I am not quite sure"*: BYU, DeMille to Cecilia deMille Presley, 12-6-55, box 461, f. 5.

468 *By the time they were through:* Paul Mandell, "Parting the Red Sea and Other Miracles," *American Cinematographer,* April 1983.

468 *"I worked on that picture":* Ibid.

470 *"At our first meeting":* Ann del Valle to S.E.

471 *"I thought at the time":* Walter Mirisch to S.E.

472 *In his address:* MOMA, Joe Hyams, "This Is Hollywood" "Don't Make Fun of Silent Films," *Herald Tribune,* 2-5-56.

473 *"Oh, it's nothing":* Wilcoxon, p. 265.

473 *"Anne has reserved":* BYU, Cole to DeMille, 12-30-55, box 461, f. 1.

473 *"The whole picture":* Heston, *Actor's Life,* p. 10.

474 *The exhibitor's manual:* Exhibitor's manual courtesy of Jeff Joseph and Martin Hart.

474 *"He treated her":* Ann del Valle to S.E.

475 *"Cecilia ran things":* David Friedman to S.E.

475 *"There had to be 100":* Cecilia deMille Presley to S.E.

475 *"Even if it was only":* Essoe and Lee, p. 285.

476 *"You're not going to wipe out":* Essoe and Lee, pp. 235–36.

477 *"a man of action":* Thomson, p. 311.

477 *"a certain cheapness":* Michael Browning to S.E.

477 *"It's the traditional":* First part, *Photoplay,* Martin Scorsese interview; second part quoted in Paul Mandell, "Parting the Red Sea and Other Miracles," *American Cinematographer,* April 1983.

479 *"The circus picture":* BYU, autobiography files, box 17, f. 47.

479 *"It was a giant":* Rock Brynner to S.E.

Chapter 23

Page

480 *"Children liked him":* Richard deMille to S.E.

481 *"I am of this opinion":* BYU, Milbank to DeMille, 1-2-57, box 493, f. 6.

481 *"Streams of celluloid":* MOMA, "DeMille Barn Restoration Begun," *Classic Images,* no. 92, February 1983.

481 *"He never seemed":* James V. D'Arc, "So Let It Be Written . . . : The Creation of Cecil B. DeMille's Autobiography," *Literature/Film Quarterly,* vol. 14, no. 1, 1986.

482 *"I think this fellow":* BYU, 6-3, no year, but probably 1957, box 30, f. 1.

482 *"Actually, I feel closer":* MOMA, "DeMille on DeMille," *Time,* undated but 1958.

483 *At lunch:* Robert Osborne to S.E.

483 *" 'The Lord giveth' ":* BYU, provisionally dated 1957 by "C" (Florence Cole?), box 133, f. 2.

483 *"I was not frightened":* BYU, autobiography files, 7-8-57, box 10, f. 24.

483 *"Tell him how much":* Myrent and Langlois, pp. 185–86.

484 *On October 31:* BYU, box 203, f. 4.

484 *In the margins:* BYU, first draft script for *The Buccaneer,* box 745, f. 5.

485 *"Is that so":* Wilcoxon, p. 325.

485 *"You're not gonna":* Quinn, pp. 263–64.

485 *"I was wild":* Richard deMille to S.E.

485 *"Yul hated Tony's":* Wilcoxon, p. 327.

485 *Jesse Lasky Jr. would come:* Pat Silver Lasky to S.E.

486 *"When you first expressed":* BYU, Noerdlinger to DeMille, 7-13-57, box 748, f. 10.

486 *DeMille's notes:* BYU, *Buccaneer* script dated 9-10-57, box 748, f. 3.

486 *"It was a big":* Claire Bloom to S.E.

486   *DeMille's breathing*: BYU, box 171, f. 23.

487   *"Well, Ben-Hur's the part"*: Heston, *Arena*, pp. 177–78.

487   *"A couple of times"*: Kenny Miller to S.E.

487   *"He was fascinating"*: Ann del Valle to S.E.

488   *"The point to get over"*: BYU, DeMille to Wilcoxon, 10-9-57, box 750, f. 2.

488   *"I'd be drawing"*: John Jensen to S.E.

488   *"When DeMille shouted"*: Wilcoxon, p. 334.

488   *"had become moody"*: Lasky Jr., p. 330.

488   *Frank Freeman had sent a memo*: BYU, Freeman to Wilcoxon, 2-20-58, box 750, f. 3.

489   *"the film is a fair"*: Claire Bloom to S.E.

489   *"The one man in the world"*: BYU, Quinn to DeMille, 4-9-58, box 750, f. 3.

489   *DeMille's company*: BYU, box 753, f. 6.

489   *"Look, DeMille was old"*: Elmer Bernstein to S.E.

490   *deeply in debt*: Betty Lasky to S.E.

490   *When she died*: BYU, box 220, f. 10.

490   *"Am I a stockholder"*: BYU, box 493, f. 17.

491   *"Get the needles"*: BYU, 2-4-57, box 491, f. 12.

491   *The price was*: Memo of the Paramount-MCA deal courtesy of David Pierce.

492   *"I have the advantage"*: BYU, DeMille to Ruth Stuart, 5-13-58, box 495, f. 10.

492   *"We've been married"*: DeMille to Max Rasbach, 4-28-58, p. 12, box 20, f. 12.

493   *He saw pay television*: BYU, box 19, f. 2.

493   *In New York he stayed*: Itinerary and meetings with Jacobson are at BYU, box 493, f. 20.

493   *"He said to tell me"*: Hedy Lamarr to S.E.

493   *"Dear Cecil"*: Berg, pp. 483–84.

493   *an elevator was installed*: Memo regarding DeMille's health, 7-18-58, DeMille FBI file.

493   *"While Mr. DeMille"*: DeMille memo, 8-6-58, DeMille FBI file.

494   *He started giving some thought*: BYU, memo, July 1958, box 1040, f. 2.

494   *"Treacy–please order"*: BYU, DeMille to Russel Treacy, 9-9-58, box 171, f. 23.

494   *"Dear Cecilia"*: BYU, 11-7-58, box 173, f. 26.

495   *"he was almost Oriental"*: Maltin, *Hollywood*, p. 129.

495   *Essentially, it concerned*: BYU, Noerdlinger transcript, p. 14; Wilcoxon, p. 340.

495   *reading C. S. Lewis's*: BYU, memo, 12-23-58, box 1040, f. 7.

495   *"The brain is the wire"*: BYU, DeMille lunch notes, 11-11-58; also 6-4-58, box 1040, f. 8.

496   *"Henry [Noerdlinger] says"*: BYU, undated note, box 1040, f. 8.

496   *"I had to stand there"*: Ann del Valle to S.E.

496   *Max Jacobson*: BYU, night wire, 12-5-58, box 491, f. 12.

496   *He was attended*: BYU, itinerary, box 749, f. 6.

496   *"I noticed that you allowed"*: I want to thank Betty Lawson at AADA for scouring the archives for DeMille's remarks.

497   *A recording*: The tape of *Don McNeill's Breakfast Club* on 12-11-58 is at BYU.

497   *"When he came back"*: Ann del Valle to S.E.

498   *DeMille sent her*: BYU, DeMille to Reynolds, 11-2-58, box 495, f. 2.

498   *"Do you think"*: BYU, box 497, f. 18.

498   *In DeMille's mind*: BYU, notes on *On My Honor*, box 1043, f. 8.

498   *"He was very frail"*: Orrison, p. 190.

499   *"We never really"*: Quinn, p. 269.

499   *"He never really recovered"*: Cecilia deMille Presley to S.E.

499   *"He was enduring"*: Richard deMille to S.E.

499   *"If I had to do it over"*: BYU, DeMille, autobiography files, 8-57, box 20, f. 12.

501   *"I was deeply saddened"*: Hoover to deMille, 1-21-59, DeMille FBI file.

501   *"The death of a man"*: Heston, *Actor's Life*, p. 65.

501   *"I should have thanked him"*: Charlton Heston to S.E.

502   *When the polished mahogany*: MOMA, "DeMille Is Entombed in $250,000 Mausoleum," *New York Herald Tribune*, 1-24-59.

502   *Donald Hayne spoke*: *Autobiography*, p. 439.

502   *"There were a lot of people"*: *Photoplay*, A. C. Lyles interview.

502   *The night after*: Ann del Valle to S.E.

Epilogue

Page

505   *"I once asked him"*: Essoe and Lee, p. 284.

505   *"He was the undeniable"*: MOMA, "Cecil B. DeMille," *New York Times*, Bosley Crowther, 1-25-59.

506   *The estate inventory*: DeMille estate inventory, Los Angeles County.

506   *"One reason the will"*: Richard deMille to S.E.

507   *Clara Beranger had died*: Both Beranger's and Bauchens's obituaries derive from MOMA: "Mrs. Cecil B. DeMille, 87, Film Maker's Widow, Dies," *New York Herald Tribune*, 7-19-60; "Anne Bauchens, 85, Won 1940 Film Editing Oscar," *New York Times*.

507   *"Very heavy"*: Pat Silver Lasky to S.E.

507   *"Well, Cecilia"*: Cecilia deMille Presley to S.E.

508   *"the contrast between"*: Courtesy of Robert Gottlieb.

509   *A gold money clip*: MOMA, Suzanne Daley, "Memories of DeMille Go on Auction Block," *New York Times*, 10-19-88.

509   *"DeMille knew how to do it"*: Silvester, p. 488, quoting Brodsky and Weiss, *The Cleopatra Papers*.

509   *"I prefer to call"*: Wagner, pp. 160–61.

510   *"Cecil B. DeMille lived at an"*: Agnes deMille, *Portrait Gallery*, pp. 190–91.

511   *"the greatest showman"*: Zukor, p. 296.

511   *"Forget the beautiful"*: Lasky Jr. to Brownlow, Kevin Brownlow archives.

511   *"He could be"*: Agnes deMille, *Portrait Gallery*, p. 194.

512   *"DeMille presented"*: I have combined two paragraphs, the first from Scorsese, p. 75, the second from the *Photoplay* interview with Martin Scorsese.

513   *Gloria Swanson visited*: Bernard Drew, "William Holden," *American Film*, February 1977.

BIBLIOGRAPHY

Abel, Richard. *Americanizing the Movies and "Movie-Mad" Audiences, 1910–1914.* Berkeley: University of California Press, 2006.

Aberth, John. *A Knight at the Movies: Medieval History on Film.* New York: Routledge, 2003.

Adamson, Joe. *Byron Haskin.* Metuchen, N.J.: Scarecrow, 1984.

Altman, Rick. *Silent Film Sound.* New York: Columbia University Press, 2004.

Apps, Jerry. *Ringlingville USA.* Madison: Wisconsin Historical Society Press, 2005.

Balshofer, Fred, and Arthur Miller. *One Reel a Week.* Berkeley: University of California Press, 1967.

Bardeche, Maurice, and Robert Brasillach. *The History of Motion Pictures.* New York: Norton, 1938; rpt., 1970.

Barrios, Richard. *Screened Out.* New York: Routledge, 2003.

Barsacq, Leon (edited by Elliott Stein). *Caligari's Cabinet and Other Grand Illusions.* Boston: New York Graphic Society, 1976.

Basinger, Jeanine. *Silent Stars.* New York: Knopf, 1999.

Basquette, Lina. *Lina: DeMille's Godless Girl.* Fairfax, Va.: Denlinger's, 1990.

Beardsley, Charles. *Hollywood's Master Showman: The Legendary Sid Grauman.* New York: Cornwall, 1983.

Beauchamp, Cari. *Joseph P. Kennedy Presents: His Hollywood Years.* New York: Knopf, 2009.

——. *Without Lying Down: Frances Marion and the Powerful Women of Early Hollywood.* New York: Scribner, 1997.

Beauchamp, Cari (ed.). *Adventures of a Hollywood Secretary.* Berkeley: University of California Press, 2006.

Behlmer, Rudy. *Henry Hathaway.* Lanham, Md.: Scarecrow, 2001.

Behlmer, Rudy (ed.). *Memo from David O. Selznick.* New York: Viking, 1972.

Berg, A. Scott. *Goldwyn.* New York: Knopf, 1989.

Bergman, Andrew. *We're in the Money.* New York: New York University Press, 1971.

Bernstein, Matthew. *Walter Wanger: Hollywood Independent.* Berkeley: University of California Press, 1994.

Birchard, Robert S. *Cecil B. DeMille's Hollywood.* Lexington: University of Kentucky Press, 2004.

Bodeen, DeWitt. *From Hollywood.* South Brunswick, N.J.: A. S. Barnes, 1976.

——. *More from Hollywood.* South Brunswick, N.J.: A. S. Barnes, 1977.

Bogdanovich, Peter. *Who the Devil Made It.* New York: Knopf, 1997.

——. *Who the Hell's in It.* New York: Knopf, 2004.

Bojarski, Richard, and Kenneth Beals. *The Films of Boris Karloff.* Secaucus, N.J.: Citadel, 1974.

Bonadio, Felice. *A. P. Giannini.* Berkeley: University of California Press, 1994.

Bowen, Thomas. "Cecil B. DeMille and the Tiburon Island Adventure." In *Journal of the Southwest*, vol. 46, no. 3 (Autumn 2004), Tucson: University of Arizona, 2004.

Bowser, Eileen (ed.). *Film Notes.* New York: Museum of Modern Art, 1969.

Boyd, Grace Bradley, and Michael Cochran. *Hopalong Cassidy: An American Legend.* York: Gemstone, 2008.

Brady, Frank. *Citizen Welles.* New York: Scribner's, 1989.

Britting, Jeff. *Ayn Rand.* New York: Overlook, 2004.

Brown, Karl. *Adventures with D. W. Griffith.* New York: Farrar, Straus & Giroux, 1973.

Brownlow, Kevin. *Behind the Mask of Innocence.* New York: Knopf, 1990.

——. *Hollywood: The Pioneers.* London: Collins, 1979.

——. *Mary Pickford Rediscovered.* New York: Abrams, 1999.

——. *The Parade's Gone By.* New York: Knopf, 1968.

——. *The War, the West, and the Wilderness.* New York: Knopf, 1979.

Buhle, Paul, and Dave Wagner. *Radical Hollywood.* New York: Free Press, 2002.

Callow, Simon. *Charles Laughton: A Difficult Actor.* New York: St. Martin's, 1988.

——. *Orson Welles, Vol. 2: Hello Americans.* New York: Viking, 2006.

Card, James. *Seductive Cinema: The Art of Silent Film.* New York: Knopf, 1994.

——. *Tribute to Gloria Swanson.* Rochester: Eastman House, 1966.

Cardiff, Jack. *Magic Hour—The Life of a Cameraman.* London: Faber & Faber, 1996.

Ceplair, Larry, and Steven Englund. *The Inquisition in Hollywood.* Berkeley: University of California Press, 1983.

Chierichetti, David. *Edith Head.* New York: HarperCollins, 2003.

——. *Hollywood Costume Design.* New York: Harmony, 1976.

——. *Mitchell Leisen: Hollywood Director.* Los Angeles: Photoventures, 1995.

Coe, Brian. *The History of Movie Photography.* New York: New York Zoetrope, 1981.

Coffee, Lenore. *Storyline.* London: Cassell, 1973.

Coghlan Jr., Frank. *They Still Call Me Junior.* Jefferson, N.C.: McFarland, 1993.

Coleman, Herbert. *The Hollywood I Knew.* Lanham, Md.: Scarecrow, 2003.

Coursodon, Jean-Pierre (ed.). *American Directors*, Vol. 1. New York: McGraw-Hill, 1983.

Cowie, Peter. *John Ford and the American West.* New York: Abrams, 2004.

Crafton, Donald. *The Talkies.* New York: Scribner's, 1997.

Curtis, James. *Between Flops: A Biography of Preston Sturges.* New York: Harcourt Brace Jovanovich, 1982.

——. *W. C. Fields.* New York: Knopf, 2003.

Davis, Ronald. *Duke: The Life and Image of John Wayne.* Norman: University of Oklahoma Press, 1998.

——. *The Glamour Factory.* Dallas: Southern Methodist University Press, 1993.

——. *William S. Hart: Projecting the American West.* Norman: University of Oklahoma Press, 2003.

——. *Words into Images: Screenwriters on the Studio System.* Jackson: University Press of Mississippi, 2007.

deMille, Agnes. *Martha: The Life and Work of Martha Graham.* New York: Random House, 1991.

——. *Portrait Gallery.* Boston: Houghton Mifflin, 1990.

——. *Where the Wings Grow.* Garden City: Doubleday, 1978.

——. *Dance to the Piper.* Boston: Little, Brown, 1952.

DeMille, Cecil B. *The Autobiography of Cecil B. DeMille*. Englewood Cliffs, N.J.: Prentice Hall, 1959.

deMille, Richard. *My Secret Mother—Lorna Moon*. New York: Farrar, Straus & Giroux, 1998.

deMille, William. *Hollywood Saga*. New York: Dutton, 1939.

Deutelbaum, Marshall (ed.). *"Image" on the Art and Evolution of the Film*. New York: Dover, 1979.

Dmytryk, Edward. *It's a Hell of a Life but Not a Bad Living*. New York: Times Books, 1978.

———. *Odd Man Out: A Memoir of the Hollywood Ten*. Carbondale: Southern Illinois University Press, 1996.

Doherty, Thomas. *Pre-Code Hollywood*. New York: Columbia University Press, 1999.

Doyle, G. R. *Twenty-five Years of Films*. London: Mitre, 1936.

Drew, William M. *Speaking of Silents*. Vestal: Vestal, 1989.

Dunning, John. *The Encyclopedia of Old-Time Radio*. New York: Oxford University Press, 1998.

Durgnat, Raymond, and Scott Simmon. *King Vidor, American*. Berkeley: University of California Press, 1988.

Easton, Carol. *No Intermission: The Life of Agnes deMille*. Boston: Little, Brown, 1996.

Edelman, Rob, and Audrey Kupferberg. *Angela Lansbury*. Secaucus, N.J.: Citadel, 1999.

Edwards, Anne. *The DeMilles: An American Family*. New York: Abrams, 1988.

Eldridge, David. *Hollywood's History Films*. London: Tauris, 2006.

Endres, Stacey, and Robert Cushman. *Hollywood at Your Feet*. Los Angeles: Pomegranate, 1992.

Essoe, Gabe, and Raymond Lee. *DeMille: The Man and His Pictures*. New York: Castle, 1970.

Everson, William K. *American Silent Film*. New York: Oxford University Press, 1978.

Eyles, Allan. *John Wayne*. South Brunswick, N.J.: A. S. Barnes, 1979.

Eyman, Scott. *Ernst Lubitsch: Laughter in Paradise*. New York: Simon & Schuster, 1993.

———. *Five American Cinematographers*. Metuchen, N.J.: Scarecrow, 1987.

Fairbanks Jr., Douglas. *Salad Days*. New York: Doubleday, 1988.

Farrar, Geraldine. *Such Sweet Compulsion*. New York: Greystone, 1938.

Feiler, Bruce. *America's Prophet: Moses and the American Story*. New York: Morrow, 2009.

Fell, Gong, et al. *Before Hollywood: Turn-of-the-Century American Film*. New York: Hudson Hills, 1987.

Fields, Ronald J. *W. C. Fields by Himself*. Englewood Cliffs, N.J.: Prentice Hall, 1973.

Finch, Christopher, and Linda Rosenkrantz. *Gone Hollywood*. Garden City: Doubleday, 1979.

Fine, Marshall. *Accidental Genius: The Life of John Cassavetes*. New York: Miramax, 2005.

Fountain, Leatrice Gilbert, with John Maxim. *Dark Star*. London: Sidgwick & Jackson, 1985.

Fraser, George MacDonald. *The Hollywood History of the World*. New York: Morrow, 1988.

Garnett, Tay, and Fredda Dudley Balling. *Light Your Torches and Pull Up Your Tights*. New Rochelle, N.Y.: Arlington House, 1973.

Geist, Kenneth. *Pictures Will Talk*. New York: Scribner's, 1978.

Giesen, Rolf. *Special Effects Artists*. Jefferson, N.C.: McFarland, 2008.

Gilbert, Julie. *Opposite Attraction: The Lives of Erich Maria Remarque and Paulette Goddard*. New York: Pantheon, 1995.

Gish, Lillian. *The Movies, Mr. Griffith and Me*. Englewood Cliffs, N.J.: Prentice Hall, 1969.

Goldenson, Leonard, with Marvin Wolf. *Beating the Odds*. New York: Scribner's, 1991.

Goodman, Ezra. *The Fifty Year Decline and Fall of Hollywood*. New York: Simon & Schuster, 1961.

Gomery, Douglas. *The Hollywood Studio System*. New York: St. Martin's, 1986.

Gottlieb, Robert. *Reading Dance*. New York: Pantheon, 2008.

Grieveson, Lee, and Peter Kramer (eds.). *The Silent Cinema Reader*. London: Routledge, 2004.

Gutner, Howard. *Gowns by Adrian*. New York: Abrams, 2001.

Haberski Jr., Raymond J. *Freedom to Offend: How New York Remade Movie Culture*. Lexington: University Press of Kentucky, 2007.

Hambley, John, and Patrick Downing. *The Art of Hollywood*. London: Thames, 1979.

Hampton, Benjamin B. *History of the American Film Industry*. New York: Dover, 1931; rpt., 1970.

Haney, Lynn. *Gregory Peck: A Charmed Life*. New York: Carroll & Graf, 2004.

Hardwicke, Sir Cedric, and James Brough. *A Victorian in Orbit*. Garden City: Doubleday, 1961.

Hart, William S. *My Life East and West*. New York: Benjamin Blom, 1929.

Harvith, John, and Susan Harvith. *Karl Struss: Man with a Camera*. Bloomfield Hills, Mich.: Cranbrook, 1976.

Haskell, Molly. *From Reverence to Rape*. New York: Holt, Rinehart & Winston, 1974.

Henabery, Joseph E. *Before, In and After Hollywood*. Lanham, Md.: Scarecrow, 1997.

Henderson, Mary. *Mielziner: Master of Modern Stage Design*. New York: Back Stage, 2001.

Henderson, Robert. *D. W. Griffith: His Life and Work*. New York: Oxford University Press, 1972.

Henning, Robert. *Destined for Hollywood: The Art of Dan Sayre Groesbeck*. Santa Barbara: Santa Barbara Museum of Art, 2001.

Heston, Charlton. *The Actor's Life: Journals, 1956–1976*. New York: Dutton, 1978.

——. *In the Arena*. New York: Simon & Schuster, 1995.

Hickerson, Jay. *The Lux Radio Theatre Log*. Hamden, Conn.: Hickerson, 1996.

Higashi, Sumiko. *Cecil B. DeMille and American Culture: The Silent Era*. Berkeley: University of California Press, 1994.

Higham, Charles. *Cecil B. DeMille*. New York: Scribner's, 1973.

——. *Hollywood Cameramen*. Bloomington: Indiana University Press, 1970.

Horne, Gerald. *Class Struggle in Hollywood*. Austin: University of Texas Press, 2001.

Jablonski, Edward. *Alan Jay Lerner*. New York: Holt, 1996.

Jacobs, Diane. *Christmas in July: The Life and Art of Preston Sturges*. Berkeley: University of California Press, 1992.

Jacobs, Lewis. *The Rise of the American Film*. New York: Teacher's College Press, 1968.

Johnston, Alva. *The Great Goldwyn*. New York: Random House, 1937.

Jura, Jean-Jacques, and Rodney Norman Bardin II. *Balboa Films: A History and Filmography of the Silent Film Studio*. Jefferson, N. C.: McFarland, 1999.

Kantor, Michael, and Laurence Maslon. *Broadway: The American Musical*. New York: Bulfinch, 2004.

Kazan, Elia. *Kazan on Directing*. New York: Knopf, 2009.

——. *A Life*. New York: Knopf, 1988.

Keyes, Evelyn. *Scarlett O'Hara's Younger Sister*. Secaucus, N.J.: Lyle Stuart, 1977.

Knight, Arthur, and Eliot Elisofon. *The Hollywood Style*. London: Macmillan, 1969.

Kobal, John. *The Art of the Great Hollywood Portrait Photographers*. New York: Knopf, 1980.

——. *People Will Talk*. New York: Knopf, 1985.

Koszarski, Richard. *An Evening's Entertainment*. New York: Scribner's, 1990.

——. *Hollywood Directors, 1914–1940*. New York: Oxford University Press, 1976.

——. *Von: The Life and Films of Erich von Stroheim*. New York: Limelight, 2001.

Kotsilibas-Davis, James. *The Barrymores: The Royal Family in Hollywood*. New York: Crown, 1981.

——. *Great Times, Good Times: The Odyssey of Maurice Barrymore*. Garden City: Doubleday, 1977.

Koury, Phil. *Yes, Mr. DeMille*. New York: Putnam, 1959.

Lally, Kevin. *Wilder Times: The Life of Billy Wilder*. New York: Holt, 1996.

Lambert, Gavin. *Nazimova*. New York: Knopf, 1997.

Lamour, Dorothy, with Dick McInnes. *My Side of the Road*. Englewood Cliffs, N.J.: Prentice Hall, 1980.

Lasky, Bessie Mona. *Candle in the Sun*. Los Angeles: DeVorss, 1957.

Lasky, Jesse, with Don Weldon. *I Blow My Own Horn*. Garden City, N.Y.: Doubleday, 1957.

Lasky Jr., Jesse. *Whatever Happened to Hollywood?* New York: Funk & Wagnalls, 1975.

Leider, Emily W. *Dark Lover: The Life and Death of Rudolph Valentino*. New York: Farrar, Straus & Giroux, 2003.

LeRoy, Mervyn, with Dick Kleiner. *Take One*. New York: Hawthorn, 1974.

Levy, Emanuel. *George Cukor: Master of Elegance*. New York: Morrow, 1994.

Lockwood, Charles. *Dream Palaces: Hollywood at Home*. New York: Viking, 1981.

Long, Bruce. *William Desmond Taylor: A Dossier*. Metuchen, N.J.: Scarecrow, 1991.

Long, Robert Emmet. *Broadway, The Golden Years: Jerome Robbins and the Great Choreographer-Directors, 1940 to the Present*. New York: Continuum, 2001.

Louvish, Simon. *Cecil B. DeMille: A Life in Art*. New York: St. Martin's, 2008.

Love, Bessie. *From Hollywood with Love*. London: Elm Tree, 1977.

Lowrey, Carolyn. *The First One Hundred Men and Women of the Screen*. New York: Moffat, Yard, 1920.

Macdonald, Kevin. *Emeric Pressburger: The Life and Death of a Screenwriter*. London: Faber & Faber, 1994.

MacGowan, Kenneth. *Behind the Screen: The History and Techniques of the Motion Picture*. New York: Delacorte, 1965.

Madsen, Axel. *William Wyler*. New York: Crowell, 1973.

Maltin, Leonard. *The Art of the Cinematographer*. New York: Dover, 1978.

Maltin, Leonard (ed.). *Hollywood: The Movie Factory*. New York: Popular Library, 1976.

Mandelbaum, Howard, and Eric Myers. *Screen Deco*. New York: St. Martin's, 1985.

Marill, Alvin H. *Samuel Goldwyn Presents*. South Brunswick, N.J.: A. S. Barnes, 1976.

Marion, Frances. *Off with Their Heads*. New York: Macmillan, 1972.

Marmorstein, Gary. *Hollywood Rhapsody*. New York: Schirmer, 1997.

Marubbio, M. Elise. *Killing the Indian Maiden: Images of Native American Women in Film*. Lexington: University Press of Kentucky, 2006.

Marx, Arthur. *Goldwyn*. New York: Norton, 1976.

Marx, Samuel. *Mayer and Thalberg: The Make-Believe Saints*. New York: Random House, 1975.

Mast, Gerald. *A Short History of the Movies*. New York: Macmillan, 1986.

May, Lary. *Screening Out the Past: The Birth of Mass Culture and the Motion Picture Industry*. New York: Oxford University Press, 1980.

McBride, Joseph. *Frank Capra: The Catastrophe of Success*. New York: St. Martin's, 2000.

———. *Hawks on Hawks*. Berkeley: University of California Press, 1982.

McCandless, Barbara, Bonnie Yochelson, and Richard Koszarski. *New York to Hollywood: The Photography of Karl Struss*. Fort Worth: Amon Carter Museum, 1995.

McCann, Richard Dyer. *The First Film Makers*. Metuchen, N.J.: Scarecrow, 1989.

McCarthy, Todd. *Howard Hawks*. New York: Grove, 1997.

McCarthy, Todd, and Charles Flynn. *Kings of the Bs*. New York: Dutton, 1975.

McCartney, Laton. *The Teapot Dome Scandal*. New York: Random House, 2008.

McClelland, Doug. *Forties Film Talk*. Jefferson, N.C.: McFarland, 1992.

McGilligan, Patrick. *Alfred Hitchcock: A Life in Darkness and Light*. New York: ReganBooks, 2003.

———. *Film Crazy*. New York: St. Martin's, 2000.

McGilligan, Pat (ed.). *Backstory 2*. Berkeley: University of California Press, 1986.

McLean, Adrienne, and David Cook (eds.). *Headline Hollywood*. New Brunswick, N.J.: Rutgers University Press, 2001.

Meyers, Jeffrey. *Gary Cooper: American Hero*. New York: Morrow, 1998.

Morris, Michael. *Madam Valentino: The Many Lives of Natacha Rambova*. New York: Abbeville, 1991.

Munn, Michael. *John Wayne: The Man Behind the Myth*. New York: New American Library, 2004.

Myrent, Glenn, and Georges Langlois. *Henri Langlois: First Citizen of Cinema*. New York: Twayne, 1995.

Navasky, Victor S. *Naming Names*. New York: Hill & Wang, 2003; 3rd ed.

Newsom, Iris (ed.). *Wonderful Inventions: Motion Pictures, Broadcasting and Recorded Sound at the Library of Congress*. Washington, D.C.: Library of Congress, 1985.

Norman, Marc. *What Happens Next: A History of American Screenwriting*. New York: Harmony, 2007.

Oller John. *Jean Arthur: The Actress Nobody Knew*. New York: Limelight, 1997.

Orrison, Katherine. *Written in Stone: Making Cecil B. DeMille's Epic* The Ten Commandments. Lanham, Md.: Vestal, 1999.

Parish, James Robert, and Don Stanke. *The Swashbucklers*. New Rochelle, N.Y.: Arlington House, 1976.

Parrish, Robert. *Growing Up in Hollywood*. New York: Harcourt Brace Jovanovich, 1976.

Peters Jr., House. *Another Side of Hollywood*. Madison, Wisc.: Empire, 2000.

Peters, Margot. *The House of Barrymore*. New York: Knopf, 1990.

Phillips-Fein, Kim. *Invisible Hands: The Making of the Conservative Movement from the New Deal to Reagan*. New York: Norton, 2008.

Pickford, Mary. *Sunshine and Shadow*. Garden City: Doubleday, 1955.

Plummer, Christopher. *In Spite of Myself*. New York: Knopf, 2008.

Powell, Michael. *Million Dollar Movie*. New York: Random House, 1995.

Pratt, George. *Spellbound in Darkness*. Greenwich, Conn.: New York Graphic Society, 1973.

Price, Victoria. *Vincent Price: A Daughter's Biography*. New York: St. Martin's, 1999.

Primack, Bret (ed.). *The Ben Hecht Show*. Jefferson, N.C.: McFarland, 1993.

Quinn, Anthony, with Daniel Paisner. *One Man Tango*. New York: HarperCollins, 1995.

Quirk, Lawrence J. *Claudette Colbert*. New York: Crown, 1985.

Ramirez, Joan Antonio. *Architecture for the Screen*. Jefferson, N.C.: McFarland, 2004.

Ramsaye, Terry. *A Million and One Nights*. New York: Simon & Schuster, 1964.

Rand, Ayn. *Journals of Ayn Rand* (edited by David Harriman). New York: Dutton, 1997.

Raymond, Emilie. *From My Cold, Dead Hands: Charlton Heston and American Politics*. Lexington: University Press of Kentucky, 2006.

Reinhartz, Adele. *Jesus of Hollywood*. New York: Oxford University Press, 2007.

Ringgold, Gene, and DeWitt Bodeen. *The Complete Films of Cecil B. DeMille*. Secaucus, N.J.: Citadel, 1969.

Rivkin, Allen, and Laura Kerr. *Hello, Hollywood*. Garden City: Doubleday, 1962.

Roberts, Randy, and James S. Olson. *John Wayne: American*. New York: Free Press, 1995.

Robinson, Edward G., and Leonard Spigelgass. *All My Yesterdays*. New York: Hawthorn, 1973.

Rooney, Mickey. *Life Is Too Short*. New York: Ballantine, 1991.

Rosenberg, Bernard, and Harry Silverstein. *The Real Tinsel*. New York: Macmillan, 1970.

Roud, Richard. *Cinema: A Critical Dictionary*, Vol. 1. New York: Viking, 1980.

Sadoul, Georges (edited by Peter Morris). *Dictionary of Filmmakers*. Berkeley: University of California Press, 1972.

Schary, Dore. *Heyday*. Boston: Little, Brown, 1979.

Scorsese, Martin, with Michael Henry Wilson. *A Personal Journey with Martin Scorsese Through American Movies*. New York: Miramax/Hyperion, 1997.

Scott, Evelyn F. *Hollywood: When Silents Were Golden*. New York: McGraw-Hill, 1972.

Semenov, Lillian Wurtzel, and Carla Winter. *William Fox, Sol M. Wurtzel and the Early Fox Film Corporation: Letters, 1917–1923*. Jefferson, N.C.: McFarland, 2001.

Server, Lee. *Screenwriter: Words Become Pictures*. Pittstown: Main Street, 1987.

Sherman, Eric. *Directing the Film*. Boston: Little, Brown, 1976.

Shipman, Nell. *The Silent Screen and My Talking Heart*. Boise, Idaho: Hemingway Western Studies Center, 1987.

Shorris, Sylvia, and Marion Abbott Bundy. *Talking Pictures*. New York: New Press, 1994.

Silvester, Christopher (ed.). *The Grove Book of Hollywood*. New York: Grove, 1998.

Sito, Tom. *Drawing the Line: The Untold Story of the Animation Unions from Bosko to Bart Simpson*. Lexington: University Press of Kentucky, 2006.

Slide, Anthony. *Nitrate Won't Wait*. Jefferson, N.C.: McFarland, 1992.

——. *Selected Film Criticism, 1912–1920*. Metuchen, N.J.: Scarecrow, 1982.

——. *Selected Film Criticism, 1921–1930*. Metuchen, N.J.: Scarecrow, 1982.

——. *Selected Film Criticism, 1931–1940*. Metuchen, N.J.: Scarecrow, 1982.

——. *Selected Film Criticism, 1941–1950*. Metuchen, N.J.: Scarecrow, 1983.

Slide, Anthony, and Edward Wagenknecht. *Fifty Great American Silent Films, 1912–1920*. New York: Dover, 1980.

Smith, Gary Allen. *Epic Films*. Jefferson, N.C.: McFarland, 2004, 2nd ed.

Spears, Jack. *Hollywood: The Golden Era*. New York: Castle, 1971.

Sperber, A. M., and Eric Lax. *Bogart*. New York: Morrow, 1997.

Springer, John Parris. *Hollywood Fictions*. Norman: University of Oklahoma Press, 2000.

Staggs, Sam. *Close-up on Sunset Boulevard*. New York: St. Martin's, 2002.

Stevens Jr., George (ed.). *Conversations with the Great Moviemakers of Hollywood's Golden Age*. New York: Knopf, 2006.

Sturges, Preston. *Preston Sturges by Preston Sturges*. New York: Simon & Schuster, 1990.

Swindell, Larry. *Screwball: The Life of Carole Lombard*. New York: Morrow, 1975.

Talmey, Allene. *Doug and Mary and Others*. New York: Macy-Masius, 1927.

Thomas, Bob. *Thalberg: Life and Legend*. Garden City: Doubleday, 1969.

Thomas, Bob (ed.). *Directors in Action*. Indianapolis: Bobbs-Merrill, 1973.

Thomas, Tony. "Sam Wood," in *Hollywood Professionals*, Vol. 2. New York: A. S. Barnes, 1974.

Thomson, David. *Hollywood*. New York: Dorling Kindersley, 2001.

Torrence, Bruce. *Hollywood: The First Hundred Years*. New York: New York Zoetrope, 1982.

Turner, George (ed.). *The ASC Treasury of Visual Effects*. Hollywood: American Society of Cinematographers, 1983.

Usai, Paolo Cherchi, and Lorenzo Codelli (eds.). *The DeMille Legacy*. Pordenone, Italy: Le Giornate del Cinema Muto, 1991.

Vieira, Mark. *Sin in Soft Focus: Pre-Code Hollywood*. New York: Abrams, 1999.

von Sternberg, Josef. *Fun in a Chinese Laundry*. New York: Macmillan, 1965.

Wagner, Walter. *You Must Remember This*. New York: Putnam's, 1975.

Wakeman, John (ed.). *World Film Directors*, Vol. 1. New York: H. W. Wilson, 1987.

Walker, Alexander. *Vivien: The Life of Vivien Leigh*. New York: Weidenfeld & Nicolson, 1987.

Walsh, Raoul. *Each Man in His Time*. New York: Farrar, Straus & Giroux, 1974.

Weddle, David. *If They Move . . . Kill 'Em: The Life and Times of Sam Peckinpah*. New York: Grove, 1994.

Welles, Orson, and Peter Bogdanovich. *This Is Orson Welles*. New York: HarperCollins, 1992.

Wertheim, Arthur Frank. *Vaudeville Wars: How the Keith-Albee and Orpheum Circuits Controlled the Big Time and Its Performers.* New York: Palgrave Macmillan, 2006.

Wilcoxon, Henry, with Katherine Orrison. *Lionheart in Hollywood.* Metuchen, N.J.: Scarecrow, 1991.

Williams, Tennessee. *Memoirs.* Garden City: Doubleday, 1975.

Wilmeth, Don, and Christopher Bigsby, (eds.). *The Cambridge History of American Theater,* Vols. 1–3. New York: Cambridge University Press, 1998–2000.

Wlaschin, Ken. *The Silent Cinema in Song, 1896–1929.* Jefferson, N.C.: McFarland, 2009.

Wright, Basil. *The Long View.* London: Secker & Warburg, 1974.

Young, Freddie. *Seventy Light Years: A Life in the Movies.* New York: Faber & Faber, 1999.

Youngerman, Joseph C. *My Seventy Years at Paramount Studios and the Directors Guild of America.* Los Angeles: Directors Guild of America, 1995.

Youngkin, Stephen. *The Lost One: A Life of Peter Lorre.* Lexington: University Press of Kentucky, 2005.

Zollo, Paul. *Hollywood Remembered.* New York: Cooper Square, 2002.

Zolotow, Maurice. *Billy Wilder in Hollywood.* New York: Putnam's, 1977.

——. *Shooting Star: A Biography of John Wayne.* New York: Simon & Schuster, 1974.

Zukor, Adolph, with Dale Kramer. *The Public Is Never Wrong: My Fifty Years in Motion Pictures.* New York: Putnam's, 1953.

INDEX

555